ELEVEN MADISON PARK

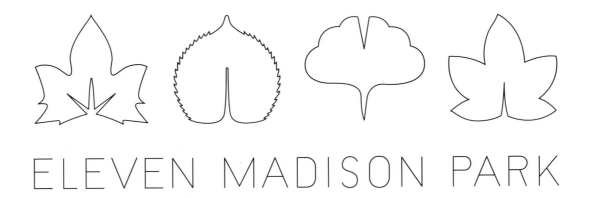

# ELEVEN MADISON PARK

## THE COOKBOOK

DANIEL HUMM          WILL GUIDARA

FOREWORD BY DANNY MEYER

PHOTOGRAPHY BY FRANCESCO TONELLI

LITTLE, BROWN AND COMPANY

NEW YORK   BOSTON   LONDON

# CONTENTS

# FOREWORD
## BY
## DANNY MEYER

Restaurants are a lot like children: they're fun to conceive, challenging to bring into the world, and they generally reward you with abundant triumph and occasional hardship as the years progress. Their personalities are essentially imprinted upon delivery, and about the most impact you can have as a parent/patron is to imbue them with nonnegotiable family values and character, expose them to the best possible education, teach them to care for their health, correct their mistakes consistently and calmly, guide them through inevitable bouts of adversity, avoid causing undue damage to their self-esteem, and love them every step of the way.

After enough years have passed, and if you've done your best work, the gift and thanks you get is a healthy, independent adult whose time has come to live life with autonomy and independence — founded upon your values, but with a distinctive personal stamp and style.

So it has been with Eleven Madison Park.

It is late 1996 and I hear about an exciting-sounding restaurant opportunity in a one-million-square-foot building I've never stepped foot in, towering over a derelict park any sane New Yorker has always steered clear of. But I'm intrigued — perhaps even more so because that park has a storied past and miles of potential. It's nearly impossible to comprehend a tour of the enormous space, as it's currently a makeshift construction office — a warren of desks, metal toolboxes, and equipment. The entire art deco building is getting a multimillion-dollar makeover.

Three towering thirty-foot windows are glazed over in purple film, making it impossible to see Madison Square Park — which is not such a bad thing because at this point in time there's not much you want to see in that park anyway. But the grandness and sheer cubic volume of space is beyond impressive, and all I can think about is the word "brasserie." This space is dying to be a giant nightly party with the most solid possible brasserie cooking, and the goal is to create an irresistible restaurant that will be even more fun and tastier than the French standard. We will update and refine traditional brasserie fare by cooking benchmark versions of well-known dishes — like cassoulet, choucroute, *soupe à l'oignan, cuisses de grenouilles,* pot-au-feu, coq au vin, *côte de boeuf,* and so on. And no brasserie on earth will ever welcome its guests with a warmer sense of hospitality than we will in this establishment.

After an entire year of negotiating with the building's owner, MetLife, we sign a lease and then design a restaurant that will turn out even more beautifully than I'd imagined (Bentel and Bentel architects astonish me with their understanding of the landmark building by creating a place that retires the brass in brasseries). I don't know it yet, but this will become the most expensive restaurant I've ever built, a combination of high design, complicated construction, and the taxing requirements of a space that's on the National Register of Historic Places.

We bring on board a very talented chef, Kerry Heffernan, who deftly updates brasserie fare for the new century ahead of us. It is November 1998 and the restaurant is at last open for guests. The room is stately and stunning, far more urbane than we'd ever dreamed. The restaurant bustles from the outset, attracting early crowds who devour dinners of *frisée aux lardons,* skate *grenobloise,* and chocolate soufflé. Early reviews are in: Eleven Madison Park receives four enthusiastic stars from the *Daily News*; then two middling stars from the *New York Times*; next, a spot on *Esquire*'s list of America's Best New Restaurants; and at last a cover story in the *Wine Spectator* spotlighting New York's best new eateries.

After the early glow subsides, business is solid enough but rarely spectacular. On Monday nights many of the restaurant's 180 seats go empty; each day of the week grows busier, and by Fridays and Saturdays the waitlist for reservations is a mile long. People are trying to tell us something, but we can't quite hear what it is. Why do they love — even crave — the place on date night, and avoid it at the beginning of the week? This is not supposed to have become a special-occasion restaurant, but that is precisely how people are using it.

The ups and downs of business cause a collective adversity that actually invigorates the staff. They become tighter as a family unit because the challenge of inconsistent business is something they are working through together. The staff is strong and talented; their hearts are big. They earn Eleven Madison Park its first James Beard Award, for Outstanding Service in America. Then, with hallowed placement in the Zagat Survey, Eleven Madison Park breaks solidly into the "Top 20" among New Yorkers' Favorite Restaurants.

The restaurant becomes the de facto headquarters for the new Madison Square Park Conservancy — adopting the upkeep and programming of its namesake park as its chief cause. Next it joins the fight against hunger by embracing and supporting the work of Share Our Strength. On September 11, 2001, the restaurant instinctively shifts into active community mode, setting up a makeshift kitchen in the basement of the 69th Regiment Armory to serve emergency meals to the families of victims and early responders.

To be sure, EMP (as it is now lovingly known) has developed a legion of devoted loyalists. But there is an undercurrent of disaffection among some, especially in the "foodie world," who feel it is not living up to its potential. It's neither boisterous nor enough fun to be considered a brasserie. Rather than feeling like an overachieving brasserie, it eats like an underachieving grand restaurant. It seems the restaurant's satisfying comfort food is the wrong piece of art for the grand frame that is the architectural bones of the place. In 2005, the *New York Times* restaurant critic Frank Bruni adds to this sentiment and gives EMP its second two-star review. At least the restaurant has now earned its first four *New York Times* stars: too bad it has taken two reviews from two separate reviewers to achieve them!

There is some good news. By the end of the year, the restaurant has at last paid off its mountain of bank debt — the longest it has ever taken us to reach that milestone. This is the time investors wait for, as cash distributions can at last begin. The new Zagat Survey comes out and the restaurant reaches number 13 among New Yorkers' Favorites — not at all bad considering there are more than 26,000 eating establishments in New York!

However, emboldened to listen to my own gut, I decide that now is the time to start from scratch — to break the vase and form a new one. I ask my business partner, Richard Coraine, to scour the country in search of a chef who still has most of his or her career ahead — and who has the culinary chops necessary to turn jaded New York palates into apostles of EMP. I want to find someone who has never cooked in New York, who has yet to become a household name among its food-obsessed.

Eventually, Richard steers me to one restaurant, San Francisco's Campton Place, where a twenty-nine-year-old Swiss-born chef, Daniel Humm, is turning heads nightly with dishes that appear far simpler than they taste. I visit one night and cut into a pristine but rather plain-looking torchon of foie gras, only to have its center ooze a puddle of unctuous maple syrup. Brilliant. My suckling pig — deboned and reformed into a mini block topped with the finest crackling skin — is alone worth the trip.

Six months of gentle coaxing ensue, after which Daniel Humm chooses at last to move to New York to take over the kitchen at Eleven Madison Park. We hire a new general manager as well — someone who has run one of the country's leading temples of cooking — also from beyond New York. One by one, staff members decamp — leaving just a handful of the originals. Their cheese has been moved in a big way.

We reduce the restaurant's seating count from 180 to 168, and then further to 120 or so. This will help the kitchen to cook at Daniel's level, and it sends a signal to our guests that we mean for the experience to change. This is no longer a neo-brasserie. It is a grand restaurant. Gone are the French fries, the *côte de boeuf* for two, and the sandwiches at lunch. The only food that remains from the original Eleven Madison Park are the delicate *gougères* guests are served alongside their aperitif.

We're convinced it will pay off, because surely this will earn Eleven Madison Park its elusive third star from the *New York Times*; this is how guests have always told us they want to use the restaurant. During Daniel's first weeks he is often despondent — certain that he's made a mistake in coming to New York. The restaurant is too large, New Yorkers don't understand his ways with flavored foams, it's harder than he thought to find cooks who can cook his food, and the growing season for pristine produce is so much longer and better in the Bay Area than it is here.

Daniel respects the restaurant's general manager, but their stylistic chemistry is lacking. I decide to make a management move, and concerned that the restaurant not lose its distinctive culture of generous warmth — even while refining its offerings — I recruit one of our own young stars, twenty-six-year-old Will Guidara, who has worked for us at Tabla (fresh out of Cornell), and later, following a stint outside Union Square Hospitality Group, has opened our very busy and excellent cafes (Cafe 2 and Terrace 5) at the Museum of Modern Art. It takes some serious convincing to get Will to move from the museum to Eleven Madison Park. But after two meetings with Daniel, tasting his food, sizing up his own aspirations, Will chooses his path, and it is EMP.

Within several short months, the restaurant begins to recapture the fancy of foodies. Chefs from other restaurants are showing up for the first time in years. Influentials from the food blogosphere eat and weigh in almost nightly. The *New York Observer* grants EMP a three-and-a-half-star review, and shortly thereafter the restaurant at last earns its first three-star review from Frank Bruni in the *New York Times*. Business heats up and morale soars.

Will and Daniel ask for a meeting with me to describe their boldest plan to date. They show me what it would take to get four stars from the *Times,* shower me with all the reasons it is important to go all the way, and ask for my advice and permission for sharing this with the other Union Square Hospitality Group partners. "This restaurant has never been satisfied with its current point of success. We've always been about endless reinvention. This is our time," they say. The financial projections look solid — if further down the road than we'd all hoped — and I'm completely taken with the notion of reinventing the classic four-star experience for a new generation. Less starch, more human, every bit as delicious.

Around a year before we finally earn that fourth star, the three of us have dinner in Brooklyn one night and discuss a future in which there is even more autonomy — ownership — for Will and Daniel. They want to begin their own restaurant company to do their own thing — but also want to remain at Eleven Madison Park. Our conversations take place with growing frequency over the next months. Their entrepreneurial zeal is exciting to me (having opened Union Square Cafe at age twenty-seven, because I just had to), and I completely understand where they are coming from.

I want them to go for it, to follow their collective passion. But the trouble is that I cannot fathom or square in my mind being colleagues at Eleven Madison Park and rivals elsewhere at the same time. That is not healthy for our relationship, nor is it fair to Eleven Madison Park or its employees. So we talk and talk some more, until finally we conclude that the very best outcome is to take a page from so many great European restaurants — where the original patron hands the restaurant over to his protégé.

The restaurant is ready for its independence, for an autonomous life built upon the character of its family, the thumbprint of its genetic makeup — and the very specific and beautiful personality its leaders, Will and Daniel, have instilled it with. From my viewpoint, my partners and I have done our most responsible jobs as parents, and the proof is in the family celebration acknowledging that Eleven Madison Park is ready to ride forward under the irrepressible and irresistible leadership of Will and Daniel.

The future of Eleven Madison Park is blindingly bright — and so long as it sustains its personality trait of never ever resting on any laurel, I cannot wait to return and return.

In the meantime, you and I have this gorgeous cookbook. Some of us will cook from it; and when we don't, all of us can savor the beauty of Daniel's cooking, which jumps off these pages, and dig into the ongoing story of a dynamic and majestic restaurant.

# HOW TO USE
# THIS BOOK

Over the past two years, as we have been writing this book, the question that has come up most frequently is "Will people actually be able to cook from this book?"

The simple answer is yes-ish.

If you never cook, this is probably a book that should stay on your coffee table. Many recipes require a significant time commitment, a certain level of skill, a reasonably equipped kitchen, and a healthy dose of persistence.

That said, every recipe has been tested multiple times both by members of our team and by friends of the restaurant. If you follow them exactly, they will work, and you will be rewarded for your efforts.

A few notes to help you navigate:

The recipes are organized by season and are intended to be cooked in the season in which they're presented. Some of these seasonal ingredients can be difficult to locate, although we have listed sources in the back to facilitate your search. Others, including edible flowers, wild herbs, and other garnishes, accentuate a dish but certainly aren't essential.

The portions of each recipe are sized to be a part of a multicourse meal. Each recipe serves eight. If you intend to serve any of these dishes on their own, or as a part of a shorter meal, the recipe will serve four.

In the back of the book are recipes for all of the "basics," which are referenced in nearly every recipe. These encompass the building blocks of our food and include pickles, oils, dressings, gels, purees, stocks, jus, smoked items, crumbles, granolas, doughs, sorbets, ice creams, and butters.

If you are not feeling ambitious enough to attempt one of these recipes in its entirety, you can still make a great dish even if you omit one or two components. Many of the dishes have several variations on a single ingredient, and no one will judge you if you choose to make only a few. Additionally, feel free to treat any of the "basics" in the back of the book as individual recipes to be used in dishes of your own.

*Sous vide* means "under vacuum." It requires two pieces of equipment: a Cryovac machine and an immersion circulator. Sources for both can be found in the back of this book. In the restaurant, we use *sous vide* quite a bit, at times because it ensures consistency, in other cases because it yields a better result. Throughout the book, where possible, we have recommended suitable alternatives to *sous vide* cooking. In cases where we haven't, it's because the recipe truly requires the technique.

Cooking *sous vide* can raise certain safety concerns. In order to avoid the risk of bacteria-related illnesses in those recipes that call for *sous vide* preparation, cook all meats at the specified temperatures for the specified amount of time.

A few of the recipes call for the use of liquid nitrogen to freeze things very quickly. When possible, we've included an alternate technique. To acquire liquid nitrogen, contact an industrial gas supplier. They will often rent you an insulated dewar, which is necessary to hold the nitrogen. Because liquid nitrogen is so cold (-321°F), it can cause very serious burns. Use care and wear goggles when handling it. Avoid using glass bowls, as they can break from the shock. Carefully transfer the liquid nitrogen to an insulated container (such as a Styrofoam cooler) instead of working with it directly from the dewar. Do not store the liquid nitrogen in a fully sealed container, as the pressure from the gas can build quickly and cause a sealed container to explode.

Bitter almonds, their seeds, and extracts can be poisonous if not processed to remove toxic chemicals. Obtain processed bitter almonds for culinary use from a reliable source, such as those listed in the back of the book.

Unless otherwise stated, rely on the following rules:

Eggs are extra large and organic
Butter is unsalted
Flour is all-purpose
Sugar is granulated
Herbs are fresh
Salt is kosher
Pepper is ground fresh
Wine is dry
Gelatin is gold
Cream is heavy
Milk is whole
Foie gras is grade-A duck (about 2 pounds)

We have often listed specific quantities of salt in the recipes. However, seasoning is a personal thing. Feel free to use more or less, based on your palate.

Finally, if at any point you are confused, frustrated, or require further clarification on any of these recipes, feel free to send us an email at cookbook@elevenmadisonpark.com. We are here if you need us.

MILES DAVIS

IN THE SUMMER OF 2006, Daniel and I got together for dinner at a restaurant called Crispo on West 14th Street in New York City. It wasn't the first time we had met, but we were no more than acquaintances up to that point. Now, as the idea of joining him at Eleven Madison Park was officially on the table, it was time to get to know one another.

DANIEL WAS BORN IN 1976 in Strengelbach, Switzerland, and grew up in a small town just outside of Zurich. He has had a passion for food his entire life. As a child, he shopped at the produce market with his mother, Brigitte, who would cook both lunch and dinner for the entire family every day. He always loved it there, the frenetic energy, the constantly changing selection of fresh fruits and vegetables. The farmers were kind to him and would give him tastes of all the different foods, slices of apples and peaches, teaching him what they were and how to know when they were perfectly ripe. When he was eight years old, he started spending his summers helping out around that market, arriving at 4:00 a.m. to greet the delivery trucks from Italy, Spain, France, Germany, and Holland, pushing carts filled with their goods from one stand to another. His relationships with the farmers slowly turned into friendships, and his next summers were spent working with them on their farms. He would pick cherries and strawberries, apples and walnuts. He learned to milk cows.

At age eleven, he turned to kitchens to fill his summers and secured his first position as a commis. Watching the cooks work with the same food that he had been helping to grow on the farms just one year earlier fascinated him, and he immediately fell in love. This made his father incredibly nervous. Roland was an amazing role model, a hardworking architect in Zurich, and was responsible for instilling that same work ethic and a sense for quality in Daniel at an early age. Although he always taught Daniel that the most important part of a job was really loving it, he never saw cooking as a real profession. He desperately wanted Daniel to follow in his footsteps, insisting that he accept an internship at his firm one year and at another local architecture firm the next. But it didn't take; office life definitely did not suit Daniel. He could never sit still for that long. He longed to return to restaurants. He didn't seem to like anything else.

He especially didn't like school. In Switzerland, at age fifteen, students decide between two paths — either to continue with formal schooling or select a trade and pursue an apprenticeship, a three-year program in which they work four days a week and go to classes on the fifth. By that age, Daniel had been focusing so much of his attention on the kitchen that his grades had suffered, to the extent that continuing with formal schooling was no longer an option. The only thing he could do was pursue an apprenticeship in cooking. His life as a chef had officially begun.

It was during this same time that Daniel joined the Junior Swiss National Mountain Biking Team. He has always been a serious athlete, and the four years of intensive training he was put through while on that team helped give him the discipline and endurance required for the long hours he was spending in the kitchen. Eventually, he had to choose between the two paths, and he left the team to focus on cooking, though to this day he continues to be a competitive athlete.

For Daniel's apprenticeship, he chose the Kurhotel im Park in Schinznach-Bad, where he worked through every station of its restaurant kitchen, applying himself in a way he never had before. At the end of the three-year apprenticeship, he faced a week of testing before graduation. Daniel, someone who had never gotten better than a C in any of his "regular" classes, did better on that test than anyone else in the entire country that year.

He spent the next few years working in Relais & Chateaux and other five-star hotels throughout Switzerland before finally landing a job with Gérard Rabaey at his three–Michelin star Le Pont de Brent on Lake Geneva, where Daniel would spend the next few years of his life.

It was not easy. Daniel worked eighteen hours each day and lived with other cooks a few blocks away from the restaurant in housing arranged by the chef. The restaurant was his entire life. He did nothing but work. It was physically and emotionally exhausting — his hands swelled from butchering fish, his head pounded from constantly getting screamed at — and all for very little money. There were times he considered walking away, but his passion for cooking, and his need to prove his father wrong, made it impossible for him to quit. Thankfully he didn't, because in those years he developed the foundation upon which he would build his career as a chef. Rabaey was a machine who worked constantly and never compromised on anything. Daniel learned about organization and precision, seeing for the first time what it really meant to be committed to excellence.

After that experience, however, he was burned out and decided to "take some time off" by accepting his first chef job at a small country restaurant called Gasthaus zum Gupf. It was a forty-five-seat restaurant whose aspirations were much different from those at Le Pont de Brent. It was a simple place. It didn't exist for the sake of stars or accolades.

Daniel settled in gently. He didn't try to reshape the cuisine, but he put many of the lessons he had just learned to work — refining the menu as opposed to reshaping it. He was also learning how to be a chef for the first time, managing a team of people, learning the challenges of being in charge. While it was in no way easy, things were somewhat relaxed; there was much less pressure.

Then suddenly — and to this day Daniel isn't sure how it happened — people started to take notice. Just eight months after his arrival at this small restaurant in the middle of the Swiss Alps, Daniel earned his first Michelin star and was named Discovery of the Year by Gault Millau, the most respected restaurant guide in Switzerland. Immediately, a restaurant that was hardly on the map was full every single night, with gourmands from all over the country coming to see what the fuss was about.

With the increased attention came much higher expectations, which Daniel wanted to live up to. He realized that the menu needed to evolve, that the time to relax was over, and that he needed to step it up. Taking that country menu and truly reshaping it into his own is how Daniel really began to develop his culinary style.

About a year later the next major change in his life took place, coming in the form of a man named Paul Zuest. Paul is from Switzerland but has run hotels in America for years. At the time, he was running Campton Place Hotel in San Francisco, whose restaurant needed a new chef. Campton Place restaurant had been home to some star chefs over the years — Bradley Ogden, Laurent Manrique, Todd Humphies, Jan Birnbaum — and he wanted to continue the legacy. He began a search for someone young and talented who could take the helm.

Through a friend of his, Hans-Jörg Schmid, a regular at Gasthaus zum Gupf, Paul found Daniel. Daniel was skiing with his parents when he received the call. Paul quickly introduced himself and asked Daniel if he wanted to move to California. Daniel's instinct was to politely decline. He had never imagined living in America, didn't speak a word of English, and things in Switzerland were going really well. Paul, however, proved to be persistent, and he eventually convinced Daniel to visit California and check things out.

Over the course of a week Paul introduced Daniel to San Francisco. The two explored the city; spent time at the Campton Place; ate at Chez Panisse, Michael Mina, and Gary Danko and traveled to Napa Valley for a meal at the French Laundry. Daniel fell in love.

In July 2003 Daniel got a one-year J1 student visa and moved to America. Things at Campton Place happened in much the same way as they had in Switzerland. People immediately took notice of the changes at the restaurant and there was an excitement in the city about the new Swiss chef. Shortly after his arrival, Daniel was named a *Food & Wine* magazine Best New Chef, and Michael Bauer of the *San Francisco Chronicle* re-reviewed the restaurant, elevating it from two to three and a half out of four stars. The buzz about Campton Place had started and the dining room was full.

Over the course of the next year, the restaurant did anything but slow its pace. People traveled from across the country to taste Daniel's food, to experience his bold flavors and his melding of modern and classic techniques. With things in the kitchen continuing to heat up came the necessity for things in the dining room to follow suit. The restaurant strove to push itself to evolve, to elevate the service to the same level as the food, to constantly and persistently improve. And improve they did, so much so that Michael Bauer had no choice but to return. In August 2005, just two years after his previous review, he gave Campton Place four stars, saying that Daniel was "the brightest star to arrive in California since Thomas Keller." It was big news in the culinary world. The restaurant exploded overnight.

It was actually just a few weeks before that review came out that Danny Meyer's longtime business partner, Richard Coraine, sat down for dinner in the dining room at Campton Place. Danny had recently decided that Eleven Madison Park needed to be reborn. The restaurant had been a commercial success for seven years, having been conceived to be a New York brasserie, tipping its hat both to Paris and to New York at the turn of the past century.

Eleven Madison Park's early success (including the James Beard Award for Outstanding Service in America) established it as one of the most popular restaurants in New York. But being an award-winning brasserie wasn't enough. The restaurant's majestic design, urbane setting, and gorgeous architectural bones fueled a growing desire on the part of the dining public that the restaurant offer a far grander and more refined dining experience. In order to achieve that level, many elements of this evolving restaurant would have to change. It would have to create for itself a new identity, one that would maintain its place

as a beloved New York eatery and that would also give it the capability to sail into uncharted waters.

Danny's sense was that the chef to lead that charge was not currently cooking in New York, and he assigned Richard the task of searching America to find him. Richard visited nearly forty restaurants in four months, traveling to Boston, Philadelphia, Virginia, South Carolina, Atlanta, Miami, Chicago, New Orleans, Dallas, Houston, Denver, Phoenix, Las Vegas, and Los Angeles before finally landing in San Francisco. There, he visited seven restaurants in three days, and on his last night in the city he showed up at Campton Place for a 10:00 p.m. reservation. He ordered the tasting menu but knew that his search was over by the second course. He called Danny at 2:00 a.m. to give the news. Just a week later, Danny flew out to San Francisco to see for himself. In January 2006, Daniel moved to New York.

The move to Eleven Madison Park was the hardest transition of Daniel's career. With a restaurant that was much bigger than he was used to, more than three times the size of Campton Place, he immediately felt overwhelmed. Additionally, the kitchen staff he inherited was not trained to cook food of his caliber, and with a dining room that was always busy, there never seemed to be enough time to do anything about it. The pressure of New York was intense; its spotlight was harsh and unforgiving. Many times within the first year he wondered whether he had made a mistake.

With time, it also became clear that Daniel didn't have the partner he needed to move the restaurant forward. He needed someone in the dining room who shared his level of ambition, someone whose desire to create something imaginative and exceptional would fuel the restaurant from within. Just a few months after Daniel's arrival, the search for a new general manager who could embody this need began. Danny's restaurants have always been rooted in the culture of the company, a culture that can't be learned overnight. Whenever possible, he always looks to hire from within. Danny asked Daniel if there was anyone in the company he would be interested in working with. Daniel's response, even though we had met only fleetingly, was "What about Will?"

**I WAS BORN AND RAISED** in Sleepy Hollow, New York. With the exception of a brief interest in becoming an astronaut and a lifetime love for the drums, I've always known I wanted to be in the restaurant business. My dad, Frank, is an exceptional restaurateur, and when I was young he would take me to work on the weekends, always leaving me with one of the cooks or servers, who would give me some basic task to keep me busy and out of the way. It was the energy of restaurants that attracted me, with people everywhere busily and collectively working to create an experience. When I was old enough, I started getting real restaurant jobs each summer — running food, busing tables, cooking, hosting, and so on.

By the end of high school I had no doubt that the restaurant business was for me, and I enrolled at Cornell University's Hotel School. In spite of the bitterly cold winters in Ithaca, New York, I loved my four years there and all of the opportunities that the university presented to me. I spent a summer as a busboy at Spago Beverly Hills and another as a server at Tribeca Grill. As graduation drew near, I knew that I wanted to move to New York City to work in a restaurant, but I wasn't sure which

one. So my friend Brian Canlis and I traveled to the city and spent an entire day going from restaurant to restaurant.

We worked our way uptown from Tribeca, having a snack or a glass of wine at each place before moving on. We stopped at Nobu, Montrachet, Chanterelle, Zoë, Gotham Bar and Grill, Gramercy Tavern, Union Pacific, Tabla and Eleven Madison Park (neighboring Danny Meyer restaurants), Alain Ducasse, Daniel, Café des Artistes, and more. Of the group, something about Tabla and Eleven Madison Park stood out. It felt natural for me to be in their dining rooms.

I returned to school excited to learn more about them and for the first time started getting to know who Danny Meyer was. It didn't take me long to realize that he was the guy I wanted to work for. I made several calls until I was able to land an interview with the same person who would find Daniel just a few years later, Richard Coraine.

Ironically, my interview with Richard took place at Eleven Madison Park, though he ended up offering me a job at Tabla. I was twenty-one years old working in one of New York's hottest restaurants. I worked for two years as a maitre d' at Tabla, learning about Danny's approach to hospitality and loving every minute of it. But I knew I needed to learn the business side of restaurants as well, and eventually I moved on to become a purchaser and then a financial controller at a much larger, more corporate company called Restaurant Associates. My passion was never in accounting, but my time there was instrumental in building my foundation.

A couple of years later, I ran into Danny in Union Square on a day off. That brief conversation on the street led to another in which Danny presented me with the opportunity to help open the restaurants at the Museum of Modern Art. I loved working in that environment. It was unbelievably stimulating to be surrounded by art, even though I knew very little about it. The constantly changing exhibits, the cinema, the permanent collection, all inspired me to take a more creative approach to everything I was doing.

As with any opening, it was intense in the beginning. But, in the interest of full disclosure, life got pretty cushy after a few years. As far as restaurant jobs go, I wasn't working that much; things were running incredibly smoothly; I had most nights free. But that summer, in 2006, Danny asked me to sit down to discuss a new opportunity he wanted me to consider: to become the general manager of Eleven Madison Park, where Daniel Humm had just taken over the kitchen.

**THE DINNER AT CRISPO WAS FANTASTIC.** Straightaway we realized that we have a mutual love of pasta, and we gorged on it that night. As we got to know each other, we understood that in spite of our many differences we actually have a lot in common. We discussed our individual aspirations and what we each imagined for Eleven Madison Park. Daniel was engaging, his passion palpable, and we talked for hours. At around 4:00 a.m., while drinking beers at a Dominican bar just down the street, we decided we would give it a go.

There was a synergy between Daniel and me from day one, and we immediately started making progress. Just months after we began working together, we received our first review, written by Moira Hodgson in the *New York Observer*. It was really good. In it she acknowledged

that a significant shift had taken place at the restaurant, that exciting things were afoot. But right at the end, she said that the restaurant needed "a bit of Miles Davis." We love jazz, most music for that matter, so something about this comment resonated with us, even though we had absolutely no idea what she meant.

Her review actually came at the perfect time. We knew that we wanted to change a lot about the restaurant, but we had yet to develop a true direction. We knew that we wanted to be better — we had aspirations of getting four stars in the *New York Times,* of becoming one of the best restaurants in New York — but that was all we knew. In the beginning, that was enough, and many of the decisions were obvious. We knew we needed to reduce the number of seats, to heighten the level of service, to change the menu, to train the cooks, to change the china, the glassware, the silver . . . these things were clear. But to continue to evolve, we were going to need a better sense of what exactly we wanted to be. We needed language to help define our culture and guide the many changes we were about to make. Moira had presented us with a gift.

We started listening to a lot more Miles Davis and began to realize what an amazing career he had had and the impact he had made on jazz. He approached music with a completely fresh perspective. He knew all the rules but selectively broke them. He was technically perfect but always added a sense of himself to the music. Moreover, with each consecutive album, he seemed to reinvent himself. After the success of *Kind of Blue,* he could have continued recording albums just like it for the rest of his career. But instead, in the years that followed, he started experimenting with electric jazz, completely changing, and challenging, the listening experience. The fact that the same person who recorded *Kind of Blue* later recorded *Bitches Brew* is almost inconceivable. Miles was the man.

We started reading as many articles as we could find about Miles and eventually came up with a list of the eleven words we found most commonly used to describe him. This list included: Cool, Endless Reinvention, Inspired, Forward Moving, Fresh, Collaborative, Spontaneous, Vibrant, Adventurous, Light, and Innovative. That list became our inspiration. We printed a large sign with the words and our logo and placed it in our office, where it still hangs today. In brainstorming ideas we continue to reference those words. They hold us accountable; we look at them every single day. Miles Davis became a significant part of our foundation.

# COLLABORATIVE

AFTER FINDING INSPIRATION from Miles Davis, and the list of words that described him, we realized that there was merit in looking in other unexpected places. We started by studying the success of some of the corporate giants we were most drawn to: Apple, American Express, JetBlue. With our list of words in mind, we tried to figure out what it was that made these companies great.

The first of the words that jumped out at us was "collaborative." It was almost as if that word were the key to all the others on the list. We found that each of these companies would, to varying degrees, get a collection of people together for strategic planning, to consider their future, to decide where they wanted to go and what they needed to do to get there. Then we looked at our team, our *entire* team, and started to wonder why it had taken us so long to figure this out. There we were, surrounded by so many young, bright, and energetic people, yet we had never allowed them to have an organized voice. We started to imagine what we would be capable of accomplishing if we did; it was a pretty powerful idea.

So in January 2007, we started doing what so many had done before us. We held our first planning meeting, where all 140 members of our team got together during the first week of the year. While each consecutive year would have a mission statement, this first year simply posed a question: what do we want to embody? We needed to define our core values, to determine our nonnegotiables, to figure out what it was that we wanted to represent.

We split the team into ten groups spread throughout our dining room, challenging each to brainstorm. Each gathered around a notebook, frantically writing down ideas, getting excited by some, arguing about others. Daniel and I spent the day walking from group to group, listening to their respective processes, careful not to contribute — this was their time.

Eight hours went by, and at the end of that afternoon, as each group presented their thoughts, it was clear that it had worked. We came up with a list of four words: hospitality, excellence, education, and passion. Not one of them, on its own, was groundbreaking, but if we could embody them all simultaneously, we would be capable of doing great things.

## HOSPITALITY

When we talk about hospitality we talk about *genuine* hospitality, about the idea that we want to be a group of people who derive true pleasure from doing nice things for others — not for financial gain, or some sort of karmic bump, but just because the act itself makes our days better. We often reference the idea of running up the street to pick up and return someone's dropped scarf and the unbelievable ability that has to brighten your day.

## EXCELLENCE

We define excellence as being the culmination of thousands of details executed perfectly. We understand that true perfection is unattainable. But rather than be discouraged by that fact, we find inspiration in trying to get as close to it as possible. We also believe that excellence comes with accountability and that in order to improve it is our job to help hold one another to the highest standard possible. One of the first English phrases that Daniel learned after moving to America was "Make it nice." It was the way he first learned to communicate the idea of striving for excellence. This phrase has grown to be a big part of our culture, and a sign with those three words hangs in our kitchen. We say it to one another constantly.

## EDUCATION

We serve doctors and lawyers and bankers every day, all of whom require secondary or tertiary education to do what they do, neither of which is required in the restaurant business. But we decided that we would make Eleven Madison Park into our graduate school, building a culture of education — based on both teaching and learning. For it to be sustainable, it would require everyone on the team to contribute. If all of us focused on learning from one another, and on teaching one another, we could all grow exponentially.

## PASSION

Nothing is more motivating than passion. It is the thing that compels people to be hospitable, to strive for excellence, and to constantly look to learn, not because these are part of their job but because they are naturally inclined to pursue them on their own. What we do is like running a marathon, except it never ends, and there is an entire team of people running together. This can slow you down, but if everyone truly believes in the spirit of the endeavor, such that when one person gets tired the rest of the group helps to pick them up, it can make you move so much more quickly.

WE ALSO TALKED ABOUT NOBILITY, and the sense of it that we had started to feel. Too often the restaurant business is seen as a lesser profession, with parents lamenting when their children decide to pursue it as a career, or with some guests looking down on their waitstaff. That day we realized that what we were doing was noble. Restaurants are an art form, both theatrical and visual. When approached the right way, they enable you to enrich people's lives, either by creating one of their most lasting memories or in giving them a break from their reality. This was some heavy stuff, and with it came a sense of responsibility and pride.

Finally, at the end of the meeting, after the staff had left, we took our entire management team for Korean fried chicken just up the block at a place called Mad for Chicken. Our first visit there was amusing. It is located in what looks and feels like a random apartment building on Fifth Avenue. We walked in, found that the elevator was broken, walked up two flights of stairs, and opened a random door to find a fairly modern and bustling fried-chicken restaurant and bar. We went through several buckets of chicken and more OB Lager than I care to remember. We exchanged stories about the day, talked about the people whose enthusiasm had surprised us, argued over who came up with one idea or another. It was my first time eating Korean fried chicken but certainly not my last; we have been back every year since.

It's probably clear at this point that the meeting got us pretty fired up. Spending a day together, all of us, talking about what we wanted to become . . . we couldn't wait to get started. We immediately began functioning on a whole new level, with the entire team working together

in a much more integrated and passionate way. In our pursuit of education we started a series of classes on Wednesday afternoons called Happy Hour, in which each week we would slightly intoxicate ourselves learning about wines, spirits, and beers. We started another program called Notes from the Kitchen, in which each week someone from the staff was assigned a farm, ingredient, or technique. He or she would then write a paper about it and present it to the entire team before service on Saturday night.

Several wine-tasting groups were established, meeting nearly every day of the week in the morning before lunch service. We arranged regularly scheduled field trips to local farms, wineries, and breweries, where our team would get to bond while learning about the products we were serving. We started writing the first of what would become a series of magazines for our guests — educational newsletters of a sort, written and edited by several members of our team and exploring one topic at a time, whether related to wine, cocktails, or food. All of these programs still exist, and in the time since we have started many more.

**IN THE TRUE SPIRIT OF COLLABORATION,** we started an ownership program. We found that our team craved more influence over the direction of the restaurant, and with our ambitious goals, we knew we needed everyone's involvement and help. We also recognized the degree to which feeling a sense of ownership can motivate people to work that much harder. Danny always gave us complete autonomy, and it inspired to invest ourselves completely in the restaurant.

Although initially hesitant, as we are each a bit controlling, we decided to trust in the power of delegation and we empowered our team. We relinquished control over many areas of the restaurant — the beer program, the spirits program, the cheese program, team building, linens, music, coffee, tea, china, glass, silver, recipe testing. The list goes on. We were still involved in everything, but we gave autonomy, inspiring each to strive to make their area of ownership the best it could be.

Suddenly, by increasing the number of people with control over all the different areas of the restaurant, we found ourselves capable of doing much more, and doing it all much better. One of our assistant servers, who was running the tea program, flew herself to Las Vegas to attend the World Tea Expo. The kitchen server in charge of the beer program did an internship at Sixpoint brewery in Brooklyn. One of the owners of the liquor program engaged a team to work with a local distillery in making our own bitters.

All of these changes began to take place in the month following the meeting, and during that same time we received a piece of positive affirmation — our first re-review by Frank Bruni in the *New York Times,* in which we received three stars. This was Frank Bruni's second review of the restaurant; the first came before our arrival in February 2005, when he had given the restaurant two stars.

The three-star review was gratifying and, for the first time, showed that our work was starting to pay off. It acknowledged the change in the food as being the reason for the re-review. Bruni said that meals at the restaurant had "hit highs they never came close to in the past." It felt good, and although we knew that three stars was not our destination, it showed that the city was starting to take notice of what we were up to. That night, we began a tradition that we have diligently maintained ever since: we threw a giant party to celebrate.

**WE LOVE PARTIES.** There are few things better than loosening our ties, drinking copious amounts of Champagne, and listening to loud music long after the last guest has left the dining room. We are a very young group of people. At the time most of us were in our twenties, younger than many would expect to be running a restaurant like Eleven Madison Park. While we take what we do very seriously, we try not to take ourselves too seriously. We work hard, but we also play hard, and whenever there is an excuse to have a good time, whether it is to celebrate our successes or to console ourselves when things just don't work out, we take it.

It feels really good when our entire team can raise a glass, maybe get a little out of control, and act our age.

**IN FACT, IT WAS ONLY A FEW MONTHS LATER,** in June, when we found ourselves doing it again. Daniel, then twenty-nine, had been nominated by the James Beard Foundation for Rising Star Chef of the Year, an award you can win only while in your twenties. We were thrilled to see him on the list and weeks in advance made the arrangements to attend. Daniel and I put on our tuxedos, had a glass of Champagne in our bar, and headed uptown to Lincoln Center for our first outing as a team.

It's an overwhelming scene, going to the awards. You walk up the red carpet alongside all the people you have looked up to your entire career. It's difficult to feel as though you belong when you are in the presence of the likes of Thomas Keller, Jean-Georges Vongerichten, Eric Ripert, and many other prominent chefs. Camera flashes were going off all around us as photographers from every major press outlet documented the evening.

It's important to note that none of them were taking *our* pictures, but it was exhilarating nonetheless. We wanted to win badly, not only for Daniel but for the entire restaurant. We wanted something to continue the momentum we had gained from the review months earlier, and we truly believed he deserved it. We waited patiently for the ceremony to begin, as Rising Star Chef is the first award to be announced. We were confident but incredibly nervous. When the envelope was finally opened and the announcement made, we experienced our first real disappointment.

The first time you deal with adversity is a defining moment, because the way you react says a lot about your character. Daniel had lost, and it didn't feel good. But one of our regulars once told us that he liked to drink his best bottles of wine on his worst days, rather than the other way around, because they helped to cheer him up. That idea has always resonated with us. In an effort not only to console ourselves but also to celebrate how close we had come to winning, we did what we had done just a few months earlier when we were feeling great. We threw another party.

We headed back downtown. Richard Coraine, one of the partners in the restaurant, took the keys to the wine cellar and started opening bottles. Our sommeliers were sabering bottles of Champagne, and Daniel Boulud was in the kitchen roasting foie gras. Nearly everyone we knew stopped by. It was a night to remember. Our entire team celebrated late into that night in spite of the defeat. It was one of the most significant bonding moments we've had.

Once we cleaned up the restaurant and reopened for service, we remembered that things were actually going quite well. With the *Times* review, the Beard nomination, and general excitement by word of mouth, the dining room was full most nights and we were having

small restaurant that was mostly empty but looked promising, so we gave it a try. It was the most unassuming of the restaurants we visited. We had some cured meats, a few pastas, and a couple of good bottles of wine. As the meal was winding down, the owner of the restaurant came to the table with a bottle of grappa and some glasses. He poured just a bit for each of us, left the bottle on the table, and, in his broken English, told us it was a gift from him, that we should drink as much as we'd like.

He didn't know who we were. He was just giving a gift to a few foreigners who had walked into his restaurant. We sat there for a few more hours, passing the bottle around the table, telling stories, brainstorming ideas for Eleven Madison Park, and enjoying one another's company. In spite of the fact that we were thousands of miles from New York City, it felt like we were at home.

We wanted to re-create this feeling in the restaurant, and it was the first idea that we implemented when we got back. Throughout a meal in our dining room, our team of servers works hard to ensure that the guest hardly has to raise a finger. We are always there to pour more wine, to provide you with everything you need to enjoy your meal. However, at the very end of the meal we bring a bottle of a local eau-de-vie or some other digestif to the table, pouring only a taste for each guest, leaving the bottle on the table, and encouraging guests to help themselves to as much as they like. We learned that night in Alba that the sense of graciousness, community, and comfort that comes with passing a bottle around the table is palpable. We love making that one of the lasting memories of a dinner at Eleven Madison Park.

**THE HOLIDAY SEASON IN NEW YORK CITY** is the busiest time of the year for restaurants, and things at Eleven Madison were booming. It was the last season before the recession started, people were ordering big wines, the private dining rooms were full every night. Times were good, and before we knew it the year was over. In November, however, something significant happened: we opened for Thanksgiving for the first time ever.

The decision was first made for financial reasons. We wanted to close for the first few days of January, and in order to do so we needed to make up for the lost revenue. However, we ended up discovering that spending that holiday together also had a profound impact on the culture of the restaurant.

Since so many of us lived so far away from our families, Thanksgiving had a tendency to be a lonely day. Spending it together with a group of people who were starting to feel like family, in spite of the fact that we were at work, felt really good. The kitchen made sure to have plenty of leftovers, and that night, after the last guest left the restaurant, we sat down for our Thanksgiving dinner. We opened several bottles of wine, put on some music, took over the dining room, and ate and drank together for hours.

While we spend a lot of time together both in and out of the restaurant, it was the first time we had ever sat down, all of us together, for a real dinner. It was great. Staff meals in restaurants are often called "family meals." That Thanksgiving was the first time that the name seemed totally appropriate. It's become one of our favorite traditions.

the best financial year the restaurant had ever had. Things were smooth enough that we were able to break away for a couple of weeks, the start of another tradition: taking a vacation.

Each year, Daniel and I take a trip together. It's a chance to get inspired by what other people around the world are doing, to be able to think about the restaurant without the distractions of the day-to-day, to continue to get to know each other so that we can continue growing as a team, and just to have a good time. This first trip was to Piedmont for truffle season. We went with both our executive sous chef and wine director at the time, Jason Franey and John Ragan. In addition to consuming more white truffles in one week than we could possibly have prepared ourselves for, we visited the wineries and homes of some of the great Barolo producers: an afternoon with Maria-Teresa Mascarello, a morning tasting with Antonio Gaja, a decadent dinner with Roberto Conterno. We ate at some memorable restaurants — fire-roasted goat at the eccentric Da Cesare, a multicourse lunch with the chef in the kitchen at La Ciau del Tornavento. We even spent a rather hazy night or two at Alba's only nightclub.

One evening, we went into town to find a place to eat. We found a

# SPRING

*For me, spring has always represented a new beginning — fresh ideas, inspiration, and renewed focus. Each April, as the weather starts to turn, I get excited about the new menu, going to the greenmarket each week, talking to the farmers, anxiously awaiting the first green asparagus, garden peas, and ramps.*

*Our inspirations come from everywhere: classic dishes, the change in seasons, traveling around the world, walking through the market, even from a color, an experience, a memory, or something I learned from my mentor, Gérard Rabaey.*

*Our baked potato is very classic. It's served with caviar, crème fraîche, and chives, but in an unfamiliar way. Our garden peas are about the transition from winter into spring, with the pea soup representing rebirth and the buttermilk a late snowfall.*

*Traveling to Spain when I was younger, and eating gazpacho later, led us to our version of the soup with strawberries. Seeing fresh farm eggs at the Union Square Greenmarket, I started to imagine how to serve them: ramps…frogs legs…the color green…jamón Ibérico.*

*My first chef job was at Gasthaus zum Gupf, in Switzerland, where we had our own suckling pig farm and had to use the entire animal, an experience that inspired me to create a tasting menu devoted to suckling pig at Eleven Madison. I have fond memories from growing up of drinking a glass of warm milk with a spoonful of honey before bed. We reimagined it as a dessert. And as for my mentor, the turbot is an homage to him. We use all sorts of peas. I remember his love for all their variations. Every morning, he was the first at the market so he could get the smallest and sweetest garden peas, sugar snap peas, and snow peas.*

| POTATO | GARDEN PEA | STRAWBERRY | IBÉRICO HAM |
| ASPARAGUS | CRAB | TUNA | FOIE GRAS |
| EGG | RICOTTA | TURBOT | SKATE |
| JOHN DORY | LANGOUSTINE | LOBSTER | POUSSIN |
| RABBIT | CHICKEN | SUCKLING PIG | VEAL |
| BEEF | LAMB | CHÈVRE | RHUBARB |
| MILK | FRAIS DES BOIS | MINT | CHOCOLATE |

# HORS D'ŒUVRES

STURGEON SABAYON
323

LOLLIPOPS
322

ASPARAGUS AND CAVIAR
323

BUTTER RADISHES
323

FOIE GRAS SABLÉ WITH STRAWBERRY
324

ASPARAGUS AND CRAB
325

# POTATO
## ICE CREAM WITH CRÈME FRAÎCHE AND OSETRA CAVIAR

*Serves 8*

### POTATO CHIPS

1 large Yukon Gold potato
2 tablespoons Clarified Butter (see page 370)
1 1/2 teaspoons salt

Thinly slice the potato using a French mandoline with a wavy blade. To create a waffled chip, slice the potato once, turn it 90 degrees, and slice again. Repeat. Cut each slice with a ring cutter, approximately 1 inch in diameter. Place the potato slices in ice water for about an hour to rid them of any excess starch and to prevent oxidation.

Preheat the oven to 380°F. Remove the potatoes from the water and pat dry using a kitchen towel. Turn over a rimmed baking sheet and line the underside with parchment paper. Lay the potato slices on the parchment paper and brush lightly with the Clarified Butter. Cover with another piece of parchment paper and place another rimmed baking sheet, right side up, on top of the potatoes. Weigh down with a cast-iron skillet to keep the potatoes flat. Bake for 10 minutes or until golden brown. Remove from the oven and allow the potatoes to cool between the pans before seasoning with salt.

### WHIPPED CRÈME FRAÎCHE

1 cup crème fraîche
1 teaspoon salt
1 teaspoon lime juice

Place the crème fraîche, salt, and lime juice in a bowl set over ice or in the cold bowl of a stand mixer. Whip for 4 minutes or until the crème fraîche stands at a soft peak.

### TO FINISH

Whipped Crème Fraîche
4 ounces osetra caviar
Potato Ice Cream (see page 369)
16 chive tips
16 chive blossoms
Potato Chips

Scoop 1 teaspoon of Whipped Crème Fraîche onto a plate. Using the side of a spoon, drag the Crème Fraîche across the plate. On top of the Crème Fraîche, place 1 quenelle of caviar (1/2 ounce) and 1 quenelle of Potato Ice Cream side by side. Garnish with 2 chive tips, 2 chive blossoms, and a Potato Chip. Repeat with the remaining ingredients, to serve 8.

# GARDEN PEA
## CHILLED SOUP WITH MINT, BUTTERMILK, AND PROSCIUTTO

*Serves 8*

**PEA SOUP**

1/2 cup chopped scallions, green parts only
4 cups shelled English peas
1 cup buttermilk
4 tablespoons olive oil
2 tablespoons salt
10 leaves mint

Bring a large pot of salted water to a boil. Add the scallions and cook for about 30 seconds. Using a slotted spoon, transfer them to a bowl of ice water, and drain. Add the peas to the boiling water and cook for 3 to 4 minutes. Transfer to a bowl of ice water and drain. In a blender, puree the scallions with the peas, buttermilk, olive oil, salt, mint leaves, and 6 cups water. Blend on high until smooth and then pass through a chinois. Chill over ice and then refrigerate.

**BUTTERMILK SNOW**

1 quart buttermilk
1 1/2 tablespoons salt
1 pinch cayenne pepper
Liquid nitrogen (optional)

In a mixing bowl, combine the buttermilk with the salt and cayenne. Line a large metal bowl with acetate. Fill the bowl halfway with liquid nitrogen and then carefully pour the buttermilk into the liquid nitrogen. As it freezes it will start to become brittle. Quickly transfer the frozen buttermilk to a food processor and grind. The finished Buttermilk Snow will be powdery. Reserve in the freezer.

Alternatively, pour the buttermilk-and-cayenne mixture into a pan and freeze until completely solid. When ready to serve, scrape the frozen buttermilk with a fork to create the Buttermilk Snow.

**PROSCIUTTO BUTTER**

1 cup prosciutto trimmings
2 pounds butter

In a small pot over medium-low heat, render the prosciutto trimmings until all of the fat has been released. Add the butter and bring to 160°F. Steep for 2 hours in a warm place, such as near a warm oven or stove. Strain and keep warm.

**PROSCIUTTO CRISPS**

10 brick dough sheets
2 cups melted Prosciutto Butter
1 pound prosciutto, sliced paper thin

Brush 1 side of a brick dough sheet with the Prosciutto Butter. Place 5 slices of the prosciutto in the middle of the sheet, leaving 1 inch around the edges. Place another sheet of brick dough on top, forming a sandwich, and brush with Prosciutto Butter once again. Repeat with the remaining 8 sheets of brick dough to create 4 more sandwiches. Refrigerate for 1 hour to set the Prosciutto Butter.

Preheat the oven to 325°F. Line an upside-down 13-by-18-inch rimmed baking sheet with parchment paper. Remove the brick and prosciutto sandwiches from the fridge one at a time and, working quickly, cut them into 6-by-3/4-inch strips. Put the strips on the parchment paper and place another piece of parchment on top, along with another 13-by-18-inch rimmed baking sheet. Weigh the baking sheet down with a cast-iron skillet and bake for 15 to 20 minutes. The strips should be golden brown and crispy. Cool the crisps at room temperature and store between paper towels in an airtight container.

**TO FINISH**

Pea Soup
8 teaspoons Buttermilk Gel (see page 347)
Prosciutto Crisps
16 leaves mint
48 mint blossoms
24 pea tendrils
Buttermilk Snow

Pour 1/4 cup of the Pea Soup into a small bowl. Place 5 dots of Buttermilk Gel onto a Prosciutto Crisp. Arrange 2 mint leaves, 6 mint blossoms, and 3 pea tendrils on the Crisp. Garnish the soup with the Buttermilk Snow and place the Crisp across the edge of the bowl. Repeat with the remaining ingredients, to serve 8.

# STRAWBERRY
## GAZPACHO WITH BASIL, BLACK PEPPER, OLIVE OIL, AND GUANCIALE

*Serves 8*

### GAZPACHO

1 tablespoon plus 1/2 cup extra-virgin olive oil
2 cloves garlic, crushed but kept whole
1 1/2 cups whole grain bread, crusts removed, cut into 1-inch cubes
2 sprigs thyme
6 cups strawberries, hulled and quartered
2 1/4 cups English cucumber, peeled, seeded, and diced
1 1/4 cups diced red bell pepper
3/4 cup diced green bell pepper
6 tablespoons tomato juice
3 tablespoons red wine vinegar
1 1/2 teaspoons salt
Tabasco sauce

Heat a small sauté pan over medium-high heat. Coat the bottom with 1 tablespoon of the olive oil and add 1 clove of garlic. When the garlic begins to sizzle, add the bread cubes. Toss occasionally until the bread begins to color, being careful not to burn. Add the thyme and continue to toss until the bread is golden brown. Transfer the bread to a large bowl. Discard the garlic and thyme.

Add the strawberries, cucumber, peppers, remaining garlic clove, remaining 1/2 cup of olive oil, tomato juice, vinegar, and salt to the bowl. Toss to combine and cover tightly with plastic wrap. Marinate at room temperature for 3 to 6 hours. Puree the ingredients and their juices in small batches in a blender on high speed until very smooth. Strain through a chinois and chill in the refrigerator until very cold. Taste and season, if necessary, with Tabasco sauce and additional salt and red wine vinegar.

### CROUTONS

2 tablespoons extra-virgin olive oil
2 cloves garlic, crushed but kept whole
2 cups diced (1/4 inch) whole grain bread, crusts removed
3 sprigs thyme
1/2 teaspoon salt

Heat a small sauté pan on medium-high heat. Coat the bottom with the olive oil and add the garlic. When the garlic begins to sizzle, add the diced bread. Toss occasionally until the bread begins to color, being careful not to burn. Add the thyme and continue to toss until the bread is golden brown. Quickly transfer to a baking sheet lined with paper towels. Discard the garlic and thyme and season with the salt. Once cool and dry, store in an airtight container lined with paper towels for up to 1 day.

### STRAWBERRY CONFIT

16 small strawberries, hulled and halved lengthwise
1 1/2 teaspoons extra-virgin olive oil, plus more for storing
1 tablespoon confectioners' sugar

Preheat the oven to 195°F. Line a rimmed baking sheet with a silicone baking mat. Toss the halved strawberries in the olive oil to coat them lightly. Place them cut side down on the silicone mat and dust with the confectioners' sugar. Bake for 1 1/2 hours. Flip the strawberries and bake them for an additional 30 minutes. The strawberries should be deep maroon and tender but still hold their shape. Cool then on the silicone mat before storing in a flat, airtight container that has been coated with olive oil to keep them hydrated. The Confit can be made 3 days ahead and stored in the refrigerator.

### TO FINISH

Gazpacho
Black pepper
Strawberry Confit
Croutons
*Fleur de sel*
Basil (bush, opal, and flowering varieties)
1/4 pound *guanciale,* thinly sliced
Extra-virgin olive oil

Pour the cold Gazpacho into 8 chilled bowls. Season with a single grind of pepper. Arrange the Strawberry Confit and Croutons on the Gazpacho. Season with *fleur de sel.* Garnish with basil and a slice of *guanciale* and finish with olive oil.

# IBÉRICO HAM
## THINLY SLICED WITH GREEN SALAD

*Serves 8*

### BLANCHED VEGETABLES
1 cup shelled garden peas
1/2 cup shelled fava beans
24 small sugar snap peas
24 small green asparagus,
   bottom inch trimmed on the bias
2 bunches broccoli rabe, bottom inch trimmed
   and any excess leaves removed

Bring a pot of salted water to a boil. Add the peas to the boiling water, cooking until they are bright green, about 3 to 4 minutes. Remove with a slotted spoon and transfer to a large bowl filled with ice water. This helps maintain the vegetables' vibrant color. Once cold, remove the peas from the water, transfer to a bowl, and refrigerate. Repeat with the fava beans (they will take 1 to 2 minutes to cook), snap peas (1 to 2 minutes), asparagus (3 to 4 minutes), and broccoli rabe (3 to 4 minutes).

### HAM BROTH
2 teaspoons butter
2 shallots, peeled and thinly sliced
1 clove garlic, crushed but kept whole
Jamón Ibérico trim (reserved from Jamón Ibérico)
1/4 cup white wine
2 cups Chicken Stock (see page 356)
1 bay leaf
5 black peppercorns

Heat the butter in a saucepan over medium heat until it begins to foam. Reduce the heat to low and add the shallots and garlic. Sweat over low heat until tender, 6 to 7 minutes. Add the Jamón Ibérico and continue to sweat for 3 to 4 minutes. Add the white wine and reduce until almost dry. Add the Chicken Stock and bring to a simmer. Add the bay leaf and peppercorns, cover, remove from the heat, and steep for 45 minutes in a warm place, such as near a warm oven or stove. Strain through a chinois and chill over ice.

### JAMÓN IBÉRICO
1/2 pound Ibérico ham

On a rotating deli slicer, thinly slice the ham into 24 translucent sheets. Store in between sheets of parchment paper and wrap with plastic to prevent it from drying out. Thinly slice any remaining ham and reserve for the Ham Broth.

### BABY FENNEL
2 tablespoons butter
12 baby fennel bulbs, halved lengthwise
4 tablespoons white wine
4 teaspoons freshly grated orange zest
1 teaspoon fennel seeds
1 1/2 cups Ham Broth

Melt the butter in a small saucepan over medium heat. Add the fennel and sweat for 2 to 3 minutes. Add the wine, orange zest, and fennel seeds, and simmer for 2 to 3 more minutes. Add the Ham Broth and simmer slowly for 10 minutes or until the fennel is tender.

### CUCUMBER RELISH
1 English cucumber, peeled and seeded
1 tablespoon almond oil
1 tablespoon white balsamic vinegar
Salt

Mince the cucumber to "caviar" consistency. Place the minced cucumber in cheesecloth and wring out any excess moisture, reserving the flesh. Toss with the almond oil and vinegar, and season with salt to taste.

### BROCCOLI RABE COUSCOUS
2 bunches broccoli rabe

With a sharp pair of scissors, trim the tips off of the broccoli rabe stalks. They should resemble tiny grains of couscous once trimmed.

### RAW VEGETABLES
4 large green asparagus, bottom woodsy ends trimmed
4 baby zucchini
32 green almonds
1 cup milk

Finely shave the green asparagus and the zucchini into thin ribbons on a mandoline or with a vegetable peeler.
   Using a sharp paring knife, cut around the edge of each almond, being careful to keep the nut in the center intact. Remove the raw almond from its green husk. Place the almonds in the milk to prevent oxidation.

### HERBS
24 leaves mint
24 leaves lemon balm
16 ramp leaves
24 fennel fronds
24 pea shoots

Pick and carefully wash all of the herbs. Dry and set aside.

### GREENS
8 heads Bibb lettuce
24 leaves miner's lettuce
24 leaves celery
24 leaves wood (clover) sorrel

Pick and carefully wash all of the greens. Dry and set aside.

### TO FINISH
1/2 cup Ham Broth
Blanched Vegetables
1 tablespoon butter
Broccoli Rabe Couscous
2 tablespoons almond oil
Raw Vegetables
Baby Fennel
Greens
Herbs
1 cup White Balsamic Vinaigrette (see page 346)
1/3 cup Almond Gel (see page 347)
1/3 cup Fennel Puree (see page 351)
Cucumber Relish
Jamón Ibérico

Warm the Ham Broth in a sauté pan over medium heat. Add the Blanched Vegetables and warm through. Add the butter, tossing to glaze.
   Lightly toss the Broccoli Rabe Couscous in the almond oil. Toss the Blanched Vegetables, Baby Fennel, Raw Vegetables, Greens, and Herbs in the White Balsamic Vinaigrette.
   Place 2 teaspoons (across from each other) of the Almond Gel off center on a warm plate. In a small saucepan over low heat, warm the Fennel Puree. Place 2 teaspoons of the Fennel Puree opposite the Almond Gel (also across from each other). Arrange the vegetables on top.
   Place a teaspoon each of the Cucumber Relish and the Broccoli Rabe Couscous on the plate separately next to the vegetables. Lay the Jamón Ibérico over the vegetables and finish with the Greens and Herbs.

## FROZEN ASPARAGUS MOUSSE

2 tablespoons butter
2 cloves garlic, crushed but kept whole
1/4 cup diced shallot
4 cups diced (1/4 inch) green asparagus
4 cups diced (1/4 inch) white asparagus
Scant 1/2 cup white wine
8 cups cream
2 tablespoons salt
1 $N_2O$ charger
Liquid nitrogen
*Fleur de sel*

Melt the butter in a large sauté pan. Add the garlic and shallots and sweat until translucent. Add the green and white asparagus and sweat until tender. Deglaze the pan with the white wine and reduce until almost dry. Add the cream, bring to a simmer, and remove from heat. Cover and steep for 2 hours. Strain and season with salt.

In a whipped-cream canister, charge 4 cups of the asparagus base with the $N_2O$ charger. Release half of the charged mixture into a stainless-steel bowl lined with acetate. Ladle liquid nitrogen on the top of the foam until it is frozen, then release the other half on top of the frozen foam. Continue ladling the liquid nitrogen over the foam until it is completely frozen. Turn the frozen foam out onto a baking sheet and break it apart into large chunks. Season with *fleur de sel* to taste and store in the freezer.

## DEHYDRATED ALMOND MILK CRISP

4 cups bitter almond seeds
1 quart milk
3 drops bitter almond extract
3/4 cup glucose syrup

Preheat the oven to 275°F. Toast the almond seeds in the oven for 12 minutes, until golden brown. In a saucepan, bring the milk to a simmer. Add the seeds, remove from the heat, cover, and steep in a warm place, such as near a warm oven or stove, for 3 hours. The liquid should not dip below 145°F as it steeps. Strain and season with the extract. Stir in the glucose.

Reduce the oven to 175°F and line a 9-by-13-inch rimmed baking sheet with acetate. Bring the steeped milk to 170°F and remove from the heat. Using a hand blender, froth the milk. Spoon the foam onto the prepared baking sheet, being sure to fill it. Place the baking sheet immediately into the warm oven and dry overnight or for 8 to 9 hours. Allow to cool to room temperature before breaking it into pieces. Store the dehydrated foam in a sealed, airtight container.

## ALMOND MILK SNOW

4 cups bitter almond seeds
1 quart milk
3 drops bitter almond extract
1 teaspoon salt
Liquid nitrogen (optional)

Preheat the oven to 275°F. Toast the almond seeds in the oven for 12 minutes, until golden brown. In a saucepan, bring the milk to a simmer. Add the toasted seeds, remove from the heat, cover, and steep in a warm place, such as near a warm oven or stove, for 3 hours. The liquid should not dip below 145°F as it steeps. Strain and season with the extract and salt.

Line a large metal bowl with acetate. Fill the bowl halfway with liquid nitrogen and carefully pour the almond milk into the liquid nitrogen. As it freezes it will start to become brittle. Quickly transfer the frozen almond milk to a food processor and grind. The finished Almond Milk Snow will be powdery. Store in the freezer.

Alternatively, pour the almond milk into a shallow baking dish and freeze until completely solid. When ready to serve, scrape the frozen almond milk with a fork to create the Almond Milk Snow.

## SHRIMP

1 cup white wine
1 tablespoon sliced shallot
1 cup cold butter, diced
2 teaspoons lime juice
2 teaspoons salt
1/4 teaspoon cayenne pepper
24 sweet Maine shrimp (about 1/2 pound)

In a small pot, reduce the white wine with the shallots until 3 tablespoons remain. Reduce the heat to low and whisk in the butter a few cubes at a time. Once all of the butter has been added and emulsified, season with the lime juice, salt, and cayenne. Strain. Keep in a warm place, such as near a warm oven or stove, at 140°F.

Peel and devein the shrimp and rinse thoroughly in cold water. Pat dry and season with salt. Poach the shrimp in the beurre blanc for 45 seconds, until just cooked. Transfer the shrimp to a paper towel to drain. Serve immediately.

## TO FINISH

20 green asparagus, bottom woodsy ends trimmed
8 white asparagus, bottom woodsy ends trimmed
32 asparagus buds
3 tablespoons Almond Vinaigrette (see page 345)
8 tablespoons Lobster Crumble (see page 363)
Frozen Asparagus Mousse
16 pea tendrils
Shrimp
Dehydrated Almond Milk Crisp
40 anise hyssop blossoms
32 leaves anise hyssop
Almond Milk Snow

Bring a pot of salted water to a boil. Add 16 of the green asparagus and cook for 3 to 4 minutes. Transfer with a slotted spoon to a bowl of ice water. Repeat with all of the white asparagus, cooking for 8 minutes. Transfer to the ice water. Repeat with the asparagus buds, cooking for 30 seconds. Transfer to the ice water. Once the cooked asparagus are cold, drain and dry on paper towels. Shave the remaining 4 asparagus with a vegetable slicer or mandoline. In a medium bowl, dress all of the asparagus, buds, and shaves with the Almond Vinaigrette. Place a spoonful of Lobster Crumble on the bottom of the plate. Top with Frozen Asparagus Mousse. Garnish the Mousse with the blanched white and green asparagus, pea tendrils, shaved asparagus, Shrimp, Dehydrated Almond Milk Crisp, 5 anise hyssop blossoms, and 4 anise hyssop leaves. Immediately before serving, place 1 tablespoon of Almond Milk Snow on top of the salad. Repeat with the remaining ingredients, to serve 8.

# CRAB
## SALAD WITH PICKLED DAIKON RADISH AND VIOLA FLOWERS

*Serves 8*

### CRAB SALAD

1 pound shelled peekytoe crab
4 tablespoons Mayonnaise (see page 371)
2 tablespoons diced (1/8 inch) daikon radish
2 tablespoons finely sliced chives
2 tablespoons diced (1/8 inch) Granny Smith apple
4 teaspoons lime juice
1/4 teaspoon *piment d'Espelette*
Salt

Pick through the crab, discarding any remaining bits of shell. Pat off any excess moisture with a paper towel. In a large bowl, gently fold together the crab, Mayonnaise, radish, chives, apple, lime juice, *piment d'Espelette,* and salt until combined. Taste for seasoning and adjust if necessary.

### TO FINISH

Crab Salad
Pickled Daikon (see page 341)
200 viola leaves
8 tablespoons Crustacean Mayonnaise (see page 371)
8 teaspoons Daikon Vinaigrette (see page 345)
Lobster Roe Oil (see page 345)
1 teaspoon Lobster Roe Powder (see page 371)
40 sprigs dill

Place 2 teaspoons of Crab Salad on a Pickled Daikon round. On a separate daikon round, place 5 viola leaves. Flip the second daikon round onto the first so that the viola leaves and crab are sandwiched between them. Repeat with the remaining daikon rounds, Crab Salad, and viola leaves. Place 5 daikon-crab rounds in a circle on a plate, garnishing with dots of Crustacean Mayonnaise and the Daikon Vinaigrette. Place a small amount of Lobster Roe Oil and Lobster Roe Powder in the middle. Finish the plate with 5 dill sprigs and viola leaves. Repeat with the remaining daikon-crab rounds, to serve 8.

# TUNA
## MARINATED WITH ASPARAGUS, EGG YOLK, AND SORREL

*Serves 8*

### ASPARAGUS

Peel of 2 lemons
4 tablespoons lemon juice
4 sprigs thyme
4 bay leaves
4 tablespoons butter
3/4 cup plus 2 tablespoons salt
32 jumbo white asparagus,
     bottom woodsy ends trimmed

In a medium pot, combine the lemon peel, lemon juice, thyme, bay leaves, butter, and salt with 8 quarts water. Bring to a simmer over medium heat. Using a vegetable peeler, carefully peel the asparagus to the base of the tip. Add the peeled asparagus to the simmering liquid and cook for 10 minutes or until tender. Remove from the heat and cool over ice in the cooking liquid.

### CRISPY EGG YOLK

16 eggs
1 teaspoon salt
2 tablespoons milk
1 cup flour
1 cup brioche bread crumbs
8 cups canola oil

Using an immersion circulator, bring a water bath to 145°F. Add 12 of the eggs in their shells. Maintain the temperature of the water for 45 minutes. Remove the eggs from the water and cool to room temperature. Crack the eggs and separate the white from the yolk. Place the yolks in a small mixing bowl and whisk together with the salt until smooth and creamy. Spoon the mixture into a pastry bag and pipe into 2-piece magnetic molds (1-inch diameter). Freeze the yolks overnight. Once frozen, pop the yolks out of the molds.

Make an egg wash by whisking together the remaining 4 eggs and the milk. Dredge the frozen egg yolks first in the flour, then in the egg wash, and then in the brioche crumbs, making sure that the breading is even and smooth.

Heat the oil to 350°F. Fry the dredged yolks until golden brown and just warm in the center, 1 to 2 minutes.

### TUNA-WRAPPED ASPARAGUS TIPS

1 1/2 pounds sashimi-grade tuna
Asparagus
3/4 cup Lemon Oil (see page 345)
1 1/2 teaspoons *fleur de sel*

Cut the tuna into 3-inch-by-1/8-inch-thick squares. Place a tuna square between 2 sheets of plastic wrap and gently pound the fish with a mallet until it is about 1/16 inch thick. Repeat with the remaining squares. Trim the tuna pieces so that they are 4 inches long. Carefully wrap the tuna around the Asparagus, leaving the tip exposed. Brush the tuna with Lemon Oil and season with *fleur de sel*.

### TO FINISH

8 tablespoons Sorrel Puree (see page 353)
Tuna-Wrapped Asparagus Tips
Spring Vegetable Vinaigrette (see page 346)
16 leaves green sorrel
32 Oxalis blossoms
8 leaves wood (clover) sorrel
Crispy Egg Yolk

Spoon 1 tablespoon of the Sorrel Puree onto a plate. With the side of the spoon, drag it 4 inches across the plate. Place 2 Tuna-Wrapped Asparagus Tips along the line of the puree. Spoon 1 1/2 teaspoons of the Vinaigrette over the asparagus and tuna. Punch the green sorrel with a 1-inch ring cutter. Garnish with 2 green sorrel circles, 4 Oxalis blossoms, and a leaf of wood sorrel. Finish with the Crispy Egg Yolk. Repeat with the remaining ingredients, to serve 8.

# FOIE GRAS
## TERRINE WITH GREEN ASPARAGUS, MINER'S LETTUCE, AND BLACK TRUFFLES

*Serves 8*

### FOIE GRAS TERRINE

One 2-pound lobe grade-A foie gras
1 tablespoon salt
1/2 teaspoon pink curing salt
1 teaspoon sugar
1/2 teaspoon white pepper
2 teaspoons Madeira
1 teaspoon Cognac
1 cup sliced black truffles

Bring the foie gras to room temperature to soften. Separate the main lobes and remove the veins with tweezers and a paring knife. Season the foie gras with the salt, pink salt, sugar, and white pepper, and place it in a *sous vide* bag. Add the Madeira and Cognac to the bag. Cover one side of the foie gras with the black truffle slices. Seal the bag and marinate the foie gras in the refrigerator for 24 hours.

Place the bag of marinated foie gras in a water bath. Using an immersion circulator, maintain the water at 140°F for 10 minutes and then place it in an ice bath for 2 to 3 minutes. Do not allow the fat to solidify. When the foie gras is slightly cooler than room temperature, remove it from the bag and carefully separate the truffles. Reserve the truffles. Pass the cooked foie gras and rendered fat through a fine-mesh tamis. Whip the foie gras with a rubber spatula until it is re-emulsified. Place the whipped foie gras onto a sheet of acetate. Place another sheet of acetate on top and roll the foie gras using a rolling pin or a dough sheeter until it is 1/2 inch thick. Chill the foie gras in the refrigerator for 2 hours. Transfer the foie gras from the refrigerator to a cutting board and remove the top layer of acetate. Place a 3-by-5-1/2-inch rectangular mold over the foie gras and gently press down to punch out a rectangle. Repeat, leaving the mold around the second rectangle. Trim away any excess. You should be left with 2 identical rectangles. Save the trim for another use. On top of the foie gras rectangle inside the mold, lay the sliced truffles as flat as you can without overlapping. Take the other rectangular block of foie gras and place it on top of the truffles in the mold. Slightly press the terrine together without denting the foie gras and smooth the edges against the wall of the terrine to create a seal. Cover and place the terrine in the refrigerator to chill.

### ASPARAGUS GELÉE

3 cups thinly sliced green asparagus
3 cups loosely packed spinach
1 1/2 teaspoons salt
7 sheets gelatin

Bring a pot of salted water to a boil and add the asparagus. Cook for 1 minute or until bright green. Using a slotted spoon, transfer the asparagus to a bowl of ice water. Add the spinach to the boiling water and cook for 20 to 30 seconds or until wilted. Transfer the spinach to the ice water. Drain the asparagus and the spinach and puree them in a blender with 1 cup ice and 2 cups water. Blend on high speed for about 30 seconds, until smooth but slushy. Line a colander with 10 layers of cheesecloth. Set the colander over a bowl. Pour the icy puree over the cheesecloth and allow it to drain for 2 hours. The liquid will slowly drip through the cheesecloth as the ice melts, yielding a clear green liquid. Season with salt.

Bloom the gelatin by placing the sheets in a bowl of ice water for 10 minutes, until pliable. Measure 2 cups of the asparagus-spinach liquid. Warm 1/4 cup of that liquid in a small pot over low heat. Remove the gelatin from the cold water, squeeze to remove excess moisture, and stir into the warm liquid until the gelatin is completely melted. Add the other 1 3/4 cups liquid and stir to combine evenly. Strain immediately out of the pot and into another container to prevent the Gelée from turning brown. Let the liquid cool but not gel at this point.

Pour the cool Asparagus Gelée on top of the Foie Gras Terrine. Ensure that the Terrine is level so that the Gelée is even. Refrigerate for 1 hour to set the Gelée.

### SAUCE

1/4 cup black truffle juice
1/2 cup Chicken Jus (see page 356)
1 tablespoon lemon juice
1/2 teaspoon salt
1 tablespoon extra-virgin olive oil

Reduce the truffle juice in a small saucepan over low heat to 2 tablespoons. Stir in the Chicken Jus and season with lemon juice and salt. Cool to room temperature and stir in the olive oil.

### TO FINISH

28 green asparagus
24 slices black truffle
Foie Gras Terrine
Extra-virgin olive oil
*Fleur de sel*
Sauce
8 teaspoons Black Truffle Puree (see page 350)
32 leaves miner's lettuce
32 miner's lettuce flowers
Brioche (see page 364), toasted

Trim 24 of the asparagus to 3 inches in length and peel the bottom 3/4 inch evenly with a paring knife. Bring a pot of salted water to a boil and add the trimmed asparagus, cooking for 4 minutes. Transfer with a slotted spoon to a bowl of ice water. Once cold, drain and dry the asparagus on paper towels. Trim the woodsy ends of the remaining 4 asparagus. Shave them with a vegetable peeler or on a mandoline. Punch the black truffle slices with a 1/2-inch round cutter.

Transfer the Foie Gras Terrine to a cutting board and carefully remove the mold from the foie gras by running a paring knife along the edge and lifting up gently. Using a sharp chef's knife, cut it into 1/4-inch-thick slices. Trim off the rough edges and brush the slices lightly with olive oil. Season with *fleur de sel* and place a slice on each of 8 chilled plates. Garnish with the shaved asparagus and blanched asparagus. Sauce each plate with the Sauce. Place dots of Black Truffle Puree around the foie gras and cover the dots with the truffle slices. Garnish each dish with 4 miner's lettuce leaves and 4 flowers. Serve with slices of toasted Brioche.

# EGG
## POACHED WITH FROG LEGS, RAMPS, AND VIN JAUNE

*Serves 8*

### POACHED EGGS
8 organic eggs

Set up a water bath with an immersion circulator set to 145°F. Add the eggs in their shells to the water and circulate the water for 45 minutes.

Alternatively, set a pot of water over medium heat. Once it reaches 145°F, add the eggs. Using a thermometer, monitor the temperature of the water, maintaining it at 145°F for 45 minutes.

Remove the eggs from the water and keep at room temperature.

### VIN JAUNE BEURRE BLANC
2 cups *vin jaune*
2 tablespoons minced ramp bottoms
1 pound cold butter, cut into 1-inch cubes
4 teaspoons sherry vinegar
4 teaspoons salt
1/2 teaspoon cayenne pepper

In a small saucepan set over medium heat, reduce the *vin jaune* with the ramps until 3 tablespoons of liquid remain. Once reduced, lower the heat and begin to slowly whisk in the butter. Once all of the butter has been added and emulsified, season with sherry vinegar, salt, and cayenne. Strain through a chinois and keep in a warm place, such as near a warm oven or stove.

### FROG LEG RAGOUT
2 pounds frog legs
1 teaspoon salt
1/2 cup plus 2 tablespoons Vin Jaune Beurre Blanc
1/4 cup shelled sugar snap peas

Remove the muscles from the frog legs, using a paring knife. Clean all of the veins and tendons from the meat and season with salt.

Heat the Vin Jaune Beurre Blanc in a small sauté pan over medium heat. Add the frog legs, making sure that the sauce does not get too hot, which will cause it to separate and become greasy. Poach the frog legs in the sauce until slightly firm but still supple, about 1 to 2 minutes. At the last minute, add the shelled snap peas to the Ragout and remove from heat.

### TO FINISH
Poached Eggs
1 tablespoon salt
1 1/2 teaspoons *fleur de sel*
8 ramp leaves
Frog Leg Ragout
64 chive blossoms
Vin Jaune Beurre Blanc

To reheat the eggs, heat 6 cups water in a saucepan over medium heat. Once it reaches 160°F, add the salt. Crack the eggs into the water and heat for 4 to 5 minutes. Drain with a slotted spoon and place in the center of a shallow bowl. Season with the *fleur de sel* and garnish with a ramp leaf. Spoon the Ragout around the egg and garnish with 8 chive blossoms. Finish the plate with a tablespoon of Beurre Blanc around the Ragout. Repeat with the remaining ingredients, to serve 8.

# RICOTTA
## GNOCCHI WITH VIOLET ARTICHOKES AND SMOKED PORK

*Serves 8*

### GNOCCHI
7 cups cow's milk ricotta
2 eggs
3 cups grated Parmesan, loosely packed
1 cup flour
1 teaspoon salt
6 cups semolina flour

Line a colander with cheesecloth and place it in a large bowl. Place the ricotta in the cheesecloth and cover with more cloth. Place a bowl on top of the wrapped ricotta and weigh down with a cast-iron skillet or heavy can. Refrigerate, allowing the pressed ricotta to drain and dry overnight. The next day, unwrap and measure 5 1/2 cups ricotta. Reserve any remaining ricotta for another use. Blend the measured ricotta with the eggs in a food processor until very smooth and completely incorporated. In a large bowl, fold together the blended ricotta, Parmesan, flour, and salt. Transfer to a piping bag and line a baking sheet with parchment paper. Pipe 1-inch mounds onto the parchment paper. Refrigerate for 4 hours.

Pour 2 cups of the semolina into a 1 1/2- to 2-inch-deep pan. With your hands, roll the cheese mixture into smooth balls. Place them in the semolina and cover completely with the remaining 4 cups semolina. It is important that the Gnocchi are covered so that as they rest, the semolina absorbs any moisture from the ricotta and a pasta shell forms. Refrigerate overnight.

### ARTICHOKES BARIGOULE
4 tablespoons lemon juice
8 baby artichokes
2 tablespoons olive oil
2 cloves garlic, crushed but kept whole
2 teaspoons salt
2 cups white wine
2 sprigs thyme
1 sprig rosemary

Place the lemon juice in a large bowl filled with ice water. Peel away the outer leaves of the artichoke until reaching the light yellow leaves. Cut off the top 1/2 inch of an artichoke and, with a sharp paring knife or vegetable peeler, turn the artichoke and remove the woodsy stem. Cut the turned artichoke into slices and submerge in the lemon water as you continue cleaning the remaining artichokes.

Heat 1 tablespoon of the olive oil in a large sauté pan over high heat. Drain the artichokes and add them, along with the garlic, to the pan. Sauté for 1 minute and season with salt. Remove from the heat and add the wine. Return to the heat, bring to a boil, and add the remaining olive oil, the thyme, and the rosemary. Cover and continue to cook over medium-high heat until the artichokes are tender, about 7 minutes. Remove from the heat and let the artichokes cool in their liquid.

### TO FINISH
8 tablespoons Artichoke Puree (see page 350)
Gnocchi
2 tablespoons butter
24 taggiasca olives, pitted
Artichokes Barigoule
Smoked Pork Jerky (see page 359)
24 leaves sylvetta arugula
24 Elephant Garlic Chips (see page 371)

Warm the Artichoke Puree in a small saucepan.

Remove the Gnocchi from the semolina flour. Bring a large pot of salted water to a boil and cook the Gnocchi for 2 minutes. Meanwhile, warm the butter with a tablespoon of the pasta cooking water in a sauté pan. Gently remove the Gnocchi from the water and drain. Add them to the butter and lightly toss together for 30 seconds. Be careful when handling the Gnocchi, as they are very delicate and will fall apart when handled roughly.

In a separate sauté pan, over medium heat, toss together the olives and Artichokes Barigoule.

Spoon a tablespoon of the Artichokes Puree into the base of a warm bowl. Place 3 Gnocchi, 3 olives, and 3 artichoke slices on top. Using a microplane grater, shave the cold Smoked Pork over the Gnocchi. Garnish with 3 arugula leaves and 3 Elephant Garlic Chips. Repeat with the remaining ingredients, to serve 8, noting that you will have leftover Gnocchi. Any leftover Gnocchi may be frozen for 2 to 3 days.

# TURBOT
## POACHED WITH GARDEN PEA NAGE AND LEMON THYME

*Serves 8*

### TURBOT
2 tablespoons butter, softened
1 tablespoon minced shallots
Eight 3-ounce fillets turbot, skinned
1 1/2 tablespoons salt
1 quart Fish Fumet (see page 356)
6 sprigs lemon thyme

Preheat the oven to 250°F. Brush the bottom of a gratin dish with 1 tablespoon of the butter. Sprinkle the minced shallots over the butter. Season the fish with the salt and place on top of the shallots. Pour the Fish Fumet into the gratin dish, covering the fillets a quarter of the way up the dish. Add the lemon thyme. Brush a sheet of parchment paper with the remaining 1 tablespoon butter. Cover the dish with the parchment, butter side down. Bake for 25 to 30 minutes or until tender, occasionally basting the fish with the Fumet. Remove the fish from the cooking liquid and keep warm. Reserve the cooking liquid along with any additional Fumet for the Nage.

### GLAZED VEGETABLES
32 sugar snap peas
1/2 cup shelled fava beans
32 haricots verts
1 cup shelled garden peas
8 garden peas, in their shells
16 spring onions
3 tablespoons Chicken Stock (see page 356)
1 1/2 teaspoons salt
4 tablespoons butter

Bring a pot of salted water to a boil. Add the sugar snap peas and cook for 1 to 2 minutes. Remove with a slotted spoon and transfer to a large bowl filled with ice water. Repeat with the fava beans (1 to 2 minutes), haricots verts (2 to 3 minutes), shelled and unshelled garden peas (3 to 4 minutes), and spring onions (3 to 4 minutes). Once cool, drain and dry on paper towels. With a small pair of scissors, carefully trim around the edges of the unshelled peas to remove the top shell and expose the peas. Be sure to leave the peas attached to the shell.

Heat the Chicken Stock in a large sauté pan over medium heat and bring to a simmer. Add all of the blanched vegetables and season with salt. Add the butter and toss. As the butter melts and emulsifies, it will glaze the vegetables evenly. Be careful not to overcook the vegetables or reduce the glaze, as the emulsion will break and make the vegetables greasy. Remove the vegetables from the pan with a slotted spoon and reserve warm on a paper towel to remove any excess glaze.

### NAGE
3 1/2 cups Fish Fumet cooking liquid
1/2 teaspoon saffron
1 pinch cayenne pepper
4 sprigs lemon thyme
5 tablespoons cold butter, diced
2 tablespoons lemon juice
4 tablespoons peeled and diced (1/8 inch)
     red bell pepper
1/2 teaspoon salt

Strain the Fumet cooking liquid through a fine-mesh chinois into a saucepan. Add the saffron and cayenne and reduce by half over medium heat. Add the thyme, remove from the heat, and steep for 10 minutes. Strain through the chinois. Add the butter and lemon juice and emulsify with a hand blender. Stir in the red pepper and season with salt.

### TO FINISH
Turbot
1 teaspoon *fleur de sel*
Glazed Vegetables
Nage
16 sprigs lemon thyme

Place a turbot fillet in the middle of a warm bowl and sprinkle with *fleur de sel*. Arrange the glazed sugar snap peas, fava beans, haricots verts, shelled garden peas, and spring onions around the fillet. Spoon 1/4 cup of the Nage around the fish. Garnish with a garden pea pod and 2 lemon thyme sprigs. Repeat with the remaining ingredients, to serve 8.

# SKATE
## ROASTED WITH LEMON, CAPERS, AND BROWN BUTTER

*Serves 8*

### SKATE

4 skate wing fillets, 6 ounces each
12 tablespoons canola oil
Salt
1 cup flour
4 tablespoons cold butter
1 lemon

Stack 2 skate wings together so that they mirror each other. Place them in a *sous vide* bag and vacuum-seal. Repeat with the other 2 wings. Place in a water bath maintained at 145°F by an immersion circulator and cook for 4 minutes. Transfer the sealed bags to an ice bath to cool. Heat 2 large sauté pans over high heat with 6 tablespoons canola oil in each one. Remove the skate wings from the bags, pat dry, and season with salt. Dredge in the flour, patting off any excess. Just before the oil begins to smoke, add the skate wings (1 stack in each pan) and lower the heat to medium-high. Sauté until golden brown on one side, about 4 minutes. Flip the fish and baste with the oil to evenly brown, about 3 more minutes. Drain the oil, add the butter, and continue basting for 2 minutes. Remove from the heat and squeeze the lemon over the skate. Remove the fish from the pans and place on paper towels to remove excess oil. Slice each wing in half and then in half again and trim the ends to make eight 3-ounce pieces.

Alternatively, begin by heating 2 large sauté pans over high heat with 3 tablespoons canola oil in each one. Stack 2 skate wings together so that they mirror each other. Season the skate wings with salt, dredge in the flour, and pat off any excess. Continue as indicated above, noting that the stacked skate wings may come apart as they cook. (The *sous vide* technique ensures that the wings will stay together.)

### LEMON BEURRE BLANC

1 cup lemon juice
1/2 shallot, thinly sliced
1/4 cup cream
1 pound cold butter, cut into 1-inch cubes
1 tablespoon salt
1 1/2 teaspoons capers
1/2 teaspoon caper brine

Place the lemon juice and shallot in a saucepan over medium heat. Reduce the juice to 2/3 cup. Add the cream and reduce to 1/2 cup. Turn the heat down, and slowly whisk in the cold butter several pieces at a time. Pass through a fine-mesh chinois. Season the butter with the salt, capers, and brine. Keep warm.

### BROWN BUTTER POWDER

1/3 cup butter
4 tablespoons milk powder

In a small saucepan over medium heat, melt the butter. Add the milk powder, stirring often as the milk solids begin to brown. When evenly browned, strain through a chinois, reserving the solids. Turn the solids out onto a paper towel and pat to remove any excess butter. Reserve the milk solids in a dry, airtight container.

### VEGETABLES

16 spring onions
16 pieces celery heart
16 baby onions
8 baby leeks
32 sea beans
2 tablespoons Brown Butter (see page 370)
Salt
16 green almonds

Bring a pot of salted water to a boil. Add the spring onions and cook for 1 minute. Transfer with a slotted spoon to a bowl of ice water. Repeat with the celery heart (20 seconds), baby onions (20 seconds), baby leeks (1 minute), and sea beans (1 minute). Once they are cold, drain and dry all of the vegetables. Dress them in the Brown Butter and season with salt. Using a sharp paring knife, cut around the edge of a green almond, being careful to keep the almond in the center intact. Remove the raw almond from its green husk. Repeat with the remaining almonds.

### TO FINISH

Skate
Vegetables
24 slices toasted almond
16 white strawberries
16 green strawberries, hulled and sliced
32 leaves nasturtium
Lemon Beurre Blanc
Brown Butter Powder

Place the Skate in the center of a dinner plate and arrange the Vegetables around the fish. Garnish the plate with 6 slices toasted almond, 2 white strawberries and 2 sliced green strawberries, and 4 nasturtium leaves. Finish with the Lemon Beurre Blanc and Brown Butter Powder. Repeat with the remaining ingredients, to serve 8.

# JOHN DORY
## SEARED WITH VARIATIONS OF GARLIC AND CRAYFISH

*Serves 8*

### CITRUS BEURRE BLANC
1/2 cup grapefruit juice
1/3 cup orange juice
2 tablespoons lemon juice
1 pound cold butter, cut into 1-inch cubes
1 tablespoon salt

In a saucepan over medium heat, combine the grape-fruit juice, orange juice, and lemon juice. Reduce the juices so that 1/4 cup remains. Reduce the heat to low and slowly whisk in the cold butter until all of it is fully emulsified. Season with salt.

### JOHN DORY
4 tablespoons canola oil
Eight 4-ounce John Dory fillets, skinned
1 tablespoon salt
2 tablespoons butter
1/2 cup Citrus Beurre Blanc
Smoked Maldon salt

Heat 2 large sauté pans over medium-high heat and add 2 tablespoons oil to each of the pans. Pat the fish dry with a paper towel and season with salt on both sides. Just before the oil begins to smoke, put 4 fillets in each pan — the side where the bones were should be facing up — pressing the fillets lightly in the center with a fish spatula to remove air pockets. Rotate the fish 180 degrees when it releases itself from the pan to ensure even color. When the fish is three quarters of the way cooked through, after about 2 to 3 minutes, add 1 tablespoon butter to each pan and remove from the heat. Baste the fish off the heat for 2 minutes, making sure not to overcook it. Remove the fish from the pan, flip it so that the seared side is up, and blot any excess oil with a paper towel. Dress the fish with Citrus Beurre Blanc and season each piece of fish with a few crystals of the smoked Maldon salt.

### CRAYFISH
32 crayfish (about 1 pound)
1 cup Citrus Beurre Blanc
1 teaspoon salt

Bring a pot of salted water to a boil. Add the crayfish to the water and cook for 2 minutes. Transfer with a slotted spoon to a bowl of ice water. Once the crayfish are cold, remove the tails and reserve the bodies for the Crayfish Bisque. Peel, trim, and devein the tails. In a small pot, heat the Beurre Blanc to 145°F. Add the crayfish and warm through. Remove the crayfish to a paper towel to drain and keep in a warm place, such as near a warm oven or stove. Season with salt.

### CRAYFISH BISQUE
1 tablespoon canola oil
Crayfish bodies and shells from 1 pound whole crayfish
1 tablespoon butter
1/4 cup diced fennel
2 tablespoons grated ginger
2 cloves garlic, crushed but kept whole
1 tablespoon flour
1/2 cup tomato juice
2 tablespoons Noilly Prat
2 tablespoons Cognac
1/4 teaspoon saffron
2 quarts Lobster Stock (see page 356)
5 sprigs tarragon
3 pods cardamom
1 pod star anise
1/2 cup crème fraîche
1 tablespoon lobster roe
2 tablespoons lime juice
1 tablespoon salt
1 pinch cayenne pepper

In a medium pan over high heat, heat the canola oil. Add the crayfish bodies and shells, crushing them with a large wooden spoon as they toast. When the shells are lightly browned, pour off the oil and add the butter. Lower the heat to medium and add the fennel, ginger, and garlic and cook until tender, about 7 minutes. Sprinkle in the flour and sweat for another 3 minutes, stirring. Add the tomato juice, Noilly Prat, Cognac, and saffron, and reduce to about 3/8 cup. Add the Lobster Stock and reduce to about 1 quart. Make a sachet with the tarragon, cardamom, and star anise, and add it to the stock. Simmer for 30 minutes. In a small bowl, whisk the crème fraîche and lobster roe together. Remove and discard the sachet from the sauce. Strain the sauce through a chinois and then puree the hot liquid, along with the lobster roe and crème fraîche, in a blender on high. Finish with lime juice, salt, and cayenne. Pass through a fine-mesh chinois and keep hot.

### BLACK GARLIC CIRCLES
2 heads fermented black garlic

Peel the garlic and pass the cloves through a fine-mesh tamis. Coat 2 sheets of acetate with vegetable spray. Place the garlic between the sheets and, using the palm of your hand, flatten. Use a rolling pin or a dough sheeter to evenly roll the black garlic into a 1/16-inch-thick sheet. Chill in the refrigerator for 1 hour.

Preheat the oven to 125°F. Peel off the top sheet of acetate and bake the garlic for 4 hours. The garlic sheet should be very dry. You can also use a dehydrator to dry the garlic sheet overnight. Once dry, use a 1/2-inch round cutter to punch out even circles.

### TO FINISH
1 cup Smoked Potato-Garlic Puree (see page 353)
John Dory
Crayfish Bisque
Crayfish
Black Garlic Circles
2 tablespoons olive oil
Pickled Spring Garlic Batons (see page 343)
16 Elephant Garlic Chips (see page 371)
8 stalks spring garlic, shaved
16 sprigs flowering chervil
1 teaspoon Lobster Roe Powder (see page 371)

Spoon 2 tablespoons of the Smoked Potato-Garlic Puree against the left-hand side of a 4-inch ring mold. Using a small spoon, make one fluid motion three quarters of the way around the mold. Lift the mold from the plate.

Place a fillet of John Dory between the beginning and end of the Puree. Gently spoon 2 tablespoons of the Crayfish Bisque between the fillet and the Puree, creating a small bowl for the Bisque.

Space 3 of the Crayfish evenly along the Puree. Brush 3 Black Garlic Circles with olive oil. Place 2 of the Black Garlic Circles on the Crayfish and 1 on the bottom left corner of the John Dory. Place 2 Pickled Spring Garlic Batons on the edge of the Black Garlic, garnishing the Crayfish.

Finish with 2 Elephant Garlic Chips, shaved raw spring garlic, 2 sprigs flowering chervil, and a small line of Lobster Roe Powder above the John Dory. Repeat with the remaining ingredients, to serve 8.

# LANGOUSTINE
## SLOW-COOKED WITH CAULIFLOWER, RAISINS, AND GREEN ALMONDS

*Serves 8*

### LANGOUSTINES
8 medium langoustines (just over 1 pound total)

Peel and devein each langoustine, using a small pair of tweezers. Place a small bamboo skewer through the length of the langoustine. This ensures that the tail stays straight during the cooking process. Refrigerate.

### BROWN BUTTER BEURRE BLANC
2 cups white wine
2 pounds cold butter, cut into 1-inch cubes
1/4 cup Brown Butter (see page 370)
2 tablespoons lime juice
1 1/2 tablespoons salt

Reduce the white wine to about 1/2 cup in a medium saucepan over medium heat. The wine should begin to take on a golden color. Slowly whisk in the diced butter, 3 to 4 cubes at a time, stirring constantly to emulsify. When three quarters of the butter has been emulsified, slowly pour in the Brown Butter, stirring constantly. Continue to whisk in the rest of the cold butter. Finish with lime juice and salt, and keep in a warm place, such as near a warm oven or stove.

### CAULIFLOWER PANNA COTTA
2 heads cauliflower
8 cups half-and-half
1 tablespoon agar-agar (7 grams)
3 tablespoons salt

Cut the cauliflower into small pieces and place in a medium pot. Pour the half-and-half over the cauliflower and bring to a simmer. Once it simmers, remove from the heat and cover. Steep for 1 hour.

Strain the liquid into a medium pot and keep warm. Discard the cauliflower.

In a large saucepan, whisk the agar-agar into 3/4 cup cold water and bring to a simmer, cooking for 5 minutes. Bring 6 cups of the cauliflower base to a simmer over medium heat. Once the agar-agar is completely hydrated in the boiling water, whisk the cauliflower base into it, season with the salt, and strain through a fine-mesh chinois.

Line a 13-by-18-inch rimmed baking sheet with acetate and pour the strained mixture into the baking sheet. It will be about 3/8-inch thick. Refrigerate for 1 hour. Once set, cut with a 1 1/2-by-4-inch rectangular mold, to yield 8 rectangles.

### CRUSTACEAN NAGE
2 quarts Lobster Stock (see page 356)
1 tablespoon butter
1/2 cup diced fennel
1/4 cup grated ginger
1 clove garlic, crushed but kept whole
1/4 teaspoon saffron
1 vanilla bean, split lengthwise
1/4 cup Cognac
1/4 cup Noilly Prat
1/2 cup tomato juice
5 sprigs tarragon
3 pods cardamom
1 pod star anise
1/2 cup crème fraîche
1 tablespoon lobster roe
2 tablespoons lime juice
1 1/2 tablespoons salt
1 pinch cayenne pepper

In a medium saucepan over medium heat, reduce the stock by half. Melt the butter in another medium saucepan. Add the fennel, ginger, garlic, saffron, and vanilla pod and seeds, and sweat for 4 minutes. Deglaze the pan with the Cognac and reduce until almost dry. Add the Noilly Prat and reduce again until almost dry. Add the tomato juice and reduced Lobster Stock and bring to a simmer. Combine the tarragon, cardamom, and star anise in a sachet and steep in the sauce for 10 to 15 minutes.

Remove and discard the sachet. In a blender, puree the sauce. Add the crème fraîche and lobster roe, blending until smooth. Strain through a fine-mesh chinois, and season with the lime juice, salt, and cayenne.

### RUM RAISINS
2 cups dark rum
1 cup golden raisins

In a small saucepan, over medium heat, reduce the rum by half. Once reduced, pour the rum over the golden raisins. Rehydrate the raisins at room temperature for 6 hours.

### TO FINISH
Brown Butter Beurre Blanc
Langoustines
Cauliflower Panna Cotta
8 cauliflower florets
5 teaspoons almond oil
1/4 teaspoon *fleur de sel*
24 green almonds
Rum Raisins
32 leaves celery
Crustacean Nage

Preheat the oven to 300°F. Place the Brown Butter Beurre Blanc in a sauté pan and bring to 145°F. Place langoustines in the sauce and gently baste until warm in the center. It is important to be gentle when cooking the langoustines as they are very delicate and can fall apart if handled incorrectly. Remove the langoustines from the butter and gently pull out the skewers.

While the langoustines are cooking, place the Cauliflower Panna Cotta rectangles on a baking sheet and warm for 1 minute in the oven. Place the Panna Cotta in the middle of a shallow bowl. Gently place a Langoustine on top. Thinly slice the cauliflower florets on a mandoline. Dress the slices with 1 teaspoon of the almond oil and *fleur de sel*. Using a sharp paring knife, cut around the edge of the almonds, being careful to keep the almond in the center intact. Remove the raw almond from its green husk. Garnish the Langoustine along the back with 3 cauliflower slices, 1 tablespoon Rum Raisins, 3 green almonds, and 4 celery leaves. Spoon the Crustacean Nage around the Panna Cotta, covering the bottom of the bowl. Repeat with the remaining Langoustines, to serve 8. Finish each bowl with 1/2 teaspoon almond oil.

# LOBSTER
## POACHED WITH CARROTS AND VADOUVAN GRANOLA

*Serves 8*

## LOBSTER

8 (1 1/4-pound) live lobsters

Fill a large stockpot with water and bring the water to 150°F. Add 2 of the lobsters, and cook for 7 minutes, maintaining the temperature of the water at 150°F. Remove the tails from the lobsters and transfer them to an ice bath. Return the knuckles and claws to the water and continue cooking for 7 more minutes. Transfer the knuckles and claws to the ice bath. Repeat with the remaining lobsters. When the tails, knuckles, and claws are completely cool, carefully remove the meat from the shells, making sure to keep the meat intact. Refrigerate.

## ORANGE BEURRE BLANC

4 cups white wine
4 cups orange juice
1/2 cup cream
2 1/2 pounds cold butter, cut into 1-inch cubes
1 1/2 tablespoons salt
1 tablespoon *piment d'Espelette*

Reduce the white wine in a saucepan to 1 cup. In a separate saucepan reduce the orange juice and the cream to just over 1 cup. Stir the reduced wine into the orange juice mixture and place the pan over low heat. Slowly whisk in the butter, 3 or 4 cubes at a time. Stir slowly and constantly. When the butter is completely emulsified, add the salt and *piment d'Espelette*. Keep warm at 155°F.

## GLAZED BABY CARROTS AND SUGAR SNAP PEAS

16 baby carrots, green tops intact
1/2 cup Chicken Stock (see page 356)
2 tablespoons butter
1/2 teaspoon salt
8 sugar snap peas
1 teaspoon lime zest

Trim the tops of the carrots, leaving 1/2 inch of green, and reserve. Place the carrots in a medium sauté pan over medium heat along with the Chicken Stock, butter, and salt. Cover and simmer for 7 minutes, until the carrots are tender and glazed. In the meantime, bring a pot of salted water to a boil. Add the snap peas and cook for 1 to 2 minutes. Transfer with a slotted spoon to a bowl of ice water. Once the peas are cold, drain and dry them. Add the blanched sugar snap peas to the glazed carrots, tossing to glaze the peas. Finish with the lime zest. Cool to room temperature.

## CITRUS SABAYON

1 quart Lobster Stock (see page 356)
2 1/2 cups orange juice
1 cup grapefruit juice
1/4 cup lime juice
2 tablespoons diced ginger
2 cups butter, melted
5 eggs
2 egg yolks
2 tablespoons salt
2 $N_2O$ cartridges

In a saucepan over medium heat, reduce the Lobster Stock to 2 cups. Add all the citrus juices and reduce over medium heat to just under 2 cups. Add the ginger and reduce until 1 cup remains. Strain the reduction and pour into a whipped-cream canister. Add the melted butter, eggs, egg yolks, and salt. Charge with 2 $N_2O$ cartridges. Place in a 145°F water bath and cook for 1 hour.

## TO FINISH

Orange Beurre Blanc
Lobster
*Fleur de sel*
16 baby carrot tops (reserved from Glazed Baby Carrots and Sugar Snap Peas)
1 red carrot
1 teaspoon olive oil
8 tablespoons Yellow Carrot Puree (see page 350)
Vadouvan Granola (see page 364)
Glazed Baby Carrots and Sugar Snap Peas
8 coriander blossoms
Citrus Sabayon

Heat the Orange Beurre Blanc to 145°F and add the lobster tails (and knuckles and claws, if using) for 5 to 10 minutes or until warmed through. Remove from the Beurre Blanc and sprinkle lightly with *fleur de sel*.

Bring a pot of salted water to a boil. Add the carrot tops and cook for 30 seconds. Transfer with a slotted spoon to the bowl of ice water. Once cool, drain.

Using a vegetable peeler or mandoline, make thin ribbons from the red carrot. Toss the ribbons with the olive oil and 1/4 teaspoon *fleur de sel*.

Warm the Yellow Carrot Puree in a small saucepan over low heat. Spoon the Puree onto a plate and pull with a spoon toward the right. At the top of the Puree, sprinkle a line of Vadouvan Granola (about 2 1/2 inches). Place a lobster tail (2 knuckles and 2 claws) on top of the Granola. At the bottom of the Puree, delicately place 2 glazed carrots, 2 carrot tops, a sugar snap pea, and a red carrot ribbon. Top with a coriander blossom. At the last minute, expel 1 to 2 tablespoons of the Citrus Sabayon over the lobster tail (and claws). Repeat with the remaining ingredients, to serve 8.

*Note: At the restaurant, we use the claws and knuckles in other dishes. If you're preparing only one lobster recipe, plate the dishes with the claws, knuckles, and tails.*

# POUSSIN
## EARTH AND OCEAN

*Serves 8*

### POUSSIN ROULADES

4 whole poussins
2 nori sheets
2 teaspoons salt

Remove the breasts from a poussin, using a sharp boning knife. Lay the breast skin side up and gently separate the skin from the breast, peeling it back to reveal the flesh. Cut a small rectangle (3/4 inch by 2 3/4 inch) of nori and place it on top of the breast. Pull the skin back over the nori and breast to cover. Season the bottom of the breast with 1/4 teaspoon salt. Repeat with the remaining breasts. Roll the poussin breasts tightly in plastic wrap and tie the ends with butcher's twine or the plastic wrap itself to create a small roulade. Cook the poussins in a water bath maintained at 145°F by an immersion circulator for 15 minutes. Remove and discard the plastic wrap and keep the breasts warm until ready to serve.

### VIN JAUNE BEURRE BLANC

2 cups *vin jaune*
1 tablespoon minced shallots
1 pound cold butter, cut into 1-inch cubes
4 teaspoons sherry vinegar
4 teaspoons salt
1/2 teaspoon cayenne pepper

In a small saucepan set over medium heat, reduce the *vin jaune* with the shallots until 3 tablespoons of liquid remain. Lower the heat and begin to slowly whisk in the butter. Once the mixture has emulsified, season with the sherry vinegar, salt, and cayenne. Strain the Beurre Blanc through a chinois and keep in a warm place, such as near a warm oven or stove.

### HAWAIIAN PRAWNS

16 Hawaiian blue prawns (U10, about 1/2 pound total), shelled
1 teaspoon salt
Vin Jaune Beurre Blanc

Remove the veins from the prawns, using a small knife or tweezers. Season the prawns with the salt. Bring the Beurre Blanc to 145°F and poach the prawns in the Beurre Blanc for 2 minutes.

### LEMON CHICKEN JUS

1 ounce kombu
1/2 cup Lobster Stock (see page 356)
2 cups Chicken Jus (see page 356)
4 teaspoons lemon juice

Soak the kombu in cold water for 2 hours. Rinse well and pat dry. Bring the Lobster Stock to a simmer and reduce by half. Add the Chicken Jus and reduce to 1 3/4 cups. Add the kombu, remove from the heat, and steep for 20 minutes. Strain the sauce through a chinois and season with the lemon juice.

### CHANTERELLES

56 small chanterelles
2 tablespoons butter
1 tablespoon minced Shallot Confit (see page 371)
2 teaspoons salt

Clean the chanterelles of all dirt with a paring knife and scrape any discoloration from the stems. Trim the bottoms and rinse thoroughly. Spread the chanterelles on a paper towel to dry. Melt the butter in a medium sauté pan over medium heat until it begins to foam. Add the chanterelles and sauté until tender. Add the Shallot Confit and toss. Season with the salt and keep warm.

### TO FINISH

16 Mendocino bladderwrack
16 Mendocino grapestone
16 succulent miru (also called codium fragile)
16 sea beans
Poussin Roulades
1/4 cup Brown Butter (see page 370)
1 teaspoon *fleur de sel*
Hawaiian Prawns
Chanterelles
Pickled Seaweed (see page 343)
Vin Jaune Beurre Blanc
Lemon Chicken Jus

Bring a pot of salted water to a boil. Add the Mendocino bladderwrack, Mendocino grapestone, succulent miru, and sea beans. Cook for 2 minutes and then transfer with a slotted spoon to a bowl of ice water. Once cool, drain. Trim off the ends of the Poussin Roulades on the bias. Slice the Roulades in half on the bias, making 2 equal diamond-shaped pieces. Brush with Brown Butter and season with *fleur de sel*. Place the 2 pieces across from each other on a warm plate. Trim the ends of the Hawaiian Prawns and place 2 next to the Poussin Roulades. Arrange 7 Chanterelles around the plate and sauce with the Beurre Blanc and 1 teaspoon of the Lemon Chicken Jus. Finish the plate with sea beans and seaweed, pickled and fresh. Repeat with the remaining ingredients, to serve 8.

# RABBIT
## FANTASY
## WITH BACON
## AND MUSTARD

*Serves 8*

2 young rabbits, 3 to 4 pounds each, skinned and
    gutted, heads removed

Remove the kidneys from the rabbits; set aside. Lay the
rabbit on its back with the legs facing toward you and,
using a boning knife, remove the hind legs. Turn the
rabbit so that the shoulders are facing you. Remove the
forelegs. With the rabbit still on its back, use scissors
to remove the rib cage. Turn the rabbit over onto its
stomach; it should lay flat with the neck facing you.
With a boning knife, working through the back, remove
the 2 loins, following along the backbone. With a
cleaver, cut the bones into 1 1/2-inch pieces. Repeat
with the other rabbit.

### RABBIT LOIN

4 young rabbit loins
6 ounces double-smoked slab bacon,
    thinly sliced (1/16 inch)
2 tablespoons salt
1 tablespoon canola oil

Preheat the oven to 350°F. Line a rimmed baking
sheet with parchment paper. Trim the loins to about
3 1/2 inches long. Remove all fat and silver skin. Layer
the bacon slices horizontally so that they are barely
overlapping. Layer enough bacon slices to completely
wrap a loin. Repeat to make 3 more bacon sheets.
Refrigerate the bacon until it is cold and firm. Season
the rabbit loin with salt. Tightly roll the rabbit in the
bacon, cutting off any excess bacon. Heat the oil in a
sauté pan over medium heat. Sear the bacon-wrapped
rabbit on all sides, and then place the pan in the oven
for 3 minutes. Remove the rabbit from the pan and let
it rest for 10 minutes.

## RABBIT THIGHS

4 young rabbit legs
One 2-pound lobe grade-A foie gras, chilled
Salt
8 Swiss chard leaves, stems removed
1 pound caul fat, thoroughly rinsed
4 tablespoons canola oil
4 tablespoons butter

Using a boning knife, trim off one of the lower legs so that only the thigh remains. Reserve the meat from the shank for use in the Crépinette and the bones for the Jus (see next recipe). Carefully, using scissors, bone the thigh while keeping the leg intact. This will provide a pocket for the foie gras. Do not cut through the meat. Remove the veins and cartilage from the joint area. Repeat with the remaining legs.

Separate the main lobes of foie gras with your hands. Using tweezers, carefully remove the large and small veins from both sides, being careful not to tear the foie gras or cut it into larger pieces. Refrigerate until cold. Using a hot, sharp knife, cut it into 1-inch-by-1-inch-by-2-inch blocks. Place the blocks on a baking sheet, season with salt, and refrigerate until very cold again.

Bring a large pot of salted water to a boil. Add the Swiss chard leaves and cook until just wilted. Using a slotted spoon, transfer them to an ice bath. Drain the Swiss chard and dry the leaves completely on a paper towel. Cut the leaves into 3 1/2-inch-by-2-1/2-inch rectangles. Place the chard leaves, rib side down, on a cutting board. Place a block of seasoned foie gras on the chard and roll until the foie gras is covered. Trim any excess chard leaf that may be protruding from the back. Fold the sides down as if wrapping a present. Refrigerate to keep the foie gras very cold.

Place a foie gras package into the pocket in the rabbit thigh. Spread out the caul fat on a cutting board. Place the thigh on the fat horizontally. Roll the thigh tightly in the fat, being careful not to crush or misshape the foie gras. Wrap the thigh until all sides are covered. Cut the fat off from the back side so that the seal is on the bottom of the thigh. Refrigerate until ready to cook.

Preheat the oven to 350°F. Heat 2 tablespoons of oil in each of 2 cast-iron sauté pans until it just begins to smoke. Season the thighs with salt and place 2, seal side down, in each pan. Lower the heat to medium and cook for 3 minutes. Flip and cook for 3 more minutes. Place the pans into the oven and cook for 3 minutes. Flip and continue cooking for 3 more minutes. Remove from the oven, add 2 tablespoons of butter to each pan, and baste for 2 minutes. Remove the rabbit from the pan and let it rest for 8 minutes.

## RABBIT CRÉPINETTES

4 young rabbit shoulders
4 ice cubes
2 teaspoons butter
2 tablespoons diced (1/8 inch) shallot
1/2 cup diced (1/8 inch) mustard greens
1 egg yolk
1 teaspoon chopped thyme leaves
1 teaspoon chopped parsley
1 teaspoon salt
1/2 teaspoon black pepper
1/2 pound caul fat, thoroughly rinsed
2 tablespoons canola oil
1 1/2 cups Rabbit Jus (see page 357)

Preheat the oven to 350°F. Remove the meat from the shoulders and pass through a meat grinder set on the smallest dial. While grinding the meat, add the ice throughout and 1 cube at the very end to push out any remaining meat. Place the meat in a bowl set over ice. In a small pan over medium heat, melt the butter. Sweat the shallot until it's soft, add the mustard greens, and sauté until wilted. Allow to cool to room temperature. Add the egg yolk to the meat and mix with gloved hands. Add the sautéed shallots and mustard greens, as well as the thyme and parsley. Season with salt and pepper. Refrigerate the mixture until it is cold. Lay out a sheet of caul fat on a cutting board. Place 1 tablespoon of the meat in the middle of the fat. Cut out a square of fat 3 inches around the meat. Carefully wrap the caul fat around the meat, creating a circular patty, or Crépinette. Season with salt and pepper and refrigerate. Repeat to make 7 more. Heat 1 tablespoon of oil in each of 2 medium oven-safe sauté pans over medium-high heat until it begins to smoke. Add 4 Crépinettes to each pan, seal side down, and render until golden brown. Flip the Crépinettes and render the top side. Once browned on both sides, pour off the fat and add 3/4 cup of Rabbit Jus to each pan. Reduce the Jus by half and place the pans in the oven for 3 minutes. Remove from the oven and baste the Crépinettes with the Jus until completely glazed and shiny.

## RABBIT SAUCE

2 tablespoons canola oil
4 pounds rabbit bones from 2 whole young rabbits
2 cups diced (1/2 inch) onions
1 cup diced (1/2 inch) carrots
1 cup diced (1/2 inch) celery
3 sprigs thyme
1 bay leaf
2 cups red wine
1 gallon Chicken Stock (see page 356)
1 teaspoon salt

Heat the oil in a medium pot until it just begins to smoke. Add the bones and roast until dark golden brown. Lower the heat to medium. Add the onions, carrots, and celery and sweat for 10 minutes. Add the thyme and bay leaf and deglaze with red wine. Reduce until almost dry. Add the Chicken Stock and reduce to about 1 quart over medium heat. Strain into a smaller saucepan and reduce to 1 cup. Season with salt and keep in a warm place, such as near a warm oven or stove.

## RABBIT KIDNEYS

1 cup extra-virgin olive oil
4 young rabbit kidneys
1 teaspoon salt
*Fleur de sel*

In a saucepan, bring the olive oil to 140°F. Remove any fat or membrane from the kidneys; trim away any blood spots. Season the kidneys with salt and cook in the olive oil for 7 minutes. Remove from the oil and allow to rest for 3 minutes. Slice in half and season with *fleur de sel* when ready to serve.

## TO FINISH

8 teaspoons Dijon mustard
4 Rabbit Thighs, halved lengthwise
4 Rabbit Loins, cut to yield 6 slices each
8 Rabbit Crépinettes
4 Rabbit Kidneys, halved
32 pieces mustard cress
32 mustard flowers
8 teaspoons Pickled Red Mustard Seeds (see page 342)
Rabbit Sauce
Chives

Spread 1 teaspoon Dijon mustard on a warm plate. Place a slice of Rabbit Thigh and 3 slices of Loin on the plate around the mustard. Place a Crépinette in the middle of the plate and 2 Kidney halves on the sides. Garnish the plate with 4 pieces mustard cress, 4 mustard flowers, and 1 tablespoon Pickled Red Mustard Seeds. Sauce the dish with 2 tablespoons of Rabbit Sauce and finish with chives. Repeat with the remaining ingredients, to serve 8.

# CHICKEN
## POACHED WITH BLACK TRUFFLES, ASPARAGUS, MORELS, AND VIN JAUNE

*Serves 8*

### CHICKEN

2 whole organic chickens, 3 pounds each
2 ounces black truffles
1 tablespoon salt
1/2 pound butter, cut into 1-inch cubes
4 sprigs thyme

Carefully remove the skin from a chicken. Start by scoring the skin around the ankles and cutting up the back of the legs from the score toward the cavity. Gently peel the skin toward the neck using your fingers to help separate it from the flesh. If done correctly, the skin should come off in one piece. Reserve. Remove the breasts (without any bones) and the legs from the chicken. Bone the legs and cut the meat into even pieces. Repeat with the second chicken. Reserve the leg pieces from 1 of the chickens for the sauce; reserve the remaining leg pieces and the bones for stock.

Thinly slice the truffles on a truffle slicer or on a mandoline. Cut a deep pocket lengthwise into each breast (it should go about three quarters of the way into the breast) and fill each pocket with 1/2 ounce thinly sliced black truffles. Press the breasts back together to return them to their original shape.

Season the chicken with the salt, wrap with plastic to help maintain shape, and place each breast into a small *sous vide* bag. Add a cube of butter to each bag as well as 1 thyme sprig. Vacuum-seal the bags, making tight packages. Place in a water bath maintained at 145°F by an immersion circulator for 30 to 35 minutes. Remove the packages from the water bath and keep them warm until ready to serve.

Alternatively, you can wrap the seasoned breast along with a cube of butter and a thyme sprig in a second layer of plastic wrap. Tie a knot on each end (either with the plastic wrap itself or with a piece of butcher's twine) to seal the ends. The packets can then be poached in a pot of water that is kept at 145°F for 30 to 35 minutes. Remove the packages from the water bath and keep them warm until ready to serve.

### VEGETABLES

12 large white asparagus
24 green pencil asparagus, bottom inch trimmed on the bias
2 tablespoons butter
1 teaspoon minced shallot
24 small morels, stems trimmed, thoroughly rinsed
2 teaspoons salt

Trim off the bottom woodsy end of the white asparagus, and, using a vegetable peeler, carefully peel them to the base of the tips. Bring a pot of salted water to a boil. Add the white asparagus and cook for 7 to 8 minutes. Remove with a slotted spoon and transfer to a bowl of ice water. Add the green asparagus to the boiling water and cook for 2 minutes. Remove with a slotted spoon and transfer to a bowl of ice water. Once cold, cut the white asparagus in half lengthwise. Cut the green asparagus into 1 1/2-inch-long pieces.

Heat a large sauté pan over medium heat and add the butter. Sweat the shallot until translucent. Add the morels and sauté for 30 seconds to 1 minute, just to cook them through. Season with the salt and keep warm until ready to serve.

### VIN JAUNE SAUCE

2 tablespoons canola oil
Chicken leg meat (from 1 chicken)
2 tablespoons butter
1 1/2 cups morels, stems trimmed, thoroughly rinsed, sliced
1/4 cup diced shallots
2 teaspoons salt
1 1/2 cups *vin jaune* or dry sherry
1 cup Chicken Jus (see page 356)
3 teaspoons lemon juice
2 tablespoons cream

Heat the oil in a sauté pan until it is very hot but not yet smoking. Add the chopped chicken leg meat and sauté until golden brown. Drain the oil from the pan and return the pan with the legs to the heat. Add the butter and then the morels and shallots. Add 1 teaspoon of salt and sweat the vegetables, mushrooms, and chicken. Deglaze the pan with *vin jaune* or dry sherry and reduce to 1/2 cup. Add the Chicken Jus and continue to reduce to 1 cup liquid. Strain the sauce through a fine-mesh chinois into a saucepan and continue to reduce the sauce by half, leaving just over 1/2 cup sauce. Remove from the heat and season with the remaining teaspoon salt and the lemon juice. Whisk the cream in a cold bowl to soft peaks. Just before serving, whisk the whipped cream into the sauce.

### CHICKEN SKIN CHIPS

Skin of 2 whole chickens (reserved from Chicken)
1/2 cup salt
1 ounce black truffle, shaved
1/2 cup Clarified Butter (see page 370)

Toss the chicken skins with the salt and cure on a rimmed baking sheet for 1 hour in the refrigerator.

Preheat the oven to 350°F. Rinse the skins thoroughly for 5 minutes under cold running water to remove the salt. Dry between 2 kitchen towels. Use a knife to scrape off all excess fat and flesh from the skin.

Place a sheet of parchment paper on an upside-down 13-by-18-inch rimmed baking sheet. Brush the parchment with 1/4 cup Clarified Butter. Place one skin, skin side down, on the parchment and neatly place the shaved truffle on the fat side, completely covering it in a single layer. Place the other skin on top and brush it with the remaining Clarified Butter. Place another piece of parchment on top and a 13-by-18-inch rimmed baking sheet on top of the parchment. It is important that both baking sheets are very flat. Weigh the baking sheets with 2 cast-iron pans and bake for 10 minutes. Remove from the oven, uncover, and cut into 1-inch-by-4-inch rectangles. Return to the baking sheet, cover, and weight. Cook for 10 more minutes, until golden brown and crispy. Cool uncovered.

### TO FINISH

1 cup Chicken Stock (see page 356)
8 tablespoons butter
2 ounces black truffles
Vegetables
32 morels, stems trimmed, thoroughly rinsed
Breasts from 2 chickens, halved and trimmed
8 tablespoons Potato Mousseline (see page 353)
Vin Jaune Sauce
Chicken Skin Chips

Warm the Chicken Stock and butter in a small sauté pan. Using a very sharp knife, cut the truffles into 1/4-inch dice. Add the diced truffles, Vegetables, and morels to the Chicken Stock and toss constantly to glaze. Arrange 3 white asparagus halves on the bottom of a warm plate. Insert the green asparagus pieces into the bottoms of the morels and place 4 around the white asparagus. Neatly place a chicken breast half on top of the white asparagus. Warm the Potato Mousseline over low heat and spoon 1 tablespoon next to the chicken. Garnish with 1 tablespoon Vin Jaune Sauce. Gently lean a Chicken Skin Chip against the breast and place 5 cubes truffle around the plate to finish. Repeat with the remaining ingredients, to serve 8.

# SUCKLING PIG

*Served in four courses*

# SUCKLING PIG
## TÊTE DE COCHON WITH RADISHES

*Serves 8*

### BRINED PIG HEAD
4 cups salt
1 suckling pig head, split, brain removed

Combine the salt and 2 1/2 gallons water in a large pot and bring to a boil over high heat. Cool over ice. Transfer to a nonreactive container and add the pig head. Refrigerate, covered, for 12 hours. Drain and rinse the head under cool running water for 5 minutes.

### TÊTE DE COCHON COOKING LIQUID
3 sprigs thyme
1 bay leaf
8 black peppercorns
1 cup white wine
1/4 cup diced celery
1/4 cup diced carrot
1/4 cup diced onion
4 tablespoons curing salt
4 tablespoons salt
Brined Pig Head
4 suckling pig feet

Preheat the oven to 300°F. Tie the thyme, bay leaf, and black peppercorns together in cheesecloth to make a sachet. Put the sachet in a large pot, along with the wine, celery, carrot, onion, curing salt, salt, pig head, pig feet, and 3 gallons water. Cover and cook in the oven for 6 1/2 hours or until the meat is falling off the bone. Remove from the oven and allow the meat to rest in its liquid for 45 minutes.

### TÊTE DE COCHON TORCHON
Cooked pig head
1/2 cup sherry vinegar
1 1/2 tablespoons salt

Remove the head from its cooking liquid and strain the liquid through a chinois lined with cheesecloth. Cool the cooking liquid over ice immediately. While the head is still hot, pick the tender pink meat from the face and place in a bowl. Remove the fat from the face and freeze half of it for 30 minutes. Discard the rest of the fat. Once the fat is cold, cut it into a small dice. Gently mix together the picked meat, diced fat, sherry vinegar, and salt, being very careful not to overwork. The mixture should be cohesive but not homogenous.

Measure out an arm's length of cheesecloth and wet it under warm running water. Wring out any excess moisture and fold it into a 12-inch square. Place the meat mixture 4 inches in on the long edge closest to you. Shape into a log measuring 2 1/2 by 6 inches. Fold the cheesecloth over the top of the meat and roll tightly, being sure to keep the excess ends of cheesecloth straight. Pinch the ends of the roll to ensure they are tight while rolling. Once all the cheesecloth is rolled around the meat, tie off each end with butcher's twine, making it as tight as possible. Place the tied Torchon into a deep-sided dish.

Bring 1 gallon of the reserved cooking liquid to a simmer. Pour the hot liquid over the Torchon, cool over ice, and refrigerate for 24 hours. Unwrap the Torchon and rewrap it tightly in plastic wrap. Store in the refrigerator.

### POMMERY MAYONNAISE
1/2 cup Mayonnaise (see page 371)
1 tablespoon sherry vinegar
1 tablespoon whole grain mustard
1/2 teaspoon salt

In a small bowl, mix together the Mayonnaise, sherry vinegar, mustard, and salt. Transfer to a squeeze bottle and store in the refrigerator.

### BABY RADISHES
1 cup baby spring radishes
1 tablespoon olive oil
2 teaspoons lemon juice
1 pinch *fleur de sel*

Toss the radishes, olive oil, lemon juice, and *fleur de sel* in a bowl. Place the radishes on a paper towel to drain any excess liquid.

### TÊTE DE COCHON GELÉE
1 cup egg whites, approximately 8
1/2 cup julienned carrots
1/2 cup julienned onion
1/4 cup julienned celery
2 sprigs thyme
1 bay leaf, julienned
2 tablespoons salt, plus more to taste
1 quart Tête de Cochon Cooking Liquid, skimmed, strained, and chilled
1/2 cup sherry vinegar
8 sheets gelatin

Whisk the egg whites in a mixing bowl to soft peaks. Fold in the carrots, onion, celery, thyme, bay leaf, and 2 tablespoons salt. Whisk in the Tête de Cochon Cooking Liquid and the sherry vinegar. Pour the mixture into a tall, narrow pot and set over medium heat. Bring the mixture to bare simmer. The egg white mixture will float to the top, creating a raft. Once the raft has floated to the top, use the edge of a 2-ounce ladle to carefully scoop out a small piece of the raft, forming a hole in the center. Baste the raft with the liquid simmering through the hole. After 45 minutes, ladle the liquid through the hole into a chinois lined with cheesecloth. The consommé should be very clear. Discard the raft.

Measure out 4 cups of the consommé. Season the consommé with salt to taste. Bloom the gelatin by placing the sheets in a bowl of ice water for 10 minutes. Once they are pliable, remove them from the cold water, squeeze to remove excess moisture, and stir them into the warm consommé. Pour into a small container and refrigerate until set, about 4 hours.

### TO FINISH
Tête de Cochon Torchon
Sherry Vinaigrette (see page 346)
Pommery Mayonnaise
16 slices cornichon
Baby Radishes
Pickled Breakfast Radishes (see page 341), sliced
Pickled White Pearl Onions (see page 343)
Tête de Cochon Gelée
32 leaves garden mizuna
2 tablespoons freshly grated horseradish
*Fleur de sel*

Cut the Torchon into 3/8-inch-thick slices and dress with the Sherry Vinaigrette. Place 1 slice in the center of a plate. Dot the Pommery Mayonnaise around it. Delicately arrange 2 cornichon slices, Baby Radishes, Pickled Breakfast Radish slices, and Pickled Onion quarters around the Torchon, leaving a 1/2-inch space around it. Using a small spoon, scoop out a small dollop of Tête de Cochon Gelée and place it next to the Torchon. Finish with 4 mizuna leaves, horseradish, and *fleur de sel*. Repeat with the remaining ingredients, to serve 8.

# SUCKLING PIG
## BELLY WITH PEAS, MINT, AND LETTUCE

*Serves 8*

### PORK BELLY
1 1/2 cups salt
1 tablespoon curing salt
5 black peppercorns
5 sprigs thyme
2 bellies (from one 30-pound suckling pig)

In a large pot, combine the salt, curing salt, peppercorns, thyme, and 16 cups water. Bring to a boil, remove from the heat, transfer to a large plastic container, and chill over ice. Add the pork belly to the brine, cover, and refrigerate for 24 hours.

Remove the pork belly from the brine and rinse thoroughly under cold water. Dry the pork belly with a kitchen towel.

### SOUS VIDE COOKING METHOD
Place the pork belly into a *sous vide* bag and vacuum-seal. Place in a water bath maintained at 135°F by an immersion circulator for 48 hours. Remove from the water bath and cool in a large ice bath.

Preheat the oven to 350°F. Once the belly is cold, remove it from the bag and trim the pork belly into 2 long pieces. Heat a cast-iron skillet over medium heat and sear the pork belly, fat side down, for about 3 minutes, or until the fat begins to brown. Place the skillet in the oven for 5 to 6 minutes or until the belly is warm throughout. Remove from the oven and slice immediately into eight 1 1/2-by-4-inch slices.

### CONVENTIONAL COOKING METHOD
3 sprigs thyme
1 bay leaf
8 black peppercorns
1 cup white wine
1/4 cup diced celery
1/4 cup diced carrot
1/4 cup diced onion
4 tablespoons curing salt
4 tablespoons salt

Preheat the oven to 300°F. Tie the thyme, bay leaf, and black peppercorns in cheesecloth to make a sachet. In a large pot, combine the sachet, white wine, celery, carrots, onion, curing salt, and salt, along with the brined pork belly and 12 quarts water. Cover and cook in the oven for 4 hours.

Carefully remove the pork belly from the liquid and place it on a 13-by-18-inch rimmed baking sheet lined with parchment paper. Be sure to remove any vegetables or herbs that have stuck to the meat and skin. Place another piece of parchment paper on top of the pork belly and place another 13-by-18-inch rimmed baking sheet on top. Place a heavy pan or cast-iron skillet on top of the baking sheet to lightly flatten the belly, making sure the weight is evenly distributed. Refrigerate, weighted, for 12 hours.

Preheat the oven to 350°F. Once the pork belly is pressed and cool, remove the skin with a knife. Trim the belly into 2 long pieces. Heat a cast-iron skillet to medium heat and sear the belly, fat side down, for about 3 minutes, or until the fat begins to brown. Place the skillet in the oven for 5 to 6 minutes or until the belly is warm throughout. Remove from the oven and slice immediately into eight 1 1/2-by-4-inch slices.

### VEGETABLE RAGOUT
1/2 cup shelled garden peas
12 white pearl onions
8 baby carrots
1 tablespoon butter
1 teaspoon salt
1/4 cup Chicken Stock (see page 356)

Bring a pot of salted water to a boil. Add the garden peas and cook for 3 to 4 minutes. Using a slotted spoon, transfer the peas to a bowl of ice water. Repeat with the onions (4 to 6 minutes) and the carrots (3 to 4 minutes). Once cold, strain the blanched vegetables. Cut the pearl onions in half lengthwise and the carrots in thirds.

Melt the butter in a small sauté pan over medium heat. Add the vegetables and the salt and toss lightly. Add the Chicken Stock, bringing it to a simmer, allowing the butter to emulsify. Transfer the vegetables to a paper towel to remove excess glaze. Keep warm.

### ONION MINT JUS
2 teaspoons butter
2 spring onions, minced
1/2 clove garlic, minced
4 tablespoons white balsamic vinegar
1/2 cup Veal Jus (see page 357)
4 sprigs mint

Melt the butter in a small saucepan over medium-low heat. Add the onions and garlic and sweat until tender. Add the vinegar and reduce by half. Add the Veal Jus and mint, remove from the heat, and steep for 20 minutes. Strain through a fine-mesh chinois and keep warm until ready to serve.

### TO FINISH
4 tablespoon Pea Puree (see page 352)
Pork Belly
Vegetable Ragout
24 small Bibb lettuce hearts
4 tablespoons Buttermilk Dressing (see page 344)
16 sprigs mint
16 pea shoots
Onion Mint Jus

Warm the Pea Puree in a small saucepan over low heat.

Spoon 1/2 tablespoon onto a plate and place a rectangle of the Pork Belly in the middle. Surround with 1 1/2 tablespoons of Vegetable Ragout. Dress the Bibb lettuce hearts lightly with Buttermilk Dressing and place them 3 around the plate. Garnish with 2 mint sprigs and 2 pea shoots. Finish with the Jus around the meat. Repeat with the remaining ingredients, to serve 8.

# SUCKLING PIG
CONFIT OF
SHOULDER WITH
ONIONS AND
RHUBARB

*Serves 8*

### CARAMELIZED CIPOLLINI ONIONS
8 *cipollini* onions, peeled
1 cup white wine
1 tablespoon salt
4 tablespoons sugar
1 cup Chicken Stock (see page 356)
1 tablespoon Chicken Jus (see page 356)

In a saucepan, combine the onions with the wine and salt. Bring to a simmer and cook halfway, about 2 to 3 minutes. Remove from heat. Strain the onions. Heat the sugar in a heavy-bottomed saucepan. Cook until it is a deep caramel color. In a small saucepan over low heat bring the Chicken Stock and Chicken Jus to a simmer. Add to the sugar and bring to a simmer. Whisk to dissolve any solidified sugar. Simmer until the sauce is reduced to a glaze. Add the onions to the glaze and simmer for 3 minutes over low heat until onions are tender. Keep warm.

### BABY LEEKS
16 young leeks, peeled, roots trimmed
20 to 25 chives
1 tablespoon Chicken Stock (see page 356)
1 tablespoon butter
1 pinch salt

Bring a pot of salted water to a boil. Add the leeks and cook until tender, 1 to 2 minutes. Transfer with a slotted spoon to a bowl of ice water. Add the chives to the boiling water and cook for 10 to 15 seconds. Transfer with a slotted spoon to the ice water. Tie 2 leeks together with chives on both ends, taking care because the chives are delicate and may break. Bring the Chicken Stock with the leeks to a simmer in a sauté pan. Add the butter, tossing to emulsify, and glaze the leeks. Season with salt.

### SUCKLING PIG CONFIT
2 shoulders and 2 butts from one 30-pound suckling pig, bone in, skin on
1 cup salt, plus more to taste
14 sprigs thyme
8 quarts duck fat
8 black peppercorns
1 bay leaf
1 pinch black pepper
2 tablespoons canola oil
2 tablespoons Brown Butter (see page 370)

Rub the pork with 1 cup of the salt and 12 of the thyme sprigs and refrigerate for 4 hours.

Preheat the oven to 300°F. Warm the duck fat in a large pan until it is melted. Rinse the pork with cold water and pat dry. Place the pork in a baking dish and add the melted duck fat, 2 remaining thyme sprigs, peppercorns, and bay leaf, covering the entire shoulder. Cover and cook in the oven for about 6 hours, until the meat starts falling off the bone. Remove from the oven and allow to rest, uncovered, for 45 minutes.

Line a large baking sheet with parchment paper. Carefully remove the pork from the duck fat and place, skin side down, on the baking sheet. Strain the fat through a chinois and allow to separate. Reserve the liquid and chill the fat for another use. Pick the meat from the legs, keeping the skin intact. Discard the bones. Place the meat in a large mixing bowl. Gently scrape the fat from the skin so that it is less than 1/8-inch thick. Line a 13-by-18 rimmed baking sheet with parchment paper and cover the parchment paper with the skin (outer side down) without overlapping. Be sure that there are no holes and that it completely covers the bottom of the baking sheet. Season the picked meat with the reserved liquid, the ground pepper, and salt to taste. The meat should be moist but not wet. Spread the meat evenly on the skin. It should be about 1 inch thick. Cover with parchment paper and place another 13-by-18-inch rimmed baking sheet on top. Weigh down with a cast-iron skillet to flatten. Refrigerate for 24 hours.

Preheat the oven to 350°F.

Cut the pork into 1 3/4-by-2-inch rectangles. Heat 1 tablespoon canola oil in each of 2 large oven-safe sauté pans set over high heat. When the oil begins to smoke, place 4 of the rectangles, skin-side down, in each pan. Lower the heat to medium-low and render for 1 1/2 minutes. Transfer the pans to the oven and roast for 7 to 8 minutes, until warmed through and the skin is crisp. Remove from the pan and brush the skin with the Brown Butter.

### BLACK PEPPER JUS
3 tablespoons sugar
3 tablespoons Banyuls vinegar
4 tablespoons red wine
1/2 cup minced rhubarb
2 teaspoons Tellicherry peppercorns
1 teaspoon fennel seeds
1 cup Veal Jus (see page 357)
1/4 teaspoon salt

Heat the sugar in a heavy-bottomed saucepan. Cook until it is a deep caramel color. Remove from the heat and add the Banyuls vinegar to stop the cooking. Return to medium heat and reduce by half. Add the red wine, rhubarb, peppercorns, and fennel seeds. Reduce to a jam consistency. Add the Veal Jus and bring to a simmer. Remove from the heat, season with salt, and steep in a warm place such as near a warm oven or stove, for 20 minutes. Strain and keep warm.

### RHUBARB CHUTNEY
2 teaspoons butter
1 cup finely diced (1/8 inch) Granny Smith apples
4 tablespoons sugar
4 tablespoons pomegranate juice
2 tablespoons glucose syrup
4 cups chopped rhubarb
1 tablespoon white balsamic vinegar
1 pinch salt

In a large pot, cook the butter with the apples until the apples are translucent. Cool over ice immediately.

In a separate pan, combine the sugar, pomegranate juice, and glucose. Bring to a boil and reduce just slightly. Add the rhubarb and vinegar and reduce until thick. Cool over ice.

Combine the rhubarb mixture with the apples and season with salt.

### TO FINISH
Rhubarb Chutney
Suckling Pig Confit
Onion Puree (see page 352)
Baby Leeks
Caramelized Cipollini Onions
Black Pepper Jus

Place a quenelle of the Rhubarb Chutney on a plate. Place the Confit next to it and garnish with the Onion Puree, Baby Leeks, and Cipollini Onions and finish with the Black Pepper Jus. Repeat with the remaining ingredients, to serve 8.

# SUCKLING PIG
## ROASTED RACK WITH MORELS, FAVA BEANS, AND MARJORAM

*Serves 8*

### SUCKLING PIG RACKS

2 racks (from one 30-pound suckling pig, frenched)
1 tablespoon salt
2 tablespoons canola oil
2 cloves garlic, crushed but kept whole
4 sprigs marjoram
2 tablespoons butter

Preheat the oven to 300°F. Season the pork with the salt. Heat the canola oil in a large oven-safe sauté pan and sear the racks, fat side down, until golden brown, 1 to 2 minutes. Add the garlic to the pan and roast in the oven for 5 minutes. Remove from the oven, add the marjoram and butter, and baste with the melted, browning butter for about 1 minute. Finally, flip the racks so that they are fat side up and return to the oven to continue roasting for 3 to 4 more minutes, or until golden brown. Let the meat rest for 10 minutes.

### MOREL PANNA COTTA

1 teaspoon butter
2 tablespoons minced double-smoked bacon
1 1/2 teaspoons minced shallot
1 1/2 teaspoons minced garlic
1/4 cup fresh morels, thoroughly rinsed
2 tablespoons dried morels,
    soaked in warm water and rinsed
4 cups half-and-half
2 sprigs thyme
1 tablespoon dry sherry
1 tablespoon salt
2 teaspoons agar-agar (4.6 grams)

Heat the butter in medium saucepan over medium heat. Add the bacon, shallot, and garlic, and sweat for 5 minutes. Add the fresh and dried morels, and continue to sweat for 5 minutes. Add the half-and-half, thyme, and sherry and bring to a simmer. Remove from the heat, cover, and steep in a warm place, such as near a warm oven or stove, for 1 hour. Strain through a fine-mesh chinois and season with salt.

Place 4 cups of the panna cotta liquid on the stove and bring to a slow simmer without boiling. In a large saucepan, whisk together 1/2 cup cold water with the agar-agar. Bring to a boil over medium heat and whisk constantly for 5 minutes. Pour the hot panna cotta into the agar-agar mixture and bring to a simmer, whisking for 1 minute. Strain through a fine-mesh chinois into a 9-by-13-inch rimmed baking sheet lined with acetate. Chill in the refrigerator for 1 hour.

### MOREL CREAM

1 tablespoon butter
1 cup morels, including any available trim,
    thoroughly rinsed and roughly chopped
1 tablespoon finely diced shallots
1 cup cream
1 teaspoon salt

In a small pot, melt the butter over medium heat. Sweat the morels and shallots for 2 minutes. Deglaze with the cream and bring to a simmer. Remove from the heat, cover, and let infuse for 45 minutes. Season with salt and strain.

### MOREL AND FAVA BEAN RAGOUT

4 cups shelled fava beans
2 cups small morels, stems trimmed, thoroughly rinsed
1 tablespoon butter
2 tablespoons minced double-smoked bacon
2 teaspoons minced shallots
1/2 teaspoon salt

Bring a pot of salted water to a boil. Add the fava beans and cook for 1 to 2 minutes or until bright green and tender. Remove with a slotted spoon and transfer to a large bowl filled with ice water. Drain the beans and peel the remaining layer off each one. Dice three quarters of the beans into 1/8-inch pieces and reserve the rest for garnish. Dice half of the morels into 1/8-inch pieces. Reserve the rest for garnish.

Melt the butter in a sauté pan and sweat the bacon and the shallots. Add the diced morels and sauté for 2 minutes before adding the diced fava beans. Season with the salt and remove from the heat.

### MARBLE POTATOES

32 marble potatoes
4 cups olive oil
3 cloves garlic, crushed but kept whole
2 sprigs thyme
2 tablespoons canola oil
1 tablespoon butter
2 sprigs marjoram
*Fleur de sel*

Preheat the oven to 275°F. Place the unpeeled potatoes in a baking dish with the olive oil, 2 of the garlic cloves, and the thyme and cover with aluminum foil. Roast the potatoes in the oven for 1 hour and 30 minutes. Remove from the oven and cool the potatoes in the oil to room temperature. Once cool, strain, reserving the oil. Peel the potatoes with a paring knife and return them to the strained olive oil. The potatoes can be stored in the olive oil for up to 4 hours.

Heat the canola oil in a large sauté pan over high heat. Strain the potatoes from the olive oil, add them to the pan, and cook for 5 minutes, constantly turning the potatoes with a spoon or tongs to brown them evenly. Drain and discard the oil. Add the butter, marjoram, and the remaining garlic clove, turning the potatoes for 2 more minutes, or until evenly golden brown. Drain on paper towels and season with *fleur de sel*.

### PORK JUS WITH GUANCIALE

1 tablespoon canola oil
1 cup pork trimmings (from the racks, shoulder,
    and belly), diced (1/4 inch)
1/2 cup white wine
1 cup Veal Jus (see page 357)
8 sprigs marjoram
1 teaspoon salt
1/4 cup minced *guanciale*

Heat the canola oil in a medium saucepan and sauté the pork trimmings until golden brown. Drain and discard any oil from the pan and then deglaze with the white wine. Reduce the wine by half and add the Veal Jus. Add the marjoram and simmer for 10 minutes. Strain and reduce by half. Season with the salt. Heat a sauté pan over medium heat and add the *guanciale,* lower the heat, and render until browned. Strain and stir the rendered fat into the sauce.

### TO FINISH

2 tablespoons butter
Morels (reserved from the Morel and Fava
    Bean Ragout)
Blanched fava beans (reserved from Morel and
    Fava Bean Ragout)
1/3 cup Morel Cream
1 teaspoon Chicken Stock (see page 356)
Morel Panna Cotta
Morel and Fava Bean Ragout
Suckling Pig Racks
Marble Potatoes
Pork Jus with Guanciale
24 marjoram tips

Preheat the oven to 300°F. Heat 1 tablespoon of the butter in a sauté pan. Add the morels and fava beans and sauté for just under 30 seconds. Add the Morel Cream and toss to coat. Heat the Chicken Stock with the morels and fava beans. When it comes to a simmer, add the remaining tablespoon butter and toss to glaze.

Using a 2-inch round cutter, cut the Panna Cotta. Leave the ring cutter around the Panna Cotta and cover the top with the warm Morel and Fava Bean Ragout. Place into the oven for 3 minutes to bring to temperature. Once hot, place in the middle of a warm plate. Repeat with the remaining Panna Cotta, to serve 8.

After letting the pork racks rest, cut in between the bones in one fluid motion to make chops. Place 2 slices of the rack on opposite sides of the Panna Cotta. Place 4 potatoes in various spots around each plate and garnish with the glazed morels and fava beans. Finish the plates with the Pork Jus and 3 marjoram tips.

# VEAL
## BLANQUETTE WITH CRAYFISH AND TARRAGON

*Serves 8*

### SAUCE

32 crayfish
1 tablespoon butter
1/4 cup morels, stems trimmed, thoroughly rinsed
1 tablespoon diced (1/8 inch) shallot
3 cups Lobster Stock (see page 356)
2 cups Veal Jus (see page 357)
1 cup cream
2 sprigs tarragon
2 teaspoons lemon zest
2 tablespoons lemon juice
2 teaspoons salt

Bring a pot of salted water to a boil. Add the crayfish to the water and cook for 2 minutes. Transfer with a slotted spoon to a bowl of ice water. Once the crayfish are cold, remove the tails. Peel and devein the tails and reserve for the final assembly.

Melt the butter in a large saucepan over medium heat. Add the crayfish bodies and stir while crushing with a wooden spoon. Add the morels and shallot and sweat until soft. Add the Lobster Stock and reduce to 1 1/2 cups. Add the Veal Jus and reduce to 2 1/2 cups. Bring to a simmer and add the cream. Add the tarragon and lemon zest, remove from the heat, cover, and steep for 20 minutes. Strain through a chinois. Season with the lemon juice and salt.

### VEAL GLAZE

2 cups Veal Jus
1 cup cream
1 teaspoon salt

Combine the Veal Jus, cream, and salt in a small saucepan set over medium heat. Reduce by half and strain through a chinois.

### VEAL TENDERLOIN

2 veal tenderloins
Salt
1 cup flour
4 tablespoons canola oil
1 cup Veal Glaze

Cut the tenderloins into 1-inch cubes. Season with salt, dredge in flour, and pat off any excess. Heat the canola oil in a sauté pan over high heat. Sear the veal to medium rare on 4 sides, about 1 minute per side, or until evenly browned. Remove from the heat, drain, and discard any excess oil. Add the glaze to the pan and baste the veal until medium. Rest in a warm place, such as near a warm oven or stove, for 10 minutes.

### BLANCHED VEGETABLES

1/2 cup shelled fava beans
1/3 cup shelled English peas
24 baby carrots (8 orange, 8 yellow, 8 Thumbelina)
16 green asparagus, woodsy ends trimmed
16 sugar snap peas
8 red pearl onions, peeled
8 white pearl onions, peeled

Bring a pot of salted water to a boil. Add the fava beans and cook for 1 to 2 minutes. Transfer with a slotted spoon to a bowl of ice water. Repeat with the English peas (3 to 4 minutes), the baby carrots (3 to 4 minutes), the asparagus (3 minutes), the snap peas (1 to 2 minutes), and the red and white pearl onions (3 to 4 minutes). Once the vegetables are cool, drain and pat dry.

### TO FINISH

1/4 cup butter
24 morels, stems trimmed, thoroughly rinsed
Blanched Vegetables
Crayfish tails (reserved from Sauce)
1/3 cup Chicken Stock (see page 356)
Veal Tenderloin
1 tablespoon thinly sliced chives
Sauce
4 teaspoons Tarragon Oil (see page 345)
16 pea tendrils
16 sprigs tarragon

Melt the butter in a large sauté pan over medium heat. Add morels to the pan and sauté for 1 minute. Add the Blanched Vegetables to the pan along with the crayfish tails. Add the Chicken Stock and warm through. Toss lightly to glaze. Place 3 veal cubes in a warm, shallow bowl. Place the glazed vegetables and 4 crayfish tails on and around the veal. Sprinkle with the chives. Blend the Sauce with a hand blender to aerate. Then sauce the plate around the veal, being careful not to cover the vegetables. Drizzle 1/2 teaspoon Tarragon Oil around. Garnish with 2 pea tendrils and 2 tarragon sprigs. Repeat with the remaining ingredients, to serve 8.

# BEEF
## ROASTED RIB EYE WITH ASPARAGUS, PARMESAN, AND BONE MARROW

*Serves 8*

### ROASTED RIB EYE

2 pounds boneless beef rib eye
1 1/2 tablespoons salt
1 tablespoon canola oil
8 tablespoons butter
2 cloves garlic, crushed but kept whole
1/2 bunch thyme (about 8 sprigs)

Preheat the oven to 300°F. Slice the beef into 4 even steaks and season them with salt. Heat a heavy cast-iron pan over medium-high heat. Add the canola oil to the pan. Just before the oil begins to smoke, add the butter, garlic, and thyme and reduce the heat to medium-low, allowing the butter to foam and brown. Add the steaks to the pan and baste for 2 to 3 minutes with the butter, flipping the steaks often. Remove the steaks from the pan and save the butter, garlic, and thyme for basting. Place the steaks on a roasting rack and roast in the oven for 3 minutes. Flip the steaks and baste them with the reserved butter. Roast for another 3 minutes. Remove from the oven, flip the steaks, and pour the remaining butter with garlic and thyme over them. Allow the steaks to rest for 10 minutes before cutting, just before serving, into 1-inch-thick slices.

### PARMESAN-CRUSTED ASPARAGUS

1 cup brioche bread crumbs
1/2 cup butter, softened
1/3 cup grated Parmesan cheese
1 teaspoon salt
8 jumbo green asparagus

In a bowl, mix the bread crumbs with the butter, using a rubber spatula. Mix in the Parmesan and salt. Place the crust between 2 sheets of parchment paper and, using a rolling pin, roll to a thickness of 1/16 inch. Refrigerate until very cold, about 1 hour.

Preheat the broiler. Trim the asparagus to 4 inches in length and peel the bottom 1/2 inch evenly with a paring knife. Bring a pot of salted water to a boil and add the asparagus, cooking for 3 to 4 minutes. Remove with a slotted spoon and transfer to a bowl of ice water. Once cold, drain and dry the asparagus on paper towels. Cut 8 pieces of crust into 1/4-inch-by-3-inch rectangles. Work quickly so that the butter does not melt and the crust is easier to handle. Remove the parchment and lay a crust rectangle on top of each asparagus spear, leaving the asparagus tips uncovered. Place the crusted asparagus under the broiler for 45 seconds, until the crust is golden brown.

### SAUCE BORDELAISE

1 tablespoon diced bone marrow
1 teaspoon thyme leaves
1 teaspoon diced (1/8 inch) shallot
1/2 teaspoon salt
1 cup Veal Jus (see page 357)

Preheat the broiler. Toss the bone marrow with the thyme and shallot and season with the salt. Roast briefly under the broiler to just warm the marrow. Remove from the oven when the marrow is slightly melted and the aromas are released from the thyme. Heat the Veal Jus in a small saucepan over medium heat. Just before serving, add the marrow with the shallot and thyme to the jus. Serve immediately.

### TO FINISH

3 jumbo green asparagus
8 slices shaved Parmesan
Roasted Rib Eye
Parmesan-Crusted Asparagus
40 chive blossoms
8 chive buds
Sauce Bordelaise

Trim the woodsy ends of the raw asparagus on the bias. Using a vegetable peeler, make thin asparagus ribbons. Using a 1-inch round cutter, punch out disks from the Parmesan slices. Place 1 slice of beef on a plate. Place a Parmesan-Crusted Asparagus next to it, creating a V-shape. Garnish the meat with a shaved Parmesan disk, 5 chive blossoms, and 1 chive bud. Place 1 shaved asparagus ribbon on the plate. Spoon 1 tablespoon of the Sauce Bordelaise between the meat and the asparagus. Repeat with the remaining ingredients, to serve 8.

# LAMB
## HERB-ROASTED WITH LETTUCE, MORELS, AND MUSTARD SEEDS

*Serves 8*

### BRAISED LAMB SHANKS

One 750-milliliter bottle red wine
3 pounds spring lamb shanks
1 carrot, diced
1 stalk celery, diced
1 white onion, diced
1/2 celery root, diced
1 shallot, minced
Salt
1/4 cup canola oil
1 teaspoon tomato paste
8 cups Chicken Stock (see page 356)
2 cups Lamb Jus (see page 356)
5 sprigs thyme
1 bay leaf

In a large nonreactive container, combine the wine with
the lamb, carrot, celery, onions, celery root, and shallot.
Marinate in the refrigerator for 48 hours.

Preheat the oven to 300°F. Remove the shanks
from the marinade and pat them dry and season with
salt. Strain the marinade, reserving the liquid and the
vegetables. In a large saucepan, bring the liquid to a
simmer, skimming off any fats and impurities that rise
to the top. Heat the oil in a large straight-sided pan
and sear the shanks until evenly browned. Remove the
shanks from the pan and pour off the excess oil. Add
the reserved vegetables and sweat over medium heat.

Add the tomato paste and sweat for 2 minutes.
Deglaze the pan with the simmering liquid. Add the
Chicken Stock, Lamb Jus, thyme, and bay leaf, bring to
a simmer, and return the lamb shanks to the pan. Bring
to a simmer, skimming the liquid. Cover and braise in
the oven for 3 1/2 hours, or until the lamb is tender and
falling off the bone.

Gently remove the shanks from the pan and strain
the braising liquid. Reduce the liquid until it coats the
back of a spoon. Pick the meat from the bones and
place it in a large mixing bowl. Gently pull the meat
to shred it slightly. Fold in a few tablespoons of the
reserved braising liquid just to moisten the shredded
meat. Season with salt.

## MOREL CREAM

1 tablespoon butter
1 cup morels, including any available trim, thoroughly rinsed and roughly chopped
1 tablespoon finely diced shallots
1 cup cream
1 teaspoon salt

In a small pot, melt the butter over medium heat. Sweat the morels and shallots for 2 minutes. Deglaze with the cream and bring to a simmer. Remove from the heat, cover, and let infuse for 45 minutes. Season with salt and strain.

## LAMB FILLING

1 cup Braised Lamb Shanks
1 cup goat cheese
3 tablespoons grated pecorino
3 tablespoons thinly sliced mint
1 tablespoon sheep's milk yogurt
1 teaspoon salt
1/2 teaspoon black pepper

Finely chop the braised lamb. Stir in the goat cheese and pecorino and then fold in the mint and the yogurt. Season with the salt and pepper. Transfer to a pastry bag for piping.

## TORTELLINI

Pasta Dough (see page 364)
Lamb Filling
3 egg whites, lightly whisked

Remove the pasta dough from the refrigerator to allow it to soften slightly. Set up a pasta roller as per the manufacturer's instructions. Flatten the pasta with a rolling pin until it can fit through the widest setting on the pasta machine. Run the Pasta Dough through the machine, gradually decreasing the thickness until the thinnest setting is reached. Run the pasta twice on the thinnest setting. Lay the pasta sheet flat and cut into 1-foot lengths. Using a 2 1/2-inch round cutter, cut out circles of pasta dough. Place 1/4 teaspoon of the Lamb Filling directly in the middle of a circle. Brush the edges of the circle lightly with the egg-white wash. Fold the pasta over the filling, forming a semicircle, and remove all air pockets by pressing the bubbles to the edge of the pasta. Using both thumbs and index fingers, pick up the tortellino and face the straight edge away from you. Brush the left corner with a touch of egg-white wash. Push the middle of the pasta inward and up, creating a point. Then fold the right corner over the top of the left and press together gently. Repeat. Line a baking sheet with a linen napkin and place the completed tortellini on top. Cover with another linen napkin and keep in a cool place until ready to cook.

## LAMB SWEETBREADS

1 pound lamb sweetbreads
1 cup Lamb Jus (see page 356)
1/2 teaspoon salt
1/2 cup flour
4 cups canola oil

Using scissors, trim the sweetbreads into 3/4-inch pieces, removing any fat and blood. Soak the sweetbreads in ice water in the refrigerator overnight. Reduce the Lamb Jus by half and cover to keep warm. Drain and dry the sweetbreads, season them with the salt, and dredge them in the flour. In a large sauté pan, heat the canola oil to 375°F. Pat off any excess flour and fry the sweetbreads for 4 minutes. Drain them on paper towels. Toss the drained sweetbreads in the reduced Lamb Jus just before serving.

## RACK OF LAMB

2 racks spring baby lamb, frenched
Salt
Black pepper
2 tablespoons canola oil
4 tablespoons butter
4 sprigs thyme
2 cloves garlic, crushed but kept whole

Preheat the oven to 300°F. Wrap and cover each lamb bone tightly with a small piece of aluminum foil. Season the racks with salt and pepper. Heat the canola oil in a large cast-iron skillet over high heat and sear the lamb fat side down. Render the fat for 2 minutes, until golden brown. Flip the racks and sear the meat for 1 to 2 minutes. Once the racks are evenly browned on all sides, transfer to a roasting rack and roast in the oven for 5 to 6 minutes. Return the lamb to the cast-iron skillet, fat side up, return to the stove, and add the butter, thyme, and garlic. Baste the meat with the foamy hot butter for 2 to 3 minutes, rotating the meat to ensure even cooking. Rest in a warm place, such as near a warm oven or stove, for 10 to 15 minutes. Slice the lamb just before serving.

## RENDERED LAMB FAT

1 1/2 pounds lamb fat, frozen

Grind the frozen lamb fat in a meat grinder or have your butcher do it. Place the lamb fat and 1/4 cup water in a medium pot over low heat. Render the fat, making sure not to achieve any color. Once all of the water has been cooked out and the fat is completely rendered, strain through a fine-mesh chinois, reserving the liquid fat.

## LAMB SAUCE

2 cups Lamb Jus (see page 356)
3 sprigs mint
2 tablespoons Rendered Lamb Fat
3 tablespoons Pickled Yellow Mustard Seeds (see page 342)
1/2 teaspoon salt

Heat the Lamb Jus in a small pot. Remove from the heat, add the mint, and steep for 5 minutes. Strain and then stir in the Rendered Lamb Fat and Pickled Yellow Mustard Seeds. Season with salt.

## TO FINISH

1 tablespoon butter
32 morels, thoroughly rinsed
Salt
Tortellini
Morel Cream
8 Romaine lettuce hearts
Rack of Lamb
16 petite lettuce hearts
Buttermilk Dressing (see page 344)
Lamb Sweetbreads
Lamb Sauce

Bring a pot of salted water to a boil. Heat the butter in a large sauté pan over medium heat. Add the morels, season with salt, and sauté until just tender. Add the Tortellini to the boiling water and cook for 3 to 4 minutes. As the Tortellini cook, add the Morel Cream to the morels. Drain the Tortellini and add them to the morels. Add the Romaine lettuce hearts to the boiling water and cook until just wilted. Drain the lettuce well and add to the morels and Tortellini. Toss to glaze evenly.

On a warm plate, place 1 slice Rack of Lamb. Arrange the glazed Romaine, morels, and Tortellini next to the lamb. Brush the petite lettuce hearts with Buttermilk Dressing. Garnish the plate with the dressed petite lettuce and the Lamb Sweetbreads and spoon the Lamb Sauce between the garnish and the lamb. Repeat with the remaining ingredients, to serve 8.

# CHÈVRE
## WITH PISTACHIO
## AND WILD GREENS

*Serves 8*

### CANDIED PISTACHIOS
1/2 cup shelled pistachios
1 cup sugar
1 tablespoon glucose syrup

Preheat the oven to 300°F. Place the pistachios on a rimmed baking sheet and toast in the oven for 8 to 10 minutes. Combine the sugar, glucose, and 1 table-spoon water in a small heavy-bottomed saucepan over medium heat and cook to a light caramel (about 300°F). Add the pistachios and coat evenly with the caramel. Separate the pistachios on a rimmed baking sheet lined with a silicone baking mat while they're still warm and roll each individual nut in your hand to create a smooth, round outer shell. Cool to room temperature.

### PISTACHIO BUTTER
2 cups shelled pistachios
1 tablespoon salt
1/2 cup pistachio oil

Preheat the oven to 300°F. Place the pistachios on a rimmed baking sheet and toast in the oven for 8 to 10 minutes. Combine the toasted pistachios and salt in a food processor. Chop the pistachios in the processor and slowly drizzle in the oil until the mixture reaches the consistency of a loose, crunchy peanut butter. Transfer to a blender and blend on high speed until you have a smooth paste. Pass the paste through a fine-mesh tamis and cool to room temperature.

### TO FINISH
8 leaves baby green kale
8 leaves salad burnet
8 leaves red ribbon sorrel
8 leaves lovage
1 tablespoon Lemon Vinaigrette (see page 346)
Pistachio Puree
4 ounces fig leaf–wrapped chèvre
4 ounces chestnut leaf–wrapped chèvre
4 ounces ash-wrapped chèvre
Candied Pistachios

In a small bowl, lightly toss the kale, salad burnet, sorrel, and lovage in the Lemon Vinaigrette.

Place 1 tablespoon Pistachio Butter on a plate and spread evenly in one motion. Slice each chèvre into 8 even pieces. Arrange 1 piece of each on and around the Puree. Garnish with the Candied Pistachios and 1 of each green. Repeat with the remaining ingredients, to serve 8.

# RHUBARB
## SLOW-COOKED WITH CELERY AND SHEEP'S MILK YOGURT SORBET

*Serves 8*

### RHUBARB STICKS
2 stalks rhubarb
1 tablespoon sugar
1/2 cup rhubarb juice (from about 2 cups
    sliced rhubarb)

Preheat a combination steam oven to 150°F. In a *sous vide* bag, vacuum-seal the rhubarb stalks with the sugar and juice. Steam in the oven for 18 minutes. Shock in a bowl of ice water. Remove the rhubarb from the bag and peel off the outer layer. Cut into 2-inch-long matchsticks with each end cut on the bias.

### RHUBARB GELÉE
5 sheets gelatin
1 vanilla bean
1/2 cup rhubarb juice (from about 2 cups
    sliced rhubarb)
1 tablespoon sugar

Bloom the gelatin by placing it in a bowl of ice water for 10 minutes, until pliable. Line a 9-by-13-inch rimmed baking sheet with acetate and coat with vegetable spray. Wipe off excess spray with a paper towel. Using a paring knife, split the vanilla bean and scrape out the seeds. Combine the rhubarb juice, sugar, and vanilla seeds in a small saucepan over low heat. Squeeze the gelatin sheets to remove excess moisture and stir them into the warm juice mixture. Strain through a chinois. Cool the liquid over ice slightly to a syrupy consistency. This will help suspend the vanilla seeds. Be careful not to allow the gelatin to chill too much or it will begin to set. Pour the mixture onto the prepared baking sheet and refrigerate for 1 hour to set. Cut into 3-inch squares.

### SHEEP'S MILK YOGURT FOAM
1/2 cup skim milk
1/3 cup sheep's milk yogurt
1/3 cup half-and-half
1 1/2 teaspoons soy lecithin
1/4 teaspoon salt

Using a hand blender, combine the milk, yogurt, half-and-half, soy lecithin, and salt. Strain through a chinois and refrigerate.

### TO FINISH
Sheep's Milk Yogurt Sorbet (see page 367)
1 stalk celery
Sheep's Milk Yogurt Foam
Black Pepper Crumble (see page 361)
Rhubarb Sticks
Rhubarb Gelée
Rhubarb Gel (see page 348)
Vanilla Oil (see page 345)
8 baby celery
16 celery leaves

Transfer the Sheep's Milk Yogurt Sorbet to a piping bag and pipe into eight 3-inch-by-1-inch cylindrical molds. Return to the freezer for 1 hour.

Using a vegetable peeler, shave the celery into thin ribbons. Using a hand blender, blend the top of the Sheep's Milk Yogurt Foam. Let stand for 1 minute to stabilize the foam. Place the Black Pepper Crumble on a diagonal in the middle of a plate. Behind it, place the Rhubarb Sticks, celery ribbons, and a spoonful of the Sheep's Milk Yogurt Foam. Unmold the sorbet from the cylinders. Place a cylinder of Sorbet on top of the Crumble, and the Rhubarb Gelée on top of the Sorbet cylinder. Place a dot of Rhubarb Gel on the left and the Vanilla Oil around the edge of the Gel. Finish with the baby celery and celery leaves and serve immediately. Repeat with the remaining ingredients, to serve 8.

# MILK
## AND HONEY

*Serves 8*

### DEHYDRATED MILK FOAM

2 1/2 cups milk
1/2 cup glucose syrup

Preheat the oven to 175°F. Line a 9-by-13-inch rimmed baking sheet with acetate. In a medium saucepan, heat the milk and glucose until just under a boil. Remove from the heat and froth with a hand blender. Scoop the foam out with a large spoon onto the prepared baking sheet. Dry in the oven overnight, or for 8 to 9 hours. Allow the foam to cool before breaking it into small pieces. Store in an airtight container.

### MILK SNOW

2 1/2 cups milk
Liquid nitrogen (optional)

Line a large metal bowl with acetate. Fill the bowl halfway with liquid nitrogen and carefully pour the milk into the liquid nitrogen. As it freezes it will start to become brittle. Quickly transfer the frozen milk to a food processor and grind. The finished Milk Snow will be powdery. Reserve in the freezer.

Alternatively, pour the milk into a shallow pan and freeze until completely solid. When ready to serve, scrape the frozen milk with a fork to create Milk Snow and garnish the plate.

### CHAMOMILE HONEY

2 cups honey
1 cup dried chamomile flowers

Bring the honey to 190°F in a saucepan set over medium heat. Add the flowers, remove from the heat, and steep for 15 minutes. Return to medium heat, bring to 190°F, and strain.

### MILK SORBET WITH TUACA HONEY CENTERS

1 cup Chamomile Honey
3 tablespoons Tuaca
Liquid nitrogen
Milk Sorbet (see page 367)

Stir together the Honey and Tuaca. Fill 1 1/4-inch demi-sphere flex molds with the Tuaca honey. It is easiest to do this with a squeeze bottle. Ladle the nitrogen over the top of the molds until a thin frozen layer forms. Dip the mold into the nitrogen repeatedly until the spheres are frozen solid.

Scoop the Milk Sorbet into 2-inch demisphere flex molds and smooth into the mold with a spoon. Push a frozen Tuaca Honey Center into the middle of each demisphere of Sorbet. Cover the Honey Center with excess Sorbet to encase the honey completely. Place the entire flex mold into liquid nitrogen for 30 seconds. Remove from the liquid nitrogen and let rest for 1 minute. Unmold the demispheres and place in the freezer for at least 1 hour before serving. This will let the Frozen Honey Centers return to a liquid state.

### TO FINISH

Dehydrated Milk Foam
Milk Sorbet with Tuaca Honey Centers
Milk Snow
Maldon salt
Bee pollen

Place a tablespoon of the Dehydrated Milk Foam in the center of a plate. Place 1 Milk Sorbet with Tuaca Honey Center onto the Milk Foam. Spoon 4 tablespoons of Dehydrated Milk Foam over the top of the right-hand side of the Milk Sorbet demisphere. Spoon 4 tablespoons of Milk Snow over the opposite side. Sprinkle with Maldon salt and bee pollen. Repeat with the remaining ingredients, to serve 8. Serve immediately.

# FRAISE DES BOIS
## VACHERIN WITH LEMON PARFAIT AND BASIL

*Serves 8*

## LEMON PARFAIT

1 cup cream
Zest of 2 lemons
3 tablespoons crème fraîche
1 egg white
3 tablespoons sugar

Bring the cream to a simmer in a saucepan over medium heat, and then add the lemon zest. Remove from the heat and steep for 15 minutes. Strain through a chinois and chill. In a cold bowl, whip the crème fraîche to soft peaks. Add 2 tablespoons of lemon cream, reserving and chilling the rest. Rewhip the crème fraîche mixture, if necessary, to achieve soft peaks.

In a small bowl, whip the egg white until you can see traces of the whisk. Add the sugar and whip to stiff, glossy peaks. Fold into the crème fraîche mixture. Line a 5-inch-by-1-inch cylindrical mold with acetate. Transfer the parfait to a piping bag and pipe a third of the way up from the base. Freeze.

## BASIL PARFAIT

2 cups loosely packed basil leaves
1/2 cup cream
3 tablespoons crème fraîche
1 egg white
3 tablespoons sugar

Bring a pot of water to a boil. Add the basil and cook until just wilted, 10 to 15 seconds. Drain and transfer to a bowl of ice water. Once cold, place the blanched basil in a clean, dry towel and squeeze out any excess moisture. In a small saucepan over low heat, warm the cream without allowing it to boil. In a blender, puree the basil with the warm cream. Strain though a chinois and chill. In a cold bowl, whip the crème fraîche to soft peaks. Add 2 tablespoons of the basil cream, rewhipping, if necessary, to achieve soft peaks.

In a small bowl, whip the egg white until you can see traces of the whisk. Add the sugar and whip to stiff, glossy peaks. Fold into the crème fraîche mixture. Transfer the parfait to a piping bag and pipe 1 inch of the Basil Parfait on top of the frozen Lemon Parfait. Freeze.

Repeat the Lemon Parfait recipe using the reserved lemon cream. Pipe on top of Basil Parfait to fill the mold. Freeze.

## FRENCH MERINGUE TEARS

2 egg whites
1/2 cup sugar

Preheat the oven to 175°F and line a baking sheet with parchment paper. In a small bowl, whip the egg whites until you can see traces of the whisk. Add the sugar and whip to stiff, glossy peaks. Transfer to a piping bag and pipe 1 3/4-inch-long teardrops onto the parchment paper. Let dry for at least 2 hours or overnight in the oven. The teardrops should be dry and crispy. Cool to room temperature. Crush any imperfect tears and any leftover tears for use in the plating of the dessert. Store the tears and the crushed meringue in separate airtight containers.

## STRAWBERRY SYRUP

10 cups strawberries, hulled and quartered
1 1/4 cups sugar

In a large heat-resistant bowl, toss together the strawberries and sugar. Let sit at room temperature for 20 minutes. Bring a large saucepan of water to a simmer over medium heat. Set the bowl of strawberries over the water, ensuring that the water does not touch the bottom of the bowl. Cover and cook for 2 hours. When the color has left the berries and a lot of syrup has formed, strain through 10 layers of cheesecloth. Chill over ice and then refrigerate.

## STRAWBERRY GELÉE

3 sheets gelatin
1 cup Strawberry Syrup
1/4 teaspoon citric acid

Bloom the gelatin by placing the sheets in a bowl of ice water for 10 minutes, until pliable. In a small pan over low heat, warm the Strawberry Syrup. Remove the gelatin from the cold water, squeeze to remove excess moisture, and stir into the warm liquid until the gelatin is completely melted. Line a 6-by-9-inch pan with acetate and coat with vegetable spray. Wipe out any excess spray with a paper towel. Pour the Gelée into the prepared pan. Refrigerate for 1 hour. Once set, cut into 1/2-inch cubes.

## TO FINISH

Crushed meringue
    (reserved from French Meringue Tears)
Lemon Basil Parfait
Basil Gel (see page 347)
Lemon Gel (see page 348)
Strawberry Gel (see page 348)
Strawberry Gelée
16 tristar strawberries, diced (1/4 inch)
Strawberry Sorbet (see page 367)
8 micro purple basil leaves
16 sprigs basil
32 basil blossoms
French Meringue Tears
8 white strawberries
32 *fraise des bois* or wild red strawberries

Place a spoonful of crushed meringue in the middle of a plate and put the frozen Lemon Basil Parfait on top. Garnish the plate with random dots of the gels. Place the Strawberry Gelée cubes and diced strawberries around the dot clusters. Place the Strawberry Sorbet next to the Parfait and on top of the crushed meringue. Finish with all 3 types of basil, the Meringue Tears, the white strawberries, and the *fraise des bois*. Repeat with the remaining ingredients, to serve 8. Serve immediately.

# MINT
## VARIATIONS WITH CHOCOLATE

*Serves 8*

### LEMON CHOCOLATE SPRAY

2 cups (8.6 ounces) Valrhona Caraïbe chocolate
    (66 percent), chopped
2 cups cocoa butter
2 tablespoons Lemon Oil (see page 345)

Melt the chocolate with the cocoa butter and Lemon Oil. Strain. Fill a spray gun with the mixture.

### CHOCOLATE MOUSSE

1 1/2 sheets gelatin
1 cup (4.3 ounces) plus 1/4 cup (1 ounce) Valrhona
    Araguani chocolate (72 percent), chopped
1 1/4 cups cream
1 egg
4 egg yolks
1/3 cup sugar

Bloom the gelatin by placing the sheets in a bowl of ice water for 10 minutes, until pliable. Squeeze out the excess moisture. In the meantime, melt 1 cup of the chocolate over a double boiler and set aside in a warm place, such as near a warm oven or stove. In a cold bowl, whip the cream to very soft peaks. Keep in the refrigerator. In a separate bowl, combine the egg, egg yolks, and sugar and whisk over a double boiler until very warm and the sugar is dissolved. Add the bloomed gelatin to the warm egg mixture. Transfer to the bowl of a stand mixer fitted with the whisk attachment and whip on high speed until pale yellow and a ribbon forms. Cool to room temperature and then fold into the chocolate, very slowly to avoid lumps. Then fold in the cream.

Line a 9-by-13-inch rimmed baking sheet with acetate. Spread the mousse onto the acetate into a thin, even layer. Freeze for 3 hours. Melt the remaining 1/4 cup chocolate over a double boiler. Set aside to cool. Once the mousse is frozen, coat the mousse with a thin layer of the melted chocolate. Allow the chocolate to set and then invert it onto a baking sheet. Peel off the acetate and cut the mousse into various triangle shapes. Return to the freezer for 1 hour. Spray with the Lemon Chocolate Spray. Freeze until ready to use.

### CHOCOLATE CARAMEL TUILES

1/4 cup glucose syrup
2 tablespoons poured white fondant
1/2 cup (2.15 ounces) Valrhona Araguani chocolate
    (72 percent), chopped

Preheat the oven to 300°F. Line a rimmed baking sheet with a silicone baking mat. Cook the glucose syrup and the fondant in a heavy-bottomed saucepan to 320°F. Remove the pan from the heat, add the chocolate, mix well to melt, and pour onto the silicone mat. Place another silicone mat on top and roll out with a rolling pin to help the mixture cool quickly. Place it in the oven until remelted and flexible. Using an offset spatula, stretch the Tuile to create thin, transparent pieces. It may be necessary to return the Tuile to the oven to soften it again. Cool and keep in an airtight container.

### CRYSTALLIZED MINT LEAVES

1/2 teaspoon canola oil
8 leaves mint
1/4 cup superfine sugar

Tightly cover a plate with plastic wrap and rub the plastic wrap with the canola oil. Place the mint leaves on the plate and cover with another sheet of plastic wrap. Smooth out the plastic wrap to push out any air bubbles. Microwave on high for about 1 minute and then again for about 30 seconds. The exact times will vary depending on the the microwave. The mint leaves should be completely dry but not brown.

Remove the top piece of plastic wrap. Dust the leaves with half of the superfine sugar. Flip the leaves over, place on a parchment-lined baking sheet and dust the other side with the remaining superfine sugar. Keep dry in an airtight container.

### TO FINISH

1/2 cup crème fraîche, whipped
Chocolate Chip Cookie Crumble (see page 361)
Peppermint Sorbet (see page 367)
Spearmint Sorbet (see page 367)
Lemon Mint Sorbet (see page 367)
8 tablespoons coarsely ground chocolate chips
Chocolate Mousse
Chocolate Caramel Tuiles
Crystallized Mint Leaves
8 sprigs lemon mint
8 sprigs flowering peppermint
16 sprigs flowering mint
Chocolate Gel (see page 348)

Spoon 2 teaspoons whipped crème fraîche onto a plate and pull them across with the back of a spoon. Place 1 teaspoon Chocolate Chip Cookie Crumble on the plate and place a quenelle of Peppermint Sorbet on top. Repeat with another teaspoon of the Crumble and the Spearmint Sorbet and then a teaspoon of Crumble and the Lemon Mint Sorbet. Sprinkle 1 tablespoon chocolate chips on the plate. Arrange 2 pieces of Chocolate Mousse and 3 Chocolate Caramel Tuiles around the sorbets. Garnish with a Crystallized Mint Leaf, a lemon mint sprig, a flowering peppermint sprig, 2 flowering mint sprigs, and 3 drops Chocolate Gel. Repeat with the remaining ingredients, to serve 8.

# CHOCOLATE
# AND MILK

*Serves 8*

## DEHYDRATED MILK FOAM

2 cups milk
5 tablespoons glucose syrup

Preheat the oven to 175°F. Line a 9-by-13-inch rimmed baking sheet with acetate. In a medium saucepan, heat the milk and glucose until just under a boil. Remove from the heat and froth with a hand blender. Scoop the foam out with a large spoon onto the prepared baking sheet. Dry in the oven overnight, or for 8 to 9 hours. Allow the foam to cool before breaking it into pieces. Store the dehydrated foam in an airtight container.

## DEHYDRATED CHOCOLATE MOUSSE

3 ounces Valrhona Equatoriale chocolate
  (55 percent), chopped
1 1/2 ounces Valrhona Coeur de Guanaja chocolate
  (80 percent), chopped
5 egg whites
3 tablespoons sugar
2 egg yolks

Preheat the oven to 150°F and line a 13-by-18-inch rimmed baking sheet with acetate. Melt the chocolate over a double boiler until just barely warm, remove from the heat, and reserve in a warm place, such as near a warm oven or stove. In a stand mixer fitted with the whisk attachment, whip the egg whites until you can see traces of the whisk. Add the sugar and whip to medium peaks. Incorporate the yolks into the chocolate while the meringue is whipping. Once the meringue is whipped, thoroughly whisk a small amount of the meringue into the chocolate. Using a rubber spatula, fold the rest of the meringue into the chocolate. Once fully incorporated, spread the chocolate mousse out onto the prepared baking sheet. Dry in the oven overnight or for 8 to 9 hours, allowing the mousse to dehydrate. Remove from the oven and cool at room temperature. Break into pieces and store in an airtight container.

## FROZEN CHOCOLATE FOAM

2 sheets gelatin
3 ounces Valrhona Equatoriale chocolate
  (55 percent), chopped
2 ounces Valrhona Coeur de Guanaja chocolate
  (80 percent), chopped
1/4 cup sugar
2 tablespoons milk powder
1/4 teaspoon salt
2/3 cup milk
3 $N_2O$ cartridges
Liquid nitrogen

Bloom the gelatin by placing the sheets in a bowl of ice water for 10 minutes, until pliable. Line a deep pan with acetate. Place the chocolates into a medium mixing bowl. Combine the sugar, milk powder, and salt, in a medium bowl. Combine the milk and 2/3 cup water in a small saucepan over low heat until warm. Slowly add the warm liquid into the sugar mixture. Return to the saucepan and bring to a light simmer. Remove the gelatin from the cold water and squeeze to remove excess moisture. Pour the simmering mixture over the chocolate, add the bloomed gelatin, and stir, allowing the chocolate to melt. Emulsify with a hand blender. Strain through a chinois and chill. Fill a whipped-cream canister two thirds full and load with the $N_2O$ chargers. Expel into the prepared pan. Ladle liquid nitrogen over the mousse to freeze. Reserve the mousse in the freezer.

## BROWNED MILK SOLIDS

1/3 cup butter
4 tablespoons milk powder

In a small saucepan over medium heat, melt the butter. Add the milk powder, stirring often as the milk solids begin to brown. When evenly browned, strain through a chinois, reserving the solids. Turn the solids out onto a paper towel and pat to remove any excess butter. Reserve the milk solids in a dry, airtight container.

## AERATED CHOCOLATE

1 pound Valrhona Equatoriale chocolate
  (55 percent), chopped
6 tablespoons grapeseed oil
3 $N_2O$ cartridges

Line a 9-by-13-inch rimmed baking sheet with acetate and place in the freezer. Combine the chocolate and oil together in a whipped-cream canister. Place the canister into an 82°F water bath maintained by an immersion circulator and temper for 1 1/2 hours. Charge the melted chocolate with the $N_2O$ chargers. Expel the foam onto the prepared baking sheet. Return to the freezer and freeze until completely set, about 30 minutes. Break into pieces of various sizes and store in a cool, dry, airtight container.

## DULCE DE LECHE

One 14-ounce can sweetened condensed milk

Bring a large pot of water to a boil over high heat. Carefully place the can of condensed milk into the boiling water. Lower the heat to medium and cook, completely covered in the boiling water bath, for 2 hours. Carefully remove the can from the boiling water and shock in an ice-water bath. Once completely cool, open the can and transfer the Dulce de Leche to another container.

## TO FINISH

Dulce de Leche
Dehydrated Milk Foam
Aerated Chocolate
Dehydrated Chocolate Mousse
1/2 cup crème fraîche, whipped
Caramelized White Chocolate Sorbet (see page 366)
Frozen Chocolate Foam
Browned Milk Solids
Maldon salt

In the upper right-hand corner of the plate, spoon 1 tablespoon Dulce de Leche and pull it across the plate to the left-hand bottom corner using a small offset spatula. Place the Dehydrated Milk Foam around the bottom right of the Dulce de Leche. Place the Aerated Chocolate and Dehydrated Chocolate Mousse around the top left of the Dulce de Leche. Use a squeeze bottle to make 4 dots of the whipped crème fraîche around the plate and spoon 1 tablespoon in the middle. Spoon a quenelle of the Caramelized White Chocolate Sorbet and lay it on top of the crème fraîche. Place the Frozen Chocolate Foam on both sides of the quenelle. Finish with the Browned Milk Solids and Maldon salt. Repeat with the remaining ingredients, to serve 8. Serve immediately.

# MIGNARDISES

CARROT MACARONS
334

CHOCOLATE PALETTE
WITH CARAMEL AND SEA SALT
335

PASSION FRUIT BASIL PAVLOVAS
335

# ENDLESS REINVENTION

**THERE IS A NERVOUS EXCITEMENT** each time we start a new year. The restaurant is closed for at least a couple days at the beginning of January, and everyone returns to work relaxed and recharged, looking forward to seeing one another. When we gathered together for our annual planning meeting in January 2008, we knew that there were many challenges ahead. We would spend hours discussing them but decided first to spend time reflecting on everything that had happened the year before.

We laid out a large piece of paper, ten feet long by three feet wide, gave everyone a colored marker, and collectively wrote down all the things we had done in 2007. Not all of it was serious (there were definitely a few jokes at my expense), but it gave us another way to celebrate our work. Trying to remember all the things that had happened created community, and it created pride, as we realized how many things, both big and small, we had accomplished.

Our Mission Statement for the year, which Daniel and I presented to the team at the beginning of the meeting, was "to become the four-star restaurant for the next generation." What did it mean? Well, we wanted four stars, but at the time there were only five in a city of 22,000 restaurants that had that distinction. We realized that in order to join that exclusive group, we needed to figure out what it was that would distinguish us.

People of our generation are increasingly being drawn to more casual restaurants, avoiding places they perceive as stuffy, sacrificing a certain amount of excellence in the pursuit of comfort. We imagined an environment with impeccable food and service, but one that was relaxed, with no dress code, where people of all ages would fill the dining room each night. It was going to be a year defined by Endless Reinvention.

**THE MOST SIGNIFICANT IDEA** that came out of that day still helps to define everything we do: balance. It began as a concept in conversations among our chefs discussing recipes, about technique, flavor combinations, and what makes a dish work. With food, as with music, there is not much that hasn't been done before — but a chef's job is to infuse a dish with his own personality and to ensure that there is appropriate balance among the ingredients. Balance in the textures on the plate, in the combination of flavors, and in the use of temperature. Restaurants are no different. The dining experience is really just one giant recipe with thousands of ingredients. Our job is to decide which ingredients to use and in what proportion. In the end, it all comes down to balance.

## BALANCE

### CLASSIC AND MODERN

We strive to be timeless, while also defining a time. As we have made changes over the years we always make sure that if we add an element of modernity to the experience, we also introduce something more classic. We truly believe that striking this balance is critical; if you are too classic, you run the risk of becoming irrelevant; if you are too modern, you risk not having enough soul.

### GOING OUT AND COMING HOME

We love all the elements of the dining experience that add a sense of luxury, the things that make it very clear that you are out at a restaurant about to experience a world-class meal: a thick wine list, gleaming silver, never having to lift a finger. However, we want to make you feel at home, for the experience to be reminiscent of going to a friend's place for dinner. Over the years we have introduced elements into the dining experience that are a bit more casual, because of the feelings they evoke. We endeavor to offer a polished, yet familiar, style of service.

### WORKING HARD AND HAVING FUN

This is one of the things we find ourselves talking about most with our team, even now. Losing balance in either direction can be deadly. If you focus too much on having fun, you'll never be the best. If you focus too much on excellence, you lose your spark. It's only possible to be truly great if you enjoy what you do. It is crucial to make sure that as hard as you work to excel, you never stop loving your job. Morale in a restaurant, or any culture for that matter, is a difficult thing to maintain. With the highs and lows, as well as all the hard work, it can quickly slip away from you. It is important to maintain a healthy balance if you want to stay in control.

**OUR APPLICATION TO RELAIS & CHÂTEAUX** marked the beginning of the year. Daniel had grown up cooking in the kitchens of Relais & Châteaux hotels and had for a long time wanted to be the chef of a restaurant in the association. We had considered applying for quite a while, decided that the time was right, and went to Danny to let him know of our intentions. Danny, who also had a history with Relais & Châteaux through work his father did in Europe, was sensitive about the idea. Thinking that we were not quite ready, he asked that we wait another year to apply.

We were disappointed; our confidence was shaken. We tried to let it go, we tried to move on, but it was weighing on us. It just didn't feel right to give up so easily. Eventually, feeling restless, we went back to Danny to plead our case one more time, to try and change his mind. He patiently listened to everything we had to say and told us to give it a shot.

Within a week, we hastily put together and submitted the application and began anxiously awaiting a response. When we finally did hear back, it was in the form of an email: because we had waited so long to apply, we had just missed the deadline. There were suggestions that our application had been well received, and we were encouraged to reapply the following year. The news was initially crushing, and once again we struggled to accept it. In one last-ditch effort, we reached out to Daniel Boulud, who had initially urged us to apply, and asked his advice. He invited us to Restaurant Daniel the following afternoon to talk.

We sat in the small private dining room overlooking the kitchen and asked him if there was anything he could do to help. He considered things for a while and then picked up the phone and called Patrick O'Connell and Thomas Keller, both of whom are Relais & Châteux Grand Chefs. He explained the situation and asked them for their support.

Within a week, all three chefs came into the restaurant to eat, to see if the experience was worthy of a recommendation. Apparently it was, because they all followed with letters to the president of the organization on our behalf, explaining why they thought he should reconsider. We heard from him soon thereafter, letting us know that he would accept our application after all.

Over the next two weeks, a string of unknown inspectors was dispatched to the restaurant to further evaluate the experience. Every night we'd scan the dining room, trying to figure out which one of the guests was there to judge us, something we never figured out. It was incredibly stressful, and one very long month later we got the call saying we had been accepted. Getting to hang the bronze Relais & Châteaux plaque in front of our restaurant made us proud. The experience showed us the incredible power of persistence and determination. It's one of the most important lessons we've learned.

**OUR CONFIDENCE WAS AT A NEW HIGH,** and you could feel it in both the dining room and the kitchen. Service was getting better and better, as was the food, and we were much more in control. As we continued to improve, however, we found that the physical restaurant was holding us back in many ways. In the dining room, the fact that every table was a banquette prevented us from granting the many requests for round tables. It also gave the room too much of a masculine and clubby feel. The dining room chairs were original to the opening of the restaurant, and with the longer experience we were now delivering, they needed to be slightly bigger and more comfortable. The design of the service areas didn't suit the ways in which they were now being used, additional wine storage was required, and we craved a lounge where guests could enjoy hors d'oeuvres or a digestif. In the kitchen, we needed several new pieces of equipment so that the menu could continue to evolve. We still didn't have many things that would have come with a new restaurant kitchen: a combi oven, a Pacojet, a Hold-o-mat, and more. All of these things needed to be done and it was going to take some cash.

So we set up a meeting with Danny and his partners, Paul Bolles-Beaven, Richard Coraine, Michael Romano, and David Swinghamer, and made a proposal. We outlined all the different things we wanted to change about the restaurant, doing everything we could to convince them that it was a necessary step in its evolution. We even boldly, and foolishly, as it was somewhat out of our control, stated that if they funded this project, we would deliver a four-star restaurant. We had absolutely no idea how they would react. We finished the meeting by telling them how much it would cost and then held our breath as we patiently waited for a response. It took a few weeks before they got back to us, but when they eventually did, Danny said yes.

It would take a couple months of planning before the renovation could actually happen. But during that time, at the beginning of April, we took our first trip with Danny. We spent a week together in London, to bond and to check out the dining scene. We toured Neal's Yard Dairy, had one of the best grilled-cheese sandwiches of our lives at Borough Market, and had our first-ever meal at the legendary River Café. At the end of the week, Danny needed to leave for Portugal, but he already had a plan for how we would spend our last two days in London. He sent us to Paris . . . for lunch.

Taillevent was the original inspiration for Eleven Madison Park, and since we were so close he insisted that we experience it. It was an amazing meal, not because any one detail was so earth-shattering, but because of how it all felt: for such a high-end restaurant, it was an incredibly comfortable place to be. Physically, it was very similar to many stuffier restaurants of its caliber, but there was something different about the vibe there. The staff had a great sense of humor and they didn't seem to take themselves too seriously. During that meal, embarrassingly, my napkin kept slipping off my lap onto the floor. Each time, as expected, they brought me a new one on a silver tray. It was starting to get a bit uncomfortable until the last time I did it, when the server once again brought a new napkin, this time with a big smile on his face and a clothespin resting on the napkin. It was absolutely hilarious, and I didn't drop my napkin again for the rest of the lunch. They embodied the balance between hospitality and excellence more effectively than anywhere we had ever been. We were inspired.

**JUST A FEW WEEKS AFTER OUR RETURN,** the renovation took place. Our new dining room felt more elegant, more spacious, and more refined; and our guests appreciated the change. We were incredibly motivated and worked tirelessly, but at times it was too much. We were starting to lose balance, and it was becoming unhealthy. That became clear one day when we had a powerful — albeit somewhat humorous — wake-up call. One afternoon, one of our cooks left work at 4:00 p.m. after her lunch shift had ended. Just four hours later, as we were in the middle of our dinner rush, she ran back into the kitchen under the impression that she had overslept for her shift the next morning. She had somehow managed to lose track of when one day ended and the next began.

We had a meeting with our team shortly thereafter, addressing the need to regain balance between working hard and having fun. We had to refresh our conviction in the way we wanted to go about achieving our goals, and we did. It was as if we pressed a reset button, something we've had to do many times since. The challenge in managing a culture is that you are always on the verge of losing balance. You can never stop paying attention to it. We had realized its importance earlier that year, but maintaining it was another challenge entirely. We struggle with it to this day.

**COME JUNE,** we were once again dressed in tuxedos, sipping Champagne in our bar, and getting ready to head to Lincoln Center for the James Beard Awards. This time, we were nominated for the Outstanding Wine Service Award. We were slightly less confident after our loss the year before, but we really believed we deserved it. So we waited with bated breath for nearly the entire night, until the envelope was opened and the announcement finally made. This time, however, we won.

John Ragan, Daniel, and I went to the stage to accept the award together. We were then escorted backstage to have a glass of Champagne with the other winners. It was the first time any of us had experienced anything like it.

**FALL BROUGHT WITH IT AN EXCITING ANNOUNCEMENT.** The Michelin Guide, the most respected dining guide in France, was coming to New York. It was a great time for the entire city. Many of our great chefs are from Europe, and the chance to finally be awarded one, two, or three coveted Michelin stars was thrilling.

Every chef I know combed the Internet for the week leading up to its release, hoping that some blog would leak the results. But none did, and it wasn't until that morning that we were able to get our hands on a guide. We were confident that we would get one star, no more, no less. While our ultimate aspirations were for more, for now we were just really looking forward to being on that list. We read and reread the list a few times until it finally sunk in. We hadn't gotten a single star. This was by far our biggest disappointment to date. I was hurt, but Daniel was crushed.

Although some argue that the Guide's influence in America is minimal, globally it means a lot. It was tough to travel around the world having to tell people that we didn't even have one star. After the initial disappointment wore off, we began looking at it as something to strive toward, something to motivate us to work harder. We earned our first star in the 2010 Guide, and we are going to continue climbing until we get more.

**IN NOVEMBER** we took our second trip with Danny, to our first Relais & Châteaux congress, the association's annual gathering, where we would be officially inducted into the organization. It took place in Vienna and was a wonderfully surreal experience. There we were, surrounded by some of the best chefs, restaurateurs, and hoteliers in the world. Hundreds of people got together to attend lectures, cocktail parties, and dinners. Daniel got to reconnect with some of the chefs he had apprenticed for when he was younger, and we both relished the feeling of being a part of something much bigger than ourselves.

We spent four days together in Vienna before Danny returned to New York and Daniel and I traveled to Switzerland. There, we ate at some incredible restaurants, experienced Zurich's nightlife, and I got to see where Daniel was from. He toured me through Zurich, showing me the city's sites and some of the bars he frequented growing up. He even took me to experience one of Switzerland's temples of gastronomy, the legendary Rochat, the restaurant passed down to its chef, Phillipe Rochat, by its former chef and owner, Fredy Girardet.

That was an important week for our relationship. I spent time with his parents, met his daughter, Justine, and went out for drinks with his childhood friends. Daniel is like a brother to me. Spending time together in the place that he calls home was a powerful experience.

# SUMMER

*During the summer we're at the markets almost every day. Summer is abundant with fruits and vegetables and requires you to be in close touch with the farmers. The seasons within the season pass quickly; to get produce at its peak, you need to pay attention.*

*When I was growing up, my mom did all the cooking at home, and she bought her ingredients from nearby farms. We also had a garden where we grew some of our own tomatoes, beans, herbs, and raspberries. We even had a cherry tree.*

*To my chagrin, summer meant spending time in that garden, while all my friends were having fun on the beach. I would also help in the kitchen — not actually cooking, just doing the boring stuff: washing greens, cleaning vegetables, peeling garlic, pitting cherries. Although there was something beautiful about cleaning vegetables that had just come out of the ground, I couldn't stand the smell of my hands after peeling enough garlic to make pesto, and it took forever to pit enough cherries to make one jar of jam.*

*As a child I never understood the reasoning behind all this extra work. But my mom always said that you could taste the difference, that when you cook it's all about the ingredients. When I started eating at friends' houses, or even in restaurants, I realized why she was so adamant about it. I started to really appreciate my mom's cooking. I loved coming home from school for lunch, trying to guess by the smell what was on the table. I'm so thankful to have learned these lessons so early because the ingredients we use, and the relationships we have with farmers, are truly the core of what we do.*

*In the summer I get so excited about heirloom tomatoes, all the varieties of cucumbers, melons, and summer squashes. The recipes are light and refreshing. Many dishes have a Mediterranean feel — the smoked couscous salad or the poached turbot and ratatouille — while the glazed duck with lavender and peaches is reminiscent of Provence.*

| CAVIAR | CORN | YOGURT | COUSCOUS |
| TOMATO | WATERMELON | CUCUMBER | AVOCADO |
| FOIE GRAS | RABBIT | JOHN DORY | COD |
| TURBOT | LOUP DE MER | BLACK BASS | SCALLOP |
| LOBSTER | CHICKEN | DUCK | PORK |
| VEAL | LAMB | FROMAGE BLANC | MALT |
| CHERRY | BERRIES | APRICOT | CHOCOLATE |

# HORS
# D'ŒUVRES

SALMON GALETTE WITH DILL AND HORSERADISH
326

RICE CRACKER WITH CUCUMBER AND HAMACHI
326

SWEETBREAD CORNET
327

# CAVIAR
## BUTTERMILK, BUCKWHEAT, AND BORAGE

*Serves 8*

### BUCKWHEAT CRISPS

1/2 cup sugar
1/2 cup egg yolks, about 6
2/3 cups butter, softened
1 1/2 cups buckwheat flour
1/3 cup flour
1 1/2 teaspoons baking powder
1 teaspoon salt

Preheat the oven to 350°F. In a stand mixer fitted with the whisk attachment, whip the sugar and egg yolks on high speed until the mixture forms pale yellow ribbons. Change to the paddle attachment and add the butter. Slowly add the buckwheat flour, flour, baking powder, and salt. Mix until well incorporated, noting that the dough will be soft. Roll the dough between 2 pieces of parchment paper to a 1/4 inch thickness. Transfer to a rimmed baking sheet, remove the top layer of parchment, and bake until risen and beginning to brown, about 20 minutes. While still warm, cut into rough pieces. Lower the oven temperature to 175°F. Return the Crisps to the oven for 30 minutes to dehydrate.

### BUTTERMILK GELÉE

11 sheets gelatin
2 cups buttermilk
Salt
2 lemons

Bloom the gelatin by placing it in a bowl of cold water for 10 minutes. In the meantime, warm 1/2 cup of the buttermilk in a small saucepan without bringing it to a boil. Squeeze the sheets of gelatin to remove any excess moisture. Stir into the warmed buttermilk, then whisk in the rest of the cold buttermilk and season with salt to taste. Coat four 9-by-13-inch plastic trays with vegetable spray, wiping off any excess. Pour about 3/4 cup of the buttermilk mixture into each tray, yielding a 1/16-inch-thick gelée, and zest the lemons with a microplane grater evenly over the gelée. Refrigerate for 1 hour, until set. Cut into 3 1/2-by-3/4-inch strips.

### QUAIL YOLKS

10 quail-egg yolks

Bring a small saucepan of salted water to 170°F. Add the quail-egg yolks and slowly poach for 4 minutes. Remove with a slotted spoon to a bowl of cold salted water.

### KASHA

1/2 cup kasha or buckwheat
2 cups canola oil
Salt

Preheat the oven to 175°F. In a medium saucepan, boil the kasha in 4 cups water for 7 to 10 minutes, until tender. Strain and lay out evenly on a rimmed baking sheet. Dehydrate in the oven for 20 to 25 minutes, until dry. In a medium saucepan, heat the oil to 390°F. Fry the kasha until puffed and crispy. Drain on paper towels and season with salt to taste.

### TO FINISH

8 tablespoons Buttermilk Gel (see page 347)
Quail Yolks
*Fleur de sel*
Buckwheat Crisps
8 tablespoons osetra caviar
Buttermilk Gelée strips
Kasha
16 borage blossoms
16 leaves borage

For each serving, spoon 1 tablespoon of Buttermilk Gel on a plate and pull it to the left with a spoon. Place a Quail Yolk on top of the dollop. Season with *fleur de sel*. Arrange pieces of Buckwheat Crisp on the plate alongside the Gel. Lay 1 tablespoon of caviar under the yolk. Lay a Buttermilk Gelée strip so that it crosses over the caviar and the Gel. Garnish with the Kasha, 2 borage blossoms, and 2 borage leaves.

# CORN
## CHILLED SOUP WITH LOBSTER

*Serves 8*

### CORN BISQUE
3/4 cup butter
1/2 cup chopped fennel
3 tablespoons chopped ginger
2 cloves garlic
3 tablespoons Cognac
1/4 cup dry vermouth
1 1/4 cups tomato juice
1 teaspoon saffron
1 1/2 cups Lobster Stock (see page 356)
1 1/4 cups corn juice (from 2 1/2 quarts corn kernels)
2 pods star anise
10 pods cardamom
4 sprigs tarragon
3 tablespoons crème fraîche
2 tablespoons lobster roe
2 tablespoons lime juice
1 1/2 tablespoons salt
Cayenne pepper

In a medium pot, melt the butter. Sweat the fennel, ginger, and garlic until tender. Deglaze the pan with the Cognac and reduce until almost dry. Add the vermouth and reduce until almost dry. Then add the tomato juice and saffron and reduce by half. Add the Lobster Stock and corn juice and simmer for 10 minutes. To make a sachet, wrap the star anise, cardamom, and tarragon in a piece of cheesecloth and tie together with butcher's twine. Drop the sachet in the liquid, remove from the heat, and steep for 10 minutes. Remove and discard the sachet. In a small bowl, whisk together the crème fraîche and the lobster roe. Puree the hot Bisque in a blender. With the blender running on high speed, add the lobster roe and crème fraîche mixture, blending thoroughly. Strain through a fine-mesh chinois. Season with the lime juice, salt, and cayenne and chill over ice.

### CORN BAVAROIS
2 cups cream
1 tablespoon salt
1 pinch cayenne pepper
6 sheets gelatin
1 tablespoon butter
1 tablespoon diced shallots
1/2 cup corn juice (from 1 quart corn kernels)
2 teaspoons lime juice

In a cold bowl, whip the cream to soft peaks. Season with the salt and cayenne and reserve in the refrigerator.

Bloom the gelatin by placing the sheets in a bowl of ice water for 10 minutes. Once they are pliable, remove them from the cold water and squeeze to remove excess moisture. In the meantime, melt the butter in a medium saucepan over medium heat. Add the shallots and sweat until translucent. Add the corn juice and lime juice and cook, whisking constantly, until thickened. Stir in the bloomed gelatin, transfer to a blender, and puree on high speed. Strain through a fine-mesh chinois and chill over ice to just below room temperature, being careful not to allow the gelatin to set.

Working very quickly, whisk a third of the corn mixture into the reserved whipped cream. Then, using a rubber spatula, gently fold the whipped-cream mixture, in 2 parts, into the rest of the corn mixture. Chill over ice for 4 hours.

### BREAD TUILES
1/2 loaf Brioche (see page 364)
1 cup melted Clarified Butter (see page 370)
Salt

Preheat the oven to 300°F. With a serrated knife, remove the crust from the bread. Cut the loaf into 4-inch-long pieces and tightly wrap the individual pieces in plastic. Freeze for 1 hour. Using a rotating deli slicer or a sharp knife, slice the bread into 1/16-inch slices. Use a 1 1/2-inch round cutter to punch the bread into circles. Use a large round pastry tip (11/16-inch opening) to punch smaller holes inside the rounds just below center to create offset round cutout. Line an upside-down 13-by-18-inch rimmed baking sheet with parchment paper. Brush the parchment with melted Clarified Butter. Arrange the bread neatly on top of the butter and season with salt. Brush another piece of parchment paper with the Clarified Butter and place it on top of the bread, butter side down. Place another very flat 13-by-18-inch baking sheet on top. Weigh down with a cast-iron skillet and bake for 10 to 12 minutes, until golden brown.

### LOBSTER
4 (1 1/4-pound) live lobsters

Fill a large stockpot with water and bring the water to 150°F. Add 2 of the lobsters, and cook for 7 minutes, maintaining the temperature of the water at 150°F. Remove the tails from the lobsters and transfer them to an ice bath. Return the knuckles and claws to the water and continue cooking for 7 more minutes. Transfer the knuckles and claws to the ice bath. Repeat with the remaining lobsters. When the tails, knuckles, and claws are completely cool, carefully remove the meat from the shells, making sure to keep the meat intact. Refrigerate.

### TO FINISH
Pickled Baby Corn (see page 341)
Lobster claws
Lobster knuckles
1/4 cup White Balsamic Vinaigrette (see page 346)
Corn Bavarois
8 quail-egg yolks
48 corn kernels
Bread Tuiles
16 sprigs baby tarragon
16 sprigs dill
Corn Bisque

Dress the Pickled Baby Corn and Lobster claws and knuckles in the White Balsamic Vinaigrette. Place 2 quenelles of Corn Bavarois in a bowl. Place a claw and a knuckle around them along with 1 quail-egg yolk. Top with 6 corn kernels, 1 slice Pickled Baby Corn, 2 Bread Tuiles, and 2 sprigs each baby tarragon and dill. Pour 1/4 cup Bisque around the garnish. Repeat with the remaining ingredients, to serve 8.

*Note: At the restaurant, we use the tails in other dishes. If you're preparing only one lobster recipe, plate the dishes with the claws, knuckles, and tails.*

# YOGURT
## APRICOTS, CURRY, AND PICKLED ONIONS

*Serves 8*

### APRICOT CONFIT

4 apricots
1/4 cup olive oil
1 teaspoon salt
2 teaspoons confectioners' sugar
10 sprigs thyme
Grapeseed oil

Preheat the oven to 350°F. Cut the apricots in half and discard the pits. In a large bowl, toss the apricots with the oil and salt and dust with the sugar. Line a rimmed baking sheet with parchment paper. Place the apricot halves on the parchment paper, cut side down. Roast for 20 minutes, until you can easily remove the skin, but cool to room temperature before peeling. Peel, lower the temperature to 200°F, cover with the thyme, and bake for 2 hours.

### CANDIED APRICOTS

16 dried apricots
4 cups white wine
1 cup sugar
1 teaspoon salt
5 sprigs thyme

Using a 3/4-inch ring cutter, punch the apricots into coins. Combine the wine, sugar, and salt in a medium saucepan and reduce by half. Add the thyme and apricot coins and continue to reduce until the liquid is syrupy. Cool the apricots to room temperature in their syrup.

### GREEK YOGURT MOUSSE

3 sheets gelatin
1 cup cream
2 cups skim milk
1 cup Greek yogurt
1 tablespoon plus 1 teaspoon salt
2 N$_2$O cartridges

Bloom the gelatin by placing the sheets in a bowl of ice water for 10 minutes. In the meantime, warm the cream without boiling it in a small saucepan over medium heat. Squeeze the gelatin sheets to remove any excess moisture and stir them into the warm cream. Whisk in the skim milk, Greek yogurt, and salt. Transfer the mixture to a whipped-cream canister and charge with the N$_2$O cartridges, shake well, and chill.

### GREEK YOGURT FOAM

1 cup skim milk
2 tablespoons Greek yogurt
1 tablespoon sugar

Combine the milk, yogurt, and sugar in a small pot and heat to 180°F. When ready to serve, froth with a hand blender until foamy.

### TO FINISH

Greek Yogurt Mousse
Apricot Confit
Curry Granola (see page 364)
Candied Apricots
Greek Yogurt Foam
8 sprigs salad burnet
16 sprigs flowering dill
16 leaves micro tarragon
8 sprigs micro mint
8 leaves micro basil
48 edible flowers, such as violas, garlic flowers,
    or citrus coriander blossoms
Pickled Red Pearl Onion Slivers (see page 343)

Pipe 1/4 cup of Greek Yogurt Mousse into a bowl. Place a Confit Apricot half and a mound of Granola next to each other on the side of the bowl. Place 2 Candied Apricots in the middle. Froth the Greek Yogurt Foam with a hand blender. Spoon the foam around the Apricots and Granola. Garnish with a sprig of the salad burnet, 2 flowering dill sprigs, 2 leaves tarragon, a leaf each mint and basil, and 6 flowers. Repeat with the remaining ingredients, to serve 8.

# COUSCOUS
## SALAD WITH TOMATOES, CUCUMBERS, AND MELON

*Serves 8*

### GREEK LABNE

1 cup Greek yogurt
Olive oil

Line a colander with 10 layers of cheesecloth. Place the colander in a large bowl, making sure that there is room between the bottom of the colander and the bowl. Strain the yogurt through the cheesecloth for 2 days in the refrigerator. Roll the strained yogurt into small balls about 1/2 inch in diameter and store in the refrigerator in olive oil to cover.

### CHERRY TOMATO CONFIT

24 cherry tomatoes
1/2 cup extra-virgin olive oil, plus more for storing
1/2 teaspoon salt
1/2 teaspoon sugar

Preheat the oven to 200°F. Bring a large pot of salted water to a boil. Prick each tomato with a cake tester or the tip of a knife. Add the tomatoes to the boiling water and cook for 3 to 4 seconds. Transfer to a bowl of ice water and, once cold, remove the skins of the tomatoes, using a sharp paring knife. Be careful not to cut into the flesh. Toss the tomatoes in 1/2 cup of the olive oil, the salt, and the sugar. Place on a rimmed baking sheet lined with parchment paper and bake for 2 hours, until slightly shriveled and reduced in size by a quarter. Reserve the tomatoes in olive oil and store covered at room temperature.

### CUCUMBER CAVIAR

1 English cucumber, peeled, halved, and seeded
1 tablespoon olive oil
1 tablespoon white balsamic vinegar
Salt

Mince the cucumber to "caviar" consistency. Place the minced cucumber in cheesecloth and wring out any excess moisture, reserving the flesh. Toss with the olive oil and vinegar and season with salt to taste.

### YOGURT SAUCE

1 cup Greek yogurt
2 tablespoons lemon juice
1 tablespoon salt

In a small bowl, whisk together the yogurt and the lemon juice. Season with the salt and reserve in the refrigerator.

### OLIVE POWDER

1 cup taggiasca olives, pitted

Wrap a microwave-safe plate in plastic. Rinse the olives to remove any excess oil and dry thoroughly with paper towels. Finely chop the olives and place them on the plastic-wrapped plate. Microwave on high for 2 minutes and check to see if they are crispy. If they are not, microwave in 30-second intervals until they are.

### COMPRESSED MELON

1 honeydew melon
1 cantaloupe

Peel and seed the melons. Slice them into 1/8-inch-thick slices. Vacuum-seal in *sous vide* bags and compress.

### VEGETABLE SALAD

8 sea beans
Compressed Melon
2 radishes, shaved
1 fennel bulb, shaved
24 sprouting chickpeas
24 sprigs purslane
2 tablespoons Lemon Vinaigrette (see page 346)

Bring a pot of salted water to a boil. Add the sea beans and cook for 1 minute. Transfer to a bowl of ice water and, once cool, drain. Toss the blanched sea beans, Compressed Melon, radishes, fennel, chickpeas, and purslane in the Lemon Vinaigrette.

### TO FINISH

Yogurt Sauce
Smoked Couscous (see page 359)
Cucumber Caviar
Vegetable Salad
Cherry Tomato Confit
Olive Powder
Greek Labne
16 sprigs bush basil
8 basil blossoms
24 sprigs baby cilantro
16 leaves mint
8 buds flowering marjoram
32 nasturtium petals

Place 2 teaspoons of the Yogurt Sauce on each plate. Drag the yogurt across the plate with an offset spatula. Spread 1/2 cup Smoked Couscous along the plate. Garnish with 1 tablespoon Cucumber Caviar, 5 Compressed Melon slices, 2 radish shaves, 1 fennel shave, 3 Confit Cherry Tomatoes, a sprinkle of Olive Powder, a Greek Labne ball, 3 sprouting chickpeas, 2 bush basil sprigs, 1 basil blossom, 3 cilantro sprigs, 1 blanched sea bean, 2 mint leaves, 3 purslane sprigs, 1 flowering marjoram bud, and 4 nasturtium petals.

# TOMATO

*Served in four courses*

# TOMATO
## TEA WITH LEMON THYME

*Serves 8*

**TOMATO TEA**

4 leaves lemon verbena
3 sprigs lemon thyme
Peel of 1 lemon
1 pod star anise
1 1/2 teaspoon salt
4 cups Tomato Water (see page 371)

Combine the lemon verbena, thyme, lemon peel, star anise, and salt in a bowl. Bring the Tomato Water to a simmer and pour over the herb mixture. Steep for 5 minutes. Strain and chill.

**TO FINISH**

8 bunches flowering lemon thyme
8 raffia pieces, each 6 inches long
Tomato Tea

Tie small bouquets of flowering lemon thyme with raffia and put 1 bouquet in each of 8 teacups. Heat the Tomato Tea to 185°F and pour 2 to 3 ounces into each cup over the lemon thyme bundles.

# TOMATO
## GELÉE WITH CHÈVRE, HERBS, AND SAFFRON

*Serves 8*

3 1/2 sheets gelatin
2 cups Tomato Water (see page 371)
4 tablespoons soft chèvre
8 sprigs bush basil
24 saffron threads
40 sprigs salad burnet
8 sprigs sea cress
Basil blossoms
24 dill blossoms
8 sprigs purslane
4 teaspoons Saffron Oil (see page 345)
*Fleur de sel*

Place 8 shallow bowls in the refrigerator to chill. Bloom the gelatin by placing the sheets in ice water for 10 minutes, until pliable. In the meantime, warm 1/4 cup of the Tomato Water in a small saucepan over low heat. Remove the gelatin from the ice water and squeeze out the excess moisture. Stir the gelatin into the warm Tomato Water until melted. Combine the melted gelatin with the remaining cold Tomato Water. Quickly pour the Tomato Water into the chilled bowls to 1/4 inch thick and refrigerate for 1 hour to set. Make sure that the bowls are level to ensure that the gelée sets straight. In each bowl, place six 1/4-teaspoon-sized dollops of chèvre randomly around the gelée. Place several of each herb, blossom, and green on top. Finish with 1/2 teaspoon Saffron Oil and *fleur de sel*.

# TOMATO
## CLOUD
## WITH BASIL

*Serves 8*

# TOMATO
## SALAD WITH
## MOZZARELLA
## ICE CREAM

*Serves 8*

### TOMATO CLOUD

4 sheets gelatin
1 cup Tomato Water (see page 371)
1 tablespoon salt

Bloom the gelatin by placing the sheets in a bowl of ice water for 10 minutes, until pliable. Warm 1/4 cup Tomato Water in a small pot over low heat and season with the salt. Squeeze out any excess moisture from the gelatin and stir into the warm Tomato Water. Once the gelatin has melted, add the remaining Tomato Water.

Pour into the bowl of a stand mixer fitted with the whisk attachment. Secure a bowl of ice water under the mixing bowl and whip the Tomato Water mixture on high speed until it is like a stiff meringue and cloudlike.

Alternatively, pour the Tomato Water mixture into a bowl. Set that bowl over another bowl of ice. Mix with an electric hand mixer until it is like a stiff meringue and cloudlike.

Place four 4-inch ring molds on a 13-by-18-inch rimmed baking sheet lined with acetate. Coat the molds with vegetable spray and wipe off any excess with a paper towel. Spoon the Cloud into the molds and smooth out with an offset spatula. Refrigerate for 1 hour to set. Remove the ring molds and cut the Clouds in half when ready to serve.

### TO FINISH

64 cherry tomatoes, various shapes and colors
Olive oil
*Fleur de sel*
25-year-old balsamic vinegar
24 sprigs bush basil
Pickled Red Onion Rings (see page 343)
Tomato Cloud halves

Bring a large pot of salted water to a boil. Prick each cherry tomato with a cake tester or the tip of a knife. Add the tomatoes to the boiling water and cook for 3 to 4 seconds. Transfer to a bowl of ice water and, once cold, remove the skins, using a sharp paring knife. Be careful not to cut into the flesh. Toss the tomatoes in olive oil and season with *fleur de sel*. Place 8 tomatoes in the bottom of a bowl and drizzle with the aged balsamic vinegar. Arrange 3 bush basil sprigs on top, as well as 5 Pickled Onion Rings. Top with a Tomato Cloud half. Repeat with the remaining ingredients, to serve 8.

### CHERRY TOMATO CONFIT

16 cherry tomatoes
1/2 cup extra-virgin olive oil, plus more for storing
1/2 teaspoon salt
1/2 teaspoon sugar

Preheat the oven to 200°F. Bring a large pot of salted water to a boil. Prick each tomato with a cake tester or the tip of a knife. Add the tomatoes to the boiling water and cook for 3 to 4 seconds. Transfer to a bowl of ice water and, once cold, remove the skins of the tomatoes, using a sharp paring knife. Be careful not to cut into the flesh. Toss the peeled tomatoes in 1/2 cup of the olive oil, the salt, and the sugar. Place on a rimmed baking sheet lined with parchment paper and bake for 2 hours, until slightly shriveled and reduced in size by a quarter. Reserve the tomatoes in olive oil and store covered at room temperature.

### TO FINISH

10 ounces buffalo mozzarella
2 large red heirloom tomatoes
2 large yellow heirloom tomatoes
2 large green heirloom tomatoes
1/4 cup White Balsamic Vinaigrette (see page 346)
*Fleur de sel*
Mozzarella Ice Cream (see page 369)
Cherry Tomato Confit
Provençal Granola (see page 364)
8 sprigs flowering basil
40 leaves bush basil
Extra-virgin olive oil
25-year-old balsamic vinegar

Roughly chop the buffalo mozzarella until it is the size of large curds. Using a small apple corer, punch 8 rounds out of each heirloom tomato. Drizzle the tomato cylinders with White Balsamic Vinaigrette and season with *fleur de sel*. Lay 3 cylinders of dressed tomato (one of each color) in the center of a plate. Spoon 1 tablespoon chopped mozzarella onto each plate. Scoop 1 quenelle of Mozzarella Ice Cream onto the mozzarella. Place 2 Confit Tomatoes on either side of the Ice Cream. Garnish with the Provençal Granola, 2 sprigs flowering basil, and 5 leaves bush basil. Sauce the plate lightly with olive oil and a few drops of balsamic vinegar. Repeat with the remaining ingredients, to serve 8.

# WATERMELON
## CEVICHE
## WITH SCALLOP,
## LOBSTER,
## AND CALAMARI

*Serves 8*

### WATERMELON JUICE
1 large seedless red watermelon, 7 to 8 pounds

Remove all rind from the flesh of the watermelon; reserve the rind to make the pickles. Cut the flesh into 2-inch pieces. Puree the watermelon pieces in batches in a blender. Strain the pureed watermelon through 10 layers of cheesecloth. Allow to strain for 2 hours.

### WATERMELON GELÉE
10 sheets gelatin
1/2 cup lime juice
1 tablespoon salt
1 1/2 cups Watermelon Juice

Bloom the gelatin by placing the sheets in a bowl of ice water for 10 minutes, until pliable. Prepare four 9-by-13-inch plastic trays by coating with vegetable spray and then wiping away excess. In a small pot over low heat, warm half of the lime juice. Squeeze out any excess moisture from the gelatin and stir into the warm lime juice. When the gelatin has melted, remove from the heat and combine with the Watermelon Juice and salt. Do not cook the Watermelon Juice. Add the remaining lime juice. Strain the Gelée and then quickly pour about 3/4 cup into each prepared tray, yielding a 1/16-inch-thick Gelée. Chill for 1 hour in the refrigerator until set. Punch circles with a 6-inch ring cutter. Remove with an offset spatula when ready to serve.

### TAPIOCA
1 cup tapioca pearls
1 cup yuzu juice
Salt

Bring the tapioca and 1 gallon water to a boil in a medium pot and cook until tender, 30 to 35 minutes. Strain and rinse under cold water. Place in a plastic container. Pour the yuzu juice over the pearls, making sure the pearls are covered. Season with salt and marinate for 20 minutes. Then drain.

### DEHYDRATED WATERMELON
2 pounds red seedless watermelon
2 pounds yellow watermelon
Olive oil

Preheat the oven to 200°F. Line a baking sheet with parchment paper. Remove the flesh from the rind. Cut the flesh into 1-inch-by-1-inch-by-5-inch rectangles, then slice the rectangles into very thin (1-inch square) chips. Coat the chips in olive oil and neatly place on the prepared sheet tray. Bake for 3 hours.

### WATERMELON SAUCE
1 cup Watermelon Juice
1/2 cup lime juice
1/8 teaspoon xanthan gum (0.3 grams)
1 tablespoon Lemon Oil (see page 345)
1 teaspoon salt

In a small bowl, whisk together the Watermelon Juice, lime juice, and xanthan gum. Whisk in the Lemon Oil, whisking until the xanthan gum is completely dissolved. Season with the salt.

### MARINATED SHELLFISH
2 (1-pound) live lobsters
Watermelon Sauce
6 sea scallops
3 calamari tubes, cut into strips
1 cup sweet Maine shrimp, peeled

Remove the tails from the live lobsters, press the tails firmly against a flat surface, and insert a 6-inch skewer through each of the tails to keep them flat. Freeze for 1 hour. Once frozen, remove the shells from the tails and slice the meat into 1/8-inch-thick slices. Brush with the Sauce.

Preheat a steam oven to 210°F. Place the scallops on a wire rack and steam in the oven for 2 minutes. Chill immediately. Once cool, punch with a 1-inch ring cutter and thinly slice. Marinate in the Sauce for 5 minutes.

Bring a pot of water to a boil. Blanch the calamari for 1 minute; transfer to a bowl of ice water, dry, and marinate in the Sauce for 5 minutes.

Rinse and dry the shrimp. Reserve in the Sauce.

### TO FINISH
Marinated Shellfish
Watermelon Sauce
Watermelon Gelée
Tapioca
Dehydrated Watermelon
Pickled Watermelon Rind (see page 343)
16 dill blossoms
16 sprigs chervil
16 sprigs sea cress
16 leaves mint
16 sprigs bush basil

Alternating between the two, place lobster and scallop slices in a 5 1/2-inch circle in the middle of each plate. Place a few pieces of calamari and Maine shrimp in the middle of the lobster and scallop ring so that they barely overlap. Drizzle the seafood with the Watermelon Sauce and cover with the Watermelon Gelée. Place the Tapioca, Dehydrated Watermelon, and Pickled Watermelon Rind on top and garnish with 2 each of the dill blossoms, chervil, sea cress, mint, and bush basil. Repeat with the remaining ingredients, to serve 8.

# CUCUMBER
## VARIATION WITH SLOW-COOKED CHAR AND SMOKED CRÈME FRAÎCHE

*Serves 8*

### ARCTIC CHAR

1 (3-pound) arctic char, filleted, pinbones and
   skin removed
Salt
1 cup extra-virgin olive oil

Place the char in a plastic container. Cover completely
with salt and let cure in the refrigerator for 1 hour.
Rinse thoroughly in cold water and pat dry. Preheat the
oven to 140°F. Place the char in a roasting pan, skin
side down, and brush with olive oil. Bake for 15 minutes.
Brush with olive oil again and return to the oven
for another 15 to 20 minutes, or until the fish begins
to flake.

### CUCUMBERS

2 Persian cucumbers
5 lemon cucumbers
White Balsamic Pickling Liquid (see page 343)
8 cucamelons (Mexican gherkins)

Cut 1 Persian cucumber in half lengthwise and slice on
a mandoline into 1/8-inch-thick strips. Cut the other
in half and slice into rounds. Store in ice water. Cut the
lemon cucumbers in wedges and place in a *sous vide*
bag with the Pickling Liquid. Vacuum-seal. Cut the
cucamelons in half lengthwise and store in ice water.

### TO FINISH

1/3 cup Smoked Crème Fraîche (see page 359)
1/2 cup Everything Crumble (see page 362)
Arctic Char
Extra-virgin olive oil
Cucumbers
16 teaspoons char roe
16 sprigs bronze fennel
40 sprigs salad burnet
8 tablespoons freshly grated horseradish

Spoon 2 teaspoon-sized dollops Smoked Crème
Fraîche on a plate and place a tablespoon of Everything
Crumble between them. Break the Arctic Char up
with a fork and arrange it on and around the Crumble.
Garnish with the Cucumbers, 2 teaspoons char
roe, 2 bronze fennel sprigs, 5 salad burnet leaves,
and 1 tablespoon grated horseradish. Repeat with
the remaining ingredients, to serve 8.

# AVOCADO
## ROULADE WITH PRAWNS AND WOOD SORREL

*Serves 8*

## POACHED PRAWNS

1 cup white wine
1 cup orange juice
3/4 cup chopped fennel
3/4 cup chopped celery
1/2 cup sliced leeks
3 cloves garlic, peeled
1 tablespoon orange zest
1 tablespoon salt
1 teaspoon fennel seeds
1 teaspoon coriander seeds
1 teaspoon black pepper
1 pod star anise
1 1/2 pounds Hawaiian blue prawns
   (U10, about 15 total), peeled and deveined

Prepare a court bouillon in a medium saucepan
by combining all of the ingredients, except for the
prawns, with 3 cups water. Bring to a boil over medium
heat and simmer for 20 minutes. Remove from the
heat and cool the liquid to 140°F. Add the prawns to
the warm liquid and poach for 4 to 5 minutes, until
they start to become firm and pink. Chill the prawns
in their poaching liquid over ice.

## PRAWN SALAD

Poached Prawns
2 tablespoons peeled and diced (1/8 inch)
   Granny Smith apple
1 tablespoon diced (1/8 inch) avocado
2 teaspoons chopped tarragon
1 1/2 tablespoons Mayonnaise (see page 371)
1 tablespoon Greek yogurt
1 tablespoon crème fraîche
2 teaspoons lime juice
1 1/2 tablespoons salt
1 pinch cayenne pepper

Remove the cold prawns from the court bouillon and
cut into small dice (1/8 inch). In a large mixing bowl,
combine the diced prawns with the apple, avocado,
and tarragon. In a separate bowl, mix the Mayonnaise
with the yogurt, crème fraiche, and lime juice, and fold
gently into the prawns with a rubber spatula. Season
with the salt and cayenne.

## AVOCADO ROULADES

8 ripe but firm avocados, cold
Prawn Salad
5 tablespoons Lemon Oil (see page 345)
*Fleur de sel*

Quarter an avocado. (To avoid oxidation, work with only
1 avocado at a time.) Discard the pit and peel each
quarter. Discard any bruised or dark sections. Using a
mandoline or a very sharp knife, thinly slice the quarters. On a piece of parchment paper, shingle the slices
in the order that they were sliced, in even, overlapping
layers. Place the avocado sheet in a 6-inch-by-8-inch
*sous vide* bag and vacuum-seal. The compression helps
the slices adhere to one another and prevents oxidation. Repeat with the remaining avocados. Remove the
avocado sheets from the bags and spread the Prawn
Salad down the center of the avocado slices. Roll like
a cigar. Make sure that the ends of the roulade are
clean and even. Brush the roulades with Lemon Oil
and season with *fleur de sel*.

## GREEK YOGURT SAUCE

1 cup Greek yogurt
1 tablespoon lime juice
1 1/4 teaspoons salt
1 pinch cayenne pepper

Combine the yogurt and lime juice in a small bowl.
Season with the salt and cayenne. Reserve the Yogurt
Sauce in a squeeze bottle in the refrigerator.

## TO FINISH

Greek Yogurt Sauce
Avocado Roulades
16 leaves wood (clover) sorrel
24 leaves red-veined sorrel
40 Oxalis blossoms
Lobster Roe Oil (see page 345)
Lobster Roe Powder (see page 371)

Place 2 dots of Greek Yogurt Sauce on each plate.
Pull the dots across the plate with a small spoon in
opposite directions. Place a Roulade in the center of
the plate and garnish with the 2 wood sorrel leaves,
3 red-veined sorrel leaves, and 5 Oxalis blossoms.
Finish with a few drops of Lobster Roe Oil and a pinch
of Lobster Roe Powder. Repeat with the remaining
ingredients, to serve 8.

# FOIE GRAS CRÈME BRÛLÉE WITH SUMMER BERRIES AND PICKLED BEETS

*Serves 8*

### MARINATED FOIE GRAS

One 2-pound lobe grade-A foie gras
1 tablespoon salt
1/2 teaspoon pink curing salt
1 teaspoon sugar
1/2 teaspoon white pepper
2 teaspoons Madeira
1 teaspoon Cognac

Bring the foie gras to room temperature to soften. Separate the main lobes and remove the veins with tweezers and a paring knife. Pass the foie gras through a tamis and season with the salt, pink salt, sugar, and white pepper, and place in a *sous vide* bag. Add the Madeira and Cognac, seal the bag, and marinate in the refrigerator for 24 hours. Remove the foie gras from the refrigerator and allow it to come to room temperature. Transfer to a large mixing bowl and whip with a rubber spatula to re-emulsify. Chill in the refrigerator.

### FOIE GRAS CUSTARD

3 1/2 cups Sauternes
1 1/2 cups cream
1/2 cup Chicken Jus (see page 356)
1 3/4 cups Marinated Foie Gras, cold and broken into 1-inch pieces
2 eggs
2 egg yolks
1 1/2 teaspoons salt
4 teaspoons sugar

Preheat the oven to 325°F. In a medium saucepan over medium heat, reduce the Sauternes to just under 1 cup. Add the cream and Chicken Jus and bring to a boil. Remove from the heat. Immediately add the Marinated Foie Gras and blend thoroughly with a hand blender. Pass through a chinois and cool to room temperature. Whisk in the eggs and yolks and pass through a chinois again. Season with the salt.

Cut eight 3 1/2-inch squares of parchment paper. Cut eight 4 1/2-inch squares of aluminum foil. Center a parchment square on top of a foil square. Place a 2 3/4-inch ring mold on top of the parchment paper and wrap the aluminum foil and parchment paper tightly around the base of the ring mold. Repeat with 7 more ring molds and the remaining parchment paper and aluminum foil squares. Place the molds, aluminum foil side down, on a 9-by-13-inch rimmed baking sheet. Pour 1/3 cup of the Foie Gras Custard into each mold. Pour 2 cups hot water in the baking sheet around the molds. Cover with aluminum foil and bake for about 15 minutes. Remove from the oven and chill in the refrigerator until set, about 3 hours.

Dust each Custard with 1/2 teaspoon sugar and carefully shake off any excess. Tilt a ring mold on its side and gently peel away the aluminum foil and parchment paper. Place the Custard, still in its ring mold, on a plate. Caramelize the sugar with a blow torch until golden. Use a paring knife to cut around the edges of the mold before lifting to remove it. Repeat with the remaining Custards.

### BERRY SALAD

32 pink currants
16 black currants
24 golden raspberries
16 black raspberries
8 green gooseberries
24 sprigs organic watercress
16 sprigs salad burnet
2 tablespoons White Balsamic Vinaigrette (see page 346)

In a small bowl, toss together the currants, berries, and greens with the White Balsamic Vinaigrette.

### TO FINISH

1/2 cup Chicken Jus Vinaigrette (see page 345)
Foie Gras Custards
Maldon salt
Berry Salad
Pickled Red Beets (see page 341)

Warm the Chicken Jus Vinaigrette in a small saucepan over low heat. Season the Foie Gras Custards with with Maldon salt. Garnish with 4 pink currants, 2 black currants, 3 golden raspberries, 2 black raspberries, 1 green gooseberry, 3 watercress sprigs, 2 salad burnet sprigs, and the Pickled Beets. Spoon the warm Chicken Jus Vinaigrette around the Custard to finish. Repeat with the remaining ingredients, to serve 8.

# RABBIT
## RILLETTE
## WITH CHERRIES,
## PISTACHIOS, AND
## VIOLET MUSTARD

*Serves 8*

### RABBIT CONFIT
3 pounds rabbit legs
Salt
6 sprigs thyme
1 gallon duck fat

Lay the rabbit legs in a single layer in a roasting pan and cover them completely with salt. After 2 hours, remove the legs from the salt and rinse under cold water. Preheat the oven to 275°F. Pat the legs dry and place then in a large pan with the thyme. Melt the duck fat over low heat in a large saucepan. Add the legs to the duck fat along with the thyme. The legs should be completely covered in the duck fat. Cover with aluminum foil and cook in the oven for 2 to 2 1/2 hours, or until the legs come cleanly apart. Cool the legs in the fat and, once cool, pick the meat from the bone, keeping it in large pieces.

### MARINATED FOIE GRAS
One 2-pound lobe grade-A foie gras
1 tablespoon salt
1/2 teaspoon pink curing salt
1 teaspoon sugar
1/2 teaspoon white pepper
2 teaspoons Madeira
1 teaspoon Cognac

Bring the foie gras to room temperature to soften. Separate the main lobes and remove the veins with tweezers and a paring knife. Pass the foie gras through a tamis, season with the salt, pink salt, sugar, and white pepper, and place in a *sous vide* bag. Add the Madeira and Cognac, seal the bag, and marinate in the refrigerator for 24 hours. Remove the foie gras from the refrigerator and allow it to come to room temperature. Transfer to a large mixing bowl and whip with a rubber spatula to re-emulsify.

## CHERRY VINEGAR

1 1/2 cups pitted Bing cherries
1 cup white balsamic vinegar

Vacuum-seal the cherries and vinegar in a *sous vide* bag. Cook in a water bath maintained by an immersion circulator at 170°F for 25 minutes. Transfer the bag to a bowl of ice water. Marinate in the refrigerator overnight. Strain through a fine-mesh chinois, reserving only the liquid.

## CHERRY CONSOMMÉ

5 pounds Bing cherries, pitted
1/2 cup sugar

Place the cherries, 2 cups water, and sugar in a large metal bowl, and place it over a large saucepan. Cook over medium-low heat for 3 hours. Strain through cheesecloth and chill the liquid over ice.

## CHERRY AND VIOLET MUSTARD GELÉE

3 sheets gelatin
1 cup Cherry Consommé
1/3 cup violet mustard

Bloom the gelatin by placing the sheets in a bowl of ice water for 10 minutes, until pliable. In the meantime, warm the Consommé in a small saucepan over low heat. Squeeze the gelatin to remove excess moisture and stir into the warm Consommé. Stir in the mustard and pass through a chinois.

## RABBIT RILLETTE

2 cups Rabbit Confit
3/4 cup Marinated Foie Gras
1/4 cup butter
1/4 cup cream
1 tablespoon Dijon mustard
1 1/2 teaspoons salt
1/4 teaspoon white pepper
Cherry and Violet Mustard Gelée

Allow the Rabbit Confit, Marinated Foie Gras, and butter to come to room temperature. Combine them in a mixing bowl and then add the cream, mustard, salt, and pepper, being careful not to overwork the mixture. The rabbit pieces should remain as whole as possible.

Roll the Rillette between 2 sheets of parchment paper to 3/4-inch thickness. Using an 8-inch square mold, cut the Rillette, keeping the mold around it. Pour 3/4 cup of the Gelée evenly on top of the Rillette and refrigerate 4 hours to set.

Once set, dip a knife into warm water and slice the Rillette into 5-inch-by-1/2-inch slices.

## PISTACHIO-COATED CHERRIES

2 sprigs lemon verbena
7 sheets gelatin
2 cups Bing cherries, pitted
1 1/2 cups dried sour cherries
1 cup flour
3 egg yolks
2 cups finely ground pistachios
8 cups canola oil

Wrap the lemon verbena in cheesecloth and tie together with butcher's twine. Bloom the gelatin by placing the sheets in a bowl of ice water for 10 minutes, until pliable. Vacuum-seal the cherries, dried cherries, and lemon verbena sachet in a *sous vide* bag. Cook in a water bath maintained at 170°F by an immersion circulator for 10 minutes. Coat a 2-piece magnetic mold (1 inch in diameter) with vegetable spray. Remove the cherries from the bag and discard the lemon verbena. Transfer the cherries to a blender. Squeeze the gelatin to remove excess moisture and puree with the cherries while still warm. Pass through a fine-mesh tamis and pipe into the prepared mold. Chill in the refrigerator for 4 hours.

Place the flour, egg yolks, and ground pistachios in separate bowls. Remove the cherries from the mold and dredge them first in flour, then in the yolks, and then in the ground pistachios. In a medium saucepan, heat the oil to 375°F. Fry the cherries for 20 seconds, until golden.

## CANDIED PISTACHIO

1/2 cup shelled pistachios
1 cup sugar
1 tablespoon glucose syrup

Preheat the oven to 300°F. Place the pistachios on a rimmed baking sheet and toast in the oven for 8 to 10 minutes. Combine the sugar, glucose, and 1 tablespoon water in a small, heavy-bottomed saucepan over medium heat and cook to a light caramel (about 300°F). Add the pistachios and coat evenly with the caramel. Separate the pistachios on a rimmed baking sheet lined with a silicone baking mat while still warm, and roll each individual nut in your hand to create a smooth, round outer shell. Cool to room temperature.

## PISTACHIO BUTTER

2 cups shelled pistachios
1 1/2 teaspoons salt
1/2 cup pistachio oil

Preheat the oven to 300°F. Place the pistachios on a rimmed baking sheet and toast in the oven for 8 to 10 minutes. Cool to room temperature. Combine the toasted pistachios and salt in a food processor. Chop the pistachios in the processor and slowly drizzle in the oil until the mixture reaches the consistency of a loose, crunchy peanut butter. Transfer to a blender and puree on high speed until it is a smooth paste. Pass the paste through a fine-mesh tamis and cool to room temperature.

## PISTACHIO YOGURT

1 cup Greek yogurt
1/2 cup Pistachio Butter
1 teaspoon salt

Combine the yogurt, Pistachio Butter, and salt in a mixing bowl. Reserve in a squeeze bottle.

## BREAD CRISPS

1 loaf Pistachio Nut Bread (see page 373)

Freeze the bread for 1 hour. Preheat the oven to 220°F. Slice the bread to 1/16 inch on a rotating deli slicer or with a sharp knife. Toast in the oven for 17 to 20 minutes.

## MARINATED RAINIER CHERRIES

2 cups sugar
2 cups white balsamic vinegar
1 cup Rainier cherries, with stems, pitted

Bring the sugar and 2 cups water to a boil and chill over ice. Add the vinegar and the cherries and marinate in the refrigerator for 4 hours.

## TO FINISH

Rabbit Rillette
Bread Crisps
Marinated Rainier Cherries
Pistachio-Coated Cherries
Candied Pistachios
1/2 cup ground pistachios
Pistachio Yogurt
16 Pickled White Pearl Onions (see page 343)
Cherry Vinegar
Olive oil
32 leaves mizuna

Place 1 slice of the Rabbit Rillette in the middle of a plate. Place 2 Bread Crisps at opposite angles against the Rillette. Arrange 2 Marinated Cherries, 1 Pistachio-Coated Cherry, 3 Candied Pistachios, 1 tablespoon ground pistachios, 6 dots Pistachio Yogurt, and 2 Pickled White Pearl Onions on the plate. Sauce with the Cherry Vinegar and olive oil. Finish with 4 mizuna leaves. Repeat with the remaining ingredients, to serve 8.

# JOHN DORY
## SEARED WITH SWEET CORN, CHANTERELLES, AND LEMONGRASS

*Serves 8*

### SUMMER NAGE WITH SWEET CORN

1 quart Tomato Water (see page 371)
1 quart Fish Fumet (see page 356)
1/4 cup plus 1/2 pound cold butter, cut into 1-inch cubes
1/2 cup chopped lemongrass
2 tablespoons chopped shallots
2 tablespoons chopped ginger
2 cups corn juice (from 4 quarts corn kernels)
3 sprigs basil
1 1/2 tablespoons lime juice
1 tablespoon salt
Cayenne pepper

In 2 separate saucepans, reduce the Tomato Water and Fish Fumet to 2 cups each. Melt 1/4 cup of the butter in a medium pot and sweat the lemongrass, shallots, and ginger together until tender and translucent. Add the reduced Tomato Water and reduced Fumet, and reduce the liquid to 3 cups. Add the corn juice and simmer for 5 minutes. Remove from the heat, add the basil, and steep for 10 minutes. Discard the basil, and transfer the liquid to a blender. Puree on high and strain through a chinois. Using a hand blender, blend in the remaining 1/2 pound cold butter to emulsify. Season with the lime juice, salt, and cayenne to taste.

### JOHN DORY

4 tablespoons canola oil
Eight 4-ounce John Dory fillets
1 tablespoon salt
2 tablespoons butter

Heat 2 large sauté pans over medium-high heat and add 2 tablespoons of oil to each of the pans. Pat the fish dry with a paper towel and season with salt on both sides. Just before the oil begins to smoke, put 4 fillets in each pan — the side where the skin was should be facing down — pressing the fillets lightly in the center with a fish spatula to remove air pockets. Rotate the fish 180 degrees when it releases itself from the pan in order to ensure even color. When the fish is three quarters of the way cooked through, after about 2 to 3 minutes, add 1 tablespoon butter to each pan and remove from the heat. Baste the fish off the heat for 2 minutes, making sure not to overcook it. Remove the fish from the pan and blot any excess oil with a paper towel.

### BABY RADISHES AND CORN

32 baby radishes, washed, green tops intact
1 1/2 cups corn kernels
2 tablespoons Chicken Stock (see page 356)
3 tablespoons butter
1 teaspoon salt

Bring a pot of salted water to a boil. Add the radishes and corn, cooking for 1 minute. Transfer to a bowl of ice water and, once cool, drain. Heat the Chicken Stock in a sauté pan. Add the radishes, corn, and butter, and toss to glaze. Season with salt.

### CHANTERELLES

60 small chanterelles
2 tablespoons butter
1/2 cup Chicken Stock (see page 356)
2 teaspoons salt

Clean the chanterelles of all dirt with a paring knife and scrape any discoloration from the stems. Trim the bottoms and rinse thoroughly. Spread the chanterelles on a paper towel to dry. Melt the butter in a large sauté pan over medium heat. Add the chanterelles and sauté for 1 minute. Add the Chicken Stock and bring to a simmer. Reduce until the mushrooms are glazed. Season with the salt.

### CORN POWDER

1 cup freeze-dried corn

Place corn into a spice grinder and grind to a fine powder.

### TO FINISH

John Dory
Baby Radishes and Corn
Summer Nage with Sweet Corn
8 teaspoons Lemongrass Oil (see page 345)
4 baby radishes, shaved
Chanterelles
8 teaspoons freeze-dried corn
Corn Powder
Lime zest

Place a piece of John Dory in the middle of a plate. Create a rectangle around the fish with the Baby Radishes and Corn. Spoon the Summer Nage between the fish and radishes. Garnish with 1 teaspoon Lemongrass Oil, shaved radishes, and Chanterelles. Place 1 teaspoon of the freeze-dried kernels in a line below the sauce and sprinkle with Corn Powder and lime zest.

# COD
## POACHED CHEEKS WITH BELL PEPPERS AND PIMENT D'ESPELETTE

*Serves 8*

### RED PEPPER NAGE

1/4 cup extra-virgin olive oil
2 1/2 cups diced (1/2 inch) red bell pepper
1 cup sliced onion
1 tablespoon minced garlic
1/8 teaspoon saffron
1 cup white wine
5 cups Fish Fumet (see page 356)
1 tablespoon cornstarch
8 leaves basil
2 tablespoons lemon juice
1 1/2 tablespoons salt
1 teaspoon *piment d'Espelette*

Heat the olive oil in a large saucepan over low heat. Add the garlic, onion, pepper, and saffron, and cook over low heat until the vegetables are soft and golden. Raise the heat to high and add the white wine. When the wine comes to a boil, reduce the heat and simmer until the wine is almost dry and the peppers are glazed in the pan. Add the Fumet to the vegetables and bring to a simmer. Dissolve the cornstarch in 2 1/2 tablespoons water to make a slurry. When the Fumet comes to a simmer, thicken the liquid with the cornstarch slurry and continue to simmer for 20 minutes. Remove from the heat and add the basil. Steep for 15 minutes and then remove the basil. Puree the sauce in a blender until smooth. Strain through a chinois and season with lemon juice, salt, and *piment d'Espelette*.

### PEPPER CONFIT

8 cups canola oil
8 baby yellow bell peppers
8 baby red bell peppers
8 baby orange bell peppers
2 poblano peppers
2 cups olive oil
5 sprigs thyme
3 cloves garlic, crushed but kept whole

In a large saucepan, bring the canola oil to 425°F. Add all the peppers, being careful to not allow the oil to overflow or splatter, and cook for 15 to 20 seconds. Drain and place in a large bowl. Cover with plastic wrap until cool. Remove and discard the skin from the peppers.

Preheat the oven to 250°F. In a medium oven-safe pot, combine all the peeled peppers and the olive oil, thyme, and garlic. Place the pot in the oven for 1 1/2 hours, or until the peppers are tender. Slit the sides of the peppers and remove the seeds.

### POTATO CHIPS

2 cups peeled and diced Idaho potatoes
1 tablespoon salt
*Piment d'Espelette*

Preheat the oven to 175°F. Place the potatoes in a medium pot and cover with cold water. Bring to a simmer, cooking until the potatoes are tender and almost falling apart. In the meantime, line an inverted rimmed baking sheet with parchment paper. Drain the potatoes, but reserve the cooking water. Place the cooked potatoes in a blender with the salt and enough of the cooking water, 3 to 4 tablespoons, so that the potatoes spin. Blend until smooth and creamy. Using an offset spatula, spread the potatoes paper thin on the baking sheet and generously sprinkle with *piment d'Espelette*. Dehydrate in the oven for 8 to 10 hours. Cool to room temperature, break into small pieces, and store in an airtight container.

### COD CHEEKS

16 cod cheeks, cleaned
2 pounds salt
6 cups olive oil
10 sprigs thyme
2 cloves garlic, crushed but kept whole

Cover the cod cheeks in salt and cure in the refrigerator for 20 minutes. Rinse thoroughly under cold water and pat dry. Combine the oil, thyme, and garlic in a medium pot and warm over medium heat to 155°F. Add the cod cheeks and poach for 6 minutes, until tender.

### TO FINISH

Cod Cheeks
*Fleur de sel*
Pepper Confit
Potato Chips
8 purslane tips
8 garlic blossoms
16 dill blossoms
8 nasturtium leaves
8 nasturtium petals
Red Pepper Nage

Place 2 Cod Cheeks on a plate and season with *fleur de sel*. Lay the Pepper Confit on and around the cheeks and garnish with a Potato Chip. Finish the plate with 1 purslane tip, 1 garlic blossom, 2 dill blossoms, 1 nasturtium leaf, and 1 nasturtium petal, and spoon the Red Pepper Nage all around. Repeat with the remaining ingredients, to serve 8.

# TURBOT
POACHED
WITH ZUCCHINI,
SAFFRON FUMET,
AND TARRAGON

*Serves 8*

## TURBOT
10 baby zucchini
8 turbot fillets, 5 ounces each
Salt

Using a mandoline, shave the baby zucchini into paper-thin coins. Bring a pot of salted water to a boil. Add the zucchini slices and blanch for 10 to 15 seconds. Transfer to a bowl of ice water. Once cold, pat dry. Season the turbot fillets with salt. Starting at the top right corner of the fish, layer the zucchini like scales all the way across and down, covering the whole fillet. Place in a *sous vide* bag and vacuum-seal.

## RATATOUILLE-STUFFED SQUASH BLOSSOMS
6 yellow bell peppers
6 red bell peppers
4 medium zucchini
3 tablespoons olive oil
3 cloves garlic, crushed but kept whole
3 sprigs thyme
1 1/2 teaspoons salt
1 teaspoon lemon juice
8 squash blossoms

Peel, seed, and remove any veins from all the bell peppers. Cut the skin off the zucchini, leaving a little more than 1/16 inch of flesh attached; discard the center and seeds. Dice the yellow peppers, the red peppers, and the zucchini (all 1/8 inch), keeping the vegetables separate.

In a small sauté pan, heat 1 tablespoon of the olive oil with 1 clove of garlic. Once the garlic begins to sizzle, add the diced yellow bell pepper and 1 thyme sprig, and sauté for 1 minute. Remove from the pan and cool over ice. Discard the garlic. Repeat this process for the red pepper and zucchini.

Once all of the vegetables have been sautéed and cooled, mix them together and season with the salt and lemon juice. Remove the stamen from the inside of the squash blossoms. Carefully pull back the tips of the blossoms and fill with 1 1/2 tablespoons of the pepper-and-zucchini filling.

## SAFFRON FUMET
1 tablespoon butter
1/4 cup sliced shallots
2 teaspoons saffron
1 1/4 cups white wine
1 1/4 cups vermouth
2 cups Fish Fumet (see page 356)
2 cups cream
1 1/2 teaspoon salt
1 teaspoon lemon juice
1 tablespoon tarragon leaves, sliced on the bias
1 tablespoon diced (1/8 inch) red bell pepper

In a medium pot over medium heat, melt the butter and sweat the shallots with the saffron until tender. Deglaze with the white wine and vermouth and reduce until almost dry. Add the Fish Fumet and reduce by half. Add the cream and reduce to about 1 1/2 cups. Season with salt and lemon juice, and pass through a chinois. Stir in the tarragon and red bell pepper.

## FLOWER AND HERB BOUQUETS
12 full-length chives
8 sprigs chervil
8 sprigs thyme
8 sprigs tarragon
8 sprigs flowering garlic

Bring a small saucepan of salted water to a boil. Add the chives and cook for 15 to 20 seconds, or until wilted. Transfer the chives to a bowl of ice water to stop the cooking and help them retain their bright green color. Once cold, remove from the water and gently squeeze in a kitchen towel to remove any excess moisture.

In one hand, grasp together a chervil sprig, a thyme sprig, a tarragon sprig, and a flowering garlic sprig. Wrap a blanched chive around the base of the sprigs, encircling the bottoms 3 times with the chive. Secure with a double knot. Trim the bottom of the herbs to make a 3/4- to 1-inch-long bundle. Repeat with the remaining herbs.

## TO FINISH
1/4 cup plus 2 tablespoons olive oil
Ratatouille-Stuffed Squash Blossoms
2 tablespoons Chicken Stock (see page 356)
Salt
Turbot
*Fleur de sel*
Saffron Fumet
8 Flower and Herb Bouquets
8 teaspoons Tarragon Oil (see page 345)
*Piment d'Espelette*

Preheat the oven to 350°F. Warm 2 tablespoons of the oil in a large oven-safe sauté pan over medium heat. Add the Squash Blossoms and the Chicken Stock, season with salt, and baste with the oil and Stock for 30 seconds. Transfer the pan to the oven and roast for 3 minutes until warmed through. Baste with the liquid once again.

Cook the Turbot in a water bath maintained at 135°F by an immersion circulator. Remove the Turbot from the *sous vide* bags and trim the edges with a sharp knife. Brush with the remaining 1/4 cup olive oil and sprinkle with *fleur de sel*.

Place a Turbot fillet on a warm plate and lay a Squash Blossom next to it. Spoon the Saffron Fumet in the middle and garnish with a Bouquet. Finish with 1 teaspoon Tarragon Oil and *piment d'Espelette*. Repeat with the remaining ingredients, to serve 8.

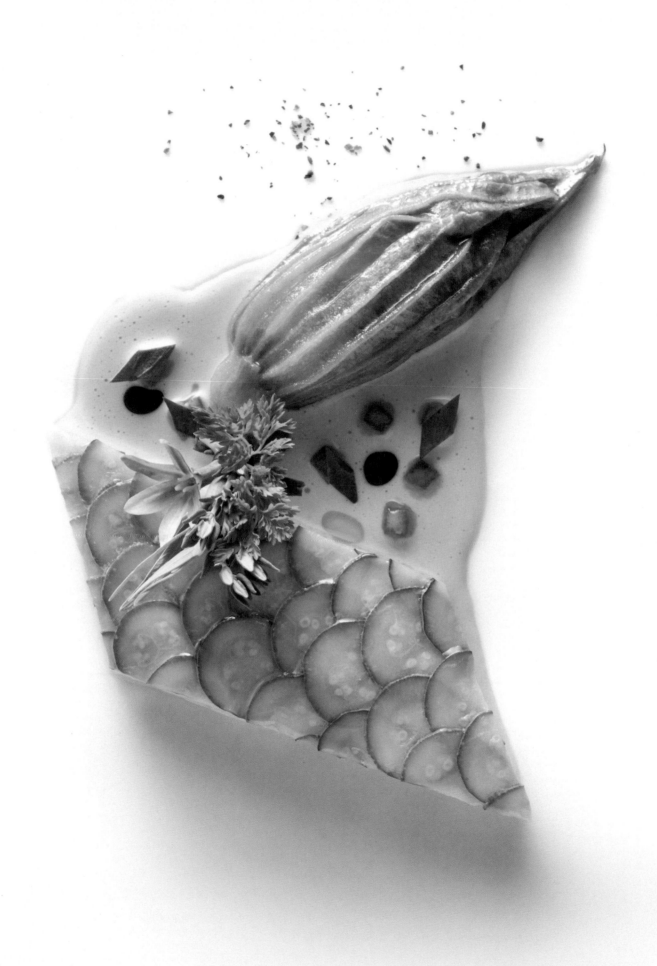

# LOUP DE MER
## SEARED WITH CANNELLINI BEANS, CHORIZO, AND SAUCE BOUILLABAISSE

*Serves 8*

### MANILA CLAMS

2 pounds clams, washed
1 tablespoon olive oil
2 cups white wine
8 sprigs thyme

Soak the clams in water for 2 hours to purge. In a very hot large sauté pan with a lid, heat the oil. Sauté the clams for 30 seconds. Add the wine and thyme, cover, and cook until all of the clams are opened, about another minute. (Discard any that don't open.) Chill over ice. Remove the clams from their shell and clean away any dirt. Trim away and discard the mantle. Strain the cooking liquid through a chinois and store the clams in their cooking liquid, noting that you will need some of this liquid in the Sauce Bouillabaisse.

### SAUCE BOUILLABAISSE

1/4 pound *loup de mer* bones
2 tablespoons olive oil
1/2 cup chopped fennel
1/4 cup sliced carrot
2 tablespoons sliced shallot
2 cloves garlic
1/8 tablespoon saffron
1/4 cup Pernod
1/4 cup white wine
1 cup canned whole peeled tomatoes
1 cup Fish Fumet (see page 356)
1 cup Chicken Stock (see page 356)
1 cup Lobster Stock (see page 356)
1/2 cup Manila Clam cooking liquid (reserved
    from Manila Clams)
Salt
Lime juice
Cayenne pepper

Using a sharp chef's knife or heavy-duty scissors, cut the fish bones into medium pieces. Heat the olive oil in a large pot. Add the fish bones and sear until lightly browned. Add the fennel, carrot, shallot, garlic, and saffron, and sweat. Deglaze the pan with the Pernod, cooking until almost dry. Add the white wine and cook until almost dry. Add the tomatoes, Fish Fumet, Chicken Stock, Lobster Stock, and Manila Clam cooking liquid. Simmer the stock mixture for 30 minutes. Puree the entire mixture in a blender until smooth. Push the mixture through a chinois. Transfer the strained mixture back to the blender and blend again. Strain through a chinois 7 to 8 times. Do not push the liquid through with a ladle; instead, tap the chinois with a spoon or swirl the liquid through. The end product should be smooth but have body. Season with salt, lime juice, and cayenne to taste.

### LOUP DE MER AND SEAFOOD

8 *loup de mer* fillets, skin on, 3 ounces each
8 Maine shrimp
3 calamari tubes, cut into strips
Salt
4 tablespoons canola oil

Season the *loup de mer,* shrimp, and calamari with salt. Heat 1 1/2 tablespoons of the oil in a large sauté pan over medium-high heat. Add 4 of the fillets, skin side down, lower the heat, and sear for 3 minutes. Turn to briefly sear the flesh side and remove from the pan. Repeat with another 1 1/2 tablespoons of oil and the remaining 4 fillets. Heat the remaining tablespoon of oil in another sauté pan over medium-high heat. Quickly cook the shrimp and calamari until just cooked through.

### TO FINISH

8 tablespoons White Bean Puree (see page 354)
Loup de Mer and Seafood
Sauce Bouillabaisse
1/4 cup diced (1/8 to 1/16 inch) dry Spanish chorizo
Manila Clams
24 sprigs bush basil
1/2 cup cooked cannellini beans (reserved from
    White Bean Puree, see page 354)
8 taggiasca olives
8 teaspoons Chorizo Oil (see page 344)

Warm the White Bean Puree in a small saucepan over low heat. Spoon 1 tablespoon of the Puree on a plate. Drag down with the back of a spoon to make a comma. Place a *loup de mer* fillet at the base of the Puree and spoon the Sauce Bouillabaisse in the groove of the Puree. Garnish with the chorizo, Manila Clams, 3 basil sprigs, 1 tablespoon beans, shrimp, calamari, 1 olive, and 1 teaspoon of the Chorizo Oil. Repeat with the remaining ingredients, to serve 8.

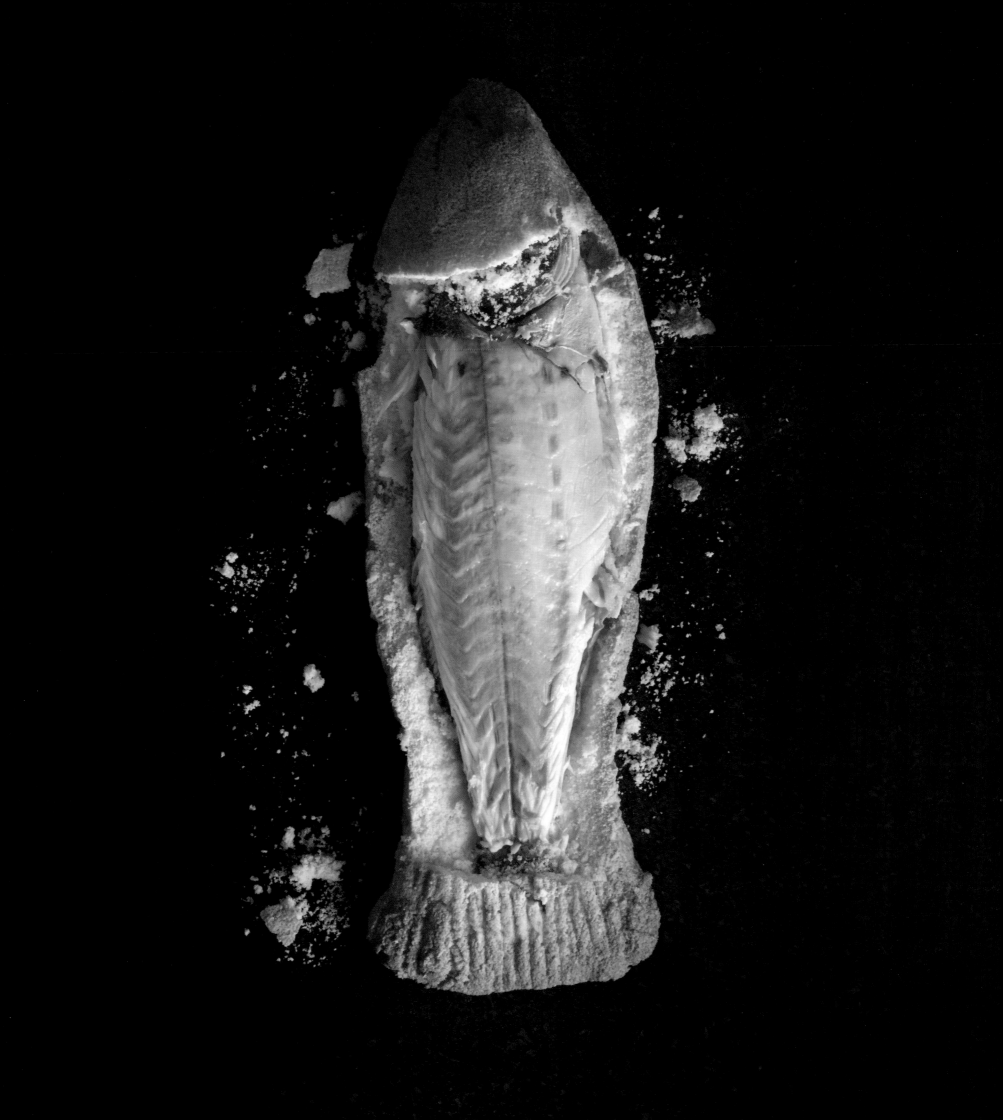

# BLACK BASS
## SALT-CRUSTED WITH ARTICHOKES, TOMATOES, AND LEMON THYME

*Serves 8*

### CREPE BATTER

2 1/4 cups milk
1 egg
1 1/4 cups flour
1 1/2 teaspoons chopped thyme
1 1/2 teaspoons chopped rosemary
1 1/2 teaspoons chopped tarragon
1 1/2 teaspoons chopped chives
1 teaspoon salt

In a large bowl, whisk together the milk, eggs, and flour. Add the herbs and salt, whisking until smooth. Heat a large sauté pan over high heat for 2 minutes. Lower the heat to low and allow the pan to cool for 4 to 5 minutes. Coat the pan with vegetable spray. Ladle 1/4 cup batter into the middle of the pan and roll the pan, spreading the batter evenly and quickly. Cook for 1 minute and flip. Cook for 30 seconds on the other side and remove from the pan. Repeat 5 more times to make a total of 6 crepes.

### SALT CRUST

24 egg whites
4 1/2 pounds salt

In a stand mixer fitted with the whisk attachment, whip the egg whites until they reach medium peaks. Lower the speed to the lowest setting and add the salt. Once the salt is incorporated, remove from the mixer and allow to rest in the refrigerator for 1 hour.

### BLACK BASS

3 sprigs rosemary
3 sprigs parsley
3 sprigs thyme
3 whole black bass, scaled and gutted,
    2 1/2 pounds each
1 lemon, thinly sliced into 6 slices

Preheat the oven to 375°F. Place 1 sprig each of rosemary, parsley, and thyme and 2 lemon slices into the cavity of each fish. Lay out 2 crepes so that they overlap and place the fish on top. Wrap the fish in the crepes. Line a baking sheet with parchment paper and spread a 1/4-inch layer of the Salt Crust on the parchment. The layer should be longer and wider than the fish. Place the fish-filled crepe on top of the crust. Using an offset spatula, spread an even, smooth crust on top of the fish, making sure that it is completely covered. Use the edge of an offset spatula to create fish "scales." Repeat with the remaining ingredients. Place the fish into the oven and cook for 7 to 8 minutes. Rotate the fish and cook for another 8 minutes. Remove from the oven and allow to rest for 5 minutes.

### ARTICHOKES BARIGOULE

2 tablespoons lemon juice
20 baby artichokes
4 tablespoons olive oil
2 cloves garlic
2 teaspoons salt
2 cups white wine
2 sprigs thyme
1 sprig rosemary

In a large bowl, stir the lemon juice with 1 gallon water. Cut off the top of an artichoke and remove the outer leaves. Turn the artichoke with a sharp paring knife or vegetable peeler and remove the stem. Quarter the turned artichoke lengthwise and reserve in the water with lemon juice as you turn and stem the remaining artichokes.

Heat 2 tablespoons of the olive oil in a saucepan over medium-high heat. Drain the artichokes and add them and the garlic to the pan. Sauté for 1 minute and season with some of the salt. Remove the pan from the heat and add the wine. Return to the heat and bring to a boil, adding the remaining 2 tablespoons olive oil, the thyme, and the rosemary. Cover and continue to cook over medium-high heat until the artichokes are tender, 2 to 3 minutes. Season with the remaining salt, remove from the heat, and cool the artichokes in their liquid. Reserve 10 of the Artichokes Barigoule for the Diced Vegetables.

### CURRY SPICE

1 tablespoon pink peppercorns
1 tablespoon white peppercorns
1 tablespoon Madras curry powder
1 tablespoon cumin seeds
1 teaspoon cloves
1 teaspoon nutmeg
1/4 cinnamon stick

In a small sauté pan over medium heat, toast all of the spices until fragrant. Grind together in a spice grinder and reserve in a dry place.

## MUSSELS

3 pounds mussels
2 tablespoons olive oil
2 shallots, sliced
2 cups white wine
1 cup parsley leaves and stems
1 teaspoon saffron
1 sprig thyme

Remove any beard from the mussels and rinse them well under cold running water. Heat a large sauté pan until very hot and add the oil. Add the mussels and shallots and sauté on high heat to toast lightly. Add the white wine, parsley, saffron, and thyme, and cover. Cook over high heat until just over three quarters of the mussels are opened. Strain over a colander set over a bowl and allow to cool to room temperature. Strain the liquid through a fine chinois and reserve. Pick all the mussels that have opened from the shells and store in the reserved liquid. (Toss any mussels that don't open.)

## TOMATO FONDUE

8 beefsteak tomatoes
2 cups extra-virgin olive oil
Peel of 1 lemon
16 sprigs lemon thyme
1 1/2 tablespoons salt
3 tablespoons lemon juice

Preheat the oven to 400°F. Slice the tomatoes in half crosswise and remove all of the seeds. Line a rimmed baking sheet with parchment paper and lay the tomatoes, cut side down, on the parchment. Bake for 10 minutes, until the skin starts to release from the flesh. Peel the tomatoes and transfer them to a medium saucepan with the olive oil, lemon peel, 8 of the lemon thyme sprigs, and a pinch of salt to start the release of the water in the tomatoes. Place the saucepan over very low heat and cook for about 4 hours, until all the liquid has evaporated and the tomatoes are falling apart and slightly sweet. Remove the lemon thyme sprigs from the Tomato Fondue. Pick the leaves from the remaining 8 lemon thyme sprigs and stir them in. Season with the remaining salt and the lemon juice.

## DICED VEGETABLES

1/4 cup fava beans
1/4 cup peeled and diced (1/8 inch) red bell pepper
10 Artichokes Barigoule, diced (1/8 inch)
1/4 tablespoon diced (1/8 inch) taggiasca olives
2 tablespoons olive oil

Bring a pot of salted water to a boil. Add the fava beans and cook for 2 minutes. Transfer to a bowl of ice water. Once cool, drain and peel. Cut into 1/8-inch dice. Add the bell pepper to the water and cook for 30 seconds. Transfer to a bowl of ice water and, once cool, drain. Combine the fava beans, Artichokes Barigoule, olives, peppers, and olive oil in a small bowl.

## TO FINISH

Canola oil, for frying
Mussels
1/4 cup flour
Salt
Curry Spice
Black Bass
8 tablespoons Artichoke Puree (see page 350)
Tomato Fondue
Artichokes Barigoule
Diced Vegetables
24 sprigs sea cress

In a medium saucepan, heat the canola oil to 400°F. Dredge the Mussels in the flour, shaking off any excess. Add the oil and fry for 20 to 30 seconds, until crispy. Remove with a slotted spoon and drain on paper towels. Sprinkle with salt and Curry Spice. Remove the top layer of Salt Crust, not allowing the salt and the flesh of the fish to come into contact. Fold the Crepe back to expose the fish. Peel away the skin and scoop out a portion of the fish. Place it in the center of a plate. Warm the Artichoke Puree in a small saucepan over low heat and place a tablespoonful next to the fish. Spoon a little bit of the Tomato Fondue on top and around the fish. Garnish with the fried Mussels, Artichokes Barigoule, Diced Vegetables, and 3 sea cress springs. Repeat with the remaining ingredients, to serve 8, noting that once you've scooped out the flesh from one side of the fish, you can discard the herbs and lemon and grasp the backbone. In one motion, pull it out of the fish to reveal the other half of the fish's flesh.

# SCALLOP
## MINESTRONE WITH CORN AND FLAGEOLETS

*Serves 8*

### MINESTRONE

2 tablespoons extra-virgin olive oil
1 1/2 cups diced (1/4 inch) zucchini
1/2 cup diced (1/4 inch) carrots
1/4 cup diced (1/4 inch) celery root
2 tablespoons minced leeks
1 tablespoon minced onion
1 clove garlic, minced
1 teaspoon tomato paste
1/2 cup white wine
1 quart Chicken Stock (see page 356)
1 1/2 cups diced (1/4 inch) tomatoes
1/2 cup diced (1/4 inch) potatoes
1 cup thinly sliced basil
1/4 cup thinly sliced mint
1/4 cup lemon juice
1 tablespoon salt
1 teaspoon *piment d'Espelette*
2 tablespoons cold butter

Heat the olive oil in a saucepan and add the zucchini, carrots, celery root, leeks, onion, and garlic, sweating for about 10 minutes without browning. Add the tomato paste and sweat for 2 more minutes. Add the white wine and reduce by half. Add the Chicken Stock, diced tomatoes, and potatoes, and simmer over low heat for 30 minutes. Remove from the heat and add the basil and mint. Season with the lemon juice, salt, and *piment d'Espelette*, and let infuse for 20 minutes. Strain through a fine-mesh chinois and reduce the remaining broth by a third. Add the cold butter and emulsify with a hand blender.

### GARGANELLI PASTA

1 pound Pasta Dough (see page 364)

Remove the pasta dough from the refrigerator to allow it to soften slightly. Set up a pasta roller as per the manufacturer's instructions. Flatten the pasta with a rolling pin until it can fit through the widest setting on the pasta machine. Run the dough through the pasta machine, gradually decreasing the thickness until the thinnest setting is reached. Run the pasta twice on this setting. Cut into 1-inch squares. Barely moisten 1 corner of the pasta square with water. Using a thin dowel (1/8 inch thick) or a chopstick, roll the pasta corner to corner, keeping the pasta tightly wound around the dowel. Firmly press the pasta together as you roll to help the dough stick to itself. It is helpful to roll on a *garganelli* board to create ridges and bind the dough to itself. Pull the hand-rolled piece of pasta off the dowel and repeat until all of the pasta squares are rolled. (The *garganelli* will look similar to ridged penne.) It may be necessary to flour the dowel lightly to prevent the pasta from sticking. The *garganelli* can be kept refrigerated on a semolina-lined baking sheet or can be air-dried.

### COCO BEANS

1 cup dried coco beans (French navy beans)
2 sprigs thyme
1 tablespoon black pepper
3 bay leaves
2 tablespoons olive oil

Soak the beans overnight in water. Wrap the thyme, pepper, and bay leaves in cheesecloth and tie together with butcher's twine. Strain the beans, place them in a medium saucepan, and cover with 3 inches water. Add the herb sachet and simmer for 1 to 1 1/2 hours, until tender. Cool the beans in their liquid.

### TO FINISH

2 cups shelled *flageolet* beans
Garganelli Pasta
1 tablespoon Chicken Stock (see page 356)
1 red bell pepper, peeled and diced (1/8 inch)
1/4 cup corn kernels
Coco Beans
1/3 cup butter
12 sea scallops
2 tablespoons canola oil
Salt
Minestrone
Marjoram
Chocolate mint
8 squash blossoms
Olive oil

Bring a pot of salted water to a boil. Add the *flageolets* and cook for 4 minutes. Remove with a slotted spoon and transfer to a bowl of ice water. Once cool, drain and peel. Add the Garganelli to the boiling salted water and cook for 3 to 4 minutes. Drain. Heat the Chicken Stock in a sauté pan. Add the bell pepper, corn, Coco Beans and *flageolets,* Garganelli, and butter, and toss to glaze. Cut the scallops in half with a crinkle-cut knife, creating 24 thin rounds. In a sauté pan, heat the canola oil. Season the scallops with salt and sear the crinkle-cut side for 45 seconds, until golden. Punch with a 1-inch ring cutter. Spoon the glazed vegetables and Garganelli into 8 bowls. Aerate the minestrone with a hand blender and spoon into the bowls. Nestle 3 scallop halves, crinkle-cut side up, into each bowl of minestrone. Garnish with the marjoram, chocolate mint, squash blossoms, and olive oil.

# LOBSTER
## LASAGNA WITH SUMMER FLOWERS AND LEMON VERBENA

*Serves 8*

### LOBSTER

4 (1 1/4-pound) live lobsters

Fill a large stockpot with water and bring the water to 150°F. Add 2 of the lobsters, and cook for 7 minutes, maintaining the temperature of the water at 150°F. Remove the tails from the lobsters and transfer them to an ice bath. Return the knuckles and claws to the water and continue cooking for 7 more minutes. Transfer the knuckles and claws to the ice bath. Repeat with the remaining lobsters. When the tails, knuckles, and claws are completely cool, carefully remove the meat from the shells, making sure to keep the meat intact. Refrigerate.

### LASAGNA

1 pound Pasta Dough (see page 364)
2 egg whites
1/2 cup leaves chervil, loosely packed
1/2 cup Johnny-jump-up petals

Roll the dough with a rolling pin until it is a manageable width for a pasta machine. Gradually roll out the dough until the number 1 setting on the pasta machine has been reached. Brush half of the sheet with egg whites and arrange the chervil and flower petals in a tight pattern over the egg-washed side. Keep the other half clean. Fold the clean half of the pasta over the side with the chervil and flowers and press down gently. Run it through the pasta machine at the number 1 setting 3 times and then once at setting 1/2 (between 0 and 1). Cut the pasta into 6-inch-by-3 1/2-inch rectangles. Store the pasta in the refrigerator on a baking sheet between layers of linen.

### LEMON VERBENA LOBSTER EMULSION

1 tablespoon lobster roe
3 tablespoons cream
8 cups Lobster Stock (see page 356)
1 tablespoon cornstarch
1/2 cup loosely packed lemon verbena
Cayenne pepper
Salt
Lime juice

Pass the lobster roe through a tamis and combine it with the cream. In a large saucepan, reduce the Lobster Stock over medium heat to 4 cups. Combine 1/2 cup cold water with the cornstarch to make a slurry. Bring the Lobster Stock to a boil and add the slurry. Simmer for about 5 minutes, remove from the heat, add the lemon verbena, and infuse for 15 minutes. Strain through a chinois. Transfer the hot liquid to a blender and carefully blend on high speed. Slowly add the roe mixture to the blender and season with cayenne, salt, and lime juice. Strain through a chinois.

### LEMON VERBENA BEURRE BLANC

4 cups white wine
3 cups orange juice
1/2 cup cream
3 pounds cold butter, cut into 1-inch cubes
3 stalks lemon verbena
1 1/2 teaspoons *piment d'Espelette*
3 tablespoons salt

Reduce the white wine in a saucepan to 1 cup. Add the orange juice and cream and reduce to just over 2 cups. Reduce the heat to low and slowly whisk in the butter, 3 or 4 cubes at a time. Stir slowly and constantly. Once fully emulsified, add the lemon verbena stalks, remove from the heat, and steep for 5 minutes. Strain through a fine-mesh chinois. When the butter is completely emulsified, add the salt and *piment d'Espelette*. Keep warm at 155°F.

### SQUASH AND ZUCCHINI

7 yellow pattypan squash
4 green pattypan squash
3 baby zucchini
2 teaspoons Lemon Oil (see page 345)
Salt
1/4 cup Chicken Stock (see page 356)
1/4 cup butter

Cut 4 of the yellow pattypan squash and the 4 green pattypan squash into quarters. Using a mandoline, shave the remaining 3 yellow pattypan squash and the baby zucchini. Bring a pot of salted water to a boil. Add the squash quarters and cook for 3 minutes. Shock in ice water and, once cold, drain. Dress the yellow pattypan and zucchini shaves with the Lemon Oil and season with salt. Heat the Chicken Stock in a saucepan and add the squash quarters. Add the butter and toss to glaze.

### TO FINISH

Lobster
Lemon Verbena Beurre Blanc
*Fleur de sel*
Lasagna
1/2 cup Chicken Stock (see page 356)
3/4 cup butter
Zucchini Puree (see page 354)
Squash and Zucchini
8 viola flowers
16 sprigs chervil
8 sprigs dill
Lemon Verbena Lobster Emulsion
1/4 cup olive oil
1 teaspoon Lobster Roe Powder (see page 371)

Cut the lobster tails in half lengthwise. Place the lobster tails, knuckles, and claws into the Lemon Verbena Beurre Blanc and heat at 155°F for 5 to 8 minutes, until warmed through. Remove the lobster from the Beurre Blanc and sprinkle lightly with *fleur de sel*. Bring a pot of salted water to a boil and blanch the Lasagna for 2 to 3 minutes. While the pasta is boiling, heat the Chicken Stock in 2 separate sauté pans over medium heat. Remove the Lasagna from the boiling water and divide between the 2 sauté pans. Add the butter, tossing to glaze the sheets evenly. Warm the Zucchini Puree in a small pan over low heat. Spoon the Puree into the bottom of a bowl. Alternate Lobster and Lasagna in layers over the Puree. Place the Squash and Zucchini around. Garnish with a viola flower, 2 chervil sprigs, and 1 dill sprig. Briefly aerate the Lemon Verbena Lobster Emulsion with a hand blender and spoon around the dish. Finish with a drizzle of olive oil and 1/8 teaspoon Lobster Roe Powder. Repeat with the remaining ingredients, to serve 8.

# CHICKEN
## ROASTED WITH CHANTERELLES, CORN, AND FARRO

*Serves 8*

### CHICKEN BREASTS
4 boneless chicken breasts, skin on
2 teaspoons salt
4 sprigs thyme

Season the chicken evenly on both sides with salt.
Place 1 sprig thyme on the skinless side of the breasts.
Place each breast in a *sous vide* bag and vacuum-seal.
Cook in a water bath maintained at 145°F by an immersion circulator for 25 to 30 minutes.

### CORN PUDDING
2 cups corn juice (from 4 quarts of corn kernels)
3 tablespoons mascarpone
3/4 teaspoon salt

Heat the corn juice in a medium saucepan over
medium-high heat while whisking constantly. As the
starches in the corn juice start to thicken, turn the heat
down slightly to avoid scorching. Whisk until it reaches
a pudding-like thickness. When the pudding is done
cooking, remove it from the heat and whisk in the mascarpone. Season with the salt.

### FARRO
2 tablespoons olive oil
2 tablespoons minced shallot
1 pound farro
1/4 cup white wine
10 cups Chicken Stock (see page 356)
1 tablespoon salt
4 sprigs thyme

Heat the olive oil in a large saucepan over low heat.
Sweat the shallots in the oil until translucent. Add the
farro and toast lightly. Deglaze the pan with the white
wine and bring to a boil. Add the Chicken Stock and
season with the salt. Bring to a boil and reduce the heat
to a simmer. Add the thyme and simmer for 1 1/2 hours,
until the farro is tender and the liquid is absorbed.
Remove the thyme and cool over ice.

## COCKSCOMB

1/2 pound cockscombs
1 clove garlic, crushed but kept whole
5 sprigs thyme
4 cups duck fat

Preheat the oven to 300°F. Rinse the cockscombs to remove any blood. Pat dry and place in a medium pan with the garlic and thyme. Melt the duck fat in a large saucepan over low heat. Pour over the cockscombs and cover the pan. Place in the oven for 3 hours, until tender. Cool to room temperature in the fat. Once cool, strain, discarding the garlic, thyme, and duck fat. Dice (1/8 inch) the cockscombs.

## SWEET CORN AND FARRO RAGOUT

2 cups Farro
1/2 cup corn kernels
1/4 cup Chicken Stock (see page 356)
3/4 cup Corn Pudding
2 tablespoons Cockscomb
2 tablespoons minced Shallot Confit (see page 371)
1 1/2 teaspoons salt
1 tablespoon sliced chives

In a medium pan over medium heat, heat the cooked Farro with the corn and Chicken Stock. When the corn kernels become slightly tender, add the Corn Pudding, Cockscomb, and Shallot Confit. Cook the Ragout until it has reached the consistency of risotto. Season with the salt and finish with the chives.

## CHICKEN SAUCE

2 cups Chicken Jus (see page 356)
1 tablespoon butter
1/2 cup diced foie gras
1 shallot, chopped
1 tablespoon Banyuls vinegar

Place the Chicken Jus in a small saucepan over medium heat and reduce by half. In a small sauté pan set over low heat, melt the butter. Add the foie gras and shallot, and sweat. Once the Jus is reduced, add the melted foie gras and the sweated shallots. Add the Banyuls vinegar and strain.

## VIN JAUNE SABAYON

2 cups *vin jaune*
5 egg yolks
2 eggs
1 pound butter, melted
1 tablespoon salt
1 tablespoon lime juice
2 N$_2$O cartridges

In a small pot over medium heat, reduce the *vin jaune* by half. Combine the egg yolks, eggs, butter, salt, lime juice, and *vin jaune* in a large bowl. Pour it into a whipped-cream canister. Charge the base with the N$_2$O cartridges. Place in a water bath and maintain at 145°F with an immersion circulator for 1 hour before serving.

## CHICKEN FRICASSEE

20 chanterelles
1 tablespoon canola oil
1/2 cup diced onion
1/4 cup diced carrot
1/4 cup diced celery
Salt
2 chicken legs
1 cup white wine
1 quart Chicken Stock (see page 356)
1 sprig thyme
5 black peppercorns
1 bay leaf
2 tablespoons butter
1/4 cup Chicken Jus (see page 356)
3/4 cup Vin Jaune Sabayon
1/4 cup sliced chives
24 sprigs purslane
1/2 cup corn kernels

Clean the chanterelles of all dirt with a paring knife and scrape any discoloration from the stems. Trim the bottoms and rinse thoroughly. Spread the chanterelles on a paper towel to dry.

Preheat the oven to 325°F. Heat the oil in a straight-sided sauté pan over medium heat. Add the onion, carrot, and celery, and sweat without browning. Season the chicken with salt. Add the chicken to the pot and allow it to sweat without browning. Add the wine and reduce for 3 minutes to cook out the alcohol. Add the Chicken Stock, thyme, peppercorns, and bay leaf. Cover and stew in the oven for 40 to 45 minutes. The chicken is done when a fork can easily remove the flesh from the bones. Remove from the oven and allow to rest for 15 minutes. While the chicken is still warm, pick the meat from the bones. In a sauté pan, heat the butter. Add the chanterelles and sauté over medium heat. Add the Chicken Jus and the shredded chicken meat. Season with salt to taste, fold in the Sabayon, and, at the last minute, fold in the chives. Garnish with the purslane and corn.

## CHANTERELLES

60 small chanterelles
2 tablespoons butter
1/2 cup Chicken Stock (see page 356)
2 teaspoons salt

Clean the chanterelles of all dirt with a paring knife and scrape any discoloration from the stems. Trim the bottoms and rinse thoroughly. Spread the chanterelles on a paper towel to dry.

Melt the butter in a large sauté pan over medium heat. Add the chanterelles and sauté for 1 minute. Add the Chicken Stock and bring to a simmer. Reduce until the mushrooms are glazed. Season with the salt.

## TO FINISH

2 tablespoons canola oil
Chicken Breasts
1/4 cup Brown Butter (see page 370)
*Fleur de sel*
Sweet Corn and Farro Ragout
1 tablespoon sliced chives
8 tablespoons Chanterelle Puree (see page 351)
Chicken Sauce
Chanterelles
24 purslane tips
8 teaspoons Pickled Corn (see page 341)
Chicken Fricassee

Divide the canola oil between 2 large sauté pans and heat over high heat. Place 2 breasts in each pan, skin side down, and lower the heat to medium-low. Sear and render the fat from the skin for 2 minutes, until golden and crisp. Remove from the pan and allow to rest for 1 minute. Trim off the sides and slice each breast in half lengthwise. Brush with Brown Butter and season with *fleur de sel.*

Place the chicken breast in the middle of the plate, offset to the right. Place a large spoonful of Ragout in a line above the breast, in the middle, offset to the left. Pull the Chanterelle Puree from the top right of the plate to the left. Sauce the plate with the Chicken Sauce and garnish with the Chanterelles. Finish with 3 purslane tips and 1 teaspoon Pickled Corn. Serve the Fricassee on the side. Repeat with the remaining ingredients, to serve 8.

# DUCK
## LAVENDER-GLAZED WITH FENNEL AND PEACHES

*Serves 8*

### DUCK SPICE
1 cup Szechuan peppercorns
1 cup dried coriander seeds
1/2 cup cumin seeds
1 cup dried lavender flowers

In a spice grinder, grind the Szechuan peppercorns, coriander, and cumin until roughly ground. Transfer to a bowl and stir in the lavender flowers.

### ROASTED DUCKS
2 Muscovy ducks, head on
2 cups lavender honey
Salt
Duck Spice

Dry the ducks completely with paper towels. Use meat hooks to hang them by their necks in a refrigerator with good air circulation. Allow to age and dry for a minimum of 8 days and a maximum of 14 days. When ready to cook, preheat a convection oven to 375°F. Remove and discard the neck, feet, and wing tips, and truss the ducks with butcher's twine. Rub thoroughly with honey, being sure to coat all of the skin. Season with salt, then coat evenly with the Duck Spice. Place on a roasting rack and roast for 8 minutes. Rotate the duck and return it to the oven for another 8 to 9 minutes. Remove from the oven, and rest for 12 to 15 minutes before carving.

### DUCK SAUCE
3 lemons
4 limes
2 oranges
3/4 cup sugar
3 pods star anise
1 tablespoon butter
2 cups Duck Jus (see page 356)
1/2 teaspoon raspberry vinegar
1/2 teaspoon salt

Zest and juice the lemons, limes, and oranges. Combine the juices in one bowl and the zests in another. Place the sugar in a medium saucepan over medium heat. Caramelize to a very deep amber color. Add the star anise and the citrus juices to stop the cooking. Reduce by three quarters, or until thick and syrupy. Add the zest and butter and chill. In a separate pot, heat the Duck Jus and add 1 1/2 tablespoons of the citrus syrup. Season with the vinegar and salt.

### COMPRESSED PEACHES
3 very firm but ripe peaches
1/4 cup Sauternes

Cut the peaches into quarters and slice each quarter into thin half-moons. Arrange the peaches in a *sous vide* bag and add the Sauternes. Vacuum-seal and allow them to marinate. Remove them from the bag when ready to serve.

### PEACH CONFIT
8 large peaches
2 tablespoons olive oil
2 tablespoons lime juice
Salt
Black pepper
1 tablespoon confectioners' sugar

Preheat the oven to 200°F. Cut each peach into quarters. Slice cut each quarter into 3 half-moons. You should have 12 wedges per peach. Dress with olive oil, lime juice, and salt. Line a rimmed baking sheet with parchment paper. Arrange the wedges on the parchment and sprinkle with pepper and the confectioners' sugar. Bake for 45 minutes.

### FENNEL TEARS
2 fennel bulbs
1/2 cup white wine
2 tablespoons Pernod
3 pods star anise
1/4 teaspoon fennel seeds
4 pieces lemon peel
1/2 teaspoon salt

Pull apart the fennel petals and trim the tops and the bottoms to make even widths. Cut them into 1 1/2-by-3/4-inch isosceles triangles. Using a paring knife, round of the bottoms to form tear shapes. Trim them to 1/8-inch thickness.

Combine the white wine, Pernod, star anise, fennel seeds, and lemon peel in a small saucepan over medium heat and reduce by half. Add 1/4 cup water and the salt.

Place the Fennel Tears and 1/4 cup of the cooking liquid in a *sous vide* bag. Vacuum-seal and steam at 195°F for 35 minutes. Transfer to a bowl of ice water. Once cool, remove the Fennel Tears from the bag.

### TO FINISH
8 tablespoons Fennel and Potato Puree (see page 352)
Roasted Ducks
Brown Butter (see page 370)
*Fleur de sel*
Compressed Peaches
Peach Confit
Fennel Tears
Duck Sauce

Warm the Fennel and Potato Puree in a small saucepan over low heat. Carve the breasts off of the roasted ducks. Slice into even pieces and brush with Brown Butter and season with *fleur de sel*. Put 2 duck slices on a plate. Spoon the Fennel and Potato Puree onto the plate and garnish with the Compressed Peaches and Peach Confit and the Fennel Tears. Finish with the Duck Sauce. Repeat with the remaining ingredients, to serve 8.

# PORK
## ROASTED RACK WITH ONIONS AND CHERRIES

*Serves 8*

### PORK RACK

1 rack (from one 50-pound) pig, frenched
Salt
2 tablespoons canola oil
5 tablespoons butter
5 sprigs thyme
2 cloves garlic

Preheat the oven to 300°F. Place a roasting rack in the oven to preheat. Season the pork with salt. In a large sauté pan, heat the oil over high heat. Sear the rack, fat side down, in the oil until it is evenly browned, about 2 minutes. Add the butter, thyme, and garlic and baste for another 2 minutes. Transfer to the preheated roasting rack and roast in the oven for 35 to 40 minutes, basting with butter every 5 minutes. Remove from the oven and allow to rest for 10 to 15 minutes.

### CHERRY PORK SAUCE

1 tablespoon canola oil
1/4 cup *guanciale,* diced (1/8 inch)
1 cup sugar
1 quart Bing cherries, pitted
5 pods star anise
1 cup red wine
1/2 cup balsamic vinegar
3 cups Chicken Jus (see page 356)
Salt

In a sauté pan, heat the oil over medium heat and add the *guanciale.* Render the fat from the *guanciale* for 5 minutes. Strain, reserving the rendered fat.

In a saucepan over medium heat, cook the sugar to a dark caramel. Add the cherries and the star anise and cook until the cherries are soft. Deglaze with the red wine and balsamic vinegar, stirring to dissolve the sugar. Reduce to a glaze. Chill over ice.

Reduce the Chicken Jus over medium heat to 2 cups and whisk in 2 tablespoons of the glaze. Stir in the rendered fat and season with salt to taste.

### ROASTED ONION PETALS

1 white onion, skin on
Salt
Olive oil

Preheat the oven to 325°F. Toss the onion with salt and olive oil and wrap in aluminum foil. Roast in the oven for 3 hours or until the onion is tender but still holds its shape. Cool to room temperature. Quarter the onion, remove the skin, and separate the onion into individual petals. Cut each petal into 1/2-inch-thick strips.

### ONIONS AND CHERRIES

2 scallions, white and light green parts only
1 teaspoon olive oil
Salt
1/4 cup Chicken Stock (see page 356)
Roasted Onion Petals
8 baby scallions
16 Bing cherries, pitted
1 tablespoon butter

Shave the scallions with a vegetable peeler, and dress them with the olive oil and salt. Heat the Chicken Stock in a sauté pan over medium heat. Add the Onion Petals, baby scallions, and pitted cherries. Toss to combine and add the butter, tossing to glaze.

### TO FINISH

Pork Rack
Brown Butter (see page 370)
*Fleur de sel*
8 tablespoons Onion Puree (see page 352)
Onions and Cherries
16 Pickled Rainier Cherries (see page 342)
8 teaspoons Pickled Yellow Mustard Seeds
    (see page 342)
8 slices shaved *guanciale*
24 leaves mizuna
Cherry Pork Sauce

Slice the Pork Rack in between the bones to yield 8 chops. Brush the cut side of a pork chop with Brown Butter and season with *fleur de sel.* Warm the Onion Puree in a small saucepan over low heat and spoon onto a plate. Place the pork chop on the plate and arrange the glazed Onion Petals, 2 glazed cherries, and 1 glazed baby scallion below the pork chop. Place 2 Pickled Cherry pieces between the glazed cherries. Scatter the Pickled Yellow Mustard Seeds and 2 scallion shaves around the plate and lay a piece of *guanciale* over a glazed cherry. Finish the plate with 3 mizuna leaves and the Cherry Pork Sauce. Repeat with the remaining ingredients, to serve 8.

# VEAL
## VARIATIONS WITH SUMMER BEANS, VIOLET MUSTARD, AND SAVORY

*Serves 8*

### BRINED VEAL TONGUE

1 cup salt
2 tablespoons pink curing salt
1 teaspoon black pepper
6 cloves
4 juniper berries
4 allspice berries
1 bay leaf
4 cups ice
2 veal tongues

In a large pot, bring 8 cups water, salt, pink curing salt, bay leaf, black pepper, cloves, juniper berries, allspice, and bay leaf to a boil. Remove from the heat, add the ice, and chill. Add the veal tongues and brine for 4 days in the refrigerator.

### BRAISED VEAL TONGUE

8 black peppercorns
3 sprigs thyme
1 bay leaf
1 cup white wine
1/4 cup diced celery
1/4 cup diced carrot
1/4 cup diced onion
2 tablespoons pink curing salt
2 tablespoons salt
2 Brined Veal Tongues

Make a sachet by wrapping the peppercorns, thyme, and bay leaf in cheesecloth and tying the ends together with butcher's twine. In a large pot, combine the sachet, white wine, celery, carrot, onion, curing salt, salt, and 2 gallons water. Bring to a simmer. Add the veal tongues and cover. Set over medium heat, bring to a simmer, and cook for 2 1/2 to 3 hours. The veal tongue is done when a knife can be inserted easily. Cool the tongue in the braising liquid. Peel away the thick outer skin before thinly slicing.

### VEAL SWEETBREADS

1 pound veal sweetbreads
1 cup Veal Jus (see page 357)
1/2 teaspoon salt
1/2 cup flour
4 cups canola oil

Using scissors, trim the sweetbreads into 3/4-inch pieces, removing any fat and blood. Soak the sweetbreads in ice water in the refrigerator overnight. Reduce the Veal Jus by half and cover to keep warm. Drain and dry the sweetbreads, season them with salt, and dredge them in the flour. Pat off any excess. In a large sauté pan, heat the canola oil to 375°F. Fry the sweetbreads for 4 minutes and then drain them on paper towels. Toss the drained sweetbreads in the reduced Veal Jus just before serving.

## VEAL RACK

Four 1-inch-thick veal loin steaks
1 tablespoon salt
2 tablespoons canola oil
4 tablespoons butter
4 cloves garlic, crushed but kept whole
6 sprigs savory
1/4 cup Brown Butter (see page 370)

Preheat the oven to 300°F. Season veal steaks with salt. Heat 2 sauté pans over high heat with 1 tablespoon oil in each pan. Sear the veal, fat side down, for 1 to 2 minutes. Reduce the heat to medium-low and continue to cook the meat. Add 2 tablespoons butter, 2 garlic cloves, and 3 sprigs of savory to each pan and baste the steaks with the butter for 30 to 40 seconds on each side.

Remove the steaks from the pan and place on a roasting rack. Roast in the oven for 7 minutes, flip the steaks, add the Brown Butter, and baste. Roast for another 7 minutes. Remove the steaks from the oven and allow them to rest for 5 minutes. Slice the steaks on a bias, 3/4 to 1 inch thick.

## VIOLET MUSTARD

1 cup violet mustard
1/4 cup crème fraîche

In a small bowl, whisk together the mustard with the crème fraîche.

## TOMATO CONFIT

10 plum tomatoes
1/4 cup olive oil
2 cloves garlic, peeled and thinly sliced
5 sprigs thyme
1 teaspoon salt

Preheat the oven to 200°F. Bring a pot of salted water to a boil. Score a small x in each of the tomatoes with a sharp knife and add them to the water. Cook for 10 to 15 seconds or until the skin begins to peel away from the flesh. Transfer to a bowl of ice water and, once cool, peel. Cut the tomatoes in half lengthwise and remove and discard the seeds. In a large bowl, toss the tomato halves with the olive oil, garlic, thyme, and salt. Lay the tomatoes face down on a rimmed baking sheet lined with parchment paper. Bake for 1 1/2 hours. Flip the tomatoes and continue to cook for an additional 1 1/2 to 2 hours or until the tomatoes are no longer soft and wet. Be careful not to dry them too much — they should not be dehydrated and leathery.

## SAVORY CREAM

1 cup Chicken Stock (see page 356)
1 cup cream
1 1/2 teaspoons roughly chopped savory leaves

In a medium saucepan, reduce the Chicken Stock by half. Add the cream and reduce by half. Remove from the heat and add the savory. Steep for 10 minutes, strain, and chill.

## SUMMER BEANS

1 cup fresh chickpeas
8 sprigs thyme
4 bay leaves
20 black peppercorns
1 bunch parsley
1 cup fresh shelled cranberry beans
1 cup fresh shelled coco beans (French navy beans)
1 cup fresh shelled black turtle beans
1 cup fresh shelled cannellini beans
1/4 cup olive oil
1/4 cup salt

Bring a pot of salted water to a boil. Add the chickpeas and cook for 2 to 3 minutes. Transfer to a bowl of ice water and, once cool, drain. Make a sachet by wrapping 2 thyme sprigs, 1 bay leaf, 5 peppercorns, and 2 to 3 parsley sprigs in a piece of cheesecloth. Tie the cheesecloth with butcher's twine. Repeat 3 more times. Place the cranberry beans, coco beans, black turtle beans, and cannellini beans in separate medium saucepans, add a sachet, 1 tablespoon olive oil, and 1 tablespoon salt to each, and cover with 3 inches of water. Cover, bring to a boil, and reduce to a simmer. The beans will need to cook for 15 to 20 minutes. Cool the cooked beans in their cooking liquid.

## RENDERED MARROW FAT

12 (2 1/2-inch) beef marrow bones

Soak the bones in water for about 30 minutes. Once the marrow is soft, carefully push it out of the bone. Cut the bone marrow cylinders into 1/2-inch pieces. Place the bone marrow and 1/4 cup water in a medium pot over low heat. As the marrow cooks, the fat will render out. Completely render the marrow, making sure not to achieve any color. Once all of the water has been cooked out and the marrow is completely rendered, strain through a fine-mesh chinois, reserving only the rendered marrow fat. Reserve for use in the Marrow Vinaigrette.

## VEAL SAUCE

1 tablespoon canola oil
1 pound veal trim, cut into 1/2-inch pieces
1 shallot, thinly sliced
1/2 cup white wine
1 quart Veal Jus (see page 357)
6 sprigs savory

Heat the oil in a saucepan over high heat. Add the veal trim and brown for 2 to 3 minutes. Add the shallot, lower the heat to medium, and cook until tender. Deglaze with the wine and reduce to 1/4 cup. Add the Veal Jus and bring to a slimmer. Skim off any fats or impurities that rise to the top. Simmer over low heat for 30 minutes, strain, and then reduce to 2 cups. Add the savory and let steep for 5 minutes. Strain.

## BEAN RAGOUT

16 haricots verts, trimmed and cut into 1-inch pieces
8 Romano beans, trimmed and cut into 1-inch diamonds
8 yellow wax beans, trimmed and cut into 1-inch pieces
Savory Cream
Summer Beans
1 tablespoon butter
Salt

Bring a pot of salted water to a boil. Add the haricots verts, Romano beans, and yellow wax beans, and cook for 3 to 4 minutes. Drain and transfer to a bowl of ice water. Once cold, drain. Heat the Savory Cream in a sauté pan over medium-low heat. Add the Summer Beans, blanched haricots verts, blanched Romano beans, and blanched yellow wax beans. Toss to combine and add the butter to glaze. Season with salt to taste.

## TO FINISH

Marrow Vinaigrette (see page 346)
Braised Veal Tongue
Veal Rack
Brown Butter (see page 370)
Bean Ragout
Tomato Confit
Veal Sweetbreads
Veal Sauce
20 sprigs savory
Violet Mustard

Heat the Marrow Vinaigrette in a medium saucepan over medium heat. Add the tongue slices to warm through. Lay a Veal Rack slice on a plate and brush the cut side with Brown Butter. Curl the sliced tongue and arrange around the rack. Spoon the Bean Ragout, 1 Confit Tomato, and 4 sweetbread pieces around the meat. Sauce with the Veal Sauce and finish the dish with savory and Violet Mustard. Repeat with the remaining ingredients, to serve 8.

# LAMB
## HERB-ROASTED WITH EGGPLANT, SHEEP'S MILK YOGURT, AND CUMIN

*Serves 8*

### LAMB LOIN

2 lamb loins from one 5-pound saddle of lamb
2 teaspoons salt
1 tablespoon canola oil

Preheat the oven to 300°F. Trim the fat from the lamb loins, leaving 1/4 inch of fat. Season with the salt. Heat the oil in a large sauté pan over medium-high heat. Sear the loins, fat side down, and continue to render the fat for 6 to 8 minutes, depending on the amount of fat. Turn the loins and sear the other side. Remove the loins from the pan and place on roasting rack, fat side up. Roast in the oven for 15 minutes. Remove from the oven and allow to rest for 15 minutes.

### RENDERED LAMB FAT

1 1/2 pounds lamb fat, frozen

Grind the frozen lamb fat in a meat grinder or have this done by your butcher. Place the lamb fat and 1/4 cup water in a medium pot over low heat. Render the fat, making sure not to achieve any color. Once all of the water has been cooked out and the fat is completely rendered, strain through a fine-mesh chinois.

### MOROCCAN-SPICED LAMB JUS

3 cups Lamb Jus (see page 356)
1 teaspoon cumin seeds
1 tablespoon crushed coriander seeds
1/2 cup Rendered Lamb Fat
1 teaspoon paprika
1 tablespoon salt
1 teaspoon sugar

In a small saucepan over medium heat, reduce the Lamb Jus to 2 cups. Heat a small sauté pan over medium heat. Add the cumin seeds and toast until fragrant, about 20 seconds. Repeat with the crushed coriander. In a small saucepan, heat the Rendered Lamb Fat to 325°F. Remove from the heat and add the toasted cumin seeds, toasted coriander, paprika, and reduced Lamb Jus. Steep for 20 minutes. Strain and season with the salt and sugar.

### LAMB SWEETBREADS

1 pound lamb sweetbreads
1 cup Lamb Jus (see page 356)
1/2 teaspoon salt
1/2 cup flour
4 cups canola oil

Using scissors, trim the sweetbreads into 3/4-inch pieces, removing any fat and blood. Soak the sweetbreads in ice water in the refrigerator overnight. Reduce the Lamb Jus by half and cover to keep warm. Drain and dry the sweetbreads, season them with the salt, and dredge them in the flour. Pat off any excess. In a large sauté pan, heat the canola oil to 375°F. Fry the sweetbreads for 4 minutes and then drain them on paper towels. Toss the drained sweetbreads in the reduced Lamb Jus just before serving.

### CUMIN DUST

1/2 cup cumin seeds

Heat a small sauté pan over medium heat. Add the cumin seeds and toast until fragrant, about 20 seconds. Once cool, place in a spice grinder and grind to a fine powder.

### TO FINISH

Lamb Loins
Brown Butter (see page 370)
*Fleur de sel*
3 tablespoons White Eggplant Puree (see page 354)
8 tablespoons Sheep's Milk Gel (see page 348)
Lamb Sweetbreads
Moroccan-Spiced Lamb Jus
16 borage leaves
16 borage blossoms
16 Elephant Garlic Chips (see page 371)
8 Pickled Baby Eggplants (see page 341)
Cumin Dust
Pickled Red Pearl Onions (see page 343)
Crushed black pepper

Trim the ends of the Lamb Loins. Slice them down the center lengthwise and crosswise, yielding 4 strips from each loin, approximately 3 inches by 3/4 inch each. Brush them with Brown Butter and sprinkle them with *fleur de sel*. Warm the White Eggplant Puree in a small saucepan over low heat and pull a spoonful across a plate. Pull a spoonful of the Sheep's Milk Gel opposite the White Eggplant Puree. Place a strip of lamb on the plate and arrange the Lamb Sweetbreads around it. Sauce with the Moroccan-Spiced Lamb Jus and garnish with 2 borage leaves, 2 borage blossoms, the Elephant Garlic Chips, and a Pickled Baby Eggplant. Finish with the Cumin Dust, Pickled Red Pearl Onions, and crushed black pepper. Repeat with the remaining ingredients, to serve 8.

# FROMAGE BLANC
## INSPIRED BY YELLOW

*Serves 8*

### GOLDEN BEETS

5 baby golden beets, peeled
3/4 cup Chicken Stock (see page 356)
1/2 cup white balsamic vinegar
1 tablespoon salt

Seal all of the ingredients in a *sous vide* bag and cook in a water bath maintained at 185°F by an immersion circulator for 2 hours, until tender when pierced with a knife. Cool the beets in their cooking liquid. Once cold, strain the beets.

Alternatively, preheat the oven to 375°F. Combine all of the ingredients in a baking dish and cover with aluminum foil. Roast until the beets are tender when pierced with a knife, 40 to 45 minutes. Remove from the oven and cool the beets in their liquid. Once cold, strain the beets.

### TO FINISH

La Faisselle *fromage blanc*
24 golden raspberries
1 apricot, cut into 8 slices
1 cup golden currants
Pickled Cantaloupe (see page 341)
Pickled Golden Beets (see page 341)
Golden Beets, cut into 8 slices each
Yellow Beet Vinaigrette (see page 346)
24 sprigs yellow Swiss chard
*Fleur de sel*
Extra-virgin olive oil

Remove the colander of *fromage blanc* from the container and strain for 30 minutes to drain excess liquid. Dress the raspberries, apricots, currants, Pickled Cantaloupe, Pickled Golden Beets, and Golden Beets in the Vinaigrette. Place the *fromage blanc* in the center of a plate. Scatter the dressed fruits and beets on either side of the *fromage blanc*. Place 3 Swiss chard sprigs on top. Finish with *fleur de sel* and a drizzle of extra-virgin olive oil.

# MALT
## SORBET WITH OLIVE OIL AND BLACK PEPPER

*Serves 8*

### MALT FRENCH MERINGUE

2 egg whites
1/3 cup sugar
1 1/2 tablespoons malted milk powder

Line an inverted baking sheet with acetate. Preheat the oven to 175°F. In the metal bowl of a stand mixer, whip the egg whites until very soft peaks form. Slowly add the sugar and continue to whip to stiff, glossy peaks. Fold in the malted milk powder, a little at a time. Thinly spread the meringue onto the acetate and dry overnight in the oven. Peel off the acetate. Save the large pieces of meringue for the tuiles used in the plating of the dessert and crush the small pieces to use as a crumble underneath the sorbet. Store the tuiles and the crumble separately in airtight containers.

### OLIVE OIL EMULSION

5 tablespoons glucose syrup
3 egg yolks
1/4 teaspoon salt
1 cup olive oil

In a small saucepan, heat the glucose until it is liquid. Transfer it to the bowl of a food processor and, with the motor running, add the egg yolks and the salt. Slowly stream in the oil to emulsify. Store the emulsion in the refrigerator.

### TO FINISH

Olive Oil Emulsion
Yogurt Gel (see page 348)
2 teaspoons cracked black pepper
Maldon salt
Malt French Meringue
Malted Milk Sorbet (see page 367)

Spread 1 teaspoon Olive Oil Emulsion onto a plate. Squeeze 1 tablespoon Yogurt Gel onto the plate and spread it slightly with an offset spatula. Sprinkle 1/4 teaspoon black pepper and a pinch of Maldon salt on top. Place 1 tablespoon Malt French Meringue crumble in the middle of the plate and rest a quenelle of the Malted Milk Sorbet on top of the crumble. Top the Sorbet with a Malt French Meringue tuile. Repeat with the remaining ingredients, to serve 8.

# CHERRY
## CRUMBLE
## WITH PISTACHIO

*Serves 8*

## PISTACHIO PASTE

2 cups shelled pistachios
3/4 cup confectioners' sugar
1 tablespoon salt
3/4 cup pistachio oil

Preheat the oven to 300°F. Place the pistachios on a rimmed baking sheet and toast in the oven for 8 to 10 minutes. Combine the toasted pistachios, sugar, and salt in a food processor. Chop the pistachios in the processor and slowly drizzle in the oil until the mixture reaches the consistency of a loose, crunchy peanut butter. Transfer to a blender and blend on high speed until it is a smooth paste. Pass the paste through a fine-mesh tamis and cool to room temperature.

## CANDIED PISTACHIOS

1/2 cup shelled pistachios
1 cup sugar
1 tablespoon glucose syrup

Preheat the oven to 300°F. Place the pistachios on a rimmed baking sheet and toast in the oven for 8 to 10 minutes. Combine the sugar, glucose, and 1 tablespoon water in a small heavy-bottomed saucepan over medium heat and cook to a light caramel (about 300°F). Add pistachios and coat evenly with the caramel. Separate the pistachios on a rimmed baking sheet lined with a silicone baking mat while they're still warm and roll each individual nut in your hand to create a smooth, round outer shell. Cool to room temperature.

## CHERRY SYRUP

4 cups Bing cherries, pitted
1/2 cup dried sour cherries
1/4 cup sugar

Crush the Bing cherries using gloved hands. Place the Bing cherries, dried cherries, and sugar in a deep saucepan over medium-high heat. Add 2 cups water. Bring to a boil and simmer for about 1 hour. Strain through cheesecloth. The resulting syrup should be slightly thick. Cool over ice.

## REHYDRATED SOUR CHERRIES

1/4 cup dried sour cherries
1/4 cup Cherry Syrup

Place the cherries and syrup in a small saucepan. Add enough water to barely cover the cherries. Bring to a boil, remove from the heat, and cover with plastic wrap. Set aside to rehydrate for 1 hour. Cool.

## PISTACHIO PASTE POWDER

3 cups tapioca maltodextrin
1/4 cup Pistachio Paste
1 1/2 tablespoons confectioners' sugar
1 pinch salt

Whisk together the tapioca maltodextrin, Pistachio Paste, confectioners' sugar, and salt in a bowl until powdery.

## PISTACHIO SPONGE CAKE

1 cup Pistachio Paste
7 eggs plus 1 yolk
3/4 cup sugar
1/3 cup flour
1 teaspoon salt
3 N$_2$O cartridges

Preheat the oven to 200°F. Puree the Pistachio Paste, eggs plus yolk, sugar, flour, and salt in a blender. Strain through a chinois and place in a whipped-cream canister. Charge with the N$_2$O chargers and shake well. To test the batter, expel a small amount into a bowl. If it does not have the consistency of a mousse, shake it again, let it rest for 5 to 10 minutes, and test again. Once it is ready, fill 6 microwave-safe pint containers halfway with batter (about 1 cup per container) by expelling the batter directly into them. Let sit for 10 minutes. Cook the cakes one at a time in the microwave, about 1 minute per cake, depending on your microwave. Allow the cakes to rest and cool completely.

## GLAZED CHERRIES

1/2 cup Cherry Syrup
12 Bing cherries

In a small sauté pan set over medium heat, reduce the Cherry Syrup by half. Add the cherries and toss to glaze. Halve 4 of the glazed cherries and keep the rest whole.

## TO FINISH

Pistachio Paste
Rehydrated Sour Cherries
8 pitted Bing cherries, halved
4 pitted Rainier cherries, halved
Candied Pistachios
Pistachio Crumble (see page 363)
Pistachio Ice Cream (see page 369)
Cherry Granola and Crumble (see page 362)
Pistachio Paste Powder
Cherry Sorbet (see page 366)
Maldon salt
Pistachio Sponge Cake
Glazed Cherries, 8 whole and 8 halves

Brush 1 tablespoon of the Pistachio Paste diagonally across a plate. On the left end of the brushstroke, place 3 drained Rehydrated Sour Cherries, 2 Bing cherry halves, 1 Rainier cherry half, and 3 Candied Pistachios. Spoon 1 tablespoon of the Pistachio Crumble on the plate. Place a quenelle of Pistachio Ice Cream on top of the Crumble on a diagonal opposite the Pistachio Paste. Cover the quenelle evenly with 1 tablespoon of the Cherry Granola, 1 tablespoon of the Cherry Crumble, and 1 tablespoon of Pistachio Paste Powder. Place a small quenelle of Cherry Sorbet on the right side of the Pistachio Ice Cream. Sprinkle with a few crystals of Maldon salt, and lay a Pistachio Sponge Cake between the Ice Cream and Sorbet. Place a whole Glazed Cherry and halved Glazed Cherry on the upper right corner of the plate. Repeat with the remaining ingredients, to serve 8.

# BERRIES
## SALAD WITH BALSAMIC VINEGAR AND OLIVE OIL

*Serves 8*

### RASPBERRY YOGURT

1 cup raspberries
1 1/2 teaspoons sugar
1 cup Greek yogurt

In a blender, puree the raspberries with the sugar until smooth. Pass the puree through a fine-mesh tamis. Whisk together the puree and the Greek yogurt until thoroughly combined. Chill.

### LEMON YOGURT

1 cup Greek yogurt
1 teaspoon sugar
2 tablespoons lemon zest

In a small bowl, whisk together the yogurt and the sugar. Fold in the lemon zest. Allow to infuse for 3 hours and then pass through a fine-mesh tamis to remove the lemon zest.

### BALSAMIC FRENCH MERINGUE

3 egg whites
3/4 cup sugar
2 tablespoons freeze-dried strawberry powder
3 tablespoons balsamic vinegar powder
1 tablespoon white vinegar powder

Line an inverted baking sheet with acetate. Preheat the oven to 150°F. In the metal bowl of a stand mixer, whip the egg whites to soft peaks. Stream in the sugar and continue to whip until full, stiff, and glossy peaks form. Meanwhile, sift together the strawberry powder and balsamic vinegar powder. Fold the mixture into the egg whites a little at a time, being careful not to deflate the meringue. Thinly spread the meringue, about 1/8 inch thick, on the acetate-lined baking sheet. Dry in the oven overnight. Once dried, peel off the acetate into 16 tuiles, sprinkle with the white vinegar powder, and store in an airtight container in a cool, dry place.

### OLIVE OIL POWDER

3 cups tapioca maltodextrin
1/3 cup extra-virgin olive oil
1/4 cup confectioners' sugar
1/2 teaspoon salt

Mix the tapioca maltodextrin, oil, sugar, and salt in a food processor. Store in a cool, dry place.

### RASPBERRY BEADS

2 cups red raspberries
1/2 gallon liquid nitrogen (optional)

Immerse the raspberries in the liquid nitrogen for 15 seconds. Once frozen, remove. Quickly break apart the raspberries to separate the individual beads. Store in the freezer until ready to use. Alternatively, the raspberries can be frozen for 3 hours, until firm, then quickly broken apart to separate the individual beads.

### TO FINISH

Raspberry Yogurt
Lemon Yogurt
Black Pepper Crumble (see page 361)
Buttermilk Olive Oil Sorbet (see page 366)
Olive Oil Powder
Blackberry Sorbet (see page 366)
16 strawberries
16 red raspberries
16 black raspberries
24 golden raspberries
16 green gooseberries
24 blackberries
3/4 cup red currants
1/4 cup black currants
1 tablespoon olive oil
Raspberry Beads
Balsamic French Meringue
1 teaspoon Maldon salt
16 sprigs lemon mint

Spoon 1 tablespoon of the Raspberry Yogurt onto a plate and pull it across with the back of the spoon. Repeat with 2 separate tablespoons of the Lemon Yogurt. Place 1 tablespoon of Black Pepper Crumble on the plate and place a quenelle of Buttermilk Olive Oil Sorbet on top. Place 1 tablespoon of Olive Oil Powder on the plate and place a quenelle of Blackberry Sorbet on top. Toss the berries and currants in the olive oil. Arrange 1 teaspoon of Raspberry Beads, 2 strawberries, 2 red raspberries, 2 black raspberries, 3 golden raspberries, 2 green gooseberries, 3 blackberries, 10 red currants, and 4 black currants all around. Place 2 Balsamic French Meringue tuiles on top of each sorbet. Sprinkle with Maldon salt and garnish with 2 lemon mint sprigs. Repeat with the remaining ingredients, to serve 8.

# APRICOT
# AND ALMONDS

*Serves 8*

## CANDIED OLIVES
1/2 cup taggiasca olives, pitted
1 1/2 cups sugar
1 1/2 tablespoons salt

Bring a pot of salted water to a boil. Add the olives and cook for 30 seconds. Transfer to a bowl of ice water. Once cool, drain and repeat. In the meantime, combine 1/2 cup of the sugar with 1/2 cup water in a small saucepan and bring to a boil. Add the blanched olives to the sugar and water, bring the mixture back up to a boil, and continue to simmer. Add another 1/2 cup sugar to the olives and cook over low heat for 30 minutes. Add the remaining 1/2 cup sugar and cook for another 30 minutes. Cool to room temperature. Set aside 16 olives for plating and use the rest for the Dehydrated Olives.

## DEHYDRATED OLIVES
Remaining Candied Olives

Preheat the 200°F. Finely chop the Candied Olives. Line a baking sheet with a silicone baking mat and sprinkle the chopped olives onto the mat. Bake for 3 to 4 hours, until crunchy and dry. Cool to room temperature and then crumble.

## APRICOT TAPIOCA TUILES
1/2 cup large tapioca pearls
1/2 cup Apricot Puree (see page 350)
4 cups canola oil
1 tablespoon Maldon salt
2 tablespoons Dehydrated Olives

Preheat the oven to 200°F. Line a baking sheet with acetate. In a medium saucepan, bring 1 gallon water to a boil. Add the tapioca, lower the heat, and simmer for 30 to 35 minutes, until the pearls are soft. Strain the cooked tapioca and rinse under cold water. Blend 1/3 cup of the cooked tapioca with the Apricot Puree. Pass the mixture through a fine-mesh tamis. Spread the mixture onto the acetate-lined baking sheet and dry in the oven for 3 hours, until dry. Once the tapioca is dry, break into 8 large pieces.

Heat the oil to 375°F. Using a spider skimmer to hold a Tuile, fry the Tapioca Tuile for 5 seconds, or until lightly golden brown but still orange. Carefully remove it from the oil and bend it slightly into a wave shape while it is still hot. Repeat with the remaining Tuiles. Sprinkle with Maldon salt and Dehydrated Olives.

## TOASTED ALMOND BAVAROIS
1 cup sliced almonds
3 cups milk
2/3 cups sugar, divided
5 tablespoons pastry cream powder
1 egg
2 egg yolks
2 sheets gelatin
1/4 cup butter, softened
1 cup cream

Preheat the oven to 350°F. Place the almonds on a baking sheet and toast for 6 to 7 minutes, until fragrant. In a medium saucepan, bring the milk to just under a boil. Remove from the heat and add the toasted almond slices. Steep for 30 minutes. Strain the almonds from the milk. Dissolve 1/3 cup of the sugar into 2 cups of the toasted-almond milk. In a bowl, combine the pastry cream powder and the remaining 1/3 cup sugar. Mix the egg and egg yolks into the pastry cream powder and sugar mixture. Slowly add the hot almond milk to the egg mixture, whisking constantly. Transfer to a medium saucepan and cook over medium-high heat, stirring constantly. Bring to a boil and continue to cook for 5 minutes. The pastry cream should be shiny and sweet and should not taste of starch.

Bloom the gelatin by placing the sheets in a bowl of ice water for 10 minutes, until pliable. Squeeze to remove excess moisture. Remove the pastry cream from the heat and allow it to stop boiling before stirring in the bloomed gelatin sheets. Stir in the butter and pass the warm pastry cream through a fine-mesh tamis.

Place a sheet of plastic wrap directly over the pastry cream and cool to room temperature. Once the pastry cream is completely cool, place 2 cups in the bowl of a stand mixer fitted with the paddle attachment. Mix until completely smooth and soft. Scrape down the sides of the bowl. Switch to the whisk attachment and drizzle in the cream. Whip the mixture for 1 minute on high speed, until the pastry cream is light and fluffy. Store in the refrigerator.

## MALDON SALT STREUSEL
1 3/4 cups flour
3/4 cup almond flour
3/4 cup sugar
1 tablespoon Maldon salt
1/2 teaspoon salt
3/4 cup cold butter, diced

Preheat the oven to 350°F. Line a baking sheet with parchment paper. In the bowl of a stand mixer, combine the flour, almond flour, sugar, Maldon salt, and salt. Gradually add the butter, mixing slowly until the dough comes together. Pinch off pieces of the dough to form small nuggets. Place the nuggets on the prepared baking sheet. Bake for 15 minutes, until golden brown. Keep 40 to 50 pieces whole and pulse the remaining pieces into a crumble in a food processor for use under the sorbet.

## ROASTED APRICOTS
1 bunch lemon thyme
5 bay leaves
4 ripe but firm apricots
1/2 cup sugar
1/2 cup white wine

Preheat the oven to 350°F. Scatter the lemon thyme and bay leaves over the bottom of a 9-by-13-inch rimmed baking sheet to cover. Peel, halve, and pit the apricots, and lay them, cut side down, on the lemon thyme and bay leaves. Sprinkle the sugar over the apricots and roast for 12 minutes. Add 1 cup water and the wine to the bottom of the pan and return to oven and continue to bake until the fruit is just tender. Cool to room temperature.

## TO FINISH
8 tablespoons Apricot Puree (see page 350)
Toasted Almond Bavarois
Crumbled Maldon Salt Streusel
Apricot Sorbet (see page 366)
Roasted Apricots
Maldon Salt Streusel nuggets
16 Candied Olives
Dehydrated Olives
8 sprigs flowering lemon thyme
2 teaspoons olive oil
2 teaspoons Lemon Vinaigrette (see page 346)
Apricot Tapioca Tuiles
Maldon salt

Smear 1 tablespoon of the Apricot Puree on a plate. Next to the smear, place 1 teaspoon of the Toasted Almond Bavarois. Place a scoop of crumbled Maldon Salt Streusel between the Puree and the Bavarois. Top the crumbled Streusel with a quenelle of Apricot Sorbet. Arrange a Roasted Apricot half, 4 Maldon Salt Streusel nuggets, 2 Candied Olives, 1/4 teaspoon Dehydrated Olives, and a sprig of flowering lemon thyme on the plate. Drizzle 1/4 teaspoon of the olive oil and 1/4 teaspoon of the Lemon Vinaigrette around the plate and finish with an Apricot Tapioca Tuile on top of the Sorbet and a sprinkle of Maldon salt. Repeat with the remaining ingredients, to serve 8.

# CHOCOLATE
## FLEUR DE SEL AND CARAMEL

*Serves 8*

### CHOCOLATE GANACHE CIRCLES
3/4 cup cream
3 tablespoons glucose syrup
6 ounces Valrhona Araguani chocolate (72 percent), chopped

In a small saucepan, heat the cream and glucose to just under a boil. Place the chocolate in a bowl and pour the cream mixture over the chocolate. Allow to rest for 1 minute in order to let the chocolate melt completely. Using a hand blender, blend the mixture together. Line a 9-by-13-inch rimmed baking sheet with acetate. Pour the chocolate ganache onto the lined baking sheet and refrigerate for 1 hour to set. Using a 7/8-inch ring cutter, cut 8 circles from the ganache. Repeat with a 1 1/4-inch ring cutter and a 1 1/2-inch ring cutter. You should have 24 circles altogether.

### SUCRÉE TUBES
2 tablespoons butter, softened
2 tablespoons sugar
1/2 vanilla bean, split lengthwise and scraped
1/4 teaspoon salt
Zest of 1 small orange
1 egg yolk
3/4 cup flour

In the bowl of a stand mixer fitted with the paddle attachment, cream together the butter and the sugar. Add the vanilla bean seeds, salt, orange zest, and egg yolk, mixing until smooth. Add the flour and mix until just combined. Refrigerate for 1 hour. Roll out the dough to a thickness of 1/8 inch. Cut the dough into 2-inch-by-5-inch rectangles. Save the scraps to make the Sucrée Dough Crumble. Wrap the rectangles around metal tubes that are 1 inch in diameter and 6 inches long. Refrigerate for 1 hour.

Preheat the oven to 325°F. Place the tubes on a baking sheet and bake for 10 minutes, until golden brown. Allow to cool slightly before gently removing the tubes and breaking them into large shards. Store in an airtight container.

### SUCRÉE DOUGH CRUMBLE
Sucrée Tube dough scraps

Preheat the oven to 325°F. Place the scraps from the Sucrée Tubes on a baking sheet. Bake for 6 to 8 minutes, until golden brown. Cool to room temperature before breaking it apart with your fingers. Store in an airtight container.

### COCOA NIB TUILES
1/2 cup sugar
2 tablespoons milk
2 tablespoons glucose syrup
1/3 cup butter
6 tablespoons cocoa nibs
1 tablespoon unsweetened cocoa powder

In a small saucepan bring the sugar, butter, milk, and glucose to 220°F, stirring constantly. Remove from the heat and stir in the cocoa nibs and cocoa powder, mixing until incorporated. Pour onto a sheet of parchment paper and cover with another sheet of parchment paper. Roll to 1/16 inch thick. Freeze for 1 hour.

Preheat the oven to 350°F. Place the frozen sheet onto a baking sheet and remove the top layer of parchment paper. Bake while still frozen, for 5 minutes or until any large bubbles disappear. Cool slightly before cutting 8 circles with a 1 1/4-inch ring cutter and 8 circles with a 1 1/2-inch ring cutter.

### TO FINISH
Caramel Gel (see page 347)
Chocolate Ganache Circles
Sucrée Dough Crumble
Chocolate Sorbet (see page 366)
Salted Caramel Ice Cream (see page 369)
Cocoa Nib Tuiles
Sucrée Tubes
*Fleur de sel*

Starting on the left side of the plate, spoon 1 tablespoon of the Caramel Gel, dragging it to the right about halfway across the plate. Place a 1/2-inch Chocolate Ganache Circle on the far left of the plate, a 1-inch Circle in the middle of the plate, and a 3/4-inch Circle on the far right of the plate. Mound 1 tablespoon of Sucrée Dough Crumble among the Circles. Place a quenelle of Chocolate Sorbet on top of one of the mounds and a quenelle of the Salted Caramel Ice Cream on top of the other mound. Lay a large Cocoa Nib Tuile on the Chocolate Sorbet and a small Cocoa Nib Tuile on the Salted Caramel Ice Cream. Lay a Sucrée Tube shard on each of the Chocolate Ganache Circles. Finish with *fleur de sel*. Repeat with the remaining ingredients, to serve 8.

# MIGNARDISES

PB&J
336

MANGO AND CURRY
336

CHOCOLATE AND MINT
337

VIBRANT

TOWARD THE END OF 2008, halfway through his review of the newly opened Corton, Frank Bruni wrote that it "joins the constantly improving Eleven Madison Park as a restaurant hovering just below the very summit of fine dining in New York." I was reading the review on Wednesday morning in a cab on my way to the restaurant when I saw that line. I nearly jumped out of my seat.

I was so excited that even though we hadn't seen Bruni in some time, he was still thinking about us, seemingly aware of the progress we were making. We cut that section out of the review and hung it on the wall in our office for the balance of the year, looking to it for motivation during times that we were tired, or frustrated with our progress.

When Daniel and I sat down to determine our mission statement for 2009, it seemed the obvious choice: "to reach the summit." We made T-shirts for our entire team with the four leaves of our logo hovering just above an image of a mountain range, and once again we got together for our planning meeting, first reflecting on our accomplishments from the year before and then deciding on what we would do in the year ahead.

One of the first things that came out of that meeting was a suggestion from one of our servers that we ban the terms "front of house" and "back of house." In the restaurant business, there is constant tension and friction between the people making the food and those serving it. Daniel and I are extremely close, but we felt that those terms, so often used, only perpetuated the divide between the two halves of the restaurant. We made it a rule that the words "dining room" and "kitchen" should be used instead. It was a symbolic change more than anything, and a part of what would become a continued effort to create opportunities for all of us to get to know one another better and to work together more seamlessly.

The other outcome of the meeting was the realization that we needed to work to build our brand. Although the holiday season of 2008 was busy, it was clear that January would be very different. The recession was now at its worst, at least for us, and while we needed to stay focused on continuing to improve, we also needed to work to keep the restaurant full. We knew that in a down economy it was a problem if we were perceived as being overly serious or too precious, and as we continued to strive for four stars, we knew we were running that risk. We needed to show that we were still a group of excited young people who didn't take ourselves too seriously.

To that end, we started a number of initiatives. First, seizing on the fact that our private dining rooms were often vacant, we started a series of corkage dinners, where we would pick a wine region and cook family-style feasts to accompany those wines. We charged a nominal price and invited a group of our regulars, along with some winemakers from the selected region to add caché. It felt good for the rooms to be full, gave us an opportunity to show our guests a more dressed-down version of the restaurant, and created community among the many people who had supported us over the years.

Next, we began planning our first annual Kentucky Derby Party. We invited New York into our home to watch the race in seersucker suits and big hats, to drink bourbon, eat fried chicken, and listen to bluegrass. We had two different bands, a cigar lounge, and a raw bar with oysters and moonshine mignonette. People drank mint juleps all afternoon and gathered together to watch the big race. We were intent on showing the city that although we were continuing to improve, Eleven Madison Park was still fun.

In spite of these efforts, however, the recession was taking its toll. No matter what we tried, we couldn't fill our dining room. Month after month after month, we were losing money — continuing to run a restaurant with four-star expenses but without charging four-star prices. We needed to cut costs but desperately didn't want to compromise our standards, so we got creative. In the kitchen, we would cut paper towels in half, and our cooks traded in their expensive, pure white chef toques for the skull caps most commonly worn by dishwashers. In the dining room, we ran with fewer servers, and managers became more engaged in service, everyone hustling to pick up the slack. We were trying everything we could think of, but continued to operate at a loss.

Things were getting scary. There were times when we started to realize that we might have to change our course considerably. We had worked so hard to get to where we were, and suddenly, due to circumstances beyond our control, it was starting to feel like it was all for naught. Beloved restaurants throughout Manhattan were closing: Chanterelle, Café des Artistes, Fiamma, Fleur de Sel, Country. We were nervous. We were starting to feel desperate. We didn't know what to do.

THEN SOMETHING HAPPENED: one night, completely out of the blue, when, as had become the norm, our dining room was only half full, Frank Bruni walked through our revolving door. Now, to be clear, in spite his efforts to remain anonymous, we knew who he was. Like every restaurant in New York, we had a picture of him hanging in the kitchen. But knowing who the important restaurant reviewers are doesn't mean a thing. You can't suddenly become something you're not.

It is difficult to explain the physical, mental, and emotional reaction we all had when we realized he was there. We were at once excited, nervous, scared, and sick to our stomachs, praying with our entire beings that we wouldn't mess up. We freaked out at first, but eventually calmed down, focused, and delivered an experience that we were proud of. The next few months were the most stressful of our entire lives, constantly wondering if and when he would show up again. This was our chance, maybe our last.

It was a month or more before he returned, and then a month before his next visit after that. Then, within the course of a few weeks, he visited us several more times. We had figured it was going to lead to *something*, but it was taking so long that we were starting to lose faith. Then, finally, during the first week of August, we received the call from the *New York Times* telling us that we were being reviewed. The paper calls you in advance because it needs to send a photographer in to take pictures to accompany the review, but you have no idea whether it will be positive or negative until it is posted online the night before the printed paper is released.

That night, August 8, 2009, we went through service anxiously awaiting the news, constantly running back to the office to go online to see whether the review had yet been posted. I was drizzling olive oil tableside over an appetizer of gnocchi when a single diner, one of our regulars, finally pulled up the review on his iPhone. He leapt out of his chair, thrust his phone into the air, and yelled, "Four stars!" into the dining room. The restaurant erupted. Everything became a blur.

I rushed into the office where Daniel, members of our team, and I crowded around the computer reading the review, giant smiles across our faces, laughing, embracing. The headline read, "A Daring Rise to the Top," and in it Bruni chronicled our rise from two, to three, and then to four stars, saying that he "watched an improved, excellent restaurant…make yet another unnecessary advance." He "fell in love gradually, not all at once…." We had done it.

Danny showed up not too much later, glowing with pride. I saw him before he even walked through the door, ran out, and gave him a big hug. The first thing he did was ask me for my cell phone. He took it and immediately called my dad, wanting to share the moment with him and congratulate him on the role he had played in making it happen. My dad and Danny represent the two mentors in my life. It was an incredible moment for me.

The party that night was bigger than any we had thrown before; we had a DJ on call, just in case the news was good, and we raged in celebration into the night. Dom Pérignon was flowing like water and T-shirts with our four leaves and four stars were passed out to everyone on the staff. The next day, when we opened for lunch service, there were Riedel Champagne flutes on the sidewalks lining Madison Avenue, a few pieces of broken glass were still scattered through the dining room, and somehow a homeless man in the park had found and was wearing one of our four-star shirts.

Bottles of Champagne and giant bouquets of flowers arrived every day for the next week from all over the world. Each of the four-star restaurants in New York sent us something to welcome us to the club, and all of our regulars came to celebrate what their support had helped us achieve. Suddenly everything had changed. Our dining room was full every night, our team was reenergized, all of our hard work had been rewarded. We even stopped cutting the paper towels in half, and the chefs were back to wearing their proper toques.

The increased business brought challenges, as well. We needed to hire and train about twenty-five new employees between the kitchen and the dining room, and we needed to reprogram our phone system to handle the increased traffic.

We also weren't prepared for all the naysayers, people coming to the restaurant just to prove that we didn't deserve the recognition. We felt driven to try to change their opinions. In some cases we did; in others we fell short. As hard as we had worked leading up to the review, we found that we were working even harder after it. It was clear that as proud as we were, we needed to remain focused on getting better.

THAT OCTOBER, Daniel turned thirty-two and we took a much-needed break from the restaurant to celebrate. Through our good friend Scott Kasen, we secured a table at Rao's, where we were joined by Danny, Daniel Boulud, Grant Achatz, Daniel's wife, Geneén, and a few other of our closest friends for an intimate dinner. Rao's is New York's most

difficult reservation. It has been open since 1896 and serves home-style Italian American food. When I say it's New York's hardest reservation, that's because it's not actually possible to make one. People own their tables there. Someone will have a table for four every Monday night. You don't call up and make that reservation, it's just yours, and if you don't go, you make sure someone else does. How does one come to own a table? Likely you inherited it. What happens if you don't fill your table? I would imagine no one has tried to find out.

Now, while the food is very good, the allure of Rao's comes with its history, with the difficulty of getting in, and with the way in which you order. There are no menus. One of the people who works there (in our case it was a man who introduced himself as Nicky the Vest) pulls up a barstool and tells you what they have. You don't get to hear about the pastas until you pick the antipasti, you don't get to hear about the meats until you pick the pastas, and so on. It's a conversation of sorts, which ends with Nicky ultimately deciding what you are going to eat.

We loved it. It felt like I was at my grandma's house for dinner. The menu, the thing that represented the fact that this was a business transaction, had been removed. It felt so good. We left that dinner convinced that we needed to get rid of the menus at our restaurant, that the entire process should be a dialogue. When the effects of the wine eventually wore off, we realized that this might be a bit too extreme, but we knew there was something in the idea. We wouldn't figure out what until the following year, but it planted the seed of an idea in us.

SHORTLY THEREAFTER, in November, we left for our annual trip, this time to Biarritz for the Relais & Châteaux congress, but by way of Paris, where we experienced some of the city's most recognized restaurants. That week we ate at L'Ambroisie, L'Astrance, L'Arpège, and the infamous L'Ami Louis. It was the first time for both of us at L'Arpège and L'Ami Louis, where we experienced Alain Passard's mastery of vegetables at the former and impeccable roast chicken at the latter. It was my first time at L'Ambroisie, which is one of Daniel's favorite restaurants in the world.

Located on Place des Vosges, L'Ambroisie is one of the most beautiful restaurants I've ever seen. One of the main distinctions between it and its Parisian counterparts is that L'Ambroisie is entirely à la carte, but it is as classic a restaurant as they come. It's classic in its look, in its service, and especially in its food. The cuisine there is not breaking any boundaries, but each dish nears perfection, having more focus on the individual ingredients than most restaurants of its caliber. While a plate might have only three or four elements, the technique is exceptional, and the ingredients are of the highest quality. Daniel took me there because he has always been enamored of this focus, the confidence it takes to create such a seemingly simple menu, but do it so well that the restaurant can still be considered one of the best in the world.

It was also on this trip that I met Yannick Alléno and Florence Cane for the first time. Yannick is the exceptional chef of the three-star Le Meurice in Paris, and he and Florence are partners in the group that manages restaurants serving his food all over the world. Daniel had become close friends with each of them over the years, first meeting

them in New York and later spending a week with them in Paris, staying with Yannick and *staging* at Le Meurice. My getting to know them was a meaningful experience. In the two of them, I saw a partnership and friendship reminiscent of the one Daniel and I share. They are ambitious and focused, and they love what they do. They will be giving you sage advice one moment and have you laughing out loud the next. They are an inspiring duo, and in the years since have become some of our closest advisers.

WITH THE RELAIS & CHÂTEAUX CONGRESS in Biarritz and so close to the Spanish border, it presented us with an opportunity to cross over to San Sebastián a couple times to experience Akelarre and Mugaritz, two of the much more modern "molecular" restaurants that Spain has become known for. We first went to Akelarre, where we saw a lobster dish cooked tableside in a coffee siphon, an unexpected presenta-

tion that would later inspire the evolution of our coffee program. At the beginning of our meal at Mugaritz, we were brought for a tour of the test kitchen. It was a wonderful experience even for the two of us, who have spent our entire lives in kitchens; it reminded us how powerful it can be to invite people behind the scenes and into your home, to break down the barrier between the kitchen and the dining room, to make people feel much more a part of the restaurant. While these restaurants were far from what we were looking to create at Eleven Madison Park, their forward-moving approaches were inspiring. In balancing what we learned from them and their much more classical counterparts in Paris, we returned to New York with a new dose of inspiration.

# AUTUMN

*The fall is my favorite time in New York. I love the weather, watching the leaves change in Madison Square Park, and the energy that starts to build in our dining room. It brings new ingredients and a different style of cooking. Flavors are earthier and stronger, dishes are bolder.*

*I like to surprise people, but without sacrificing the sense of comfort. I work very closely with my sous chefs to develop new dishes. We often talk about how a dish has to first come from your heart and then your mind. It's not interesting if it's not also delicious. It should be something innovative that people can still really connect with.*

*Early in my career I would use too many different techniques and ingredients in one dish, thinking that the more challenging, the better. The dishes ended up being more about me than about my guests. "See what I can do?" Today, I believe less is more. Everything on the plate needs to make sense, and above all it needs to taste good. By focusing on fewer ingredients, but using several different preparations, you can really accentuate the flavors.*

*In the beet dish, we use three different kinds of beets, each roasted, pickled, and as a sauce. With poached prawns, we serve butternut squash roasted, glazed, as a puree, and as a bisque. The beef has the tenderloin as the main component, the bone marrow for the crust, the oxtail as a braise. Our philosophy is to highlight each ingredient: beets should taste like beets, squash like squash, beef like beef.*

|  |  |  |  |
|---|---|---|---|
| CAVIAR | CHICKEN | BEET | PORCINI |
| BAY SCALLOP | SEA URCHIN | LANGOUSTINE | FOIE GRAS |
| CAULIFLOWER | ENDIVE | CARROT | WHITE TRUFFLE |
| SNAPPER | SOLE | LOUP DE MER | PRAWN |
| LOBSTER | GUINEA FOWL | PORK | VEAL |
| BEEF | GAME | HOBELCHÄS | CASSIS |
| APPLE | HAZELNUT | SWEET POTATO | CHOCOLATE |

# HORS D'ŒUVRES

SEA URCHIN TOAST
328

OYSTER VICHYSSOISE
330

POACHED EGG WITH CHICKEN AND WHITE TRUFFLES
329

# CAVIAR
## FANTASY OF EGGS

*Serves 8*

### POACHED EGG YOLKS

10 eggs
3 tablespoons salt

Set up a water bath with an immersion circulator set to 145°F. Add the eggs in their shells and circulate the water at 145°F for 45 minutes. Transfer to a bowl of ice water and cool for 10 minutes.

Alternatively, set a pot of water over medium heat. Once it reaches 145°F, add the eggs. Using a thermometer, monitor the temperature of the water, maintaining it at 145°F for 45 minutes. Transfer to a bowl of ice water and cool for 10 minutes.

In the large bowl, dissolve the salt into 4 quarts of ice water. Remove the eggs from the water. Working with 1 egg at a time, crack the egg gently and remove from the shell. Hold the cooked egg in one hand and gently run cold water over the egg. The egg white should easily pull away from the yolk. Gently place the yolk in the seasoned ice-water bath. Repeat with the remaining eggs. Hold in the water bath until ready to use.

### SEA URCHIN BAVAROIS

4 sheets gelatin
2 1/2 cups cream
1 tablespoon butter
2 tablespoons minced shallots
6 ounces sea urchins (about 1 cup)
2 tablespoons Cognac
2 teaspoons lime juice
1 tablespoon salt
1 pinch cayenne pepper

Bloom the gelatin by placing the sheets in a bowl of ice water for 10 minutes, until pliable. In a stand mixer fitted with the whisk attachment, whip 2 cups of the cream to soft peaks. Reserve over an ice bath in the refrigerator.

Heat the butter in a small sauté pan over medium heat and sweat the shallots until soft and translucent, about 2 minutes. Add half of the sea urchins to the pan and sweat for 1 minute. Deglaze the pan with the Cognac and reduce for 2 minutes. Add the remaining 1/2 cup cream and the lime juice. Squeeze out the excess moisture from the gelatin and stir it into the sea urchin mixture until it is melted. Transfer the mixture to a blender, add the remaining sea urchins, and puree until smooth. Season with salt and cayenne. Pass the mixture through a fine-mesh chinois and chill over ice, stirring constantly to keep the gelatin from setting.

Remove the whipped cream from the refrigerator. Keeping it over the ice bath, quickly incorporate a third of the sea urchin mixture into the whipped cream with a rubber spatula. Then fold the whipped cream into the sea urchin mixture in 2 parts. Be sure they are fully and evenly incorporated.

Allow the Bavarois to set over ice in the refrigerator for 3 hours. Just before serving, whisk the Bavarois to achieve a smooth, buttery texture.

### BREAD CRISPS

1 loaf white bread
1/4 cup Clarified Butter (see page 370)
1 teaspoon salt

Trim the crust from the bread and freeze the loaf overnight. Prepare 32 pieces of parchment measuring 3 by 2 1/2 inches, 8 copper tubes (3 inches in length and 1/2 inch in diameter), and 16 paper clips. On a rotating deli slicer or with a sharp knife, thinly slice 16 pieces of bread. Trim the slices so that they are 3 by 2 1/2 inches. Brush 2 pieces of the parchment paper with the Butter and sandwich the trimmed bread between the buttered sides of parchment. Repeat with the remaining bread slices.

Preheat the oven to 350°F. Wrap the parchment and bread slices around the copper tubes and fix them to the tube with paper clips on both ends. Toast the bread slices in the oven for 12 to 15 minutes, until golden brown. Allow the Bread Crisps to cool slightly before gently removing the paper clips. Slide the Bread Crisps off the tubes and remove the parchment paper. Season with the salt.

### TO FINISH

Poached Egg Yolks
16 hearts baby gem lettuce
1/2 cup Buttermilk Dressing (see page 344)
1/4 cup sliced chives
Sea Urchin Bavarois
16 pieces sea urchin
1/2 cup osetra caviar
24 sprigs dill
Bread Crisps

Place 1 Poached Egg Yolk on a plate, slightly off center. Dress 2 heads baby gem lettuce with 1 teaspoon Buttermilk Dressing and sprinkle with sliced chives. Place a dressed lettuce head on either side of the Yolk. Spoon 2 quenelles of Sea Urchin Bavarois on the plate and arrange a piece of sea urchin next to each quenelle. Arrange the caviar, 3 dill sprigs, and 2 Bread Crisps on the salad. Use a hand blender to foam the remaining Buttermilk Dressing and spoon 1 teaspoon of the foam around the Yolk and Bavarois. Repeat with the remaining ingredients, to serve 8.

# CHICKEN
## VELOUTÉ WITH BRIOCHE AND BLACK TRUFFLES

*Serves 8*

### VEAL SWEETBREADS

1 pound veal sweetbreads
1/2 teaspoon salt
1/2 cup flour
4 cups canola oil

Using scissors, trim the sweetbreads into 3/4-inch pieces, removing any fat and blood. Soak the sweetbreads in ice water in the refrigerator overnight. Drain and dry the sweetbreads, season them with the salt, and dredge them in the flour pat off any excess. In a large saucepan, heat the canola oil to 375°F. Fry the sweetbreads for 4 minutes and drain them on paper towels.

### CHICKEN VELOUTÉ

1 tablespoon canola oil
2 chicken legs, each cut into 2 pieces
1 cup diced white onion
1/2 cup diced celery
1/2 cup diced leeks
16 cups Chicken Stock (see page 356)
6 sprigs thyme
3 stems parsley
1 bay leaf
1/2 cup butter, room temperature
1/2 cup flour
1/4 cup sherry
2 tablespoons salt
2 tablespoons lemon juice
1 pinch cayenne pepper
1/2 cup crème fraîche

In a medium saucepan, heat the canola oil over medium-high heat. Add the chicken legs, skin side down, and sear until golden, about 10 minutes. Pour off any excess oil. Add the onion, celery, and leeks and sweat until soft and translucent, about 5 minutes. Add the Chicken Stock, thyme, parsley stems, and bay leaf. Simmer until reduced by half, about 1 1/2 hours. In the meantime, mix together the soft butter and flour. The result should be the consistency of cookie dough. Once the soup is reduced by half, whisk in the butter-flour mixture until fully incorporated. Bring the soup to a simmer, stirring constantly to prevent it from burning. Simmer for 20 minutes to cook out the starchy flavor. The butter-flour mixture will thicken the soup and at this point, the soup should coat the back of a spoon. Strain the soup through a chinois and season with the sherry, salt, lemon juice, and cayenne. Whisk in the crème fraîche. Keep the soup covered and hot until ready to serve.

### CHICKEN

1 skinless, boneless chicken breast
1/2 teaspoon salt
1 sprig thyme

Season the chicken evenly on both sides with the salt. Place the thyme on the tenderloin side of the breast. Place the breast in a *sous vide* bag and vacuum-seal. Cook in a water bath maintained at 145°F by an immersion circulator for 25 to 30 minutes. Remove the chicken breast and cut into 1/4-inch cubes.

### TRUFFLE BAVAROIS

4 sheets gelatin
1 cup black truffle juice
2 1/2 cups cream, divided
1 1/2 teaspoons salt

Bloom the gelatin by placing the sheets in a bowl of ice water for 10 minutes, until pliable. In the meantime, reduce the truffle juice in a small saucepan until 1/2 cup remains. Squeeze the gelatin to remove any excess moisture and stir it into the reduced truffle juice. In a mixing bowl, whip 2 cups of the cream to soft peaks. Add the remaining 1/2 cup cream to the truffle juice and strain. Chill over ice, stirring constantly to prevent the gelatin from setting. Whisk the truffle mixture into the whipped cream until completely smooth. Season with the salt. Cover with plastic wrap and refrigerate for 3 hours to set.

Once the Bavarois is set, whip it with a whisk until smooth. The result should be smooth and glossy. Keep in the refrigerator until ready to serve.

### TO FINISH

Veal Sweetbreads
Chicken
2 large black truffles, broken into a rough crumble
Truffle Bavarois
8 small celery leaves
Chicken Velouté
Brioche (see page 364), toasted
8 tablespoons Black Truffle Butter (see page 371)

Arrange the Veal Sweetbreads, cubed Chicken, and black truffle crumble in 8 warm bowls. Drop a quenelle of Truffle Bavarois into each bowl and garnish with a sprig of celery leaf. Blend the Chicken Velouté with a hand blender and pour it into the bowls. Serve immediately accompanied by slices of toasted Brioche and Truffle Butter.

# BEET
## SALAD WITH CHÈVRE FRAIS AND CARAWAY

*Serves 8*

### ROASTED BEETS

1 1/2 to 2 pounds large red beets
1 1/2 to 2 pounds large Chioggia beets
1 1/2 to 2 pounds large golden beets
1/2 cup olive oil
1/2 cup salt
4 tablespoons sugar
3 cups red wine vinegar

Preheat the oven to 400°F. Wash the beets thoroughly under running water. Trim off the top and bottom of each beet. Toss in the olive oil, salt, and sugar, coating evenly. Separate the beets by color and place them in 3 individual roasting pans. Pour 1 cup red wine vinegar and 1 cup water in each pan. Cover the pans with aluminum foil and roast for 30 minutes. Remove the beets from the oven, uncover, and, using tongs, turn them over in their liquid. Cover them again and continue roasting for another 30 minutes or until the beets are tender when pierced with a knife. Once the beets are done, uncover them and cool them in their cooking liquid. Peel the beets, cut them crosswise into 1/2-inch slices, and punch the slices with ring cutters of varying sizes.

### GOAT CHEESE MOUSSE

1 1/2 cups skim milk
1 cup chèvre
3/4 cup cream
2/3 cup sheep's milk yogurt
2 tablespoons lime juice
2 tablespoons salt
1 N$_2$O charger

In a medium bowl, whisk together the milk, chèvre, cream, and yogurt. Season with lime juice and salt and continue to whisk until thoroughly combined. Transfer the mousse to a whipped-cream canister and charge with the N$_2$O cartridge.

### CARAWAY TUILES

2 tablespoons caraway seeds
2/3 cup rye flour
1/2 cup flour
1 teaspoon baking soda
1/2 cup butter, melted
3/4 cup glucose syrup
4 egg whites

In a small sauté pan over medium heat, toast the caraway seeds for 1 minute, until fragrant. Allow to cool before grinding in a spice grinder. Sift together the rye flour, flour, caraway seeds, and baking soda. Place in the bowl of a stand mixer fitted with the whisk attachment. With the mixer running on medium speed, slowly add the butter. In a small saucepan over low heat, heat the glucose syrup so that it is runny and add it to the mixer. Once the butter and glucose are thoroughly incorporated, pour in the egg whites. Whip until the batter becomes slightly puffy. Pass the batter through a fine-mesh tamis and refrigerate for 1 hour.

Preheat the oven to 250°F. Line an 18-by-26-inch baking sheet with a silicone baking mat. Spread the Tuile batter evenly and thinly, using 3 different round stencils, measuring 1 1/4 inches, 1 1/2 inches, and 2 inches in diameter to create 10 Tuiles of each size. You can create your own stencils from thin sheets of acetate. Bake for 10 minutes. Allow the Tuiles to cool completely at room temperature and gently remove them with an offset spatula. Store in an airtight container.

### TO FINISH

Roasted Beets
2 tablespoons olive oil
*Fleur de sel*
Caraway Tuiles
Goat Cheese Mousse
3 tablespoons Beet Vinaigrette (see page 345)
3 teaspoons Rye Crumble (see page 364)
32 dill blossoms

Brush the Roasted Beet slices with olive oil and sprinkle with *fleur de sel*. Place 5 slices of varying color and size on each plate. Rest 1 of each size Tuile on the beets. Expel 3 tablespoon-sized dollops of Goat Cheese Mousse in between the Beets. Spoon the Beet Vinaigrette around and finish with the Rye Crumble and dill blossoms. Repeat with the remaining ingredients, to serve 8.

# PORCINI
## SALAD WITH AUTUMN GREENS AND PEANUTS

*Serves 8*

**POACHED PORCINI ON BREAD ROUNDS**

2 cups white wine

1 cup olive oil

2 tablespoons white balsamic vinegar

1 tablespoon minced shallots

1 tablespoon salt

8 peppercorns, crushed

2 cloves

1 bay leaf

8 porcini mushrooms

1 loaf white bread, frozen

1 egg

In a medium saucepan, combine the wine, oil, vinegar, shallots, salt, peppercorns, cloves, and bay leaf. Reduce the wine for 5 minutes to cook out the alcohol. Add the porcini mushrooms and cover with a cartouche (lid made of parchment paper). Simmer for 20 minutes. Remove the mushrooms from the poaching liquid and drain them on paper towels. Cut the porcinis in half lengthwise.

Using a rotating deli slicer or a sharp knife, thinly slice the bread, about 1/8 inch thick, to yield at least 16 slices. Use a 3 1/2-inch ring cutter to cut rounds from the slices. Beat the egg with 1 teaspoon water to make an egg wash. Dip the cut side of a poached porcini in the egg wash and adhere the porcini half to a bread round. Repeat with the remaining porcinis and bread rounds.

**TO FINISH**

Poached Porcini on Bread Rounds

1 teaspoon Clarified Butter (see page 370)

8 teaspoons Peanut Puree (see page 353)

16 sprigs chervil

8 green frilly mustard greens

8 red frilly mustard greens

8 red sorrel leaves

8 baby green kale

8 green orach leaves

8 red orach leaves

8 parsley leaves

8 teaspoons Peanut Vinaigrette (see page 346)

24 slices from 4 porcini mushrooms

Pickled Porcini Mushrooms (see page 342)

2 teaspoons coarsely ground toasted, salted peanuts

To toast the Poached Porcini on Bread Rounds, heat the Clarified Butter in a sauté pan over high heat. Place the Porcini, bread side down, in the pan and quickly toast the bread until it is golden brown, 1 to 2 minutes. Remove immediately and place on paper towels. Work quickly but gently so that the porcinis stay glued to the bread.

Spread 1 teaspoon of the Peanut Puree on a plate. In a small bowl, toss the greens in the Peanut Vinaigrette and arrange 1 of each leaf on the plate. Place 3 raw porcini slices, 2 Pickled Porcini mushroom slices, and 2 toasted Poached Porcini on Bread Rounds on the plate. Dot with a few drops of Peanut Vinaigrette. Finish the plate with 1/8 teaspoon ground peanuts. Repeat with the remaining ingredients, to serve 8.

# BAY SCALLOP
CEVICHE WITH
RADISHES AND
PERSIMMON

*Serves 8*

### COMPRESSED RADISHES
1 green radish
1 daikon radish
2 tablespoons olive oil
1 teaspoon salt

On a mandoline, slice the radishes paper thin. Cut the green radish slices into half-moons and place the half-moon slices, 1 tablespoon of the olive oil, and 1/2 teaspoon of the salt in a *sous vide* bag. Vacuum-seal and hold in the bag until ready to serve.

Punch the daikon radish slices into rounds using a 1 1/4-inch ring cutter. Place the punched daikon radishes, the remaining 1 tablespoon olive oil, and the remaining 1/2 teaspoon salt in a *sous vide* bag. Vacuum-seal and hold in the bag until ready to serve.

### BAY SCALLOPS
1 pound bay scallops
1 tablespoon Lemon Oil (see page 345)
Salt

Rinse the scallops in cold water and remove any muscles that are still attached.

Toss the bay scallops with the Lemon Oil to coat and season with salt.

### TO FINISH
3 ripe persimmons
8 tablespoons Persimmon Puree (see page 353)
Bay Scallops
Pickled Persimmons (see page 342)
Compressed Radishes
Pickled Watermelon Radishes (see page 343)
24 slices baby radish
Persimmon Vinaigrette (see page 346)
5 ounces daikon radish sprouts
8 baby radishes
Hawaiian sea salt

Cut the persimmons into 1/4-inch slices and punch out rounds with a 1 1/4-inch ring cutter. Place 1 streak of the Persimmon Puree down the center of plate. Arrange 3 persimmon rounds, 6 dressed Bay Scallops, 3 Pickled Persimmon wedges, Compressed Radishes, Pickled Watermelon Radishes, and 3 baby radish slices on the plate. Spoon 1 tablespoon of the Persimmon Vinaigrette on top of the salad. Place 3 small bunches of sprouts and 1 baby radish on the plate. Finish with Hawaiian sea salt. Repeat with the remaining ingredients, to serve 8.

# SEA URCHIN SALAD WITH LOBSTER, SCALLOPS, AND POTATO

*Serves 8*

### SEA URCHIN SAUCE
1/3 cup (2 1/2 ounces) sea urchins
2 tablespoons lemon juice
1/2 cup grapeseed oil
2 teaspoons salt
1 1/2 teaspoons soy lecithin

In a food processor, puree the sea urchins with the lemon juice. Slowly stream in the oil, blending until fully incorporated. Blend in 3/4 cup water, the salt, and the soy lecithin. Refrigerate until ready to serve.

### STEAMED SCALLOPS
8 sea scallops

Steam the scallops in a combination steam oven at 185°F for 2 minutes. Allow the scallops to cool completely. Trim off the ends of the scallops and then slice in half lengthwise. Punch each scallop with a 1 1/4-inch ring cutter. Refrigerate.

### BRAISED POTATOES
1 large russet potato
4 cups Chicken Stock (see page 356)
1/2 cup white balsamic vinegar
1 tablespoon Pernod
8 black peppercorns
6 pods star anise
2 cloves
1 tablespoon salt

Slice the potatoes into 1/4-inch slices. With a 1 1/4-inch ring cutter, punch out rounds from the slices. Hold in cold water until ready to cook. In a medium straight-sided pot, combine the remaining ingredients and the potato rounds. Bring the mixture to a simmer over medium heat and reduce the heat to low. Simmer the potatoes until they are tender, 7 to 10 minutes. Cool the potatoes over ice in their cooking liquid. Keep the potatoes in their cooking liquid until ready to serve.

### BRAISED FENNEL
3 fennel bulbs
1/3 cup orange juice
1/4 cup Chicken Stock (see page 356)
2 tablespoons olive oil
2 strips (1 by 3 inches) orange zest
1 teaspoon salt

Slice the fennel bulbs lengthwise 1/4 inch thick. In a medium bowl, whisk together the remaining ingredients to make the braising liquid. Combine the fennel slices and the braising liquid in a *sous vide* bag and vacuum-seal. Steam the fennel slices in a combination steam oven at 185°F for 45 minutes. Chill in an ice bath and reserve in the bag until ready to serve.

### FENNEL WINGS
1 fennel bulb
1 tablespoon extra-virgin olive oil
1/4 teaspoon salt

Trim away the top and bottom of the fennel bulb and quarter it. Thinly slice the fennel bulb lengthwise on a mandoline so that the slices are less than 1/16 inch thick. Trim each slice with a paring knife on a curved bias so that they resemble wings. Prepare at least 24 slices. Combine the fennel "wings," olive oil, and salt in a *sous vide* bag and vacuum-seal. Keep in the bag until ready to serve.

### TO FINISH
Steamed Scallops
24 lobster knuckles (see page 99, for example)
1 tablespoon Lemon Oil (see page 345)
1/4 teaspoon salt
Braised Potatoes
Braised Fennel
Fennel Wings
24 sea urchin tongues
40 sprigs lemon balm
24 sprigs petite tarragon
16 sprigs fennel fronds
1 tablespoon minced tarragon
1 tablespoon minced lemon balm
1 1/2 teaspoons minced shallots
1 teaspoon White Balsamic Vinaigrette (see page 346)
Sea Urchin Sauce
Lobster Roe Powder (see page 371)

In a mixing bowl, gently toss the Steamed Scallops, lobster knuckles, Lemon Oil, and salt.

Arrange 2 pieces of Steamed Scallops, 3 pieces of Braised Potatoes, 2 pieces of Braised Fennel, 3 lobster knuckles, 3 Fennel Wings, and 3 sea urchin tongues on a plate. Lay 5 sprigs lemon balm, 3 sprigs tarragon, and 2 fennel fronds on top.

In a small mixing bowl, whisk together the chopped tarragon, chopped lemon balm, shallots, and White Balsamic Vinaigrette. Garnish the plate with 1/4 teaspoon of the mixture.

With a hand blender, froth the Sea Urchin Sauce. Spoon 3 tablespoons of the Sauce onto the plate and finish with a pinch of Lobster Roe Powder. Repeat with the remaining ingredients, to serve 8.

# LANGOUSTINE
## TERRINE WITH VEGETABLES À LA GRECQUE

*Serves 8*

## LANGOUSTINES

8 medium langoustines (just over a pound total)

Bring 1 gallon water to a rolling boil. While the water is heating, place the langoustines in a heatproof container. Pour the boiling water over the langoustines and let stand for 2 minutes. Remove the langoustines from the hot water and remove the tails and claws. Place the tails in the ice bath and return the claws to the hot water. Let the claws stand in the hot water for another minute and then shock in the ice bath. Reserve the langoustine heads for the Saffron Consommé. When the tails and claws are completely cool, carefully remove the meat from the shells, making sure to keep the meat intact. Reserve the shells for the Consommé. Keep the langoustine meat in the refrigerator until ready to make the Langoustine Terrine.

## SAFFRON CONSOMMÉ

1 tablespoon canola oil
Cleaned langoustine heads and shells
1 shallot, sliced
1 carrot, diced (1/2 inch)
1 stalk celery, diced (1/2 inch)
1 fennel bulb, sliced
1 1/2 tablespoons fennel seeds
1/2 cup Pernod
2 cups white wine
1 quart Fish Fumet (see page 356)
1 teaspoon saffron
3 egg whites
10 stems parsley
1 tablespoon salt

Heat the oil in a medium saucepan over medium heat. Add the langoustine heads and shells and sweat for 3 minutes. Add the shallot, carrot, celery, and fennel and sweat the vegetables until tender, 5 minutes. Add the fennel seeds and toast for 1 minute. Deglaze the pan with Pernod, reduce by half, and add the white wine. Reduce by half to ensure that all the alcohol is cooked out. Add the Fish Fumet and saffron and bring to a simmer. Simmer over low heat for 30 minutes, strain through a chinois, and chill over ice.

Whisk the egg whites in a mixing bowl until they are foamy. Whisk the whipped whites into the chilled stock, add the parsley stems, transfer the mixture to a tall, narrow pot, and set the pot over medium heat. Bring the mixture to a bare simmer for 5 minutes, being careful not to disturb the egg whites. The egg whites and parsley stems will float to the top, creating a raft. Once the raft has floated to the top, use the edge of a 2-ounce ladle to carefully scoop out a small piece of the raft, forming a hole in its center. The hole should be large enough to accommodate the ladle. Baste the raft with the simmering liquid every 5 minutes. When the Consommé is clear, after about 30 minutes, ladle the Consommé through the hole into a fine-mesh chinois lined with cheesecloth and season with the salt. The Consommé should be very clear. Discard the raft and keep the Consommé warm.

## LANGOUSTINE TERRINE

12 sheets gelatin
1/4 cup diced (1/8 inch) carrot
1/4 cup diced (1/8 inch) celery
1/4 cup diced (1/8 inch) leek greens
4 cups warm Saffron Consommé
1/2 teaspoon dill
1 tablespoon salt
Langoustine tails

Bloom the gelatin by placing the sheets in a bowl of ice water for 10 minutes, until pliable. In the meantime, bring a large pot of salted water to a boil and add the carrot. Cook for 2 minutes, until tender. Transfer to a bowl of ice water. Repeat with the celery and leek. Drain. Squeeze the excess moisture from the gelatin and dissolve the gelatin in the Saffron Consommé. Add the carrot, celery, leek, and dill and season with the salt.

Stir the liquid over ice until the gelatin begins to set slightly, causing the vegetables to suspend in the liquid. Pour into a 4-cup triangle terrine mold lined with plastic wrap. Fill the mold three quarters of the way full. Add the cooked langoustine, belly side up. Fill the mold with the remaining gelée and allow to set in the refrigerator for 4 hours. Store in the refrigerator until ready to slice.

## VEGETABLES À LA GRECQUE

1 tablespoon olive oil
32 baby carrots
8 baby fennel bulbs
1/2 cup white wine
1 teaspoon coriander seeds
1/2 teaspoon saffron
1/2 teaspoon salt
8 baby white scallions
8 baby red scallions

Heat the olive oil in a medium sauté pan over medium heat, add the baby carrots and the baby fennel, and gently sauté for 2 minutes. Add 2 tablespoons of the wine and the coriander and saffron and gently simmer the carrots and the fennel, adding more wine as needed so that the pan does not dry out completely. Simmer the vegetables until they are tender but still crunchy, about 10 to 15 minutes total. Season with the salt. Chill the vegetables in the cooking liquid until ready to serve.

Bring a pot of salted water to a boil. Add the white and red scallions, cooking for 2 minutes, until just tender. Transfer to a bowl of ice water and, once cold, drain. Toss them with the carrots and fennel for a few seconds to combine.

## TO FINISH

Langoustine Terrine
Olive oil
1 tablespoon *fleur de sel*
Langoustine claws
Escabèche Vinaigrette (see page 345)
Vegetables à la Grecque
32 coriander blossoms
8 leaves celery
32 sprigs tarragon

Slice 3 pieces of the Langoustine Terrine with a knife and place the slices on a plate. Brush with the olive oil and season with *fleur de sel*. Dress the claws in 1 tablespoon of the Vinaigrette and place them around the terrine slices. Sauce with 1 teaspoon of the Vinaigrette and finish with the Vegetables à la Grecque, 4 coriander blossoms, a celery leaf, and 4 sprigs tarragon. Repeat with the remaining ingredients, to serve 8.

# FOIE GRAS
## TERRINE WITH PLUMS AND BITTER ALMOND

*Serves 8*

### MARINATED FOIE GRAS
One 2-pound lobe grade-A foie gras
1 tablespoon salt
1/2 teaspoon pink curing salt
1 teaspoon sugar
1/2 teaspoon white pepper
2 teaspoons Madeira
1 teaspoon Cognac

Bring the foie gras to room temperature to soften. Separate the main lobes and remove the veins with tweezers and a paring knife. Pass the foie gras through a tamis, season with the salt, pink salt, sugar, and white pepper, and place in a *sous vide* bag. Add the Madeira and Cognac, seal the bag, and marinate in the refrigerator for 24 hours. Remove the foie gras from the refrigerator and allow it to come to room temperature. Transfer to a large mixing bowl and whip with a rubber spatula to re-emulsify. Place between 2 sheets of acetate and pat down to create a rough rectangle. Chill in the freezer for 15 minutes. The foie gras should be cold enough to be rolled out without breaking but not so warm that it is a loose puree. Roll the foie gras to 3/4 inch thick. Chill in the refrigerator for 1 hour, until firm.

Cut the foie gras into 8 rectangles that are just under 3/4 by 3/4 by 2 3/4 inches. Then cut those blocks in half lengthwise to form 16 even rectangular pieces of chilled foie gras. Store in the refrigerator between acetate until ready to serve.

### REDUCED PLUM WINE
Three 750-milliliter bottles sweet Japanese plum wine

In a large saucepan, reduce the wine by half over medium-low heat. Chill over ice.

### PLUM CONSOMMÉ
5 1/2 pounds red or black plums, pitted and thinly sliced
2 cups Reduced Plum Wine
1/3 cup sugar
1/3 cup *umeboshi* vinegar
1 teaspoon salt

In a double boiler over medium-low heat, combine the plums, 2 cups water, Reduced Plum Wine, sugar, vinegar, and salt. Cook covered for 3 hours. Strain through cheesecloth and chill the liquid over ice.

### PLUM GELÉE
10 sheets gelatin
3/4 teaspoon agar-agar (1.5 grams)
2 1/4 cups Plum Consommé
1 tablespoon salt

Bloom the gelatin by placing the sheets in a bowl of ice water for 10 minutes, until pliable. In the meantime, whisk the agar-agar into the cold Plum Consommé. Place over medium heat and simmer for 5 minutes to hydrate fully. Squeeze the gelatin of any excess moisture and stir it into the Plum Consommé mixture until melted. Stir in the salt. Cool to just above room temperature. Prepare one 13-by-18-inch plastic tray with vegetable spray, wiping off any excess with a paper towel. Pour the Plum Consommé mixture into the plastic tray to form a thin layer that is about 1/16 inch thick. Chill on a level surface in the refrigerator for 1 hour. Use a 1-inch ring cutter to cut rounds of the Gelée. Carefully remove the rounds with an offset spatula. Reserve on acetate in the refrigerator.

### BITTER ALMOND TUILE
1/2 cup glucose syrup
1/3 cup poured fondant
1 cup bitter almonds, chopped
1 tablespoon *fleur de sel*

Preheat the oven to 325°F. In a small saucepan over medium heat, cook the glucose, 1/2 cup water, and fondant to a light blond caramel. Pour onto a silicone baking mat and cool to room temperature. Break the hard caramel into small pieces and grind with the bitter almonds in a spice grinder until the mixture is a fine powder. Sprinkle evenly with a sifter onto the silicone mat and bake in the oven for 2 minutes. Remove from the oven, sprinkle with *fleur de sel*, and continue to bake until light golden brown, 7 to 10 minutes. While the Tuile is still hot, cut with an adjustable pastry cutter to 1-by-3-inch rectangles. You will need 24 total, but be sure to prepare plenty of extras and handle them carefully, as they are very delicate.

### COMPRESSED PLUM
2/3 cup Reduced Plum Wine
1/4 cup *umeboshi* vinegar
1 teaspoon salt
4 fresh plums

In a small bowl, combine the Reduced Plum Wine, vinegar, and salt. Cut 2 of the plums into 1/2-inch cubes and 2 into thin half-moon slices. Lay out the plum pieces evenly in *sous vide* bags, pour in 3 tablespoons of the liquid, and vacuum-seal. Remove the Compressed Plum from the bags when ready to use.

### TO FINISH
16 rectangles Marinated Foie Gras
2 tablespoons plus 1 teaspoon Lemon Oil
    (see page 345)
24 pieces Bitter Almond Tuile
*Fleur de sel*
8 teaspoons Plum Puree (see page 353)
16 lily bulb petals
Compressed Plum
16 rounds Plum Gelée
16 leaves baby purple shiso
24 leaves baby green shiso
8 teaspoons Bitter Almond Crumble (see page 361)
4 teaspoons Plum Wine Gel (see page 348)

Brush the sides of the Foie Gras with 2 tablespoons of the Lemon Oil. Sandwich the Foie Gras between the 3 Tuiles to form a "triple-decker sandwich" and season with *fleur de sel*. Set aside. Spoon 1 teaspoon Plum Puree on a plate and pull with a spoon. Place the foie gras sandwich on the Puree. Dress the lily bulbs in the remaining 1 teaspoon Lemon Oil. Arrange the Compressed Plum, 2 lily bulb petals, 2 rounds Plum Gelée, 2 leaves purple shiso, and 3 leaves green shiso on the plate around the sandwich. Drop 1 teaspoon Crumble on one end of the sandwich and squeeze 3 dots Plum Wine Gel onto the plate. Season with additional *fleur de sel* and repeat with the remaining ingredients, to serve 8.

# CAULIFLOWER
## ROASTED WITH GRAPES, ALMONDS, AND CURRY

*Serves 8*

## ROASTED CAULIFLOWER

1 head cauliflower
1/4 cup Curry Oil (see page 344)
1/4 cup Brown Butter (see page 370)
1 tablespoon salt

Slice 4 cross sections of the cauliflower, measuring 3/8 inch thick each. The cross sections should have the florets intact. Cut each slice in half lengthwise, yielding 8 pieces. Reserve the remainder of the cauliflower to use in the Cauliflower Puree (see "To Finish").

To roast the cauliflower, preheat the oven to 300°F. Heat 2 large oven-safe sauté pans over high heat and divide the Curry Oil and Brown Butter between the 2 pans. Place 4 pieces of cauliflower in each pan and lower the heat to medium. Sear the cauliflower for about 4 minutes on each side so that both sides are evenly browned, continuously basting the cauliflower with the hot Curry Oil and Brown Butter. Transfer the 2 pans to the oven and roast until the cauliflower is cooked through and dark golden brown, about 10 minutes. Season with the salt.

## SOUS VIDE CAULIFLOWER

1 head cauliflower
1/4 cup Curry Oil (see page 344)
1/4 cup Brown Butter (see page 370)
1 teaspoon salt

Slice 4 cross sections of the cauliflower, measuring 3/8 inch thick each. The cross sections should have the florets intact. Use a 1 1/4-inch ring cutter to punch out 16 cauliflower rounds from the slices that include florets and stem. Trim 16 florets from the remaining cauliflower. Save all other trim for the Cauliflower Puree (see "To Finish") and the Cauliflower Couscous. Place the rounds and 2 tablespoons Curry Oil, 2 tablespoons Brown Butter, and 1/2 teaspoon salt in a *sous vide* bag and vacuum-seal. Place the cauliflower florets and the remaining 2 tablespoons Curry Oil, 2 tablespoons Brown Butter, and 1/2 teaspoon salt in another *sous vide* bag and vacuum-seal. Steam the bags of cauliflower in a combination steam oven at 185°F for 20 minutes, until tender. Transfer to a bowl of ice water.

## CAULIFLOWER COUSCOUS

2 cups cauliflower trim (from the heads purchased for the Roasted and Sous Vide Cauliflower)
1 tablespoon Brown Butter (see page 370)
2 teaspoons lemon juice
1/2 teaspoon salt

Finely chop the cauliflower trim so that it resembles the size and texture of couscous. Place in a small mixing bowl and season with the Brown Butter, lemon juice, and salt. Refrigerate until ready to use.

## CURRIED RAISINS

1 teaspoon canola oil
1 1/2 cups thinly sliced Granny Smith apple
1/4 cup thinly sliced shallots
1 teaspoon Madras curry powder
1 pod star anise
10 black peppercorns
1/3 cup white port
1 kaffir lime leaf
1 tablespoon salt
1/4 cup golden raisins

In a medium straight-sided sauté pan, heat the canola oil over medium heat. Add the apple and shallots and sweat until translucent, without caramelizing, about 10 minutes. Add the curry powder, star anise, and peppercorns, and toast with the apples and shallots for 1 minute. Deglaze the pan with the port and reduce until the pan is almost dry. Add 2 cups water and the kaffir lime leaf and bring to a boil. Remove from the heat and steep for 10 minutes. Season with the salt. Place the golden raisins in a heatproof container. Strain the hot liquid over the raisins. Cool to room temperature. Keep the raisins in their liquid until ready to serve.

## CARROT CURRY SAUCE

1 tablespoon canola oil
2 cups thinly sliced carrots
1 cup thinly sliced white onion
1 tablespoons thinly sliced ginger
1 teaspoon Madras curry powder
1/4 cup white wine
1/2 cup canned whole peeled tomatoes, drained
3 1/2 teaspoons coriander seeds
1 1/2 teaspoons cumin seeds
2 1/2 cups Chicken Stock (see page 356)
1 1/2 teaspoons salt

In a large saucepan, heat the canola oil over medium heat. Add the carrots, onion, and ginger and sweat the vegetables until the carrots are fork-tender, about 15 minutes. Add the curry powder and toast for 1 minute. Deglaze the pan with the white wine and reduce until almost dry. Add the tomatoes, cooking until they are almost dry, about 3 minutes. Meanwhile, in a small sauté pan, toast the coriander and cumin until fragrant, about 2 minutes. Add the toasted spices and Chicken Stock to the vegetables and bring to a slow simmer. Simmer for 45 minutes. Strain the sauce and reduce it to 1 1/2 cups. Season with salt and chill over ice.

## DEHYDRATED GRAPES

2 cups sugar
32 seedless red grapes

Preheat the oven to 150°F or set a dehydrator to 125°F. Line a rimmed baking sheet with parchment paper.

In a large straight-sided sauté pan, combine the sugar and 2 cups water and bring to a low simmer until the sugar is completely dissolved. Add the grapes and remove from the heat. Steep for 5 minutes, remove from the syrup, and transfer them to the prepared baking sheet. Dehydrate the sugared grapes in the oven for 2 hours or in the dehydrator for 4 hours.

## TO FINISH

8 tablespoons Cauliflower Puree (see page 351)
8 teaspoons Curry Raisin Puree (see page 353)
Carrot Curry Sauce
2 tablespoons Curry Oil (see page 344)
Sous Vide Cauliflower
2 tablespoons Chicken Stock
2 tablespoons butter
Salt
Roasted Cauliflower
Curried Raisins
Dehydrated Grapes
32 Marcona almonds
Cauliflower Couscous
Madras curry powder
16 sprigs celery leaves

In 3 small pots over low heat, reheat the Cauliflower Puree, Curry Raisin Puree, and Carrot Curry Sauce. Add the Curry Oil to the Carrot Curry Sauce. Open the bags of Sous Vide Cauliflower, pour off the liquid, and reserve it. Using 2 medium sauté pans, heat 1 tablespoon of the Chicken Stock in each over medium heat and add equal amounts of the cooking liquid from the Sous Vide Cauliflower. Bring to a simmer and add the cauliflower discs to one pan and the florets to the other. Add 1 tablespoon butter to each pan and reduce to glaze, about 2 to 3 minutes. Season with salt to taste. Spoon Cauliflower Puree and Curry Raisin Puree on a plate. Place a Roasted Cauliflower cross section on top of the Purees. Arrange 2 cauliflower rounds, 2 cauliflower florets, 3 Curried Raisins, 4 Dehydrated Grapes, 4 Marcona almonds, and a spoonful of Cauliflower Couscous around the Roasted Cauliflower. Finish the plate with 1 tablespoon Carrot Curry Sauce, a dusting of Madras curry powder, and 2 sprigs celery. Repeat with the remaining ingredients, to serve 8.

# ENDIVE
## BRIOCHE-CRUSTED WITH GRUYÈRE, HAM, AND PEARS

*Serves 8*

### SAFFRON COOKING LIQUID

1 tablespoon canola oil
4 cups endive trim from 12 heads yellow endive
    (see Braised Endives method)
3/4 cup thinly sliced shallots
1/2 cup thinly sliced ginger
1/3 cup white wine
1/4 cup vermouth
2 tablespoons Pernod
2 pinches saffron
1 tablespoon salt

Heat the oil in a large saucepan over medium heat. Add the endive, shallots, and ginger and sweat until they are soft, about 10 minutes. Deglaze with the wine, vermouth, and Pernod. Add the saffron and reduce by half. Add 4 cups water and the salt and reduce over medium heat until 2 cups remain. Strain through a fine-mesh chinois and chill until ready to use.

### DICED EGG YOLK

20 egg yolks (*sous vide* method) or 10 eggs
    (conventional method)
1 teaspoon salt

Whisk 20 yolks in a large bowl until combined. Season with the salt. Place a 9-by-13-inch rimmed baking sheet in a *sous vide* bag and vacuum-seal. Pour the yolks onto the sealed sheet and steam in a combination steam oven for 10 minutes at 180°F. Chill in the refrigerator. Once chilled, dice the yolks into 1/4-inch pieces.

Alternatively, you can place 10 eggs in their shells in a pot of cold water. Place the pot over medium-high heat and bring to a simmer. Simmer for 12 minutes, remove from the heat, and transfer the eggs to a bowl of ice water for 10 minutes. Peel, discard the whites, and dice the yolks into 1/4-inch pieces. Season with 1/2 teaspoon salt.

### BRAISED ENDIVES

12 heads yellow endive
2 tablespoons salt
3 tablespoons Saffron Cooking Liquid

Halve the endives lengthwise and remove the outer leaves until the endives are 3 1/2 inches long. Trim the bottom of the endives so that they are rounded and uniformly shaped. Reserve the trim for the cooking liquid. Season both sides of the endives with the salt.

Place in a *sous vide* bag with the Saffron Cooking Liquid and vacuum-seal. Steam the endives in a combination steam oven for 25 to 30 minutes at 185°F. Make sure the endives are fully cooked, as they will turn black if they are only partially done. Transfer the endives in their bags to an ice bath. When cool, remove the endives from the *sous vide* bags and reserve the cooking liquid.

Alternatively, place the endives in a single layer in a straight-sided sauté pan. Season with the salt and cover with the Saffron Cooking Liquid and then a cartouche (lid made of parchment paper). Bring to a simmer over medium-high heat and cook for 25 to 30 minutes or until tender when pierced with a knife. Transfer the endives and their liquid to a bowl and cool over ice. Store them in the liquid. You'll use 16 halves for the Brioche-Crusted Endives and the remaining 8 for the Seared Endives.

### BRIOCHE-CRUSTED ENDIVES

1 hard-boiled egg
1 1/4 cups brioche bread crumbs
1/2 cup butter, softened
1/3 cup shredded Gruyère (about 1.2 ounces)
1/4 cup finely sliced chives
2 tablespoons minced black truffles
1 tablespoon diced (1/8 inch) ham
1 teaspoon salt
16 Braised Endive halves

Peel the egg, discard the white, and finely crumble the yolk. In a bowl, mix the crumbled egg yolk with the bread crumbs, butter, Gruyère, truffles, chives, and ham. Season with the salt. Place the dough between 2 sheets of parchment paper and use a rolling pin to roll the crust to 1/8 inch thick. Chill the crust until firm and trim to the shape of the endive. Top the flat, cut side of each Braised Endive with a piece of the crust.

### MUSHROOM SAUCE

3 tablespoons butter
2 shallots, thinly sliced
1 1/2 pounds button mushrooms, thinly sliced
1 tablespoon tomato paste
2/3 cup plus 1 teaspoon sherry
10 sprigs thyme
1 cup dried black trumpet mushrooms
1/8 teaspoon xanthan gum (0.3 grams)
1 teaspoon salt
1 teaspoon sherry vinegar
1 1/2 tablespoons olive oil

In a small sauté pan, heat the butter over medium heat. Add the shallots and sweat until soft and translucent, about 5 minutes. Add the button mushrooms and sauté until they are soft and begin to brown, about 15 minutes. Add the tomato paste and cook with the shallots and mushrooms for 3 minutes, or until a crust forms on the bottom of the pan. Deglaze the pan with 2/3 cup of the sherry, and reduce until almost dry, about 5 minutes.

Add 4 cups water, the thyme, and the dried black trumpet mushrooms and bring to a simmer. Simmer over low heat for 45 minutes. Strain, discarding the mushrooms and reserving the liquid. Reduce the liquid by half in a saucepan. Whisk in the xanthan gum to thicken the sauce. Season with the salt, sherry vinegar, and the remaining teaspoon of sherry. Break the sauce by topping with the olive oil.

### GRUYÈRE SAUCE

2/3 cup white wine
5 black peppercorns
2 cups cream
2 cups shredded Gruyère (7 ounces)
1 1/2 teaspoons flour
1 tablespoon salt

In a small saucepan, combine the white wine with the black peppercorns and reduce the wine until 1/3 cup remains. In the meantime, reduce the cream in a small saucepan over medium-low heat until just under 1 1/4 cups remain. Once the wine is reduced, strain it and whisk it into the reduced cream. Remove from the heat. Toss the Gruyère with the flour and whisk it into the sauce. Use a hand blender to emulsify the sauce fully. Season with the salt.

### SEARED ENDIVES

1 1/2 tablespoons canola oil
8 Braised Endive halves
1 1/2 teaspoons salt

In a large sauté pan over high heat, heat the canola oil until just before it begins to smoke. Pat the Braised Endive halves dry on a paper towel and season the cut sides with the salt. Place them cut side down in the hot pan, reduce the heat to medium, and sear until they are golden brown and warmed through, 3 to 4 minutes. Do not turn over. Remove the Endives from the pan.

### ENDIVE LEAVES

16 leaves yellow endive
1 teaspoon White Balsamic Vinaigrette (see page 346)

Halve the leaves lengthwise. Trim the bottoms so that you are left with 1 1/4-inch tips. Pare off the edges to create smooth, sail-shaped leaves. Gently toss in the Vinaigrette.

### TO FINISH

16 Brioche-Crusted Endives
Gruyère Sauce
8 Seared Endives
1/4 cup diced (1/4 inch) ham
1/4 cup diced (1/4 inch) black truffles
1/4 cup Diced Egg Yolk
1/4 cup diced (1/4 inch) Gruyère
32 slices red Anjou pear
Endive Leaves
40 leaves salad burnet
Mushroom Sauce

Preheat the broiler. Place the Brioche-Crusted Endives, crust side up, on a rimmed baking sheet. Broil for 5 minutes on the middle rack to brown the crust and heat the endives.

Place a streak of Gruyère Sauce down the center of a plate. Arrange 2 Brioche-Crusted Endives and 1 Seared Endive on the plate. Scatter the ham, truffles, Egg Yolk Dice, and Gruyère around the endives. Arrange 4 pear slices, 4 Endive Leaves, and 5 salad burnet leaves among the endives. Finish the plate with the Mushroom Sauce. Repeat with the remaining ingredients, to serve 8.

# CARROT
## ROASTED IN DUCK FAT WITH CUMIN AND WHEAT BERRIES

*Serves 8*

### OVEN-ROASTED CARROTS

8 orange carrots
1/4 cup olive oil
1 tablespoon salt

Preheat the oven to 375°F. Wash the carrots thoroughly, leaving the skin on. Coat the carrots with the oil and season with the salt. Place the carrots on a roasting rack and roast until tender, about 45 to 50 minutes, depending on the size of the carrots. Keep at room temperature until ready to serve.

### DUCK FAT–ROASTED CARROTS

3 cups duck fat
8 heirloom carrots (such as Purple Haze and Dragon)
4 sprigs thyme
4 cloves garlic, crushed but kept whole
2 sprigs rosemary
1 tablespoon butter
1 teaspoon salt

Preheat the oven to 250°F. Melt the duck fat in a large straight-sided oven-safe pan over medium heat. Add the carrots and transfer to the oven. Roast the carrots for 2 hours, basting and rotating every 15 minutes. The carrots should be very tender. Drain most of the duck fat from the pan and transfer the pan to the stove. Continue to roast the carrots over high heat. Add the thyme, garlic, rosemary, butter, and salt, basting until the butter is browned. Drain the carrots on paper towels and reserve the browned butter to reheat the carrots.

### WHEAT BERRIES

1 cup diced (1/4 inch) onion
1/2 cup diced (1/4 inch) celery
1/2 cup diced (1/4 inch) carrots
3 cloves garlic, crushed but kept whole
2 strips lemon zest
8 cups Chicken Stock (see page 356)
1 1/2 cups wheat berries
1/4 cup Lemon Vinaigrette (page 346)
1 1/2 tablespoons salt

Tie the onions, celery, carrots, garlic, and lemon zest in a piece of cheesecloth to make a sachet. Combine the sachet, Chicken Stock, and wheat berries in a medium saucepan and bring up to a simmer over medium heat. Simmer the wheat berries until they are tender but maintain their shape, about 1 hour and 30 minutes to 2 hours. Strain the wheat berries through a chinois and discard the sachet. While still warm, season the wheat berries with the Lemon Vinaigrette and salt.

### CARROT SAUCE

4 cups carrot juice (from about 16 large carrots)
1/2 cup mascarpone
2 tablespoons Dijon mustard
1 1/2 teaspoons Cumin Oil (see page 344)
2 tablespoons lemon juice
1 1/2 teaspoons salt

In a medium saucepan over medium heat, reduce the carrot juice until 1 1/2 cups remain. Strain the juice through a fine-mesh chinois. Transfer to a blender, and, with the blender running, add the mascarpone, mustard, and Cumin Oil. Season with the lemon juice and salt.

### TO FINISH

Oven-Roasted Carrots
Duck Fat–Roasted Carrots
1/2 cup Carrot Puree (see page 350)
8 teaspoons Date Puree (see page 351)
Wheat Berries
Carrot-Duck Crumble (see page 361)
Pickled Dates (see page 341)
32 sprigs carrot tops
Carrot Sauce

Slice the Oven-Roasted and Duck Fat–Roasted Carrots lengthwise to 1/4-inch-thick pieces. Alternate the carrots so that there are 2 pieces of Oven-Roasted Carrots and 2 pieces of Duck Fat–Roasted Carrots per portion. Trim the carrots with a round ring cutter measuring 5 inches in diameter.

Warm the Carrot Puree in a small saucepan over low heat. Spoon 1 tablespoon of the Carrot Puree down the center of a plate. Spread 1 teaspoon of the Date Puree next to the Carrot Puree. Place 1 portion of the Roasted Carrots on top. Spoon 2 tablespoons of Wheat Berries across the Carrots. Sprinkle with 2 teaspoons of the Carrot-Duck Crumble and 2 Pickled Dates. Garnish with 4 sprigs carrot tops and finish the plate with 3 tablespoons of the Carrot Sauce. Repeat with the remaining ingredients, to serve 8.

# WHITE TRUFFLE TORTELLINI WITH FONTINA CHEESE AND CHESTNUTS

*Serves 8*

## FONTINA TORTELLINI

1/2 cup semolina flour
1 pound Pasta Dough (see page 364)
2 cups Fontina Filling
1 egg white

Line a 9-by-13-inch rimmed baking sheet with the semolina. Remove the Pasta Dough from the refrigerator to allow it to soften slightly. Set up a pasta roller as per the manufacturer's instructions. Flatten the pasta with a rolling pin until it can fit through the widest setting on the pasta machine. Run the Pasta Dough through the machine, gradually decreasing the thickness until the thinnest setting is reached. Run the pasta 3 times on the thinnest setting. Trim the pasta to 14-inch-long sheets. As you work, keep the pasta covered with plastic wrap to prevent the sheets from drying out.

Work with 1 sheet of pasta at a time. Cut the sheet lengthwise into a long strip measuring 2 inches in width and 14 inches in length. Starting 1 inch from the left edge of the pasta strip, pipe 1/4-teaspoon dollops of the Fontina Filling, 2 inches apart, down the middle of the pasta strip. You should have about 7 dollops of filling per strip. Lightly brush the top edge of the pasta with egg white. Fold the bottom up over the filling, lining it up with the top edge and encasing the filling. Gently press down between each bump of filling to seal it inside the pasta. Using a knife, cut between the bumps to create rectangles measuring 2 inches wide by 1 inch long. To form the tortellini, dab the bottom left corner of the rectangle with a little egg white. Push gently in the center and pull the bottom right corner of the pasta over the bottom left and pinch together to hold the shape. It should look like a little hat with a point of filling in the middle and two points of pasta on the sides. Place the finished tortellini onto the semolina. Repeat with the remaining sheets of pasta. Keep covered with a linen cloth in the refrigerator until ready to cook.

## FONTINA FILLING

2/3 cup white wine
5 black peppercorns
2 cups cream
7 ounces fontina cheese, shredded
1 tablespoon salt

In a small saucepan over medium heat, combine the white wine and black peppercorns. Reduce until 1/3 cup remains. Meanwhile, in a separate saucepan over medium heat, reduce the cream by half. Whisk the reduced wine and cream together, remove from the heat, and strain into another small saucepan. Use a hand blender to melt in the shredded cheese. Season with the salt and chill over ice. Transfer the filling to a piping bag and refrigerate until ready to use. When ready to pipe the filling, allow the filling to soften to room temperature.

## CHESTNUT FOAM

1 1/2 pounds fresh chestnuts
1 tablespoon canola oil
1/2 cup Cognac
4 cups cream
1 tablespoon White Truffle Butter (see page 371)
2 teaspoons salt
1 1/2 teaspoons sugar

Preheat the oven to 350°F. Score a small *x* in the hard outer shell of the chestnuts with a paring knife and place on a baking sheet. Roast in the oven for 10 to 15 minutes, until they are lightly browned and the peel begins to curl away. Cool to room temperature and peel away both layers of skin. In a food processor, coarsely grind the chestnuts. Heat the oil in a large sauté pan over medium-high heat until hot but not smoking. Add the ground chestnuts and toast until dark brown. Remove from the heat and deglaze the pan with the Cognac. Return to medium heat and reduce until the pan is almost dry. Cover the ground chestnuts with cream and bring to a simmer. Remove from the heat, cover, and steep for 20 minutes. Strain, and season the chestnut-infused cream with White Truffle Butter, salt, and sugar.

## CHESTNUT SHAVES AND CRUMBLE

16 fresh chestnuts
2 tablespoons butter
Salt

Using a paring knife, score a small *x* in the hard outer shell of the chestnuts. Peel the chestnuts so that only the white flesh is left. Using a mandoline, shave 4 of the chestnuts and reserve the shaves for garnish.

With your hands, break apart the remaining 4 chestnuts into large chunks, about 1/4 inch in size. In a small sauté pan over medium heat, heat the butter until it begins to foam. Add the chestnut chunks and toast them until golden brown, about 2 minutes. Season with salt. Drain the toasted chestnuts on a paper towel.

## TO FINISH

Fontina Tortellini
2 tablespoons White Truffle Butter (see page 371)
8 tablespoons Chestnut Puree (see page 351)
Chestnut Shaves and Crumble
White truffle
Chestnut Foam
1/4 pound Castelmagno cheese, crumbled

Bring a large pot of salted water to a rolling boil. Add the Tortellini, cook for 2 minutes, drain (reserving 1 tablespoon pasta cooking water), and transfer to a medium sauté pan. Add the pasta cooking water to the pan and glaze over low heat with 2 tablespoons White Truffle Butter. Warm the Chestnut Puree in a saucepan over low heat, whisking constantly to ensure that it is smooth. Place a 6-inch ring mold on a plate, and trace a streak of Chestnut Puree inside the mold. Place 12 cooked Tortellini in the center of the streak. Arrange the Chestnut Shaves and Crumble on top of the Tortellini and shave white truffles on top. Using a hand blender, froth the Chestnut Foam and spoon it on top of the Tortellini. Finish with Castelmagno cheese. Repeat with the remaining ingredients, to serve 8.

# PINK SNAPPER
POACHED WITH
PEARS, PARSNIPS,
AND RAZOR CLAMS

*Serves 8*

### RAZOR CLAMS

1 tablespoon olive oil
24 razor clams
1 medium shallot, thinly sliced
1 tablespoon thinly sliced ginger
2 sprigs parsley
1/3 cup white wine
2 cups Fish Fumet (see page 356)

Heat the oil in a large saucepan over high heat until it is very hot and begins to shimmer in the pan. Add the razor clams and sauté on high heat for 10 seconds. Add the shallot, ginger, and parsley and sweat for 10 seconds. Add the white wine and stir. Allow the white wine to reduce to evaporate the alcohol, about 30 seconds. Add the Fish Fumet and cover the pan with a lid. Allow the clams to cook for a little more than 1 minute. Transfer the contents of the pot to a mixing bowl and chill over ice.

Strain the cooking liquid and reserve 2 cups for the Pear-Parsley sauce. (Do not discard the rest.) When the clams are chilled, remove the meat from the shells and trim away all but the cleaned neck, or "siphon." Discard the shells and the body, reserving only the neck, and store the clams in the remaining reserved cooking liquid until ready to serve.

### PARSNIPS

3 parsnips, peeled
1 cup Chicken Stock (see page 356)
3/4 cup butter
1 1/2 teaspoons salt

Starting with the larger end of the parsnips, slice them lengthwise into 1/8-inch thick strips on a mandoline, avoiding the woody center. Trim the slices on a bias to 2-inch-by-3/4-inch-long strips. To cook the parsnips, combine them with the Chicken Stock, butter, and salt in a large shallow pan. Cover with a cartouche (lid made of parchment paper) and bring to a simmer over medium heat. Be sure that the parsnips are in an even layer. Slowly simmer the parsnips until tender, about 20 minutes. Keep warm in the butter glaze until ready to serve.

### PEARS

2 tablespoons pear vinegar
2 tablespoons lime juice
2 red Anjou pears
1 1/4 teaspoons salt
1 tablespoon butter

Whisk together the pear vinegar, lime juice, and 2 tablespoons water. On a mandoline, slice the pears to 1/4 inch thick, 8 slices total. Season the pear slices with 1 teaspoon of the salt and place them in a *sous vide* bag. Add 3 tablespoons of the pear vinegar mixture and vacuum-seal. Steam the pears at 185°F for 10 minutes and immediately chill in an ice bath.

Heat a medium sauté pan over medium heat. Add the cooking liquid along with the pear slices to just warm through. Add the butter and reduce to glaze. Season with the remaining 1/4 teaspoon salt. Drain the pears on a paper towel.

### POACHED PINK SNAPPER

8 cups Chicken Stock (see page 356)
5 cloves garlic, peeled and halved lengthwise
5 sprigs thyme
1 1/2 tablespoons plus 1 1/2 teaspoons salt
1/2 cup cornstarch
Eight 3-ounce pink snapper fillets
2 teaspoons *fleur de sel*

Preheat the oven to 300°F. To make the poaching liquid, combine the Chicken Stock, garlic, and thyme in a medium pot and bring to a rolling boil. Season with 1 1/2 tablespoons of the salt. In a mixing bowl, whisk together 1/2 cup water and the cornstarch. When the Chicken Stock is at a full boil, whisk in the cornstarch mixture and boil for 3 minutes to cook out the starch. Strain into a deep baking dish and allow to cool to 145°F. Place the baking dish in the oven to keep the poaching liquid warm.

Season the snapper on both sides with the remaining 1 1/2 teaspoons salt. Place the fillets in the poaching liquid and poach until the fish can be easily pierced with the tip of a knife, 8 to 10 minutes. Using a fish spatula, remove the fillets from the poaching liquid and drain them on paper towels. Rest the fish for 1 minute and season with *fleur de sel*.

### PEAR-PARSLEY SAUCE

2 cups Razor Clam Cooking Liquid (see Razor Clams, left)
2 cups packed parsley leaves
1 pound Anjou pears, peeled, cored, and diced
1/4 cup fresh green apple juice
2 teaspoons salt
1 pinch cayenne pepper
1/8 teaspoon xanthan gum (0.3 gram)
2 tablespoons Parsley Oil (see page 345)

Reduce the Razor Clam Cooking Liquid until 1 cup remains. Transfer to a bowl and chill over ice. Bring a pot of salted water to a boil. Add the parsley and cook for 10 to 15 seconds. Transfer to a bowl of ice water, and, once cold, squeeze out the excess water. Transfer the reduced Razor Clam Cooking Liquid to a blender, along with the parsley and pears. Blend until smooth and strain the mixture through a chinois, being sure to not press the mixture down. Allow the liquid to drain and discard the puree. Keep cold until ready to serve. Season with the apple juice, salt, and cayenne. Whisk in the xanthan gum and dissolve completely in the liquid. Finish with the Parsley Oil.

### TO FINISH

1 tablespoon Chicken Stock (see page 356)
Razor Clams
1 tablespoon butter
1/4 teaspoon salt
1/2 cup Parsnip Puree (see page 352)
Poached Pink Snapper
Parsnips
Pears
1/2 cup Parsnip Crumble (see page 363)
1/4 cup grated horseradish
16 sprigs parsley
Pear-Parsley Sauce

Heat the Chicken Stock in a medium sauté pan over medium heat. Add the Razor Clams and the butter, reducing and tossing to glaze. Season with the salt.

On a plate, spoon 1 tablespoon of the Parsnip Puree. Place 1 snapper fillet on top of the Puree and arrange 3 Parsnips, 1 glazed Pear, and 3 pieces of glazed Razor Clams on the plate. Garnish with 1 tablespoon Parsnip Crumble, 1 teaspoon grated horseradish, and 2 sprigs parsley. Finish the plate with 1 tablespoon of the Pear-Parsley Sauce. Repeat with the remaining ingredients, to serve 8.

# SOLE
## POACHED WITH MUSHROOMS AND SPINACH

*Serves 8*

### POACHED DOVER SOLE
Eight 1 1/2-ounce skinless fillets Dover sole
2 teaspoons salt
2 tablespoons butter, room temperature
*Fleur de sel*

Place the fillets skin side up on a baking sheet and
sprinkle with salt. Stack 2 fillets together (skin side
to skin side) and repeat with the remaining fillets. You
should have 4 stacks of sole fillets. Place the stacked
fillets in 4 separate *sous vide* bags, add 1 1/2 teaspoons
butter to each one, and vacuum-seal. Place the bags
in an ice bath and allow the fillets to set for 4 hours.
Cook in a water bath maintained at 135°F by an immersion circulator for 6 to 8 minutes. Remove the fillets
from the bags, trim the edges, and cut the stacks in half
on the bias to yield 2 portions per stack. Sprinkle with
*fleur de sel*.

## POACHED MATSUTAKE MUSHROOMS

8 matsutake mushrooms
1 tablespoon butter
2 tablespoons diced shallots
2 cups white wine
2 sprigs thyme
1 tablespoon salt

Rinse the matsutake mushrooms. Use a paring knife to peel the skin from the mushroom stems and caps, being careful to keep the mushrooms intact. Save the trim for the Matsutake Mushroom Sabayon. In a small saucepan, melt the butter over low heat and sweat the shallots until tender and translucent, about 3 minutes. Deglaze the pan with the white wine and reduce by half. Add 1 cup water, and bring to a simmer. Add the thyme, salt, and mushrooms. Cover and simmer over low heat until the mushrooms are fully tender, about 1 hour. Add water as necessary to keep the mushrooms submerged in liquid. Remove the mushrooms from the poaching liquid and drain on paper towels until ready to use. Reserve the poaching liquid to reheat the mushrooms and to glaze the beech mushrooms in the Sautéed Mushrooms.

## MATSUTAKE MUSHROOM SABAYON

2 tablespoons plus 2 cups butter, melted
1 pound matsutake mushrooms, thoroughly rinsed and thinly sliced (plus any trim reserved from Poached Matsutake Mushrooms)
1/2 cup chopped white onion
1/4 cup chopped celery
1/4 cup chopped celery root
1 1/2 cups white wine
2 sprigs thyme
3 white peppercorns
1 clove
1 bay leaf
5 eggs
2 egg yolks
1 tablespoons salt
2 N$_2$O cartridges

In a medium saucepan, warm the 2 tablespoons butter over medium heat. Add the mushrooms and sweat until they are soft, about 10 minutes. Add the onion, celery, and celery root, and continue to sweat for 5 minutes. Deglaze the pan with white wine and reduce until the pan is almost dry. Cover the mushrooms with 4 cups water and add the thyme, peppercorns, clove, and bay leaf. Simmer over low heat for 45 minutes. Strain, reserving the liquid and discarding the solids. Transfer the liquid to a small pot and reduce until 1 cup remains. Using a hand blender, mix the liquid with the remaining 2 cups melted butter, the eggs, and the egg yolks. Season with the salt. Transfer to a whipped-cream canister and charge with the N$_2$O cartridges. Place the canister in a water bath maintained at 145°F by an immersion circulator for 1 hour, shaking the canister occasionally.

## SAUTÉED MUSHROOMS

16 chanterelle mushrooms
2 cups black trumpet mushrooms
8 shiitake mushrooms
1 tablespoon canola oil
1/2 teaspoon salt plus more to taste
1/4 cup Chicken Jus (see page 356)
2 teaspoons plus 1 tablespoon butter
Black pepper
1 (4-ounce) package beech mushrooms
1/2 cup matsutake poaching liquid
Poached Matsutake Mushrooms

To clean the chanterelles, rinse them thoroughly and allow them to dry at room temperature. Use a sharp knife and scrape the stems so that they are smooth. To clean the black trumpet mushrooms, pull them apart and rinse under cold running water, being sure to remove any dirt. Allow them to dry on paper towels. Remove and discard the stems from the shiitake mushrooms and thinly slice the caps.

Heat the oil in a medium sauté pan over high heat. Add the chanterelle mushrooms and sauté for 2 minutes. Add the shiitake mushrooms and sauté for 1 minute. Add the black trumpet mushrooms and sauté for 1 minute. Season with the 1/2 teaspoon salt and add the Chicken Jus. Reduce the Jus until the mushrooms are evenly coated, add 2 teaspoons of the butter, and toss to glaze. Season with salt and pepper.

Trim the beech mushroom caps so that each mushroom has a 1/4-inch stem. In a medium sauté pan, heat the liquid from the Poached Matsutake Mushrooms. Add the trimmed beech mushrooms and season with salt. Add the Poached Matsutake Mushrooms and the remaining 1 tablespoon butter, tossing to glaze and warm through, about 3 minutes.

## TO FINISH

1 tablespoon butter
1 tablespoon diced (1/8 inch) shallots
8 ounces baby spinach, stems removed (about 8 cups loosely packed)
1 teaspoon salt
8 tablespoons Chanterelle Puree (see page 351)
Poached Dover Sole
Sautéed Mushrooms
16 slices shaved raw matsutake mushrooms
8 tablespoons Chicken Jus (see page 356)
Matsutake Mushroom Sabayon

Heat the butter in a large sauté pan over low heat. Sweat the shallots for 3 minutes, raise the heat to high, add the spinach, and season with the salt. Toss the spinach and quickly remove it from the pan. Drain the sautéed spinach on a paper towel.

Reheat the Chanterelle Puree in a small saucepan over low heat. Spoon a streak of Chanterelle Puree down the center of a plate. Place a portion of Sole on top of the Chanterelle Puree. Arrange the sautéed spinach and Sautéed Mushrooms around the Sole. Place 2 slices of raw matsutake mushroom on the Sole. Spoon Chicken Jus around the mushrooms and finish by expelling the Matsutake Sabayon over the Sole. Repeat with the remaining ingredients, to serve 8.

# LOUP DE MER
## SEARED WITH PORCINI, SWEET POTATO, FIGS, AND JAMÓN IBÉRICO

*Serves 8*

### POACHED DRIED FIGS

2 1/2 cups white port
2 pods star anise
2 sprigs thyme
5 black peppercorns
8 dried white Iranian figs
1 tablespoon Chicken Stock (see page 356)
1 tablespoon butter

In a small saucepan over medium heat, reduce the port to 1 cup. Add the star anise, thyme, and black peppercorns, remove from the heat, and allow the spices to infuse for 20 minutes. Strain, discarding the spices, and add the Iranian figs to the warm liquid. Marinate the figs in the port until they are tender, about 30 minutes. Cool over ice and store in the liquid until ready to glaze.

To glaze, drain the figs from their liquid. Heat the Chicken Stock in a medium sauté pan over medium heat. Add the figs and the butter, reducing the sauce to a glaze.

### ROASTED FIGS

8 black Mission figs
1/2 cup sugar
1 tablespoon canola oil

Preheat the oven to 350°F. Remove the stems from the figs and cut them in half lengthwise. Spread the sugar out onto a plate and press the cut side of the figs into the sugar. Heat a medium oven-safe sauté pan over high heat and add enough canola oil to just coat the bottom of the pan. Using a paper towel, blot any excess oil from the pan. Sear the figs, cut side down, to caramelize the sugar, about 1 minute. Flip the figs and transfer the pan to the oven. Roast for 1 minute.

### ROASTED PORCINI MUSHROOMS

8 porcini mushrooms
2 tablespoons canola oil
1/2 cup butter
5 sprigs thyme
1 teaspoon salt

Cut the mushrooms in half lengthwise. Heat the oil in a sauté pan over medium-high heat. Sear the mushrooms cut side down for about 1 minute. Add the butter, thyme, and salt to the pan. Once the butter is melted, tilt the pan and baste the mushrooms with the foamy butter until tender. Drain on a paper towel.

### FIG JUS

1 tablespoon canola oil
1 pound *loup de mer* bones
8 black Mission figs
2 pods star anise
1 shallot, thinly sliced
1/4 cup minced *guanciale*
1/4 cup Banyuls vinegar
3 cups Chicken Jus (see page 356)
1 teaspoon salt

Heat the canola oil in a large, straight-sided pan set over high heat. Add the *loup de mer* bones and sear until golden on all sides, 1 to 2 minutes. Remove the bones from the pan but do not discard, and pour out any excess oil. Lower the heat to medium and add the figs, star anise, shallots, and *guanciale,* sweating until the shallots are translucent and the fat is rendered from the *guanciale,* 4 to 5 minutes. Deglaze with the vinegar. Return the bones to the pan along with the the Chicken Jus. Bring to a simmer and simmer for 20 minutes. Strain through a large-mesh chinois and season with the salt.

### LOUP DE MER

Eight 4-ounce fillets *loup de mer*, skin on
Salt
1 tablespoon canola oil

Trim the fillets and season them with salt. Heat the oil in a large sauté pan over medium-high heat until hot but not smoking. Sear the fish, skin side down. Be sure the pan is hot enough, or the fish will stick to the pan. Lower the heat to medium-low and press the fillets down with a metal spatula as they begin to curl, to keep them flat. Render the skin for 3 to 4 minutes, until crisp. Flip the fillets and sear the other side briefly. Remove the fish from the pan and rest, skin side up, on a rack.

### TO FINISH

8 tablespoons Sweet Potato Puree (see page 354)
Loup de Mer
Roasted Figs
Poached Dried Figs
16 slices Pickled Porcini Mushrooms (see page 342)
Roasted Porcini Mushrooms
8 slices porcini mushroom
1 tablespoon olive oil
16 slices Ibérico ham
Fig Jus
16 leaves lamb's-quarter

Spoon 1 tablespoon of Sweet Potato Puree onto a plate and pull down the center with a small spoon. Place a seared fillet of *Loup de Mer* in the center of the plate. Arrange 2 Roasted Fig halves, 1 glazed Poached Dried Fig, 2 Pickled Porcini Mushroom slices, 2 Roasted Porcini Mushroom halves, 1 raw porcini mushroom slice dressed with olive oil, and 2 Ibérico ham slices around the fish. Finish with plate with 1 tablespoon Fig Jus and garnish with 2 lamb's-quarter leaves. Repeat with the remaining ingredients, to serve 8.

# PRAWN
## POACHED WITH BUTTERNUT SQUASH AND BACON

*Serves 8*

## BUTTERNUT SQUASH BISQUE

3 tablespoons butter
1 pound peeled and diced (1/2 inch) butternut squash
    (about 4 cups)
1/2 cup thinly sliced fennel
1 teaspoon thinly sliced ginger
3 cloves garlic, crushed but kept whole
1/4 cup flour
1/4 cup vermouth
2 tablespoons Cognac
2/3 cup tomato juice
6 cups Lobster Stock (see page 356)
1 pod star anise
6 pods cardamom
1/2 cup tarragon leaves
1 1/2 tablespoons lobster roe
1 tablespoon crème fraîche
1/2 cup butternut squash juice (from 1 quart peeled
    and diced butternut squash)
1 tablespoon plus 1 teaspoon salt
2 teaspoons lime juice
1/8 teaspoon cayenne pepper

In a large saucepan, melt the butter over medium heat. Add the squash, fennel, ginger, and garlic and sweat until soft, about 15 minutes. Once the vegetables are soft, sprinkle in the flour and stir together to make a roux. Cook the roux for 5 minutes to cook out the starch.

Deglaze the pan with vermouth and Cognac and reduce until the pan is almost dry. Add the tomato juice and reduce the juice by half, about 2 minutes. Add the Lobster Stock, anise, and cardamom and simmer until reduced to approximately 3 1/3 cups, about 30 minutes. Remove from the heat and add the tarragon. Cover and steep for 5 minutes. Strain through a fine-mesh chinois.

In a separate bowl, whisk together the lobster roe and crème fraîche. Transfer the bisque to a blender and puree on high speed. Slowly incorporate the lobster roe mixture while the bisque is still hot. Blend the bisque on high for 5 minutes and strain through a chinois again. Season with butternut squash juice, salt, lime juice, and cayenne.

## BACON CRISPS

1 pound double-smoked bacon (6 by 6 inches), skin
    removed and frozen

Preheat the oven to 325°F. Line a rimmed baking sheet with parchment paper. Thinly slice the bacon on a deli slicer to 1/16-inch thick. Place the bacon slices on a baking rack and set the rack on the prepared baking sheet. Bake for 15 to 20 minutes, until crisp.

Alternatively, you can use high-quality, thinly sliced store-bought bacon and bake as instructed above.

## COCO BEANS

1 cup dried coco beans (French navy beans)
3 bunches parsley stems
3 sprigs thyme
1 bay leaf
5 black peppercorns
3 tablespoons olive oil
3 tablespoons salt
1/2 cup Chicken Stock (see page 356)
2 tablespoons butter

Soak the dried beans in plenty of water overnight. When ready to cook, drain the beans of their soaking liquid. Make a sachet by wrapping the parsley, thyme, bay leaf, and peppercorns in a piece of cheesecloth. Tie the ends together with butcher's twine. Place the beans and the sachet in a large saucepan. Cover with 3 inches water and add the olive oil and salt. Bring to a simmer, reduce the heat to low, cover with a cartouche (lid made of parchment paper), and simmer for 1 to 1 1/2 hours. When the beans are cooked, remove from the heat and allow them to cool in the cooking liquid. Before glazing, drain the liquid from the coco beans. To glaze the coco beans, heat the Chicken Stock in a sauté pan, add the coco beans, and warm through. Add the butter and reduce to glaze.

## BEURRE BLANC

4 cups white wine
3 cups orange juice
1/2 cup cream
3 pounds cold butter, cut into 1-inch cubes
3 tablespoons salt
1 1/2 teaspoons *piment d'Espelette*

Reduce the white wine in a saucepan over medium heat to 1 cup. Add the orange juice and cream and reduce to 2 cups. Set over low heat and slowly whisk in the butter, 3 to 4 cubes at a time. Stir slowly and constantly. When the butter is completely emulsified, add the salt and *piment d'Espelette*. Keep warm at 155°F.

## BUTTERNUT SQUASH WEDGES

1 base end (about 3 inches) of a butternut squash
3 tablespoons butter
3 sprigs thyme
1 1/2 teaspoons salt
1 tablespoon canola oil

Peel, halve, and scoop the seeds from the squash. Cut each half into four 1/2-by-2-inch wedges. Use a paring knife to trim the squash so that the sides and corners are smooth. Place the wedges in a *sous vide* bag with the butter, thyme, and salt, and vacuum-seal. Steam the butternut wedges for 17 to 20 minutes at 185°F. Cool in an ice bath. Heat the oil in a large sauté pan over medium heat. Add the Butternut Squash Wedges and sear until caramelized. Remove from the pan and drain on paper towels.

## TOASTED PUMPKIN SEEDS

2 cups raw shelled pumpkin seeds (also called *pepitas*)
1/2 teaspoon salt

Preheat the oven to 350°F. Place the pumpkin seeds on a baking sheet and toast them for 8 minutes. Season with salt and cool at room temperature. Store the pumpkin seeds in a cool, dry container.

## PRAWNS

Beurre Blanc
32 ruby red prawns, shelled and deveined

In a large saucepan, bring the Beurre Blanc to 135°F and poach the prawns in the Beurre Blanc for 6 to 7 minutes.

## TO FINISH

8 tablespoons Butternut Squash Puree (see page 350)
Prawns
Butternut Squash Wedges
Pickled Butternut Squash Diamonds (see page 341)
Coco Beans
Bacon Crisps
Butternut Squash Bisque
Toasted Pumpkin Seeds
1/4 cup pumpkin seed oil
*Fleur de sel*

Warm the Butternut Squash Puree in a small saucepan over low heat. Spoon the Butternut Squash Puree onto a plate and pull across with a small spoon. Arrange 4 Prawns, 1 Butternut Squash Wedge, 2 Pickled Butternut Squash Diamonds, Coco Beans, and 3 Bacon Crisps around the Puree. Using a hand blender, foam the Butternut Squash Bisque and spoon it onto the plate. Finish with Toasted Pumpkin Seeds, 1 teaspoon pumpkin-seed oil, and *fleur de sel*. Repeat with the remaining ingredients, to serve 8.

# LOBSTER
## POACHED WITH FENNEL, ORANGE, AND PERSIMMONS

*Serves 8*

### LOBSTER

4 (1 1/4-pound) live lobsters

Fill a large stockpot with water and bring the water to 150°F. Add 2 of the lobsters, and cook for 7 minutes, maintaining the temperature of the water at 150°F. Remove the tails from the lobsters and transfer them to an ice bath. Return the knuckles and claws to the water and continue cooking for 7 more minutes. Transfer the knuckles and claws to the ice bath. Repeat with the remaining lobsters. When the tails, knuckles, and claws are completely cool, carefully remove the meat from the shells, making sure to keep the meat intact. Refrigerate.

### BRAISED FENNEL

2 cups white wine
3 pods star anise
1/4 teaspoon fennel seeds
4 pieces lemon peel
2 teaspoons salt, plus more to taste
2 large fennel bulbs
2 tablespoons butter

To make the fennel cooking liquid, combine the white wine, 1/4 cup water, star anise, fennel seeds, and lemon peel in a medium saucepan over medium heat. Reduce the liquid until 1 cup remains. Season with the 2 teaspoons salt, strain, and chill. Trim the fennel, leaving 1 inch of the tops intact. Slice the fennel lengthwise 1/4 inch thick. Place the sliced fennel in a *sous vide* bag with the cooking liquid and vacuum-seal. Cook in a water bath maintained at 185°F by an immersion circulator for 45 to 50 minutes. Chill in an ice bath and keep in the *sous vide* bag until ready to serve.

Heat a large sauté pan over medium heat with 3 tablespoons of the fennel cooking liquid. Add the Braised Fennel and warm through, about 4 minutes. Add the butter and reduce slowly to glaze. Season with salt.

### COMPRESSED FENNEL

1 fennel bulb
1 tablespoon olive oil
1/2 teaspoon salt

Cut the fennel bulb into quarters. Using a mandoline, slice the fennel quarters 1/16 inch thick. Trim the fennel pieces with a paring knife so that they resemble small wings. Place the fennel wings, olive oil, and salt in a *sous vide* bag and vacuum-seal. Keep the Compressed Fennel in the *sous vide* bag until ready to serve.

### BEURRE BLANC

4 cups white wine
3 cups orange juice
1/2 cup cream
3 pounds cold butter, cut into 1-inch cubes
3 tablespoons salt
1 1/2 teaspoons *piment d'Espelette*

In a large saucepan over medium heat, reduce the white wine to 1 cup. Add the orange juice and the cream and reduce to 2 cups. Turn down the heat to low and whisk in the butter, 4 or 5 cubes at a time. Stir constantly. Once all the butter is added, pulse with a hand blender to fully emulsify. Season with salt and *piment d'Espelette*. Keep warm at 155°F.

### TO FINISH

Lobster tails
Beurre Blanc
1 teaspoon *fleur de sel*
2 persimmons, peeled
8 tablespoons Fennel and Potato Puree (see page 352)
Braised Fennel
Pickled Persimmons (see page 342)
Compressed Fennel
16 fennel fronds
4 teaspoons Lobster Roe Oil (see page 345)
2 teaspoons Lobster Roe Powder (see page 371)

Cut the lobster tails in half lengthwise. Place them in the Beurre Blanc at 155°F degrees for 7 to 8 minutes, until warmed through. Remove the lobster from the Beurre Blanc and sprinkle lightly with *fleur de sel*.

Slice the persimmons to 1/4-inch slices and punch with a 2-inch ring cutter.

Spoon 1 tablespoon Fennel Potato Puree onto a plate and spread with an offset spatula. Place 1 piece of Braised Fennel on top and arrange 1/2 lobster tail, 3 Pickled Persimmon wedges, 1 persimmon round, 1 Compressed Fennel wing, and 2 fennel fronds on top. Spoon the Beurre Blanc beside the Compressed Fennel and Lobster and garnish with a few drops of Lobster Roe Oil. Sprinkle with Lobster Roe Powder. Repeat with the remaining ingredients, to serve 8.

*Note: At the restaurant, we use the claws and knuckles in other dishes. If you're preparing only one lobster recipe, plate the dishes with the claws, knuckles, and tails.*

# GUINEA FOWL
## ROASTED WITH PARSNIPS, BLACK TRUMPET MUSHROOMS, AND OATS

*Serves 8*

## GUINEA FOWL

2 whole guinea fowl
1 1/2 tablespoons salt
4 sprigs thyme
2 tablespoons canola oil
2 tablespoons Brown Butter (see page 370)
*Fleur de sel*

Remove the breasts from the guinea fowl and reserve the legs and carcass for the Guinea Fowl Sauce. Trim away any excess fat or blood from the breasts and season them with the salt. Place 1 sprig thyme on the skinless side of each breast. Place each breast in a *sous vide* bag and vacuum-seal. Cook in a water bath maintained at 145°F by an immersion circulator for 25 minutes. Remove the bags from the water and let the cooked guinea fowl rest in the bags for 15 minutes. Remove from the bags and pat dry with a paper towel.

Divide the canola oil between 2 large sauté pans and heat over high heat until just before the oil begins to smoke. Place 2 breasts in each pan, skin side down, and lower the heat to medium-low. Sear and render the fat from the skin for 2 minutes, until golden and crisp. Remove from the pan and allow to rest for 1 minute. Just before serving, trim off the sides and slice each breast in half lengthwise. Brush with Brown Butter and season with *fleur de sel*.

## POACHED GRAPES

24 seedless green grapes
2 1/2 cups Riesling
1 tablespoon salt
3 pods star anise
1 teaspoon fennel seeds
1 tablespoon butter

To peel the grapes, use a paring knife to pull the skin away from the flesh, starting where the grape is connected to the stem. Be careful not to cut through flesh. Combine the Riesling and 1/2 cup water in a medium saucepan and reduce by half. Remove from the heat and add the salt, star anise, and fennel seeds. Infuse for 30 minutes. Strain. Add the grapes and marinate at room temperature for 2 hours. Strain the grapes, reserving both the grapes and the liquid. Heat 1 tablespoon of the liquid in a sauté pan over medium heat. Add the grapes and warm through. Add the butter, reducing to a glaze.

## GUINEA FOWL SAUCE

2 tablespoons canola oil
2 1/2 pounds guinea fowl legs and carcasses (reserved from Guinea Fowl), cut into 2-inch pieces
1 3/4 cups red *verjus*
2 cups seedless red grapes
1 quart Chicken Stock (see page 356)
2 cups Chicken Jus (see page 356)
1 1/2 tablespoons diced (1/8 inch) foie gras

Heat the oil in a straight-sided sauté pan over medium high heat. Add the guinea fowl bones and cook for 25 to 30 minutes, turning the bones until they are golden brown and caramelized. Deglaze the pan with the *verjus*, scraping up any crust that has formed on the bottom of the pan. Add the grapes, cooking until they are tender, about 10 minutes. Add the Chicken Stock and Chicken Jus, and bring the mixture to a simmer. Simmer on low heat for 30 minutes, skimming away any impurities or fats that rise to the top. Strain and reduce until the sauce coats the back of a spoon, about 1 3/4 cups. In the meantime, melt the foie gras in a small sauté pan over medium-low heat. Strain, discarding the solids and adding the foie gras fat to the sauce. Strain again and keep warm until ready to serve.

## DEHYDRATED GRAPES

2 cups sugar
32 seedless red grapes

Preheat the oven to 175°F. Line a rimmed baking sheet with parchment paper.

In a medium straight-sided sauté pan, combine the sugar and 2 cups water and bring to a low simmer until the sugar is completely dissolved. Add the red grapes and remove from the heat. Steep for 5 minutes, remove the grapes from the syrup, and transfer them to the prepared baking sheet. Dehydrate the sugared grapes in the oven for 2 hours. Remove from the oven and cool to room temperature. You can also use a dehydrator set at 125°F to dehydrate the grapes for 3 hours.

## MUSHROOMS

2 cups black trumpet mushrooms
2 tablespoons butter
2 tablespoons Chicken Stock (see page 356)
Salt

To clean the black trumpet mushrooms, pull then apart and rinse under cold running water, being sure to remove any dirt. Allow them to dry on paper towels.

Heat the butter in a large sauté pan over medium heat until it begins to foam. Add the mushrooms and sauté until tender, 3 to 4 minutes. Add the Chicken Stock, season the mushrooms with salt, and cook until the Stock is reduced and the mushrooms are glazed. Drain on a paper towel.

## TO FINISH

8 tablespoons Parsnip Puree (see page 352)
Guinea Fowl
Poached Grapes
Dehydrated Grapes
Mushrooms
8 tablespoons Oat Crumble (see page 363)
Guinea Fowl Sauce

Warm the Parsnip Puree in a small pot over low heat. Pull 1 tablespoon of Puree down the center of a plate. Place 1 piece Guinea Fowl right below the Puree and arrange 3 Poached Grapes, 4 Dehydrated Grapes, Mushrooms, and Oat Crumble on the plate. Finish with the Sauce. Repeat with the remaining ingredients, to serve 8.

# PORK
## BRAISED NECK WITH SWEET POTATO, PLUMS, AND AMARETTI

*Serves 8*

### PORK NECK

1 1/2 cups salt
1/2 teaspoon pink curing salt
Large loin from 1 pork neck, boned (ask your butcher for the large loin from a fresh pork neck for *coppa*, Italian cured specialty meat)

In a large pot, bring 1 gallon of water to a boil with the salts. Chill over ice. Transfer to a nonreactive container and add the loin. Cover and refrigerate for 12 hours.

Remove the pork from the brine, pat dry with paper towels, and roll tightly in plastic wrap to maintain its shape during cooking. Tie off each end tightly. Place into a *sous vide* bag and vacuum-seal. Place in a water bath maintained at 142°F by an immersion circulator for 24 hours. Chill in ice water for 4 hours. Remove the pork from the bag and plastic wrap and pat dry. Trim into an even cylinder. Rewrap in plastic wrap, place in a *sous vide* bag, and vacuum-seal. Keep in the refrigerator until ready to use.

### SWEET POTATO PARISIENNE

1 large sweet potato (about 1 1/2 pounds), peeled
1/4 cup butter
1 teaspoon salt
1/2 cup Chicken Stock (see page 356)
1 sprig thyme

Use a #15 Parisian spoon or melon baller (1/2 inch in diameter) and scoop 32 balls from the sweet potato. In a small saucepan, melt 1 tablespoon of the butter over medium heat. Add the potato balls and salt and sweat for 3 minutes. Add the Chicken Stock and thyme and bring to a simmer. Cover and simmer for about 20 minutes, until tender. Add the remaining butter and continue simmering until the potatoes are glazed, about 2 more minutes.

### DRIED PLUMS IN TEA

1 1/2 teaspoons allspice berries
1 1/2 teaspoons black peppercorns
1/2 teaspoon cloves
1/4 teaspoon juniper berries
1 pod star anise
1/2 stick cinnamon
1 1/3 cups red wine
1 1/3 cups red port
1/4 cup sugar
1/4 cup Earl Grey tea leaves
8 dried plums
1 cup Chicken Jus (see page 356)
1 tablespoon butter

In a small saucepan over medium heat, toast the allspice, peppercorns, cloves, juniper berries, anise, and cinnamon for 1 minute. Remove from the heat and add the red wine, port, and sugar. Return to the heat and simmer over medium heat until reduced by half. Remove from the heat, add the tea leaves, and steep for 5 minutes. Place the dried plums in a heatproof container and strain the hot liquid over them. Wrap with plastic wrap and cool to room temperature.

Strain, reserving both the liquid and the plums. Combine the liquid and Chicken Jus in a small saucepan and reduce until it is the consistency of honey. Place the plums in the glaze, add the butter, and warm over low heat when ready to serve.

### PORK SAUCE

2 tablespoons canola oil
1 cup finely minced *guanciale*
2 tablespoons minced shallots
3 plums, diced (1 1/2 cups)
6 dried plums, diced (1/2 cup)
1 sprig thyme
1/2 teaspoon salt
1 quart Chicken Jus (see page 356)
1 1/2 teaspoons Banyuls vinegar

In a medium saucepan, heat 1 tablespoon of the canola oil over medium heat and add the minced *guanciale*. Render the fat from the *guanciale* for 5 minutes. Strain, reserving the rendered fat. Heat the remaining canola oil in another sauté pan. Add the shallots, diced plums, diced dried plums, thyme, and salt, and sweat until the dried plums are soft, about 5 minutes. Add the Chicken Jus and lower the heat to a simmer. Simmer until reduced by half, about 40 minutes. Strain, top with the rendered fat, and season with the Banyuls vinegar.

### TO FINISH

Pork Neck
2 tablespoons canola oil
1 cup flour
1/2 cup Chicken Jus (see page 356)
10 scallions, peeled
3 tablespoons butter
2 tablespoons Chicken Stock (see page 356)
Sweet Potato Parisienne
Pickled Plums (see page 342)
*Fleur de sel*
Black pepper
8 tablespoons Sweet Potato Puree (see page 354)
1/2 cup chopped chives
Dried Plums in Tea
8 teaspoons Amaretti Crumble (see page 361)
Pork Sauce

Slice the Pork Neck into eight 1/2-inch slices. Heat 2 large sauté pans over medium-high heat with 1 tablespoon canola oil in each. Dredge each slice of Pork Neck in flour and dust off any excess. Place 4 slices of Pork Neck into each pan and sauté until caramelized, about 2 minutes on each side. Heat 2 additional sauté pans over medium heat with 1/4 cup Chicken Jus in each. Transfer 4 slices of caramelized Pork Neck to each one and baste with the Jus to glaze.

Bring a saucepan of salted water to a boil. Add 8 of the scallions and cook for 1 minute. Transfer to a bowl of ice water and, once cold, drain. On a mandoline or with a vegetable peeler, shave the remaining 2 scallions so that you have at least 8 scallion shaves. Heat 2 small sauté pans with 1 tablespoon butter and 1 tablespoon Chicken Stock in each pan. Add the Sweet Potato Parisienne to one pan and the blanched scallions to the other pan, swirling the pans to glaze the vegetables.

In a small sauté pan, sear the Pickled Plums, flesh side down, for 15 seconds. Add the remaining tablespoon of butter to glaze. Serve the plums, flesh-side up, and sprinkle with *fleur de sel* and pepper.

Warm the Sweet Potato Puree in a small saucepan over low heat and spoon 1 tablespoon onto a plate. Drag it to the right. Place a slice of Pork Neck on the Puree and season with chives, *fleur de sel,* and pepper. Place a Pickled Plum on top and a Dried Plum in Tea next to it. Lay a glazed scallion across the Pork Neck, and finish with the Sweet Potato Parisienne, a scallion shave, Amaretti Crumble, and Pork Sauce. Repeat with the remaining ingredients, to serve 8.

# VEAL
GLAZED
SWEETBREADS
WITH SMOKED
POTATOES,
CHESTNUTS, AND
WHITE TRUFFLES

*Serves 8*

## GNOCCHI

3 pounds large russet potatoes, scrubbed
4 tablespoons salt
2 cups flour, plus more for dusting
1 cup butter, softened
8 egg yolks
1/3 cup grated Parmesan
1 pinch nutmeg

Place the potatoes in a large saucepan and cover with cold water. Add 2 tablespoons of the salt and bring to a simmer over medium heat. Cook until tender when pierced with a knife, 45 minutes to 1 hour. Once the potatoes are cooked, remove the pan from the heat but keep the potatoes in the water to keep them hot as you peel them. Working quickly with 1 potato at a time, use a paring knife to peel off the skin. Pass the peeled, warm potato through a medium tamis onto a baking sheet lined with parchment paper. Repeat with the remaining potatoes, making sure that as they pass through the tamis they fall in a single layer instead of mounding. This will ensure that the potatoes are fluffy and light, as opposed to wet and dense. Wrap in a kitchen towel and cool to room temperature.

When the potatoes are cool, measure out 8 cups without packing them as you measure. Dust a work surface with flour and spread the potatoes out in an even layer. Evenly layer 1 1/2 cups of the flour and all of the butter, egg yolks, Parmesan, nutmeg, and the remaining 2 tablespoons salt, on the potatoes in even layers. Using a pastry cutter or dough scraper, combine together with a cutting motion. Do not knead the dough. Continue to cut the dough until the ingredients are fully incorporated, adding a little of the remaining 1/2 cup flour as necessary to help keep the pastry cutter from sticking to the dough.

Flatten the dough to a 3/4-inch thickness and transfer to a baking sheet lined with parchment paper. Cover with plastic wrap and refrigerate for at least 2 hours.

When ready to form the gnocchi, dust your work surface with flour. Remove the dough from the baking sheet and cut it into 3/4-inch-wide strips. Roll the strips into long ropes. Do not use too much force when rolling. Line up the ropes of dough and cut them into 3/4-inch pillows. Roll each pillow into a sphere. Roll the balls of dough down the back of a fork, gently pressing with the tip of your thumb, to create a ridged front and a dimpled back. Place the gnocchi on a baking sheet lined with parchment paper and lightly floured. Refrigerate until ready to cook, up to 8 hours.

## VEAL SWEETBREADS

1 pound veal sweetbreads
1 cup Veal Jus (see page 357)
1/2 teaspoon salt
1/2 cup flour
4 cups canola oil

Using scissors, trim the sweetbreads into 1-inch pieces, removing any fat and blood. Soak the sweetbreads in ice water in the refrigerator overnight. In a small saucepan, reduce the Veal Jus by half and cover to keep warm. Drain and dry the sweetbreads, season them with the salt, and dredge them with the flour. Pat to remove excess flour. In a saucepan, heat the oil to 375°F. Fry the sweetbreads for 4 minutes and then drain them on paper towels. Toss the drained sweetbreads in the reduced Veal Jus at the last minute.

## PARMESAN FOAM

1 tablespoon butter
1 tablespoon minced shallots
1/3 cup white wine
1/2 cup Chicken Stock (see page 356)
5 1/2 ounces Parmesan cheese, cut into cubes, plus 1/4 cup grated
2 cups cream
1 tablespoon plus 1 teaspoon salt
2 tablespoons lemon juice

In a small saucepan over low heat, melt the butter. Add the shallots and sweat until soft and translucent, about 3 minutes. Add the white wine and reduce by three quarters. Add the Chicken Stock and the cubed Parmesan and reduce the mixture by half. Add the cream and bring to a slow simmer. Strain, add the grated Parmesan, and puree the mixture with a hand blender. Season with the lemon juice and salt. Keep hot until ready to use.

## CHESTNUT SHAVES AND CRUMBLE

16 fresh chestnuts
2 tablespoons butter
Salt

Using a paring knife, score a small x in the hard outer shells of the chestnuts. Peel the chestnuts so that only the white flesh is left. Using a mandoline, shave 8 of the chestnuts and reserve the shaves for garnish.

With your hands, break apart the remaining 8 chestnuts into large chunks, about 1/4 inch in size. In a small sauté pan over medium heat, heat the butter until it begins to foam. Add the chestnut chunks and toast them until golden brown, about 2 minutes. Season with salt. Drain the toasted chestnuts on a paper towel.

## SMOKED POTATO CONFIT

24 marble potatoes
4 cups plus 2 tablespoons Smoked Butter (see page 359), melted
2 sprigs thyme
3 cloves garlic, crushed but kept whole
2 tablespoons Chicken Stock (see page 356)
1 tablespoon White Truffle Butter (see page 371)
*Fleur de sel*

Preheat the oven to 275°F. Place the unpeeled potatoes in a baking dish with the 4 cups Smoked Butter, thyme, and garlic and cover with aluminum foil. Roast the potatoes in the oven for 1 hour and 15 minutes. Remove from the oven and cool the potatoes in the Butter to room temperature. Once cool, strain, reserving the Butter. Peel the potatoes with a paring knife and return them to the strained Butter, reserving at room temperature until ready to use. Heat the Chicken Stock in a large sauté pan over medium heat. Drain the potatoes and add them to the pan to warm through. Add the remaining 2 tablespoons Smoked Butter and White Truffle Butter, tossing to glaze. Drain on paper towels and season with *fleur de sel*.

## TO FINISH

Gnocchi
1/4 cup White Truffle Butter (see page 371)
3/4 cup Smoked Potato Puree (see page 353)
Veal Sweetbreads
Smoked Potato Confit
1 white truffle, shaved
Shaved Parmesan
Chestnut Shaves and Crumble
Parmesan Foam

Bring a large pot of salted water to a rolling boil. Cook the Gnocchi for 3 minutes. Heat the White Truffle Butter in a large sauté pan over medium-high heat. Drain the Gnocchi and glaze them in the White Truffle Butter. Warm the Smoked Potato Puree in a small saucepan over low heat. On a plate, spoon 2 streaks (1 1/2 tablespoons total) of the Smoked Potato Puree. Arrange 4 Veal Jus–glazed Sweetbreads, 3 glazed confit potatoes, and 5 Gnocchi on the plate. Lay the white truffle shaves, 4 Parmesan shaves, and 8 Chestnut Shaves on and around the Sweetbreads and Gnocchi. Finish the plate with the Chestnut Crumble and a few teaspoons of Parmesan Foam. Repeat with the remaining ingredients, to serve 8.

# BEEF
## ROASTED TENDERLOIN WITH BONE MARROW CRUST, SWISS CHARD, AND CHANTERELLES

*Serves 8*

## BRAISED OXTAIL

2 pounds beef oxtail
3 white onions, diced
2 carrots, diced
2 stalks celery, diced
1/2 celery root, diced
Three 750-milliliter bottles red wine
Salt
1/4 cup canola oil
1/4 cup tomato paste
8 cups Veal Stock (see page 357)
4 sprigs thyme
2 bay leaves

Place the oxtails in a nonreactive container with the onions, carrots, celery, and celery root. Add the red wine, cover, and refrigerate for 48 hours.

Preheat the oven to 275°F. Remove the oxtails from the marinade and pat them dry. Season with salt. Strain the marinade, reserving the liquid and the vegetables separately. In a large saucepan, bring the liquid to a simmer, skimming off any fats and impurities that rise to the top. Heat the oil in a large straight-sided pan. Add the reserved vegetables and sweat over medium heat. Add the tomato paste and sweat for 2 minutes. Deglaze the pan with the simmering liquid. Add the Veal Stock, thyme, and bay leaves, bring to a simmer, and return the oxtails to the pan. Bring to a simmer, skimming the liquid. Cover and braise in the oven for 4 hours or until the meat is tender and falling from the bone. Remove the meat from the braising liquid and pick the meat from the bones. Strain the liquid and reduce to a glaze. Add the picked meat back to the liquid and glaze. Chill.

## BEEF

2 pounds beef tenderloin
Salt
1 sprig thyme

Season the beef with salt and place in a *sous vide* bag with the thyme. Vacuum-seal and cook in a water bath maintained at 145°F by an immersion circulator for 25 to 30 minutes. Chill in an ice-water bath, remove from the bag, and cut into 8 portions.

## THYME AND GARLIC BUTTER

4 tablespoons butter
5 sprigs thyme
2 cloves garlic, crushed but kept whole

In a small saucepan over medium heat, warm the butter until the milk solids begin to brown. Add the thyme and garlic, remove from the heat, and cool to 150°F.

## BONE MARROW CRUST

1 tablespoon plus 1 cup butter, softened
2 tablespoons minced shallots
1/4 cup thyme leaves
1/4 cup chopped parsley
2 cups brioche bread crumbs
3/4 cup diced bone marrow
1 teaspoon salt

Heat the 1 tablespoon butter in a sauté pan. Add the shallots and sweat for 5 minutes over low heat. Add the thyme and parsley and mix thoroughly. Remove from the heat and cool. Combine with the bread crumbs and then fold in the remaining 1 cup butter. Fold in the bone marrow and season with the salt. Place the mixture between 2 sheets of parchment paper and roll to 1/8 inch thick. Keep cool. Punch out 8 crust disks to fit the top of the beef tenderloin portions.

## CRUSHED POTATOES

2 pounds fingerling potatoes, peeled
Salt
1/2 cup extra-virgin olive oil
1/2 cup sliced chives

Put the potatoes in a medium saucepan and cover with cold water. Season with salt and bring to a simmer over medium heat. Simmer until tender, about 30 to 35 minutes. Strain. Return the potatoes to the saucepan and crush with a fork, adding in the extra-virgin olive oil. Stir in the chives and season with salt.

## RENDERED MARROW FAT

Twelve 2 1/2-inch beef marrow bones

Soak the bones in water for about 30 minutes. Once the marrow is soft, carefully push it out of the bone. Cut the bone marrow cylinders into 1/2-inch pieces. Place the bone marrow and 1/4 cup water in a medium pot over low heat. Render the marrow, making sure not to brown it. Once all of the water has been cooked out and the marrow is completely rendered, strain through a fine-mesh chinois, reserving only the liquid fat.

## BORDELAISE SAUCE

4 cups Veal Jus (see page 357)
1 tablespoon olive oil
1 tablespoon minced shallots
1 tablespoon thyme leaves
1/4 cup Rendered Marrow Fat
1/2 teaspoon salt

In a small saucepan over medium heat, reduce the Veal Jus to 2 cups. Heat the oil in a small saucepan over medium heat. Add the shallots and sweat. Add the reduced Jus, bring to a simmer, and add the thyme leaves. Break the sauce with the Rendered Marrow Fat and season with the salt.

## TO FINISH

112 small chanterelles
16 large Swiss chard leaves
2 tablespoons Chicken Stock (see page 356)
2 tablespoons butter
5 sprigs thyme
1 clove garlic, crushed but kept whole
Salt
Braised Oxtail
Beef
Thyme and Garlic Butter
Bone Marrow Crust
*Fleur de sel*
Crushed Potatoes
Bordelaise Sauce
16 sprigs baby yellow chard

Clean the chanterelles of all dirt with a paring knife and scrape any discoloration from the stems. Trim the bottoms and rinse thoroughly. Spread the chanterelles on paper towels to dry.

Bring a pot of salted water to a boil. Add the large Swiss chard leaves and cook for 15 to 20 seconds. Transfer to a bowl of ice water, and, once cold, strain. In a sauté pan over medium heat, warm 1 tablespoon of the Chicken Stock with the Swiss chard. Add 1 tablespoon of the butter, tossing to glaze. In another sauté pan, melt the remaining 1 tablespoon butter. Add the chanterelles, thyme, and garlic, sweating until the chanterelles are tender. Add the remaining 1 tablespoon Chicken Stock, reducing until almost dry. Season with salt and discard the thyme and the garlic. Lay out 8 glazed Swiss chard leaves and place 1 1/2 tablespoons of the warm Braised Oxtail in the center of each leaf. Wrap the leaf around the Oxtail to create a small bundle. Roll each piece of Beef in the Thyme and Garlic Butter. Top with a Bone Marrow Crust disk. Broil on high for 1 minute until golden. Slice the beef in half lengthwise. Brush the cut sides of the Beef with Thyme and Garlic Butter and sprinkle with *fleur de sel*. Spoon the 1 tablespoon of Crushed Potatoes on a plate. Place the Bone Marrow Crusted Beef on top. Spoon the chanterelles around the beef and place a Swiss chard bundle and a glazed Swiss chard leaf above the beef. Finish the plate with the Bordelaise Sauce and garnish with 2 baby yellow chard sprigs. Repeat with the remaining ingredients, to serve 8.

# GAME

*Served in four courses*

# WILD BOAR
# AND FOIE GRAS
# TORCHON
# WITH JUNIPER

*Serves 8*

### MARINATED FOIE GRAS

One 2-pound lobe grade-A foie gras
1 tablespoon salt
1/2 teaspoon pink curing salt
1 teaspoon sugar
1/2 teaspoon white pepper
2 teaspoons Madeira
1 teaspoon Cognac

Bring the foie gras to room temperature to soften. Separate the main lobes and remove the veins with tweezers and a paring knife. Pass the foie gras through a tamis, season with the salt, pink salt, sugar, and white pepper, and place in a *sous vide* bag. Add the Madeira and Cognac, seal the bag, and marinate in the refrigerator for 24 hours. Remove the foie gras from the refrigerator and allow it to come to room temperature. Transfer to a large mixing bowl and whip with a rubber spatula to re-emulsify. Place between 2 sheets of acetate and pat down to create a rough rectangle. Chill in the freezer for 15 minutes. The foie gras should be cold enough to be rolled out without breaking but not so warm that it is a loose puree. Roll to 3/4 inch thick. Refrigerate until ready to roll the Torchon.

### WILD BOAR

2 pounds bone-in wild boar shoulder
One 750-milliliter bottle red wine
1 carrot, diced
1 stalk celery, diced
1 white onion, diced
1/2 celery root, diced
10 black peppercorns
4 cloves
1 teaspoon juniper berries
2 allspice berries
Salt
1/4 cup canola oil
1/4 cup tomato paste
1 quart Veal Stock (see page 357)
2 sprigs thyme
1 bay leaf
1 teaspoon balsamic vinegar
Black pepper

Place the wild boar in a nonreactive container and add the red wine, carrot, celery, onion, and celery root. Make a sachet by wrapping the peppercorns, cloves, juniper berries, and allspice in cheesecloth. Tie together with butcher's twine and add to the marinade. Cover and marinate in the refrigerator for 48 hours.

Preheat the oven to 275°F. Strain the boar, reserving the liquid, the vegetables, and the sachet. Pat the boar dry and season with salt. In a large saucepan, bring the reserved liquid to a simmer, skimming any fats and impurities as they rise to the top. Heat the oil in a large straight-sided oven-safe pot over medium heat. Sear the boar until browned on all sides. Remove from the pan and set aside. Pour out the excess fat from the pan. Add the reserved carrot, celery, onion, and celery root and sweat until tender, 10 minutes. Add the tomato paste and sauté for 5 minutes. Return the boar to the pan and deglaze with the simmered liquid. Add the Veal Stock, thyme, bay leaf, and the reserved sachet, and bring to a simmer. Skim the liquid of any fats and impurities that rise to the top. Cover and braise in the oven for 3 1/2 hours, until the meat is tender and falling from the bone. Remove from the oven and allow to rest for 45 minutes. Remove the meat from the braising liquid and pick it apart. Strain the liquid and reduce in a saucepan over medium heat to a glaze. Add the picked boar back to the liquid and gently stir to glaze. Season with the balsamic vinegar and salt and pepper to taste.

Lay out a double layer of plastic wrap on a smooth, clean surface. Spread the boar onto the plastic wrap in a roughly 1-by-12 inch rectangle. Fold the plastic wrap up over the meat and roll it tightly. Make sure the edges are clean and straight. Roll the boar in the plastic wrap. As you roll, use a cake tester to poke holes in the plastic to remove air pockets. Tighten as you roll, being sure that the roll does not exceed 1 inch in diameter. Tightly tie one end of the plastic wrap and twist the other end to compact the boar. Tie the second end to finish. Chill the rolled boar in ice water until it is a solid log.

### WILD BOAR AND FOIE GRAS TORCHON

Wild Boar
Marinated Foie Gras

Using a damp towel, wipe down a smooth and spacious work surface. Lay out 3 long sheets (about 3 feet long each) of plastic wrap so that they overlap slightly. Wipe the plastic wrap with a damp towel. Place the Foie Gras on top of the plastic wrap and peel off both layers of the acetate. Trim the edges of the Foie Gras with a dough scraper (being careful not to cut through the plastic wrap) so that the Foie Gras measures the same length as the roll of Wild Boar. Save the trim for another use. Unwrap the plastic from the Wild Boar roll and place it 1 inch from the bottom edge of the Foie Gras. Hold up the bottom edge of the plastic wrap and roll the Foie Gras over the Boar halfway. Use your hand to gently mold and adhere the Foie Gras to the Boar. Pull up the plastic wrap again and pull the Foie Gras completely over the Boar. Pull back slightly to make sure the rest of the Boar is sticking to the Foie Gras. There will be excess Foie Gras at the top of the roll. Use a dough scraper to trim off the excess Foie Gras in a straight, clean line.

At the seam of the roll, use a dough scraper to cut the Foie Gras at a 45-degree angle to make it flush along the seam. Using the plastic, roll the Foie Gras over to seal the roll. Smooth the edge and mold the roll into an even cylinder. There should be no Boar poking out of the ends of the Foie Gras roll; if there is any excess, trim it away.

Cut off the plastic wrap at the bottom of the roll so that only 1 inch of excess remains. Pull up the plastic wrap and completely roll it over the Torchon. Pinch the plastic wrap at the ends of the Torchon and roll by holding the ends of the plastic. Use a cake tester to poke holes to remove any air pockets. Roll again to press out more air. Tie both ends of the Torchon tightly and trim the excess plastic.

Place the Torchon in an ice bath to allow to set for 4 hours.

### HERB RELISH

1/4 cup minced parsley
1/4 cup minced shallots
1/4 cup minced Brussels sprouts
2 teaspoons White Balsamic Vinaigrette (see page 346)

In a small bowl, mix together the parsley, shallots, and minced Brussels sprouts with the White Balsamic Vinaigrette.

## VEGETABLE SALAD

8 baby turnips, green tops intact
2 1/2 teaspoons White Balsamic Vinaigrette (see page 346)
2 Brussels sprouts, leaves separated
8 leaves baby Russian kale
8 tiny beets, green tops intact

Bring a pot of salted water to a boil. Holding the turnips by their tops, submerge just the turnips in the water. Hold them in the water for 4 minutes without submerging the green tops. Dip the tops in the water, then transfer the turnips to a bowl of ice water. Once cool, drain and toss in 1 teaspoon of the White Balsamic Vinaigrette. Add the Brussels sprout leaves to the water, cook for 10 to 15 seconds, and transfer to the bowl of ice water. Once cool, drain and dress with 1/2 teaspoon of the White Balsamic Vinaigrette.

Add the Russian kale to the water and cook for 10 to 15 seconds. Transfer to a bowl of ice water, and, once cool, drain. Holding the beets by their tops, submerge just the beets in the water. Hold them in the water for 12 to 15 minutes without submerging the green tops. Dip the tops in the water, then transfer the beets to a bowl of ice water. Once cool, drain and toss in the remaining 1 teaspoon White Balsamic Vinaigrette.

## TO FINISH

Wild Boar and Foie Gras Torchon
*Fleur de sel*
Herb Relish
Pickled Minced Butternut Squash and Butternut Squash Balls (see page 341)
4 black Mission figs, pulp only
40 huckleberries
Pickled Matsutake Mushrooms (see page 342)
24 leaves red orach
8 sprigs amethyst clusters (the fruit of the beautyberry plant)
Vegetable Salad
8 teaspoons Juniper Berry Crumble (see page 362)
Game Vinaigrette (see page 346)

With a sharp knife, cut the Torchon into 1/2-inch-thick slices. Use a 2 1/2-inch ring cutter to punch the slices and reserve the foie gras trim for another use. Place a slice of Torchon off center on a plate and sprinkle with *fleur de sel*. On top of the Torchon, spoon 1 teaspoon Herb Relish, using a 1-inch ring cutter as a mold. Arrange 2 spoonfuls of the Minced Pickled Butternut Squash and 2 spoonfuls of the fig pulp onto the plate. Arrange 5 huckleberries, Pickled Matsutake Mushrooms, 3 leaves red orach, 2 large and 2 small amethyst clusters, Pickled Butternut Squash Balls, 1 Russian kale leaf, 3 Brussels sprout leaves, 1 tiny beet, and 1 turnip around the Torchon. Finish the plate with the Juniper Crumble and Game Vinaigrette. Repeat with the remaining ingredients, to serve 8.

# HARE
# À LA ROYALE

*Serves 8*

## SAUCE POIVRADE

20 juniper berries
6 allspice berries
1 clove
1/2 teaspoon black peppercorns
1 cup red wine
1 cup red currants
1 1/2 cups Chicken Stock (see page 356)
1 1/2 cups Chicken Jus (see page 356)
4 sprigs thyme
1 bay leaf
3 tablespoons pig blood
1 tablespoon cornstarch
1 teaspoon Dijon mustard
1 teaspoon salt
1/4 ounce Valrhona Araguani chocolate (72 percent), chopped (about 1 tablespoon)

In a sauté pan set over medium heat, toast the juniper berries, allspice, clove, and black peppercorns. Add the red wine and reduce until the pan is almost dry. Add 1/2 cup of the currants and crush into the spices.

Transfer the mixture to a medium saucepan and add the Chicken Stock, Chicken Jus, thyme, and bay leaf. Simmer until the sauce coats the back of a spoon. In a small bowl, whisk together the pig blood, cornstarch, and mustard and whisk the mixture into the boiling sauce. Simmer for 5 minutes to cook out the starch. Season with the salt and chocolate and stir in the remaining 1/2 cup currants. Keep warm until ready to use.

## BLACK TRUFFLE TOAST

2 black truffles
1 loaf Brioche (see page 364)
1/4 cup Clarified Butter (see page 370)
1 teaspoon *fleur de sel*

On a mandoline, thinly slice the black truffles. Trim the crusts off the Brioche and cut into eight 1/4-inch-thick triangles measuring 2 3/4 by 2 1/2 by 3/4 inches. In a small sauté pan, heat 2 teaspoons of the Clarified Butter. Add 2 pieces of the Brioche, toasting on one side until golden brown. Repeat with the remaining Clarified Butter and Brioche pieces.

On a piece of acetate, lay out the black truffle slices, overlapping slightly, about 3 1/2 inches long and 1 inch wide for each portion, making 8 portions total. Place the toasted Brioche (toasted side down) on the truffle slices. Using a paring knife, trim the black truffle so that there are no overhanging truffle slices. Carefully flip the Brioche over so that the truffles are on top. Sprinkle with *fleur de sel*.

## WILD HARE RAGOUT

1 whole hare, skinned and gutted, head removed
One 750-milliliter bottle red wine
1 carrot, chopped
1 stalk celery, chopped
1 white onion, chopped
10 black peppercorns
4 cloves
1 teaspoon juniper berries
2 allspice berries
Salt
2 tablespoons canola oil
1 tablespoon tomato paste
4 cups Chicken Jus (see page 356)
2 sprigs thyme
1 bay leaf

Rinse the hare and pat it dry. Remove the legs and use a heavy knife to cut the torso in half crosswise. You will now have six pieces. Place the hare in a large nonreactive container and cover with the red wine, carrot, celery, and onion. Make a sachet by wrapping the peppercorns, cloves, juniper berries, and allspice in cheesecloth. Tie together with butcher's twine and add to the marinade. Cover and marinate in the refrigerator for 48 hours.

Preheat the oven to 275°F. Strain the hare, reserving the liquid, the vegetables, and the sachet. In a large saucepan, bring the liquid to a simmer, skimming of any fats and impurities that rise to the top. Pat the hare dry and season with salt. Heat the oil in a large straight-sided oven-safe pot over medium heat. Sear the hare until browned on all sides, about 10 minutes. Remove from the pot and pour off any excess oil. Add the reserved carrot, celery, onion, and celery root and sweat for 10 minutes. Add the tomato paste and cook with the vegetables for 3 minutes. Deglaze with the simmered liquid. Add the Chicken Jus, thyme, bay leaf, and the reserved sachet. Bring to a simmer and return the hare to the pot.

Cover and transfer to the oven. Braise the hare in the oven until the meat comes off the bones, about 2 hours and 30 minutes. Once the hare is cooked, remove from the oven and allow to rest, uncovered, for 30 minutes. Remove the hare from the cooking liquid. Strain the liquid and transfer it to a straight-sided pan. Reduce to a glaze over medium heat, skimming frequently. Meanwhile, pick the meat from the bones. Shred the meat with your hands and chill until the cooking liquid is reduced.

Add the shredded meat to the liquid to make the Ragout. Simmer the meat with the cooking liquid for 20 minutes and season with 1 teaspoon salt.

## POTATO MOUSSELINE ESPUMA

1 pound La Ratte fingerling potatoes, peeled
1 tablespoon plus 1 teaspoon salt
3 cups cream
1 tablespoon Brown Butter (see page 370)
2 N$_2$O cartridges

Place the potatoes and 1 tablespoon of the salt in a medium saucepan and cover with cold water. Bring to a simmer over medium-low heat and cook until tender, 30 to 35 minutes. In the meantime, reduce the cream in a small saucepan over medium heat until 2 cups remain. Drain the cooked potatoes and transfer to a blender. Puree the hot, reduced cream and Brown Butter with the potatoes. Blend on high for 2 minutes and season with the remaining 1 teaspoon salt. Strain through a chinois and transfer the potatoes to a whipped-cream canister. Charge with the N$_2$O cartridges and hold in a water bath maintained at 145°F by an immersion circulator until ready to serve.

## FOIE GRAS TORCHON

One 2-pound lobe grade-A foie gras
1 tablespoon salt
1/2 teaspoon pink curing salt
1 teaspoon sugar
1/2 teaspoon white pepper
2 teaspoons Madeira
1 teaspoon Cognac

Bring the foie gras to room temperature to soften. Separate the main lobes and remove the veins with tweezers and a paring knife. Pass the foie gras through a tamis, season with the salt, pink salt, sugar, and white pepper, and place in a *sous vide* bag. Add the Madeira and Cognac, seal the bag, and marinate in the refrigerator for 24 hours. Remove the foie gras from the refrigerator and allow it to come to room temperature. Transfer to a large mixing bowl and whip with a rubber spatula to re-emulsify. Cover with plastic wrap and refrigerate for 15 to 20 minutes, until cool but not firm.

Using a damp towel, wipe down a smooth and spacious work surface. Lay out 3 long sheets (about 3 feet long each) of plastic wrap such that they overlap slightly. Wipe the plastic wrap with a damp towel. Spoon the foie gras in a line onto the plastic wrap so that it is about 11 inches long and a little less than 2 inches wide. Fold the plastic wrap over the foie gras and roll tightly to make a cylinder measuring 2 inches in diameter. As you roll the cylinder, poke several small holes in the roll with a cake tester and roll again to squeeze out any air bubbles. Tie off the ends tightly and trim the excess plastic wrap. Place the Torchon in ice water to set completely, about 3 hours.

## TO FINISH

Wild Hare Ragout
Sauce Poivrade
Foie Gras Torchon
Potato Mousseline Espuma
Black Truffle Toast

Spoon the Wild Hare Ragout into a small bowl. Top with 2 tablespoons of Sauce Poivrade. Using a sharp knife, slice the Torchon 1/8 inch thick. Place a Torchon slice on top of the Ragout. Expel the Potato Mousseline Espuma on top. Repeat with the remaining Ragout, Torchon, and Potato, to serve 8. Serve each with the Black Truffle Toast.

# SQUAB
## ROASTED WITH CABBAGE AND APPLES

*Serves 8*

## SQUAB BREASTS

4 whole squabs
3 tablespoons salt
16 sprigs thyme
2 tablespoons canola oil

Remove the breasts and legs from the squabs. Reserve the squab legs for the Farce, the bodies for the Sauce, and the livers for the Mousse. Remove any excess fat from the breasts and legs, but do not remove the skin.

Preheat the oven to 300°F. Place a roasting rack in the oven to preheat. Season the breasts with the salt. Place 2 squab breasts and 2 sprigs thyme in a *sous vide* bag and vacuum-seal. Repeat with the remaining breasts. Cook the breasts in a water bath maintained at 145°F by an immersion circulator for 10 minutes and transfer to a bowl of ice water. When ready to serve, remove the breasts from the bags and pat them dry. Heat 2 large sauté pans over medium-high heat with 1 tablespoon of oil in each pan. Place 4 breasts in each of the hot pans, skin side down, to brown and crisp the skin, 45 seconds to 1 minute. Transfer the squab breasts to the preheated roasting rack, skin side up. Finish cooking the squab breasts in the oven, 5 to 7 minutes. Remove the squab from the oven and allow to rest for 5 minutes before slicing as directed under "To Finish."

## BRAISED RED CABBAGE WITH APPLES

2 pounds red cabbage
5 tablespoons butter
1 Granny Smith apple, peeled and grated
1 1/2 teaspoons thinly sliced shallots
1 1/2 teaspoons red wine vinegar
1 1/2 cups red wine
1/2 cup sugar
1 1/2 tablespoons salt
Black pepper

Peel the leaves off the cabbage, remove the thick veins, and cut the leaves into approximately 2-inch squares. Melt 3 tablespoons of the butter in a small sauté pan and sweat the apple and shallots until soft, about 10 minutes. Transfer to a blender and puree until smooth.

Preheat the oven to 350°F. In a large, oven-safe, straight-sided sauté pan, heat the red wine vinegar over low heat, add the cabbage, and sweat for 10 minutes. Add the apple and shallot puree and cover with a cartouche (lid made of parchment paper). Continue to simmer over low heat for 20 minutes. In a small bowl, whisk together the red wine, sugar, and salt. Add 2 tablespoons of the mixture to the cabbage and stir to combine. Cover and transfer the pan to the oven. Stir the cabbage every 20 minutes, adding 2 tablespoons of the red wine mixture each time. This will take about 2 hours total. As the cabbage becomes completely tender, transfer the pan from the oven to the stove and cook uncovered over low heat until the liquid has reduced. Add the remaining 2 tablespoons butter, tossing until the cabbage is glazed. Chill the cabbage in its liquid over ice.

## SAVOY CABBAGE

1 head Savoy cabbage
2 tablespoons Chicken Stock (see page 356)
2 tablespoons butter
1 pinch nutmeg

Peel apart the cabbage, discarding the outermost leaves. Pull away 16 leaves, using only the green leaves closest to the core. Cut the leaves into approximately 2-inch squares. Bring a large pot of salted water to a boil. Add the cabbage and cook for 2 minutes. Transfer to a bowl of ice water and, once cold, drain.

Heat the Chicken Stock in a sauté pan over medium heat. Add the cabbage and warm through. Add the butter, reducing to a glaze. Finish with the nutmeg.

## RED WINE GLAZE

10 black peppercorns
5 cloves
3 pods star anise
2 allspice berries
1 cinnamon stick
4 cups red wine
2 cups red port
1 cup red wine vinegar
2/3 cup sugar

In a small saucepan over medium heat, toast the peppercorns, cloves, star anise, allspice, and cinnamon for 1 minute. Remove from the heat and add the red wine, port, vinegar, and sugar. Reduce over medium heat until the consistency of syrup. Strain the glaze and keep warm.

## SQUAB LIVER MOUSSE

Livers from the 4 squabs, plus enough chicken livers
    to make 1 pound total
1 pound butter
3 tablespoons salt
1 cup minced shallots
1/4 cup minced celery heart
1/4 cup minced garlic
1/2 cup red port
2 teaspoons pink curing salt
1 cup cream
1 teaspoon Dijon mustard
1 pinch nutmeg

Rinse the livers in ice water and trim off all fat and veins. Pat dry and refrigerate until ready to use.

In a small sauté pan, heat 1/2 cup of the butter over medium heat until it is foamy but not browned. Cut the rest of the butter into cubes and keep at room temperature. Season the livers with 1 teaspoon of the salt and lightly sear the livers in the foamy butter. Flip them over and continue cooking until medium. Remove the livers from the pan.

Add the minced shallots, celery heart, and garlic to the pan and gently sweat the vegetables over low heat until they are tender but not browned. Season with 1 teaspoon of the salt. Add the port and pink salt to the pan and allow the alcohol to evaporate. Whisk in the cream and mustard and bring the mixture to a slow simmer. Remove from the heat.

Place the seared livers in a blender and puree on high speed. Gradually incorporate the cooked vegetables and the hot liquid from the pan. Add the room-temperature butter, a few cubes at a time. Season the Mousse with the nutmeg and the remaining 2 tablespoons plus 1 teaspoon salt. While the Mousse is still hot, strain it through a chinois and chill.

## MARINATED FOIE GRAS

One 2-pound lobe grade-A foie gras
1 tablespoon salt
1/2 teaspoon pink curing salt
1 teaspoon sugar
1/2 teaspoon white pepper
2 teaspoons Madeira
1 teaspoon Cognac

Bring the foie gras to room temperature to soften. Separate the main lobes and remove the veins with tweezers and a paring knife. Pass the foie gras through a tamis, season with the salt, pink salt, sugar, and white pepper, and place it in a *sous vide* bag. Add the Madeira and Cognac, seal the bag, and marinate in the refrigerator for 24 hours. Remove the foie gras from the refrigerator and allow it to come to room temperature. Transfer to a large mixing bowl and whip with a rubber spatula to re-emulsify. Transfer to a *sous vide* bag, vacuum-seal, and refrigerate.

## SQUAB FARCE

16 squab legs
1/4 cup sugar
1 1/3 cups plus 1/2 teaspoon salt
1 teaspoon black pepper
5 sprigs thyme
4 cups duck fat
1 cup chicken livers
1 tablespoon butter
2 tablespoons Marinated Foie Gras,
    at room temperature
1/3 cup Squab Liver Mousse
1 tablespoon diced (1/16 inch) shallot
1 teaspoon sherry vinegar
1 teaspoon finely minced parsley

Place the squab legs in a nonreactive container. Cover with the sugar, 1 1/3 cups of the salt, the black pepper, and the thyme, and cure in the refrigerator for 1 hour.

Preheat the oven to 300°F. In a medium saucepan over medium heat, melt the duck fat. In the meantime, rinse the salt cure off of the squab legs and pat dry. Transfer to a deep baking dish and pour the melted fat over them. Cover with aluminum foil and cook in the oven for 1 hour or until the meat is falling from the bone. Cool the squab legs in the duck fat at room temperature and then refrigerate. Store in the fat until ready to use.

When ready to use, preheat the oven to 300°F. Heat the legs to remelt the duck fat. Gently remove the squab legs, peel off the skin, and pull the meat from the bones, being careful to remove every pinbone. Discard the skin and bones. Chop the squab meat into 1/4-inch pieces.

Rinse the livers in ice water, trim off all fat and veins, and pat dry. Heat the butter in a large sauté pan over medium heat until it begins to foam. Season the livers with the remaining 1/2 teaspoon salt and sear them on both sides until cooked to medium, about 1 minute on each side. Drain on paper towels and cool in the refrigerator. Once chilled, cut into 1/8-inch pieces.

In a large bowl, use a rubber spatula to fold together the chilled livers, Marinated Foie Gras, 1/4 cup of the chopped squab legs, Squab Liver Mousse, shallot, vinegar, and parsley. Place the mixture into a piping bag and keep refrigerated until ready to use. Before serving, soften the Farce at room temperature.

## SQUAB SAUCE

2 tablespoons canola oil
Squab bones from 4 bodies, cut into 1-inch pieces
5 medium shallots, thinly sliced
6 cloves garlic
1 Granny Smith apple, peeled and diced
1/4 head red cabbage, thinly sliced,
    plus 1/2 cup thinly sliced
1 cup red wine
1/4 cup red wine vinegar
2 quarts Chicken Stock (see page 356)
2 1/2 cups Chicken Jus (see page 356)
1 cup Calvados
1 cup cabbage juice (from 1/2 large head of
    red cabbage)
1 sprig thyme
1 1/2 tablespoons diced (1/8 inch) foie gras
1 tablespoon butter
1 teaspoon salt

Heat the canola oil in a large, straight-sided sauté pan over high heat. Add the squab bones and roast for 5 minutes, until evenly browned. Pour off any excess oil. Reduce the heat to low and add the shallots and garlic, sweating until soft and translucent, about 3 minutes. Add the apple and cabbage and sweat until tender, about 10 minutes. Deglaze with the Calvados, reduce by half, and add the red wine. Reduce the liquid until it is almost dry, about 15 minutes. Add the vinegar and cabbage juice and reduce by half. Add the Chicken Stock and Chicken Jus and bring to a simmer. Simmer on low for 45 minutes, skimming frequently. Reduce over medium heat to 2 cups. Add the thyme and simmer for 5 minutes.

In a small sauté pan over medium-low heat, melt the foie gras. Strain, discarding the solids and adding the foie gras fat to the sauce. Stir in the butter and season with salt.

## APPLE CHIPS

1 Lady apple

Thinly slice the apple on a mandoline to 1/16 inch thick.

Place the sliced apple into the dehydrator and dehydrate for 8 to 10 hours.

Alternatively, preheat the oven to 175°F. Place the apples slices on a baking sheet lined with a silicone baking mat and dehydrate in the oven for 2 hours or until dry.

## BREAD CRISPS

1/4 loaf country bread

Preheat the oven to 200°F. Thinly slice the bread on a rotating deli slicer or with a sharp knife, to produce 8 slices. Place the bread slices on a baking sheet lined with parchment paper. Bake in the oven until the bread is dried and crispy, 15 to 20 minutes.

## TO FINISH

Squab Breasts
1/2 cup Brown Butter (see page 370)
*Fleur de sel*
Black pepper
Braised Red Cabbage with Apples
Red Wine Glaze
Squab Farce
Bread Crisps
8 tablespoons White Apple Puree (see page 350)
Savoy Cabbage
24 Pickled Dehydrated Apples (see page 342)
Apple Chips
Squab Sauce
16 leaves baby Russian kale

Slice the Squab Breasts in half lengthwise and brush with Brown Butter. Season with *fleur de sel* and black pepper. In a large sauté pan over medium heat, glaze the Braised Red Cabbage with Apples in 1/4 cup of the Red Wine Glaze. Spread 1 tablespoon of Squab Farce on the tip of each Bread Crisp.

Warm the White Apple Puree in a small saucepan over low heat. On each plate, spoon a streak of White Apple Puree down the center. Place a Squab Breast on top. Arrange the Braised Red Cabbage, glazed Savoy Cabbage, 3 Pickled Dehydrated Apples, and 1 Apple Chip around the squab. Finish with the Squab Sauce, 2 kale leaves, and a Bread Crisp with Squab Farce.

# VENISON
## GLAZED WITH PEAR AND BLACK TRUMPET MUSHROOMS

*Serves 8*

## JUNIPER SALT

2 tablespoons juniper berries
1/3 cup salt

In a small sauté pan over medium heat, toast the juniper berries until fragrant. Grind the toasted juniper to a powder in a spice grinder. Combine the powder with the salt and reserve in an airtight container.

## VENISON

1 venison loin, 1 1/2 to 2 pounds, cut in half crosswise
1/4 cup Juniper Salt
6 sprigs thyme
2 cups Venison Jus (see page 357)
2 tablespoons canola oil
4 tablespoons butter
8 juniper berries

Season the venison loin lightly with a few teaspoons of the Juniper Salt. Place 2 sprigs thyme on each loin half, and tightly roll the 2 halves with thyme in plastic wrap. Place the venison into individual *sous vide* bags and vacuum-seal. Cook the venison in a water bath maintained at 145°F by an immersion circulator for 25 minutes. Remove from the water and allow to rest for 10 minutes. In the meantime, reduce the Venison Jus in a large straight-sided sauté pan over medium-low heat until it is the consistency of honey. Heat 2 large sauté pans with 1 tablespoon oil in each over high heat. Remove the venison from the bags and remove the plastic wrap and thyme. Pat dry with paper towels. Place a venison portion in each pan and quickly sear on all sides, about 1 minute total. Add 2 tablespoons of butter to each, as well as a thyme sprig and 4 cracked juniper berries. Baste the venison for 30 seconds. Roll the venison in the reduced Venison Jus and sprinkle with the remaining Juniper Salt.

## SAUCE POIVRADE

20 juniper berries
6 allspice berries
1 clove
1/2 teaspoon black peppercorns
1 cup red wine
1 cup huckleberries
1 1/2 cups Chicken Stock (see page 356)
1 1/2 cups Venison Jus (see page 357)
4 sprigs thyme
1 bay leaf
3 tablespoons pig blood
1 teaspoon cornstarch
1 teaspoon Dijon mustard
1 teaspoon salt
1/4 ounce Valrhona Araguani chocolate (72 percent),
   chopped (about 1 tablespoon)

In a sauté pan set over medium heat, toast the juniper berries, allspice, clove, and black peppercorns for 2 minutes, until fragrant. Add the red wine and reduce until the pan is almost dry. Add 1/2 cup of the huckleberries and crush into the spices.

Transfer the mixture to a medium saucepan and add the Chicken Stock, Venison Jus, thyme, and bay leaf. Simmer, and reduce, until the sauce coats the back of a spoon. In a small bowl, whisk together the pig blood, cornstarch, and mustard and whisk the mixture into the simmering sauce. Simmer for 5 minutes to cook out the starch. Season with the salt and chocolate and strain through a chinois. Stir in the remaining 1/2 cup huckleberries. Keep warm until ready to use.

## PEAR COOKING LIQUID

1 cup Sauternes
1/4 cup sugar
2 tablespoons cup pear brandy
1 tablespoon salt
8 juniper berries
4 cloves

In a small saucepan over low heat, combine the Sauternes, sugar, brandy, salt, juniper, and cloves. Reduce by half and then chill over ice.

## POACHED PEARS

8 red Anjou pears, peeled
1/2 cup Pear Cooking Liquid

Slice the pears lengthwise to retain only the center 1/4-inch-thick portions, being sure to keep the stem attached. Reserve the rest of the pear for another use. Place the pear slices in a *sous vide* bag with the Pear Cooking Liquid and steam at 165°F for 15 minutes. Chill in an ice bath. Remove the cooked pears from the bag and reserve the Cooking Liquid. Core the hearts of the pears with a 1 1/2-inch ring cutter. Place the pears on a rimmed baking sheet lined with parchment paper. Reduce the Pear Cooking Liquid in a small saucepan over low heat until 1/4 cup remains. Keep warm until ready to use.

## BLACK TRUMPET DUXELLE

1 cup diced black trumpet mushrooms (1/8 inch)
1 cup diced double-smoked bacon (1/8 inch)
1 teaspoon raspberry vinegar
1 cup diced onion (1/8 inch)
1/2 teaspoon salt

To clean the black trumpet mushrooms, pull them apart and rinse under cold running water, being sure to remove any dirt. Allow them to dry on paper towels.

In a small sauté pan over low heat, render the bacon until it begins to caramelize, about 10 minutes. Add the raspberry vinegar and cook for 1 minute. Add the onion and sweat until soft and translucent, about 3 minutes. Add the black trumpet mushrooms and sweat until tender, another 4 minutes. Season with the salt.

## BACON PANNA COTTA

2 pounds double-smoked bacon, diced (1/4 inch)
2 quarts half-and-half
1 tablespoon agar-agar (3.5 grams)

Combine the diced bacon with the half-and-half in a medium saucepan and bring to a simmer over medium heat. Reduce the heat to low and steep for 45 minutes. Skim away any rendered fat and strain. Reserve the bacon-infused liquid and chill over ice. Whisk the agar-agar into 3 cups of the cold bacon cream and bring to a simmer in a medium saucepan over medium heat. Simmer for 5 minutes to be sure the agar-agar is hydrated. Line a 9-by-13-inch rimmed baking sheet with acetate. Strain the mixture and pour it into the baking sheet to 1/4 inch thick and chill, level, in the refrigerator for 1 hour to set.

Once the panna cotta is set, use a 1 1/2-inch ring cutter to cut rounds out of the Panna Cotta. Remove the rounds with a small offset spatula. Insert the rounds into the cored hearts of the Poached Pears.

## BRUSSELS SPROUTS

32 baby green Brussels sprouts
1 teaspoon White Balsamic Vinaigrette (see page 346)
Salt
2 tablespoons Chicken Stock (see page 356)
2 tablespoons butter
2 sprigs thyme

Peel off the outer leaves from the Brussels sprouts. Toss 24 of the leaves in the White Balsamic Vinaigrette with a pinch of salt.

Bring a pot of salted water to a boil. Add the baby Brussels sprouts and cook for 3 to 4 minutes. Transfer to a bowl of ice water, and, once cold, drain. Heat a medium sauté pan over medium heat and add the Chicken Stock. Add the baby Brussels sprouts and warm through, about 1 minute. Add the butter and thyme and toss to glaze. Season with salt to taste.

## BLACK TRUMPET MUSHROOMS

1 cup black trumpet mushrooms
2 tablespoons butter
2 teaspoons minced shallots
2 sprigs thyme
2 tablespoons Chicken Stock (see page 356)
1/2 teaspoon salt

To clean the black trumpet mushrooms, pull them apart and rinse under cold running water, being sure to remove any dirt. Allow them to dry on paper towels.

Heat the butter in a medium sauté pan over medium heat. When it begins to foam, add the shallots and sweat until translucent. Add the black trumpet mushrooms and the thyme and sauté for about 3 minutes. Add the Chicken Stock, season with the salt, and cook until the stock is reduced and the mushrooms are glazed.

## TO FINISH

1/4 cup Pear Cooking Liquid
1/2 cup butter
Poached Pears with Bacon Panna Cotta
Black Trumpet Duxelle
Venison
1/2 cup Brown Butter (see page 370)
Juniper Salt
Black Trumpet Mushrooms
Brussels Sprouts
Sauce Poivrade

Heat 2 large sauté pans over low heat. Add 2 tablespoons of the Pear Cooking Liquid to each pan and whisk in 2 tablespoons butter to each to form a glaze. Carefully add the Poached Pears with Bacon Panna Cotta and spoon the sauce over to glaze and reheat them. Do not heat the pan too much, or the panna cotta will melt. Once warm, remove the Pears from the pans and, using a 1 1/2-inch ring cutter as a mold, spoon 1 teaspoon of the Black Trumpet Duxelle onto the Bacon Panna Cotta and flatten slightly.

Place 1 glazed Poached Pear with Bacon Panna Cotta in the center of a plate. Slice off the 2 ends of each Venison portion and then slice each into 4 even pieces. Halve each piece crosswise. Brush the cut sides with Brown Butter and season with Juniper Salt.

Place the Venison on the Pear. Arrange the Black Trumpet Mushrooms and glazed Brussels Sprouts on the plate. Garnish with 3 dressed Brussels Sprout leaves and finish with the Sauce Poivrade. Repeat with the remaining ingredients, to serve 8.

# HOBELCHÄS
## SHAVED WITH APPLES AND CHESTNUTS

*Serves 8*

8 fresh chestnuts
24 thin slices Hobelchäs
24 leaves parsley
24 thinly sliced Granny Smith apple (half-moon shapes)
24 pieces thinly sliced Granny Smith apple (1 1/4-inch rounds)
16 celery leaves
8 teaspoons Red Wine Apple Puree (see page 353)

Using a paring knife, score a small *x* in the hard outer shells of the chestnuts. Peel the chestnuts so that only the white flesh is left and then thinly slice them.

Arrange 3 slices Hobelchäs on a plate. Scatter the chestnuts, parsley, apples, and celery leaves on and around the cheese. Smear 1 teaspoon Red Wine Apple Puree next to the cheese. Repeat with the remaining ingredients, to serve 8.

# CASSIS
## KIR ROYALE

*Serves 8*

### LEMON MERINGUE

3 egg whites
3/4 cup sugar
Zest of 1 lemon

Preheat the oven to 175°F. In a stand mixer fitted with the whisk attachment, whip the egg whites until foamy. Slowly incorporate the sugar and continue to whip the egg whites until they are glossy and hold stiff peaks. Using a spatula, fold in the lemon zest. Transfer to a piping bag fitted with a 1/2-inch round tip. Line a baking sheet with parchment paper and pipe tubes of meringue that are the length of the baking sheet onto the paper. Place them in the oven overnight to dehydrate. Break the meringue into small pieces and reserve them in an airtight container.

### CHAMPAGNE FOAM

3 sheets gelatin
1 1/2 cups Champagne
1/2 cup sugar
4 egg whites
1 tablespoon citric acid
3 $N_2O$ cartridges

To bloom the gelatin, place the sheets in a bowl of ice water for 10 minutes, until soft. In a small saucepan over medium heat, warm the Champagne with the sugar until the sugar is dissolved. Squeeze the gelatin to remove excess moisture and melt into the warm Champagne. Chill over ice until just cold but not set. Using a hand blender, mix the Champagne mixture with the egg whites and citric acid. Strain the mixture through a sifter (not a chinois). Fill a whipped-cream canister two thirds full with the mixture and charge with the $N_2O$ cartridges. Refrigerate until ready to use.

### SUGAR TUILE

1/2 cup poured fondant
1/4 cup glucose syrup

Combine the fondant, glucose, and 1/2 cup water in a small saucepan over medium heat. Cook until the sugar is a light caramel. Pour the cooked sugar onto a silicone baking mat and allow it to cool to room temperature. Once cool, break into pieces and grind in a spice grinder to a fine powder.

Preheat the oven to 325°F. Sift a thin layer of the sugar powder onto a rimmed baking sheet lined with a silicone baking mat and bake for 10 minutes. Cool to room temperature and break into shards. Reserve in a cool, dry place.

### TO FINISH

8 teaspoons Lemon Gel (see page 348)
Lemon Meringue
8 teaspoons black currants
Cassis Sorbet (see page 366)
Champagne Foam
Sugar Tuile

On the bottom of a plate, squeeze 1 teaspoon of the Lemon Gel. Spoon 1 tablespoon of the Lemon Meringue pieces and 1 teaspoon of the black currants on top of the Gel. Place 1 quenelle of the Cassis Sorbet on top. Expel 1 1/2 tablespoons Champagne Foam on top of the Sorbet and finish with a piece of the Sugar Tuile. Repeat with the remaining ingredients, to serve 8.

# APPLE
## AND CARAMEL

*Serves 8*

**TOFFEE SAUCE**
1 quart cream
3 cups milk
1 1/2 cups dark brown sugar
1/2 cup butter
1 1/2 teaspoons salt

In a large saucepan over medium heat, combine the
cream with 2 cups of the milk, the brown sugar, butter,
and salt. Bring the mixture to a boil and reduce by half.
The color of the reduction should be a deep tan. Add the
remaining 1 cup milk, strain, and keep in a warm place,
such as near a warm oven or stove.

## TOFFEE PUDDING CAKE

1 1/2 teaspoons baking soda
2 cups flour
2 teaspoons baking powder
1 cup butter
3/4 cup sugar
Zest of 1 lemon
1/2 vanilla bean, split lengthwise and scraped
1 teaspoon salt
4 eggs
Toffee Sauce

Preheat the oven to 350°F. Combine 1 cup water with the baking soda in a small pot and bring to a boil over medium heat. Set aside to cool. In a mixing bowl, stir together the flour and baking powder. In a stand mixer fitted with a paddle attachment, cream together the butter and sugar. Once the butter and sugar are combined, add the lemon zest, vanilla bean seeds, and salt. Add the eggs, one at a time, allowing each one to be incorporated before adding the next. The mixture will appear curdled. Mix in half of the flour mixture and stream in the baking soda mixture. Continue to mix and make sure that the liquid is absorbed. Scrape down the sides of the bowl. Mix in the remaining flour mixture. Line a 9-by-13-inch rimmed baking sheet with parchment paper and coat with vegetable spray. Pour the cake batter into the prepared baking sheet and smooth the top with an offset spatula. Bake until golden and the center of the cake springs back when touched, about 25 minutes. Cool and cut into 1-by-2-inch rectangles.

Reduce the oven temperature to 275°F. Place the rectangles on a wire rack and warm in the oven for 5 minutes. Spoon the Toffee Sauce over the cakes, making sure that all sides are coated. Return the coated cakes to the oven and bake for another 5 minutes. Cool to room temperature.

## WALNUT CHUTNEY

1 cup walnuts
1 1/2 tablespoons sugar
1 1/2 teaspoons walnut oil
1 teaspoon salt
1/2 cup almond flour

Preheat the oven to 275°F. Bring a pot of salted water to a boil. Add the walnuts and cook for 30 to 45 seconds. Transfer to a bowl of ice water, and, once cool, transfer to a baking sheet. Toast the walnuts in the oven for 15 minutes or until dry. While the walnuts are still warm, puree them in a food processor with the sugar, walnut oil, and salt. The resulting mixture should be coarse yet still hold its shape when pressed. Roll the walnut chutney into 1/2-teaspoon-sized balls and then roll them in the almond flour. Once they've all been rolled, roll once more in the almond flour.

## CARAMEL LIQUID

1 1/4 cups plus 1/3 cup sugar
1 cup warm apple cider
1 vanilla bean, split lengthwise and scraped

Place 1 1/4 cups of the sugar in a saucepan over medium-high heat and cook to a very dark caramel. Add the apple cider and continue to boil until the caramel dissolves. Add the remaining 1/3 cup sugar and the vanilla bean seeds and continue to boil for 2 more minutes to dissolve the sugar. Remove from the heat, steep for 20 minutes, and strain through a chinois.

## CARAMEL GLAZE

1/2 cup Caramel Liquid
3/4 cup apple cider
3/4 cup cream
1 tablespoon iota carrageenan (14.5 grams)
1/2 teaspoon salt
1/8 teaspoon xanthan gum (0.4 gram)

In a saucepan over medium heat, combine the Caramel Liquid with the apple cider, cream, iota carrageenan, salt, and xanthan gum. Bring to a rolling boil and continue to boil until the mixture is loose, about 10 minutes. Keep melted over low heat.

## POACHED FUJI AND GRANNY SMITH APPLES

Juice of 2 lemons
6 Fuji apples
3 Granny Smith apples
1 quart apple cider
1 cup Caramel Liquid
Caramel Glaze

In a large bowl, combine the lemon juice with 8 cups water. Quarter 2 of the Fuji apples and trim each quarter into six-sided oblongs. You should have 8 pieces total. Place the oblongs in the lemon water. Peel the remaining apples and use a 3/4-inch melon baller to extract 32 balls from the Fuji apples. Use a 1/2-inch melon baller and extract 16 balls from the Granny Smith apples. To poach the apples, place the apple cider and Caramel Liquid in a medium pot. Add the apple oblongs and balls and bring the liquid to a slow simmer over medium-low heat. Simmer for 30 minutes, remove from the heat, and hold in the liquid until ready to serve.

Just before serving, dip the Granny Smith apple balls in the melted Caramel Glaze, dip them back into the Caramel Liquid, and then transfer to a baking sheet lined with acetate.

## WALNUT TOFFEE

1 cup sugar
1/2 cup light brown sugar
1/2 cup butter
1/3 cup glucose syrup
1/3 cup milk powder
1 tablespoon salt
1 cup walnuts, toasted and cooled

Combine the sugar, brown sugar, butter, glucose syrup, milk powder, salt, and 2 tablespoons water in a small saucepan. Cook over medium heat, stirring constantly until the mixture reaches 295 to 300°F. Pour onto a baking sheet lined with parchment paper and cool to room temperature. Once cool, grind in a food processor. Grind the walnuts separately and combine with the ground toffee. Store in an airtight container.

## TO FINISH

8 tablespoons Granny Smith Apple Puree (see page 350)
Toffee Pudding Cake
Poached Fuji and Granny Smith Apples
Walnut Chutney
8 teaspoons Caramel Gel (see page 347)
Walnut Toffee
Maldon salt
Granny Smith  Apple Ice Cream (see page 368)

Spread 1 tablespoon of the Granny Smith Apple Puree onto a plate to create an elongated S-shape. Place the glazed Toffee Pudding Cake in the center of the Puree. Arrange 1 Poached Fuji Apple oblong, 2 glazed Poached Granny Smith Apple balls, and 4 Poached Fuji Apple balls around the cake. Arrange 2 Walnut Chutney balls on either side. Dot 1 teaspoon Caramel Gel around the cake and place 1 teaspoon Walnut Toffee on top of the cake. Sprinkle with a few grains of Maldon Salt. Spoon a quenelle of the Granny Smith Apple Ice Cream on top of the Walnut Toffee. Repeat with the remaining ingredients, to serve 8.

# HAZELNUT
## AND GRAPES

*Serves 8*

## PISTACHIO TUILE

3/4 cup sugar
2/3 cup butter
1/3 cup glucose syrup
1/4 cup milk
1 cup finely ground pistachio nuts

In a medium saucepan, bring the sugar, butter, glucose, and milk to 220°F, stirring constantly. Remove from the heat and stir in the ground pistachios. Allow the mixture to cool slightly. Scoop 1/4 cup of the Tuile batter onto a sheet of parchment paper. Cover with another sheet of parchment paper and roll the Tuile very thin, about 1/8 inch thick. Repeat with another 1/4 cup of batter. Freeze for 8 hours or overnight until it becomes hard.

Preheat the oven to 350°F. When ready to bake, transfer to a baking sheet, peel off the top layer of parchment paper, and bake for 6 to 8 minutes.

## CHESTNUT PASTRY CREAM

1 sheet gelatin
1 1/2 cups Sweetened Chestnut Puree (see page 351)
1 1/4 cups cream
1 1/4 cups milk
2/3 cup sugar
1/2 cup pastry cream powder
1/2 teaspoon salt
1 vanilla bean, split lengthwise and scraped
1 egg
3 egg yolks
1/4 cup butter, softened

Bloom the gelatin by placing the sheet in a bowl of ice water for 10 minutes, until pliable. Combine the Chestnut Puree, cream, milk, and 1/3 cup of the sugar in a medium saucepan and heat to just under a boil. In another bowl, combine the pastry cream powder, the remaining 1/3 cup of sugar, and the vanilla seeds. Whisk in the egg and egg yolks.

Slowly whisk the hot milk into the egg mixture. Bring to a boil, whisking constantly, and cook for 2 minutes. The pastry cream will thicken quickly, so whisk it vigorously. Remove from the heat, and allow it to cool slightly. Squeeze the gelatin to remove excess moisture and stir the gelatin into the warm cream mixture, along with the butter. Whisk until the pastry cream is smooth and combined. Pass through a tamis and refrigerate until cold.

## CHESTNUT BAVAROIS

3 cups Chestnut Pastry Cream
1 cup cream

In a stand mixer fitted with the whisk attachment, break up the Chestnut Pastry Cream. Slowly incorporate the cream and whip until the mixture is light and fluffy and forms peaks. Keep the Bavarois refrigerated until ready to use.

## HAZELNUT MERINGUES

3 egg whites
3/4 cup sugar
1 cup finely ground Hazelnut Crumble (see page 362)

Preheat the oven to 200°F. In a stand mixer fitted with the whisk attachment, whip the egg whites until foamy and sprinkle in the sugar. Continue to whip the egg whites until they are glossy white and form firm peaks. Fold in the finely ground Hazelnut Crumble using a rubber spatula. Transfer the Meringue to a piping bag fitted with a 1/2-inch round piping tip. Line a baking sheet with parchment paper and pipe on varying sizes of Meringue. Dry the Meringues overnight in the oven.

## HAZELNUT PAVLOVAS

3 egg whites
3/4 cup sugar
1 cup finely ground Hazelnut Crumble (see page 362)

Preheat the oven to 300°F. In a stand mixer fitted with the whisk attachment, whip the egg whites until foamy and sprinkle in the sugar. Continue to whip the egg whites until they are glossy white and form firm peaks. Fold in the finely ground Hazelnut Crumble using a rubber spatula. Transfer the meringue to a piping bag fitted with a 1/2-inch round piping tip. Line a baking sheet with parchment paper and pipe on varying sizes of meringue. Dry the meringues in the oven for 20 to 30 minutes. They will have thin shells and soft centers. Cool and keep in a cool, dry, airtight container.

## REHYDRATED GOLDEN RAISINS

1/2 cup Sauternes
1/4 cup golden raisins

In a small saucepan over medium-low heat, reduce the Sauternes by half. Add the raisins to the hot, reduced Sauternes and cover. Remove from the heat and allow the raisins to steep in the Sauternes for 2 hours to fully rehydrate.

## RIESLING POACHED WHITE GRAPES

1 cup seedless green grapes
2 cups Riesling

To peel the grapes, use a paring knife to pull the skin away from the flesh, starting where the grape is connected to the stem. Be careful not to cut through flesh. In a small saucepan, bring the Riesling up to a boil. Add the peeled grapes and simmer for 5 minutes. Remove from the heat and steep for 10 minutes. Chill over ice and keep covered and refrigerated until ready to use.

## DEHYDRATED GRAPES

1 cup sugar
1 cup small seedless red grapes
1 cup champagne grapes

In a small saucepan, combine the sugar and 1 cup water and bring to a boil over medium heat. Remove from the heat and add all the grapes. Steep for 5 minutes. Drain the grapes and spread them out onto a baking sheet lined with a silicone baking mat.

Place in a 125°F dehydrator for 3 hours.

Alternatively, dry the grapes in a 175°F oven for 2 hours.

The grapes will be slightly dehydrated but still juicy. Refrigerate until ready to use.

## TO FINISH

Chestnut Puree (see page 351)
Chestnut Bavarois
Hazelnut Meringues
Hazelnut Pavlovas
Hazelnut Crumble (see page 362)
Pistachio Crumble (see page 363)
Riesling Poached White Grapes
Dehydrated Grapes
8 Rehydrated Golden Raisins
24 seedless red grapes
8 hazelnuts, thinly sliced to 1/16 inch thick
Golden Raisin Puree (see page 353)
1 cup Yogurt Gel (see page 348)
Hazelnut Sorbet (see page 367)
Pistachio Ice Cream (see page 369)
Pistachio Tuile

Spoon 2 streaks of Chestnut Puree and 3 dots of Chestnut Bavarois on a plate. Top 2 of the Bavarois dots with Hazelnut Meringues and the third with a Hazelnut Pavlova. Place a spoonful of Hazelnut Crumble on 1 streak of Chestnut Puree and a spoonful of Pistachio Crumble on the other streak of Puree. Arrange 2 Riesling Poached White Grapes, 4 Dehydrated Grapes, 1 Rehydrated Golden Raisin, 3 red seedless grapes, and 4 hazelnut slices on the plate. In a mixing bowl, combine 1/4 cup Golden Raisin Puree with 1 tablespoon Yogurt Gel until fully incorporated and transfer to a squeeze bottle. Squeeze 3 dots of the mixture, as well as 3 dots of the Yogurt Gel, next to the grapes. Finish with a quenelle of Hazelnut Sorbet and a quenelle of Pistachio Ice Cream and top with a piece of Pistachio Tuile. Repeat with the remaining ingredients, to serve 8.

# SWEET POTATO BEIGNET WITH CHOCOLATE AND CHESTNUT HONEY

*Serves 8*

### CHESTNUT HONEY GANACHE

2 2/3 cups cream
2/3 cup chestnut honey
4 cups chopped Valrhona Guanaja chocolate
     (70 percent)
1/2 cup butter, softened

Heat the cream and honey in a medium saucepan over medium heat to just under a boil. Place the chocolate in a metal bowl. Pour the hot cream-and-honey mixture over the chocolate and emulsify the mixture with a hand blender. Blend in the softened butter. Line a 9-by-13-inch rimmed baking sheet with acetate. Pour the warm chocolate mixture onto the prepared baking sheet and refrigerate for 3 hours. Remove from the refrigerator, invert onto a cutting board, and remove the acetate. Using a warm knife, cut the chocolate into rectangles measuring 1/2 inch by 1/2 inch by 3 inches. Refrigerate until ready to serve.

### PÂTE À CHOUX

1 cup milk
2/3 cup butter, cut into cubes
2 tablespoons sugar
3 tablespoons salt
1 vanilla bean, split lengthwise and scraped
1 cup flour
5 eggs

In a medium saucepan over medium heat, combine 2/3 cup water with the butter, milk, sugar, salt, and vanilla bean in a medium pot. Bring the mixture to a boil and add the flour all at once. Stir vigorously with a wooden spoon until the flour has been combined and continue to cook for 5 more minutes. Transfer the dough to a stand mixer fitted with the paddle attachment and mix for 1 minute to cool. Add the eggs, one at a time, and mix until fully incorporated. Refrigerate until cold.

### ORANGE FOAM

1 orange, such as Valencia
1 3/4 cups milk
1/3 cup sugar
2 tablespoons chestnut honey
2/3 cup half-and-half
2 tablespoons lemon juice
2 teaspoons soy lecithin
1 teaspoon salt

Zest the orange with a microplane grater. In a small saucepan over medium heat, combine the orange zest with the milk, sugar, honey, and 1/2 cup water. Simmer for 45 minutes. Remove from the heat and steep for another 20 minutes. Strain the zest from the liquid. Chill the liquid over an ice bath. Add the half-and-half, lemon juice, lecithin, and salt, and use a hand blender to combine. Strain. Keep the liquid cold until ready to use.

### ROASTED SWEET POTATOES

4 large sweet potatoes

Preheat the oven to 400°F. Place the potatoes on a rimmed baking sheet and roast for 2 hours. Allow the sweet potatoes to cool slightly, peel off the skin, and puree the roasted flesh in a food processor. Reserve the puree for the Pommes Dauphine and Sweet Potato Sauce.

### SWEET POTATO SAUCE

1 cup Roasted Sweet Potatoes
1 vanilla bean, split lengthwise and scraped
1/2 cup Simple Syrup (see page 371)
1/4 cup lemon juice

In a blender, mix the Roasted Sweet Potatoes with the vanilla bean seeds. Slowly incorporate the Simple Syrup, blending until completely smooth. Pass the puree through a fine tamis. Mix in the lemon juice.

### POMMES DAUPHINE

2 cups Roasted Sweet Potatoes
3/4 cup sugar
1 teaspoon salt
1 1/2 cups cold Pâte à Choux
3/4 cup (3.2 ounces) Valrhona Caraïbe chocolate
     (66 percent), finely chopped
1 cup panko bread crumbs
1 vanilla bean, split lengthwise and scraped
4 cups canola oil

In a sauté pan over medium heat, combine the Roasted Sweet Potatoes, 1/4 cup of the sugar, and the salt. Dry the Sweet Potatoes for 5 minutes, stirring frequently. Cool the puree over ice.

In a medium bowl, mix together the Sweet Potatoes with the Pâte à Choux. Stir in the chocolate and transfer the mixture to a piping bag. Line a baking sheet with parchment paper and pipe 1-tablespoon mounds onto the parchment paper. Freeze the piped dough until firm but not solid, about 30 minutes. When ready to use, roll the piped dough into balls. If the dough is too hard, it may be necessary to allow it to soften a bit before rolling it. Coat the balls in panko.

In a food processor, combine the remaining 1/2 cup sugar and the vanilla bean seeds to make vanilla sugar. In a large pot, heat the oil to 320°F. Deep-fry the balls for 5 minutes, in batches, being careful not to crowd the pan. Transfer the fried Dauphines to paper towels to drain. Roll in the vanilla sugar and serve warm.

## ORANGE PÂTE DE FRUIT

1 cup orange juice
1/4 cup plus 2/3 cup sugar
1 tablespoon apple pectin
1/4 cup glucose syrup
1 teaspoon citric acid
1 drop orange food coloring

Reduce 2/3 cup of the orange juice in a small sauce-pan over medium heat until 1/3 cup remains. Add the remaining 1/3 cup orange juice and warm through. In a small bowl, stir together 1/4 cup of the sugar with the pectin and whisk the mixture into the orange juice. Bring to a boil. Whisk in the remaining 2/3 cup sugar and the glucose syrup, bring to a boil, and continue to boil over medium heat until the mixture reaches 217°F. Add the citric acid and food coloring and continue to cook until the mixture reaches 221°F. Line a 9-by-9-inch baking dish with parchment paper and pour in the mixture. Cool the Pâte de Fruit at room temperature overnight to allow it to set. When ready to use, cut the Pâte de Fruit into 1/8-inch cubes.

## TO FINISH

Sweet Potato Sauce
Cocoa Nib Crumble (see page 362)
Chestnut Honey Ganache
1 teaspoon Maldon salt
Orange Pâte de Fruit
Brown Butter Ice Cream (see page 368)
Orange Foam
Pommes Dauphine

Drop a teaspoon of Sweet Potato Sauce onto the upper left corner of a plate and drag across at an angle toward the lower right-hand corner of the plate. Cover the tip end of the sauce with 1 tablespoon Cocoa Nib Crumble. Place a Chestnut Honey Ganache rectangle in the middle of the sauce streak. Using a blowtorch, lightly torch the Ganache until shiny. Place a large flake of Maldon salt on the upper left-hand corner of the Ganache. Top with a piece of Orange Pâte de Fruit. Place a quenelle of Brown Butter Ice Cream on top of the Cocoa Nib Crumble. Using a hand blender, aerate the Orange Foam and top the ice cream with a small scoop. Place a warm Pomme Dauphine on top of the Sweet Potato Sauce in the upper left-hand corner. Repeat with the remaining ingredients, to serve 8.

# CHOCOLATE PALETTE WITH PEANUTS AND POPCORN ICE CREAM

*Serves 8*

## PEANUT BUTTER SHORTBREAD

1/4 cup butter, softened
1/4 cup creamy peanut butter
3/4 cup almond flour
1/2 cup confectioners' sugar
3/4 cup flour
1 tablespoon cream

In a stand mixer fitted with the paddle attachment, beat the butter and peanut butter on medium speed until creamy. Add the almond flour and confectioners' sugar, and mix until combined. Incorporate the flour in 3 additions. Drizzle in the cream, mixing until the dough comes together. Roll the dough between 2 sheets of parchment paper to a 1/4-inch thickness.

Preheat the oven to 350°F. Coat a 9-by-13-inch rimmed baking sheet with vegetable spray and line it with parchment paper. Line the prepared pan evenly with the dough, making sure the dough covers the entire pan. Prick it all over with a fork. Refrigerate for 10 minutes. Bake for 12 minutes, until light golden brown. Cool to room temperature.

## SALTED CARAMEL

1/4 cup cream
1 tablespoon glucose syrup
2 tablespoons sugar
1/4 ounce Valrhona Jivara chocolate (40 percent), finely chopped (about 1 tablespoon)
1/4 teaspoon salt
1/2 vanilla bean
1 tablespoon butter

Warm the cream and glucose in a small saucepan and set aside. Place the sugar in a small, heavy-bottomed saucepan over medium heat, and heat until the sugar becomes a dark caramel. Remove from the heat and deglaze with the warm cream and glucose to keep the caramel from burning. Return the pan to the stove and bring back to a simmer over medium heat. Cook until the temperature has risen to 220°F. Let the caramel cool to 185°F and add the chocolate and salt. Let the mixture cool to 95°F. Split the vanilla bean and scrape the seeds into the mixture. Mix in the butter with a hand blender. Cool to room temperature.

## CHOCOLATE PEANUT BUTTER CRISP

2 1/2 ounces Valrhona Jivara Lactée chocolate (40 percent), finely chopped
1/2 ounce Valrhona Araguani chocolate (72 percent), finely chopped (about 2 tablespoons)
1 teaspoon butter
2 tablespoons creamy peanut butter
1/3 cup *feuilletine*

In a double boiler, gently melt the chocolates with the butter, stirring with a rubber spatula. Add the peanut butter and stir to incorporate evenly. Remove from the heat and gently fold in the *feuilletine* so as to keep it intact. Cool to room temperature.

## CHOCOLATE PEANUT BUTTER MOUSSE

1/4 cup cream
1 1/2 ounces Valrhona Caraïbe chocolate (66 percent)
1 tablespoon creamy peanut butter
1 egg
1 tablespoon sugar

In a cold bowl, whip the cream to soft peaks. Melt the chocolate and peanut butter over a double boiler. In a separate bowl, whisk together the egg and the sugar. Set over a double boiler, whisking constantly, until very warm. Whip until the egg mixture is lightened in color and forms ribbons. Using a rubber spatula, fold the egg mixture into the chocolate and peanut butter. Finish by folding in the whipped cream.

## CHOCOLATE GLAZE

2 sheets gelatin
1/3 cup milk
1/3 cup cream
1/3 cup Simple Syrup (see page 371)
2 tablespoons glucose syrup
8 ounces *pâte à glacer brune*
2 1/2 ounces Valrhona Caraïbe chocolate (66 percent), chopped

Bloom the gelatin by placing the sheets in a bowl of ice water for 10 minutes. Once they are pliable, remove them from the cold water and squeeze to remove excess moisture. Bring the milk, cream, Simple Syrup, and glucose to just under a boil, and add the bloomed gelatin. Place the *pâte à glacer brune* and chocolate in a bowl and slowly pour in the cream mixture. Let rest for 1 to 2 minutes. Combine with a whisk, strain through a chinois, and then cool to room temperature.

## CHOCOLATE PEANUT BUTTER PALETTES

1/2 cup creamy peanut butter, room temperature
Peanut Butter Shortbread
Chocolate Peanut Butter Crisp
Salted Caramel
1/2 cup chopped peanuts
Chocolate Peanut Butter Mousse
Chocolate Glaze

Spread the peanut butter on top of the Peanut Butter Shortbread, making it as smooth as possible. Freeze, allowing the peanut butter to set for 30 minutes. Spread the Chocolate Peanut Butter Crisp as evenly and as smoothly as possible on top of the frozen peanut butter. Freeze for 15 minutes. Then spread the Salted Caramel on top of the crisp, making sure to work very quickly before the caramel sets. Spread the chopped peanuts across the top of the caramel. Place a sheet of parchment paper on top and, using a small rolling pin, evenly roll the peanuts into the layers to make the surface flat and even. With the parchment paper still on top, freeze for 15 minutes. Remove from the freezer and peel off the parchment paper. Spread the Chocolate Peanut Butter Mousse very evenly across the peanuts, making sure it is very smooth. Freeze for 1 hour.

Remove the palette from the freezer. Working quickly and very carefully, place a sheet of parchment on top of the Mousse and flip it upside down onto a cutting board to unmold. Be careful to keep the palette in one piece. Flip the palette back onto its shortbread side and refreeze for 20 minutes. Remove from the freezer and, working quickly, cut the palette into 1 1/4-inch-by-4-inch rectangles. Freeze for 30 minutes. In the meantime, transfer the Glaze to a confectionery funnel (also called a sauce gun). Place a rack on top of an aluminum-foil-lined 13-by-18-inch rimmed baking sheet. Remove the Chocolate Peanut Butter Palettes from the freezer and place on the rack. Slowly release the Glaze from the confectionery funnel over the Palettes in even strokes. Once the Palettes have been completely enrobed in the glaze, refrigerate until ready to serve.

## NIB SYRUP

2 tablespoons cocoa nibs
2 tablespoons glucose syrup

Bring 1/2 cup water to a boil in a small saucepan over medium heat and add the cocoa nibs. Remove from the heat, cover, and steep for 20 minutes. Strain through cheesecloth. Transfer the liquid to a new pot and stir in the glucose. Reduce over medium heat by a third. Cool to room temperature.

## CARAMEL POPCORN
## AND CARAMEL POPCORN POWDER

2 tablespoons popcorn kernels
2 teaspoons canola oil
1/2 cup sugar
2 tablespoons butter
1 tablespoon light corn syrup
1/2 cup finely chopped peanuts
1/4 teaspoon salt

Preheat the oven to 325°F. Place the kernels and the oil in a deep saucepan over medium heat and cover. Periodically shake the pot to rotate the kernels and ensure even popping. When the popping slows, remove the pot from the heat and allow the popping to finish. Once the popcorn has popped, place it on a rimmed baking sheet. In a small, heavy-bottomed saucepan, bring the sugar, butter, corn syrup, and 2 tablespoons water to a boil and cook, stirring periodically, until a medium caramel color is reached. Pour the caramel onto the popcorn and sprinkle with the peanuts. Stir the caramel and salt into the popcorn with a heat-resistant spatula until the caramel begins to stiffen. Place the popcorn in the oven for 5 minutes or just until the caramel softens again. Stir. Repeat this process 4 to 5 times, until the popcorn is completely and evenly coated. Spread the caramel popcorn out onto a silicone baking mat and let it cool to room temperature. In a spice grinder, grind a quarter of the popcorn to a powder. Reserve the Caramel Popcorn and Caramel Popcorn Powder separately in airtight containers.

## CHOCOLATE SPIRALS

1 pound Valrhona Caraïbe chocolate (66 percent)

Melt the chocolate over a double boiler until hot to the touch, about 120°F, stirring often. Note that chocolate burns easily, so keep your eye on it to avoid burning. Once the chocolate is fully melted and hot, remove it from the heat. Cool over an ice bath, stirring gently but constantly and moving it on and off the bath, slowly working the temperature down. When the chocolate is still liquid but is cold to the touch, about 84 to 88°F, it will now be at the correct working temperature and "in temper." Place a 9-by-13-inch piece of acetate on top of a 13-by-18-inch sheet of parchment paper. Spread a thin layer of the tempered chocolate on top of the acetate. Once it sets enough to touch without leaving a mark, you can begin to cut it. Score the chocolate at 1/8-inch intervals, cutting lengthwise across the top of the chocolate with a small paring knife and a ruler as your guide. After the sheet of chocolate has been cut, place another 13-by-18-inch sheet of parchment paper on top and roll the stack around a rolling pin in a diagonal direction until the rolling pin is completely wrapped in the chocolate sheet of acetate. Set the chocolate spiral in the refrigerator for 5 to 10 minutes. Gently pull the rolling pin from the center of the chocolate tube and gently pull the 2 sheets of parchment paper from the outsides of the tube. Starting at one corner of the tube, pull away the acetate, working carefully but quickly to remove the acetate and avoid breakage. Separate the spirals from one another onto a sheet tray. Store in a cool room or refrigerator.

## TO FINISH

Nib Syrup
Chocolate Peanut Butter Palettes
Edible gold leaf
Caramel Popcorn Powder
Popcorn Ice Cream (see page 369)
Caramel Popcorn
Unsweetened cocoa powder
Chocolate Spirals

Place a line of Nib Syrup across a plate. Gently lay a Palette on the plate, at a 90-degree angle to the line of Syrup, barely touching it. Garnish it with a small piece of gold leaf. Spoon a small mound of Caramel Popcorn Powder against the Palette. Lay a quenelle of Popcorn Ice Cream on top of the Powder and place the Caramel Popcorn on top of the Palette. Sprinkle a tiny pinch of cocoa powder around the Caramel Popcorn Powder and place a Chocolate Spiral on top of the Palette and Ice Cream. Repeat with the remaining ingredients, to serve 8, and serve immediately.

# MIGNARDISES

WHITE CHOCOLATE TRUFFLE
337

CARAMEL APPLE
338

COFFEE BEIGNETS
338

# FORWARD MOVING

ON A FLIGHT BACK from a trip I took to India for a friend's wedding, I started reading a book that Danny had given me called *The Perfectionist,* by Rudolph Chelminski. It's about the life of the legendary chef Bernard Loiseau, but it starts with a brief, incredibly inspiring history of haute cuisine and the chefs and restaurateurs that affected its evolution.

It is overwhelming to consider how many restaurants have existed in the world throughout the last hundred years, but when you narrow that down to those that have had some sort of lasting, significant impact, the list becomes a good deal shorter. Daniel and I love learning about and teaching our staff about the history of these restaurants. We believe that you need to know where you come from in order to evolve, and we have been inspired by the people and places that have helped to shape our industry.

We have enormous respect for Fernand Point of La Pyramide, the father of modern French cuisine; for Fredy Girardet, who pioneered the use of stocks instead of flour to thicken sauces; for Alain Chapel, one of the leaders of nouvelle cuisine, who maintained three Michelin stars from 1973 until his death in 1990; for Michel Bras, a master of plating, one of the first to embrace the idea of foraging, with his famous "Gargouillou," an ever-changing salad composition of forty to fifty ingredients; for Albert Stockli, of the Four Seasons, who along with Joe Baum gave rise to the concept of American fine dining; for Alice Waters of Chez Panisse, who gave birth to the "farm to table" movement; for Ferran Adrià of El Bulli, who changed the culinary landscape with his pioneering of molecular gastronomy; and for many more. We find it highly motivating to read about these people and the ways in which they have helped define their respective generations.

Daniel and I felt confident that Eleven Madison Park had become a great restaurant, but it started to become apparent to us that we had yet to develop our own point of view. The years leading up to now had been about being inspired by others. This one needed to be about making our own impact. When our entire staff gathered together for our planning meeting on January 3, 2010, we presented the goal that will remain for the lifetime of the restaurant: to help define our time.

Our team brainstormed for hours, but the energy was different from that of years past. The day was about changing our mind-set, challenging ourselves to take risks, compelling ourselves to think differently, no longer limiting our ideas. This year's to-do list was short: to shift our perspective; to be groundbreaking.

MARCH BROUGHT WITH IT two pieces of news. First, an Eleven Madison Park baby was born. Daniel's wife, Geneén, gave birth to their first daughter, Vivienne Marcelle. Then, a few weeks later, we were incredibly surprised to get a letter that we had long hoped to receive. We had made it onto the San Pellegrino list of the 50 Best, the world's most influential international ranking of restaurants. It was a huge honor to be recognized for the first time on the global stage, although we wouldn't know exactly which number we were on the list until the awards ceremony. So in late April, Daniel and I boarded a plane to London.

The ceremony is much like the James Beard Awards, except here we were surrounded by chefs and restaurateurs from across the globe. To be socializing with Ferran Adrià, Heston Blumenthal, René Redzepi, and many more was exhilarating, and we sat down for the awards excited to see where on the list we would fall.

At the front of the auditorium an emcee stood before a large screen upon which his image was projected. As Daniel and I took our seats, we tried to guess how we would do. "Number 35?" "Number 40?" But after only a few preliminary announcements, the countdown began. It ended for us as quickly as it started. "Number 50 . . . Eleven Madison Park."

We had come in last place. Yes, last place in a list of the fifty best restaurants in the world, but of the people in that room, we had come in last. I could only imagine the heartbroken looks we had on our faces, though I didn't have to for very long. When I glanced up, the image of the emcee on the large screen at the front of the auditorium had been replaced with a live image of Daniel and me.

We tried to fake smiles, but I'm sure they looked contrived — our humiliated reaction was on display for the entire crowd. Rather than going out that night, we returned to our hotel early. We poured ourselves a few drinks and talked for hours. That night was a reminder that as far as we had come, we still had a long way to go, especially if we aspired do something of true significance. We looked at the restaurants on the top of that list: El Bulli, The Fat Duck, Noma. We shared the same passion that they all embodied, but they had taken risks that we had not yet had the courage to take. It was our turn. Things had to change.

First was our physical space. We are blessed with an amazing home, the original MetLife Building, an Art Deco historic landmark in New York City. When it was being erected, it was intended to be the tallest building in the world, but due to the Great Depression and a lack of funds, a building that was supposed to reach over a hundred stories was capped off at thirty-two. As a result, there actually are more elevator shafts in the building than there are floors.

Our restaurant is on the street level and boasts amazing marble floors, thirty-five-foot ceilings, and giant windows overlooking historic Madison Square Park. The space has a distinctly New York feel to it; there are not many like it anywhere. As dramatic as it is, however, we used to struggle with it, finding difficulty in creating a true sense of intimacy.

For a long time we envied the smaller dining rooms of the great restaurants in the world, with their low ceilings and carpeted floors. But it was that night, in our hotel in London, that we had a change in perspective. We finally realized how special our room really was. We began to embrace its uniqueness, wanting every guest to experience its expanse. With this change of perspective came a need to change the space. We had a lower-ceilinged dining area in the back of the room that we referred to as "the cave." That part of the dining room would need to be removed, a change that would decrease the total number of seats in the restaurant from 114 to 80.

Next was our menu. Up until that point, like many fine-dining restaurants, we were offering a prix fixe menu and a chef's tasting menu. We began to think of the former as the guest's monologue, in which they would read the menu to decide exactly what they wanted and then place their order. The latter was our monologue, in which the guest would leave things entirely in our hands and we would make all the decisions.

The beauty of the prix fixe was that the guest was empowered with control, while the tasting menu brought with it a sense of surprise that was carried through the entire meal. We started to believe that in finding balance between these two classic approaches we could discover what we believed was a better way to dine.

The result was a menu card with sixteen words, a four-course menu with four options for each course, in which each dish was listed only by its principal ingredient. The guests would retain a bit of control, helping to charter the course of their meal by selecting the ingredients that appealed to them most.

Then a dialogue with our team would follow. "Do you have any ideas or preferences, any ingredients you're not in the mood to eat today, a theme you are looking for in your meal?" Finally, in the kitchen wc would create a menu with those preferences in mind. It wouldn't be an interaction in which the guests would design their own meal, but more like a made-to-measure suit: the tailor is the expert, but you're the one who has to live with their creation. You select from the limited number of fabrics available, you communicate a general idea of what you do and do not like, and then you let them do their thing. The more we refined the idea, the more excited we got. We were onto something.

After a month of preparation, we sat down in the dining room to sample the new experience with Danny, to get his approval. We were excited, yet anxious about how he would respond. We sat together for nearly four hours, showing him all of the elements of the new experience and explaining the inspirations behind each. At the end of the meal, Danny was like a proud father, and albeit with a sense of trepidation, he gave us the go-ahead. We immediately started having meetings with our team to refine the ideas, engaged a contractor to begin the planning for the physical changes, and began talks with our graphic designer to finalize the menu design. We set our sights on September as the month when the shift would take place.

**IN JUNE** we broke from the intensity of our preparation with another celebration. Once again, dressed in tuxedos, we headed to the James Beard Awards, where Daniel would win the award for Best Chef in New York City. When his name was announced, Daniel insisted that I join him on stage to accept the award. Later, in the back of the auditorium, drinking Champagne, we glanced up at the monitor to see Wolfgang Puck announcing to everyone that the party that night was at Eleven Madison Park.

Thankfully we had a renovation coming up, because we did some serious damage to the room that night. We learned that high heels dancing on leather banquettes is a bad combination. It would be our last party for quite some time, but it was worth it.

On August 28, we had our last service before closing for the renovation. It took just over a week to complete, with contractors working 24/7. The entire team took the opportunity to get out of New York for a little while to relax and recharge before reconvening at the end of the week to clean up and prepare for service. On September 7 we reopened with our smaller dining room, our newly renovated and reconfigured kitchen, our new

menu, and a photograph of Miles Davis, as well as a list of those words hanging in our kitchen.

Journalist Oliver Strand wrote a significant piece about the changes in the *New York Times,* titled "Fixing What Isn't Broke," which came out the day after our reopening, sparking quite a bit of debate in the food community about the spirit of our evolution. While our regulars were supportive, many others, having yet to experience the changes, were not. There was quite a bit of criticism. We had tried to prepare ourselves emotionally for just that, but it was still hard to take. In our excitement about the changes, we had never really considered that the idea could fail. We started questioning the decision, wondering if we had made a mistake, but we eventually realized that we had to stop reading the blogs and just start focusing on making it work. Our goal was to take risks. Based on the response, we had done just that.

But each week was a step in the right direction, and by the beginning of November, things started to feel good. Each month, the online reservations system OpenTable releases a ranking of restaurants compiled by the reviews of its users. When you make a reservation through the system, you receive an email after your meal asking you to rate the food, service, and ambience. Over the previous two years we had never placed higher than second or third in any of these categories. In the ranking that was released in November, following our first full month with our new menu, we came in first place in every category.

Although that monthly list is only one indicator, it was deeply gratifying. We knew that we still needed more time to refine the new system, but with the release of that list and along with more and more great comments from our guests, it was becoming clear that New York had given us its seal of approval.

**NOVEMBER ALSO BROUGHT** our annual trip. This time to Tokyo, where Daniel took over the kitchens at the restaurant in the Park Hyatt Hotel for five nights of service. In spite of the difficulties we had with the jet lag, and the realization that we had an absolute inability to communicate with anyone, we found the city to be electrifying. We visited the fish market one morning, watching the auctions that take place there and seeing the degree to which the Japanese honor every piece of food. We went to the unbelievable food markets at the department stores near Shinjuku Station with our friend Chef Yoshio Takazawa and his wife, Akiko. Together, we purchased a vast array of Japanese delicacies and brought them back to his restaurant for a picnic of sorts.

We had some good meals: inspiring lunches at Les Créations de Narisawa and RyuGin a simple, pure, and confident sushi dinner at Sawada; and a series of delicious late-night snacks in neighborhoods throughout the city at ramen bars, teppanyaki restaurants, and *izakayas*. We also had some difficult ones; in one case, so as not to offend the chef, I had to smuggle food out in the warm towel I had received at the beginning of the meal. It was here in Tokyo that I also found the time and piece of mind to write the essays for this book.

It was just before this trip, however, that the most significant development in our time at Eleven Madison Park began to percolate. As I have mentioned many times, Danny Meyer is like a father to both Daniel and me. He is our mentor, our friend, and an inspiration, one of the wisest and kindest people we have ever met. With his views on enlightened hospitality, I firmly believe that he has changed the restaurant industry as we know it, and I am eternally grateful that the most formative years of my career took place as a part of his company.

But over the years, Daniel and I came to recognize that in our hearts we wanted to be entrepreneurs. Danny recognized this almost before we did, and, like any great father, decided that rather than fight it he would support it and be an instrumental part of setting us up for success. To that end, he arranged to pass the torch and sell us Eleven Madison Park. He worked with us to make the transition, helping to provide us with comfort as we considered the overwhelming prospect of owning our own business, and ultimately, he began preparing the paperwork that would make the restaurant ours.

It was hard to believe at first. It was exciting, but also emotional — akin to moving out of the house after graduation. Danny had invested in us every time we had asked anything of him, always believing in us and the spirit of our endeavor. His generosity and graciousness have always been humbling, and he continues to inspire us to become better human beings. He is one of the most important people in our lives and we love knowing that our relationship with him will only continue to grow stronger.

Moving forward, we know that we still have a long way to go. We have high aspirations, ones that will likely take a lifetime to achieve. We have learned so many lessons through both our successes and our failures, yet we know that we have so much left to discover. By focusing on staying true to our core values, always striving to maintain balance, and constantly looking to reinvent ourselves, we're pretty certain that we're moving in the right direction. But only time will tell, and the uncertainty has a beauty all its own.

# WINTER

*New York winters are cold, and they remind me of home, especially when it snows. I always end up spending more time around the stove than at the markets, as not much is really growing during those months. You pretty much know what you have to work with. The ingredients are still exciting: all the citrus, bitter greens, root vegetables, and of course the black truffles. The cold water produces the best seafood: oysters, sea urchin, lobster, and clams.*

*Winter is truly about the craft of cooking. Vegetables like celery root, sunchokes, and parsnips require real technique to make them taste good. Dishes like the cured leg of pork, the braised veal cheeks, the whole roasted chicken with stuffing underneath the skin — they require time and commitment.*

*Working my way through the kitchens of my youth, I learned that cooking is repetitive. In restaurants, many of the same tasks are done every day. I would pick herbs, cut mirepoix, and roll potato gnocchi over and over and over again. But with time I realized that no matter what role you play in a kitchen, this will never change. It's the nature of what we do. I find genuine pleasure in trying to perfect the simple tasks, with the aspiration of always getting better; working cleaner, faster, more organized, with more precision. All of this training has ultimately been about one thing: trying to master my craft, something I know I'll never quite achieve. But the craft of cooking is the path I chose, and it exhilarates me to this day. For the opportunities it has provided, and the places it has taken me, I am eternally grateful. For me, success as a chef has always been about art, science, and hard work. How much talent do you have? How much knowledge have you gained? How badly do you want it?*

| CAVIAR | MACKEREL | OYSTER | HAMACHI |
| SCALLOP | RADICCHIO | FOIE GRAS | SUNCHOKE |
| LANGOUSTINE | CELERY ROOT | POTATO | BLACK TRUFFLE |
| JOHN DORY | SKATE | PRAWN | LOBSTER |
| QUAIL | GUINEA FOWL | CHICKEN | PORK |
| BEEF | LAMB | VACHERIN | GRAPEFRUIT |
| LEMON | COCONUT | COFFEE | CHOCOLATE |

# HORS
D'ŒUVRES

GOUGÈRES
330

GOAT CHEESE AND LEMON GALETTE
330

SEA URCHIN AND GREEN APPLE
331

RAZOR CLAM WITH FENNEL
331

FOIE GRAS MACARONS
333

CHICKEN LIVER CRACKLINGS
332

# CAVIAR
## POACHED OYSTERS, CHAMPAGNE SABAYON, AND WATERCRESS

*Serves 8*

### CHAMPAGNE SABAYON
24 Beausoleil oysters
1 3/4 cups white wine
5 eggs
2 egg yolks
1/2 cup Champagne
1 pound butter, melted
2 1/2 teaspoons salt
1 pinch cayenne pepper
2 N$_2$O cartridges

Shuck the oysters, reserving both the oysters and their liquor. In a small saucepan over medium-high heat, reduce the white wine until 1/2 cup remains. Cool to room temperature. Meanwhile, combine the eggs and the egg yolks in a deep mixing bowl. Add the reduced white wine, the Champagne, and the oyster liquor. With a hand blender, slowly blend in the melted butter. Season with the salt and cayenne and blend again to fully incorporate. Transfer the Sabayon to a whipped-cream canister and charge with the N$_2$O cartridges. Place the canister in water bath maintained at 145°F by an immersion circulator for 2 hours, shaking occasionally.

### BABY LEEKS
16 baby leeks

Peel and discard the outer layers of the leeks, keeping the hearts intact. Rinse well under running water. Bring a pot of salted water to a boil. Add the leeks, cooking for 3 to 4 minutes, and then transfer to a bowl of ice water. Once cold, drain. Cut the leeks into 1-inch pieces on the bias to make diamond shapes.

### POACHED MATSUTAKE MUSHROOMS
8 matsutake mushrooms
1 tablespoon butter
2 tablespoons diced shallots
2 cups white wine
2 sprigs thyme
1 tablespoon salt

Rinse the mushrooms. Using a paring knife, peel the skin from the mushroom stems and caps, being careful to keep the mushrooms intact. In a small saucepan, melt the butter over low heat and sweat the shallots until tender and translucent, about 3 minutes. Deglaze the pan with the white wine and simmer for 4 to 5 minutes to cook out the alcohol. Add the thyme, salt, mushrooms, and 1 cup of water. Cover and simmer over low heat until the mushrooms are fully tender, about 1 hour. Remove the mushrooms from the poaching liquid and reserve the liquid. Drain the mushrooms on a paper towel before cutting into quarters.

### RAZOR CLAMS
8 razor clams
1 tablespoon olive oil
3 cloves garlic, crushed but kept whole
2 sprigs thyme
1 cup white wine
1/2 teaspoon salt

Rinse the clams well under cold running water. Heat the oil in a medium straight-sided pan over high heat. Add the clams, garlic, and thyme, and sauté for 30 seconds. Deglaze with the wine and season with the salt. Cover and cook until the clams are just open, about 5 minutes. Strain the clams and reserve the cooking liquid. Chill the clams and the liquid over ice. When the clams are chilled, remove the meat from the shells. Trim away all but the cleaned neck, or "siphon." Cut in half crosswise on a bias. Discard the shells and store the clams in the reserved cooking liquid until ready to serve.

### PUFF PASTRY CRISPS
1 sheet puff pastry

Preheat the oven to 300°F. Cut 16 triangles measuring 1 1/2 inches by 1 1/2 inches by 3/4 inch each. Place the triangles on a baking sheet lined with parchment paper and bake the pastries until the tops are golden brown, 12 to 15 minutes. Cool to room temperature. Pull the crispy tops off of the baked puff pastries and store them in an airtight container.

### TO FINISH
Razor Clam cooking liquid (reserved from Razor Clams)
32 Maine shrimp
24 shucked Beausoleil oysters (reserved from Champagne Sabayon)
Razor Clams
2 tablespoons butter
Matsutake mushroom poaching liquid (reserved from Poached Matsutake Mushrooms)
Poached Matsutake Mushrooms
Baby Leeks
1/2 cup Watercress Puree (see page 354)
40 sprigs watercress
32 sprigs dill
Puff Pastry Crisps
Champagne Sabayon
2 ounces osetra caviar

Warm 1/2 cup of the Razor Clam cooking liquid in a medium saucepan over low heat. Add the shrimp and poach for 1 minute. Remove the shrimp and add the oysters. Poach for 1 minute. Return the shrimp, oysters, and Razor Clams to the Razor Clam cooking liquid, add 1 tablespoon of the butter, and reduce to glaze.

In a small sauté pan, warm 2 tablespoons of the Matsutake mushroom poaching liquid over low heat. Add the quartered Poached Matsutake Mushrooms and the Baby Leeks and warm through. Add the remaining tablespoon butter, reducing to glaze. Drain on a paper towel.

On a plate, squeeze 3 dime-sized dollops of Watercress Puree. Arrange 4 shrimp, 2 Razor Clam pieces, 3 oysters, 4 Poached Matsutake Mushroom quarters, and 4 Baby Leeks on the plate. Garnish the plate with 5 sprigs watercress, 4 sprigs dill, and 2 Puff Pastry Crisps. With a hand blender, foam the Champagne Sabayon and spoon the foam onto the plate. Dot the plate with caviar. Repeat with the remaining ingredients, to serve 8.

# MACKEREL
## TARTARE WITH FRUIT DE MER AND SEA BEANS

*Serves 8*

### SAFFRON MUSSELS

2 pounds mussels
2 tablespoons olive oil
2 teaspoons thinly sliced ginger
2 shallots, sliced
10 stems parsley
2 cups white wine
2 teaspoons salt
1 teaspoon saffron

Remove any beard from the mussels and rinse them well under cold running water. In a large straight-sided pot, heat the olive oil over high heat. Add the ginger, shallots, parsley stems, and mussels and stir for 1 minute. Deglaze the pot with the wine and add the salt and saffron. Cover and cook until the mussels are all open, about 6 to 8 minutes. Strain the mussels, discarding any that did not open fully, and reserve the cooking liquid. Cool the mussels over ice.

When the mussels are cold, remove the meat from the shells. Strain the cooking liquid through a fine-mesh chinois and reserve the mussels in their reserved cooking liquid until ready to serve.

### RAZOR CLAMS

16 razor clams
2 tablespoons olive oil
4 cloves garlic, crushed but kept whole
4 sprigs thyme
2 cups white wine
1 teaspoon salt

Rinse the clams well under cold running water. In a large straight-sided pot, heat the olive oil over high heat. Add the garlic, thyme, and clams and sauté for 30 seconds. Deglaze the pot with the white wine and add the salt. Cover and cook until the clams are just open, 5 minutes. Strain the clams and reserve the cooking liquid. Chill the clams over ice.

When the clams are cold, remove the meat from the shells and trim away all but the cleaned neck, or "siphon." Discard the shells and the bodies, reserving only the necks. Cut them on the bias into 3 pieces each. Store in their reserved cooking liquid until ready to serve.

### SAFFRON WATER

1 cup water
1 teaspoon saffron

Bring the water to a boil. Add the saffron and reduce liquid to 1/4 cup. Strain and chill.

### SAFFRON SAUCE

2/3 cup mussel cooking liquid (reserved from Saffron Mussels)
2/3 cup razor clam cooking liquid (reserved from Razor Clams)
2 tablespoons plus 2 teaspoons lime juice
1 teaspoon salt
1 teaspoon Saffron Water
1/8 teaspoon xanthan gum (0.4g)
1 tablespoon extra-virgin olive oil

In a mixing bowl, whisk together all of the ingredients except the olive oil until the xanthan gum is fully absorbed. Add the olive oil right before serving.

### MOLLUSK FOAM

2/3 cup mussel cooking liquid (reserved from Saffron Mussels)
2/3 cup razor clam cooking liquid (reserved from Razor Clams)
1/3 cup crème fraîche
1/4 cup Mayonnaise (see page 371)
2 tablespoons lime juice
1 1/4 teaspoons salt
1 teaspoon soy lecithin

In a mixing bowl, blend together all of the ingredients with a hand blender. Reserve the foam base in the refrigerator until ready to use.

### TO FINISH

40 shelled edamame
32 sea beans
1 Spanish mackerel (2 to 3 pounds)
Saffron Mussels
24 Maine shrimp
Razor Clams
2 tablespoons Lime Vinaigrette (see page 346)
32 sprigs dill
32 pieces upland cress
Saffron Sauce
Mollusk Foam

Bring a pot of salted water to a boil. Add the edamame and cook for 1 minute. Transfer with a slotted spoon to a bowl of ice water. Repeat with the sea beans. Once cold, drain. Peel the outer membrane from the edamame. Fillet, skin, and dice the Spanish mackerel into 1/2-inch cubes so that you have 48 cubes total. Dress the diced mackerel, Saffron Mussels, shrimp, and Razor Clams in the Lime Vinaigrette. Arrange 6 pieces mackerel, 3 Saffron Mussels, 3 pieces Razor Clams, and 3 Maine shrimp on a plate. Place 4 sprigs dill, 5 edamame, 4 sea beans, and 4 pieces of upland cress on the dressed seafood. Finish the plate with 1 teaspoon Saffron Sauce and the Mollusk Foam. Repeat with the remaining ingredients, to serve 8.

# OYSTER
## GELÉE WITH POTATOES AND LEEKS

*Serves 8*

### LEEK GELÉE

3 sheets gelatin
24 Beausoleil oysters
2 1/2 cups leek greens, thinly sliced and rinsed
2 1/2 cups leek whites, thinly sliced and rinsed
2 1/2 cups packed spinach leaves
1 1/4 cups cold Fish Fumet (see page 356)
1 teaspoons salt

To bloom the gelatin, place the sheets in a bowl of ice water for 10 minutes, until pliable. Shuck the oysters, reserving the liquor. Reserve the oysters for use in the plating. Strain the liquor through cheesecloth and reserve. Bring a large pot of salted water to a boil. Add the leek greens, cooking for 4 to 5 minutes. Transfer to a bowl of ice water. Repeat with the leek whites, cooking for 6 to 7 minutes, and then the spinach, cooking for 15 to 20 seconds. Once cold, drain on paper towels. Transfer to a blender and combine with the Fish Fumet, 1 1/2 cups ice water, and the reserved oyster liquor. Blend on high speed for 30 to 45 seconds. Season with the salt and strain through cheesecloth. You should have 2 cups of liquid.

Warm 1/4 cup of the leek base in a small saucepan over medium heat. Squeeze the gelatin of excess moisture and melt into the warm liquid. Stir the mixture back into the remaining 1 3/4 cups leek base. Reserve at room temperature without allowing it to set.

### POTATO CREAM

2 tablespoons butter
1 2/3 cups leek whites, thinly sliced and rinsed
8 white peppercorns
1 bay leaf
8 medium La Ratte fingerling potatoes (just under 1 pound), peeled and sliced (1/8 inch thick)
2 teaspoons salt
2/3 cup white wine
1 cup half-and-half
1/4 cup canola oil

Melt the butter in a large saucepan over low heat. Add the leek whites and sweat until tender, about 5 minutes. Prepare a sachet by wrapping the peppercorns and bay leaf in cheesecloth and tying together with butcher's twine. Add the sachet and potatoes to the pan, season with 1/2 teaspoon of the salt, and continue to sweat over low heat for 5 minutes. Add the wine and reduce to 1/4 cup. Cover with the half-and-half and 2 cups water and bring to a simmer over medium heat. Reduce the heat to low and simmer for 25 to 30 minutes. Transfer to a blender and puree on high speed. Strain through a chinois and chill over ice. Once the puree is cold, transfer it back into a blender and blend on high speed with the canola oil. Season with the remaining 1 1/2 teaspoons salt and strain again. Keep the Potato Cream in the refrigerator.

### MIGNONETTE

1 tablespoon diced (1/8 inch) leek whites
1 tablespoon champagne vinegar
1 1/2 teaspoons crushed black pepper

In a small bowl, stir together the leeks and vinegar. Refrigerate for 2 hours, and then drain, reserving just the leeks.

### TO FINISH

1 leek, light green part only, diced (1/4 inch) and rinsed
24 shucked Beausoleil oysters (reserved from Leek Gelée)
Leek Gelée
Potato Cream
4 teaspoons extra-virgin olive oil
1/2 teaspoon *piment d'Espelette*
2 tablespoons finely sliced chives
1 teaspoon Maldon salt
Mignonette
8 tiny leeks

Bring a small saucepan of salted water to a boil. Add the diced leek and cook for 5 to 6 minutes. Transfer to a bowl of ice water and, once cold, drain. Chill 8 bowls in the refrigerator. Place 3 shucked oysters in the bottom of a bowl. Spoon 1 1/2 teaspoons of the blanched leeks around the oysters. Pour 1/4 cup Leek Gelée into each bowl and allow the gelatin to set in the refrigerator for at least 2 hours. When ready to serve, pour the chilled Potato Cream over the Leek Gelée and garnish with 1/2 teaspoon olive oil, a pinch of *piment d'Espelette*, 1/2 teaspoon sliced chives, and a pinch of Maldon salt. Spoon just under 1 teaspoon of the Mignonette over the oysters and Gelée. Finish with 1 leek. Repeat with the remaining ingredients, to serve 8.

# HAMACHI
## MARINATED WITH LEMON, FENNEL, AND HORSERADISH

*Serves 8*

1 fennel bulb, green stalks intact
3 tablespoons Lemon Oil (see page 345)
1/2 teaspoon salt
1 hamachi loin
*Fleur de sel*
8 teaspoons Meyer Lemon Puree (see page 352)
8 teaspoons Garlic Horseradish Puree (see page 352)
40 fennel fronds
Zest of 3 Meyer lemons
8 teaspoons Lemon–White Soy Vinaigrette
    (see page 346)

Separate the green stalks from the fennel bulb. On a mandoline, thinly shave the stalks into 1/16-inch thick pieces. Cut the fennel bulb in half lengthwise and thinly slice crosswise on a mandoline. Place the shaved green fennel and fennel slices in a mixing bowl and dress with 2 tablespoons of the Lemon Oil and the salt. Slice the hamachi into 1/4-inch-by-1-inch-by-3-inch pieces. Brush with the remaining Lemon Oil and season with *fleur de sel*.

Using an offset spatula, spread 1 teaspoon Meyer Lemon Puree on a plate. Arrange 3 slices of hamachi, 5 dressed fennel slices, and 4 pieces of shaved green fennel on top of the Puree. Spoon 1 teaspoon of Garlic Horseradish Puree onto the plate. Garnish with 5 fennel fronds and Meyer lemon zest strips. Finish with 1 teaspoon Lemon–White Soy Vinaigrette. Repeat with the remaining ingredients, to serve 8.

# SCALLOP
## CEVICHE WITH FENNEL, TANGERINE, AND TARRAGON

*Serves 8*

### STEAMED SCALLOPS

20 U10 scallops
1 teaspoon salt

Season the scallops on both sides with the salt. Steam the scallops in a combination steam oven for 2 minutes at 185°F. Refrigerate to chill. Trim both ends of the scallops and then cut the scallops in half to create 2 thinner pieces. With a 1 1/4-inch ring cutter, punch out circles from the scallops. Reserve all trim for the Scallop Salad and keep the scallops on ice until ready to serve.

### YUZU GELÉE

6 sheets gelatin
2/3 cup tangerine juice
1/3 cup yuzu juice
Zest from 1 tangerine
1/2 teaspoon salt

Bloom the gelatin by placing the sheets in ice water for 10 minutes, until pliable. Warm the tangerine juice, yuzu juice, and tangerine zest in a small pot over low heat without allowing it to boil. Season with the salt. Squeeze any excess moisture from the gelatin before melting it into the juice. Strain through a chinois.

Lightly spray a 9-by-13-inch plastic tray with non-stick cooking spray. Wipe with a paper towel to remove any excess. Pour about 2/3 cup of the citrus mixture into the tray. Place the tray in the refrigerator to set for 1 hour, making sure it's completely level. After 1 hour, cut the Gelée with a 1 1/4-inch ring cutter. Using an offset spatula, transfer the Gelée rounds from the tray to a clean sheet of acetate. Reserve in the refrigerator.

### FENNEL WINGS

1 fennel bulb
1 tablespoon extra-virgin olive oil
1/4 teaspoon salt

Trim away the top and bottom of the fennel bulb and quarter it. Thinly slice the fennel bulb lengthwise on a mandoline so that the slices are less than 1/16 inch thick. Trim each slice with a paring knife on a curved bias so that they resemble wings. Prepare at least 32 slices. Combine the fennel wings, oil, and salt in bowl.

### BRAISED FENNEL

1/2 cup white wine
2 tablespoons Pernod
2 pods star anise
1 teaspoon salt
1 fennel bulb

To make the fennel cooking liquid, combine the white wine, Pernod, and star anise in a small saucepan and reduce by half. Add the salt and then 1/2 cup cold water.

Cut the fennel bulb into 1/8-inch-thick slices. Combine the fennel and 3 tablespoons of the fennel cooking liquid in a *sous vide* bag and vacuum-seal. Steam the fennel in a combination steam oven at 185°F until tender, about 35 minutes. Chill in an ice bath. Remove the fennel from the bags and dice into 1/8-inch cubes.

### SCALLOP SALAD

1 1/2 cups diced (1/8 inch) scallop trim (reserved from Steamed Scallops)
1/2 cup Braised Fennel
1/4 cup diced (1/8 inch) tangerine
1 tablespoon thinly sliced tarragon
1 1/2 teaspoons thinly sliced dill
1 tablespoon diced (1/8 inch) jalapeño pepper
1 tablespoon Tangerine Vinaigrette (see page 346)
1/2 teaspoon salt

Just before serving, toss all of the ingredients together in a mixing bowl.

### TO FINISH

Steamed Scallops
Scallop Salad
Yuzu Gelée
Hawaiian pink salt
32 tangerine segments
Fennel Wings
24 leaves tarragon
24 sprigs dill
1 cup Tangerine Vinaigrette (see page 346)

On a plate, place 5 Steamed Scallop slices in a circular pattern. Top each scallop slice with 1/2 teaspoon of the Scallop Salad. Then top each portion of Scallop Salad with a circle of the Yuzu Gelée and a pinch of Hawaiian pink salt. Arrange 4 tangerine segments, 4 Fennel Wings, 3 dill sprigs, and 3 tarragon leaves around the plate. Finish with 2 tablespoons Tangerine Vinaigrette. Repeat with the remaining ingredients, to serve 8.

# RADICCHIO
## SALAD WITH MOZZARELLA, MANGO, AND BASIL

*Serves 8*

2 heads radicchio tardivo
2 mangoes, peeled and sliced into thin wedges (32
   wedges total)
3 tablespoons Lemon Vinaigrette (see page 346)
8 buffalo mozzarella, 2 ounces each
1 1/2 teaspoons coarsely ground black pepper
1 1/2 teaspoons *fleur de sel*
64 small basil leaves
3 teaspoons Basil Oil (see page 344)

Cut off the bottom of the radicchio and reserve the tips.
They should be about 3 to 4 inches long, and you should
have 112 pieces total. Place the radicchio in a mixing
bowl with the mango wedges and dress with the Lemon
Vinaigrette.

   Place a buffalo mozzarella in the center of a plate
and season it with a pinch of black pepper and a pinch
of *fleur de sel*. Arrange 4 mango wedges and 14 leaves
radicchio on the plate and garnish with 8 sprigs basil.
Spoon 1 teaspoon Basil Oil on the salad. Repeat with
the remaining ingredients, to serve 8.

# FOIE GRAS
## TORCHON WITH QUINCE AND COCOA

*Serves 8*

### MARINATED FOIE GRAS

One 2-pound lobe grade-A foie gras
1 tablespoon salt
1/2 teaspoon pink curing salt
1 teaspoon sugar
1/2 teaspoon white pepper
2 teaspoons Madeira
1 teaspoon Cognac

Bring the foie gras to room temperature to soften. Separate the main lobes and remove the veins with tweezers and a paring knife. Keep the lobes as whole as possible. In a large bowl, season the foie gras with the salt, pink salt, sugar, and white pepper. Add the Madeira and Cognac and coat evenly. Place in a *sous vide* bag in an even layered rectangle and vacuum-seal. Marinate in the refrigerator for 24 hours. Remove the foie gras from the refrigerator and allow it to soften slightly to prepare for rolling.

### QUINCE CONSOMMÉ

2 to 3 pounds quince, peeled and thinly sliced (6 cups)
1 cup pomegranate juice
1/4 cup sugar

Combine all of the ingredients in a large stainless-steel bowl with 6 cups water and cover tightly with plastic wrap. Cook over a double boiler for 3 hours and strain through a fine-mesh chinois. You should have about 8 cups consommé.

### COCOA FOIE GRAS TORCHON

Marinated Foie Gras
1/2 cup unsweetened cocoa powder
1/2 cup finely ground coriander

Using a damp towel, wipe down a smooth work surface with plenty of space. Lay out 3 long sheets (about 2 feet long each) of plastic wrap so that they overlap one another slightly. Smooth out the plastic wrap with a clean damp towel. Place the Foie Gras in a single layer on top of the plastic wrap 2 inches from the bottom edge. Combine the cocoa powder and coriander and stir to mix thoroughly. Sift an even layer of the cocoa mixture on top of the Foie Gras. Be sure to cover the Foie Gras completely with the cocoa. With your hands, break off 1- to 2-inch pieces of the Foie Gras from the top end and place them on top of one another in a line across the bottom end. The stacked Foie Gras should be in a row about 9 to 10 inches long by 3 inches wide by 3 inches tall. Pull up the bottom edge of the plastic wrap and fold over the Foie Gras, rolling it into a cylinder. Pinch the plastic wrap at the ends and roll by holding the ends of the plastic. Use a cake tester to poke holes in the plastic wrap and tighten to remove any air pockets. Roll again to press out more air. Tie both ends tightly and trim the excess plastic.

Place the cylinder in an ice bath to harden for 4 hours.

Remove from the ice water, pat dry, and vacuum-seal in a *sous vide* bag. Poach for 5 to 6 minutes in a water bath maintained at 137°F by an immersion circulator to just soften and set the roll. Transfer to an ice bath and chill for 12 hours before serving.

### QUINCE GELÉE

3 sheets gelatin
2 cups Quince Consommé
1/2 teaspoon salt

Bloom the gelatin by placing the sheets in a bowl of ice water for 10 minutes, until pliable. In a medium saucepan, reduce the consommé by two thirds and season with the salt. Squeeze the gelatin of any excess moisture and melt into the warm consommé. Divide the Gelée evenly among 8 bowls (about 1/4 cup per bowl) and refrigerate for 2 hours to set.

### QUINCE SAUCE

4 cups Quince Consommé
1 tablespoon plus 1 teaspoon extra-virgin olive oil
1/2 teaspoon salt

In a medium saucepan over medium heat, reduce the Consommé until 3/4 cup remains and it is syrupy. Stir in the olive oil and season with the salt.

### COCOA BRIOCHE

2 3/4 cups bread flour
1/3 cup sugar
2 tablespoon fresh yeast
1 tablespoon *fleur de sel*
5 eggs
1 egg yolk
2 1/4 cups butter, at room temperature, cut into cubes
1/2 cup unsweetened cocoa powder

Place the flour, sugar, yeast, and *fleur de sel* in the bowl of a stand mixer fitted with a dough hook. Mix on medium speed. In a separate bowl, whisk together 4 of the eggs, the egg yolk, and 1 tablespoon water. Gradually add the egg mixture to the dry ingredients. The dough will initially appear loose and batterlike; as the gluten develops, it will bind and start to pull away from the sides of the bowl. This process will take 15 to 20 minutes.

Once the dough pulls away from the sides of the bowl, add the butter, 1 cube at a time, and continue to mix until the dough appears silky.

Place the dough in a greased bowl, cover with plastic wrap, and allow to proof for 1 hour at room temperature. Transfer to the refrigerator and proof for an additional hour. Punch down the dough and place a piece of plastic wrap directly on the surface of the brioche. Refrigerate overnight.

Working quickly and using just a dusting of flour to keep the dough from sticking, roll the dough to about 1/2 inch thick. Sift an even layer of cocoa powder on top of the dough. Roll the dough from the bottom up and shape into a log to fit in a 5 1/2-by-13-inch loaf pan. Coat the pan with vegetable spray and transfer the dough to the pan. Evenly press the dough to completely cover the bottom of the loaf pan. Cover with plastic wrap. Proof the loaf in a warm, draft-free area of the kitchen, such as near a warm oven or stove, for 3 to 4 hours or until doubled in size.

Preheat the oven to 325°F. Beat the remaining egg and brush the top of the loaf with the beaten egg. Bake the brioche for about 1 hour or until the temperature at the center of the loaf reaches 204°F on a probe thermometer and the top is a dark golden brown.

### TO FINISH

Cocoa Foie Gras Torchon
Quince Gelée
Quince Sauce
Cocoa Brioche

With a sharp knife, cut the Torchon into 1/2-inch slices. Use a ring cutter measuring 2 1/2 inches in diameter to punch out rounds and reserve the trim for another use. Place the a Torchon round in the center of the bowl on top of the Quince Gelée. Spoon 1/2 teaspoon of Quince Sauce around the Torchon disk. Serve with a slice of toasted Cocoa Brioche. Repeat with the remaining ingredients, to serve 8.

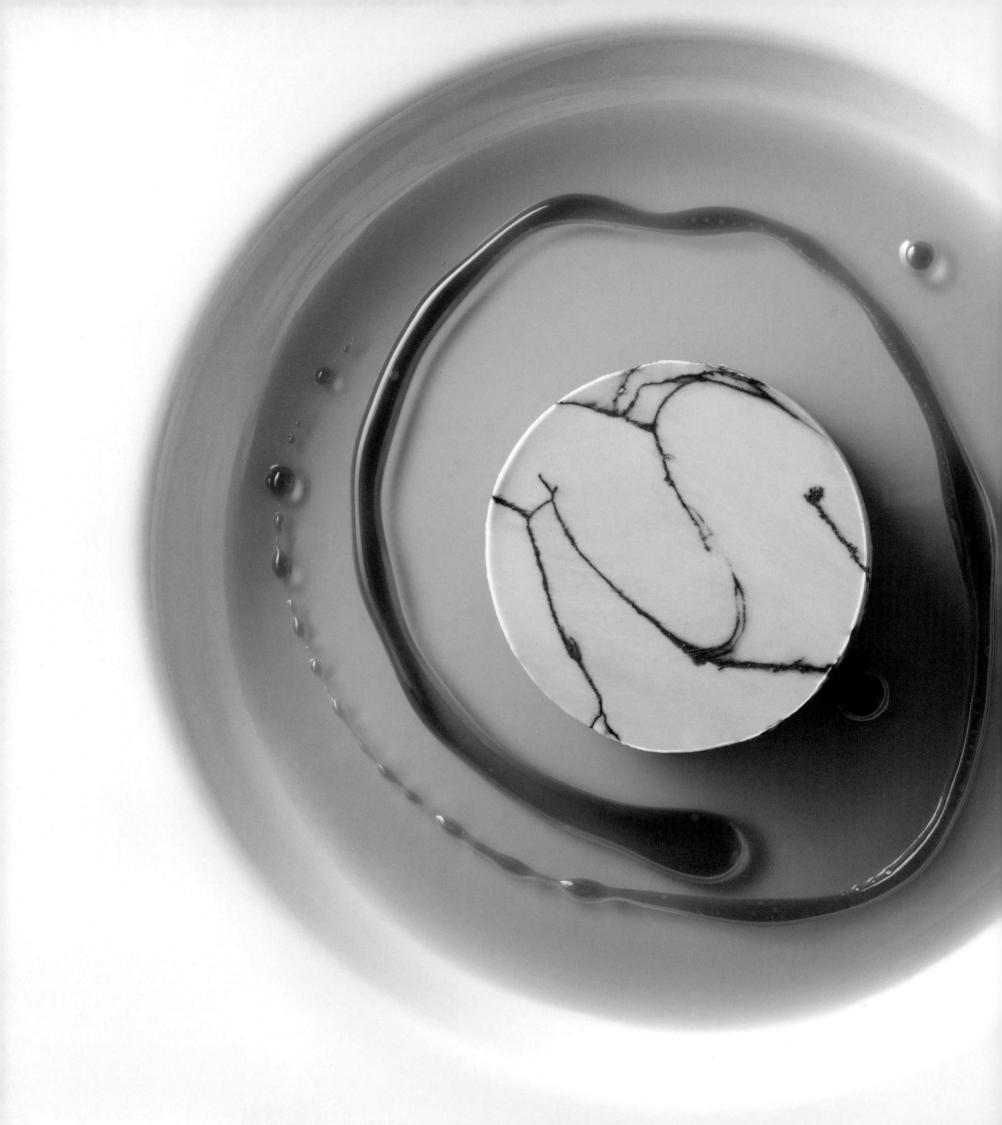

# SUNCHOKE
# ROASTED WITH WATERCRESS AND MUSTARD

*Serves 8*

### ROASTED SUNCHOKES
16 medium sunchokes
1 cup butter
8 teaspoons salt
16 sprigs thyme
4 bay leaves
8 strips (2 inches by 1/2 inch) lemon zest

Preheat the oven to 350°F. Scrub and clean the sunchokes thoroughly but do not peel them. Bring a pot of salted water to a boil and add the sunchokes. Cook for 5 minutes. Drain the sunchokes and cool to room temperature. Once cool, place 4 sunchokes in a piece of aluminum foil. Add 4 tablespoons of the butter, 2 teaspoons of the salt, 4 sprigs of the thyme, 1 bay leaf, and 2 strips of the lemon zest, and close the packet. Make 3 more packets with the remaining ingredients. Place the foil packets in a baking dish. Roast the sunchokes in the oven until they are tender, 45 to 50 minutes. Carefully remove the sunchokes from their foil packets, reserve the butter for the Sunchoke Slices and for plating the final dish, and cool the sunchokes to room temperature. Once cool, cut 8 of the sunchokes in half lengthwise, leaving the other 8 whole.

### SUNCHOKE SLICES
4 large sunchokes
10 sprigs thyme
1 1/4 teaspoons salt
2 strips (2 inches by 1/2 inch) lemon zest
4 cups Chicken Stock (see page 356)
2 tablespoons mustard powder
2 tablespoons white wine

Preheat the oven to 325°F. Scrub and clean the sunchokes thoroughly but do not peel them. Slice the sunchokes lengthwise into 1/4-inch-thick slices, yielding about 16 large slices total. In a mixing bowl, toss together the sliced sunchokes with the thyme, 1 teaspoon of the salt, and lemon zest. Transfer to a baking dish and cover with the Chicken Stock. Cover with aluminum foil and poach the sunchokes in the oven until they are tender, about 1 hour and 10 minutes, depending on the sizes of the sunchokes. Cool the sunchokes in their cooking liquid.

In a small bowl, whisk together the mustard powder and wine. Season with the remaining 1/4 teaspoon salt. Drain the Sunchoke Slices and brush them a thin layer of the mustard paste.

### LEMON BRIOCHE CRUST
2 cups brioche bread crumbs
1 tablespoon lemon zest
1 teaspoon salt
1/2 cup butter, at room temperature
Sunchoke Slices

In a large mixing bowl, toss together the bread crumbs, lemon zest, and salt. Add the butter and mix thoroughly to combine. Divide the mixture in half. Place half between 2 sheets of parchment paper and roll to 1/8 inch thick. Repeat with the other half. Chill the crust in the refrigerator for at least 2 hours before using. Once the crust is chilled, remove the top layer of parchment paper. Place the Sunchoke Slices on top of the Crust and cut the Crust to fit the Slices. Reserve in the refrigerator.

### WATERCRESS SAUCE
4 cups loosely packed watercress (5 ounces)
1/2 cup ice cubes
1/8 teaspoon xanthan gum (0.3 gram)
1 1/2 teaspoons salt
1/4 cup Lemon Oil (see page 345)

In a blender, puree the watercress with the ice and 1 3/4 cups water. Strain through a fine-mesh chinois. Return the watercress "water" to the blender. With the blender running on low speed, slowly add the xanthan gum. Season with the salt. Blend on low speed for 1 minute and then stream in the Lemon Oil to emulsify. Keep in the refrigerator.

### SUNCHOKE CHIPS
3 small sunchokes
8 cups canola oil
3/4 teaspoon salt

Thinly slice the sunchokes on a mandoline and reserve in water to prevent them from oxidizing. Meanwhile, heat the oil to 325°F. Drain the sunchoke slices and pat dry with paper towels. Fry the slices a few pieces at a time until they are golden brown, about 1 minute. Drain the chips on paper towels and season with the salt.

### TO FINISH
Sunchoke Slices
Sunchoke butter (reserved from whole
     Roasted Sunchokes)
2 cloves garlic
Roasted Sunchokes
3 sprigs thyme
24 sprigs watercress
2 teaspoons lemon juice
1/2 cup Sunchoke Puree (see page 354)
Pickled Sunchokes (see page 343)
Sunchoke Chips
4 tablespoons Pickled Yellow Mustard Seeds (page 342)
24 sprigs red watercress
Watercress Sauce

Preheat the broiler. Place the Sunchoke Slices, crust side up, on a baking sheet. Place under the broiler for 1 minute to toast the crust.

Meanwhile, melt 2 tablespoons of the sunchoke butter in a large sauté pan over medium-high heat until foamy. Add the garlic. Place the Roasted Sunchokes in the pan (the halved ones should be cut side down) and add the thyme. Baste the Sunchokes with the butter until they are heated through. Remove the Sunchokes from the pan and drain on paper towels. Add the fresh watercress to the same sauté pan and sauté with the lemon juice, until wilted, about 1 minute.

In a small saucepan, reheat the Sunchoke Puree over low heat.

On a plate, spread 1 tablespoon of the Sunchoke Puree. Place 1 Sunchoke Slice on top, 1 whole Roasted Sunchoke beside it, and 2 halves of Roasted Sunchoke on either side. Arrange 5 pieces Pickled Sunchokes, 4 Sunchoke Chips, 1 1/2 teaspoons Pickled Yellow Mustard Seeds, 3 sprigs sautéed watercress, and 3 sprigs red watercress on the plate. Finish the plate with 2 tablespoons Watercress Sauce. Repeat with the remaining ingredients, to serve 8.

# LANGOUSTINE
## MARINATED WITH CELERY ROOT AND GREEN APPLE

*Serves 8*

### GREEN APPLE SNOW

6 cups fresh green apple juice (from about 36 apples)
2 teaspoons Simple Syrup (see page 371)
2 teaspoons salt
Liquid nitrogen (optional)

Clarify the apple juice by placing it in the freezer. The sediment will settle to the bottom. Pour the juice into a clean container, leaving the sediment in the original container. Strain the juice through a coffee filter. Stir in the Simple Syrup and salt. Refrigerate until ready to freeze with liquid nitrogen.

Line a large metal bowl with acetate. Fill the bowl halfway with liquid nitrogen and carefully pour the juice into the liquid nitrogen. As it freezes, it will start to become brittle. Quickly transfer the frozen juice to a food processor and grind. The finished Green Apple Snow will be powdery. Reserve in the freezer.

Alternatively, pour the juice into a shallow baking dish and freeze until completely solid. When ready to serve, scrape the frozen juice with a fork to create the Green Apple Snow.

### CELERY CREAM

4 cups Fish Fumet (see page 356)
4 cups peeled, cored, and diced Granny Smith apples (about 2)
3 cups peeled and diced celery root (about 1/2 pound)
1/2 cup cream
1/2 cup crème fraîche
1/2 cup fresh green apple juice (from 3 to 4 apples)
4 teaspoons salt
1 teaspoon lime juice
1 pinch cayenne pepper

Combine the Fumet, apples, and celery root in a large pot, cover with a cartouche (lid made of parchment paper), and simmer over low heat until the vegetables are very tender and falling apart, about 30 minutes. Transfer to a blender and puree with the cream and crème fraîche. Strain through a fine-mesh chinois and chill over ice. Season with the apple juice, salt, lime juice, and cayenne.

### TO FINISH

8 langoustines
1 tablespoon plus 1 teaspoon Lime Vinaigrette (see page 346)
2 teaspoons salt
Celery Cream
Green Apple Snow
24 Granny Smith apple disks, 1/2 inch in diameter
24 Granny Smith apple batons, 1/8 inch by 1/8 inch by 1 1/2 inches
24 sprigs petite celery
24 celery leaves
1 teaspoon Celery Oil (see page 344)

To open the langoustines, first remove and discard the heads. With a pair of sharp scissors, start with the belly side of the langoustine and cut along the edges of the spine to remove the soft shell. With both hands, hold the edges of the spine and gently break the shell. Carefully remove the flesh, making sure to keep the red ridges on the flesh. Cut the langoustine in half and remove the veins and trim away the excess. Reserve the excess meat and dice it to make langoustine *hachée*.

Lightly dress the whole langoustines with 1 tablespoon Lime Vinaigrette and season with 1/4 teaspoon salt. Season the langoustine *hachée* with 1/2 teaspoon Lime Vinaigrette. Place 2 dressed langoustine halves and a quenelle of the seasoned langoustine *hachée* in a bowl. Pour 1/2 cup Celery Cream and spoon 2 tablespoons Green Apple Snow into the bowl. Arrange 3 apple disks, 3 apple batons, 3 celery sprigs, and 3 celery leaves on top. Garnish the bowl with 1/2 teaspoon Celery Oil. Repeat with the remaining ingredients, to serve 8.

# CELERY ROOT
## OVEN-ROASTED WITH BLACK TRUFFLES

*Serves 8*

### SALT-BAKED CELERY ROOT

4 large celery roots
2 pounds salt
12 egg whites

Preheat the oven to 375°F. Rinse the celery roots under running water, being sure to remove all dirt and grit. Keep the root ends on as they will be used for garnish. In a mixing bowl, stir together the salt and the egg whites until thoroughly combined and the mixture resembles wet sand. Line the bottom of a baking dish with 1/2 inch of the salt mixture. Place the celery root on top of the salt bed and cover with the rest of the salt mixture.

Roast in the oven until tender, about 2 1/2 hours. Remove the celery root from the salt crust and allow to cool to room temperature.

### CELERY ROOT SAUCE

4 cups finely diced celery root (about 1 1/4 pounds)
2 tablespoons canola oil
1/2 cup sliced shallots
1/2 cup diced (1/4 inch) carrots
1/2 cup diced (1/4 inch) celery
1 tablespoon tomato paste
2/3 cup red wine
1 cup truffle juice
1 1/2 teaspoons salt
1 teaspoon sherry vinegar
1/8 teaspoon xanthan gum (0.3 gram)
1 tablespoon extra-virgin olive oil

Preheat the oven to 400°F. Toss 3 cups of the celery root with 1 tablespoon of the canola oil and place on a baking sheet lined with parchment paper. Roast the celery root until dark brown, about 30 minutes. Transfer to a medium saucepan and cover with 6 cups water. Bring to a boil and remove from the heat. Cover the saucepan and allow the celery root to steep in the water for 45 minutes. Strain through a chinois, reserving the liquid.

In another medium saucepan, heat the remaining 1 tablespoon canola oil over high heat. Add the shallots, carrots, celery, and the remaining 1 cup celery root. Sauté the vegetables until they are caramelized, about 10 minutes. Add the tomato paste and continue sautéing for 5 more minutes. Deglaze the pan with the red wine and reduce until almost dry. Add the strained celery root liquid and truffle juice and simmer the mixture until approximately 1 1/2 cups remain, about 1 hour. Strain the sauce and discard the vegetables. Season with the salt and sherry vinegar and stir in the xanthan gum to thicken. Break the sauce with the olive oil.

### GREEN CELERY LEAVES AND BATONS

16 stalks celery

Bring a pot of salted water to a boil. Trim the celery, keeping the tops with their leafy greens. Peel the stalks and cut into 2-inch batons. Blanch the celery tops in the water for 2 minutes and transfer to a bowl of ice water. Add the batons and blanch for 3 minutes. Transfer to the ice bath. Once cold, drain. Using a paring knife, remove any tough stringy fibers from the batons.

### TO FINISH

Salt-Baked Celery Root
Green Celery Leaves and Batons
2 tablespoons butter
Salt
1/2 cup Smoked Celery Root Puree (see page 351)
4 black truffles, crumbled
1/2 cup Celery Root Crumble (see page 361)
*Fleur de sel*
Celery Root Sauce
16 yellow celery leaves

Trim off the root ends from the Salt-Baked Celery Root and set aside. You should have at least 40 pieces of the root ends to use for garnish. With a sharp knife, slice the Celery Root into 1/3-inch slices. Using a ring cutter measuring 2 1/2 inches in diameter, punch out circles from the slices. Trim the end pieces with the skin still on into random shapes. To glaze the Salt-Baked Celery Root, the root ends, and the Green Celery Leaves and Batons, heat 2 large sauté pans over medium heat. Add 2 tablespoons water to each pan and add the Celery Root to one pan, the Green Celery to the other. Bring to a simmer and add the butter to the pans. Season with salt and slowly reduce to glaze, about 1 1/2 minutes.

In a small saucepan over low heat, warm the Smoked Celery Root Puree. In the center of each plate, spread 1 tablespoon of the Puree and place 1 round Salt-Baked Celery Root on top. Arrange 5 pieces of the glazed root ends, 1 piece skin, 2 Celery Batons, 2 Green Celery Tops, and 7 small pieces of crumbled black truffle around the Celery Root. Spoon 1 tablespoon of the Celery Root Crumble beside it. Season with *fleur de sel* and spoon 1 tablespoon of the Celery Root Sauce onto the plate. Garnish with 2 yellow celery leaves.

# POTATO
## SMOKED WITH TRUFFLES AND PORK CRUMBLE

*Serves 8*

### MARBLE POTATO CONFIT

160 marble potatoes (about 2 1/3 pounds)
8 cups plus 2 tablespoons Smoked Butter (see page 359), melted
2 sprigs thyme
3 cloves garlic, crushed but kept whole
1 tablespoon Chicken Stock (see page 356)
*Fleur de sel*

Preheat the oven to 275°F. Place the unpeeled potatoes in a baking dish with the 8 cups Smoked Butter, thyme, and garlic and cover with aluminum foil. Roast the potatoes in the oven for 1 hour and 30 minutes. Remove from the oven and cool the potatoes to room temperature in the Butter. Once cool, strain, reserving the Butter. Peel the potatoes with a paring knife and return them to the strained Butter, keeping at room temperature until ready to use.

Heat the Chicken Stock in a large sauté pan over medium heat. Drain the potatoes and add them to the pan to warm through. Add the remaining 2 tablespoons Smoked Butter, tossing to glaze. Drain on paper towels and season with *fleur de sel*.

### TO FINISH

2 cups baby mâche leaves
2 teaspoons Buttermilk Dressing (see page 344)
1 1/2 cups Potato Mousseline (see page 353)
Marble Potato Confit
1/2 cup minced black truffle
1/4 cup Pork-Shallot Crumble (see page 363)
8 teaspoons Powdered Vinaigrette (see page 346)

Place the mâche in a mixing bowl, add the Buttermilk Dressing, and gently toss to coat.

Cut a rectangular template (measuring 2 1/2 inches by 6 inches) from a piece of acetate. Place the template on a plate, pipe 3 tablespoons of Potato Mousseline in the center, and spread evenly with an offset spatula or knife. Carefully peel off the template. Arrange 20 Marble Potatoes on top of the Potato Mousseline. Spoon 1 tablespoon minced black truffle and 1 1/2 teaspoons Pork-Shallot Crumble on top of the Potatoes. Finish with 1 teaspoon Powdered Vinaigrette and 8 sprigs of dressed mâche.

# BLACK TRUFFLE

*Served in four courses*

# BLACK TRUFFLE
## BEIGNETS

*Serves 8*

### BLACK TRUFFLE BEIGNETS

3/4 cup dried chickpeas
2 ounces (1 cup) black trumpet mushrooms
2 cups truffle juice
1 tablespoon butter
1/4 cup thinly sliced shallots
1 1/4 cups panko bread crumbs
1/2 cup thinly sliced black truffles
1 1/2 teaspoons salt
1/2 teaspoon squid ink
1/2 teaspoon baking soda
4 cups canola oil

Soak the chickpeas in water overnight. To clean the black trumpet mushrooms, pull them apart and rinse under cold running water, being sure to remove any dirt. Allow them to dry on paper towels.

In a small saucepan over medium heat, reduce the truffle juice to 2/3 cup. In a small sauté pan over medium-low heat, melt the butter and add the shallots, sweating until translucent, 3 minutes. Add the black trumpet mushrooms and sweat until they are soft and tender, 4 minutes. In a food processor, blend 1 1/4 cups of the soaked chickpeas, the reduced truffle juice, and the cooked shallot mixture. Add the bread crumbs, truffles, salt, squid ink, and baking soda. Puree until smooth.

Heat the canola oil in a large pot over medium heat to 375°F. Form balls with the dough measuring 1 1/2 inches in diameter. They should resemble black truffles and should not be perfectly round. Carefully drop the beignets into the oil, frying for about 3 minutes, until crisp. Using a slotted spoon, remove the fried beignets from the oil and drain on paper towels.

### BLACK TRUFFLE YOGURT

2 cups Greek yogurt
1 tablespoon lemon juice
2 teaspoons salt
2 tablespoons finely chopped black truffles
1 tablespoon finely sliced chives

In a medium bowl, whisk together the yogurt, lemon juice, and salt. Stir in the truffles and chives. Refrigerate until ready to use.

### TO FINISH

Black Truffle Beignets
4 cups Arborio rice (uncooked, for presentation)
Black Truffle Yogurt

Place the hot Black Truffle Beignets on a bed of Arborio rice. Place 1 1/2 tablespoons Black Truffle Yogurt in individual serving spoons to serve as a dipping sauce for the Beignets. Alternatively, the Yogurt may be served in a bowl alongside the Beignets.

# BLACK TRUFFLE
## WINTER IN PROVENCE

*Serves 8*

### POTATO MOUSSELINE ESPUMA

1 pound La Ratte fingerling potatoes, peeled and sliced
(1/8 inch thick)
1 tablespoon plus 1 teaspoon salt
3 cups cream
1 tablespoon Brown Butter (see page 370)
2 N$_2$O cartridges

Place the potatoes and 1 tablespoon of the salt in a
medium saucepan and cover with cold water. Bring to a
simmer over medium-low heat and cook until tender, 30
to 35 minutes. In the meantime, reduce the cream in a
small saucepan over medium heat until 2 cups remain.
Drain the cooked potatoes and transfer to a blender.
Puree the hot, reduced cream and Brown Butter with
the potatoes. Blend on high speed for 2 minutes and
season with the remaining 1 teaspoon salt. The mixture
should be the consistency of a thick potato soup.
Strain through a chinois and transfer the potatoes to
a whipped-cream canister. Charge with the N$_2$O cartridges and hold in a water bath maintained at 145°F
by an immersion circulator until ready to serve.

### CHÈVRE ESPUMA

1 cup goat's milk butter
3/4 cup chèvre
1/3 cup sheep's milk yogurt
3 eggs
1 egg yolk
1 tablespoon salt
2 N$_2$O cartridges

In a small saucepan, melt the butter over low heat.
Remove from the heat and allow to cool slightly. In a
mixing bowl, whisk together the chèvre, yogurt, eggs,
and egg yolk until the mixture is completely smooth.
Add the melted butter and whisk until incorporated.
Season the mixture with the salt. Transfer the mixture
to a whipped-cream canister, filling it up halfway, and
charge with the N$_2$O cartridges. Cook in a water bath
maintained at 145°F by an immersion circulator for 2
hours. Keep hot until ready to serve.

### TRUFFLE CELERY SAUCE

2 teaspoons diced (1/8 inch) green celery
3 tablespoons finely chopped black truffles
2 teaspoons thinly sliced yellow celery leaves
1/2 cup olive oil
1 teaspoon salt

Bring a small saucepan of salted water to a boil. Add
the diced celery, cooking for 45 seconds. Transfer to a
bowl of ice water and, once cold, drain. In a small mixing
bowl, combine the celery, truffles, and celery leaves.
Just before serving, add the olive oil and salt.

### TO FINISH

1/2 cup Black Truffle Puree (see page 350)
1/2 cup Celery Root Puree (see page 351)
Chèvre Espuma
Potato Mousseline Espuma
1/3 cup Truffle Celery Sauce

In 2 small saucepans set over low heat, warm the Black
Truffle Puree and Celery Root Puree. Spoon 1 tablespoon each Black Truffle Puree and Celery Root Puree
on either side of a bowl. Expel 2 tablespoons of the
Chèvre Espuma and 2 tablespoons of the Potato Mousseline Espuma between the Purees. Top the foams with
2 teaspoons of the Truffle Celery Vinaigrette. Repeat
with the remaining ingredients, to serve 8. Serve
immediately.

# BLACK TRUFFLE
POACHED TURBOT
WITH CELERY
AND TAPIOCA

Serves 8

### TURBOT MOUSSELINE
1 cup diced turbot trim (reserved from Turbot)
1 egg white
1/2 cup cream
1 teaspoon salt
1 pinch cayenne pepper
1 1/2 teaspoons diced black truffles

It is important that all of the ingredients and the bowl of the food processor are cold before beginning to prepare the Mousseline.

Place the turbot trim in the food processor and process until it is finely chopped. Add the egg white and puree until almost smooth. Scrape down the sides of the bowl to make sure the turbot is incorporated. With the food processor running, slowly incorporate the cream and salt until the mixture is smooth. Add the cayenne. Pass the mousseline through a medium tamis and fold in the truffles. Transfer to a piping bag and refrigerate until ready to use.

### TAPIOCA
1 tablespoon salt
1 cup large tapioca pearls

In a large pot, combine 1 gallon water and the salt and bring to a boil over high heat. Add the tapioca pearls and lower the heat to medium. Stir to ensure even cooking. Simmer the tapioca pearls until they are tender but still maintain a bite, about 35 to 40 minutes. Strain the tapioca and rinse under cold water to remove excess starch. Hold the tapioca pearls in cold water until ready to serve.

### TURBOT
2 whole turbot, 3 to 4 pounds each
2 medium celery roots
2 black truffles
Turbot Mousseline
2 teaspoons salt
1/4 cup butter, room temperature

Ask your fishmonger to fillet and skin the fish, saving the bones and any trim from the fish. You should have 4 fillets.

To make the "scales" on the fish, bring a saucepan of salted water to a boil. Thinly slice the celery root on a mandoline to 1/16 inch. Add the celery root slices to the water and cook for 1 to 2 minutes. Transfer to a bowl of ice water. Once cool, drain and dry the slices on paper towels. Using a ring cutter measuring 1/2 inch in diameter, cut rounds from the celery root. Thinly slice the black truffles on a mandoline to 1/16 inch and cut rounds with the same 1/2-inch ring cutter.

Lay a fillet skin side down, bone side up, and make an incision with a sharp knife down the center of the fish, being careful not to cut through to the other side. Spread the incision open with your fingers and slice an opening on the right and left sides to create a pocket. Pipe about 1 tablespoon Turbot Mousseline into the opening and carefully replace the flaps. Gently flip the fish over and arrange the celery root and truffle coins on the fish, overlapping and alternating the slices to create a scale effect. Repeat with the remaining fillets. Chill in the refrigerator to set the Turbot Mousseline and the "scales." Season both sides of the fillets with the salt and brush with the butter. Place each fillet into individual *sous vide* bags and vacuum-seal. Poach the fillets in a water bath maintained at 137°F by an immersion circulator for 7 minutes.

### VEGETABLE GARNISH
1 cup peeled and diced (1/4 inch) celery root
1 cup peeled and diced (1/4 inch) celery

Bring a pot of salted water to a boil. Add the celery root and cook for 2 minutes. Transfer to a bowl of ice water. Repeat with the celery, cooking for 3 minutes. Once cool, drain and set aside until ready to use.

### FUMET BLANC
1 tablespoon canola oil
1 pound turbot bones (reserved from Turbot), rinsed of any blood
1/4 cup thinly sliced shallots
1/4 cup diced celery
1/4 cup peeled and diced celery root
2 tablespoons diced button mushrooms
1/4 cup dry vermouth
1/4 cup white wine
8 cups ice cubes
1 cup cream
1/2 cup crème fraîche
2 tablespoons plus 1 teaspoon lime juice
2 teaspoons salt
1 pinch cayenne pepper

In a large, straight-sided pan, heat the canola oil over high heat. Dry the turbot bones on paper towels, add them to the pan, and sear for 30 to 45 seconds on each side. Remove the bones from the pan. Reduce the heat to low and add the shallots, celery, celery root, and mushrooms and cover with a cartouche (lid made of parchment paper). Sweat the vegetables until they are tender, about 5 minutes. Uncover, raise the heat to medium, and deglaze with the dry vermouth. Reduce until the pan is almost dry. Add the white wine and reduce until almost dry, but do not brown the vegetables. Return the seared bones to the pan and add the ice cubes. Bring to a simmer, skim off any fats and impurities that rise to the top, and remove from the heat. Cover with a lid and steep for 30 minutes. Strain. Return the Fumet to the pan and reduce by half. Add the cream and bring to a simmer. Using a hand blender, blend in the crème fraîche. Season with the lime juice, salt, and cayenne. Strain and keep warm until ready to use.

### TO FINISH
Turbot
2 tablespoons Fish Fumet (see page 356)
Vegetable Garnish
2/3 cup diced (1/4 inch) black truffle
Tapioca
1 tablespoon butter
1/4 teaspoon salt
Fumet Blanc

Remove the cooked Turbot from the bags and trim into 2 diamonds. Place 1 Turbot diamond in the center of a bowl. Heat the Fish Fumet in a large sauté pan over medium heat. Add the Vegetable Garnish and allow to heat through. Add the diced black truffles, the drained Tapioca, and the butter and toss to glaze evenly. Season with the salt. Spoon 1/4 cup of the glazed vegetables and Tapioca around the Turbot. With a hand blender, foam the Fumet Blanc and pour 1/4 cup around the fish. Repeat with the remaining ingredients, to serve 8.

# BLACK TRUFFLE BRAISED VEAL CHEEKS WITH PARSNIP

*Serves 8*

### BRAISED VEAL CHEEKS

8 veal cheeks, cleaned of all silver skin
1 carrot, diced (3/4 inch)
1 stalk celery, diced (3/4 inch)
1 white onion, diced (3/4 inch)
2 sprigs thyme
1 bay leaf
One 750-milliliter bottle red wine
1 1/2 teaspoons salt
1 tablespoon canola oil
1 1/2 teaspoons tomato paste
2 cups Veal Jus (see page 357)

Place the veal cheeks, carrot, celery, onion, thyme, and bay leaf in a large nonreactive container (such as plastic or glass). Cover with the wine and marinate for 48 hours in the refrigerator.

Remove the cheeks from the marinade and pat dry on paper towels. Strain the marinade, reserving the liquid and the vegetables separately. Bring the liquid to a simmer in a medium saucepan over medium heat, skimming any impurities that rise as it simmers. Strain through a chinois.

Preheat the oven to 275°F. Season the veal cheeks with the salt. Heat the oil in a large, straight-sided oven-safe pan over high heat. Sear the veal cheeks on all sides, 30 to 45 seconds per side. Remove from the pan. Drain any excess oil from the pan, lower the heat to medium, and add the strained vegetables. Sweat until tender, about 10 minutes. Add the tomato paste and sweat with the vegetables for 3 minutes. Deglaze the pan with the strained red wine and reduce by half. Add the Veal Jus and bring to a simmer. Return the seared veal cheeks to the pan, cover, and transfer to the oven. Braise in the oven until the veal is tender and can be easily pulled apart with a fork, about 2 hours.

Gently remove the veal cheeks from the braising liquid and set aside. Strain the liquid and discard the vegetables. Return the veal cheeks to the strained liquid and chill over ice. At this point, the veal cheeks can be refrigerated for up to 1 day before proceeding.

When ready to continue, remove the veal cheeks from the braising liquid. Reduce the liquid over medium heat to the consistency of a glaze, about 30 to 40 minutes. To glaze the veal cheeks, add them to the glaze, basting until heated through.

### PARSNIP AND TRUFFLES

1 large parsnip, peeled and diced (1/4 inch)
1 tablespoon Chicken Stock (see page 356)
1/4 cup diced (1/4 inch) black truffles
1 tablespoon butter
1/4 teaspoon salt

Bring a large pot of salted water to a boil. Add the diced parsnip, cooking for about 2 minutes, and transfer to a bowl of ice water. Once cool, drain.

Heat a small sauté pan over medium heat. Add the Chicken Stock and the parsnip and warm through. Add the diced truffles, butter, and salt, and reduce, tossing to glaze evenly.

### TRUFFLE JUS

2 teaspoons butter
1/2 cup finely minced shallots
1/2 cup finely minced black truffles
2 cups Madeira
4 cups Veal Jus (page 357)
1 cup truffle juice
6 sprigs thyme

In a medium straight-sided pan, melt the butter over medium heat until it begins to foam. Add the shallots and black truffles and sweat until tender, about 4 minutes. Add the Madeira and raise the heat to medium-high. Reduce the Madeira to 1 cup. Add the Veal Jus, truffle juice, and thyme and simmer over low heat until 2 cups remain. Remove the thyme and keep warm until ready to serve.

### TO FINISH

1 cup Parsnip Puree (see page 352)
Braised Veal Cheeks
Parsnip and Truffles
16 parsley leaves
Truffle Jus

Warm the Parsnip Puree in a small saucepan over medium heat. Set a 5-inch ring mold on a plate and, using a small spoon, spread 2 tablespoons Parsnip Puree along the edge of the mold. Place 1 glazed Veal Cheek at the top of the Puree. Spoon glazed Parsnip and Truffles onto the Veal Cheek and place 2 parsley leaves on top. Finish with the Truffle Jus. Repeat with the remaining ingredients, to serve 8.

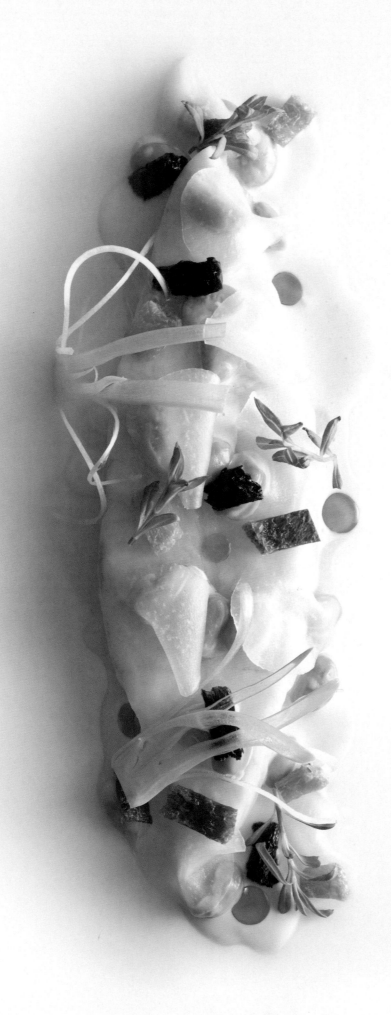

# JOHN DORY
## POACHED WITH CITRUS, DAIKON RADISHES, AND OLIO NUOVO

*Serves 8*

### DRIED CITRUS

2 pink grapefruits
2 navel oranges
2 blood oranges
2 tablespoons confectioners' sugar

Preheat the oven to 175°F. Cut off the top and bottom of the citrus fruits. Remove the rind, along with any white pith. With a paring knife, cut between the membranes to yield individual segments of fruit. Line up the segments on an acetate-lined baking sheet and sprinkle with the confectioners' sugar. Place in the oven overnight to dehydrate. Cool to room temperature. Trim the citrus into 1/2-inch pieces and store in an airtight container.

### CITRUS BEURRE BLANC

1 1/2 cups grapefruit juice
1 cup orange juice
1/2 cup lemon juice
2 pounds cold butter, cubed
1 1/2 teaspoons salt

Combine the juices in a medium straight-sided saucepan and reduce to 2 cups over high heat. Lower the heat to medium and whisk in the cubed butter, little by little, until all the butter is fully emulsified. Remove from the heat and season with the salt. Keep warm until ready to use.

### EDAMAME

2 cups shelled edamame
1 tablespoon Chicken Stock (see page 356)
1 tablespoon butter
1/2 teaspoon salt

Bring a pot of salted water to a boil. Add the edamame and cook for 2 minutes. Transfer to a bowl of ice water, and, once cold, drain. Gently peel the outer membrane off of the edamame.

Heat the edamame and Chicken Stock in a large sauté pan over medium-high heat. Once warmed through, add the butter and reduce to glaze, about 1 minute. Season with the salt.

### POACHED JOHN DORY

8 cups Chicken Stock (see page 356)
5 cloves garlic, peeled and cut in half
5 sprigs thyme
1 1/2 tablespoons plus 1 1/2 teaspoons salt
1/2 cup cornstarch
8 John Dory fillets

Preheat the oven to 300°F. To make the poaching liquid, combine the Chicken Stock, garlic, and thyme in a large pot and bring to a rolling boil. Season with the 1 1/2 tablespoons salt. In a mixing bowl, whisk together 1/2 cup water and the cornstarch. When the Chicken Stock is at a full boil, whisk in the cornstarch mixture and boil for 3 minutes to cook out the starch. Strain into a deep baking dish and allow to cool to 140°F. Place the baking dish in the oven to keep the poaching liquid warm.

Season the John Dory on both sides with the remaining 1 1/2 teaspoons salt. Place the fillets in the poaching liquid and poach until the fish can be easily pierced with the tip of a knife, 6 to 7 minutes. Using a fish spatula, remove the fillets from the poaching liquid and drain them on paper towels. Rest the fish for 1 minute.

### TO FINISH

4 scallions
Poached John Dory
Citrus Beurre Blanc
*Fleur de sel*
Pickled Daikon (see page 341)
Edamame
32 sprigs petite Spanish tarragon
Dried Citrus
8 teaspoons Daikon Vinaigrette (see page 345)
4 teaspoons *olio nuovo*

Trim off the green tops of the scallions so that 3 inches remain on the bottom. Shave the scallions on a mandoline, starting with the root end, about 1/16 inch thick. Reserve the scallion shaves in ice water until ready to serve.

Spoon 2 tablespoons of the Citrus Beurre Blanc on top of each John Dory fillet to coat evenly. Season with *fleur de sel*. Place the glazed Poached John Dory in the center of a plate. Arrange 6 Daikon Pickles and 2 tablespoons Edamame on and around the fish. Garnish with 2 scallion shaves, 4 petite Spanish tarragon sprigs, and 1 tablespoon Dried Citrus. Finish with 1 teaspoon of the Daikon Vinaigrette and 1/2 teaspoon *olio nuovo*. Repeat with the remaining ingredients, to serve 8.

# SKATE
## ROASTED WITH CURRY, COCONUT, AND SEAWEED

*Serves 8*

### GREMOLATA

2 cups parsley leaves, tightly packed
2 cups cilantro leaves, tightly packed
1 cup unsweetened shaved coconut
Zest of 1 lemon
1 small bird's-eye chili, minced
1/2 teaspoon salt

Bring a pot of salted water to a boil. Add the parsley leaves and cook for 15 seconds, until wilted. Transfer to a bowl of ice water. Repeat with the cilantro and then the coconut. Drain and dry the blanched herbs and the shaved coconut in a clean towel. Finely chop the herbs and the coconut and combine with the lemon zest, red chili, and salt.

### SKATE

Gremolata
4 skate wing fillets, 6 ounces each, cleaned and boned
6 tablespoons canola oil
1 teaspoon salt
1 cup flour

Spread about 2 tablespoons of Gremolata down the center of 1 skate wing. Stack another skate wing on top so that they mirror each other. Place the stack in a *sous vide* bag and vacuum-seal. Repeat with the other 2 fillets and refrigerate. When ready to cook, place the bags in a water bath maintained at 145°F by an immersion circulator and cook for 4 minutes. Transfer the sealed bags to an ice bath to cool. Heat 2 large sauté pans over high heat with 3 tablespoons of canola oil in each one. Remove the skate wings from the bags and season with the salt. Dredge in the flour, patting off any excess. Just before the oil begins to smoke, add 1 pair of skate wings to each pan, and lower the heat to medium-high. Sauté until golden brown on one side, about 4 minutes. Flip the fish and baste with the hot canola oil to shallow-fry and evenly brown, about 3 more minutes. Remove the fish from the pans and place on paper towels to remove excess oil. Slice each wing pair in quarters and trim the ends to make 8 even pieces.

### CURRY SAUCE

1 teaspoon canola oil
2/3 cup minced lemongrass
1 tablespoon thinly sliced ginger
2/3 cup thinly sliced leeks
4 shallots, peeled and thinly sliced
1 1/2 teaspoons Madras curry powder
1/3 cup dry white vermouth
1/4 cup white port
1/3 cup white wine
2 kaffir lime leaves
1 1/2 cups Chicken Stock (see page 356)
1 1/2 cups cream
4 tablespoons unsweetened coconut flakes
1 Granny Smith apple, peeled, cored, and diced
1/2 cup diced pineapple
1/2 banana
1/4 cup parsley leaves
1 tablespoon cold butter
1/4 cup lime juice
1 1/2 teaspoons salt
1 pinch cayenne pepper

Heat the canola oil in a straight-sided pan over medium heat. Add the lemongrass and ginger and sweat for 2 to 3 minutes. Add the leeks and shallots and sweat until they are translucent, about 3 minutes. Add the curry powder and sauté for 1 minute. Deglaze with the vermouth, port, and wine. Add the kaffir lime leaves and reduce the heat to low. Simmer the alcohol until about 1/2 cup liquid remains in the pan. Add the Chicken Stock and simmer over low heat for 5 minutes. Add the cream and coconut flakes and simmer for 10 minutes. Transfer to a blender and, while still hot, puree with the apple, pineapple, banana, and parsley. With the blender running, add the butter to emulsify. Season with lime juice, salt, and cayenne. Strain through a chinois.

### BOK CHOY

24 heads baby bok choy
3 tablespoons Chicken Stock (see page 356)
2 tablespoons butter
1/2 teaspoon salt

Peel off the outer leaves of the baby bok choy so that the hearts remain (about 2 inches in length). Bring a pot of salted water to a boil. Add the bok choy and cook for 2 minutes. Transfer to a bowl of ice water and, once cool, drain.

Warm the bok choy in the Chicken Stock in a sauté pan over medium heat. Add the butter, reducing to glaze. Season with the salt and drain on a paper towel.

### SEAWEED

1 cup dried dulse seaweed, rinsed
3 tablespoons lemon juice
2 tablespoons butter
1/4 teaspoon salt

Warm the seaweed in the lemon juice in a sauté pan over medium heat. Add the butter, reducing to glaze. Season with the salt and drain on a paper towel.

### TO FINISH

3/4 cup Meyer Lemon Puree (see page 352)
1/4 cup White Lemon Puree (see page 352)
Curry Sauce
Skate
Seaweed
Bok Choy
1/2 teaspoon Madras curry powder

In 2 separate small saucepans, heat the Meyer Lemon Puree and the White Lemon Puree over medium heat until warm. In a medium saucepan, heat the Curry Sauce over medium heat and froth with a hand blender.

Spoon 1 1/2 tablespoons Meyer Lemon Puree and 1 1/2 teaspoons of the White Lemon Puree on a plate. Place a portion of the Skate in the center of the plate. Arrange 3 pieces Seaweed and 3 Bok Choy around the Skate. Finish the plate with 3 spoonfuls of the Curry Foam and a dusting of the Madras curry. Repeat with the remaining Skate.

# PRAWN
## POACHED WITH CALAMARI AND POTATO GNOCCHI

*Serves 8*

## GNOCCHI

3 pounds russet potatoes, scrubbed
4 tablespoons salt
2 cups flour, plus more for dusting
1 cup butter, softened
8 egg yolks
1/3 cup grated Parmesan
Nutmeg

Place the potatoes in a large saucepan and cover with cold water. Add 2 tablespoons of the salt and bring to a simmer over medium heat. Cook until tender when pierced with a knife, 45 to 50 minutes. Once the potatoes are cooked, remove the pan from the heat but keep the potatoes in the water to keep them hot as you peel them. Working quickly with 1 potato at a time, use a paring knife to peel off the skin. Pass the peeled, warm potato through a medium tamis onto a baking sheet lined with parchment paper. Repeat with the remaining potatoes, making sure that as they pass through the tamis they fall in a single layer instead of mounding. This will ensure that the potatoes are fluffy and light, as opposed to wet and dense. Wrap in a kitchen towel and cool to room temperature.

When the potatoes are cool, measure out 8 cups without packing them. Dust a work surface with flour and spread the potatoes out in an even layer over the flour. Evenly layer on 1 1/2 cups of the flour and all of the butter, egg yolks, Parmesan, nutmeg and the remaining 2 tablespoons salt. Using a pastry cutter or dough scraper, combine with a cutting motion. Do not knead the dough. Continue to cut the dough until the ingredients are fully incorporated, adding as little of the remaining 1/2 cup flour as necessary to keep the pastry cutter from sticking to the dough.

Flatten the dough to a 3/4-inch thickness and transfer to a baking sheet lined with parchment paper. Cover with plastic wrap and refrigerate for at least 2 hours.

When ready to form the gnocchi, dust your work surface with flour. Remove the dough from the baking sheet and cut it crosswise into 3/4-inch-wide strips. Roll the strips into long ropes. Do not use too much force when rolling. Line up the dough ropes and cut them into 3/4-inch pillows. Roll each pillow into a sphere. Roll the dough balls down the back of a fork, gently pressing with the tip of your thumb, to create a ridged front and a dimpled back. Place the gnocchi on a baking sheet lined with parchment and lightly floured. Refrigerate until ready to cook, up to 8 hours.

## CANDIED LEMON PEEL

1 lemon
1 cup sugar

Using a vegetable peeler, peel the zest from the lemon. (Reserve the lemon segments for another use.) Cut the zest into strips measuring 1/8 inch by 3/4 inch. To blanch the lemon zest, put it in a small pot and cover with cold water. Bring to a simmer and drain. Repeat 2 more times. Combine the lemon zest, sugar, and 1 cup water in the same pot and bring to a low simmer. Cook the zest over very low heat for 2 hours. Cool in the cooking liquid and keep at room temperature.

## FINGERLING POTATO CHIPS

1/4 cup salt
5 La Ratte fingerling potatoes
Canola oil

Bring 8 cups water and the salt to a boil in a saucepan. In the meantime, slice the fingerling potatoes on a mandoline into paper-thin slices. Place the slices in a large bowl and pour the boiling water over them. Allow to cool to room temperature. In a large saucepan, bring the oil to 325°F. Remove the potato slices from the water, pat dry, and fry in batches until crisp. Drain on paper towels and cool to room temperature. Keep the potato chips in an airtight container.

## MARBLE POTATO CONFIT

40 marble potatoes (about 9 ounces)
4 cups olive oil
2 sprigs thyme
3 cloves garlic, crushed but kept whole
1 tablespoon Chicken Stock (see page 356)
2 tablespoons butter
*Fleur de sel*

Preheat the oven to 275°F. Place the unpeeled potatoes in a baking dish with the olive oil, thyme, and garlic and cover with aluminum foil. Roast the potatoes in the oven for 1 hour and 30 minutes. Remove from the oven and cool the potatoes in the oil at room temperature. Once cool, strain, reserving the oil. Peel the potatoes with a paring knife and return them to the strained olive oil, reserving at room temperature until ready to use.

Heat the Chicken Stock in a large sauté pan over medium heat. Drain the potatoes and add them to the pan to warm through. Add the butter, tossing to glaze. Drain on paper towels and season with *fleur de sel*.

## GREEN CELERY LEAVES

16 stalks celery

Bring a pot of salted water to a boil. Trim the celery and keep the tops with the leafy greens. Add the celery to the boiling water and cook for 2 minutes. Transfer to a bowl of ice water. Once cold, drain.

## ORANGE BEURRE BLANC

4 cups white wine
3 cups orange juice
1/2 cup cream
3 pounds cold butter, diced (1 inch)
3 tablespoons salt
1 1/2 teaspoons *piment d'Espelette*

Reduce the wine in a saucepan to 1 cup. Add the orange juice and cream and reduce to just over 2 cups. Reduce the heat to low and slowly whisk in the butter, 3 to 4 cubes at a time. Stir slowly and constantly. When the butter is completely emulsified, add the salt and *piment d'Espelette*. Keep warm at 155°F.

## PRAWNS

1 pound Hawaiian blue prawns, shelled
1 teaspoon salt
Orange Beurre Blanc

Using a small knife or tweezers, remove the veins from the prawns. Season the prawns with the salt. Poach the prawns in the Orange Beurre Blanc at 155°F for 3 to 4 minutes.

## CALAMARI

1 pound baby calamari, cleaned, rinsed, and dried
1/2 teaspoon salt
1 cup Orange Beurre Blanc

Season the calamari with the salt. Poach the calamari in the Citrus Beurre Blanc at 155°F for 1 minute.

## TO FINISH

Gnocchi
4 tablespoons butter
3/4 teaspoon salt
2 tablespoons Chicken Stock (see page 356)
Green Celery Leaves
1 cup Celery Root Puree (see page 351)
Zest of 1 lime
Calamari
Prawns
Marble Potatoes
24 sprigs flat-leaf parsley
Fingerling Potato Chips
Candied Lemon Peel

To cook the Gnocchi, bring a large pot of salted water to a rolling boil. Add the Gnocchi. Once they float to the top, cook them for an additional 5 to 6 seconds. Transfer the Gnocchi with 2 tablespoons of their cooking liquid to a large sauté pan over medium heat and add 2 tablespoons of the butter. Season with 1/2 teaspoon of the salt and gently reduce to glaze.

Heat the Chicken Stock in a medium sauté pan over medium heat. Add the blanched Green Celery Leaves and warm through. Add the remaining 2 tablespoons of butter and reduce to glaze. Season with the remaining 1/4 teaspoon salt.

Warm the Celery Root Puree in a small pot over low heat and stir in the lime zest. Drain the poached Calamari and Prawns on a paper towel to remove excess butter. On a plate, spoon 2 tablespoons of the warmed Celery Root Puree. Arrange 6 glazed Gnocchi, 5 Calamari, and 2 Prawns on top. Finish the plate with 2 Green Celery Leaves, 5 Marble Potatoes, 3 sprigs parsley, 5 Fingerling Potato Chips, and 4 strips Candied Lemon Peel. Repeat with the remaining ingredients, to serve 8.

# LOBSTER
## POACHED WITH BERGAMOT AND CELERY

*Serves 8*

## LOBSTER

8 (1 1/4-pound) live lobsters

Fill a large stockpot with water and bring the water to 150°F. Add 2 of the lobsters, and cook for 7 minutes, maintaining the temperature of the water at 150°F. Remove the tails from the lobsters and transfer them to an ice bath. Return the knuckles and claws to the water and continue cooking for 7 more minutes. Transfer the knuckles and claws to the ice bath. Repeat with the remaining lobsters. When the tails, knuckles, and claws are completely cool, carefully remove the meat from the shells, making sure to keep the meat intact. Refrigerate.

## ORANGE BEURRE BLANC

4 cups white wine
3 cups orange juice
1/2 cup cream
3 pounds cold butter, diced (1 inch)
3 tablespoons salt
1 1/2 teaspoons *piment d'Espelette*

Reduce the wine in a saucepan to 1 cup. Add the orange juice and cream and reduce to just over 2 cups. Reduce the heat to low and slowly whisk in the butter, 3 to 4 cubes at a time. Stir slowly and constantly. When the butter is completely emulsified, add the salt and *piment d'Espelette*. Keep in a warm place, such as near a warm oven or stove.

## BERGAMOT AND LEMON MARMALADE

1 tablespoon allspice
1 tablespoon Szechuan peppercorns
3 pods star anise
1 1/2 teaspoons fennel seeds
1/4 teaspoon cayenne pepper
4 Meyer lemons
1 bergamot
3/4 cup sugar
3 tablespoons Meyer lemon juice
1/2 teaspoon salt

To make the spice mixture, toast the allspice, Szechuan peppercorns, star anise, and fennel seeds in a small sauté pan over medium heat for about 1 minute. Grind the toasted spices in a spice grinder to a fine powder. Mix the ground spices with the cayenne and store in an airtight container until ready to use.

Slice the lemons and bergamot 1/4 inch thick and remove the seeds. Layer the lemon and three quarters of the bergamot slices on the bottom of a medium saucepan, overlapping if necessary. (Save the remaining bergamot slices for another use.) Cover the slices with cold water, bring the water up to a low simmer, and immediately drain. Repeat this process 3 times. After the slices have been blanched 3 times, return the slices to the pan, add the sugar and 2 cups water, and bring up to a low simmer. Simmer over low heat until the sugar and water cook down to a thick syrup and the lemon and bergamot slices are coated. Cool over ice. Finely chop the slices and add the Meyer lemon juice, 1/2 teaspoon of the spice mixture, and the salt.

## LOBSTER LEMONGRASS SABAYON

1 tablespoon canola oil
1 cup thinly sliced lemongrass
1/2 cup thinly sliced shallots
1/4 cup thinly sliced celery
1/4 cup Cognac
2 1/4 cups white wine
4 cups Lobster Stock (see page 356)
1 tablespoon lobster roe
1 tablespoon cream
2 cups (1 pound) butter, melted
5 whole eggs
2 egg yolks
1/4 cup lime juice
5 teaspoons salt
2 N$_2$O cartridges

Heat the oil in a large saucepan over medium heat. Add the lemongrass, shallots, and celery and sweat the vegetables until they are soft, about 5 minutes. Deglaze the pan with the Cognac and reduce until the pan is almost dry. Add the wine and reduce by half. Add the Lobster Stock and simmer over low heat for 30 minutes. Strain through a fine-mesh chinois, return the stock to the pan, and reduce until 1/2 cup remains.

In a large mixing bowl, combine the reduced stock with the butter, eggs, egg yolks, lime juice, and salt.

Mix with a hand blender and transfer the mixture to a whipped-cream canister. Fill the canister two thirds of the way full and charge with the N$_2$O cartridges. Hold the sabayon in a water bath maintained at 145°F by an immersion circulator for 2 hours.

## GLAZED CELERY

4 stalks celery
1 tablespoon Chicken Stock (see page 356)
1 tablespoon butter
1/4 teaspoon salt

Bring a pot of salted water to a boil. Peel the celery and cut it on the bias into 2 1/2-inch batons. Add the celery batons to the salted water and cook for 3 minutes. Transfer to a bowl of ice water. Using a paring knife, remove any tough, stringy fibers from the celery.

Heat the Chicken Stock in a small sauté pan over low heat. Add the blanched celery batons and bring to a simmer to warm through. Add the butter, tossing to glaze. Season with the salt.

## TO FINISH

Orange Beurre Blanc
Lobster
*Fleur de sel*
1/2 cup Celery Root Puree (see page 351)
1/2 cup Bergamot Puree (see page 350)
Bergamot and Lemon Marmalade
Glazed Celery
16 sprigs celery
Lobster Lemongrass Sabayon
Lobster Roe Powder (see page 371)

Bring the Orange Beurre Blanc to 155°F. Cook the Lobster in the warm Beurre Blanc for 8 to 10 minutes, until warmed through. Remove the Lobster from the Beurre Blanc and sprinkle lightly with *fleur de sel*.

In 2 separate saucepans over medium heat, warm the celery Root Puree and Bergamot Puree.

Spoon a streak of Celery Root Puree down the center of a plate. Place a poached Lobster at the end of the Puree. Arrange 1 tablespoon of the Bergamot and Lemon Marmalade, 1 tablespoon of the Bergamot Puree, and 2 pieces of the Glazed Celery on top. Finish the plate with 2 sprigs celery and 2 tablespoons of the Lobster Lemongrass Sabayon. Sprinkle with the Lobster Roe Powder and repeat with the remaining ingredients, to serve 8.

*Note: At the restaurant, we use the claws and knuckles in other dishes. If you're preparing only one lobster recipe, plate the dishes with the tails and claws.*

# QUAIL
## ROASTED WITH ENDIVE, DATES, AND JUNIPER

*Serves 8*

### SOY GLAZE

1 cup soy sauce
1/2 cup honey
2 tablespoons minced garlic
1/2 cup olive oil

Combine the soy sauce, honey, and garlic in a small saucepan and bring to a simmer. Reduce over very low heat for 40 minutes. Strain and stir in the olive oil.

### ENDIVES

8 red endives, halved and trimmed to 2 inches
Red Wine Endive Cooking Liquid
4 teaspoons salt
16 yellow endives, halved and trimmed to 2 inches
Saffron Cooking Liquid
2 1/2 tablespoons butter

Combine the red endives with 3 tablespoons of the Red Wine Endive Cooking Liquid and season with 2 teaspoons of the salt. Place in a *sous vide* bag and vacuum-seal. Combine the yellow endives with 3 tablespoons of the Saffron Cooking Liquid and season with the remaining 2 teaspoons salt. Place in a *sous vide* bag and vacuum-seal. Steam the endives in a combination steam oven for 25 minutes at 185°F. Chill the endives in an ice bath and hold in the bags until ready to use.

Alternatively, place the endives in 2 separate straight-sided pots. Cover with their respective cooking liquids and salt and bring to a simmer over medium heat. Cover with a cartouche (lid made of parchment paper) and simmer over low heat until they are tender, about 15 to 20 minutes. Cool the endives over ice in their cooking liquids and reserve in the refrigerator until ready to use.

To glaze the Endives (whether prepared conventionally or *sous vide*), heat 2 large sauté pans over medium heat. Add the red endives and 1 cup of the Red Wine Cooking Liquid to 1 pan. Bring to a simmer and reduce to 1 tablespoon. Add 1/2 tablespoon of the butter and reduce to glaze. Add the yellow endives and 1/2 cup Saffron Cooking Liquid to the second pan. Bring to a simmer and reduce to 1 tablespoon. Add the remaining 2 tablespoons butter and reduce to glaze. Drain the Endives on paper towels to remove excess glaze.

### ROASTED QUAIL

8 quail
1 tablespoon salt
2 tablespoon canola oil
4 tablespoons Soy Glaze

Remove the breasts, keeping the wing bones attached, from the 8 quail. Be sure to scrape the wing bones of any meat and trim the end tip. Reserve the carcass, leg, and wing bones for the Date Quail Jus. Season both sides of the quail breasts with the salt. Stack 2 breasts together, flesh side to flesh side, and trim off one of the wing bones so that the stack resembles one large breast. Repeat with the remaining quail. Gently wrap each breast stack in plastic wrap and place in individual *sous vide* bags. Vacuum-seal, refrigerate, and keep in the bags overnight so that the breasts adhere to each other.

Cook the quail in a water bath maintained at 145°F by an immersion circulator for 15 minutes. Rest the cooked quail for 5 minutes before removing from the bags and plastic wrap. When ready to sear the quail, pat them dry with a paper towel. Heat 1 tablespoon of the oil in each of 2 sauté pans over medium-high heat. Place the quail skin side down in the pans to sear the skin, about 2 minutes per side. Add 2 tablespoons of Soy Glaze to each pan and spoon over the quail. Remove from the pans and drain on a paper towel.

### ORANGE JUNIPER POWDER

Zest of 1 navel orange
1 1/2 tablespoons *fleur de sel*
2 teaspoons coarsely ground juniper berries

Tightly wrap a plate with plastic wrap and spread the orange zest on the plate. Dry the zest in the microwave at 20-second intervals until fully dehydrated, about 2 minutes total, depending on the microwave. Combine the dried zest with the *fleur de sel* and ground juniper berries. Store in an airtight container.

### PARSLEY POWDER

1/3 cup loosely packed parsley leaves

Line a microwave-safe plate with a paper towel. Place the parsley leaves in an even layer on the paper towel and cover with another paper towel. Dehydrate the parsley in the microwave at 30-second intervals until the leaves are dry, changing out the paper towels every minute, about 3 minutes total, depending on the microwave. Cool the dried parsley leaves at room temperature and grind them in a spice grinder to a fine powder. Store in an airtight container.

### RED WINE ENDIVE COOKING LIQUID

1 tablespoon canola oil
3 cups thinly sliced endive
2/3 cup thinly sliced shallots
1/3 cup thinly sliced ginger
6 cups red wine
3 cups red port
1 pod star anise
5 black peppercorns
1 clove

In a large saucepan, heat the canola oil over medium heat. Add the endive, shallots, and ginger and sweat until soft and translucent, about 10 minutes. Deglaze the pan with the wine and port. Add the star anise, peppercorns, and clove, and reduce the liquid by half. Once the liquid is reduced, strain, chill over ice, and set aside to use as the endive braising liquid.

### SAFFRON COOKING LIQUID

1 tablespoon canola oil
4 cups yellow endive trim (reserved from Endives)
3/4 cup thinly sliced shallots
1/2 cup thinly sliced ginger
1/3 cup white wine
1/4 cup vermouth
2 tablespoons Pernod
1 teaspoon saffron
1 tablespoon salt

Heat the oil in a large saucepan over medium heat. Add the endive trim, shallots, and ginger and sweat until soft, about 10 minutes. Deglaze the pan with the wine, vermouth, and Pernod. Add the saffron and reduce by half. Add 4 cups water and season with the salt. Reduce over medium heat until 2 cups remain. Strain and chill over ice.

### DATE QUAIL JUS

1 tablespoon canola oil
Quail bones (reserved from Roasted Quail), cut into 2-inch pieces
2/3 cup pitted and diced Medjool dates
1 1/2 teaspoons Madras curry powder
4 cups Chicken Jus (page 356)
1 tablespoon orange blossom water

In a large straight-sided pan, heat the canola oil over high heat. Add the quail bones and caramelize until they are golden brown on all sides, about 10 minutes. Add the dates and curry powder and sweat until the dates are tender. Add the Chicken Jus and simmer for 45 minutes. Strain the sauce and return to the pan. Continue to simmer until about 2 cups remain and the Jus coats the back of a spoon. Stir in the orange blossom water.

## ALLUMETTES

1/4 cup Clarified Butter (page 370)
1 tablespoon confectioners' sugar
1 1/2 teaspoons salt
4 large sheets phyllo dough
1 teaspoon Orange Juniper Powder
1 teaspoon Parsley Powder
1 teaspoon *piment d'Espelette*

Preheat the oven to 300°F. Warm the Clarified Butter in a small saucepan. Combine the confectioners' sugar and salt in a sifter. Working with 1 piece of phyllo dough at a time, brush the top of the dough with the melted Clarified Butter and dust with the confectioners' sugar mix. Layer another sheet of phyllo on top and repeat. After the fourth layer, cut the phyllo in half and stack the 2 pieces. Cut the phyllo into 1/3-inch-by-4-inch strips. Line an upside-down, very flat 9-by-13-inch rimmed baking sheet with parchment paper. Brush the parchment paper with Clarified Butter. Arrange the phyllo strips in a single layer on the parchment paper. Brush another piece of parchment paper with Clarified Butter and place it on top of the phyllo, buttered side down. Place another very flat 9-by-13-inch rimmed baking sheet on top. Weigh down the baking sheet with a cast-iron skillet and bake for 12 to 15 minutes, until golden brown. Mix together the Orange Juniper Powder, Parsley Powder, and *piment d'Espelette*. Sprinkle the mixture over the warm Allumettes. Cool to room temperature and store in an airtight container.

## DATE SPHERES

8 Medjool dates
1 tablespoon olive oil

Cut the dates in half lengthwise and remove the pits. Scrape away the outer skin with a paring knife. Dip your fingertips into the olive oil and roll the dates into spheres. Keep at room temperature.

## TO FINISH

8 tablespoons Orange Puree (see page 352)
Roasted Quail
Endives
Date Spheres
Allumettes
Orange Juniper Powder
Date Quail Jus

Warm the Orange Puree in a small saucepan over medium heat.

Spoon 1 tablespoon Orange Puree onto a plate and drag the spoon over the Puree to make a long streak. Place a glazed Roasted Quail breast in the center of the Puree and arrange 1 of each of the red and yellow Endive spears, 2 Date Spheres, and 1 Allumette on the plate. Sprinkle 1/4 teaspoon Orange Juniper Powder on the plate and finish with 1 teaspoon Date Quail Jus. Repeat with the remaining ingredients, to serve 8.

# GUINEA FOWL
## POACHED WITH TRUFFLES, BUTTERNUT SQUASH, PARSNIPS, AND CABBAGE

*Serves 8*

## GUINEA FOWL

4 guinea fowl breasts, skin on
2 black truffles
1 tablespoon salt
4 sprigs thyme
4 tablespoons butter

Gently peel back the skin from the guinea fowl breast, keeping it attached at one end. Scrape off any excess fat from the breast. Thinly slice the truffles on a mandoline. Layer the truffle slices on the guinea fowl breast so that the entire breast is covered. Return the skin to the breast so that it covers the truffles completely. Repeat with the remaining guinea fowl breasts. Season both sides of the breasts with the salt and place each breast in an individual *sous vide* bag along with 1 thyme sprig and 1 tablespoon butter. Vacuum-seal. Poach the breasts in a water bath maintained at 145°F by an immersion circulator for 30 minutes. Rest the breasts for 5 minutes and then remove them from the bags. Discard the thyme and slice the guinea fowl breasts in half lengthwise. Each breast will yield 2 servings.

## TRUFFLE JUS

2 teaspoons butter
1/2 cup finely minced shallots
1/2 cup finely minced black truffles
2 cups Madeira
4 cups Chicken Jus (page 356)
1 cup black truffle juice
3 sprigs thyme

In a medium straight-sided pan, melt the butter over medium heat until it begins to foam. Add the shallots and black truffles and sweat until tender, about 4 minutes. Add the Madeira and raise the heat to medium-high. Reduce the Madeira by half. Add the Chicken Jus, truffle juice, and the thyme and simmer over low heat until 2 cups remain. Remove the thyme and keep the Jus warm until ready to serve.

## SAVOY CABBAGE

1 large head Savoy cabbage
2 tablespoons Chicken Stock (see page 356)
2 tablespoons butter
1 tablespoon finely chopped black truffles
1/2 teaspoon salt

Peel away the green leaves from the cabbage and cut into 2-inch-square pieces. You should have at least 24 pieces. Bring a pot of salted water to a boil. Add the cabbage pieces and cook until tender, 2 to 3 minutes. Transfer to a bowl of ice water and, once cold, drain.

Heat the Chicken Stock and blanched cabbage in a large sauté pan over medium heat. Add the butter and reduce to glaze. Stir in the black truffles and season with the salt. Toss to coat evenly.

## TO FINISH

1/2 cup Butternut Squash Puree (see page 350)
1/2 cup Parsnip Puree (see page 352)
Guinea Fowl
Savoy Cabbage
Truffle Jus

Warm the Butternut Squash Puree and the Parsnip Puree in 2 separate saucepans over low heat.

Place the Guinea Fowl off center on the plate. Spoon 1 tablespoon of each Puree around the Guinea Fowl and arrange 3 pieces glazed Savoy Cabbage on top. Finish the plate with 1 tablespoon of the Truffle Jus. Repeat with the remaining ingredients, to serve 8.

# CHICKEN
## ROASTED WITH TRUFFLES AND LEEKS

*Serves 8*

**MARBLE POTATO CONFIT**
60 marble potatoes (about 13 ounces)
4 cups extra-virgin olive oil
15 sprigs thyme
1 head garlic, split in half crosswise
1 tablespoon Chicken Stock (see page 356)
2 tablespoons butter
*Fleur de sel*

Preheat the oven to 275°F. Place the unpeeled potatoes in a baking dish with the olive oil, thyme, and garlic and cover with aluminum foil. Roast the potatoes in the oven for 1 hour and 30 minutes. Remove from the oven and cool the potatoes to room temperature in the oil. Once cool, strain, reserving the oil. Peel the potatoes with a paring knife and return them to the strained olive oil, keeping at room temperature until ready to use.

Heat the Chicken Stock in a large sauté pan over medium heat. Drain the potatoes and add them to the pan to warm through. Add the butter, tossing to glaze. Drain on paper towels and season with *fleur de sel*.

**VIN JAUNE CREAM SAUCE**
2 tablespoons butter
1/4 cup minced shallots
1/2 cup minced black truffles
1 bunch thyme
1 cup *vin jaune*
1 cup cream
1 cup Chicken Jus (see page 356)
1/2 cup crème fraîche
1 tablespoon salt
1 pinch cayenne pepper

Heat the butter in a sauté pan over medium heat. Add the shallots, sweating until translucent. Add the truffles and thyme, sweating for 10 minutes. Deglaze the pan with the *vin jaune,* scraping the bottom of the pan. Reduce until almost dry, about 10 minutes, being careful to not burn the truffles. Add the cream and Chicken Jus and bring to a simmer for about 15 minutes. Remove from the heat, cover, and steep for 30 minutes. Whisk in the crème fraîche and season with the salt and cayenne. Strain.

## BRAISED LEEKS

8 leeks
1/3 cup butter
2 tablespoon Vin Jaune Cream Sauce
1/4 cup finely chopped black truffles
1 teaspoon salt

Trim the tops of the leeks so that about 1 inch of the green part remains. Trim off the roots. Soak the trimmed leeks in cold water for about 30 minutes and then rinse thoroughly to remove any sand. In the meantime, bring 1 gallon water to a boil. Add the leeks. Cook for 15 minutes or until tender. Transfer to a bowl of ice water and, once cold, drain.

Trim the leeks on the bias into 3 1/2-inch pieces. Slice the leeks lengthwise, leaving the bottom 1 inch intact. Fan out the layers of leeks. Heat the butter and Vin Jaune Cream Sauce in a sauté pan set over medium heat. Add the leeks and truffles, reducing to warm and glaze the leeks. Season with the salt.

## VIN JAUNE SABAYON

1 2/3 cups *vin jaune*
3 sheets gelatin
2 eggs
5 egg yolks
2 cups butter, melted
3 tablespoons salt
2 N$_2$O cartridges

In a small saucepan, reduce the *vin jaune* to 1/2 cup. Bloom the gelatin by placing the sheets in a bowl of ice water for 10 minutes, until pliable. Squeeze to remove excess moisture and melt into the reduced *vin jaune*. Combine the eggs, egg yolks, butter, salt, and *vin jaune* mixture in a large bowl. Pour into a whipped-cream canister and charge with the N$_2$O cartridges. Place in a water bath maintained at 145°F by an immersion circulator for 1 hour before serving.

## MARINATED FOIE GRAS

One 2-pound lobe grade-A foie gras
1 tablespoon salt
1/2 teaspoon pink curing salt
1 teaspoon sugar
1/2 teaspoon white pepper
2 teaspoons Madeira
1 teaspoon Cognac

Bring the foie gras to room temperature to soften. Separate the main lobes and remove the veins with tweezers and a paring knife. Pass the foie gras through a tamis, season with the salt, pink salt, sugar, and white pepper, and place it in a *sous vide* bag. Add the Madeira and Cognac, seal the bag, and marinate in the refrigerator for 24 hours. Remove the foie gras from the refrigerator and allow it to come to room temperature. Transfer to a large mixing bowl and whip with a rubber spatula to re-emulsify.

## BRIOCHE STUFFING

4 cups butter, softened
5 cups brioche bread crumbs
1 cup Marinated Foie Gras (4 ounces)
2 cups chopped black truffles
1 tablespoon salt

Combine all ingredients in a mixing bowl. Divide the stuffing between 2 piping bags.

## ROASTED CHICKEN

4 whole chickens (4 pounds each)
Brioche Stuffing
4 lemons
Salt
20 sprigs rosemary
8 cloves garlic, peeled
1 cup butter, softened

Working gently so as to not tear the skin, run your finger under the skin of the chickens, separating the skin from the meat. Be sure to leave the skin attached at the center of the sternum to maintain the shape of the breasts during roasting.

Pipe the Brioche Stuffing under the skin of the legs and breasts, distributing it evenly to maintain the shape of the chicken. Prick the lemons all over with a paring knife. Season the inside of the birds with salt and fill each cavity with 5 sprigs rosemary, 2 garlic cloves, and 1 lemon. Truss the chickens with twine and refrigerate for 1 hour to set the stuffing.

Preheat the oven to 430°F. Rub the chickens with the butter and season with salt. Place on a roasting rack and roast for about 45 minutes, rotating after 20 minutes. Rest the chickens for 15 minutes.

## CHICKEN FRICASSEE

1 cup diced (1/4 inch) leeks, white and light green parts only
Roasted Chicken legs (reserved from Roasted Chicken)
1 tablespoon butter
2 tablespoons Vin Jaune Cream Sauce
Salt
1/4 cup thinly sliced parsley
2 tablespoons finely diced black truffle
Vin Jaune Sabayon

Bring a pot of salted water to a boil. Add the leeks and cook for 3 to 4 minutes. Transfer to a bowl of ice water.

Remove the skin and stuffing from the legs and gently shred the meat into bite-sized pieces. Melt the butter in a sauté pan over medium heat. Add the Vin Jaune Cream Sauce, shredded leg meat, and leeks. Season with salt and finish with the parsley and black truffle. At the last moment, fold in the Sabayon and divide among 8 side dishes.

## TRUFFLE JUS

2 teaspoons butter
1/2 cup finely minced shallots
1/2 cup finely minced black truffles
2 cups Madeira
4 cups Chicken Jus (page 356)
1 cup black truffle juice
3 sprigs thyme
1/4 cup Marinated Foie Gras

In a medium straight-sided pan, melt the butter over medium heat until it begins to foam. Add the shallots and black truffles and sweat until tender, about 4 minutes. Add the Madeira and raise the heat to medium-high. Reduce the Madeira by half. Add the Chicken Jus, truffle juice, and the thyme and simmer over low heat until 2 cups remain. Place the Marinated Foie Gras in a small sauté pan and render for 15 minutes. Strain and reserve the rendered liquid fat. Remove the thyme and add the rendered Foie Gras fat. Keep warm until ready to serve.

## TO FINISH

Roasted Chicken breasts
Braised Leeks
Marble Potato Confit
2 large black truffles, broken into small chunks
Truffle Jus
Chicken Fricassee

Carve the breasts from the Roast Chicken. Place 1 breast on a plate and lay 1 Braised Leek next to it. Break apart the Marble Potato Confit and scatter 5 pieces around the Chicken along with 6 chunks of truffles. Finish with 1 tablespoon of the Truffle Jus. Serve with 1/2 cup Chicken Fricassee. Repeat with the remaining ingredients, to serve 8.

# PORK
## CURED WITH POTATOES AND MUSTARD

*Serves 8*

**PORK SHOULDER**

2 1/3 cups plus 4 tablespoons pink curing salt
4 cups plus 4 tablespoons salt
One 7-to-8-pound pork shoulder (from a 60-pound pig)
1 cup white wine
1/4 cup diced celery
1/4 cup diced carrot
1/4 cup diced onion
3 sprigs thyme
1 bay leaf
8 black peppercorns

Combine 2 1/3 cups of the pink curing salt, 4 cups of the salt, and 3 gallons water in a large pot and bring to a boil over high heat. Cool over ice. Transfer to a nonreactive container and add the pork shoulder. Refrigerate, covered, for 10 days. After 10 days, drain and rinse the shoulder. Place it in a large pot and add the remaining 4 tablespoons pink curing salt, the remaining 4 tablespoons salt, the wine, celery, carrot, onion, thyme, bay leaf, and peppercorns. Cover with 2 gallons water, set over low heat, and simmer the pork, uncovered, for 2 1/2 hours. Add more water as needed to make sure the pork is covered with water at all times. Remove from the heat and allow to cool to room temperature in the cooking liquid. Store in the cooking liquid until ready to serve. Trim the pork skin and fat from the pork shoulder and reserve the skin for the Crispy Pork Skin. Pull apart the muscles in the pork shoulder to yield 1- to 2-inch strips of meat.

**CRISPY PORK SKIN**

1 cup Simple Syrup (see page 371)
1 Granny Smith apple
Pork skin (reserved Shoulder from Pork),
    frozen overnight
3 shallots, thinly sliced
4 cups canola oil
1/2 cup mustard seeds
1/2 teaspoon salt

Preheat the oven to 200°F. Warm the Simple Syrup in a small saucepan without bringing it to a boil. Peel and thinly slice the apple on a mandoline and soak the slices in the warm Simple Syrup for 10 minutes. Drain the apple slices and spread them out in a single layer on a baking sheet lined with a silicone baking mat. Bake the apple slices until they are crispy, about 1 hour and 30 minutes. Do not turn off the oven. Cool the apple chips to room temperature. Cut the apple chips into 1/4-inch pieces.

　Coarsely grind the frozen pork skin in a meat grinder. Combine the ground pork skin and 1/2 cup water in a medium straight-sided pan and simmer over medium-low heat until the water has evaporated, about 30 to 40 minutes. Drain off half of the rendered pork fat and discard. Return the pan to the stove and continue to crisp the fat until golden brown, about 10 minutes. Strain and cool the crisped pork fat on paper towels. Once cooled, finely chop the pork fat and combine with the chopped apple chips.

Combine the shallots and 2 cups of the canola oil in a large straight-sided pan and fry over medium heat, stirring constantly, until the shallots are golden brown, 12 to 15 minutes. As the shallots fry, the oil should reach 265°F. Strain the shallots, drain on paper towels, and cool to room temperature. Once cooled, cut the shallots into small pieces and combine with the apple chips and crispy pork fat.

Place the mustard seeds in a small saucepan and cover with cold water. Set over medium heat and bring to a simmer. Cook the mustard seeds until tender, 15 to 20 minutes. Strain the seeds and spread them out onto a baking sheet lined with acetate. Dehydrate the seeds in the preheated oven until they are dry, about 2 hours. Heat the remaining 2 cups oil in a large saucepan to 325°F. Fry the mustard seeds for 8 to 10 seconds and drain them on paper towels. Season with the salt. Break apart the mustard seeds into individual seeds. Combine the fried seeds with the apple, shallots, and pork fat. Store the crumble in an airtight container until ready to serve.

## MARBLE POTATO CONFIT
64 marble potatoes (about 1 pound)
4 cups olive oil
2 sprigs thyme
3 cloves garlic, crushed but kept whole
1 tablespoon Chicken Stock (see page 356)
1 tablespoon butter
*Fleur de sel*

Preheat the oven to 275°F. Place the unpeeled potatoes in a baking dish with the olive oil, thyme, and garlic and cover with aluminum foil. Roast the potatoes in the oven for 1 hour and 30 minutes. Remove from the oven and cool the potatoes to room temperature in the oil. Once cool, strain, reserving the oil. Peel the potatoes with a paring knife and return them to the strained olive oil, keeping at room temperature until ready to use.

In a sauté pan over medium heat, warm the Chicken Stock with the peeled potatoes. Add the butter, tossing to glaze. Drain on a paper towel and season with *fleur de sel*.

## POACHED APPLES
1 cup Sauternes
1 tablespoon sugar
1 teaspoon salt
4 juniper berries
2 cloves
2 Gold Rush apples, peeled and cored
1 tablespoon cold butter
1/4 teaspoon salt

Combine the Sauternes, sugar, salt, juniper, and cloves in a small saucepan and bring to a simmer to melt the sugar and cook out the alcohol, about 5 minutes. Slice the apples into wedges. Combine the apple wedges and 3 tablespoons of the Sauternes mixture in a *sous vide* bag and vacuum-seal. Steam in a combination steam oven at 185°F for 9 minutes and chill in an ice bath.

When ready to serve, heat a large sauté pan over medium heat and add the apples and their cooking liquid. Simmer until the apples are warmed through and add the butter, reducing to glaze. Season with the salt and drain on a paper towel.

## PEARL ONIONS
8 white pearl onions
1 tablespoon Chicken Stock (see page 356)
1 tablespoon butter
1/4 teaspoon salt

Bring a pot of salted water to a boil. Add the onions and cook until tender, about 5 minutes. Shock the onions in an ice bath. Drain the onions, peel off the outer layer, and cut them in half. Heat the Chicken Stock in a sauté pan over medium heat. Add the onions and warm through. Add the butter, tossing to glaze, and season with the salt.

## GLAZED SAUERKRAUT
1/2 cup Sauerkraut (see page 341)
1 tablespoon Chicken Stock (see page 356)
1 tablespoon butter
1/4 teaspoon salt

Heat a small sauté pan over medium heat. Add 1/2 cup of the Sauerkraut and the Chicken Stock and simmer to warm through. Add the butter and toss, reducing to glaze. Season with the salt just before serving.

## SAUERKRAUT SAUCE
1 cup Chicken Stock (see page 356)
1 cup cream
2 cups Sauerkraut (1/2 pound) (see page 341)
2 tablespoons Sauerkraut liquid (reserved
    from Sauerkraut)
2 teaspoons salt

Combine the Chicken Stock and cream in a medium saucepan and bring to a simmer. Add the Sauerkraut and remove from the heat. Steep for 1 hour. With a hand blender, pulse the mixture to coarsely chop. Strain and discard the Sauerkraut and season the cream mixture with the Sauerkraut liquid and salt. Keep warm until ready to serve.

## PORK SAUCE
1 tablespoon canola oil
1 cup finely minced *guanciale*
4 cups Chicken Jus (page 356)
1 cup Sauerkraut (see page 341)
Ice wine vinegar

In a medium saucepan, heat the canola oil over medium heat and add the minced *guanciale*. Render the fat from the *guanciale* for 5 minutes and then strain, reserving the liquid fat.

Combine the Chicken Jus and the Sauerkraut in a medium straight-sided pot over medium heat and reduce to 2 cups. Strain the sauce and season with ice wine vinegar. Stir in 1 tablespoon of the *guanciale* fat.

## BLOOD SAUSAGE
3 links *morcilla* (Spanish blood sausage)
1 tablespoon canola oil
1/2 teaspoon salt

Remove and discard the casing from the sausages and separate them into 1-inch crumbles. Heat the oil in a small sauté pan over high heat. Add the blood sausage pieces and toss until they begin to caramelize, about 2 minutes. Season with the salt, drain on paper towels, and serve immediately.

## TO FINISH
8 tablespoons White Apple Puree (see page 350)
Pork Shoulder
Poached Apples
Marble Potato Confit
Blood Sausage
Pearl Onions
1/2 cup Glazed Sauerkraut
4 teaspoons Pickled Yellow Mustard Seeds
    (see page 342)
Sauerkraut Sauce
Pork Sauce
Crispy Pork Skin
1/3 cup grated horseradish

Warm the White Apple Puree in a small saucepan over low heat. Spoon 1 tablespoon of the White Apple Puree down the center of a plate and top with 3 pieces of the Pork Shoulder. Arrange 3 Poached Apple pieces, 8 Potatoes, 4 pieces Blood Sausage, and 2 Pearl Onion halves on and around the Pork Shoulder slices. Top with 1 tablespoon Glazed Sauerkraut and 1/2 teaspoon Pickled Yellow Mustard Seeds. Froth the Sauerkraut Sauce with a hand blender. Finish the plate with 2 tablespoons Pork Sauce, 2 tablespoons Sauerkraut Foam, 2 tablespoons Crispy Pork Skin, and 2 teaspoons grated horseradish. Repeat with the remaining ingredients, to serve 8.

# BEEF
## ROASTED WITH RED WINE–BRAISED ONIONS AND FOIE GRAS

*Serves 8*

## FOIE GRAS SLICES
## AND RENDERED FOIE GRAS FAT

One 2-pound lobe grade-A foie gras

Separate the main lobes of the foie gras and remove any of the main veins and exterior fat with tweezers and a paring knife. Slice each lobe into 3/4-inch slices and trim them, if necessary, to yield even shapes. Reserve the trim for the Rendered Foie Gras Fat.

To make the Rendered Foie Gras Fat, place the foie gras trim in a *sous vide* bag and vacuum-seal. Place the bag in a water bath maintained at 210°F by an immersion circulator and simmer until all of the fat has been rendered, 10 to 15 minutes. Remove from the bag and strain through cheesecloth. Alternatively, preheat the oven to 250°F. Place the foie gras trim in a small pan and render in the oven for 10 to 15 minutes. Strain through cheesecloth.

## ROASTED BEEF TENDERLOIN

1 beef tenderloin, trimmed of fat and silver skin
2 tablespoons salt
1/2 cup butter, at room temperature
5 cloves garlic, crushed but kept whole
10 sprigs thyme
1/4 cup Rendered Foie Gras Fat
1 1/2 teaspoons *fleur de sel*
1 1/2 teaspoons coarsely ground black pepper

Preheat the oven to 300°F. Season the beef tenderloin on all sides with the salt. In a large straight-sided pan over medium heat, melt the butter with the garlic until foamy. Lightly sear the beef on all sides in the butter, 8 to 10 seconds per side. Transfer the beef tenderloin to a roasting rack set over a rimmed baking sheet. Add the thyme to the pan of now browning butter and lightly fry. Remove from the heat and spoon a little of the butter over the beef. Transfer to a roasting rack and roast in the oven, turning and basting with brown butter every 10 minutes, until it is medium, 30 to 35 minutes. Once the beef is roasted, remove from the oven and rest for 10 minutes.

Slice the beef into 8 even portions and brush the cut sides with the Rendered Foie Gras Fat. Season each slice with the *fleur de sel* and coarsely ground black pepper.

## RED WINE–BRAISED ONIONS

2 tablespoons butter
4 cups finely diced white onion (from 3 medium onions)
4 cups red wine
4 cups red port
1/4 cup sugar
2 tablespoons red wine vinegar
2 tablespoons cornstarch
2 teaspoons salt

Melt the butter in a medium straight-sided pan over medium heat. Add the onions and sweat until translucent, about 10 minutes. Combine the red wine and port in a mixing bowl and add 4 cups of the mixture to the onions. Simmer until 2 cups remain. Add the remaining 4 cups of the wine-port mixture to the onions and reduce until 2 cups remain. Add the sugar and red wine vinegar and simmer for 3 to 4 minutes. In a small mixing bowl, whisk together the cornstarch and 1/2 cup water and whisk the slurry into the onions. Simmer for another 3 to 4 minutes to thicken and cook out the starchy flavor. The consistency of the onions should now be like pudding. Season with the salt.

## RENDERED MARROW FAT

12 (2 1/2-inch) marrow bones
4 cloves garlic, crushed but kept whole
10 sprigs thyme

Soak the bones in lukewarm water for about 30 minutes. Once the marrow is soft, carefully push it out of the bone. Cut the bone marrow cylinders into 1/2-inch pieces. Place the bone marrow and 1/4 cup water in a medium pot over low heat. Render the marrow, making sure not to achieve any color. As the marrow renders, add the garlic. Once all the water cooks out and the marrow is completely rendered, add the thyme and strain through a fine-mesh chinois, reserving the rendered fat.

## BORDELAISE SAUCE

1 tablespoon canola oil
1 pound beef trim
1 tablespoon minced shallots
1 cup red wine
4 cups Veal Jus (see page 357)
1 tablespoon thyme leaves
1/4 cup Rendered Marrow Fat
Salt

Heat the oil in a straight-sided pan over medium heat. Add the beef trim and sear until brown on all sides, 7 to 10 minutes. Reduce the heat to medium and pour out the excess oil. Add the shallots and sweat. Deglaze with the wine and reduce by half. Add the Jus, bring to a simmer, and reduce by half, skimming off any fats and impurities that rise to the top. Strain and add the thyme leaves. Break the sauce with the Rendered Marrow Fat and season with salt.

## BRIOCHE

1 loaf Brioche (see page 364)
2 tablespoons butter

Slice the Brioche about 1 inch thick. With a ring cutter measuring 3 inches in diameter, punch out rounds from the brioche slices. Heat 2 large sauté pans over medium-high heat and melt 1 tablespoon of the butter in each until it begins to foam. Place the brioche in the pans and toast on each side until golden brown, about 10 to 15 seconds per side.

## TO FINISH

2 teaspoons canola oil
Foie Gras Slices
1 tablespoon salt
1/4 cup sliced chives
1 teaspoon *fleur de sel*
Red Wine–Braised Onions
Brioche
Roasted Beef Tenderloin
Bordelaise Sauce

Heat 2 large sauté pans over medium-high heat. Add 1 teaspoon of the canola oil to each pan and turn to coat evenly with the oil. Wipe out any excess oil with a paper towel. Season the Foie Gras Slices on both sides with the salt. Place the foie gras in the hot pans (4 slices in each pan) and sear, about 1 minute on each side. The Slices should be deeply caramelized on each side yet just heated through. Be careful to not overcook. Drain the Foie Gras on paper towels and garnish each piece with about 1 teaspoon of the sliced chives and a pinch of the *fleur de sel*.

Set a ring mold measuring 4 inches in diameter in the center of a plate. Spread 3 tablespoons of the Red Wine–Braised Onions inside the ring mold and then remove the mold. Top the Onions with a piece of toasted Brioche, a slice of Foie Gras, and a slice of the Roasted Beef Tenderloin. Finish the plate with 2 tablespoons of the Bordelaise Sauce. Repeat with the remaining ingredients, to serve 8.

# LAMB
## GLAZED RIB EYE WITH PUNTARELLA, APPLES, AND VADOUVAN

*Serves 8*

### LAMB LOIN

2 lamb loins
2 tablespoons salt plus more to taste
1 teaspoon Madras curry powder
1 cup Lamb Jus (see page 356)
2 tablespoons canola oil
4 tablespoons butter
2 cloves garlic, crushed but kept whole
6 sprigs thyme

Trim the loins of all fat and sinew and round the edges to make a cylindrical shape. Pat dry with paper towels. In a mixing bowl, combine the 2 tablespoons salt and the curry. Season the lamb loins on all sides with the curry-salt mixture. Roll the lamb loins tightly in plastic wrap and tie the ends with butcher's twine or the plastic wrap itself to create a roulade. Poke small holes in the plastic wrap to release excess air pockets. Vacuum-seal the lamb loins in individual *sous vide* bags and cook them in a water bath maintained at 145°F by an immersion circulator for 30 to 35 minutes, until cooked medium. Rest the lamb loins for 10 minutes and chill in an ice bath.

Preheat the oven to 300°F. In a small saucepan, reduce the Lamb Jus over medium heat to 1/2 cup. Remove the lamb loins from the bags and cut each loin into 4 even portions. Season each cut side with salt. Divide the canola oil between 2 large oven-safe sauté pans and heat over high heat. Sear the lamb on one side for 1 minute and 30 seconds, until caramelized. Turn over and sear for 1 minute. To each pan add 2 tablespoons butter, 1 garlic clove, and 3 sprigs thyme and baste the lamb with the butter until the loins are caramelized.

Transfer the pans to the oven until each portion is warm in the middle, 2 to 3 minutes. Remove from the oven and rest the lamb on a roasting rack for 3 minutes. Just before serving, slice the portions in half and glaze in the reduced Lamb Jus.

### PUNTARELLA

1 head *puntarella*
2 tablespoons olive oil
3/4 teaspoon salt
2 tablespoons Apple Vinaigrette (see page 345)

Trim away the leaves of the *puntarella*, separating the large and small leaves. Trim the core of the *puntarella* into small pieces and toss with 1 tablespoon of the olive oil and 1/2 teaspoon of the salt. Transfer the *puntarella* cores to a *sous vide* bag and vacuum-seal. Cook the *puntarella* in a pot of boiling water until tender, about 3 minutes.

To cook the large *puntarella* leaves, heat the remaining 1 tablespoon olive oil in a large sauté pan over high heat. Add the leaves and sauté for 30 seconds. Season with the remaining 1/4 teaspoon salt. In a mixing bowl, toss the small *puntarella* leaves in the Apple Vinaigrette.

### RENDERED LAMB FAT

1 1/2 pounds lamb fat

Grind the lamb fat in a meat grinder or have this done by your butcher. Place the lamb fat and 1/4 cup water in a medium pot over low heat. Render the fat, making sure not to achieve any color. Once all the water has been cooked out and the fat is completely rendered, strain through a fine-mesh chinois, reserving the liquid fat.

### CURRY APPLE LAMB SAUCE

1 1/2 teaspoons canola oil
1 cup peeled and diced Granny Smith apple
1/2 cup thinly sliced onion
4 cups Lamb Jus (see page 356)
1/4 cup Rendered Lamb Fat
1 teaspoon *vadouvan* curry spice
2 teaspoons Apple Vinegar (see page 345)
1/2 teaspoon salt

In a medium straight-sided pan, heat the canola oil over medium heat. Add the apple and onion and sweat until tender and translucent, 8 to 10 minutes. Add the Lamb Jus and reduce the heat to low. Simmer the Lamb Jus until reduced to 2 cups. Meanwhile, heat the Rendered Lamb Fat in a small saucepan to 300°F. Add the curry and fry in the fat for 4 to 5 minutes. Strain through cheesecloth. Add 1 tablespoon of the spiced lamb fat to the Jus and season with the Apple Vinegar and salt.

### ROASTED GARLIC

1 head garlic, split into cloves and peeled
1 cup olive oil

Place the garlic in a small saucepan and cover with cold water. Bring the water to a boil and then drain. Return the garlic to the pot and add the olive oil. Simmer the garlic cloves over medium-low heat until they are tender and golden brown. Keep the garlic in the oil.

### BLACKENED LADY APPLES

4 lady apples
2 tablespoons canola oil

Preheat the oven to 300°F. Cut the apples in half and scoop out the core with a small melon baller (1/2 inch in diameter). Heat 1 tablespoon oil in each of 2 medium sauté pans over medium-high heat and place 4 apple halves, cut side down, in each pan. Caramelize the apples slightly in the pan, about 1 minute, and then transfer to the oven and roast until tender, 3 to 4 minutes.

### TO FINISH

2 tablespoons Chicken Stock (see page 356)
Puntarella
1 tablespoon butter
1/4 teaspoon salt
Lamb Loin
Roasted Garlic
Blackened Lady Apples
1/2 cup Lamb-Apple Crumble (see page 362)
Curry Apple Lamb Sauce

Heat the Chicken Stock and the Puntarella cores in a sauté pan over medium heat. Add the butter, toss to glaze, and season with the salt.

Place 2 pieces glazed Lamb Loin on a plate and arrange 3 Puntarella cores, 2 sautéed Puntarella leaves, 1 clove Roasted Garlic, and 1 Blackened Lady Apple around the Lamb. Spoon 1 tablespoon of the Lamb-Apple Crumble over each slice of lamb and garnish with 1 dressed Puntarella leaf. Finish the plate with 2 tablespoons Curry Apple Lamb Sauce. Repeat with the remaining ingredients, to serve 8.

# VACHERIN
## MONT D'OR
## WITH POTATOES
## AND MUSTARD

*Serves 8*

**MARBLE POTATO CONFIT
IN MUSTARD MARINADE**

160 marble potatoes (about 2 1/3 pounds)
8 cups olive oil
4 tablespoons plus 1/2 teaspoon salt
3 cloves garlic, crushed but kept whole
2 sprigs thyme
1 gallon Chicken Stock (see page 356)
1/4 cup red wine vinegar
3 tablespoons whole grain mustard

Preheat the oven to 275°F. Place the unpeeled potatoes
in a baking dish with the olive oil, 4 tablespoons of the
salt, garlic, and thyme and cover with aluminum foil.
Roast the potatoes in the oven for 1 hour and 30 minutes.
Remove from the oven and cool the potatoes in the oil to
room temperature. Once cool, strain, reserving the oil.
Peel the potatoes with a paring knife and return them to
the strained olive oil, keeping at room temperature until
ready to use.

   In a large pot, reduce the Chicken Stock until it is syrupy and about 1 1/2 cups remain. Stir in the vinegar and
mustard and season with the remaining 1/2 teaspoon
salt. Strain the potatoes and add them to the marinade.
Marinate in the refrigerator overnight.

**TO FINISH**

1 wheel Vacherin Mont d'Or
Marble Potato Confit in Mustard Marinade
Pickled White Pearl Onions (see page 343)
Coarsely cracked black pepper
8 teaspoons whole grain mustard
40 mixed mustard leaves

Allow the Vacherin to come to room temperature 1
hour before serving. Preheat the broiler. Transfer the
Potatoes in Mustard Marinade to a medium straight-
sided pan set over low heat. Add the Pickled White
Pearl Onions and warm until heated through. Strain,
draining the Potatoes and Onions on paper towels.
Place a spoonful of the Potatoes and Onions on a plate
and cover with 2 tablespoons Vacherin. Place under
the boiler and heat until melted, about 1 to 2 minutes.
Finish with black pepper, 1 teaspoon whole grain
mustard, and 5 mixed mustard leaves. Repeat with
the remaining ingredients, to serve 8.

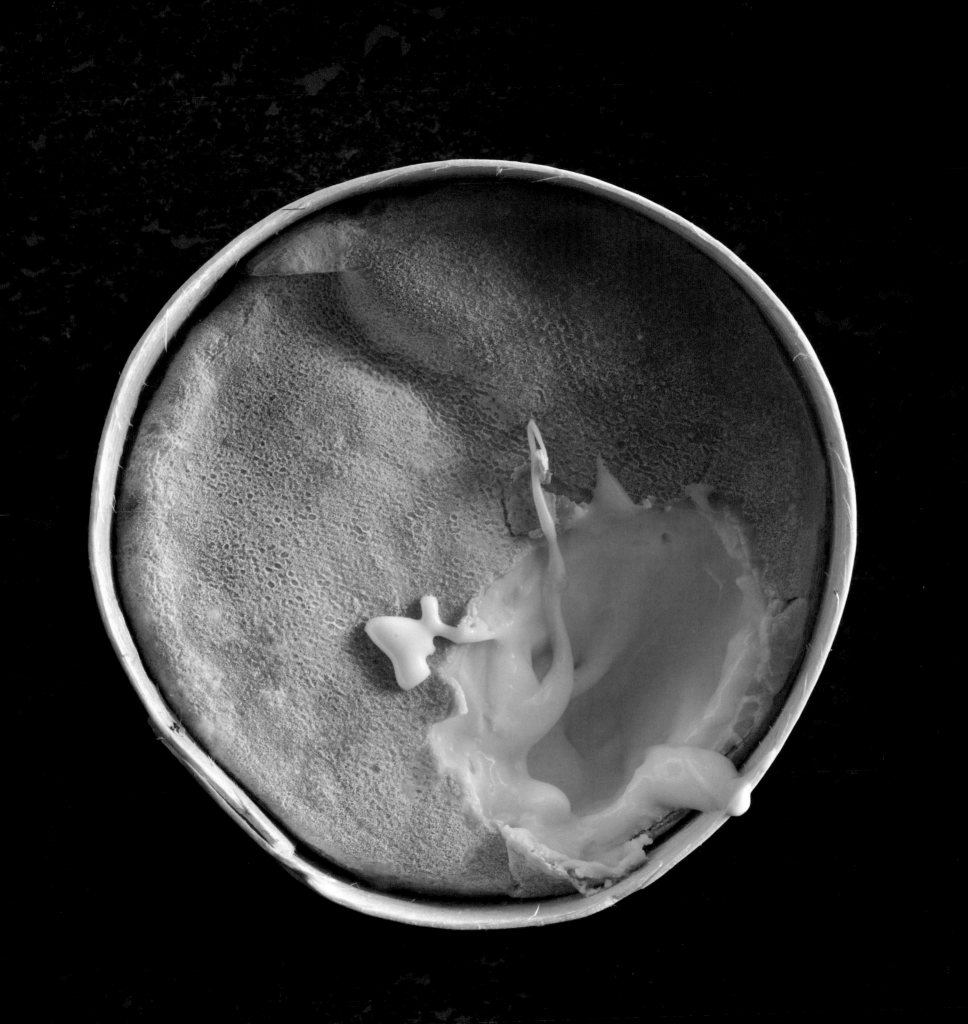

# GRAPEFRUIT
## SODA POP

*Serves 8*

### LEMON MERINGUE
Zest of 2 lemons
4 egg whites
2/3 cup sugar

Preheat the oven to 200°F. Finely chop the lemon zest and press with a paper towel to remove excess oils. In a stand mixer fitted with a whisk attachment, whip the egg whites to soft peaks. Slowly add the sugar and continue to whip until the whites reach stiff peaks. With a rubber spatula, fold in the lemon zest and transfer to a piping bag fitted with a 1/2-inch round piping tip. Pipe tubes of meringue down the length of an acetate-lined baking sheet. Dry the meringues overnight in the oven. Break the tubes into 1/4-inch pieces and reserve in an airtight container until ready to serve.

### TANGERINE FOAM
1 sheet gelatin
1 1/2 cups tangerine juice
1/2 cup sugar
5 egg whites
2 teaspoons citric acid
3 $CO_2$ cartridges

Bloom the gelatin by placing the sheet in a bowl of ice water for 10 minutes, until pliable. Combine the tangerine juice and sugar in a small saucepan and bring to just under a boil over low heat. Squeeze out excess moisture from the gelatin and melt it into the tangerine juice. Chill over ice until just cold. With a hand blender, blend in the egg whites and citric acid. Strain and chill. Transfer to a whipped-cream canister and charge with the $CO_2$ cartridges. Hold the canister in the refrigerator until ready to serve.

### POMELO BEADS
1 pomelo

Cut segments from the pomelo and, with your hands, break apart the pulp, being careful to maintain the shape of the individual beads. Freeze overnight. Take the beads out of the freezer when ready to serve.

### BLOOD ORANGE CREAM
4 blood oranges
2 tablespoons glucose syrup
7 tablespoons sugar
3 tablespoons cream
1 teaspoon citric acid
1 vanilla bean, split lengthwise and scraped

Cut off the top and bottoms from the blood oranges and trim away the peel so that none of the white pith remains. Cut into 1/2-inch cubes. Combine 3 cups of the diced blood oranges and glucose syrup in a small saucepan and bring to a simmer over low heat. Cover with a cartouche (lid made of parchment paper) and simmer until the oranges are tender, about 30 minutes. Remove the cartouche and continue to cook until the liquid is reabsorbed by the oranges. Transfer to a blender and puree on high speed until smooth. Blend in the sugar and cream and pass through a fine-mesh tamis. Stir in the citric acid and vanilla bean seeds. Chill over ice, stirring constantly. Store in the refrigerator until ready to serve.

### TO FINISH
1 pink grapefruit
2 blood oranges
Blood Orange Cream
8 teaspoons unflavored Pop Rocks
Pomelo Beads
Lemon Meringue
Liquid nitrogen
Tangerine Foam

Cut off the tops and bottoms of the grapefruit and oranges and trim away the peel so that none of the white pith remains. Using a paring knife, cut in between the membranes to reveal individual citrus segments. Cut the segments into 3/4-inch pieces. Spoon 1 teaspoon Blood Orange Cream onto the bottom of a plate. Arrange 5 pieces pink grapefruit and 5 pieces blood orange on the bottom of the plate. Spoon 1 teaspoon Pop Rocks over the citrus and top with 1 tablespoon Pomelo Beads and 1 tablespoon Lemon Meringue. Freeze the bottom part of a ladle in the liquid nitrogen. Fill the ladle with Tangerine Foam. Immerse the ladle with the Foam in the liquid nitrogen. The dome will release from the ladle. Freeze the dome for 1 minute. Carefully remove from the liquid nitrogen. Place the dome on top of the citrus and Meringue. Repeat with the remaining ingredients, to serve 8 immediately.

# LEMON
## AND POPPY SEED
## WITH GREEN OLIVES

*Serves 8*

### LEMON-POPPY CAKE

3 cups pastry flour
1 tablespoon baking powder
1 1/4 cups butter, melted
1/3 cup extra-virgin olive oil
7 eggs
2 1/4 cups sugar
Zest of 4 lemons
2 tablespoons poppy seeds
1 cup confectioners' sugar
3 tablespoons lemon juice

Preheat the oven to 325°F and line a 4-by-13-inch loaf pan with parchment paper. In a mixing bowl, combine the pastry flour and baking powder. In a separate bowl, combine the butter and olive oil. Whisk together the eggs and sugar in a stand mixer fitted with a whisk attachment until pale yellow ribbons form. Add the dry ingredients and mix until thoroughly combined. Add the lemon zest. Slowly mix in the butter-and-oil mixture and then add the poppy seeds. Pour the batter into the prepared pan.

Bake the cake until a knife inserted in the center comes out clean, 50 minutes to 1 hour. Cool the cake in the pan. In a small bowl, whisk together the confectioners' sugar and lemon juice until thoroughly combined. Transfer the cooled cake from the pan to a rack and pour the glaze over the cake, completely covering the top of the cake. Allow the glaze to set at room temperature for about 20 minutes. With a serrated knife, trim off the glazed top of the cake and reserve for garnish.

Cut the cake into 2 layers. Wrap one half in plastic wrap and freeze overnight. Cut the outer crust off of the other half and crumble. Refrigerate the crumble and the trimmed half until ready to serve.

The next day, preheat the oven to 250°F. Thinly slice the frozen cake with a sharp knife into 1/8-inch slices. Line a baking sheet with parchment paper. To crisp the Lemon-Poppy Cake slices, carefully lay the slices on the parchment paper and toast in the oven until crispy, about 10 minutes. Reserve at room temperature until ready to serve.

### CANDIED LEMON SLICES

1 Meyer lemon
1 cup Simple Syrup (see page 371)

Thinly slice the lemon and remove any seeds. Layer the lemon slices in the bottom of a medium straight-sided pan. Cover the lemon slices with 1 inch of ice and water and place over low heat. Bring to a simmer, drain, and repeat one more time. Cover the blanched lemon slices with the Simple Syrup and cook until the lemon slices are translucent and tender, 45 minutes to 1 hour.

### OLIVE OIL EMULSION

5 tablespoons glucose syrup
3 egg yolks
1/4 teaspoon salt
1 cup extra-virgin olive oil

In the bowl of a food processor, combine the glucose, egg yolks, and salt. With the motor running, slowly stream in the olive oil until the mixture thickens. Store in an airtight container in the refrigerator until ready to serve.

### LEMON CURD

3 sheets gelatin
2 1/2 cups sugar
1 1/2 cups butter, softened
8 eggs
6 Meyer lemons, zested and juiced

Bloom the gelatin by placing the sheets in a bowl of ice water for 10 minutes, until pliable. In a heatproof mixing bowl, whisk together the sugar, butter, eggs, lemon zest, and lemon juice. Set over a double boiler and cook, whisking constantly, until the mixture is thickened and reaches 180°F. Squeeze any excess moisture out of the gelatin and melt into the Curd. Strain and chill over ice.

Divide the Lemon Curd in half. Store one half of the curd in a squeeze bottle and refrigerate until ready to serve. Whip the reserved half of the Curd in a stand mixer fitted with a whisk attachment until it is light and fluffy. Transfer the whipped Curd to a piping bag.

### DEHYDRATED LEMON GLAZE

1 cup confectioners' sugar
3 tablespoons lemon juice

Preheat the oven to 200°F. Whisk the sugar and lemon juice together in a small bowl until combined and spread the glaze onto a rimmed baking sheet lined with a silicone baking mat. Bake the glaze until dry, about 1 hour. Remove from the oven and break into 1/2-inch pieces. Store in an airtight container at room temperature until ready to serve.

### SWEETENED YOGURT

1 cup Greek yogurt
1/4 cup sugar

Stir the yogurt and sugar together in a mixing bowl and fully combine. Store in a squeeze bottle in the refrigerator until ready to use.

### CANDIED OLIVES

1 cup pitted and sliced Manzanilla olives
1 cup sugar
1 teaspoon salt

Preheat the oven to 200°F and line a baking sheet with parchment paper. Place the olives on the parchment paper and dry in the oven for 3 hours, or until fully dry. Put the sugar in a medium straight-sided pan over low heat and lightly caramelize. Stir in the dried olives and salt and coat evenly with the caramel. Pour out onto a baking sheet lined with parchment paper and cool to room temperature. Grind the candied olives to a fine powder in a food processor and store in an airtight container.

### TO FINISH

Olive Oil Emulsion
Lemon Curd
Candied Lemon Slices
Sweetened Yogurt
Lemon-Poppy Cake crumble
Candied Olives
4 Castlevetrano olives, pitted and diced (1/8 inch)
Lemon-Poppy Cake glazed crumble
Dehydrated Lemon Glaze
Lemon-Poppy Cake slices
Frozen Lemon Yogurt (see page 369)
1 teaspoon Maldon salt

On the center of a plate, spread 1 teaspoon Olive Oil Emulsion and squeeze on 1 teaspoon Lemon Curd. Place 1 Candied Lemon Slice in between. Squeeze 1 teaspoon Sweetened Yogurt in the middle. Top with 1 tablespoon of Lemon-Poppy Cake crumble spread in a slight triangular shape. Pipe a small mound of whipped Lemon Curd on top of the crumble and spoon another 1 1/2 teaspoons Lemon-Poppy Cake crumble over the Curd. Sprinkle 1/2 teaspoon Candied Olive powder and 1/2 teaspoon Castlevetrano olive dice on top. Arrange 5 pieces of the Lemon-Poppy Cake glazed crumble around and accent the dish with the Dehydrated Lemon Glaze flakes. Break the crisped Lemon-Poppy Cake slices into 1 1/2-inch pieces and place on top of the crumble. Scoop a quenelle of the Frozen Lemon Yogurt, off center, on the crumble and finish with a pinch of Maldon salt. Repeat with the remaining ingredients, to serve 8.

## COCONUT-LIME YOGURT

One 2.2-pound container frozen coconut puree, thawed
3/4 cup Greek yogurt
2 tablespoons lime juice
1 1/2 teaspoons sugar

Using a ladle, skim the water off the top of the puree. You should be left with coconut solids. Combine 2/3 cup of the coconut solids with the yogurt, lime juice, and sugar in a mixing bowl. Pass through a fine-mesh tamis and store in a squeeze bottle until ready to serve.

## PASSION FRUIT CURD

2 sheets gelatin
1/3 cup frozen passion fruit puree, thawed
1/2 cup sugar
2 eggs
1/2 vanilla bean, split lengthwise and scraped
10 tablespoons softened butter, cut into cubes

Bloom the gelatin by placing the sheets in a bowl of ice water for 10 minutes, until pliable. In a heatproof mixing bowl, whisk together the passion fruit puree, sugar, eggs, and vanilla bean seeds. Cook the mixture over a double boiler, whisking constantly until thick pale yellow ribbons form. At this point, the mixture should be 180°F. Squeeze out any excess moisture from the gelatin and stir it into the curd. Cool to 122°F and whisk in the butter until fully emulsified. Strain the curd and chill over ice. Store in a piping bag fitted with a small round pastry tip.

## COMPRESSED PINEAPPLE

1 pineapple, peeled
1/2 cup coconut milk
2 tablespoons sugar

Cut the pineapple in half and reserve one half for the Caramelized Pineapple. Slice the pineapple into 1/4-inch slices. Whisk together the coconut milk, 1/4 cup water, and the sugar. Place the slices in a *sous vide* bag and add 3 tablespoons of the coconut syrup. Vacuum-seal. After 1 hour, remove the pineapples from the bag and dice them into 1/4-inch cubes, avoiding the core. Keep in the refrigerator until ready to serve.

## CARAMELIZED PINEAPPLE

1/2 pineapple (reserved from Compressed Pineapple)
1/4 cup sugar

Trim and discard the core from the pineapple and dice the fruit into 3/4-inch cubes. Just before serving, sprinkle on all sides with sugar. Hold a blowtorch 5 inches above the pineapple to caramelize the sugar.

## GREEN MANGO SALAD

1 green mango, peeled, pitted, and shredded
Zest of 1 lime
2 tablespoons lime juice
1 tablespoon Simple Syrup (see page 371)

Combine the shredded mango with the lime zest, lime juice, and Simple Syrup. Keep in the refrigerator.

## COCONUT SWISS MERINGUE

2 cups coconut powder
4 egg whites
1 1/2 cups sugar
Passion Fruit Curd

Preheat the oven to 275°F. Spread the coconut powder onto a baking sheet. Combine the egg whites and sugar in a mixing bowl and set over a double boiler, stirring constantly until the sugar is melted. Transfer the mixture to a stand mixer fitted with a whisk attachment. Whisk the mixture until stiff peaks form. Transfer the meringue to a piping bag fitted with a 1/4-inch round pastry tip and pipe quarter-sized balls onto the coconut powder. With your hands, gently roll the meringues, keeping them round, in the coconut powder. Place the powdered meringue balls onto a parchment-lined baking sheet and bake in the oven until thin hard shells form on the outside, about 10 to 12 minutes. Cool the meringues to room temperature. Poke a small hole on the bottom of each meringue ball and pipe the Passion Fruit Curd into each one. Store at room temperature until ready to serve.

## TOASTED COCONUT SLICES

1 fresh coconut

Preheat the oven to 175°F. Crack the coconut open using the back of a chef's knife. Drain and discard the water. Using a paring knife, separate the inner flesh from the hard outer brown shell. Using a vegetable peeler, peel away the thin layer of soft brown skin attached to the white flesh. You should be left with only the white flesh. On a mandoline, thinly shave the coconut into half-moon flakes. Spread onto a baking sheet lined with parchment paper and toast in the oven for 2 to 2 1/2 hours, until golden. Cool to room temperature until ready to serve.

## TO FINISH

2 ripe mangoes, peeled
Pulp of 2 passion fruits, about 1 cup total
1 ripe papaya, peeled
Coconut-Lime Yogurt
8 teaspoons Coconut Crumble (see page 362)
Coconut Swiss Meringue
Compressed Pineapple
Caramelized Pineapple
Green Mango Salad
Passion Fruit–Kaffir Lime Sorbet (see page 367)
Coconut Sorbet (see page 366)
Toasted Coconut Slices
1/4 cup coconut oil
1 teaspoon Maldon salt

Thinly slice the mangoes on a mandoline to 1/16 inch thick. With a ring cutter measuring 1 1/2 inches in diameter, cut 24 rounds from the mango slices. With a ring cutter measuring 2 1/2 inches in diameter, cut 16 rounds from the remaining mango slices. Line 8 of the larger rounds on a baking sheet lined with parchment paper. Spoon 1/4 teaspoon passion fruit pulp in the center, fold the mango rounds in half, and fold in half again. With a medium Parisian spoon or melon baller, scoop 24 balls from the papaya.

On a plate, pipe three 1/2-teaspoon dots of Coconut-Lime Yogurt and spread with an offset spatula. Spoon 1 teaspoon of the Coconut Crumble on one end and another teaspoon on the opposite end of the plate. Place 1 Coconut Swiss Meringue beside each mound of Coconut Crumble (2 for each plate). Arrange 4 pieces Compressed Pineapple dice and 2 papaya balls on the plate and drape two 1 1/2-inch rounds of mango slices on top of each papaya ball. Place the Caramelized Pineapple in the center of the plate and drape a 2 1/2 inch slice of mango on top. Place 2 piles of the Green Mango Salad on the plate and top one of the mounds with another 1 1/2-inch round mango slice. Place 1 quenelle of the Passion Fruit–Kaffir Lime Sorbet on 1 mound of the Coconut Crumble and 1 quenelle of the Coconut Sorbet on the other. Arrange 2 pieces of the Toasted Coconut Slices on top of the sorbets and finish with 1 teaspoon of the passion fruit pulp dotted randomly on the plate. Drizzle the coconut oil on the passion fruit and sprinkle with a pinch of Maldon salt. Repeat with the remaining ingredients, to serve 8.

# COFFEE
## CRISPY CANNELLONI WITH CHOCOLATE AND MILK

Serves 8

### YOGURT FOAM
1 sheet gelatin
2/3 cup cream
1/4 cup sugar
1 cup Greek yogurt
2 N$_2$O cartridges

In a small saucepan over medium heat, combine the cream and sugar and heat to just below a boil. Bloom the gelatin by placing the sheets in a bowl of ice water for 10 minutes, until pliable. Squeeze out the excess water from the gelatin and melt it into the warm milk and sugar. Strain through a chinois and combine with the Greek yogurt. Chill over ice. Place the mixture into a whipped-cream canister and charge with the N$_2$O cartridges. Keep refrigerated until ready to use.

### CHOCOLATE CARAMEL TUILES
1/3 cup poured white fondant
1/3 cup glucose syrup
3 ounces Valrhona Araguani chocolate
    (72 percent), chopped
Edible gold dust

Line a baking sheet with a silicone baking mat. In a small saucepan over medium heat, cook the fondant and glucose syrup to 320°F. Remove the pan from the heat and add the chocolate. Mix well and pour the caramel onto the silicone baking mat. Place another mat on top and roll with a rolling pin to spread the caramel thinly and help it cool quickly.

Preheat the oven to 325°F. To shape the chocolate caramel, place it between 2 silicone baking mats and put it in the oven for 5 to 7 minutes to soften. Transfer the mats to a smooth surface. Use a rolling pin to roll the Tuile between the mats so that it is almost paper-thin. Working quickly, measure and cut 3-by-4-inch pieces and roll a piece around a plastic tube that is 1 inch in diameter. Trim the caramel so it is a perfect cylinder. Set aside to cool. Repeat with the remaining pieces of caramel. You should have 8 cylinders. Brush the cylinders with edible gold dust.

### ESPRESSO MOUSSE
1 2/3 cups plus 1/4 cup black espresso,
    made from instant powder (Medaglia d'Oro)
3 tablespoons cornstarch
8 sheets gelatin
10 ounces Valrhona Araguani chocolate
    (72 percent), chopped
1 1/3 cups sugar
3 egg whites
1 cup cream

Bring 1 2/3 cups of the espresso to a boil in a small saucepan over medium heat. In a small mixing bowl, whisk together the remaining 1/4 cup cold espresso with the cornstarch. When the 1 2/3 cups espresso come to a boil, whisk in the espresso-cornstarch slurry and cook for 5 minutes to remove any starchy flavor. Bloom the gelatin by placing the sheets in a bowl of ice water for 10 minutes, until pliable. Squeeze any excess water from the gelatin and melt into the espresso. Place the chocolate in a heatproof bowl, pour the hot espresso mixture over the chocolate, and stir until fully incorporated. Cool to room temperature.

Meanwhile, make an Italian meringue by combining the sugar and 1/3 cup water in a saucepan over medium heat. Cook until the sugar is at the soft-ball stage, 239°F. While the sugar is cooking, whisk the egg whites in a stand mixer until soft peaks form. Slowly incorporate the hot sugar into the egg whites and continue to whisk until the whites are stiff, white, and slightly cooled.

Fold the meringue into the chocolate-espresso mixture. Once it is fully incorporated, set it on ice to cool slightly. While it is cooling, whisk the heavy cream to stiff peaks and fold into the cooled chocolate-espresso mixture.

Place the Mousse in piping bags and chill until ready to use.

### TO FINISH
Espresso Mousse
Chocolate Caramel Tuiles
8 teaspoons Caramel Gel (see page 347)
8 teaspoons Yogurt Gel (see page 348)
8 tablespoons Chocolate Cookie Crumble (see page 362)
Coffee Iced Milk Sorbet (see page 366)
Yogurt Foam

Pipe the Espresso Mousse into the Chocolate Caramel Tuiles until they are full and smooth the ends with an offset spatula. Drop 1 teaspoon each of the Caramel Gel and Yogurt Gel next to each other on a plate. Use an offset spatula to spread the Gels across the plate. Place a 1-tablespoon mound of Chocolate Cookie Crumble on top the Gels. Set a Mousse-filled Chocolate Caramel Tuile on the Crumble. Place a quenelle of Coffee Iced Milk Sorbet on top of the Crumble and finish with a small dollop of Yogurt Foam. Repeat with the remaining ingredients, to serve 8.

# CHOCOLATE
CRÉMEUX WITH
BANANA, YUZU,
AND SESAME

*Serves 8*

## YUZU PÂTE DE FRUIT

1 1/4 cups yuzu juice
1 1/4 cups plus 2 tablespoons sugar
1 tablespoon plus 1 teaspoon pectin
3/4 cup glucose

Place the yuzu juice in a small saucepan and warm over low heat. In a small bowl, thoroughly combine 1/4 cup of the sugar and the pectin. Whisk into the warm yuzu juice and bring the mixture up to a boil, cooking until it reaches 217°F. Combine the remaining 1 cup plus 2 tablespoons sugar and the glucose in another bowl. Slowly whisk the glucose mixture into the yuzu mixture and bring up to a second boil. Continue boiling until the temperature reaches 221°F. Pour the mixture into a rimmed baking sheet lined with parchment paper and cool to room temperature. Break the Pâte de Fruit into small pieces (about 1/4 inch). They do not have to be uniform. Cool and keep at room temperature.

## SESAME CHOCOLATE SPRAY

1 cup (4.3 ounces) Valrhona Caraïbe chocolate
    (66 percent), chopped
1 cup cocoa butter
1 tablespoon sesame oil

Combine the chocolate, cocoa butter, and sesame oil over a double boiler and and melt slowly. Strain and transfer to a spray gun.

## CHOCOLATE TAHINI FEUILLETINE

1 3/4 cups (7 ounces) Valrhona Caraïbe chocolate
    (66 percent), chopped
1 teaspoon butter
3 tablespoons tahini paste
1/2 teaspoon salt
1 1/4 cups *feuilletine*

Combine the chocolate and butter in a medium saucepan and melt over low heat. Stir in the tahini paste and salt until smooth. Fold in the *feuilletine*. Roll the mixture between 2 sheets of parchment paper until about 1/8 inch thick. Chill in the refrigerator for 2 hours. With a ring cutter measuring 2 inches in diameter, cut rounds from the Chocolate Tahini Feuilletine. Store in the refrigerator until ready to use.

## BITTERSWEET CHOCOLATE CUSTARD

3/4 cup milk
3/4 cup cream
1/4 cup sugar
4 egg yolks
1 sheet gelatin
1 1/4 cups (6 ounces) Valrhona Caraïbe chocolate
    (66 percent), chopped
Sesame Chocolate Spray

Combine the milk and cream in a medium, straight-sided pan and bring to a low simmer over low heat. In a mixing bowl, whisk together the sugar and egg yolks. Pour the hot milk slowly into the egg mixture. Return back to the pan and cook over medium heat, stirring constantly, until the mixture reaches 178°F. Bloom the gelatin by placing it in a bowl of ice water for 10 minutes, until pliable. Squeeze out any excess moisture from the gelatin and melt into the egg mixture. Strain. Place the chocolate in a large heatproof container. Pour the hot mixture over the chocolate and rest for 2 minutes to melt the chocolate. With a hand blender, emulsify the mixture. Transfer to a piping bag and pipe into mini muffin flex molds measuring 2 inches in diameter. Freeze for at least 2 hours. Unmold the custards and spray with the Sesame Chocolate Spray. Store in the refrigerator until ready to serve.

## BLACK SESAME PASTE

1 cup black sesame seeds
1/8 teaspoon salt
1/3 cup sesame oil

In a small sauté pan, lightly toast the sesame seeds over low heat. While the sesame seeds are still warm, place in a blender with the salt. Blend and slowly add the sesame oil. Puree until smooth and pass the mixture through a fine-mesh tamis.

## BANANA TAPIOCA TUILE

3 tablespoons large tapioca pearls
4 ripe bananas
4 cups canola oil
1 tablespoon sugar

Preheat the oven to 275°F. In a medium saucepan, bring 4 cups water to a rolling boil. Add the tapioca pearls and simmer until the tender, 35 to 40 minutes. Rinse the tapioca under cold running water and drain. In a blender, puree the cooked tapioca with the bananas until completely smooth. Pass through a fine-mesh tamis. With an offset spatula, spread the tuile batter onto pieces of acetate measuring 3 inches by 4 inches. Dry the tuile in the oven for about 3 hours or until completely dry. Peel the tuiles off the acetate right after removing from the oven.

Heat the oil to 375°F. Fry the tuiles for 5 to 10 seconds and drain on paper towels. Sprinkle each with the sugar.

## SESAME-AERATED CHOCOLATE

1 cup (4.3 ounces) Valrhona Caraïbe chocolate
    (66 percent), chopped
1 tablespoon sesame oil
2 N$_2$O cartridges

Line a rimmed baking sheet with acetate. Combine the chocolate and sesame oil in a whipped-cream canister. Place the canister into a water bath maintained at 83°F by an immersion circulator for 1 1/2 hours. Charge the melted chocolate with the N$_2$O cartridges. Expel the chocolate to cover the prepared baking sheet. Cover with plastic wrap and freeze overnight. Break the frozen chocolate into small pieces and reserve in the refrigerator until ready to serve.

## TO FINISH

2 large ripe bananas
1/4 cup sugar
Black Sesame Paste
Chocolate Tahini Feuilletine
Bittersweet Chocolate Custard
Sesame-Aerated Chocolate
Caramel Yuzu Gel (see page 348)
Yuzu Pâte de Fruit
Roasted Banana Sorbet (see page 367)
Banana Tapioca Tuile

With a medium Parisian spoon or melon baller, scoop 16 balls from the bananas. Place the banana balls on a baking sheet or in a heatproof dish and sprinkle them with the sugar. Using a blowtorch, caramelize the sugar on the banana balls.

Spread 1/2 teaspoon of the Black Sesame Paste down the center of a plate. Place 1 round Chocolate Tahini Feuilletine on one end of the paste and top with a Bittersweet Chocolate Custard mold. Next to the Custard and on top of the Black Sesame Paste, scoop 1 tablespoon of the Sesame-Aerated Chocolate. Squeeze 3 dime-sized dots Caramel Yuzu Gel on the plate and arrange 6 to 7 pieces of the Yuzu Pâte de Fruit next to the dots. Place 2 caramelized banana balls on the plate. Place 1 quenelle of the Roasted Banana Sorbet on the Sesame-Aerated Chocolate and top with 1 Banana Tapioca Tuile. Repeat with the remaining ingredients, to serve 8.

# MIGNARDISES

LEMON MERINGUE
339

BLACK TRUFFLE AND CHOCOLATE
338

TARTE TROPÉZIENNE
339

## 5:00 AM

Pastry cooks arrive, turn on the lights and ovens, begin brewing the first pot of coffee, and start proofing brioche for lunch and dinner service.

## 5:30 AM

The butcher arrives and sets up two large cutting boards and pans with ice, gets towels, and sharpens his knives.

Pastry cooks begin making bread dough and organize their walk-in cooler.

Pastry sous chef arrives, confirms the dessert menu for service, and organizes the day's production.

## 6:00 AM

Purchasing manager, morning sous chef, morning cooks, and prep cooks arrive.

Morning sous chef begins roasting bones for stocks.

Cooks put pots of water on to boil for blanching vegetables and organize the walk-in coolers.

Prep cooks check their prep list and distribute tasks for the day.

## 6:30 AM

Purchasing manager checks in the produce and meat delivery.

Pastry cooks begin proofing the day's bread.

Entire kitchen team assembles for the daily lunch preservice meeting to discuss production, menu changes, and staffing.

## 7:00 AM

Purees, sauces, and braises begin to fill all of the stovetops in the kitchen.

Granola production begins.

Porters and dishwashers arrive and turn on the dining-room lights.

Purchasing manager checks in the daily linen order.

## 7:30 AM

Butcher begins cutting and portioning meat to prepare for *sous vide* cooking.

Externs arrive and speak to the morning sous chef to determine their production goals for the day.

# A DAY IN THE LIFE

## 8:00 AM

Purchasing manager checks in the fish delivery, begins communicating with purveyors to confirm any second deliveries for the day, and heads out to the Greenmarket to pick up certain produce.

The prep cooks begin washing and peeling vegetables for the day.

## 8:30 AM

Morning sous chef marinates foie gras.

All purees are finished and chilled.

Florist arrives and accepts the daily flower delivery.

## 9:00 AM

Pastry cooks spin ice creams and sorbets for lunch service.

The guest-relations manager and private-dining manager arrive.

Phones are turned on and reservation books are opened.

Prep cooks cut fruit and vegetables for service.

## 9:30 AM

Butcher cuts and portions fish for service.

Morning sous chef begins fish fumet production.

Porters begin cleaning the dining room: terrazzo is buffed, brass is polished, and glass is cleaned.

The guest-relations manager creates the dining-room floor plan for lunch service by assigning captains, servers, and assistant servers to their stations.

Sommeliers arrive and practice through blind tasting of wines in one of the private dining rooms.

## 10:00 AM

Dining-room staff arrives.

Opening bartender creates a playlist, consisting of the likes of the Beatles, Jay-Z, the Rolling Stones, and Arcade Fire, to play over the sound system during dining-room setup.

Barista brews the second pot of coffee.

The entire team sits down in the bar for family meal.

Barback stocks the bar with ice, fruit, syrups, juices, and fruit for garnishes.

Lunch maître d' and anchor arrive and begin putting together notes for the afternoon's reservations.

Building security unlocks and opens the front gates.

## 10:30 AM

Meat, fish, garde-manger, and executive sous chefs arrive and have their daily sous chef meeting.

Pastry cooks begin preparing the dough for the gougères.

Line cooks begin to set up their line and stock their mise en place.

The florist details the room by changing the water in vases and replacing any imperfect flowers.

Dining-room team changes and irons every tablecloth, details every charger and water glass, and checks every napkin and menu.

Porter retrieves all supplies from storage: mason jars for granola, plastics, and extra dry goods.

Executive assistant to the chef and general manager arrives, as does the lunch dining-room manger.

Morning sous chef begins making fresh pasta for service.

## 11:00 AM

Chef moves through the stations to taste every piece of *mise en place.*

Expediter wraps all of the kitchen passes with white tablecloths for service and places a new roll of paper in every ticket printer.

Lunch hosts arrive, check the restrooms, and organize the coat-check rooms.

Guest-relations manger handwrites all birthday and anniversary cards for guests celebrating at the restaurant that day.

Maître d' and anchor lead a meeting with the executive sous chef, lunch dining-room manager, and wine director to review lunch reservations.

Line cooks finish all knife work for service.

## 11:30 AM

Porters sweep and mop the kitchen floor.

Line cooks scrub and dry all surfaces in preparation for lunch service.

Prep cooks pick herbs for lunch service.

Sous chefs give sauces and purees their final seasonings.

Dining-room team meets for the lunch preservice meeting to discuss food, wine, and service.

Chef presents all new lunch dishes to the dining-room team.

Guest-relations manager sends an email to the executive sous chef detailing all dietary restrictions and special requests for the following day.

Orange beurre blanc is emulsified for poaching lobster.

Setup playlist is turned off and the dining-room soundtrack is turned on.

The sommelier stocks the Champagne cart with Champagne and ice.

The first batch of bread begins baking.

## 12:00 PM

Maître d' unlocks the door and greets the first lunch guests.

Anchor assigns the first reservations to their tables.

Coat check and host work together to get guests comfortably settled at their tables.

Garde-manger receives the first hors d'oeuvres ticket.

Captains greet their first tables with warm towels.

## 12:30 PM

Cooks prepare and deliver hors d'oeuvres to the first few tables.

Executive sous chef and expediter receive the first order in the kitchen.

Captains discuss the menu with their guests.

Servers ring in the first orders.

## 1:00 PM

Sommelier restocks the Champagne cart with ice.

Lunch dining-room manager moves through the dining room and kitchen, supporting the team and encouraging communication.

Appetizers and entrees begin leaving the kitchen while the expediter keeps track of ticket times.

## 1:30 PM

Purchasing manager places all dry goods and dairy orders for the following day.

First desserts are prepared and brought into the dining room.

Assistant servers restock butter.

Captains and sommeliers explain dishes to the guests.

The first kitchen tour enters the kitchen with the dining-room manager.

Pastry cooks begin making bread dough for dinner service.

## 2:00 PM

Dinner cooks arrive and begin collecting their *mise en place*.

Second produce delivery arrives and is checked in by the purchasing manager to ensure quality and accuracy.

The closing dinner dining-room manager arrives, creates the dinner-service floor plan, adjusts lineup notes, and communicates with the executive sous chef to update and print menus for dinner service.

The last lunch guests are being seated in the dining room and greeted by their captains.

## 2:30 PM

The expediter and executive sous chef receive the last order in the kitchen.

The executive sous chef calls "All in." The line cooks respond with a resounding *"Oui!"*

Wine team arrives and unpacks and bins all new wine deliveries while updating the wine list for dinner service.

The final glasses of Champagne are poured.

Pastry cooks begin proofing the day's bread.

## 3:00 PM

Line cooks scrub and dry the line.

Porters take out the garbage and recycling.

Lunch line cooks pass their stations to the dinner line cooks.

Bartenders and barback juice citrus, pick herbs, and make syrups to stock the bar.

Happy Hour, the weekly wine and spirits class taught by members of the team, takes place in one of the private dining rooms.

Assistant servers change tablecloths in preparation for dinner service.

Servers clean and polish all beverage trays.

## 3:30 PM

Kitchen team assembles for their daily dinner service lineup to discuss production, menu, and promotions.

Line cooks clean and organize the walk-in coolers and rewrap all herbs.

Pastry cooks spin ice creams and sorbets for dinner service.

Dinner maître d' and anchor arrive and begin putting together notes for the evening's reservations.

The final lunch kitchen tour ends.

Assistant servers clean, polish, and stock all silver to prepare for dinner service. Servers fold napkins for dinner service.

Captains assist the last guests with their coats and escort them to the door.

## 4:00 PM

Lunch dining-room manager gathers and organizes the lunch paperwork for the accounting team.

Lunch dining-room team leaves.

Dinner dining-room team arrives.

The entire team sits down in one of the private dining rooms for family meal.

## 4:30 PM

The expediter wraps the kitchen passes with fresh linen.

Dining-room team changes and irons every tablecloth, details every charger and water glass, and checks every napkin and menu.

Dinner coat check arrives and organizes the coat-check room for service.

Dinner hosts arrive, stock the restrooms, and organize the lounge.

Sommelier stocks the Champagne cart with Champagne and ice.

Maître d' and anchor hold a meeting with the sous chefs, dining-room managers, and wine director to review the evening's reservations.

## 5:00 PM

Chef walks through the stations to taste every piece of *mise en place*.

Orange beurre blanc is emulsified for poaching lobster.

Dinner porters and dishwashers arrive.

Line cooks scrub and dry the line.

Porters sweep and mop the kitchen floor.

Closing bartender arrives.

Guest-relations manager handwrites all birthday and anniversary cards for guests celebrating at the restaurant.

Dining-room team meets for the dinner preservice meeting to discuss food, wine, and service.

Chef presents all new dishes to the dining-room team.

Pastry cooks begin baking the first batch of bread.

## 5:30 PM

Maître d' greets the evening's first dinner guests.

Anchor assigns the first reservations to their tables.

Coat check and host work together to get guests comfortably settled at their tables.

The first glasses of Champagne are being poured.

Garde-manger receives the first hors d'oeuvres ticket.

More guests begin to arrive to relax for a drink in the bar.

Kitchen servers finish folding torchons for holding hot plates.

Assistant servers fill iced-water pitchers.

Barista brews coffee and makes tea for the line cooks and sous chefs.

## 6:00 PM

Purchasing manager places the produce order for the following day.

Meat-roasting cook glazes the first duck to go into the oven.

Polisher arrives and sets up the station.

Captains explain the menu to their guests.

Sommeliers discuss the wine list.

Servers communicate with the executive sous chef to confirm guests' menus.

Cooks bring the first hors d'oeuvres to the dining room.

## 6:30 PM

The first orders of bread are brought out to the dining room.

Sommeliers retrieve bottles from the white and red wine cellars.

Dining-room managers move through the dining room and kitchen, supporting the teams and encouraging communication.

The maître d' continues welcoming guests into the restaurant and communicates with the coat check to get coats organized for the first guests.

## 7:00 PM

Night reservationist makes confirmation calls for the following evening.

Captains explain dishes to the guests.

Assistant servers crumb tables to prepare for the next course.

## 7:30 PM

The first kitchen tour begins.

The host transfers checks from the bar to the dining room.

Coat check is organizing the front closet for ticketless checking.

## 8:00 PM

Purchasing manager leaves for the evening.

Captains detail the tables before guests are seated.

The first *mignardises* are prepared and brought into
the dining room.

## 8:30 PM

Sommeliers restock the Champagne cart with ice and
polished Champagne flutes.

Garde-manger cooks clean their station to prepare for
the second seating.

Maître d' communicates with the anchor to confirm
reservations.

The coat check and hosts are assisting guests with
their coats.

The first duck leaves the kitchen and is carved in the
dining room.

## 9:00 PM

Line cooks clean their stations to prepare for the
second seating.

Assistant servers restock and stamp additional butters.

Cooks bring the first hors d'oeuvres for the second
seating into the dining room.

The dining-room manager moves through the dining
room, talking to tables and filling in when needed.

## 9:30 PM

Pastry cooks clean their station to prepare for the
second seating.

The lounge is now filled with guests relaxing over
Cognac and *mignardises*.

## 10:00 PM

The last guests are greeted by the maître d' and are
seated in the dining room.

Anchor prepares the last table list and brings it to the
executive sous chef.

Night reservationist turns off the phones.

Dining-room manager communicates with the maître d'
about kitchen tours.

## 10:30 PM

The expediter and executive sous chef receive the
last order in the kitchen.

Executive sous chef calls "All in." The line cooks
respond with a resounding *"Oui!"*

Garde-manger team begins breaking down
their station.

Opening host leaves for the evening.

## 11:00 PM

Lunch dining-room manager leaves for the evening.

Anchor completes end-of-service report and sends it to the managers.

Kitchen servers unwrap the garde-manger pass and begin folding torchons for the next day.

## 11:30 PM

Hot line cooks break down and clean their stations.

Assistant servers are resetting tables.

Servers clean and polish all beverage trays.

Captains are explaining the final savory dishes to their guests.

The last kitchen tour ends.

## 12:00 AM

Pastry cooks finish the last few dessert orders.

Assistant servers clean out the crumbing drawers.

Kitchen servers clean and polish the gueridons.

## 12:30 AM

Hot line cooks begin to leave for the evening.

The executive sous chef leaves for the evening.

Pastry sous chef details the production list for the following morning.

Polisher finishes polishing and stocking all silver.

## 1:00 AM

Porters and dishwashers sit down for their family meal.

The last *mignardises* are brought to the dining room.

Coat check organizes the last few coats in the front closet.

## 1:30 AM

The last dinner guest leaves.

Polisher finishes polishing the last water glass.

Assistant servers remove candles from the tables.

Captains organize their paperwork and complete their end-of-night report.

Barista cleans out the coffee station.

The closing dining-room manager locks the door, turns off the music and lights.

## 2:00 AM

Porters scrub the stoves.

Pastry cooks leave for the evening.

Captains, servers, and assistant servers leave for the evening.

Closing dining-room manager finishes the end-of-night report and sends it to the managers.

## 2:30 AM

Porters scrub and dry the floors and walls.

Sommeliers finish updating the wine list for the following day.

Closing dining-room manager leaves for the evening.

## 3:00 AM

Porters take out the garbage and recycling.

Building security shuts and locks the front gates.

Copper pots are cleaned and polished for the next service.

## 3:30 AM

Dishwashers finish cleaning the last plastic goods and clean their station.

Porters clean and dry the floor behind the bar and the kitchen countertops.

## 4:00 AM

Dishwashers and porters leave for the evening.

## 4:30 AM

The entire restaurant is finally empty and takes a calming breath.

## 5:00 AM

Pastry cooks arrive, turn on the lights and ovens, begin brewing the first pot of coffee, and start proofing brioche for lunch and dinner service.

# HOW ELEVEN MADISON PARK WORKS

**DINING ROOM**

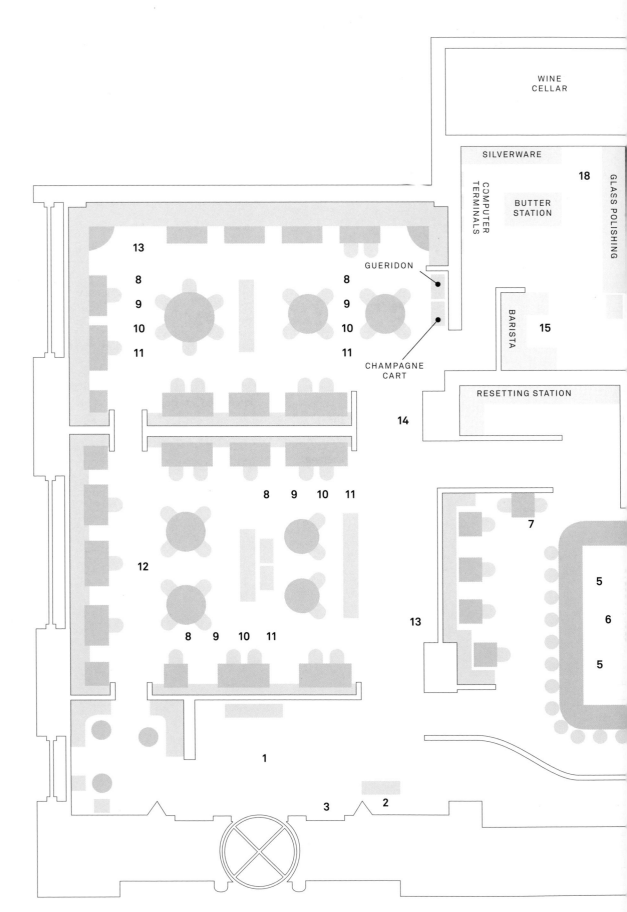

ENTRY

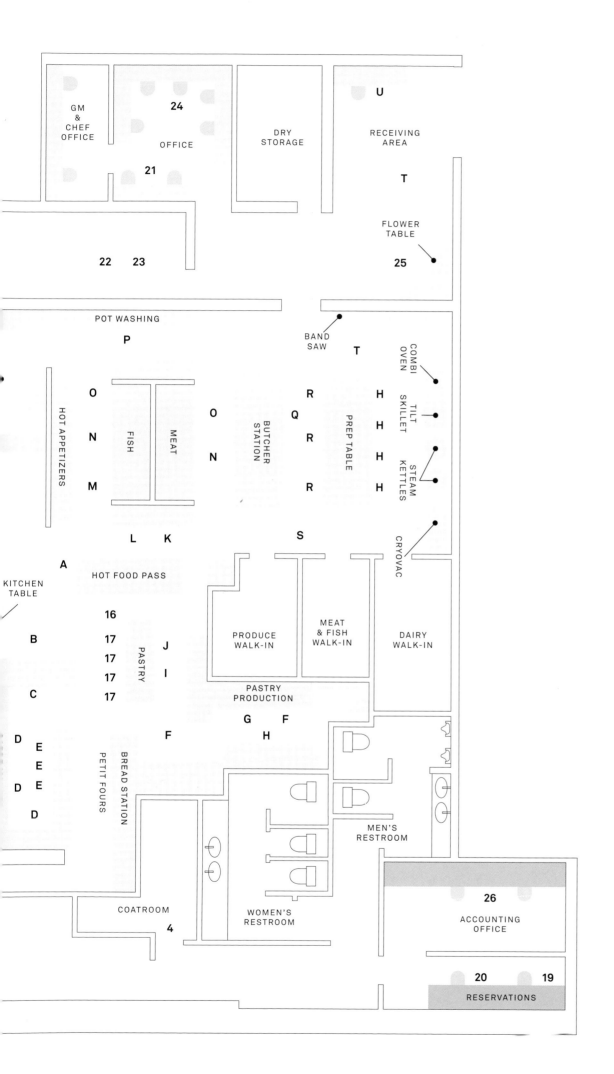

A   EXECUTIVE SOUS CHEF

B   CHEF TOURNANT

C   GARDE-MANGER SOUS CHEF

D   GARDE-MANGER COOK

E   HORS D'OEUVRES COOK

F   PASTRY PRODUCTION COOK

G   PASTRY CHEF

H   EXTERN

I   PASTRY SERVICE COOK

J   PASTRY SOUS CHEF

K   MEAT SOUS CHEF

L   FISH SOUS CHEF

M   HOT APPETIZER COOK

N   ENTREMETIER COOK

O   ROAST COOK

P   DISHWASHER

Q   BUTCHER

R   PREP COOK

S   MORNING SOUS CHEF

T   PORTER

U   PURCHASING MANAGER

1 MAÎTRE D' is responsible for warmly greeting every guest at the front door as they walk through the revolving doors. Before service, the maître'd reads through every reservation and all guest notes and does additional research on each guest so as to provide more personalized service.

2 ANCHOR is responsible for organizing the seating of the dining room during service and for the communication of information about tables to the dining room and kitchen.

3 HOSTS are primarily responsible for showing guests to their tables. They work with the anchor and maître d' to seamlessly escort guests into the dining room while gathering information to pass along to the dining-room team.

4 COAT CHECK organizes all checked coats, scarves, hats, gloves, and bags using a ticketless coat-check system. They monitor the table's progress through their meal to properly time the checked items' movement through the coat-check system.

5 BARTENDERS make all cocktails for the restaurant in addition to tending to the bar and guiding the bar guests through their drinking and dining experience.

6 BARBACK supports the rest of the bar team by ensuring that all liquors, garnishes, and juices are stocked and assists the cocktailer in maintaining the bar tables.

7 COCKTAILER tends to the bar tables and guides guests through their drinking and dining experiences.

8 CAPTAINS are in charge of the station, managing their team through all the steps of service, and guiding the guest through the dining experience. The primary contact at the table, the captains greet the guests, discuss the menu, explain the dishes as they arrive, and ensure that all members of the team are performing at the necessary level.

9 SERVERS provide communication between the captain and the kitchen. They are responsible for entering all orders into the computer, silver and glassware placement, and the delivery of all beverages from the bar to the tables.

10 ASSISTANT SERVERS maintain the tabletop. As one part of a four-person team, the assistant servers work with the server, captain, and sommelier of their team to ensure that guests are ready for the progression of courses, focusing on clearing, crumbing, and water levels.

11 SOMMELIERS are responsible for the service of all wine at the table. They help the guests navigate through the wine list, perform bottled wine service, and pour wine pairings.

12 LEAD SERVER provides additional support to the entire dining-room team. He or she begins the evening assisting the bar and then transitions to the dining room for all tableside presentations including Chemex, syphon, tea services, and duck carving.

13 DINING-ROOM MANAGERS are responsible for the daily functions of the dining room. They communicate with the executive sous chef to ensure that current menus are printed, assign teams for service, and work with the service director to plan, organize, and direct service.

14 SERVICE DIRECTOR oversees the flow of service, engages with with guests, and ensures that the dining-room staff are learning and being challenged. The service director is responsible for the development and instruction of new service points, coaching the dining-room staff through service, and the scheduling of the dining-room staff.

15 BARISTA prepares all of the coffee and espresso-based beverages for service while setting up trays for the syphon and tableside Chemex coffee preparations.

16 EXPEDITER maintains the pace of the meal for each of the tables. Without leaving the kitchen expediting pass, he or she must keep track of every table's progress. The expediter knows which guests are eating slowly, if guests are up from the table, and when wine pairings are being poured.

17 KITCHEN SERVERS alternate between delivering food to the guests and bringing information about every table's progress to the dining-room expediter.

18 POLISHER individually polishes every piece of china, glass, and silver by hand before it can be used in the dining room.

19 GUEST-RELATIONS MANAGER creates the daily reservation book, develops relationships with concierges, writes the hosts' and reservationists' schedule, and manages the guest-relations team.

20 RESERVATIONIST answers all incoming calls to the restaurant's main line. Using OpenTable, he or she fills the reservation slots while answering guests' questions about their future dining experience.

21 PRIVATE-DINING MANAGER books and organizes all events in the private-dining room. During the course of a day, he or she answers potential guests' questions, distributes private-dining information, and works with the kitchen to coordinate menus.

22 WINE DIRECTOR selects and purchases all wines for the list, works with the chef to determine the wine pairings, educates the staff on the wines, organizes all wine training, and oversees wine service.

23 CELLAR MASTER is responsible for maintaining the organization of the white and red wine cellars. They work with the wine director to properly label, stock, and bin bottles of wine as they are received.

24 EXECUTIVE ASSISTANT organizes all kitchen-observation trials for potential future employees. He or she arranges and coordinates all meetings for the chef and general manager as well as any special events.

25 FLORIST is responsible for maintaining the flowers in the dining room and for arranging flowers for private events and guests' special requests. He or she purchases flowers from the market and tends to the dining-room flowers daily to ensure their quality.

26 CONTROLLER prepares, examines, and distributes financial statements and reports for the management team. He or she executes payroll, ensures that all purveyors are being paid in a timely manner, and reviews and maintains all general ledger accounts.

**A EXECUTIVE SOUS CHEF** coordinates all menu changes with the sous chefs, dining-room managers, and the wine team. He or she works with the chef on menu research for the new dish designs. In addition, the executive sous chef writes the schedule for the kitchen team.

**B CHEF TOURNANT** is trained and proficient in every position in the restaurant. He or she supports the entire kitchen during setup and service.

**C GARDE-MANGER SOUS CHEF** produces all terrines and charcuterie. During service, he or she expedites the garde-manger line and oversees the garde-manger and hors d'oeuvres cooks.

**D GARDE-MANGER COOKS** complete the production, plating, and garnishes for all cold appetizers.

**E HORS D'OEUVRES COOKS** work on the preparation and plating of all hors d'oeuvres.

**F PASTRY PRODUCTION COOKS** are the foundation of the pastry team. They are the first to arrive in the kitchen every morning to make all bread and brioche and to portion all ingredients and garnishes for service.

**G PASTRY CHEF** coordinates all dessert menu changes with the pastry sous chefs, dining-room managers, and the wine team. He or she researches new products for future dishes and prepares and decorates all custom cakes.

**H EXTERNS** are responsible for assisting the entire kitchen team with various tasks as assigned by the sous chefs to encourage their learning and team skills. During the course of their externship, they are challenged by the sous chefs to learn and grow within their position and become stronger cooks.

**I PASTRY-SERVICE COOK** is responsible for the last-minute production and plating of all pastry dishes as the tables are ready.

**J PASTRY SOUS CHEF** oversees all production and service for pastry while helping to maintain cleanliness in the pastry station.

**K MEAT SOUS CHEF** is responsible for ordering all meats and for the plating of meat dishes during service. He or she works with the meat cooks to oversee their daily *mise en place* and to distribute current recipes.

**L FISH SOUS CHEF** is responsible for ordering all of the fish and for the plating of fish dishes during service. He or she works with the fish cooks to oversee their daily *mise en place* and to distribute current recipes.

**M HOT-APPETIZER COOK** executes all hot hors d'oeuvres and cooks all hot appetizers. He or she is responsible for producing all sabayons for service as well as the cleaning and storing of all truffles.

**N ENTREMETIER COOKS** are responsible for cooking all garnishes for hot entrees. They work in conjunction with the roast cooks to ensure that the protein and its garnishes are being finished at the same time.

**O ROAST COOKS** are responsible for all protein preparation, portioning, and cooking, as well as the finishing of sauces and *gastriques*.

**P DISHWASHERS** are responsible for washing all china, glass, silver, plastics, pots, and pans for the dining room and kitchen. They maintain the dishwashing machine to ensure that it is cleaning properly and hand-clean and polish all copper pots for service.

**Q BUTCHER** breaks down all meat and fish as it is delivered. He or she cleans and passes all foie gras and organizes and puts away all fish and meat.

**R PREP COOKS** prepare produce and juice fruits and vegetables for cooks to use in their daily *mise en place*.

**S MORNING SOUS CHEF** opens the kitchen. He or she begins by turning on all ovens and preparing the stocks. As cooks arrive, the morning sous chef organizes the daily production with the prep team and the butcher.

**T PORTER** is responsible for assisting the kitchen team with maintaining the cleanliness of the kitchen throughout the day. He or she sweeps and mops the floors in the kitchen, buffs the terrazzo in the dining room, polishes the brass throughout the restaurant, and cleans the entire kitchen after service ends.

**U PURCHASING MANAGER** is responsible for ordering all dry goods, vegetables, dairy, and other bulk products. He or she goes to the Greenmarket every day to get seasonal produce and to strengthen relationships with the purveyors and farmers. The purchasing manager receives all items as they are delivered to ensure accuracy and quality.

# HORS D'ŒUVRES

## PEA LOLLIPOPS

*Makes 32*

### MINT COCOA BUTTER
4 cups cocoa butter
2 cups loosely packed mint
2 drops mint extract

In a medium saucepan, heat the cocoa butter to 160°F. Place the mint in another saucepan and pour the cocoa butter over it. Add the mint extract and steep for 15 minutes. Strain and reserve, keeping warm.

### PEA TOPPING
2 cups freeze-dried peas
1/2 cup thinly sliced mint
1 tablespoon *fleur de sel*

Chop the freeze-dried peas until they are the size of peppercorns. Place in a fine-mesh tamis or sieve and shake out the powder. Reserve the pea powder for another use. Mix the pea bits, mint, and *fleur de sel* in a small bowl.

### TO FINISH
32 lollipop sticks, each 3½ inches long
6 lollipop molds, each with capacity for six 1 1/2-inch-diameter lollipops
Pea Ice Cream (see page 369)
Liquid nitrogen
Mint Cocoa Butter
Pea Topping

Lay the sticks in the molds and, using a small offset spatula, spread the Pea Ice Cream into the molds. Make sure that the rounds are filled entirely and evenly with ice cream and that the lollipops are the same length. Remove any excess ice cream from the edges. Freeze the lollipops for 1 hour.

Remove the molds from the freezer and dip them into the liquid nitrogen for 4 or 5 seconds to freeze the ice cream hard enough so it pops out of the molds cleanly. Be careful not to leave the molds in the nitrogen for too long, as this will cause the lollipops to be brittle and snap.

Once you've released the lollipops, dip them into the Mint Cocoa Butter. Quickly garnish with the Pea Topping before the cocoa butter sets. Keep the lollipops in the freezer until ready to serve.

## CARROT LOLLIPOPS

*Makes 32*

### CARROT COCOA BUTTER
5 cups roughly chopped carrots
6 cups cocoa butter

Process the carrots in the bowl of a food processor fitted with a steel blade until finely chopped. Stir together the carrots and the cocoa butter.

Place in a *sous vide* bag, and vacuum-seal. Place in a water bath maintained at 145°F by an immersion circulator and cook for 2 hours.

Alternatively, place the carrots and cocoa butter in a saucepan and steep at 145°F for 2 hours. Strain the mixture through a chinois and keep the cocoa butter warm.

### VADOUVAN TOPPING
1 cup buckwheat (also called kasha)
4 cups canola oil
1/2 teaspoon salt
2 teaspoons *vadouvan* curry spice
1/2 cup thinly sliced scallions, green parts only

Combine the buckwheat with 2 cups water in a saucepan and simmer for 20 minutes. Once the buckwheat is tender, drain it and spread it out on a baking sheet lined with parchment paper. Allow it to cool and dry. Once dry, bring the canola oil to 400°F in a medium saucepan. Deep-fry half the buckwheat until crispy. Strain the buckwheat and transfer it to paper towels to remove any excess oil. Repeat with the remaining buckwheat. Season with salt.

In a medium bowl, toss the buckwheat with the *vadouvan* curry and scallions.

## TO FINISH
32 lollipop sticks, each 3½ inches long
6 lollipop molds, each with capacity for six 1 1/2-inch-diameter lollipops
Carrot Ice Cream (see page 368)
Liquid nitrogen
Carrot Cocoa Butter
Vadouvan Topping

Lay the sticks in the molds and, using a small offset spatula, spread the Carrot Ice Cream into the molds. Make sure that the rounds are filled entirely and evenly with ice cream and that the lollipops are the same length. Remove any excess ice cream from the edges. Freeze the lollipops for 1 hour.

Remove the molds from the freezer and dip them into the liquid nitrogen for 4 or 5 seconds to freeze the ice cream hard enough so it pops out of the molds cleanly. Be careful to not leave the molds in the nitrogen for too long, as this will cause the lollipops to be brittle and snap.

Once you've released the lollipops, dip them into the Carrot Cocoa Butter. Quickly garnish with the Vadouvan Topping before the Cocoa Butter sets. Keep the lollipops in the freezer until ready to serve.

## WHITE ASPARAGUS LOLLIPOPS

*Makes 32*

### WHITE ASPARAGUS COCOA BUTTER
4 cups chopped white asparagus
4 cups cocoa butter

Process the asparagus in the bowl of a food processor fitted with a steel blade until very finely chopped. Stir together the asparagus and the cocoa butter.

Place the cocoa butter and asparagus in a *sous vide* bag and vacuum-seal. Place in a water bath, maintained at 145°F by an immersion circulator, for 2 hours.

Alternatively, place the asparagus and cocoa butter in a saucepan and steep at 145°F for 2 hours.

Strain the mixture through a chinois and keep the cocoa butter warm.

## DEHYDRATED GRAPEFRUIT

50 ruby grapefruit supremes, from 6 to 7
    grapefruits
1/2 cup confectioners' sugar

Preheat the oven to 175°F. Line a 13-by-
18-inch baking sheet with acetate. Line
up the supremes in even rows on the
acetate. Dust evenly with the confectioners' sugar and place in the oven to dry
overnight or for 8 to 9 hours. Remove
the grapefruit from the oven and cut
into 1/4-inch squares. If the pieces are
still too moist, return the oven for 2 to 3
more hours, or until the desired dryness
is reached. The pieces should feel like
raisins — dry on the outside but with a
bit of moisture in the center.

### TO FINISH

54 asparagus buds
32 lollipop sticks, each 3 1/2 inches long
6 lollipop molds, each with capacity
    for six 1 1/2-inch-diameter lollipops
White Asparagus Ice Cream (see
    page 369)
Liquid nitrogen
White Asparagus Cocoa Butter
Dehydrated Grapefruit

Bring a saucepan of salted water to a
boil. Add the asparagus buds and cook
for 30 seconds. Drain and transfer to a
bowl of ice water. Once cold, drain, and
dry on paper towels.

Lay the sticks in the molds and, using
a small offset spatula, spread the White
Asparagus Ice Cream into the molds.
Make sure that the rounds are filled
entirely and evenly with ice cream and
that the lollipops are the same length.
Remove any excess ice cream from the
edges. Freeze the lollipops for 1 hour.

Remove the molds from the freezer and
dip them into the liquid nitrogen for 4 or
5 seconds to freeze the ice cream hard
enough so it pops out of the molds cleanly.
Be careful to not leave the molds in the
nitrogen for too long, as this will cause the
lollipops to be brittle and snap.

Once you've released the lollipops,
dip them into the white Asparagus
Cocoa Butter. Quickly garnish with the
Dehydrated Grapefruit and asparagus
buds before the cocoa butter sets.
Keep the lollipops in the freezer until
ready to serve.

## BUTTER RADISHES

*Makes 32*

32 baby radishes, green tops intact
1 pound butter, room temperature
2 1/2 tablespoons *fleur de sel*

Gently wash the radishes in ice water,
removing any dirt from the greens.
Dry them well and trim the bottoms
of the radishes so they stand up straight
on a plate.

Temper the butter by placing it in a
bowl for a few minutes in a warm place,
such as near a warm oven or stove.
Alternatively, you can slowly warm it in
the microwave at 4-second intervals,
whisking the butter in between until it is
tempered. If it gets too hot, it will break,
becoming greasy and unusable. Once
tempered, it should have the consistency
of melted chocolate. Season with the
*fleur de sel.*

### TO FINISH

Dip the bottom half of the radishes into
the tempered butter. Dip a second time
and gently shake to remove any excess
butter from the bottom. Place on a
rimmed baking sheet lined with acetate
or wax paper. Chill the radishes in the
refrigerator until the butter is set.

## ASPARAGUS AND CAVIAR

*Makes 32*

### ASPARAGUS

Peel of 2 lemons
4 tablespoons lemon juice
4 sprigs thyme
4 bay leaves
4 tablespoons butter
3/4 cup plus 2 tablespoons salt
32 jumbo white asparagus,
    bottom woodsy ends trimmed

In a large pot, combine the lemon peel,
lemon juice, thyme, bay leaves, butter,
and salt with 8 quarts water. Bring to a
simmer over medium heat. Using a vegetable peeler, carefully peel the asparagus up to the base of the tip. Add the
peeled asparagus to the simmering liquid
and cook for 10 minutes or until tender.
Remove from the heat and cool over ice
in the cooking liquid.

### DICED EGG YOLK

20 egg yolks
1/2 teaspoon to 1 teaspoon salt

Whisk the yolks in a large bowl until
combined. Season with 1 teaspoon salt.
Place a 9-by-13-inch rimmed baking
sheet in a *sous vide* bag and vacuum-
seal. Pour the yolks onto the sealed
sheet and steam in a combination steam
oven for 10 minutes at 180°F. Chill in the
refrigerator. Once chilled, dice the yolks
into 1/4-inch pieces.

Alternatively, you can place 10 eggs in
their shells in a pot of cold water. Place
the pot over medium-high heat and bring
to a simmer. Simmer for 12 minutes,
remove from the heat, and transfer the
eggs to a bowl of ice water for 10 minutes. Peel, discard the whites, and dice
the yolks into 1/4-inch pieces. Season
with 1/2 teaspoon salt.

### TO FINISH

Asparagus
2 tablespoons Lemon Oil (see page 345)
4 ounces osetra caviar
Diced Egg Yolk
96 Pickled Red Pearl Onion Slivers (see
    page 343)
96 chive tips
96 miner's lettuce flowers

Discard the asparagus cooking liquid.
Trim all but 2 inches of the asparagus.
Reserve the bottoms for another use. In
a medium bowl, gently toss the tips in
the Lemon Oil. Place 1/2 teaspoon of the
caviar in a line on top of each asparagus
tip. Garnish each with 3 egg yolk pieces,
3 pickled onion slivers, 3 chive tips, and
3 miner's lettuce flowers.

## STURGEON SABAYON

*Makes 32*

### SMOKED STURGEON BASE

1/2 cup butter
1/2 cup thinly sliced cremini mushrooms
1 cup thinly sliced leeks
1 tablespoon salt
2 cups diced Smoked Sturgeon (see page
    359)
1/2 cup dry vermouth
1/2 cup white wine
6 1/2 cups Fish Fumet (see page 356)
3 sprigs dill
3 sprigs thyme
3 bay leaves
1 1/4 cups cream

In a medium pot over low heat, melt the
butter. Add the mushrooms and leeks
and sweat until soft and translucent.
Season with salt. Add the Smoked
Sturgeon and sweat for 1 minute. Add
the vermouth and white wine and reduce
the liquid to 1/4 cup. Once the liquid has
reduced and the alcohol has cooked off,
add the Fumet. Bring to a simmer. Tie the
dill, thyme, and bay leaves together in
cheesecloth to make a sachet. Add the
sachet to the liquid and simmer on low
for 30 minutes. Add the cream, remove
the pot from the heat, and steep for
15 minutes. Strain the mixture through
cheesecloth. Return the strained mixture
to the heat and reduce to 1 cup to con-
centrate the flavor. Skim off all of the fat
and chill the base over ice.

## SMOKED STURGEON SABAYON

2 cups Smoked Sturgeon Base
2 cups melted butter
5 eggs
2 egg yolks
1 1/2 tablespoons salt
2 1/2 tablespoons lime juice
2 $N_2O$ cartridges

Combine the Smoked Sturgeon Base with the melted butter, eggs, and egg yolks. Season with the salt and lime juice. Fill a whipped-cream canister with the mixture and charge it with the $N_2O$ cartridges. Place the canister in a water bath, maintained at 145°F by an immersion circulator, for 2 hours, shaking it periodically to ensure even incorporation.

### TO FINISH

32 Araucana eggs
1/2 pound Smoked Sturgeon, diced
  (1/4 inch) (see page 359)
Chive Oil (see page 344)
Smoked Sturgeon Sabayon

Using an egg topper, score the tops of the eggs. With a sharp paring knife, carefully remove the tops. Pour the eggs out of the shells and reserve for another use. Rinse the eggshells and use your fingers to pull away the inner membrane of each shell. Let dry.

Place 1 teaspoon of the diced Sturgeon and 1 teaspoon of Chive Oil in the bottom of an eggshell. Fill with the sabayon. Repeat with the remaining ingredients, to make 32.

# FOIE GRAS SABLÉ WITH STRAWBERRY

*Makes 32*

### STRAWBERRY CONSOMMÉ

8 pounds strawberries, hulled and sliced
1/2 cup thinly sliced ginger
1 cup sliced lemongrass
4 cups chopped rhubarb
2 cups sugar
12 black peppercorns

In a large heat-resistant bowl, toss together the strawberries, ginger, lemongrass, rhubarb, sugar, and peppercorns. Bring a large saucepan of water to a simmer over medium heat. Set the bowl over the water, ensuring that the water does not touch the bottom of the bowl. Cover and cook over medium-low heat for 2 hours. Strain through 10 layers of cheesecloth.

### BLACK PEPPER SABLÉS

4 1/2 cups butter, room temperature
12 hard-boiled egg yolks
1/2 cup almond flour
1/2 cup confectioners' sugar
4 cups flour
2 teaspoons salt
1 teaspoon black pepper

In a stand mixer fitted with the paddle attachment, beat the butter with the egg yolks, almond flour, and powdered sugar until creamy. In a separate bowl, combine the flour, salt, and pepper. Slowly combine the dry ingredients and the butter mixture, mixing until fully incorporated. The dough will be soft. Roll the dough out to an 1/8-inch thickness between 2 sheets of parchment paper set over an upside-down 18-by-26-inch baking sheet. Freeze the dough. Once frozen, cut into 1-inch-by-2 1/2-inch pieces, using an adjustable pastry cutter. Return to the freezer for an additional 30 minutes and then separate the cut Sablés from one another. Return to the freezer for another 30 minutes.

Preheat the oven to 325°F. Bake the frozen Sablés between 2 silicone baking mats for 11 minutes or until lightly golden brown. Cool to room temperature and reserve in an airtight container.

### STRAWBERRY CONFIT

32 small strawberries, hulled and halved
  lengthwise
1 tablespoon extra-virgin olive oil, plus
  more for storing
2 tablespoons confectioners' sugar

Preheat the oven to 195°F. Line a rimmed baking sheet with a silicone baking mat. Toss the strawberries in the olive oil to coat them lightly. Place them cut side down on the silicone mat and dust with the confectioners' sugar. Bake for 1 1/2 hours. Flip the strawberries and bake for an additional 30 minutes. The strawberries should be deep maroon and tender but still hold their shape. Cool them on the silicone mat before storing in a flat, airtight container that has been coated with olive oil to keep them hydrated. The confit can be made 3 days ahead and stored in the refrigerator.

### MARINATED FOIE GRAS

1 1/2 lobes grade-A foie gras (3 pounds)
1 1/2 tablespoons salt
1 teaspoon pink curing salt
1 1/2 teaspoons sugar
3/4 teaspoon white pepper
3 teaspoons Madeira
1 1/2 teaspoons Cognac

Bring the foie gras to room temperature to soften. Separate the main lobes and remove the veins with tweezers and a paring knife. Pass the foie gras through a tamis, Season with the salt, pink salt, sugar, and white pepper, and place it in a *sous vide* bag. Add the Madeira and Cognac, seal the bag, and marinate in the refrigerator for 24 hours. Remove the foie gras from the refrigerator and allow it to come to room temperature. Transfer to a large mixing bowl and whip with a rubber spatula to re-emulsify. Place between 2 sheets of acetate and pat down to create a rough rectangle. Chill in the freezer for 15 minutes. The foie gras should be cold enough to be rolled out without breaking but not so warm that it is a loose puree. Roll the foie gras to slightly less than 1/4 inch thick and cut with a 12-inch-by-12-inch metal terrine mold. Refrigerate.

### STRAWBERRY GELÉE AND FOIE GRAS TERRINE

1 cup Strawberry Consommé
1 teaspoon salt
4 sheets gelatin
Marinated Foie Gras

Heat half of the Consommé and the salt in a small saucepan. Bloom the gelatin by placing the sheets in a bowl of ice water for 10 minutes. Once they are pliable, remove them from the cold water, squeeze to remove excess moisture, and stir them into the warm liquid until the gelatin is completely melted. Combine the warm liquid with the remaining Consommé. Pour the liquid evenly over the sheeted foie gras, making sure that the terrine is level. Refrigerate for 3 hours to set the Gelée.

### TO FINISH

Strawberry Gelée and Foie Gras Terrine
Black Pepper Sablés
Strawberry Confit
64 leaves bush basil
*Fleur de sel*
Black pepper

Run a paring knife around the edge of the mold to release the terrine. Remove the terrine and clean any excess foie gras from around the edges. Reserve for another use. Cut the terrine into 3/4-inch-by-2-inch rectangular pieces using a wet chef's knife. Remove each piece of terrine and place it on a Black Pepper Sablé. Garnish with 2 pieces Strawberry Confit, 2 leaves bush basil, *fleur de sel,* and coarsely ground black pepper.

# ASPARAGUS AND CRAB

*Makes 32*

## CRAB SALAD

1 pound shelled peekytoe crab
4 tablespoons diced (1/8 inch) Granny Smith apple
6 tablespoons Mayonnaise (see page 371)
4 teaspoons lime juice
2 teaspoons finely sliced chives
1/2 teaspoon cayenne pepper
Salt

Pick through the crab, discarding any bits of shell. Pat off any excess moisture with a paper towel. In a large bowl, gently fold together the crab, apple, Mayonnaise, lime juice, chives, cayenne pepper, and salt until combined. Taste for seasoning and adjust if necessary.

## GRAPEFRUIT GELÉE

1 1/4 cups pink grapefruit juice
1 teaspoons salt
8 sheets gelatin

Coat a 13-by 18-inch rimmed plastic baking sheet with vegetable spray. Wipe with a paper towel to remove any excess. Warm 2 tablespoons of the grapefruit juice with the salt in a small saucepan over medium heat. Bloom the gelatin by placing the sheets in a bowl of ice water for 10 minutes. Once they are pliable, remove them from the cold water, squeeze to remove excess moisture, and stir them into the warm juice. Stir in the remaining grapefruit juice. Strain through a chinois and pour into the prepared baking sheet. It will be about 1/16 inch thick. Chill in the refrigerator until set, about 1 hour. Cut into 1-inch-by-3/4-inch rectangles.

## TO FINISH

Pickled White Asparagus (see page 343)
Crab Salad
Grapefruit Gelée
Anise hyssop
*Fleur de sel*

Lay out an asparagus pickle and place 1 tablespoon of the crab on the bottom. Roll the asparagus at a slight angle three quarters of the way toward the tip. Before completing the roll, place a strip of Gelée horizontally on top. Finish rolling the asparagus and garnish with the anise hyssop. Season the top of the roll with *fleur de sel*.

# CHORIZO MADELEINES

*Makes 32*

1 cup eggs, about 4
1 cup sugar
1 3/4 cups flour
1 1/2 teaspoons salt
3/4 teaspoon baking powder
1/3 cup diced (1/8 to 1/16 inch) dried chorizo
1 1/4 cups Chorizo Oil (see page 344)

In a large mixing bowl, whisk together the eggs and sugar. Add the flour, salt, baking powder and chorizo. Add the Chorizo Oil and mix until completely smooth. Transfer the batter to a piping bag and allow to rest in the refrigerator overnight.

Preheat the oven to 350°F and coat 32 madeleine molds with vegetable spray. Fill the molds one quarter full with the batter and bake for 6 minutes, until golden. Line a baking sheet with parchment paper and pop out the warm madeleines onto the tray. Serve warm.

# ZUCCHINI SABLÉ

*Makes 32*

## BLACK PEPPER SABLÉS

2 1/4 cups butter, softened
6 hard-boiled egg yolks
1/4 cup almond flour
1/4 cup confectioners' sugar
2 cups flour
1 teaspoon salt
1/2 teaspoon black pepper

In a stand mixer fitted with the paddle attachment, beat the butter with the egg yolks, almond flour, and sugar until creamy. In a separate bowl, combine the flour, salt, and pepper. Slowly combine the dry ingredients and the butter mixture, mixing until fully incorporated. The dough will be soft. Roll the dough out to a 1/8-inch thickness between 2 sheets of parchment paper set over an upside-down 18-by-26-inch baking sheet. Freeze the dough. Once frozen, cut into 1-inch-by-2-1/2-inch pieces using an adjustable pastry cutter. Return to the freezer for an additional 30 minutes and then separate the cut Sablés from one another. Return to the freezer for another 30 minutes.

Preheat the oven to 325°F. Bake the frozen Sablés between 2 silicone baking mats for 11 minutes or until lightly golden brown. Cool to room temperature and reserve in an airtight container.

## GOAT CHEESE

1/4 cup pine nuts
5 squash blossoms
1 1/2 cups chèvre
2 teaspoons salt

Preheat the oven to 300°F. Place the pine nuts on a rimmed baking sheet and toast in the oven for 8 to 10 minutes. Bring a pot of salted water to a boil. Add the squash blossoms and cook for 5 to 10 seconds. Transfer to a bowl of ice water and drain. Roughly chop the orange petals of the squash blossoms and discard the green stems and stamens. Combine the chèvre, pine nuts, and squash-blossom petals in a bowl. Mix together and season with the salt. Refrigerate for 1 hour.

## CRISPY SQUASH BLOSSOMS

10 squash blossoms
Olive oil

Wrap a microwave-safe plate tightly with plastic wrap and rub with a thin layer of olive oil. Open and arrange the blossoms evenly on the plastic and rub the tops with olive oil. Tightly wrap the entire plate and blossoms with plastic wrap and poke numerous holes around the blossoms. Work out any air bubbles between the plastic wrap. Microwave on high for 1 minute and 30 seconds. Remove the top layer of plastic wrap. Microwave on high again for another 1 minute and 30 seconds. While still warm, bend the petals gently to create a curved shape.

## TO FINISH

4 baby yellow pattypan squash
4 baby green pattypan squash
4 baby zucchini
Goat Cheese
Black Pepper Sablés
Olive oil
*Fleur de sel*
64 leaves mint
32 sprigs flowering mint
Crispy Squash Blossoms

Bring a pot of salted water to a boil. Thinly shave the yellow and green pattypan squashes and zucchini on a mandoline. Add to the water and cook for 5 seconds. Immediately shock in a bowl of ice water. Drain and pat dry. Place a 2-teaspoon quenelle of the Goat Cheese on a Sablé. Place 2 yellow pattypan slices, 1 green pattypan slice, and 1 baby zucchini slice on top. Brush with olive oil and sprinkle with *fleur de sel*. Finish with 2 mint leaves, 1 flowering mint sprig, and a Crispy Squash Blossom. Repeat with the remaining ingredients, to serve 8.

## RICE CRACKER WITH CUCUMBER AND HAMACHI

*Makes 32*

### RICE PUFFS
1 cup sushi rice
4 cups canola oil
Salt

Preheat the oven to 175°F. Combine the rice and 2 cups water in a medium saucepan over medium heat. Cover and cook until all of the water has evaporated. Remove from the heat, leaving the rice covered and allowing it to steam until very soft. Place a silicone baking mat on a flat surface. Place 1 cup of the cooked rice on the silicone mat, cover it with a sheet of acetate, and roll it to 1/8 inch thick. Remove the acetate and transfer the silicone mat with the rice to a baking sheet. Repeat with the remaining rice and bake for 2 hours, until completely dry. Heat the oil in a medium pot to 390°F. Break the rice into 3-inch pieces. Drop 2 pieces in the oil. Once they have puffed and turned white, remove them with a slotted spoon to paper towels. Season with salt while still hot. Repeat with the remaining rice chips.

### SEARED HAMACHI
1 tablespoon olive oil
1 pound hamachi loin, about
    1 1/4 inches thick
Zest of 2 lemons
Zest of 2 limes
Salt

Heat the oil in a sauté pan over high heat. Sear the hamachi on all sides for 2 to 3 seconds, until just white. It should be opaque on the outside and rare in the center. Sprinkle evenly with the lemon zest, lime zest, and salt to taste. Slice into 1/8-inch-thick pieces.

### TO FINISH
1 teaspoon *yuzu kosho*
Rice Puffs
Seared Hamachi
10 1/2 tablespoons Coconut Gel
    (see page 348)
8 Thai bird chilies, thinly sliced
8 thin slices pickled ginger
4 lemon cucumbers, each sliced into
    8 wedges
*Fleur de sel*
32 sprigs cilantro
32 sprigs flowering cilantro
32 sprigs tarragon

Place a small dot of *yuzu kosho* on a Rice Puff. Top it with a piece of Seared Hamachi, 1 teaspoon Coconut Gel, a slice of chili, a slice of pickled ginger, a cucumber wedge, and *fleur de sel*. Garnish with a sprig of cilantro, flowering cilantro, and tarragon. Repeat with the remaining ingredients, to serve 8.

## SUCRINE LETTUCE WITH KING CRAB

*Makes 32*

### KING CRAB
8 king crab legs

Bring a pot of salted water to a boil. Add the crab legs and cook for 15 to 17 minutes. To check for doneness, wiggle the smallest joint and crack it from the leg. If the cartilage comes out clean with no meat attached, the crab is ready. Transfer the crab to an ice bath. Once it's cool, harvest the meat.

Using scissors, cut along the softer back side of the legs. Pry apart the shells and remove the crabmeat, being careful to maintain the structure of the flesh. Trim the meat on the bias into thirty-two 2-inch pieces.

## LEMON CONFIT
Peel of 2 lemons
1 cup sugar

Use a paring knife to scrape any white pith from the lemon peel. Trim the peels to thirty-two 1/4 inch-by-1/8-inch diamonds. Place in a small saucepan and cover with cold water. Bring the water up to a boil, strain the lemon peels, and transfer to a bowl of ice water. Repeat this process 3 times to remove the bitterness from the peels.

Combine the sugar and 1 cup water in a small saucepan and bring to a simmer to dissolve the sugar. Place the cool lemon peels in the sugar syrup and poach the peels at 185°F for 45 minutes to 1 hour, until tender. Cool the lemon peels over ice in their cooking liquid.

### TO FINISH
32 sucrine lettuce bulbs
2 tablespoons Lemon Vinaigrette (see
    page 346)
King Crab
3 tablespoons Lemon Gel (see page 348)
3 tablespoons Crustacean Mayonnaise
    (see page 371)
3 tablespoons crème fraîche
Lemon Confit
32 leaves tarragon
32 sprigs dill

Peel off the outer leaves of the lettuce bulbs. Trim the root ends of the lettuce to remove any browning. The resulting lettuce should measure 2 1/2 inches in length. Dress the lettuce bulbs in Lemon Vinaigrette. Place a piece of King Crab on each lettuce bulb. Squeeze a drop each of Lemon Gel, Crustacean Mayonnaise, and crème fraîche on the King Crab. Place 1 slice Lemon Confit on top of the drops of Lemon Gel, 1 tarragon leaf on the Crustacean Mayonnaise, and 1 sprig dill on the crème fraîche.

## SALMON GALETTE WITH DILL AND HORSERADISH

*Makes 32*

### ALMOND TUILES
1 cup flour
3/4 cup almond flour
2 tablespoons sugar
Scant cup glucose syrup
15 tablespoons butter, melted
3/4 cup egg whites, about 6

Combine the flour, almond flour, and sugar in the bowl of a stand mixer fitted with the paddle attachment. Mix on low speed and slowly add the glucose. Once incorporated, add the melted butter, mixing until combined, and then add the egg whites. Allow the batter to rest in the refrigerator for 30 minutes.

Preheat the oven to 325°F. Thoroughly coat 2 flat, upside-down 13-by-18-inch rimmed baking sheets with vegetable cooking spray. Place a sheet of parchment paper on top of each baking sheet. Pour 1/2 cup of the batter onto one of the sheets and, using an offset spatula, spread it very thinly in fluid, even strokes. Repeat with the other baking sheet and another 1/2 cup batter. Bake until light brown, about 8 to 10 minutes, rotating the pans halfway through baking. Remove from the oven and cut into 1-inch-by-1 1/4-inch pieces, using an expanding adjustable pastry cutter that has been coated with vegetable spray. Return the sheets to the oven and continue baking until golden brown, about 1 to 2 more minutes. Remove from the oven and place another sheet of parchment paper on top of the Tuiles. Then place another baking sheet on top of the parchment. Weigh them down with a cast-iron skillet to flatten the Tuiles. Allow to cool completely before removing the weighted baking sheets and separating the Tuiles.

## HORSERADISH MOUSSE

6 cups cream
Scant cup freshly grated horseradish
22 sheets gelatin
10 ounces mascarpone
6 teaspoons salt
4 teaspoons liquid from bottled
  prepared horseradish

Place 3 1/2 cups of the cream in a small saucepan over medium heat until just warmed through (about 165°F). Remove from the heat, add the freshly grated horseradish, and cover with plastic wrap or a tight-fitting lid. Let infuse in a warm place, such near a warm oven or stove, for 1 hour. After 1 hour, the cream should be at about 120°F. Bloom the gelatin by placing the sheets in a bowl of ice water for 10 minutes. Once they are pliable, remove them from the cold water, squeeze out any excess moisture, and stir them into the warm horseradish cream, along with the mascarpone, the salt, and the liquid from the prepared horseradish. Strain through a chinois into a large bowl and cool to room temperature. In a cold bowl, whip the remaining 2 1/2 cups cream to soft peaks. Fold the whipped cream into the cooled horseradish cream in thirds. (Note that the horseradish cream must be cool to the touch to prevent the whipped cream from separating.) Evenly spread 4 cups of the mixture onto a 9-by-13-inch rimmed baking sheet lined with acetate. It will be about 3/8 inch thick. Chill in the refrigerator until set, about 4 hours. Cut into 1/4-inch-by-1 1/4-inch pieces.

## SALMON TARTARE

2 cups finely diced fresh salmon
2 tablespoons Lemon Oil (see page 345)
2 1/2 teaspoons salt
In a medium bowl, mix the diced salmon with the Lemon Oil and salt.

## TO FINISH

Horseradish Mousse
Almond Tuiles
Salmon Tartare
32 grains Maldon salt
32 sprigs dill
32 dill blossoms

Place a piece of Mousse on a Tuile so that the Mousse lies flush with the bottom edge. Sandwich the Mousse between another Tuile. Stand the sandwich upright. Carefully fill any space between the Tuiles with a tablespoon of the Salmon Tartare, making sure that the Tartare is flush with the edges of the Tuiles. Place a crystal of Maldon salt on top of the Tartare and garnish with a dill sprig and a dill blossom.

*Note: Once assembled, the Galettes may sit for about 10 minutes, after which time the Tuiles will be soft.*

# SWEETBREAD CORNET

*Makes 32*

## SWEETBREAD FILLING

1 pound veal sweetbreads
2 tablespoons canola oil
1/2 cup flour
1 1/4 cups cream
2 teaspoons butter
2 tablespoons minced shallots
3 teaspoons salt
2 tablespoons minced parsley

Soak the sweetbreads in ice water in the refrigerator overnight to purge them of any blood. Drain and dry the sweetbreads and trim them to the size of golf balls. Heat the canola oil in a sauté pan over medium heat. Dredge the sweetbreads in the flour, pat off any excess, and sauté until golden brown on all sides, 1 to 2 minutes per side. Transfer to a plate lined with paper towels and allow to cool before refrigerating. Once they are cold, finely mince the sweetbreads and place in a large bowl.

In a saucepan set over medium heat, reduce the cream by half. Remove from the heat and allow to cool slightly. Melt the butter in a sauté pan over medium heat. Add the shallots and sauté until translucent. Fold the warm cream, shallots, and salt into the sweetbreads. Cool the mixture thoroughly over ice before folding in the parsley.

## CHIVE TIES

40 full-length chives

Bring a pot of salted water to a boil. Add the chives and cook for 20 seconds, or until wilted. Transfer the chives to a bowl of ice water to stop their cooking and help retain their bright green color. Once cold, remove from the water and gently squeeze in a kitchen towel to remove any excess moisture.

## TO FINISH

2 egg whites
4 sheets brick dough
Sweetbread Filling
32 Chive Ties
2 quarts canola oil

Whisk the egg whites with a few drops of water to create a wash. Cut each round sheet of brick dough into 8 even wedges. Place 1 1/2 teaspoons Sweetbread Filling just above the point of the brick dough. Fold the point over the filling and then roll into a cornet. Brush the edge of the brick dough with the wash before completing the cornet. Pinch the dough just above the filling, leaving about 1/2 inch of brick dough exposed. Wrap the Chive Tie around the pinched part of the cornet 3 to 4 times and secure with a double knot. Repeat with the remaining brick dough and filling. Using scissors, trim the ends of the chives and the tops of the cornets.

In a medium pot, heat the canola oil to 375°F. Add half of the cornets and fry until golden brown and crispy. Transfer with a slotted spoon to a plate lined with paper towels to drain of any excess oil. Repeat with the rest of the Cornets. Serve immediately.

# BEET MARSHMALLOW

*Makes 32*

## MARSHMALLOW

8 sheets gelatin
1/2 cup red beet juice (from 2 1/2 cups
  peeled and diced beets), strained
1 1/2 tablespoons beet powder
2 teaspoons salt
2 1/2 cups isomalt
1/2 cup glucose syrup

Bloom the gelatin by placing it in a bowl with ice water for 10 minutes, until pliable. Squeeze to remove any excess moisture. In the meantime, heat the beet juice in a medium saucepan over medium heat. Add the beet powder, salt, and gelatin to the beet juice. Pour the mixture into the bowl of a stand mixer fitted with the whisk attachment.

In another saucepan, heat 1/3 cup water, isomalt, and glucose over low heat until all of the isomalt is dissolved. Continue to cook until the sugar mixture reaches 240°F. Pour the hot mixture into the beet mixture. Whip on low speed for 1 minute, then whip on high speed for 8 more minutes. Line a 9-by-13-inch rimmed baking sheet with parchment paper and coat with vegetable spray. Pour the beet mixture onto the prepared baking sheet. Smooth out evenly with an offset spatula. Spray the top lightly with vegetable spray and cover with parchment paper. Wrap with plastic wrap and refrigerate for 4 hours.

## BEET SUGAR

1 cup red wine vinegar powder
1/2 cup confectioners' sugar
2 tablespoons cornstarch
3/4 tablespoon salt
1 1/2 teaspoons beet powder

Sift all of the ingredients together and store in an airtight container in a cool, dry place.

### TO FINISH
Marshmallow
Beet Sugar

Unwrap the baking sheet of Marshmallow and remove the top layer of parchment paper. Using a fluted ring cutter (1 1/4 inches in diameter), punch individual marshmallows from the sheet. Before serving, dust each marshmallow with the Beet Sugar.

## BUTTERNUT SQUASH CANNOLI

*Makes 32*

### BUTTERNUT SQUASH MOUSSE
3 sheets gelatin
2 cups butternut squash juice
 (from 4 quarts peeled and diced
 butternut squash)
1 1/4 cups cream
Juice of 2 limes
1 1/2 teaspoons salt
1/8 teaspoon grated ginger
2 N$_2$O cartridges

Bloom the gelatin by placing the sheets in a bowl of ice water for 10 minutes, until pliable. In the meantime, reduce the butternut squash juice by half in a small saucepan over low heat. In a mixing bowl, whip the cream to soft peaks. Squeeze the gelatin sheets to remove excess moisture and stir them into the warm reduced butternut squash juice. Remove from the heat and season with lime juice, salt, and ginger. Strain through a chinois into a mixing bowl. Cool over ice, stirring constantly, until the mixture is just below room temperature. Do not allow the gelatin to begin setting.

Fold the whipped cream in 3 parts into the butternut squash mixture and transfer to a whipped-cream canister. Charge the canister with the N$_2$O cartridges and refrigerate until ready to use.

### ROASTED BUTTERNUT SQUASH
2 medium butternut squash
4 tablespoons olive oil
2 teaspoons salt

Preheat the oven to 400°F. Halve the squash lengthwise and scoop out the seeds. Place the squash halves, cut side up, in a roasting pan. Using a brush, coat with olive oil and season with salt. Cover with aluminum foil and roast for 45 to 60 minutes, until tender. Cool to room temperature. Scoop out the flesh to yield 4 cups.

### BUTTERNUT SQUASH TUILES
1 cup tapioca pearls
4 cups Roasted Butternut Squash
4 cups canola oil

Bring 8 cups water to a boil. Add the tapioca pearls and simmer for 30 to 35 minutes, until tender. Drain the tapioca and rinse under cold water. In a blender, blend 1 1/2 cups cooked tapioca with the Roasted Butternut Squash until smooth.

Preheat the oven to 200°F. Cut 32 rectangles of acetate, measuring 4 by 8 inches each. Using an offset spatula, thinly spread about 2 teaspoons of the tuile batter onto each sheet of acetate. Place the rectangles on a baking sheet and bake for 2 hours to dehydrate the Tuiles. Cool to room temperature before removing the acetate.

In a large saucepan, heat the oil to 325°F. Working quickly, fry the Tuiles, one at a time, for 10 seconds. As you remove each Tuile from the oil, immediately roll it around a copper tube measuring 1/2 inch in diameter and 3 inches in length to form a hollow cylinder. Drain off the excess oil and allow to cool. Remove the tube. Repeat this process until all 32 Tuiles are fried and shaped. The Tuiles can be kept in an airtight container for up to 6 hours.

### TO FINISH
Butternut Squash Mousse
Butternut Squash Tuiles
1/4 cup sliced chives

Expel the Mousse from the canister into a Tuile until the tube is completely filled. Smooth the ends with a spatula and sprinkle each end with chopped chives. Repeat with the remaining ingredients, to make 32 Crisps. Serve immediately after filling.

## TUNA AND FENNEL

*Makes 32*

### FENNEL COINS
1 cup white wine
4 tablespoons Pernod
2 teaspoons salt
10 fennel bulbs

To make the fennel cooking liquid, combine the white wine and Pernod in a small saucepan and reduce by half. Add the salt and then 1 cup cold water.

Trim off the tops of the fennel and carefully peel off the petals, making sure they remain intact. Use a 1 1/2-inch ring cutter to cut rounds from the petals, making sure you have at least 64 coins. Line up the fennel coins in a single layer in a *sous vide* bag and pour in the fennel cooking liquid. Vacuum-seal the *sous vide* bag and cook the fennel coins in a water bath maintained at 185°F by an immersion circulator for 35 to 40 minutes. Chill in an ice bath.

Alternatively, double the amount of cooking liquid, bring it to a boil in a saucepan, and cook the fennel coins for 15 minutes in the liquid until tender. Chill over ice.

### TUNA COINS
2 pounds sushi-grade yellowfin or
 bigeye tuna
4 tablespoons Lemon Oil (see page 345)
2 tablespoons salt

Trim the sinew from the tuna. Use a 1 1/2-inch ring cutter to cut 32 rounds from the tuna. Brush the tuna with Lemon Oil and sprinkle with salt.

### TO FINISH
Fennel Coins
Tuna Coins
32 sprigs flowering fennel
2 teaspoons fennel pollen
2 teaspoons Maldon salt

Line up 32 Fennel Coins and place a Tuna Coin onto each Fennel Coin. Top with another Fennel Coin to make small sandwiches. Place a fennel flower on top and finish with a pinch of fennel pollen and Maldon salt.

## SEA URCHIN TOAST

*Makes 32*

### MARINATED FOIE GRAS
One 2-pound lobe grade-A foie gras
1 tablespoon salt
1/2 teaspoon pink curing salt
1 teaspoon sugar
1/2 teaspoon white pepper
2 teaspoons Madeira
1 teaspoon Cognac

Bring the foie gras to room temperature to soften. Separate the main lobes and remove the veins with tweezers and a paring knife. Pass the foie gras through a tamis, season with the salt, pink salt, sugar, and white pepper, and place in a *sous vide* bag. Add the Madeira and Cognac, vacuum-seal, and marinate in the refrigerator for 24 hours. Remove the foie gras from the refrigerator and allow it to come to room temperature.

### FROZEN FOIE GRAS TORCHON
Marinated Foie Gras

Using a damp towel, wipe down a smooth and spacious work surface. Lay out 3 long sheets (about 2 feet long each) of plastic wrap so that they overlap slightly. Wipe the plastic wrap with a damp towel. Spread the Foie Gras on top of the plastic wrap in a rectangle 2 inches from the bottom edge and 12 to 13 inches in length. Pull up the bottom edge of the plastic wrap and fold over the Foie Gras, rolling it into a cylinder 1 inch in diameter. Pinch the plastic wrap at the ends and roll by holding the ends of the plastic. Use a cake tester to poke holes to remove any air pockets. Roll again to press out more air. Tie both ends of the Torchon tightly and trim the excess plastic.

Place the Torchon in an ice bath to harden for 2 hours and then place in the freezer overnight so that it is frozen solid.

## TO FINISH

1 loaf Brioche (see page 364)
1/3 cup Clarified Butter (see page 370)
8 teaspoons Lemon Gel (see page 348)
128 sea urchin tongues
Frozen Foie Gras Torchon
3 tablespoons finely sliced chives
Maldon salt

Preheat the broiler. Trim the crusts from the Brioche and cut into 32 slices, each 3 by 1 by 1/4 inch. Line up the Brioche pieces on a baking sheet lined with parchment paper and brush the tops with Clarified Butter. Toast the Brioche under the broiler until golden brown, about 1 minute. Remove from the broiler and spread 1/4 teaspoon of Lemon Gel on each piece of Brioche. Overlap 4 sea urchin tongues on top and, using a microplane grater, grate the Frozen Foie Gras Torchon in an even layer on top of the sea urchin. Finish with 1/4 teaspoon finely sliced chives and a few grains of Maldon salt.

# POACHED EGG WITH CHICKEN AND WHITE TRUFFLES

*Makes 32*

### POACHED EGGS

32 organic eggs

Set up a water bath with an immersion circulator set at 145°F. Add the eggs in their shells to the water and circulate the water for 45 minutes.

Alternatively, set a pot of water over medium heat. Once it reaches 145°F, add the eggs in their shells. Using a thermometer, monitor the temperature of the water, maintaining it at 145°F for 45 minutes.

Remove the eggs from the water and keep at room temperature for up to 2 hours.

### MUSHROOM BEURRE BLANC

4 tablespoons canola oil
2 pounds cremini mushrooms, thinly sliced
1 cup diced white onion
1/2 cup diced celery
1/2 cup diced celery root
3 cups white wine
4 sprigs thyme
1 pound cold butter, cubed
2 tablespoons salt

In a medium saucepan, heat the oil over medium heat and add the mushrooms. Sweat until tender, about 10 minutes. Add the onion, celery, and celery root and sweat for 5 minutes. Deglaze the pan with the white wine and reduce until the pan is almost dry, about 10 minutes. Add 4 cups water and the thyme and simmer for 1 hour. Strain and reduce to 1/2 cup. Slowly whisk in the cold butter until it is emulsified. Season with the salt and remove from the heat. Keep in a warm place, such as near a warm oven or stove.

### POACHED CHICKEN

4 skinless, boneless chicken breasts
1 teaspoon salt
8 sprigs thyme

Season the chicken evenly on both sides with the salt. Place 2 sprigs thyme on the tenderloin side of the breast. Place the breasts in individual *sous vide* bags and vacuum-seal. Cook in a water bath maintained at 145°F by an immersion circulator for 25 to 30 minutes. Transfer to an ice bath. Once cool, remove the chicken breast and dice into 1/4-inch cubes.

### VEAL SWEETBREADS

2 pounds veal sweetbreads
1 teaspoon salt
1 cup flour
4 cups canola oil

With a pair of scissors, trim the sweetbreads into 3/4-inch pieces, removing any fat and blood. Soak the sweetbreads in ice water in the refrigerator overnight. Drain and dry the sweetbreads, season them with the salt, and dredge them in the flour. Pat dry to remove excess flour. In a sauté pan, heat the canola oil to 375°F. Fry the sweetbreads for 4 minutes and then drain them on paper towels.

### MUSHROOM RAGOUT

3 cups chanterelle mushrooms, washed and dried
3 cups picked *maitake* mushrooms (small pieces pulled apart from a large cluster)
3 (4-ounce) packages beech mushrooms, tops only
Mushroom Beurre Blanc
Poached Chicken
1 1/2 teaspoons salt

Clean the chanterelles of all dirt with a paring knife and scrape any discoloration from the stems. Trim the bottoms and rinse thoroughly. Spread the chanterelles on paper towels to dry.

In a large sauté pan over medium heat, poach all the mushrooms in the Mushroom Beurre Blanc until tender. Add the Poached Chicken, season with the salt, and toss to glaze.

### PARMESAN FOAM

1 teaspoon butter
1 tablespoon thinly sliced shallots
1 cup white wine
1 cup Chicken Stock (see page 356)
5 ounces (1 1/4 cups) Parmesan, diced (using the rind is okay), plus 1/3 cup finely grated
2 cups cream
4 teaspoons lime juice
1 teaspoon salt
1 pinch cayenne pepper

In a medium saucepan, melt the butter over medium heat until foamy. Add the shallots and sweat until translucent, 5 minutes. Add the white wine and reduce by two thirds. Add the Chicken Stock and the diced Parmesan and simmer the mixture until it is reduced by half. Add the cream and bring to a boil. Strain. Blend in the grated Parmesan with a hand blender and season with the salt, lime juice, and cayenne. Keep hot until ready to use.

### TO FINISH

Poached Eggs
Mushroom Ragout
Veal Sweetbreads
Parmesan Foam
Shaved white truffles

Crack a Poached Egg in the bottom of a bowl. Spoon 1 tablespoon Mushroom Ragout, 2 pieces Veal Sweetbreads, and a spoonful of Parmesan Foam over the Egg. Finish with shaved white truffles. Repeat with the remaining ingredients.

## OYSTER VICHYSSOISE

*Makes 32*

### OYSTERS
32 Beausoleil oysters

Shuck the oysters. Reserve the oyster liquor for the Oyster Gelée. Wash the deep bottom half of the shells well and reserve them for plating. With a pair of sharp scissors, trim off the mantle just down to the rounded body. Keep the trimmed oysters on ice until ready to use.

### VICHYSSOISE
1/2 cup packed baby spinach (3/4 ounce)
1 tablespoon butter
1/2 cup thinly sliced leeks
1 cup peeled and diced Yukon Gold
    potatoes
1/4 cup cream
3/4 teaspoon salt
3 sheets gelatin
1 tablespoon crème fraîche

Bring a pot of salted water to a boil. Add the spinach and cook for 25 to 30 seconds, until just wilted and bright green. Transfer to a bowl of ice water and, once cold, drain. In a small, straight-sided pot, melt the butter over medium heat. Add the leeks and sweat until translucent, 3 minutes. Add the potatoes and sweat for 5 minutes. Cover with 1 cup water and reduce the heat to low. Simmer until the potatoes are tender, 15 to 20 minutes. Transfer to a blender and blend while slowly adding the cream. Season with the salt and blend in the blanched, drained baby spinach for color. Chill the soup over ice, stirring constantly to speed the cooling and to prevent a film from forming. Store the chilled soup in the refrigerator until ready to use.

To bloom the gelatin, place the sheets in a bowl of ice water for 10 minutes, until pliable. Squeeze to remove excess moisture. In a small pot, warm 2 cups of the soup over low heat without allowing it to boil. Stir in the gelatin to melt. Remove from the heat, stir in the crème fraîche, and cool to room temperature.

## OYSTER GELÉE
1 1/2 sheets gelatin
Oyster liquor (reserved from Oysters)
1 1/4 teaspoons salt

To bloom the gelatin, place the sheets in a bowl of ice water for 10 minutes, until pliable. Squeeze to remove excess moisture. Strain the oyster liquor through a coffee filter to remove any sediment. In a mixing bowl, stir together the salt and 1 cup warm water. Add enough of the salt water mixture to the oyster liquor to make 1 cup of liquid. Melt in the bloomed gelatin. Cool to room temperature.

### TO FINISH
Salt
Oyster shells (reserved from Oysters)
Pickled Leeks (see page 342)
Vichyssoise
Oysters
Oyster Gelée
4 teaspoons osetra caviar
1 bunch dill

Spread a 1/2-inch layer of salt on a rimmed baking sheet. Line up the cleaned oyster shells on the bed of salt and adjust their placement so that they are all level. Place 1/8 teaspoon of the Pickled Leeks in the bottom of each shell. Spoon 1 1/2 tablespoons Vichyssoise into each shell. Place the sheet in the refrigerator so that Vichyssoise base can set, about 1 hour. Gently place a trimmed Oyster on top of the Vichyssoise. Spoon about 1/2 teaspoon of the Oyster Gelée on top to glaze the Oysters and return them to the refrigerator to set fully, 2 hours. Just before serving, garnish each shell with about 10 beads caviar and 5 sprigs dill.

## GOUGÈRES

*Makes 32*

2/3 cup butter
1 teaspoon salt
1/8 teaspoon nutmeg
1 pinch cayenne pepper
2 cups bread flour
1 cup plus 2 tablespoons grated Gruyère
    cheese
5 eggs
1 egg yolk
1/3 cup cream
*Fleur de sel*

Preheat the oven to 425°F and line a 13-by-18-inch rimmed baking sheet with parchment paper. In a medium saucepan, bring 1 1/3 cups water to a boil with the butter, salt, nutmeg, and cayenne. Add the flour and incorporate with a spoon as the mixture thickens. Cook the dough on the stove for about 2 minutes over medium heat. Place 1 cup of the Gruyère in the bowl of a stand mixer fitted with the paddle attachment. Add the cooked dough to the cheese and mix until the dough stops steaming. In a mixing bowl whisk together the eggs, egg yolk, and cream. Add the egg mixture 1/3 cup at a time to the dough. Fully incorporate each addition before adding the next. After all of the eggs have been incorporated, transfer the dough to a piping bag fitted with a pastry tip with a 1/2-inch round opening. Pipe the Gougères into silver-dollar-sized teardrops on the prepared baking sheet. Top each Gougère with a pinch of the remaining 2 tablespoons Gruyère and a sprinkle of *fleur de sel*. Bake for 12 to 14 minutes, until golden brown. Serve warm.

## GOAT CHEESE AND LEMON GALETTE

*Makes 32*

### GOAT CHEESE MOUSSE
5 1/2 sheets gelatin
2 cups cream
1 3/4 cups chèvre, at room temperature
2 1/2 teaspoons salt

Line a 9-by-13-inch rimmed baking sheet with acetate. Bloom the gelatin by placing the sheets in a bowl of ice water for 10 minutes, until pliable. In a mixing bowl, whip 1 cup of the cream to medium peaks and reserve in the refrigerator. Heat the remaining 1 cup cream in a small saucepan. Squeeze the excess moisture from the gelatin and stir into the warm cream. Place the chèvre in a mixing bowl and whisk in the gelatin mixture until smooth. Cool to room temperature. Fold in the whipped cream until fully incorporated and season with the salt. Pour the mousse into the prepared baking sheet and smooth with an offset spatula. Cover tightly with plastic wrap and chill in a refrigerator until set, about 3 hours.

### MEYER LEMON JAM
2 Meyer lemons
1 cup sugar

Slice the lemons into 1/8-inch-thick disks. Pick out the seeds and dice the lemons, including the peel, into 1/8-inch pieces. Combine the diced lemons and sugar in a small saucepan and simmer over low heat on the smallest burner until the jam is thick, about 6 hours.

## CHEESE CRACKERS

6 ounces Gruyère cheese, shredded
   (1 1/2 cups)
3 egg whites

Preheat the oven to 300°F. Combine the cheese and egg whites in a food processor and blend until smooth. Pass the mixture through a fine-mesh tamis. With a large offset spatula, spread the batter evenly onto a silicone baking mat. Place another mat on top and, with a rolling pin, roll the batter to 1/16 inch thick. Place the stacked mats onto a baking sheet and bake for 15 minutes. Remove the top mat and cut at least 64 into 1-inch-by-2 1/4-inch rectangles, using an adjustable pastry cutter. Cover again with the silicone mat and return to the oven. Bake until golden, about 15 minutes more.

Remove the Crackers from the oven and allow them to cool to room temperature. Store in an airtight container.

### TO FINISH

Goat Cheese Mousse
Cheese Crackers
*Fleur de sel*
Meyer Lemon Jam

With a wet knife, cut the Goat Cheese Mousse into 3/4-inch-by-1 3/4-inch pieces. Sandwich a piece of Goat Cheese Mousse between 2 Cheese Crackers. Sprinkle with *fleur de sel* and top with 1/8 teaspoon of the Meyer Lemon Jam. Repeat with the remaining ingredients.

# SEA URCHIN AND GREEN APPLE

*Makes 32*

### SEA URCHIN CUSTARD

6 sheets gelatin
1 tablespoon butter
1/4 cup thinly sliced shallots
1/2 cup sea urchins (3 ounces), plus 96
   sea urchin tongues
1/3 cup Cognac
1 cup tomato juice
1 1/3 cups Lobster Stock (see page 356)
2 2/3 cups cream
1/2 cup crème fraîche
3 teaspoons lime juice
2 1/2 teaspoons salt
1 pinch cayenne pepper

Bloom the gelatin by placing the sheets in a bowl of ice water for 10 minutes, until pliable. Melt the butter in a saucepan over medium-low heat. Add the shallots and sweat until they are soft and translucent, about 5 minutes. Add the 1/2 cup sea urchins and sauté for 1 minute. Deglaze the pan with the Cognac, increase the heat to medium, and reduce the alcohol until the pan is almost dry. Add the tomato juice and reduce the liquid to 1/2 cup. Add the Lobster Stock and reduce to 1 1/2 cups. Add the cream and bring to a simmer without allowing the mixture to boil. Strain and blend in the crème fraîche. Season with the lime juice, salt, and cayenne. Squeeze the excess moisture from the gelatin and stir it into 4 cups of the warm cream mixture.

Pour 2 tablespoons of the custard base into the bottom of 32 small bowls (about 1-cup capacity) and chill in the refrigerator for 30 minutes. Place 3 sea urchin tongues on each custard and return to the refrigerator to set, about 2 hours.

## APPLE GELÉE

3 cups green apple juice (from 6 to 7
   apples)
2 sheets gelatin

To clarify the juice, place it in a container in the freezer just after juicing for about 1 hour without letting it freeze completely. The sediment will settle to the bottom. Decant the juice into a clean container and strain the decanted juice again through a coffee filter. You should have 2 cups juice.

Bloom the gelatin by placing the sheets in a bowl of ice water for 10 minutes, until pliable. Warm 1/4 cup of the clarified apple juice in a small saucepan over low heat. Squeeze the excess moisture from the gelatin and stir it into the warm apple juice. Combine with the remaining 1 3/4 cups apple juice. Cool to room temperature.

Spoon about 1 1/2 teaspoons of the Apple Gelée on top of the Sea Urchin Custard and refrigerate for at least 1 hour to let the Gelée set.

### TO FINISH

2 Granny Smith apples
Sea Urchin Custard with Apple Gelée
96 sprigs chervil
96 sprigs dill

Cut the Granny Smith apples into small batons measuring 1/16 inch by 1/16 inch by 1/2 inch, leaving on the peel. Garnish each Custard with 6 apple batons, 3 sprigs chervil, and 3 sprigs dill.

# RAZOR CLAM WITH FENNEL

*Makes 32*

### RAZOR CLAMS

32 razor clams

*Sous vide cooking method*
Rinse the clams well under cold running water. Evenly divide the razor clams between 2 *sous vide* bags and vacuum-seal. Cook in a water bath maintained at 137°F by an immersion circulator for 5 minutes. Transfer to a bowl of ice water.

Remove the razor clams from the bags. Strain any liquid that is left in the bags through a coffee filter and reserve it for the Razor Clam Gelée. Open the razor clams carefully, keeping the shells intact. Remove the meat from the shells and trim away all but the cleaned neck, or "siphon." Slice on the bias into 1/8-inch-thick slices. Scrape the shells clean and wash thoroughly.

*Conventional cooking method*
32 razor clams
2 tablespoons olive oil
4 cloves garlic, crushed but kept whole
4 sprigs thyme
2 cups white wine
1 teaspoon salt

Rinse the clams well under cold running water. In a large straight-sided pot, heat the olive oil over high heat. Add the garlic, thyme, and clams and sauté for 30 seconds. Deglaze the pot with the white wine and add the salt. Cover and cook until the clams are just open, 5 minutes. Strain the clams and reserve the cooking liquid for the Razor Clam Gelée. Chill the clams over ice.

When the clams are cold, remove the meat from the shells and trim away all but the cleaned neck, or "siphon." Slice on the bias into 1/8-inch-thick slices. Scrape the shells clean and wash thoroughly.

### DICED BACON

2 slices double-smoked bacon, 1/8 inch
thick each

In a small sauté pan over low heat, render
the bacon for about 30 minutes. Drain on
paper towels and cool to room temperature. Dice the bacon into 1/8-inch cubes.

### RAZOR CLAM GELÉE

2 sheets gelatin
1 1/2 teaspoons salt
Razor Clam Cooking Liquid (reserved
from Razor Clams)

Bloom the gelatin by placing the sheets
in a bowl of ice water for 10 minutes,
until pliable. Stir together the salt and 2
cups warm water. Warm the Razor Clam
Cooking Liquid in a small saucepan over
low heat. Add enough of the salt water
mixture to the Razor Clam Cooking Liquid
to yield 2 cups of liquid total. Squeeze the
gelatin to remove excess moisture and
melt it into the warm Razor Clam mixture.
Keep at room temperature until ready
to assemble.

### COMPRESSED FENNEL WINGS

20 bulbs baby fennel
1 teaspoon olive oil

Thinly slice the baby fennel on a mandoline and trim each slice on a curved
bias so they resemble wings. Place the
fennel "wings" in a *sous vide* bag with
the olive oil and vacuum-seal. Hold
in the bag until ready to assemble the
hors d'oeuvres.

### TO FINISH

1/2 cup Fennel and Potato Puree (see
page 352)
Razor Clams (clams and shells)
Diced Bacon
Razor Clam Gelée
4 Meyer lemons
Compressed Fennel Wings
Fennel fronds from 6 bulbs baby fennel

With an offset spatula, spread about
1 tablespoon Puree into each half of the
razor clam shells. Place the shells on a
level surface and chill in the refrigerator
for 1 hour. Dot the Puree with about 6
to 8 pieces Diced Bacon and then line the
entire length of the clam shell with 7 to
8 pieces of the sliced Razor Clam. Return
to the refrigerator and chill for another
hour. Spoon 1 teaspoon of the Razor
Clam Gelée over the Clams and Puree
to coat evenly. Return to the refrigerator to set for 30 minutes more. Spoon
another teaspoon Gelée over the Clams
and refrigerate for another hour.

 Garnish each hors d'oeuvre with
3 Compressed Fennel Wings, 2
strips Meyer lemon zest, and 3 baby
fennel fronds.

# CHICKEN LIVER CRACKLINGS

*Makes 32*

### CHICKEN LIVER MOUSSE

1 pound chicken livers
1 pound butter
3 tablespoons salt
1 cup minced shallots
1/4 cup minced celery heart
1/4 cup minced garlic
1/2 cup red port
2 teaspoons pink curing salt
1 cup cream
1 teaspoon Dijon mustard
1 pinch nutmeg

Rinse the livers in ice water and trim off
all fat and veins. Pat dry and refrigerate
until ready to use.

 In a small sauté pan, heat 1/2 cup of
the butter over medium heat until it is
foamy but not browned. Cut the rest of
the butter into cubes and keep at room
temperature. Season the livers with 1
teaspoon of the salt and lightly sear the
livers in the foamy butter. Flip them over
and continue cooking until medium.
Remove the livers from the pan.

 Add the minced shallots, celery heart,
and garlic to the pan and gently sweat
the vegetables over low heat until they
are tender but not browned. Season with
1 teaspoon of the salt. Add the port and
pink salt to the pan and allow the alcohol
to evaporate. Whisk in the cream and
mustard and bring the mixture to a slow
simmer. Remove from the heat.

 Place the seared chicken livers in a
blender and puree on high speed. Gradually incorporate the cooked vegetables
and the hot liquid from the pan. Add the
butter, a few cubes at a time. Season
the mousse with the nutmeg and the
remaining 2 tablespoons plus 1 teaspoon
salt. While the mousse is still hot, strain
it through a chinois and chill.

### CHICKEN SKIN

32 pieces chicken skin, each about 1 1/2
inches square
1 tablespoon salt

Preheat the oven to 325°F. Line a rimmed
baking sheet with parchment paper.
Rinse the skin under cold running water
and trim off any excess fat. Spread the
chicken skin out on the baking sheet
and sprinkle with the salt. Place another
sheet of parchment paper on top of the
skin and place an inverted wire cooling
rack on the chicken skin to keep it flat.
Bake for 25 minutes. The skin should be
flat and crispy. Remove from the oven
and cool completely.

### TO FINISH

Chicken Liver Mousse
Chicken Skin
16 Pickled Enoki Mushrooms (see page
342)
10 seedless red grapes, thinly sliced
32 sprigs chervil
1 bunch baby chive (rock chive) tips
1 black truffle
1-inch piece frozen foie gras

Place a quenelle of Chicken Liver Mousse
on top of a Chicken Skin square. Arrange
1 Pickled Enoki Mushroom, 1 grape slice,
1 chervil sprig, and baby chives on top
of the quenelle. Using a microplane
grater, shave the black truffle and foie
gras on top. Repeat with the remaining
ingredients, to make 32 Cracklings.

# FOIE GRAS MACARONS

*Makes 32*

### MARINATED FOIE GRAS

One 2-pound lobe grade-A foie gras
1 tablespoon salt
1/2 teaspoon pink curing salt
1 teaspoon sugar
1/2 teaspoon white pepper
2 teaspoons Madeira
1 teaspoon Cognac

Bring the foie gras to room temperature
to soften. Separate the main lobes and
remove the veins with tweezers and a
paring knife. Pass the foie gras through
a tamis, season with the salt, pink salt,
sugar, and white pepper, and place in
a *sous vide* bag. Add the Madeira and
Cognac, vacuum-seal the bag, and
marinate in the refrigerator for 24 hours.
Remove the foie gras from the refrigerator and allow it to come to room temperature. Place in a making bowl and whip
with a rubber spatula to re-emulsify.
Transfer the foie gras to a piping bag
fitted with 1/4-inch pastry tip.

### TRUFFLE MACARONS

1 1/2 cups almond flour
1 1/2 cups confectioners' sugar
1/2 cup egg whites (about 4)
1/2 teaspoon egg white powder
3/4 cup sugar
1 pinch cream of tartar
1 tablespoon ground black truffles
2 teaspoons *fleur de sel*

Blend the almond flour with the confectioners' sugar in food processor for
30 seconds. Drizzle in 1/4 cup of the egg
whites and blend to make a smooth,
wet paste. Transfer to large mixing bowl
and cover with a damp towel.

Whisk together the remaining 1/4 cup
egg whites and the egg white powder in
a stand mixer. Place the sugar in a small
copper pot. Use your hand to mix 1/4 cup
water into the sugar, making a slurry.
Make sure there are no sugar crystals
sticking to the side of the pot. Cover the
pot and place over medium heat. Bring
to a boil, uncover, and add the cream of
tartar. Do not stir. Bring the sugar mixture
to 245°F. Before the sugar reaches 245°F
(at around 240°F), whip the egg-white-
and-egg-white-powder mixture to soft
peaks. When the sugar reaches 245°F,
slowly stream the hot mixture down the
side of the mixer bowl while whipping.
Continue whipping to stiff peaks.

Position a rack in the center on the
oven and preheat it to 265°F. Line a
13-by-18-inch rimmed baking sheet with
a silicone baking mat. Remove the damp
towel from the almond-and-sugar paste.
Fold the meringue into the almond-and-
sugar paste with a rubber spatula until
smooth and well combined. Add the
ground truffles. Continue folding until
the mixture loosens — the crests and
lines from folding should disappear very
slowly. Be careful not to overfold the batter, as this will result in flat cookies. Immediately transfer the batter to a piping
bag fitted with a 1/4-inch pastry tip. Pipe
at least 64 (allowing for some breakage)
quarter-sized rounds onto the prepared
baking sheet. Sprinkle each cookie with
*fleur de sel*. Dry at room temperature
until a thin crust is formed but the cookies are still soft in the center, 30 minutes
to 1 hour, depending on the humidity in
the air. Bake for about 9 minutes, rotating
the pan halfway through. Cool completely.

### TO FINISH

Marinated Foie Gras
Truffle Macarons

Pipe 1 teaspoon of Marinated Foie Gras
on the flat side of a Truffle Macaron.
Top with the flat side of another Macaron.
Repeat with the remaining ingredients,
to make 32 hors d'oeuvres.

# MIGNARDISES

## CARROT MACARONS

*Makes 32*

### CARROT CURD

1 3/4 cups carrot juice
1 cup diced carrots
4 eggs
1/2 cup plus 2 tablespoons sugar
3/4 teaspoon salt
3 sheets gelatin
1 cup plus 2 tablespoons butter,
    softened

To make a carrot puree, combine 1 1/4 cups of the carrot juice and the diced carrots in a small saucepan over medium heat. Simmer until the carrots are tender and most of the juice is absorbed, 15 to 20 minutes. Puree in a blender with the remaining 1/2 cup carrot juice until the puree is smooth. Pass through a fine-mesh tamis and chill over ice.

In a metal bowl, combine the carrot puree, eggs, sugar, and salt. Cook in a double boiler, stirring often, until the mixture reaches 180°F. Bloom the gelatin by placing the sheets in a bowl of ice water for 10 minutes. Once they are pliable, remove from the cold water, squeeze to remove excess moisture, and stir into the warm carrot mixture until the gelatin is completely melted. Cool over ice to 105°F. Using a hand blender, blend in the butter. Pass through a tamis. Cool completely and place in a piping bag fitted with a 1/4-inch pastry tip.

### MACARONS

1 1/2 cups almond flour
1 1/2 cups confectioners' sugar
1/2 cup egg whites, approximately 4
1/2 teaspoon egg-white powder
3/4 cup sugar
1 pinch cream of tartar
1 cinnamon stick

Blend the almond flour with the confectioners' sugar in a food processor for 30 seconds. Stream in 1/4 cup of the egg whites and blend to make a smooth, wet paste. Transfer to large mixing bowl and cover with a damp towel.

Whisk together the remaining 1/4 cup egg whites and the egg-white powder in a stand mixer. Place the sugar in a small copper pot. Use your hand to mix 1 teaspoon water into the sugar, making a slurry. Make sure there are no sugar crystals stuck to the side of the pot. Cover and place over medium heat. Bring to a boil, uncover, and add the cream of tartar. Do not stir. Bring the sugar mixture to 245°F. Before the sugar reaches 245°F (at about 240°F), whip the egg white mixture to soft peaks. When the sugar reaches 245°F, slowly stream the hot mixture down the side of the mixer bowl while whipping. Continue whipping to stiff peaks.

Preheat the oven to 265°F and position a rack in the center on the oven. Line a 13-by-18-inch rimmed baking sheet with a silicone baking mat. Remove the damp towel from the almond paste. Fold the meringue into the almond paste with a rubber spatula, until smooth and well combined. Continue folding until the mixture loosens; the crests and lines from folding should disappear very slowly. Be careful not to overfold the batter, as this will result in flat cookies. Immediately transfer the batter to a piping bag fitted with 1/4-inch pastry tip. Pipe at least 64 (allowing for some breakage) quarter-sized rounds onto the prepared baking sheet. Grate the cinnamon stick over the top of the Macarons. Dry at room temperature until a thin crust is formed but the cookies are still soft in the center, 30 minutes to 1 hour, depending on the humidity. Bake for 9 minutes, rotating the pan halfway through. Cool completely.

### CINNAMON CREAM CHEESE

2 cups cream cheese
1 tablespoon cinnamon
1 tablespoon sugar

In a stand mixer fitted with the paddle attachment, paddle the cream cheese until smooth. Mix in the cinnamon and sugar. Transfer to a piping bag fitted with a scant 1/4-inch pastry tip.

### CARROT CHIPS

2 medium Thumbelina carrots
1/2 cup sugar

Preheat the oven to 175°F. Scrub the carrots clean and remove the tops with a knife. Slice the carrots paper thin on a mandoline. Bring 1/2 cup water and the sugar to a rolling boil and remove from the heat. Add the carrots to the hot syrup and let stand for 10 minutes. Lay the individual carrot slices on a silicone baking mat and place in the oven for about 5 hours or until crispy. Store in an airtight container.

### TO FINISH

Carrot Curd
Macarons
Cinnamon Cream Cheese
6 ounces Valrhona Ivoire chocolate
    (35 percent), melted
Carrot Chips

Pipe a ring of Carrot Curd on the flat side of a Macaron. Pipe a dot of Cinnamon Cream Cheese in the center of the Curd and top with the flat side of another Macaron. Melt the white chocolate in a double boiler and place in a piping bag. Pipe a dot of melted white chocolate on top of the sandwiched cookie and top with a Carrot Chip. Repeat with the remaining ingredients, to make 32 Macarons.

# PASSION FRUIT BASIL PAVLOVAS

*Makes 32*

### BASIL POWDER
1 bunch basil leaves

Tightly wrap a plate with plastic wrap. Place the basil leaves on the plastic-wrapped plate without overlapping them and wrap another sheet of plastic wrap over the leaves. With a pin or cake tester, poke a few holes in the plastic wrap. Dehydrate the basil in a microwave at 30-second intervals until the leaves are dry, about 2 to 3 minutes total, depending on the microwave. Cool the basil leaves to room temperature and grind in a spice grinder to a fine powder. Reserve in an airtight container.

### BASIL KISSES
4 egg whites
1 1/2 cups sugar
Basil Powder

Preheat the oven to 275°F. Combine the egg whites and sugar in a mixing bowl. Cook in a double boiler, stirring constantly, until the sugar is melted. Transfer to a stand mixer fitted with a whisk attachment and whip until stiff peaks form and the meringue is completely cool. Transfer the meringue to a piping bag fitted with a 1/4-inch pastry tip and pipe at least 32 (allowing for some breakage) "kisses" onto a baking sheet lined with parchment paper. With a small sieve, sift a light layer of the Basil Powder on top of the meringues. Bake until a thin hard shell forms on the outside, 10 to 12 minutes. Cool to room temperature.

### FRIED BASIL LEAVES
1 teaspoon extra-virgin olive oil
32 small basil leaves

Tightly wrap a plate with plastic wrap. With your fingertips, rub a layer of olive oil on top of the plastic wrap. Place the basil leaves facedown on the plastic wrap without overlapping them and wrap another sheet of plastic wrap over the leaves. With a pin or cake tester, poke a few holes in the plastic wrap. Microwave for 1 minute 30 seconds, rotate the plate, and microwave for another 1 to 2 minutes, depending on the microwave. While the leaves are still warm, peel off the top layer of plastic wrap and transfer the leaves to a paper towel. Store the Fried Basil Leaves in an airtight container at room temperature.

### PASSION FRUIT CURD
2 sheets gelatin
2 eggs
1/2 cup sugar
1/3 cup passion fruit puree (from frozen puree)
1/2 vanilla bean, split lengthwise and scraped
10 tablespoons butter, room temperature, cut into 1-inch cubes

Bloom the gelatin by placing the sheets in a bowl of ice water for 10 minutes, until pliable. In a mixing bowl, whisk together the eggs, sugar, passion fruit puree, and vanilla bean seeds. Cook the mixture in a double boiler, stirring often, until it reaches 180°F. Squeeze out the excess moisture from the gelatin and stir into the egg mixture. Cool to 120°F, add the butter, and use a hand blender to emulsify. Pass the Curd through a tamis and chill over ice. Transfer to a piping bag fitted with a 1/4-inch pastry tip.

### TO FINISH
32 Basil Kisses
32 small basil leaves
Passion Fruit Curd
Fried Basil Leaves

With a pair of tweezers, poke a small hole in the bottom of each Basil Kiss. Using tweezers, insert a basil leaf into the center of each Kiss. Pipe about 1/4 teaspoon of the Passion Fruit Curd into the center of each Kiss. Finish with a Fried Basil Leaf.

# CHOCOLATE PALETTE WITH CARAMEL AND SEA SALT

*Makes 32*

### CARAMELIZED WHITE CHOCOLATE
8.6 ounces (2 cups) Valrhona Ivoire chocolate (35 percent), chopped

Bring a large pot of water to a simmer over medium heat. Place the chocolate in a *sous vide* bag and vacuum-seal. Place the sealed bag in the simmering water and cook for approximately 3 hours — rotate the bag every 30 minutes to ensure even cooking — or until the chocolate takes on a medium caramel color. Cool in an ice bath. Once the chocolate has solidified, remove it from the bag, allow it to come to room temperature, and use a paring knife to break into small pieces.

### BROWNED MILK SOLIDS
1/3 cup butter
1/4 cup milk powder

In a small saucepan over medium heat, melt the butter. Add the milk powder, stirring often as the milk solids begin to brown. When evenly browned, strain through a chinois, reserving the solids. Turn out onto a paper towel and pat to remove any excess butter. Reserve in an airtight container.

### SALTED CARAMEL
1 cup sugar
1/4 cup butter
1/4 cup cream
3/4 teaspoon salt

Place the sugar in a medium saucepan and cook to a medium caramel over low heat. In a separate saucepan over low heat, combine the butter and cream, melting the butter. Slowly stream the melted butter mixture into the caramel, whisking vigorously to emulsify. Stir in the salt.

Line a 9-by-9-inch baking pan with parchment paper and coat with vegetable spray. Pour the caramel into the baking pan and allow it to cool to room temperature. Cover tightly with plastic wrap and refrigerate until hard. Once set, remove the caramel from the pan and cut into 1/4-inch pieces.

### TO FINISH
1 pound Valrhona Caraïbe chocolate (66 percent), chopped
Caramelized White Chocolate
Salted Caramel
Browned Milk Solids
Hawaiian pink salt
*Fleur de sel*
Smoked Maldon salt

Melt the chopped chocolate in a double boiler until hot to the touch, about 120°F, stirring often. Chocolate burns easily, so keep your eye on it to avoid burning. Remove from the heat and cool over ice, stirring gently and constantly, moving it on and off the ice, to lower the temperature slowly. When the chocolate is still liquid but has cooled to 84 to 88°F, the chocolate will now be at the correct working temperature and "in temper." Invert a 13-by-18-inch baking sheet and coat lightly with vegetable spray. Line with a sheet of acetate. Spoon 32 silver dollar–sized chocolate circles onto the acetate, spacing them evenly. Tap the bottom of the tray so that the mounds flatten into disks measuring 2 inches in diameter. Garnish the chocolate circles with the Salted Caramel, Browned Milk Solids, Caramelized White Chocolate, red Hawaiian salt, *fleur de sel,* and smoked Maldon salt. Allow to set in a cool room or refrigerator until hardened.

## PB&J

*Makes 32*

### MILK CHOCOLATE AND FEUILLETINE

5.4 ounces (1 1/4 cups) Valrhona Jivara chocolate (40 percent), chopped
1 3/4 cups *feuilletine*

Melt the chocolate in a double boiler and stir in the *feuilletine*. Spread out onto a baking sheet lined with parchment paper and freeze until hardened, about 4 hours. Break into pieces and grind in a food processor to a coarse powder.

### PEANUT BUTTER TRUFFLES

2 3/4 cups shelled salted jumbo peanuts
13 ounces (3 cups) Valrhona Jivara chocolate (40 percent), chopped
1/3 cup cocoa butter
6 tablespoons butter, room temperature
1 teaspoon salt
Milk Chocolate and Feuilletine

Preheat the oven to 325°F. Place the peanuts on a baking sheet and roast in the oven for 10 to 12 minutes. Keep the roasted peanuts warm. Melt 2 cups of the milk chocolate and the cocoa butter in a double boiler. Transfer the roasted peanuts to a blender and blend on high speed until they begin to form a puree. Slowly incorporate the melted chocolate and cocoa butter and continue to puree until the mixture is completely smooth. While still blending, emulsify in the butter and salt. Transfer the mixture to a large mixing bowl and allow to cool. Transfer the cooled truffle mixture to a piping bag fitted with a 1/2-inch piping tip. Line a baking sheet with parchment paper and pipe long strips of chocolate onto the parchment paper. Cut the strips into thirty-two 1-inch-long pieces and roll them into balls. If the truffle mixture becomes too soft, refrigerate for a few minutes until firm again.

Melt the remaining 1 cup milk chocolate in a double boiler. Using a fork, dip each truffle ball into the melted chocolate and quickly roll in the Milk Chocolate and Feuilletine to coat evenly. Place the truffles on a baking sheet lined with parchment paper and refrigerate until ready to serve.

### RASPBERRY PÂTE DE FRUIT

3/4 cup raspberry puree (from frozen puree)
2/3 cup raspberries
1 1/4 cups plus 2 tablespoons sugar
2 1/4 teaspoons apple pectin
1/4 cup glucose syrup
2 teaspoons citric acid

Combine the raspberry puree and raspberries in a small saucepan. Place over medium heat and bring to a boil. In a small mixing bowl, stir together 2 tablespoons of the sugar and the apple pectin. Add the pectin and sugar mixture to the hot raspberries and bring to a boil. Stir in the remaining 1 1/4 cups of sugar and the glucose and continue to boil the mixture it reaches 225°F. Add the citric acid. Pour the mixture onto a 9-by-13-inch rimmed baking sheet lined with parchment paper and cool to room temperature. Cut into thirty-two 1/2-inch-by-1-inch rectangles and freeze overnight.

### LIQUID SHORTBREAD GLAZE

2 3/4 cups flour
2 3/4 cups almond flour
1 1/2 cups cold butter, cut into 1-inch cubes
1/2 cup confectioners' sugar
1 teaspoon salt
1/2 cup grapeseed oil

Preheat the oven to 325°F. Combine the flour, almond flour, butter, sugar, and salt in the bowl of a stand mixer fitted with the paddle attachment. Mix on medium speed until small nuggets form. Transfer the shortbread to a baking sheet lined with parchment paper, press into a 1/2-inch-thick rectangles, and bake until golden brown, about 35 minutes. Halfway through baking, cut the shortbread into chunks and return to the oven to finish baking. Cool slightly at room temperature.

Grind the warm shortbread in a food processor and slowly stream in the oil. Puree until the mixture is smooth. Transfer to a blender and puree until shiny.

### TO FINISH

Peanut Crumble (see page 363)
Liquid Shortbread Glaze
Raspberry Pâte de Fruit
Peanut Butter Truffles

Spread the Peanut Crumble onto a baking sheet. Warm the Liquid Shortbread Glaze in a medium saucepan over low heat until it is warm to the touch. Using a fork, dip each frozen Raspberry Pâte de Fruit in the Liquid Shortbread Glaze and transfer to the Peanut Crumble so that the bottoms are crusted with the Crumble. Refrigerate until ready to serve and serve alongside the Peanut Butter Truffles.

## MANGO AND CURRY

*Makes 32*

### RICE PUFFS

1 cup sushi rice
4 cups canola oil
Salt

Preheat the oven to 150°F. Combine the rice and 2 cups water in a medium saucepan over medium heat. Cover and cook until all of the water has evaporated. Remove from the heat, leaving the rice covered and allowing it to steam until very soft. Place 1 cup of the cooked rice on a silicone baking mat, cover with a sheet of acetate, and roll to 1/8 inch thick. Repeat twice with the remaining rice. Remove the acetate, transfer the silicone baking mats with the rice to a baking sheet, and bake for 2 hours, until completely dry. Heat the oil in a medium pot to 390°F. Break the chips into 3-inch pieces. Drop 2 chips in the oil. Once the chips have puffed, remove with a slotted spoon to paper towels. Season with salt while still hot. Repeat with the remaining chips.

### DEHYDRATED LIME ZEST AND BEADS

1 lime

Zest the lime with a microplane grater and place the zest between 2 paper towels. Microwave the zest for 1 minute to dehydrate. Store the zest in an airtight container at room temperature until ready to use. Peel the pith from the lime and discard. Carefully separate the pulp to yield individual beads. Be careful to keep each bead intact. Place the beads in an airtight container and refrigerate.

### CURRY MANGO CURD

1 cup mango puree (from frozen puree)
1/4 cup passion fruit puree (from frozen puree)
3 eggs
2/3 cup sugar
1 tablespoon Madras curry powder
5 sheets gelatin
1 cup butter, softened
1/4 teaspoon citric acid

In a large mixing bowl, combine the mango puree, passion fruit puree, eggs, sugar, and curry. Place the bowl over a pot of simmering water, whisking until the mixture thickens and the temperature reaches 180°F. Bloom the gelatin by placing the sheets in a bowl of ice water for 10 minutes, until pliable. Squeeze the excess water from the gelatin and melt it into the mango mixture. Cool to 120°F. With a hand blender, mix in the butter until fully emulsified and season with the citric acid. Pass through a tamis and transfer the curd to a piping bag. Chill in the refrigerator for 2 hours.

### COCONUT YOGURT

Frozen coconut puree (one 2.2-pound container), thawed
3/4 cup Greek yogurt
1 1/2 teaspoons sugar

Using a ladle, skim the water from the top of the puree. You should be left with coconut solids. Combine 2/3 cup of the coconut solids with the yogurt and sugar in a mixing bowl. Pass through a fine-mesh tamis and store in a squeeze bottle until ready to serve.

1 ripe mango
3 Thai bird chilies
Rice Puffs
Dehydrated Lime Zest and Beads
Curry Mango Curd
Coconut Yogurt
32 baby cilantro leaves
2 teaspoons Maldon salt

Peel and slice the mango into 1/4-inch-thick slices. Trim the slices into 1-by-3/4-inch pieces. Slice the Thai bird chilies into 1/16-inch rings.

Dust the Rice Puffs with the Dehydrated Lime Zest. Pipe about 1/8 teaspoon of Curry Mango Curd onto each Rice Puff. Place a mango slice on top of the Curd. Garnish the mango slice with 1/8 teaspoon of Coconut Yogurt, 1 cilantro leaf, 1 slice Thai bird chili, 3 Lime Beads, and a pinch of Maldon salt.

# CHOCOLATE AND MINT

*Makes 32*

### COCOA NIB BRITTLE

1 cup cocoa nibs
1 cup sugar
2 tablespoons butter
2 tablespoons light corn syrup
1 1/2 teaspoons salt
1/2 teaspoon baking soda

Line a baking sheet with a silicone baking mat. Toast the cocoa nibs in a small sauté pan over medium heat until fragrant, about 5 minutes, and keep warm. In a medium saucepan, bring the sugar, butter, corn syrup, and 1/4 cup water to a boil. Cook the mixture until it is a light caramel. Add the salt and baking soda and mix well. Add the toasted cocoa nibs and cook for 1 minute. Pour the brittle onto the prepared baking sheet and allow it to cool to room temperature.

### MINT GANACHE

1 1/2 cups cream
2 cups packed mint leaves
1/4 cup dried peppermint
1 1/2 tablespoons glucose syrup
8.6 ounces (2 cups) Valrhona Araguani chocolate (72 percent), chopped
1 1/2 teaspoons mint extract

In a small saucepan over low heat, bring the cream to a simmer. Place the mint leaves and dried peppermint in a mixing bowl. Pour the hot cream over the mints, cover with plastic wrap, and steep for 30 minutes. Strain and discard the mint. Measure the mint-infused cream and add enough cream to yield 1 1/4 cups. Combine the mint cream and the glucose syrup in a small saucepan and warm over low heat. Place the chocolate in a mixing bowl and pour the cream mixture over it. Allow to rest for 1 minute, add the mint extract, and blend with a hand blender until fully emulsified. Pour the Mint Ganache onto a 9-by-13-inch rimmed baking sheet lined with acetate and smooth the surface with an offset spatula. Chill in the refrigerator for 2 hours.

### MINT MOUSSE

3/4 cup milk
1 cup packed mint leaves
2 tablespoons dried peppermint
1 cup plus 1 tablespoon cream
1/3 cup sugar
1 egg yolk
3 sheets gelatin
3.5 ounces Valrhona Ivoire chocolate (35 percent), chopped
1 teaspoon mint extract
Mint Ganache

In a small saucepan over low heat, bring the milk to a simmer. Place the mint leaves and dried peppermint in a mixing bowl. Pour the hot milk over the mints, cover with plastic wrap, and steep for 30 minutes. Strain and discard the mint. Measure the mint-infused milk and add enough milk to yield 1/2 cup. Stir in 1 tablespoon of the cream. In a mixing bowl, whisk together the sugar and egg yolk. In a small saucepan over low heat, warm the mint-infused milk. Slowly whisk it into the sugar and egg yolk. Transfer the mixture to a double boiler and cook, whisking constantly, until it reaches 178°F. Bloom the gelatin by

placing the sheets in a bowl of ice water for 10 minutes. Squeeze any excess moisture from the gelatin and melt into the mixture. Place the white chocolate in a mixing bowl and pour the warm mixture over it. Allow to rest for 1 minute, add the mint extract, and stir until smooth. In a medium bowl, whip the remaining 1 cup cream to soft peaks. Fold the whipped cream into the white chocolate mixture and spread over the chilled Mint Ganache. Smooth with a large offset spatula and chill in the refrigerator for 2 hours.

### MINT GELÉE

2 tablespoons dried peppermint
3 cups packed mint leaves
1/3 cup sugar
1 cup ice
2 sheets gelatin
Mint Mousse

Bring 3/4 cup water to a boil in a small saucepan over medium heat. Place the peppermint in a mixing bowl, cover with the boiling water, cover with plastic wrap, and steep for 30 minutes. Strain and discard the peppermint. Measure the mint-infused water and add enough water to yield 3/4 cup.

Bring a pot of water to a boil. Add the mint leaves and cook for 10 to 15 seconds. Transfer to a bowl of ice water. Once cold, squeeze out the excess water from the mint and transfer to a blender. Puree with the sugar, mint-infused water, and ice for about 30 seconds. Strain through cheesecloth. You should have about 1 1/2 cups liquid.

Bloom the gelatin by placing the sheets in a bowl of ice water for 10 minutes, until pliable. Warm 1/4 cup of the mint liquid in a small saucepan over medium heat. Squeeze any excess moisture from the gelatin and melt into the warm liquid. Combine with the remaining mint liquid. Slowly pour the Mint Gelée over the chilled Mint Mousse and allow the Gelée to set in the refrigerator for at least 2 hours.

### TO FINISH

Cocoa Nib Brittle
Layered Mint and Chocolate (Ganache, Mousse, and Gelée)

Break the Brittle into 1-inch shards. Cut the Layered Mint and Chocolate into 1-inch squares. Using an offset spatula, place the squares onto Cocoa Nib Brittle shards. Refrigerate until ready to serve.

# WHITE CHOCOLATE TRUFFLE

*Makes 32*

### CARAMELIZED WHITE CHOCOLATE

13 ounces Valrhona Ivoire chocolate (35 percent), chopped

Bring a large pot of water to a simmer over medium heat. Place the chocolate in a *sous vide* bag and vacuum-seal. Place the sealed bag in the simmering water and cook for approximately 3 hours — rotate the bag every 30 minutes to ensure even cooking — or until the chocolate takes on a medium caramel color. Cool in an ice bath. Once the chocolate has solidified, remove it from the bag and finely shave it. Store in an airtight container.

### TRUFFLE COATING

2 cups Sucrée Crumble (page 363)
1/2 cup finely shaved Caramelized White Chocolate
1 tablespoon finely chopped black truffle
1/2 teaspoon *fleur de sel*

In a mixing bowl, stir together all of the ingredients. Store in an airtight container.

### DIPPING CHOCOLATE

3.5 ounces Valrhona Ivoire chocolate
(35 percent)
7 tablespoons Clarified Butter (see
page 370)
1 tablespoon White Truffle Butter (see
page 371)

Melt the chocolate with the Clarified Butter and Truffle Butter in a double boiler. Keep warm on the stove.

### TO FINISH

White Truffle Ice Cream (see page 369)
Liquid nitrogen (optional)
Dipping Chocolate
Truffle Coating

Scoop 32 balls of the White Truffle Ice Cream with a 3/4-inch melon baller or Parisian spoon. Place the ice cream balls on a baking sheet lined with parchment paper and freeze overnight. Alternatively, fill a baking dish one third of the way with liquid nitrogen. Drop the ice cream balls into the liquid nitrogen to flash-freeze. Remove with a slotted spoon. With a slotted spoon, dip each frozen White Truffle Ice Cream ball into the warm Dipping Chocolate to coat evenly. Drop the coated White Truffle Ice Cream balls into the Truffle Coating and roll to coat evenly. Transfer to a baking sheet lined with parchment paper and freeze until ready to serve.

# CARAMEL APPLE

*Makes 32*

### SALTED CARAMEL

1 cup cream
1/4 cup glucose syrup
2/3 cup sugar
1/2 ounce Valrhona Jivara chocolate
(40 percent)
1 teaspoon salt
3 tablespoons butter
1 vanilla bean, split lengthwise and
scraped

Combine the cream and glucose syrup in a small saucepan and warm over low heat. In a medium straight-sided pan over medium heat, cook the sugar to a dark caramel. Slowly add the warm cream mixture and cook to 220°F. Cool the caramel mixture to 175°F and stir in the chocolate and salt. Cool to 95°F and add the butter and vanilla bean seeds. Emulsify with a hand blender. Strain the mixture through a fine-mesh chinois and transfer to a piping bag. Refrigerate until ready to use.

### CARAMEL APPLE POPS

Green Apple Sorbet (see page 366)
Salted Caramel
32 lollipop sticks, each 3 1/2 inches long

Transfer the Sorbet to a piping bag. Pipe the sorbet into thirty-two 1-inch half-sphere molds and then pipe 1/8 teaspoon of the Salted Caramel into the center of the sorbet spheres. Freeze for at least 2 hours. Unmold the sorbet and insert lollipop sticks into the center of the rounded end of the dome. Freeze for at least 2 hours.

### GREEN COCOA BUTTER

1 cup cocoa butter
4 drops oil-based green food coloring

Melt the cocoa butter in a double boiler and add the food coloring. Keep the mixture hot until ready to use.

### TO FINISH

Almond Crumble (see page 361)
Caramel Apple Pops
Green Cocoa Butter

Spread the Almond Crumble on a baking sheet. Dip the Caramel Apple Pops in the melted Green Cocoa Butter and immediately transfer to the Almond Crumble, allowing it to adhere to the flat side of the pops. Repeat with the remaining ingredients to finish 32 pops and freeze until ready to serve.

# COFFEE BEIGNETS

*Makes 32*

### BEIGNETS

Coffee Ice Cream (see page 368)
Liquid nitrogen (optional)
2 1/2 cups flour
1/3 cup sugar
1 tablespoon plus 1 teaspoon baking
powder
1 tablespoon salt
1 2/3 cups buttermilk
1/3 cup cream
1 egg

Scoop 32 balls of Coffee Ice Cream with a 3/4-inch melon baller or Parisian spoon. Place the ice cream balls on a baking sheet lined with parchment paper and freeze overnight. Alternatively, fill a baking dish one third of the way with liquid nitrogen. Drop the ice cream balls into the liquid nitrogen to flash-freeze. Remove with a slotted spoon. Store the frozen ice cream balls in the freezer until ready make the Beignet Batter.

Whisk together the flour, sugar, baking powder, and salt in a large mixing bowl. In a separate mixing bowl, whisk together the buttermilk, cream, egg, and 1/3 cup water. Slowly mix into the dry ingredients until fully incorporated. Note that the batter should be made right before it is used.

Dip the Coffee Ice Cream balls into the Beignet Batter, which should cover the ice cream completely. Place on a baking sheet lined with parchment paper and freeze overnight. Alternatively, fill a baking dish one third of the way with liquid nitrogen and add the dipped ice cream balls.

### TO FINISH

8 cups canola oil
1 cup sugar
1 vanilla bean, split lengthwise and
scraped
Beignets

Heat the oil in a large saucepan to 375°F. Meanwhile, combine the sugar and the vanilla bean seeds in a mixing bowl. Carefully drop the frozen Beignets in the oil and fry until golden brown, 30 to 40 seconds. Remove with a slotted spoon and drain on paper towels. Roll the fried Beignets in the sugar mixture. Serve immediately.

# BLACK TRUFFLE AND CHOCOLATE

*Makes 32*

### CHOCOLATE TRUFFLE COATING

2/3 cup flour
1/2 cup cocoa powder
3/4 cup sugar
1/3 cup butter
1 teaspoon salt
1 egg
1 teaspoon vanilla extract
1 tablespoon finely chopped
black truffle

Preheat the oven to 325°F. Sift the flour and cocoa powder into a mixing bowl. In a stand mixer fitted with a paddle attachment, cream the sugar, butter, and salt until fully combined. Add the egg and vanilla and continue mixing to combine. Mix in the flour and cocoa powder. Spread the dough to a 1/4-inch thickness onto a baking sheet lined with parchment paper and bake for 12 minutes. Remove from the oven and lower the temperature to 300°F. Cut the half-baked dough into chunks and return to the oven to bake until the dough is dry, 12 to 15 more minutes. Cool to room temperature and grind in a food processor to a coarse crumble. Fold in the chopped truffles and store in an airtight container in the refrigerator.

## CHOCOLATE COATING

1 cup cocoa butter
3.5 ounces (3/4 cup) Valrhona Araguani
chocolate (72 percent)

Melt the cocoa butter and chocolate
in a double boiler and keep warm on
the stove.

## TO FINISH

Chocolate Truffle Ice Cream (see page
368)
Chocolate Truffle Coating
32 slices black truffles
Chocolate Coating

Spread the ice cream in thirty-two
1 1/4-inch flat, round flex molds and
freeze overnight.

Spread a layer of the Chocolate Truffle
Coating on a baking sheet. With a ring
cutter measuring 1-inch in diameter,
punch out rounds from the truffle slices.
Remove the frozen Chocolate Truffle
Ice Cream disks from the molds and dip
them into the warm Chocolate Coating. Immediately transfer the coated
ice cream onto the Chocolate Truffle
crumble and place a truffle slice on top.
Allow the chocolate disks to set in the
freezer until ready to serve.

# LEMON MERINGUE

*Makes 32*

## LEMON CURD POPS

3 sheets gelatin
Zest and juice of 6 Meyer lemons
2 1/2 cups sugar
1 1/2 cups butter
8 eggs
Orange Sucrée Crumble (see page 363)
32 lollipop sticks, each 3 1/2 inches long

Bloom the gelatin by placing the sheets
in a bowl of ice water for 10 minutes, until
pliable. Combine the lemon zest, lemon
juice, sugar, butter, and eggs in a large
mixing bowl and cook in a double boiler,
stirring constantly, until the mixture
thickens and reaches 180°F. Squeeze
the gelatin to remove excess moisture
and melt it into the lemon mixture. Pass
the curd through a tamis into a shallow
container and freeze overnight. Scoop
32 balls of Lemon Curd with a 3/4-inch
melon baller or Parisian spoon. Roll
the balls in the Orange Sucrée Crumble
and press the Crumble into the balls
with your hands. Insert a stick into each
Lemon Curd ball to make lollipops. Hold
in the freezer.

## SWISS MERINGUE

4 egg whites
1 1/2 cups sugar

Combine the egg whites and sugar in a
mixing bowl and set over a double boiler,
stirring constantly until the sugar is
melted. Transfer the mixture to a stand
mixer fitted with the whisk attachment.
Whisk the egg whites on high speed until
stiff peaks form. The mixture should still
be slightly warm.

## TO FINISH

Lemon Curd Pops
Swiss Meringue

Dip the Lemon Curd Pops into the warm
Swiss Meringue so that the Meringue
completely enrobes the Curd. Toast the
Meringue with a blowtorch and serve
immediately.

# TARTE TROPÉZIENNE

*Makes 32*

## TROPÉZIENNES

4 cups flour
1/3 cup sugar
1 1/2 tablespoons fresh yeast
1 tablespoon lightly toasted and ground
fennel seeds
1/2 teaspoon *fleur de sel*
5 eggs
1 egg yolk
3/4 cup butter, room temperature, cut
into 1-inch cubes

Place the flour, sugar, yeast, fennel, and
*fleur de sel* in the bowl of a stand mixer
fitted with a dough hook. Combine at
medium speed. In a separate bowl, whisk
together 4 of the eggs, the egg yolk, and
1/4 cup water. Gradually add the egg
mixture to the dry ingredients. The dough
will initially appear loose and almost
batterlike. As the gluten develops, it will
bind and start to pull away from the sides
of the bowl.

Once the dough pulls away from the
sides of the bowl, add the butter, 1 cube
at a time, and continue to mix until the
dough appears silky.

Place the dough in a greased bowl,
cover with plastic wrap, and proof at
room temperature until doubled in size,
1 to 2 hours, depending on the temperature and humidity of the room. Punch
the dough down, cover with plastic
wrap again, and chill in the refrigerator
for 2 hours.

Preheat the oven to 325°F. Working
quickly and using just a dusting of flour
to keep the dough from sticking, roll
the dough into a long log and cut into 32
quarter-sized pieces. Roll each piece
into a small ball and place the dough
into silicone mini muffin molds. Rest the
dough in the refrigerator for 10 minutes.
Beat the remaining egg and brush the
dough with the egg wash. Proof at room
temperature for 10 minutes. Bake in the
oven until the tops are golden brown, 20
to 25 minutes. Cool on a wire rack.

# PERNOD SYRUP

1 cup sugar
2 tablespoons Pernod

Combine the sugar and 1 cup water in a
small saucepan and bring to a boil. Chill
over ice and add the Pernod. Refrigerate
until ready to use.

## GRAPEFRUIT CURD

4 sheets gelatin
1 1/4 cups sugar
1/2 cup grapefruit juice
6 eggs
Zest of 2 grapefruits
1 vanilla bean, split lengthwise and
scraped
2 cups butter, room temperature, cut into
1-inch cubes
2 drops grapefruit bitters

Bloom the gelatin by placing the sheets
in a bowl of ice water. Combine the sugar,
grapefruit juice, eggs, grapefruit zest,
and vanilla bean seeds in a large mixing
bowl. Place the bowl over a double boiler
and whisk until the mixture thickens
and the temperature reaches 180°F.
Squeeze the gelatin to remove excess
moisture and stir it into the grapefruit
mixture. Strain and cool to 122°F. With a
hand blender, mix in the butter until fully
emulsified and add the grapefruit bitters.
Strain through a fine-mash strainer and
cool over ice. With a hand mixer, whip on
high speed until light and fluffy. Transfer to a piping bag fitted with a 1/4-inch
pastry tip and refrigerate.

## TO FINISH

Tropéziennes
Pernod Syrup
Grapefruit Curd
Orange Shortbread Crumble (see page
363)
2 teaspoons toasted fennel seeds

Cut the Tropeziénnes in half crosswise
and soak the bottom halves in the Pernod
Syrup. Pipe the whipped Grapefruit Curd
on the cut side of each soaked Tropézienne and top with another half. Brush
with the Pernod Syrup. Top with 1/4
teaspoon of Orange Shortbread Crumble
and a pinch of fennel seeds.

## SAUERKRAUT

1 head green cabbage (2 to 3 pounds)
2 teaspoons mustard seeds
1 teaspoon coriander seeds
1 teaspoon white peppercorns
3 bay leaves
3 allspice berries
1/4 cup plus 2 tablespoons salt
4 cups white wine

With gloved hands, remove the outer leaves of the cabbage and thinly shred on a mandoline. Transfer to a clean plastic or other nonreactive container. Make a sachet by tying the mustard seeds, coriander seeds, white peppercorns, bay leaves, and allspice in a piece of cheesecloth. Bring the sachet, 1 gallon water, and salt to a rolling boil in a large saucepan over medium heat. Remove from the heat and chill over ice. Pour the chilled liquid over the shredded cabbage to cover completely. Cover with 3 layers of cheesecloth and weigh down with a clean plate or weight. Store the cabbage at room temperature, about 58°F, for 4 weeks.

After 4 weeks, strain the cabbage and reserve the liquid. Place the white wine in a medium saucepan and reduce over high heat until 1 cup remains. Bring the cabbage liquid to a rolling boil and add the reduced white wine. Strain and pour the hot liquid over the cabbage and cool to room temperature. Keep in the refrigerator.

## PICKLED GOLDEN BEETS

1 large golden beet, peeled
2 tablespoons white balsamic vinegar
1 teaspoon salt

Slice the beet paper thin on a mandoline. Use a 1 1/2-inch ring cutter to cut the slices into circles. Bring the vinegar and salt to a boil and pour the hot liquid over the beet slices. Allow to come to room temperature.

## PICKLED RED BEETS

1 medium red beet, peeled
1/2 cup white balsamic vinegar
1 1/2 tablespoons salt

Slice the beet paper thin on a mandoline. Use a 1/2-inch ring cutter to cut the beet slices into circles. Bring the vinegar and salt to a boil and pour the hot liquid over the beet circles. Cool to room temperature.

## PICKLED BABY EGGPLANTS

2 cups Tomato Water (see page 371)
8 fairytale eggplants, peeled
3 tablespoons salt

Combine the Tomato Water with the eggplants and salt in a sous vide bag. Vacuum-seal and marinate for 4 hours. Open the bag just before serving to preserve the color of the eggplant and prevent oxidation.

Alternatively, bring the Tomato Water and salt to a boil in a small saucepan. Add the eggplants and remove from the heat. Cover and steep for 8 minutes. Cool over ice, weighing down the eggplants with a plate, if necessary, to keep them submerged in the liquid.

The Pickled Baby Eggplants can be made 2 to 3 days ahead using the sous vide method and 1 day ahead using the conventional method.

## PICKLED BREAKFAST RADISHES

2 cups red wine vinegar
1 cup sugar
2 tablespoons salt
4 teaspoons fennel seeds
2 teaspoons coriander seeds
2 cups small breakfast radishes, trimmed

Combine the vinegar, sugar, salt, fennel seeds, and coriander seeds in a saucepan. Bring to a boil over medium heat and pour over the radishes. Cool to room temperature.

## PICKLED BUTTERNUT SQUASH DIAMONDS

2/3 cup white balsamic vinegar
2 tablespoons plus 2 teaspoons honey
2 tablespoons salt
10 black peppercorns
2 cloves
2 bay leaves
1 butternut squash, peeled and seeded

Combine all ingredients except the squash in a small saucepan over medium heat. Add 1 cup water. Bring to a boil, chill over ice, and strain. Using a mandoline, slice the butternut squash to paper-thin strips (4 inches long by 3/4 inch wide by 1/16 inch thick). Trim the ends of the strips on the bias.

Place the butternut squash and 1/4 cup of the chilled pickling liquid in a sous vide bag and vacuum-seal. Keep the butternut squash in the sous vide bag for at least 2 hours before serving.

Alternatively, place the butternut squash strips in a heatproof bowl. Pour 1/4 cup hot pickling liquid over them and allow to come to room temperature.

## PICKLED MINCED BUTTERNUT SQUASH AND BUTTERNUT SQUASH BALLS

2 cups white balsamic vinegar
1/2 cup honey
6 tablespoons salt
30 black peppercorns
6 cloves
6 bay leaves
1 butternut squash, peeled and seeded

In a small saucepan, bring 3 cups water to a simmer with the vinegar, honey, salt, peppercorns, cloves, and bay leaves. Using a #25 melon baller (about 1 inch in diameter), scoop 8 balls from the squash. Using a #15 melon baller (about 1/2 inch in diameter), scoop 16 balls from the squash. Place the squash balls in 2 separate saucepans with enough of the simmering liquid just to cover them. Simmer until the squash is just tender. Chill over ice and keep in the liquid until ready to use. Finely chop the remaining squash to yield 1 cup. Place it in a bowl and cover with enough of the hot liquid just to cover it. Cool to room temperature.

## PICKLED CANTALOUPE

1 cantaloupe, peeled
3/4 cup brown sugar
1/2 cup white wine
1/2 cup white balsamic vinegar
1/2 teaspoon mustard powder

Use a #15 melon baller (about 1/2 inch diameter) to scoop 24 melon balls from the cantaloupe. Combine the brown sugar, 1/2 cup water, white wine, white balsamic vinegar, and mustard powder in a small saucepan and bring to a simmer. Chill over ice.

Place the melon balls and cooled pickling liquid in a sous vide bag and vacuum-seal.

Alternatively, place the melon balls in a medium bowl. Pour the hot pickling liquid over the melon and marinate at room temperature for 1 hour.

## PICKLED CORN

1 cup fresh corn kernels
1/4 cup White Balsamic Pickling Liquid (see page 343)

Place the corn and Pickling Liquid in a sous vide bag and vacuum-seal. Allow the corn to pickle for 1 hour.

Alternatively, bring the Pickling Liquid to a boil in a small saucepan over medium heat. Place the corn in a bowl and pour the hot liquid over the kernels. Cool to room temperature.

## PICKLED BABY CORN

2 ears fresh baby corn
1/4 cup White Balsamic Pickling Liquid (see page 343)

Remove the husks from the corn and clean it of all silk. Trim off the stems. Bring a pot of salted water to a boil, add the corn, and cook for 4 minutes. Transfer to a bowl of ice water. Drain the corn and place it in a medium bowl with the Pickling Liquid. Pickle for 1 hour at room temperature. Trim off the bottom of the corn, leaving only the 1-inch tip. Slice each tip thinly on a mandoline into 4 even slices.

## PICKLED DAIKON

1 cup white balsamic vinegar
1 cup sugar
1/4 cup salt
1 jumbo daikon radish, about 3 inches in diameter

Make a pickling liquid by heating the vinegar with the sugar and salt in a small saucepan over medium heat. Thinly slice the daikon on a mandoline and cut the slices with a ring cutter that is 1 3/4 inches in diameter.

Place the daikon slices and 3 tablespoons of the pickling liquid in a sous vide bag, making sure that the slices do not overlap. Vacuum-seal.

Alternatively, bring the pickling liquid to a simmer in a small saucepan over medium heat. Place the daikon slices in a large bowl and pour the hot liquid over them. Cool to room temperature.

## PICKLED DATES

1 cinnamon stick
2 allspice berries
2 cloves
4 black peppercorns
3 juniper berries
2 cups white balsamic vinegar
1/2 cup sugar
1/4 cup salt
2 pieces orange zest (1 inch by 3 inches)
4 dates, peeled and pitted
1 teaspoon olive oil

In a medium pot, toast the cinnamon, allspice, cloves, peppercorns, and juniper over medium heat until fragrant, about 10 minutes. Add the white balsamic vinegar and bring to a boil. Stir in the sugar and salt and remove from the heat. Add the orange zest and infuse at room temperature for 1 hour. Strain through a chinois.

Quarter the dates and coat your hands with the olive oil. Roll each into small cylinders. Place them on a small rimmed baking sheet and pour 1/4 cup of the infused liquid over the dates. Marinate for 2 hours at room temperature.

## PICKLED DEHYDRATED APPLE

1 Granny Smith apple
1 teaspoon juniper berries
1 teaspoon black peppercorns
1/2 teaspoon cloves
3 pods star anise
5 allspice berries
2 cups white balsamic vinegar
1/2 cup sugar
1 tablespoon salt
1 bay leaf
1 sprig thyme

Cut the apple into 16 wedges. Use a 2-inch ring cutter to cut each wedge into a semicircle. Use a 1-inch ring cutter to cut out a smaller semicircle, thus removing the seeds and core.

Place the large apple semicircles into a dehydrator set at 125°F and dehydrate for 8 hours. The apples should still be pliable.

Alternatively, preheat the oven to 150°F. Place the apple semicircles on a baking sheet lined with a silicone baking mat and dehydrate in the oven for 3 hours.

In a small saucepan over medium heat, toast the juniper, berries, peppercorns, cloves, star anise, and allspice for 1 minute, until fragrant. Add 2 cups water and the vinegar, sugar, salt, bay leaf, and thyme and bring to a simmer. Simmer for 10 minutes and chill over ice. Strain.

To rehydrate the apples, heat 1/4 cup of the pickling liquid in a sauté pan over low heat and add the apples. Rehydrate for 1 minute and remove from the heat.

## PICKLED LEEKS

1 leek, white part only
1/2 cup White Balsamic Pickling Liquid (see page 343)

Bring a pot of salted water to a boil. Slice the leek into 1/8-inch pieces. Add the leeks to the water, cooking for 1 minute. Transfer to a bowl of ice water and once cold, drain the leeks and place in a small bowl. In a small saucepan, bring the White Balsamic Pickling Liquid to a boil and pour over the blanched leeks. Allow the leeks to marinate in the Pickling Liquid for at least 2 hours before serving.

## PICKLED ENOKI MUSHROOMS

1 bunch enoki mushrooms
3 tablespoons White Balsamic Pickling Liquid (see page 343)

Trim the enoki mushroom tops so that 1/4 inch of the stem remains.

Place the mushrooms and Pickling Liquid in a *sous vide* bag and vacuum-seal.

Alternatively, bring the Pickling Liquid to a simmer in a saucepan over medium heat. Place the mushrooms in a bowl and pour the hot liquid over them. Allow to come to room temperature.

## PICKLED MATSUTAKE MUSHROOMS

3 matsutake mushrooms
2 tablespoons White Balsamic Pickling Liquid (see page 343)

Thoroughly clean the dirt off of the matsutake mushrooms and carefully peel the sides and the cap with a paring knife. Thinly slice the mushrooms on a mandoline to just under 1/8 inch thick.

Place the slices in a *sous vide* bag with the Pickling Liquid. Vacuum-seal and allow the mushrooms to pickle for 20 minutes before removing from the bag.

Alternatively, bring the Pickling Liquid to a simmer in a saucepan over medium heat. Place the mushroom slices in a bowl and pour the hot pickling liquid over them. Allow to come to room temperature.

## PICKLED PORCINI MUSHROOMS

4 porcini mushrooms
3 tablespoons White Balsamic Pickling Liquid (see page 343)

Use a mandoline to slice the porcini mushrooms paper thin (1/16 inch), yielding 24 slices total.

Place the sliced mushrooms in a *sous vide* bag, add the Pickling Liquid, and vacuum-seal. Marinate in the bag for 30 minutes. Remove mushroom slices from the bag and dry on paper towels.

Alternatively, bring the Pickling Liquid to a simmer in a small saucepan over medium heat. Place the porcini slices in a bowl. Pour the liquid over the mushrooms. Allow to come to room temperature before drying on paper towels.

## PICKLED PERSIMMONS

2 firm persimmons, peeled
2 tablespoons White Balsamic Pickling Liquid (see page 343)

Cut each persimmon into 16 wedges.

Combine the persimmon wedges and Pickling Liquid in a *sous vide* bag and vacuum-seal. Keep the persimmons in the *sous vide* bag until ready to use.

Alternatively, bring the Pickling Liquid to a simmer in a small saucepan. Place the persimmon wedges in a bowl and pour the warm liquid over them. Allow to come to room temperature.

## PICKLED PLUMS

1 tablespoon juniper berries
1 tablespoon pink peppercorns
1 1/2 teaspoons black peppercorns
1 teaspoon allspice berries
1/2 teaspoon cloves
1 pod star anise
1/2 stick cinnamon
2 1/2 cups red wine
1 cup red wine vinegar
1/2 cup red port
1/2 cup sugar
1 tablespoon salt
1 pinch nutmeg
1 tablespoon Earl Grey tea leaves
4 Italian plums, halved and pitted

To make the pickling liquid, toast the juniper berries, pink and black peppercorns, allspice berries, cloves, star anise, and cinnamon in a small saucepan for 1 minute over medium heat. Remove from the heat and add the red wine, vinegar, port, 1 cup water, sugar, salt, and nutmeg. Return to medium heat and bring to a simmer. Reduce by half. Add the Earl Grey tea, cover, and steep for 5 minutes.

Strain the liquid into another saucepan.

Score the skin side of the plums with a paring knife. Place the plums in the bottom of a shallow dish in a single layer, cut side down. Bring the pickling liquid to a simmer over medium heat and pour the liquid over the plums. Cover and cool to room temperature. Marinate in the refrigerator for 3 days.

## PICKLED RAINIER CHERRIES

10 Rainier cherries
1 cup White Balsamic Pickling Liquid (see page 343)

Pit and quarter the cherries, place them in a bowl, and cover with the Pickling Liquid. Marinate for 30 minutes at room temperature.

## PICKLED RED MUSTARD SEEDS

1/2 cup red mustard seeds
1 cup white balsamic vinegar
2 teaspoons salt
1 teaspoon sugar

Bring a medium saucepan of water to a boil. Add the mustard seeds and cook for 30 seconds. Strain through a mesh strainer and rinse well under cold water. Transfer the seeds to a medium bowl. Bring the vinegar, salt, and sugar to a boil. Pour the liquid over the mustard seeds and allow to cool to room temperature. Cover and leave at room temperature overnight.

## PICKLED YELLOW MUSTARD SEEDS

1/2 cup mustard seeds
1 cup white balsamic vinegar
2 teaspoons salt
1 teaspoon sugar

Bring a medium saucepan of water to a boil. Add the mustard seeds and cook for 30 seconds. Strain through a mesh strainer and rinse well under cold water. Transfer the seeds to a medium bowl. Bring the vinegar, salt, and sugar to a boil in a small saucepan over medium heat. Pour the liquid over the mustard seeds and allow to cool to room temperature. Cover and leave at room temperature overnight.

## PICKLED RED ONION RINGS

7 red pearl onions, peeled
2 teaspoons salt
1 teaspoon olive oil
2 tablespoons red wine vinegar

Slice each onion into 5 or 6 coins. Separate the coins into rings, keeping only the perfect pieces. You should have about 40 rings. Season with the salt. Heat the oil in a small sauté pan. Add the onions and quickly sauté over high heat for 2 to 3 seconds. Add the vinegar and toss, steaming the onions with the vinegar. Immediately transfer the onions to a small bowl and chill over ice. Strain, discarding the liquid, and store the onions, covered, at room temperature.

## PICKLED RED PEARL ONION SLIVERS

6 red pearl onions, peeled
2 teaspoons salt
2 tablespoons olive oil
2 tablespoons red wine vinegar

Halve the onions lengthwise. Remove any of the centers that are not red. Slice each half into 5 pieces to resemble half-moons. Season with the salt. Heat the oil in a small sauté pan. Add the onions and quickly sauté over high heat for 2 to 3 seconds. Add the vinegar and toss, steaming the onions with the vinegar. Immediately transfer the onions to a small bowl and chill over ice. Strain, discarding the liquid, and store the onions, covered, at room temperature.

## PICKLED WHITE PEARL ONIONS

1 cup white balsamic vinegar
1/4 cup sugar
2 1/2 tablespoons salt
1 cup white pearl onions, peeled and quartered

Combine the vinegar, sugar, and salt in a small pot. Bring to a boil over medium heat and pour over the onions. Cool to room temperature. Reserve the pickled onions in their liquid.

## PICKLED SEAWEED

1/2 cup red *tosaka nori* (salt-packed seaweed)
1 cup white balsamic vinegar
1/4 cup salt
3 tablespoons sugar

Rinse the seaweed in cold water to remove the salt coating. Pat dry and place in a stainless-steel bowl. In a small saucepan, combine the vinegar, salt, and sugar. Bring to a boil and pour the hot liquid over the seaweed. Allow to cool to room temperature. Store the pickled seaweed in its liquid.

## PICKLED SPRING GARLIC BATONS

24 stalks spring garlic
1 cup white balsamic vinegar
3 tablespoons sugar
3 teaspoons salt

Cut the spring garlic into 1-inch batons. Place the garlic, vinegar, sugar, and salt in a saucepan over medium heat and bring to a simmer. Simmer for 5 minutes, remove from the heat, and steep at room temperature until cool.

## PICKLED SUNCHOKES

3 small sunchokes
1/4 cup White Balsamic Pickling Liquid (see right)
1/2 teaspoon salt

Scrub and clean the sunchokes thoroughly but do not peel them. Slice the sunchokes on a mandoline 1/16 inch thick. In a small saucepan over medium heat, bring the Pickling Liquid and salt to a simmer. Place the sliced sunchokes in a bowl and pour the hot liquid over them. Allow to come to room temperature and refrigerate until ready to use.

## PICKLED WATERMELON RADISHES

1 cup white balsamic vinegar
1 cup sugar
1/4 cup salt
1 watermelon radish

Make a pickling liquid by heating the vinegar with the sugar and salt in a small saucepan over medium heat. Thinly slice the radish on a mandoline and cut the slices with a ring cutter that is 1 1/4 inches in diameter.

Place the radish slices and 3 tablespoons of the pickling liquid in a *sous vide* bag, making sure that the slices do not overlap. Vacuum-seal.

Alternatively, bring the pickling liquid to a simmer in a small saucepan over medium heat. Place the radish slices in a large bowl and pour the hot liquid over them. Cool to room temperature.

## PICKLED WATERMELON RIND

Rind from 1/4 of 1 large (7 to 8 pounds) red watermelon
1 cup white balsamic vinegar
1/2 cup sugar
2 tablespoons salt

Remove and discard all of the pink flesh from the rind. Using a peeler, remove the green skin from the rind. Cut the rind into 2-inch-by-3/4-inch strips.

Place in a *sous vide* bag. Bring the white balsamic vinegar, sugar, salt, and 1/4 cup water to a boil. Chill over ice. Pour over the rind and vacuum-seal.

Alternatively, place the rind in a bowl. Pour the hot pickling liquid over the rind and cool to room temperature.

## PICKLED WHITE ASPARAGUS

1 cup white balsamic vinegar
6 tablespoons sugar
2 teaspoons salt
8 jumbo white asparagus

Make a pickling liquid by heating the vinegar with the sugar and salt in a small saucepan over medium heat. Bring the vinegar to a simmer.

Set the vinegar over ice to chill. Trim the asparagus so they are 5 inches long and, using a vegetable peeler, peel them to the base of the tip. Thinly slice the asparagus lengthwise on a mandoline.

Place the asparagus slices into a *sous vide* bag, add the pickling liquid, and vacuum-seal.

Alternatively, you can pour the warm pickling liquid over the asparagus ribbons, then allow them to cool to room temperature.

## WHITE BALSAMIC PICKLING LIQUID

1 3/4 cups white balsamic vinegar
3 tablespoons salt

In a medium bowl, stir together 1 3/4 cups water and the vinegar. Add the salt, stirring until it dissolves.

# OILS AND DRESSINGS

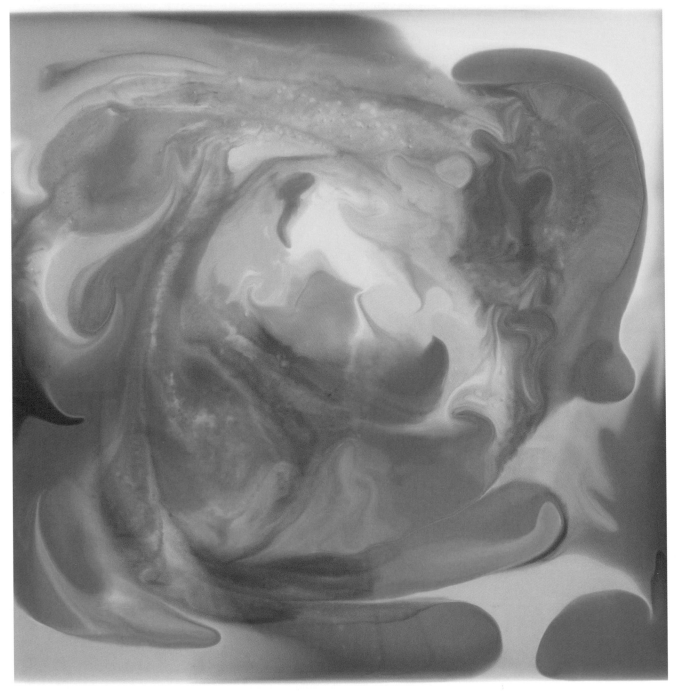

### CHIVE OIL
*Makes 1 cup*
4 cups chives, roughly chopped
1 1/2 cups grapeseed oil

Combine the chives and the oil in a blender and blend thoroughly on high speed. Transfer the mixture to a medium saucepan and cook over medium heat, whisking vigorously until the oil reaches 220°F. Chill over ice and then strain through a coffee filter.

### CHORIZO OIL
*Makes 2 cups*
5 pounds fresh chorizo
2 cups canola oil
Remove the chorizo from its casings. In a large, straight-sided sauté pan, heat 1 cup of the oil over medium heat. Add the chorizo and slowly render for 30 minutes. Add the remaining oil and continue to render for 2 hours. After 2 hours, cover the pan, remove from the heat, and allow the chorizo to steep in the oil for 3 hours. Strain the chorizo from the oil. The resulting oil should be orange and have a strong chorizo flavor and aroma. Refrigerate in an airtight container until ready to use, for up to 1 week.

### CUMIN OIL
*Makes 2 cups*
1 cup cumin seeds
2 cups canola oil

In a sauté pan, toast the cumin seeds over medium heat until fragrant, about 10 minutes. Blend the toasted cumin with canola oil and then strain the mixture through a coffee filter. Store the oil in the refrigerator until ready to serve.

### CURRY OIL
*Makes 2 cups*
2 cups canola oil
1/2 cup thinly sliced Granny Smith apple
1/3 cup thinly sliced white onion
1/2 stalk lemongrass, thinly sliced
2 tablespoons Madras curry powder
1 kaffir lime leaf

Heat 1 cup of the oil in a medium saucepan over low heat. Add the apple, onion, and lemongrass, sweating until translucent, without caramelizing, about 5 minutes. Add the curry powder and lightly toast with the vegetables for 2 minutes.

### BASIL OIL
*Makes 1 cup*
4 cups basil leaves
1 1/2 cups grapeseed oil

Combine the basil and oil in a blender and blend thoroughly on high speed. Transfer the mixture to a medium saucepan and cook over medium heat, whisking vigorously, until the oil reaches 220°F. Chill the oil over ice and then strain through a coffee filter.

### BUTTERMILK DRESSING
*Makes 2 cups*
1 cup Mayonnaise (see page 371)
1 cup buttermilk
2 tablespoons finely sliced chives
1 pinch coarsely ground black pepper
1 1/2 teaspoons salt

In a small bowl, whisk together the Mayonnaise, buttermilk, chives, and pepper. Season with the salt.

### CELERY OIL
*Makes 2 cups*
4 ounces baby celery (about 4 cups)
2 cups grapeseed oil

Combine the celery and oil in a blender and blend thoroughly on high speed. Transfer the mixture to a medium saucepan and cook over medium heat, whisking vigorously, until the oil reaches 220°F. Chill the oil over an ice bath and then strain through a coffee filter.

Add the remaining oil and the kaffir lime leaf and heat the oil to 160°F. Remove from the heat, cover, and steep for 20 minutes. Strain through a coffee filter.

## LEMON OIL
*Makes 2 cups*
20 lemons
2 1/2 cups canola oil

Zest the lemons using a microplane grater. Place the zest and oil in a saucepan over low heat. Bring the oil slowly up to 160°F. Pour the oil and zest into a jar and cover with its lid.

Line the bottom of a large saucepan with a folded kitchen towel. Place the jar on top of the towel and add enough water to the pan to come three quarters of the way up the sides of the jar. Place the saucepan over medium heat and bring the water to a simmer. Simmer for 1 1/2 hours. Carefully remove the jar from the water. Allow the oil to cool in the jar at room temperature before refrigerating overnight. The next day, strain the oil through cheesecloth. The oil may be kept, covered, in the refrigerator for up to 1 month.

## LEMONGRASS OIL
*Makes 2 cups*
5 pounds lemongrass
2 cups canola oil

Thoroughly wash the lemongrass of sand and grit. Cut the lemongrass into large pieces, place in a food processor, and coarsely chop.

In a large, straight-sided pan, heat 1 cup of the oil over low heat. Add the chopped lemongrass and gently sweat for 20 minutes. Add the remaining oil and continue to simmer for 2 hours. After 2 hours, cover the pan, remove from the heat, and allow the lemongrass to steep in the oil for 3 hours. Strain out and discard the lemongrass.

## LOBSTER ROE OIL
*Makes 1/4 cup*
2 tablespoons fresh lobster roe, still in their sacs
1/4 cup canola oil

Add the fresh sacs of lobster roe to a small pot of barely simmering water. Cook for 1 minute, until soft and red, noting that overcooking may cause the sacs

to burst. Transfer with a slotted spoon to a bowl of ice water. When cold, remove to a paper towel and pat dry. Open the roe sacs and gently rub the cooked eggs through a large-hole tamis to pop them off the membrane. Discard the membrane, place the eggs in a small bowl, and cover with the canola oil.

## PARSLEY OIL
*Makes 1 cup*
4 cups parsley leaves
1 1/2 cups grapeseed oil

Combine the parsley and oil in a blender and blend thoroughly on high speed. Transfer the mixture to a medium saucepan and cook over medium heat, whisking vigorously, until the oil reaches 220°F. Chill the oil over ice and then strain through a coffee filter.

## SAFFRON OIL
*Makes 2 cups*
4 tablespoons saffron
2 cups canola oil

Place the saffron and 2 cups water in a small saucepan and warm over medium-low heat. Reduce until almost dry. Pour the oil into the pan and lower the heat to medium-high. Cook any remaining water out of the saffron gently, being careful to not burn it. Pour into a blender and blend on high for 1 minute. Strain though a coffee filter. Cool to room temperature and reserve.

## TARRAGON OIL
*Makes 2 cups*
4 cups tarragon leaves
1 1/2 cups grapeseed oil

Bring a pot of salted water to a boil. Add the tarragon leaves and cook for 1 minute. Transfer to a bowl of ice water and, once cold, drain. Thoroughly dry the blanched leaves in a clean towel and transfer to a blender. Add the oil and blend on high speed for 3 minutes. Strain the oil through a coffee filter.

## VANILLA OIL
*Makes 1 tablespoon*
1 tablespoon olive oil
1 vanilla bean, split lengthwise and scraped

In a small bowl, mix together the oil and vanilla bean seeds until the seeds are all separated and dispersed in the oil. Strain through a chinois.

## ALMOND VINAIGRETTE
*Makes 1 cup*
1/2 cup almond oil
1/3 cup extra-virgin olive oil
1/4 cup sherry vinegar
1 teaspoon salt

In a medium bowl, whisk together all of the ingredients and reserve in a squeeze bottle.

## APPLE VINAIGRETTE
*Makes 1 cup*
3/4 cup extra-virgin olive oil
1/4 cup Apple Vinegar (see below)
1 teaspoon salt

In a mixing bowl, whisk together the olive oil, Apple Vinegar, and salt.

## APPLE VINEGAR
*Makes 2 cups*
2 cups white balsamic vinegar
1 Granny Smith apple, peeled

In a small saucepan over medium heat, bring the vinegar to a boil. Thinly slice the apple on a mandoline and transfer to a heatproof container. Pour the hot vinegar over the apple slices and steep, covered, at room temperature for 24 hours. Strain and discard the apples.

## BEET VINAIGRETTE
*Makes 2 cups*
2 cups red beet juice
1/2 cup white balsamic vinegar
1 tablespoon caraway seeds
1 teaspoon black peppercorns
1 cup raspberries
1 teaspoon salt
1/4 teaspoon xanthan gum (0.6 grams)
2 tablespoons olive oil

In a small saucepan over low heat, reduce the beet juice to 1 1/3 cups. In another small saucepan, bring the vinegar to a boil, remove from the heat, and add the caraway seeds and black peppercorns. Steep in the vinegar for 20 minutes and strain. Add the raspberries to the reduced beet juice and muddle

them with the back of a spoon. Steep for 10 minutes and strain.

Whisk together the vinegar mixture, reduced beet juice, salt, and xanthan gum, whisking until the xanthan gum is completely dissolved. Refrigerate until ready to use. Add the olive oil before serving to break the vinaigrette.

## CHICKEN JUS VINAIGRETTE
*Makes 1 cup*
1 1/2 cups Chicken Jus (see page 356)
4 tablespoons Banyuls vinegar
1 teaspoon extra-virgin olive oil
1/4 teaspoon salt

Reduce the Chicken Jus by half and whisk in the vinegar. Top with the olive oil and season with salt.

## DAIKON VINAIGRETTE
*Makes 2 cups*
1 1/2 cups Chicken Stock (see page 356)
1/2 cup daikon pickling liquid (from Pickled Daikon on page 341)
1 1/2 teaspoons honey
1 cup canola oil
1/8 teaspoon xanthan gum (0.3 gram)
1 teaspoon salt
1 pinch cayenne pepper

Combine the Chicken Stock, daikon pickling liquid, and honey in a small saucepan and reduce by half over medium heat. Chill over ice. With a hand blender, slowly emulsify the canola oil into the reduction and gradually sprinkle in the xanthan gum. The vinaigrette should be white and slightly thickened. Season with the salt and cayenne and store in a squeeze bottle at room temperature until ready to use.

## ESCABÈCHE VINAIGRETTE
*Makes 3/4 cup*
1 tablespoon canola oil
1 clove garlic, minced
1/2 shallot, diced (1/4 inch)
1/2 fennel bulb, diced (1/4 inch)
1/2 cup white wine
1 cup Fish Fumet (see page 356)
1/4 teaspoon fennel seeds
1/4 teaspoon coriander seeds
2 sprigs tarragon
2 sprigs dill
1 teaspoon saffron
1/8 teaspoon xanthan gum (0.3 grams)
1 tablespoon lime juice
2 teaspoons salt

Cayenne pepper
1 tablespoon olive oil
1 teaspoon white balsamic vinegar

Heat the canola oil in a medium saucepan over medium heat. Add the garlic, shallot, and fennel, and sweat until translucent. Add the wine and reduce by half, making sure the alcohol is cooked out. Add the Fish Fumet, fennel seeds, coriander seeds, tarragon, dill, and saffron, and reduce to 1/3 cup. Strain through a fine-mesh chinois into a medium bowl. Add the xanthan gum and whisk until dissolved. Season with the lime juice, salt, and cayenne. Reserve in the refrigerator. When ready to serve, stir in the olive oil and vinegar.

## GAME VINAIGRETTE

*Makes 2 cups*
1/4 cup juniper berries
1 teaspoon allspice berries
1 teaspoon black peppercorns
5 cloves
1/2 teaspoon fennel seeds
1 pod star anise
4 cups Chicken Jus (see page 356)
1 teaspoon pig blood
1 teaspoon cornstarch
1 tablespoon butter
1/4 cup balsamic vinegar
3/4 teaspoon salt
1 tablespoon hazelnut oil

Toast the juniper, allspice, peppercorns, cloves, fennel, and star anise in a saucepan over high heat until fragrant, about 2 minutes. Add the Chicken Jus and reduce by half. Whisk the pig blood and cornstarch together to make a slurry. Whisk the slurry into the reduced Jus and bring to a simmer for 5 minutes to cook out the starch and thicken the sauce. Whisk in the butter until it is fully incorporated. Strain the sauce and cool to room temperature. Whisk with the vinegar and salt. Finish with the hazelnut oil.

## LEMON VINAIGRETTE

*Makes 2 cups*
1 1/2 cups Lemon Oil (page 345)
1/2 cup lemon juice
1 tablespoon salt

In a mixing bowl, whisk together the Lemon Oil and lemon juice. Season with the salt.

## LEMON–WHITE SOY VINAIGRETTE

*Makes 2 1/2 cups*
1 cup Meyer lemon juice
Zest of 1 Meyer lemon
1/2 cup white soy sauce (also called *shiro shoyu*)
1/8 teaspoon xanthan gum
1 cup extra-virgin olive oil

Combine the lemon juice, lemon zest, white soy, and xanthan gum in a blender. Stream in the olive oil until fully emulsified.

## LIME VINAIGRETTE

*Makes 1 cup*
1/2 cup lime juice
1/4 cup grapeseed oil
1/4 cup olive oil
1 teaspoon salt

Whisk together all of the ingredients.

## MARROW VINAIGRETTE

*Makes 1 1/2 cups*
1/2 cup Rendered Marrow Fat (see page 143, for example)
2 teaspoons minced shallots
1/4 cup sherry vinegar
1 teaspoon chopped savory leaves
1/2 teaspoon salt

In a small saucepan over medium heat, heat the Rendered Marrow Fat. Add the shallots and sweat until translucent. Remove from the heat and add the vinegar and savory. Season with the salt and keep warm.

## PEANUT VINAIGRETTE

*Makes 1 1/2 cups*
1 cup peanut oil
1/2 cup sherry vinegar
1 teaspoon salt

Whisk together the peanut oil and sherry vinegar. Season with the salt.

## PERSIMMON VINAIGRETTE

*Makes 1 1/2 cups*
1 cup orange juice
3 tablespoons Persimmon Puree (see page 353)
4 teaspoons yuzu juice
1 1/4 teaspoons salt
1/4 cup olive oil

In a medium bowl, whisk together the orange juice, Persimmon Puree, yuzu juice, and salt. Strain the mixture

through a coffee filter. Refrigerate until ready to use. Before serving, stir in the olive oil to break the vinaigrette.

## POWDERED VINAIGRETTE

*Makes 1 1/2 cups*
2 cups tapioca maltodextrin
1/3 cup extra-virgin olive oil
3 1/2 tablespoons malt vinegar powder
2 1/2 teaspoons salt

Place the tapioca maltodextrin in a food processor and gradually add in the oil. Blend in the vinegar powder and season with the salt. Reserve in an airtight container.

## SHERRY VINAIGRETTE

*Makes 1/2 cup*
2 tablespoons olive oil
4 teaspoons sherry vinegar
2 tablespoons chopped parsley
2 tablespoons minced chives
2 tablespoons minced shallots
1/2 teaspoon salt

In a small bowl, whisk together the olive oil, sherry vinegar, parsley, chives, shallots, and salt.

## SPRING VEGETABLE VINAIGRETTE

*Makes 1 cup*
20 egg yolks
3 teaspoons salt
3 tablespoons shelled snap peas
3 tablespoons diced (1/8 inch) shallots
3 tablespoons diced (1/8 inch) carrots
3 tablespoons diced (1/8 inch) snow peas
1/2 cup Lemon Oil (see page 345)
2 tablespoons lemon juice

Whisk the yolks in a large bowl until combined. Season with 1 teaspoon of the salt. Place a 9-by-13-inch rimmed baking sheet in a *sous vide* bag and vacuum-seal. Pour the yolks onto the sealed sheet and steam in a combination steam oven for 10 minutes at 180°F. Chill in the refrigerator. Once chilled, dice the yolks into 1/8-inch pieces.

Alternatively, you can place 10 eggs in their shells in a pot of cold water. Place the pot over medium-high heat and bring to a simmer. Simmer for 12 minutes, remove from the heat, and transfer the eggs to a bowl of ice water for 10 minutes. Peel, discard the whites, and dice the yolks into 1/8-inch pieces. Season with 1/2 teaspoon of the salt.

In a small bowl, stir together the peas, shallots, carrots, snow peas, and 3 tablespoons of the diced egg yolk. Add the Lemon Oil, lemon juice, and 1 1/2 teaspoons salt. Taste for seasoning and adjust if necessary. Store at room temperature.

## TANGERINE VINAIGRETTE

*Makes 1 1/2 cups*
1 cup tangerine juice
1/4 cup yuzu juice
1 teaspoon salt
1/4 teaspoon citric acid
1/8 teaspoon xanthan gum (0.3 gram)
1/4 cup extra-virgin olive oil

In a blender, blend the tangerine and yuzu juices on low speed. Season with the salt and citric acid and gradually add in the xanthan gum with the blender running. The juice should thicken. Strain the mixture through a fine-mesh chinois and whisk in the olive oil.

## WHITE BALSAMIC VINAIGRETTE

*Makes 2 cups*
1 1/2 cups extra-virgin olive oil
1/2 cup white balsamic vinegar
1 1/2 teaspoons salt

In a mixing bowl, whisk together the oil and vinegar. Season with the salt.

## YELLOW BEET VINAIGRETTE

*Makes 1 1/2 cups*
5 baby golden beets, peeled
3 tablespoons white balsamic vinegar
1 cup beet juice (from 5 cups diced, just over 1 1/2 pounds beets)
1/4 cup orange juice
1/8 teaspoon orange blossom water
1/8 teaspoon xanthan gum (0.3 grams)
1 teaspoon salt
3 tablespoons olive oil

Combine the beets, 1 1/2 cups water, and white balsamic vinegar in a small saucepan and simmer over low heat until the beets are cooked, 35 to 40 minutes. Strain the cooked beets and reserve their cooking liquid. Combine 1 cup of the cooking liquid with the beet juice and reduce the mixture by half. Strain the reduction through a coffee filter and cool over ice. Whisk together the strained reduction, orange juice, orange blossom water, and xanthan gum, until combined. Season with the salt and stir in the olive oil.

# GELS

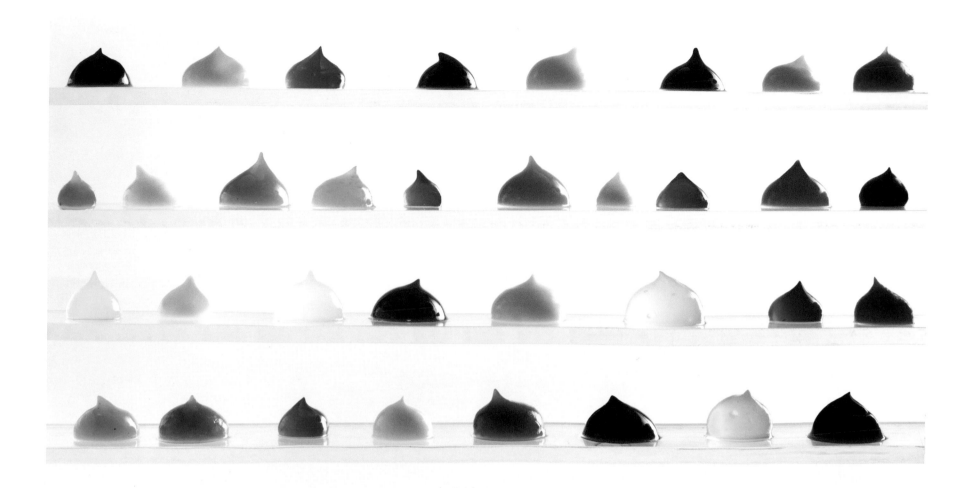

### ALMOND GEL

*Makes 4 cups*
2 cups coarsely chopped bitter almond seeds
5 cups milk
2 tablespoons agar-agar (about 14 grams)
1 teaspoon salt

Toast the almond seeds in a saucepan over medium heat until golden brown. Remove the pan from the heat, add the milk, return to the heat, and bring to a simmer. Remove from heat, cover with a tight-fitting lid, and steep for 1 hour. Strain and chill over ice. Measure 4 cups of the mixture and whisk in the agar-agar. Pour into a saucepan and bring to a simmer, whisking constantly for 5 minutes on medium heat. Season with the salt and pass through a chinois into a baking dish. Cool in the refrigerator for 1 hour or until set. Cut into small pieces and puree in a blender until smooth. Pass through a fine-mesh tamis.

### BASIL GEL

*Makes 2 cups*
4 cups basil leaves
2 1/4 cups ice
1/3 cup sugar
1 tablespoon agar-agar (7 grams)
1/4 teaspoon salt

Bring a pot of water to a boil. Add the basil and cook until just wilted, 10 to 15 seconds. Drain and transfer to a bowl of ice water. Once cold, place the blanched basil in a clean, dry towel and squeeze out any excess moisture. In a blender, puree the basil with 1 cup water and the ice until very smooth. Strain through a fine-mesh chinois. In a small saucepan, stir the sugar and agar-agar into 1/2 cup water. Place over medium heat and bring to a simmer, whisking constantly for 5 minutes to hydrate the agar-agar. Warm 1 3/4 cups of the basil liquid in a saucepan over medium heat. Whisk the warm basil liquid into the cooked agar-agar, and season with the salt. Pour the entire mixture into a baking dish and refrigerate for 1 hour. Once set, cut into small pieces and puree in a blender until smooth. Pass through a fine-mesh tamis.

### BUTTERMILK GEL

*Makes 2 cups*
2 cups buttermilk
1 teaspoon salt
1 tablespoon agar-agar (7 grams)

In a medium saucepan, whisk together the buttermilk, salt, and agar-agar. Place the pan over medium heat and bring to a boil, whisking constantly. Once it begins to boil, whisk for 2 minutes. Pour into a baking dish and refrigerate for 1 hour, until set. Cut into small pieces and puree in a blender on high speed until shiny and smooth. Pass through a fine-mesh tamis.

### CARAMEL GEL

*Makes 4 cups*
2 cups sugar
1/2 vanilla bean, split lengthwise and scraped
1 teaspoon salt
1 tablespoon agar-agar (7 grams)
1/2 cup cream

In a saucepan, combine the sugar and 1/2 cup warm water to make a slurry, being sure that there are no sugar crystals stuck to the sides of the pan. Cook the sugar slurry to a deep amber caramel over medium heat. Add 1 cup warm water to deglaze the pan. Stir in the vanilla bean seeds and salt and strain through a chinois. Set aside.

Pour 3 cups warm water and the agar-agar into a clean saucepan. Cook over medium heat for 5 minutes or until the agar-agar is dissolved. Slowly pour the caramel syrup into the agar-agar mixture. Pour into a baking dish and chill for 1 hour. Cut the gel into small pieces and puree in a blender with the cream, blending until smooth and shiny. Pass through a fine-mesh tamis.

## CHOCOLATE GEL
*Makes 2 cups*
3 cups (12.9 ounces) Valrhona Araguani chocolate (72 percent), chopped
1/4 cup unsweetened cocoa powder
1/4 cup cocoa nibs
8 egg whites
Zest of 1 lemon
1/4 cup sugar
1 tablespoon agar-agar (7 grams)
1 teaspoon salt

Combine 9 cups water with the chocolate and cocoa powder in a medium saucepan over low heat. Heat enough just to melt the chocolate completely. The mixture should be warm to the touch, not hot. In a large bowl, whisk together the nibs and egg whites until foamy. Slowly add half of the melted chocolate mixture into the whites and pour it back into the pot with the remaining melted chocolate mixture, creating a consommé. Bring to a simmer. Once a raft floats to the top of the consommé, use the edge of a 2-ounce ladle to carefully scoop out a small piece of the raft, forming a hole in the center. Baste the raft with the liquid simmering through the hole. After 30 minutes, ladle the liquid through the hole into a chinois lined with cheesecloth. Chill over ice. Strain through cheesecloth again.

Measure 2 1/4 cups of the chilled chocolate consommé and warm in a small saucepan over medium heat. Remove from the heat, add the lemon zest, and steep for 5 minutes. Strain through a chinois. Return to a small saucepan and whisk in the sugar, agar-agar, and salt. Place over medium heat, bring to a simmer, and cook for 5 minutes or until everything is dissolved. Pour the mixture into a baking dish and refrigerate for 1 hour. Once set, cut the gel into small pieces, puree in a blender until smooth and shiny, and strain through a fine-mesh tamis.

## COCONUT GEL
*Makes 2 cups*
2 cups coconut milk
1 tablespoon lime juice
1 tablespoon agar-agar (7 grams)
1 teaspoon salt

In a medium bowl, whisk together the coconut milk and lime juice. In a small saucepan, combine the agar-agar with 1/2 cup water. Place over medium heat, bring to a simmer, and whisk for 5 minutes to hydrate the agar-agar. Slowly whisk in the coconut mixture. Pour into a baking dish and refrigerate for 1 hour, until set. Once set, cut into pieces and puree in a blender blend until smooth. Season with the salt. Pass through a fine-mesh tamis.

## LEMON GEL
*Makes 4 cups*
2 cups lemon juice
2 cups Simple Syrup (see page 371)
1 1/2 tablespoons agar-agar (10.5 grams)

Strain the lemon juice through cheesecloth into a saucepan. In a separate saucepan, combine the Simple Syrup and agar-agar. Set over medium-high heat, bring to a simmer, and whisk constantly for 5 minutes. Warm the lemon juice without bringing it to a boil. Once the agar-agar is completely hydrated in the Simple Syrup, slowly whisk in the warm lemon juice. Pour into baking dish and refrigerate for 1 hour. Once set, cut into small pieces and puree in a blender until smooth. Pass through a fine-mesh tamis.

## PLUM WINE GEL
*Makes 2 cups*
3 cups sweet Japanese plum wine
1/2 cup *umeboshi* vinegar
Salt
1 tablespoon agar-agar (7 grams)

In a large saucepan, reduce the wine by half over medium-low heat. Chill over ice. Combine the 1 1/2 cups of the reduced plum wine with the vinegar and salt to taste in a small saucepan. Whisk the agar-agar into the cold liquid. Bring to a simmer over medium heat and simmer for 5 minutes until the agar-agar is completely hydrated. Pour into a baking dish and refrigerate. Once set, cut the gel into small pieces and puree in a blender until smooth. Pass through a fine-mesh tamis.

## RHUBARB GEL
*Makes 4 cups*
3 cups rhubarb juice
1/4 cup sugar
1 1/2 tablespoons agar-agar (10.5 grams)
1 cup grapefruit juice

Combine the rhubarb juice, sugar, and agar-agar in a small saucepan and bring to a simmer over medium heat, whisking for 5 minutes to hydrate the agar-agar. Warm the grapefruit juice in another small saucepan over low heat without allowing it to boil. Once the agar-agar has dissolved, whisk in the warmed grapefruit juice. Pour into a baking dish and refrigerate for 1 hour, until set. Cut into small pieces and purse a blender until smooth. Pass through a fine-mesh tamis.

## SHEEP'S MILK GEL
*Makes 2 cups*
2 cups sheep's milk yogurt
1 tablespoon agar-agar (7 grams)
1 teaspoon salt

Place the yogurt in a saucepan over low heat and warm through without bringing to a boil. In a separate saucepan, bring the agar-agar and 1 cup water to a boil, whisking constantly over medium heat to hydrate the agar-agar. Whisk in the warm yogurt and season with the salt. Strain through a chinois into a baking dish and refrigerate for 1 hour, until set. Cut into small pieces and puree in a blender until smooth. Pass through a fine-mesh tamis.

## STRAWBERRY GEL
*Makes 4 cups*
1 1/4 cups sugar
10 cups hulled and quartered strawberries
1/4 cup lemon juice
1 1/2 tablespoons agar-agar (10.5 grams)

To make strawberry syrup, sprinkle the sugar over the strawberries and let sit at room temperature for 20 minutes. In a double boiler over low heat, cook the strawberry mixture, covered, for 2 hours. When the color has left the berries and they are syrupy, strain through cheesecloth into a bowl, cover, and cool over ice.

Strain the lemon juice through cheesecloth into a small saucepan. In another saucepan, combine 4 cups of the strawberry syrup with the agar-agar. Bring to a simmer, whisking constantly over medium-low heat for 5 minutes to hy-drate the agar-agar. Warm the lemon juice briefly. Once the agar-agar is completely dissolved, slowly whisk in the warm lemon juice. Pour into a baking dish and refrigerate for 1 hour. Once set, cut into small pieces and puree in a blender until smooth. Pass through a fine-mesh tamis.

## YOGURT GEL
*Makes 4 cups*
1 cup sugar
1 tablespoon agar-agar (7 grams)
2 3/4 cups Greek yogurt

Combine 1 1/3 cups water with the sugar and agar-agar in a saucepan. Whisk over medium heat for 5 minutes until the sugar and agar-agar are dissolved. Strain the mixture into a baking dish and refrigerate for 1 hour, until set. Once the agar-agar is firm, combine it with half of the yogurt in a blender and puree until smooth. Pass the mixture through a fine-mesh tamis and fold in the remaining yogurt.

## CARAMEL YUZU GEL
*Makes 2 cups*
1 1/4 cups sugar
1 tablespoon agar-agar (7 grams)
1/2 vanilla bean, split lengthwise and scraped
1/4 cup cream
1/4 cup yuzu juice
1 teaspoon salt

In a medium straight-sided pot over medium heat, warm the sugar to a dark caramel. Add 3/4 cup water to the caramel. Bring to a boil, remove from the heat, and keep warm. In a small saucepan, combine the agar-agar and 1/2 cup water. Place over medium heat and whisk for 5 minutes while it comes to a simmer. Slowly whisk in the caramel mixture and vanilla bean seeds, transfer to a bowl, and chill over ice. Once set, cut the gel into small pieces and blend in a blender with the cream, yuzu juice, and salt. Pass through a fine-mesh tamis.

## GRANNY SMITH APPLE PUREE

*Makes 2 cups*

3 Granny Smith apples, cored and diced (1/2 inch)
1/4 cup apple cider
1/2 cup cream
1/3 cup sugar
1/2 teaspoon citric acid
1 vanilla bean, split lengthwise and scraped

In a straight-sided pan over low heat, cook the apples with the cider to keep the apples from scorching, about 30 minutes. The apples should be very tender and falling apart. Puree the apples in a blender with the cream, sugar, and citric acid. Add the vanilla bean seeds and pass through a fine-mesh tamis. Chill the puree over ice, stirring constantly to quicken the cooling and to prevent a film from forming on the Puree.

## WHITE APPLE PUREE

*Makes 2 cups*

3 tablespoons butter, plus 1/4 cup cold butter
4 cups peeled, cored, and thinly sliced Granny Smith apples (about 1 pound)
1/2 stick cinnamon
1 tablespoon sugar
3/4 cup white wine
1 tablespoon crème fraîche
1 1/2 teaspoons salt

Melt the 3 tablespoons butter in a large, straight-sided sauté pan over high heat. Add the apples and cinnamon, coat in the butter, and add the sugar. Sweat the apples over high heat without allowing them to brown, about 2 minutes. Add the white wine and 1/2 cup water. Cover with a cartouche (lid made of parchment paper). Cook the apples for another 5 minutes, until tender, and immediately puree in a blender. Add the 1/4 cup cold butter as they are blending to emulsify. Season with the crème fraîche and salt. Chill over ice.

## APRICOT PUREE

*Makes 4 cups*

2 cups sliced dried apricots
3/4 cup apricot nectar
4 cups pitted and diced fresh apricots
1/2 cup sugar
1/4 cup glucose syrup
1 tablespoon salt
Zest and juice of 1 lemon

Combine the dried apricots and nectar in a small saucepan and bring to just under a boil. Transfer to a bowl, cover with plastic wrap, and allow to rehydrate for 20 minutes. In another saucepan, combine the fresh apricots and sugar, cover, and cook over medium heat until softened but still slightly firm. Uncover and stir in the glucose. Continue to cook until all the liquid is absorbed. Stir in the salt, lemon zest, and lemon juice. Puree the apricot mixtures together in a blender and pass the puree through a fine-mesh tamis. Cool over ice.

## ARTICHOKE PUREE

*Makes 2 cups*

Juice of 3 lemons
8 artichokes
1/4 cup plus 2 tablespoons olive oil
3 cups white wine
1 garlic clove, crushed but kept whole
2 sprigs thyme
1 1/2 teaspoons salt

Pour the lemon juice into a large bowl filled with ice water. Peel away the outer leaves of an artichoke until you reach the light yellow leaves. Grab the top of the yellow leaves and pull away, revealing the prickly center leaves and thistle. Using a vegetable peeler, peel the artichoke stem and remove the tough bottom leaves. Cut the artichoke in half and, using a spoon, scoop out the prickly center leaves and choke. Cut the artichoke into small pieces and submerge them in the lemon water to keep them from oxidizing. Repeat with the remaining artichokes.

Heat 2 tablespoons of the olive oil in a large, straight-sided pan over high heat. Drain the artichokes and add them to the pan. Sauté the artichokes for 1 minute. Add the white wine and bring to a boil. Reduce the white wine to 1 1/2 cups. Add 1 1/2 cups water, the garlic, and the thyme and cover with a cartouche (lid made of parchment paper). Reduce the heat to low and simmer the artichokes until they are tender, about 15 to 20 minutes. Drain the artichokes and reserve the cooking liquid, discarding the thyme and garlic. Place the artichokes in a blender and add 1 cup of the cooking liquid. With the blender running, stream in the remaining 1/4 cup of olive oil and puree on high until smooth. Season with the salt and chill over ice.

## BERGAMOT PUREE

*Makes 2 cups*

6 Meyer lemons
6 lemons
1 bergamot
1 cup sugar
1 tablespoon butter
1 teaspoon salt

With a vegetable peeler, remove the skin from the lemons and the bergamot. With a paring knife, trim away any pith remaining on the peels. Juice the lemons and bergamot and strain the juice through a fine-mesh chinois. Place the peels in a medium pot and cover with cold water. Bring the water to a low simmer and drain immediately. Repeat this process 4 times. After the peels have been blanched 4 times, return the peels to the pot and add the sugar and 2 cups water. Bring the mixture to a low simmer over low heat and cook the peels until tender, about 45 minutes. Strain, reserving both the peels and their cooking liquid. Puree the peels in a blender with 1/3 cup of the cooking liquid and 1/2 cup of the citrus juice. Blend on high speed until smooth, about 15 minutes. Add the butter and blend to emulsify. Season with the salt.

## BLACK TRUFFLE PUREE

*Makes 2 cups*

3 tablespoons butter
2 tablespoons thinly sliced shallots
3/4 cup diced cremini mushrooms
3/4 cup diced black truffles
1/4 cup Madeira
3/4 cup truffle juice
1 1/2 tablespoons cold Black Truffle Butter (see page 371)
Salt

Melt the butter in a large sauté pan over medium heat and sweat the shallots until translucent. Add the cremini mushrooms and black truffles and sweat until tender. Deglaze with the Madeira and cook until almost dry. Add the truffle juice and reduce by half. While the mixture is still hot, puree in a blender until smooth, adding the cold Black Truffle Butter and a little hot water as necessary to keep the Puree emulsified. Run the blender for 2 to 3 minutes to create a very smooth puree. Season with salt, pass through a fine-mesh tamis, and cool over ice.

## BUTTERNUT SQUASH PUREE

*Makes 2 cups*

1 tablespoon butter plus 1/4 cup cold butter, diced (1/2 inch)
1 quart peeled and diced butternut squash
5 sprigs thyme
1 teaspoon salt

Melt the 1 tablespoon butter over medium heat in a medium straight-sided pan. Add the squash and sweat until slightly tender, about 10 minutes. Add 1 cup water and the thyme and cover with a cartouche (lid made of parchment paper). Simmer the butternut squash until tender, about 15 minutes. Remove the cartouche and continue to cook until the pan is almost dry. Discard the thyme and transfer the butternut squash to a blender. Puree on high speed and, with the blender running, add the cold butter and puree until fully emulsified. Pass through a fine-mesh tamis, season with the salt, and chill over ice.

## CARROT PUREE

*Makes 2 cups*

2 pounds carrots, peeled and diced
1 quart carrot juice
1 teaspoon salt

Combine the carrots, carrot juice, and salt in a large pot. Cover and simmer over low heat until very tender, about 15 to 20 minutes. Once tender, remove the lid and reduce the liquid until almost dry. Puree the carrots and remaining liquid in a blender on high speed until very smooth. Pass through a fine-mesh tamis. Chill over ice.

## YELLOW CARROT PUREE

*Makes 2 cups*

3/4 cup butter
4 cups peeled and thinly sliced yellow carrots (about 1 pound)
1 cup peeled and thinly sliced orange carrots (about 1/4 pound)
1 tablespoon salt

Melt the butter in a medium saucepan over medium heat. Add the carrots and the salt and sweat for 5 minutes. Add 4 cups water, cover, and cook until very tender, about 10 minutes. Strain, reserving the liquid. Puree the carrots in a blender until smooth, adding a little of the cooking liquid if necessary to blend. Pass the puree through a fine-mesh tamis and chill over ice.

## CAULIFLOWER PUREE

*Makes 2 cups*

3 cups cauliflower (or cauliflower trim), diced (1/4 inch), about 11 ounces
2 cups half-and-half
2 tablespoons Brown Butter (see page 370)
2 teaspoons salt

Place the cauliflower in a large saucepan and cover with the half-and-half. Bring the mixture to a boil over medium-high heat and reduce the heat to low. Simmer the cauliflower until tender, about 25 minutes. Drain the cauliflower, reserving the liquid. Puree in a blender, adding the cooking liquid, 1 tablespoon at a time, until the puree is smooth but not too loose. You should need about 4 tablespoons of liquid. Blend in the Brown Butter and season with the salt. Pass through a fine-mesh tamis and cool over an ice bath, stirring constantly to quicken the cooling process and to prevent a film from forming on the puree.

## CELERY ROOT PUREE

*Makes 2 cups*

1 pound celery root, peeled and diced (1/4 inch), about 3 1/2 cups
1 1/2 cups half-and-half
3 sprigs thyme
1 clove garlic, crushed but kept whole
2 tablespoons butter
2 teaspoons salt

Combine the celery root with the half-and-half in a medium saucepan and place over medium heat. Wrap the thyme and garlic in a piece of cheesecloth, tie with butcher's twine, and add to the saucepan. Bring up to just under a boil, reduce the heat to low, and simmer until the celery root is tender, about 20 to 25 minutes. Remove and discard the thyme and garlic. Strain, reserving both the celery root and the liquid. Transfer the celery root to a blender and gradually incorporate the reserved liquid as necessary until smooth but not too loose. With the blender still running, add the butter. Season with the salt. Transfer to a bowl and cool over ice, stirring constantly.

## SMOKED CELERY ROOT PUREE

*Makes 2 cups*

1 pound celery root, peeled and diced (1/4 inch), about 3 1/2 cups
2 cups half-and-half
6 sprigs thyme
1 clove garlic, crushed but kept whole
1/3 cup cold Smoked Butter (see page 359)
2 teaspoons salt

Place the celery root in a medium saucepan and cover with the half-and-half. Wrap the thyme and garlic together in a piece of cheesecloth, tie with butcher's twine, and add to the saucepan. Bring the mixture to a boil over medium-high heat, then reduce to a simmer. Cover and simmer over low heat until tender, 20 to 25 minutes. Remove and discard the thyme and garlic. Strain, reserving both the celery root and the liquid. Transfer the celery root to a blender and gradually incorporate the reserved liquid as necessary until smooth but not too loose. With the blender still running, add the Smoked Butter. Season with the salt. Transfer to a bowl and cool over ice, stirring constantly to prevent a film from forming.

## CHANTERELLE PUREE

*Makes 2 cups*

5 cups chanterelles (about 13 ounces)
1/2 cup butter, plus 1/4 cup cold butter
2 tablespoons diced shallots
1 cup button mushrooms (2 1/2 ounces)
1/4 cup white wine
1/2 cup cream
1 teaspoon salt

Clean the chanterelles of all dirt with a paring knife and scrape any discoloration from the stems. Trim the bottoms and rinse thoroughly. Spread the chanterelles on paper towels to dry. Melt the 1/2 cup butter in a large sauté pan over medium heat. Add the shallots and sweat until translucent. Add the chanterelles and button mushrooms and sweat until all of their juices have been reduced. Add the white wine and reduce until almost dry. Add 1/2 cup water and the cream and lower the heat to create a butter braise. Cook, covered, over low heat until the mushrooms are tender and the liquid is reduced yet emulsified, about 40 minutes. While still hot, puree the mixture in a blender until smooth, adding the 1/4 cup cold butter. Note that

it may be necessary to add a few tablespoons of water to the puree to achieve the desired consistency. Season with the salt, pass through a fine-mesh tamis, and chill over ice.

## CHESTNUT PUREE

*Makes 2 cups*

1/2 pound fresh chestnuts
1 1/2 teaspoons canola oil
1/4 cup Cognac
1 cup Chicken Stock (see page 356)
1/3 cup mascarpone
3/4 tablespoon sugar
1 1/2 teaspoons salt

Preheat the oven to 350°F. Using a paring knife, score a small *x* in the outer shells of the chestnuts and place them on a rimmed baking sheet. Roast in the oven for 10 to 15 minutes, until they are lightly browned and the peel begins to curl away. Cool to room temperature and peel away both layers of skin. Heat the oil in a large sauté pan over high heat until just before it begins to smoke. Add the chestnuts and toast on medium-high heat until they are dark brown, 4 to 5 minutes. Remove from the heat and deglaze the pan with the Cognac. Return to medium heat and reduce until the pan is almost dry. Cover the chestnuts with Chicken Stock, cover with a cartouche (lid made of parchment paper) and simmer over low heat until tender, about 45 minutes. Puree the chestnuts in a blender with their cooking liquid and the mascarpone. Season with the sugar and salt and pass through a fine-mesh tamis. Place a sheet of plastic wrap or parchment paper directly on the puree and cool over ice to prevent a skin from forming.

## SWEETENED CHESTNUT PUREE

*Makes 2 cups*

2/3 cup sugar
4 cups peeled frozen chestnuts, thawed
1/2 vanilla bean, split lengthwise and scraped
1 1/2 cups cream

Preheat the oven to 350°F. In a saucepan, bring 1 1/3 cups water and the sugar to a boil over medium heat. Place the chestnuts and vanilla seeds in a baking dish and pour the hot sugar-water mixture over them. Cover the baking dish with foil and bake for 1 1/2 hours. The chestnuts

should be soft and most of the liquid should be absorbed. Drain off any excess liquid from the chestnuts.

Place the cream in a blender and add 1 cup of the warm baked chestnuts. Puree the mixture on high speed until smooth and creamy. Pass the puree through a fine-mesh tamis.

## DATE PUREE

*Makes 2 cups*

1 cinnamon stick
2 allspice berries
2 cloves
4 black peppercorns
3 juniper berries
2 cups white balsamic vinegar
1/2 cup sugar
1 1/2 teaspoons salt
2 pieces orange zest (1 inch by 3 inches)
4 cups peeled and pitted dates

In a medium pot, toast the cinnamon, allspice, cloves, peppercorns, and juniper over medium heat until fragrant, about 10 minutes. Add the white balsamic vinegar and bring to a boil. Stir in the sugar and salt and remove from the heat. Add the orange zest and infuse at room temperature for 1 hour. Strain through a chinois.

Pass the dates through a large-mesh tamis and then pass them through a fine-mesh tamis. In a small pot, warm 1/4 cup of the infused liquid but do not boil. Whisk the warm liquid into the dates until fully incorporated.

## FENNEL PUREE

*Makes 2 cups*

1/4 cup fennel fronds
4 tablespoons olive oil
2 cups finely diced fennel
1 cup peeled and finely diced Yukon Gold potatoes
1 cup white wine
1 1/2 teaspoons salt

Bring a pot of salted water to a boil. Add the fennel fronds and cook for 10 to 15 seconds. Transfer to a bowl of ice water and, once cold, drain.

Heat the olive oil in a small saucepan over medium heat and add the diced fennel. Sweat for about 4 minutes, until softened. Add the potatoes and wine and bring to a boil. Add 1 cup water, continuing to cook until most of the liquid has evaporated and the vegetables are tender. Puree in a blender with the blanched fennel fronds until smooth and pass through a fine-mesh tamis. Season with the salt and chill over ice.

## FENNEL AND POTATO PUREE

*Makes 2 cups*
1/4 cup fennel fronds
2 tablespoons butter
1/2 pound fennel, diced (1/4 inch)
1/2 pound La Ratte fingerling potatoes, peeled and diced (1/4 inch)
1 1/2 teaspoons salt

Bring a saucepan of salted water to a boil. Add the fennel fronds, cooking for a few seconds, until just wilted. Transfer to a bowl of ice water and, once cold, drain. Melt the butter in a medium saucepan over medium heat. Add the diced fennel and potatoes and sweat until soft and translucent, about 15 minutes. Add 2 1/2 cups water and simmer for 25 minutes. Puree the cooked fennel and potatoes in a blender until smooth. Blend in the blanched fennel fronds and season with the salt. Pass the puree through a fine-mesh tamis and chill over ice.

## GARLIC HORSERADISH PUREE

*Makes 2 cups*
4 heads garlic
1/3 cup olive oil
1 1/2 cups peeled and diced (1/4 inch) horseradish (5 ounces)
1/3 cup white soy sauce (also called *shiro shoyu*)
2/3 cup extra-virgin olive oil

Preheat the oven to 300°F. Coat the garlic with the olive oil and wrap in aluminum foil. Place on a baking sheet and roast in the oven for 1 hour. Allow the garlic to cool slightly and peel off the husks. In a blender, puree the roasted garlic, horseradish, and the white soy. Gradually stream in the extra-virgin olive oil. Pass the puree through a fine-mesh tamis.

## MEYER LEMON PUREE

*Makes 2 cups*
12 Meyer lemons
1 cup sugar
1 tablespoon butter
1 teaspoon salt

With a vegetable peeler, peel the skin off the Meyer lemons. With a paring knife, trim away any pith remaining on the peel. Juice the lemons and strain the juice through a fine-mesh chinois. Place the lemon peels in a medium pot and cover with cold water. Bring the water to a low simmer and drain immediately. Repeat this process 2 more times. Return the peels to the pot and add the sugar and 2 cups water. Bring the mixture to a low simmer and cook the lemon peels until tender, about 45 minutes. Strain, reserving both the peels and their cooking liquid. Puree the lemon peels in a blender with 1/3 cup of the cooking liquid, 1/3 cup Meyer lemon juice, and another 1/4 cup water. Blend on high speed until smooth, about 15 minutes. Add the butter and blend to emulsify. Season with the salt.

## WHITE LEMON PUREE

*Makes 2 cups*
8 lemons
1 tablespoon cream
1 tablespoon plus 1 teaspoon sugar
1 tablespoon cold butter, cubed
1 1/2 teaspoons salt

With a vegetable peeler, remove and discard the peels from the lemons. With a paring knife, trim away any white pith from the fruit, reserving the pith. Juice the fruit, strain the juice, and reserve it for the Puree. Transfer the pith to a medium pot, cover with cold water, place over medium heat and bring to a simmer. Drain and repeat 2 more times. Transfer the blanched pith to a blender, add the cream, 5 tablespoons of the lemon juice, 1/2 cup water, and the sugar and blend on high speed until the puree is smooth. Blend in the cold butter and season with the salt. The puree will be slightly bitter. Pass the puree through a fine-mesh tamis and chill over ice, stirring constantly until cool.

## ONION PUREE

*Makes 2 cups*
7 cups thinly sliced white onions (about 2 pounds or 3 large onions)
1 tablespoon salt
5 white peppercorns
3 tablespoons butter, plus 1 tablespoon cold butter
1/2 cup white wine
1/8 teaspoon xanthan gum (0.3 grams)

Season the onions with salt and set aside. Tie the peppercorns in cheesecloth to make a sachet. Heat a sauté pan over high heat. Add the 3 tablespoons butter, onions, and the peppercorn sachet, and cook, stirring constantly, 1 to 1 1/2 minutes, being careful not to achieve any color on the onions. Add the wine and 3 tablespoons water, cover with a cartouche (lid made of parchment paper), and cook until the onions are tender. It may be necessary to add a bit more water to the pan if it begins to dry out. Once the onions are tender, remove the cartouche and reduce any liquid that is left in the pan. Puree in a blender on high speed with the xanthan gum and the 1 tablespoon cold butter. Pass through a fine-mesh chinois and cool over ice.

## ORANGE PUREE

*Makes 2 cups*
3 large Cara Cara oranges
1/2 teaspoon coriander seeds
1/2 teaspoon fennel seeds
1/2 cup sugar
1 tablespoon Curry Oil (see page 344)
1 teaspoon salt

Wash the oranges and cut off the tops and bottoms. Keep the rind on the oranges and cut them into 3/4-inch pieces. You should have about 4 cups of diced orange. Make a sachet by wrapping the coriander and fennel seeds in a piece of cheesecloth and tying with butcher's twine. Place the oranges, the sachet, and the sugar in a medium saucepan and add about 1/4 cup water. Bring to a simmer over low heat and cook until the water has reduced and the oranges are tender, 30 to 40 minutes. Remove the sachet and puree the oranges in a blender on high speed until smooth. With the blender running, add the Curry Oil and salt. Transfer to a bowl and chill the puree over ice, stirring constantly to cool rapidly and prevent a skin from forming.

## PARSNIP PUREE

*Makes 2 cups*
1/2 cup butter
1 pound parsnips, peeled and diced
1 cup half-and-half
1 teaspoon salt

In a medium sauté pan, melt the butter over medium heat. Add the parsnips and sweat until they start to break down. Add 1 1/2 cups water and cover. Continue to cook the parsnips until they are tender, about 15 minutes. Drain. Puree the parsnips in a blender and slowly incorporate the half-and-half until smooth and creamy. Season with the salt and chill over ice.

## PEA PUREE

*Makes 2 cups*
2 1/4 cups shelled garden peas (about 11 ounces)
4 ice cubes
1 teaspoon salt

Bring a pot of salted water to a boil. Add the peas and cook until tender, 3 to 4 minutes. Using a slotted spoon, transfer the peas to an ice bath. Once cold, drain the peas and shake out excess water. Puree the peas in a blender, adding the ice cubes throughout the process to keep the puree cold. Pass the puree through a fine-mesh tamis and season with the salt.

## SUGAR SNAP PEA PUREE

*Makes 2 cups*
5 cups sugar snap peas (about 1 1/2 pounds)
2 teaspoons salt

Trim any tough ends from the snap peas and remove pod strings. Bring a pot of salted water to a boil. Add the snap peas and cook until very tender, about 4 1/2 minutes. Transfer to a bowl of ice water and, once cold, drain. Puree the peas in a blender with 1/2 cup ice water and the salt. Blend until finely pureed. Pass through a fine-mesh tamis.

## PEANUT PUREE

*Makes 2 cups*

3 cups jumbo salted peanuts
1 teaspoon salt

In a food processor, puree the peanuts until they become a smooth peanut butter, about 5 minutes. Pass the puree through a fine-mesh tamis and season with the salt.

## PERSIMMON PUREE

*Makes 2 cups*

6 ripe Fuyu persimmons, peeled and quartered
2 tablespoons yuzu juice
1 1/2 teaspoons salt
1/8 teaspoon citric acid

Combine the persimmons, yuzu juice, and 1 teaspoon of the salt in a *sous vide* bag. Vacuum-seal and place in a water bath maintained at 185°F by an immersion circulator and cook for 20 minutes. Remove the cooked persimmons from the bag and puree in a blender until smooth. Pass through a fine-mesh tamis and season with the remaining 2 teaspoons salt and the citric acid. Chill over ice.

## PLUM PUREE

*Makes 2 cups*

2 tablespoons butter
1 pound fresh plums, pitted and diced
1/2 cup *umeboshi* plums, pitted
1/3 cup sugar
1/4 cup *umeboshi* vinegar
1/2 cup sweet Japanese plum wine
1 teaspoon salt

In a large pan over medium heat, melt the butter until foamy. Add the fresh and pickled plums and sugar and stew until the plums release their juices and are completely softened. Add the vinegar and the plum wine and continue to cook until the wine is reduced and the pan is almost dry. Puree the plums while hot and season with the salt. Pass through a fine-mesh tamis. Chill over ice, stirring, to ensure that a skin does not form.

## POTATO MOUSSELINE

*Makes 2 cups*

1 1/2 pounds La Ratte fingerling potatoes
1 cup cream
1/4 cup Brown Butter (see page 370)
1 teaspoon salt

Peel the potatoes and place them in a medium pot. Cover with cold water. Bring to a simmer over medium heat and cook for 25 to 30 minutes, until tender. Drain and pass through a food mill into a large bowl.

Heat the cream and Brown Butter in a small saucepan. Just before it begins to simmer, fold it into the potatoes until combined but still loose. Working quickly, pass the mixture through a fine-mesh tamis. The potatoes will become gummy if they are cold when passed through the tamis. Season with the salt and reserve in a warm place, such as near a warm oven or stove. The puree may be made 1 hour ahead of time.

## RED WINE APPLE PUREE

*Makes 2 cups*

3 Winesap apples, peeled and cored
2 cups red wine
3 tablespoons sugar
1 tablespoon plus 1 teaspoon salt

Thinly slice the apples on a mandoline. Place the slices in a medium saucepan, cover with the red wine, and simmer over low heat until all the wine is evaporated, about 1 hour. Puree in a blender until completely smooth and season with the sugar and salt. Pass through a fine-mesh tamis and chill over ice.

## SMOKED POTATO PUREE

*Makes 2 cups*

1 1/2 pounds La Ratte fingerling potatoes
1 cup cream
1 tablespoon Smoked Butter (see page 359)
1 teaspoon salt
1 tablespoon White Truffle Butter (see page 371)

Peel the potatoes and place them in a medium saucepan. Cover with cold water and bring to a simmer over medium heat. Cook until tender, about 17 to 20 minutes. In a small saucepan, bring the cream and Smoked Butter to a simmer. Season with the salt and pass through a chinois. Keep warm. Drain the potatoes and pass them through a food mill set over a large bowl. Fold in the White Truffle Butter and cream mixture. Pass through a fine-mesh tamis while still hot and cover to retain the moisture.

## SMOKED POTATO-GARLIC PUREE

*Makes 2 cups*

1 1/2 pounds La Ratte fingerling potatoes
3 cloves garlic, peeled
1 cup cream
2 tablespoons Smoked Butter (see page 359)
1 teaspoon salt

Peel the potatoes and place them in a medium pot. Cover them with cold water and bring to a simmer over medium heat. Cook until tender, about 17 to 20 minutes. In a small pot, cover the elephant garlic with cold water and bring to a simmer over medium heat. Strain and repeat two more times. Add the cream and the Smoked Butter to the garlic and bring to a simmer. Puree the hot liquid, the garlic, and the salt in a blender until smooth. Pass through a chinois and keep warm. Drain the potatoes and pass them through a food mill into a large bowl. Fold in the butter-and-cream mixture. Pass through a fine-mesh tamis while still hot and cover to retain the moisture.

## CURRY RAISIN PUREE

*Makes 2 cups*

1 1/2 cups golden raisins
1/4 cup Curry Oil (see page 344)
1 teaspoon salt

Place the raisins in a bowl. Pour hot water over the raisins and bloom at room temperature until they are soft, 2 hours. Drain, discarding the water. Puree in a blender until smooth, slowly incorporating the Curry Oil with the blender running. Season with the salt.

## GOLDEN RAISIN PUREE

*Makes 2 cups*

2 cups Sauternes
1 cup golden raisins

In a small saucepan over medium low heat, reduce the Sauternes by half. Transfer the Sauternes to a bowl and add the raisins. Cover with plastic wrap. Allow the raisins to steep in the Sauternes for 2 hours to fully rehydrate.

In a blender, puree until smooth. In a sauté pan over low heat, dry out the puree, stirring constantly, for about 3 minutes. Pass the puree through a fine-mesh tamis.

## SORREL PUREE

*Makes 2 cups*

1 1/2 pounds spinach
3 cups loosely packed sorrel leaves
1 egg yolk
1 1/2 cups canola oil
2 to 3 ice cubes
1 1/2 teaspoons salt
1 teaspoon Tabasco sauce

Bring a pot of salted water to a boil. Add the spinach and cook for 15 to 20 seconds, until wilted. Transfer to a bowl of ice water and, once cool, drain. In a blender, puree the sorrel, egg yolk, and blanched spinach. With the blender running, slowly stream in the oil along with the ice cubes to keep the puree cold and maintain its green hue. If the puree gets warm, it will turn brown. Once the puree is smooth, pass it through a tamis and chill over ice. Season with the salt and Tabasco sauce. Sorrel Puree may be made up to 1 hour ahead of time.

## SPINACH PUREE

*Makes 2 cups*

2 pounds fresh spinach
4 ice cubes
1 teaspoon salt

Bring a pot of salted water to a boil. Add the spinach, cooking for 15 to 20 seconds, until wilted. Transfer to a bowl of ice water and, once cool, drain. Puree in a blender with the ice cubes and pass through a fine-mesh tamis. Season with the salt.

## SUNCHOKE PUREE

*Makes 2 cups*

1 tablespoon butter
2 cups peeled and thinly sliced
    sunchokes
1 cup peeled and thinly sliced La Ratte
    fingerling potatoes
1 cup half-and-half
1 1/4 teaspoons salt

In a medium saucepan over medium heat, melt the butter until foamy. Add the sunchokes and potatoes, cover with a cartouche (lid made of parchment paper), and sweat until tender, about 5 minutes. Add the half-and-half and bring to a simmer. Cook, covered, until completely soft, about 15 minutes. Puree in a blender until smooth and season with the salt. Transfer to a bowl and cool the puree over ice, stirring constantly.

## SWEET POTATO PUREE

*Makes 2 cups*

1 cup butter
1 1/2 cups diced (1 inch) sweet potato
    (about 7 ounces)
1 tablespoon salt
2 cups half-and-half

In a medium saucepan over medium heat, melt the butter. Sweat the sweet potatoes until they are tender, about 10 to 15 minutes. Season with the salt. Pour in the half-and-half and cover. Simmer the sweet potatoes for 10 more minutes, being careful not to over-reduce the half-and-half. Puree the sweet potatoes in a blender until completely smooth. Pass through a fine-mesh tamis and chill over ice.

## WATERCRESS PUREE

*Makes 2 cups*

2 bunches watercress
1/4 cup olive oil
1 teaspoon salt
1/8 teaspoon xanthan gum

Bring a pot of salted water to a boil. Add the watercress and cook for 15 to 30 seconds, until wilted. Transfer to an ice bath. Once cool, squeeze out excess moisture. Puree in a blender on high with the olive oil, salt, and xanthan gum. Pass the Puree through a fine-mesh tamis and chill over ice.

## WHITE ASPARAGUS PUREE

*Makes 2 cups*

2 pounds white asparagus, bottom
    woody ends trimmed, cut into small
    pieces

Bring a pot of salted water to a boil. Add the asparagus and cook for 10 minutes, until tender. Transfer to a bowl of ice water. Once cold, drain and puree in a blender on high speed for 2 to 3 minutes, until smooth. Note that white asparagus is fibrous and needs to be blended very well. Pass through a fine-mesh tamis and chill over ice.

## WHITE BEAN PUREE

*Makes 2 cups*

2 1/2 cups dried cannellini beans
1 head garlic, halved crosswise
1 carrot, peeled and diced
1 onion, peeled and quartered
2 sprigs thyme
1 tablespoon olive oil
1 teaspoon salt

Soak the beans in water overnight. Drain the beans and place in large saucepan. Cover with 3 inches of water. Make a sachet by wrapping the garlic, carrot, onion, and thyme in a piece of cheesecloth; tie the ends with butcher's twine. Add the sachet to the beans, bring to a simmer, reduce the heat to medium, cover, and cook until tender, 40 to 45 minutes. Reserve for garnish 1/2 cup of the perfect beans that have not split. Cook the rest of the beans until they begin to fall apart, about 30 more minutes. Remove and discard the sachet and puree the beans in a blender with 1/4 cup of their cooking liquid and the olive oil. Season with salt and chill over ice.

## WHITE EGGPLANT PUREE

*Makes 2 cups*

1 teaspoon cumin seeds
3 large eggplants, peeled and diced
Juice of 1 lemon
1/4 cup canola oil
1 teaspoon salt

Heat a small sauté pan over medium heat. Add the cumin seeds and toast until fragrant, about 20 seconds. Toss the diced eggplant with the lemon juice to protect it from oxidization. Bring a pot of salted water to a boil and add the eggplant. Cook for about 10 minutes, until tender, and transfer to a bowl of ice water. Once cool, drain, place in 3 layers of cheesecloth, and squeeze out any excess moisture. Remove and discard any discolored pieces. Place the eggplant in a blender with the cumin and, with the blender running, slowly add the oil. Season with salt and pass through a fine-mesh tamis.

## ZUCCHINI PUREE

*Makes 2 cups*

2 tablespoons olive oil
4 cups seeded and thinly sliced zucchini
    (about 1 1/2 pounds)
6 mint leaves
2 tablespoons extra-virgin olive oil
1 to 2 ice cubes
1 teaspoon salt

Heat the olive oil in a large, straight-sided sauté pan over medium-high heat. Quickly sauté the zucchini, stirring frequently but otherwise keeping covered, until tender, but without browning. Cool very quickly over ice, stirring constantly to speed up the cooling process. The quick cooking and cooling help to maintain the zucchini's green color. In a blender, puree the zucchini and mint while slowly adding the extra-virgin olive oil and ice cubes to help the blending process. Season with the salt. Pass through a tamis and chill over ice.

## CHICKEN JUS

*Makes 1 quart*
10 pounds chicken wings
1/4 cup canola oil
4 cups sliced onions
2 cups diced carrots
2 cups diced celery
2 cups diced leeks
2 cups diced celery root
1/2 cup tomato paste
4 cups red wine
10 sprigs thyme
2 bay leaves
25 black peppercorns
5 pounds chicken feet
30 pounds ice cubes

Preheat the oven to 375°F. Spread the chicken wings in a single layer on 2 large rimmed baking sheets and roast in the oven until golden brown, 1 hour and 15 to 1 hour and 30 minutes, turning every 30 minutes. Heat the oil in a 20-quart stockpot over high heat. Sauté the onions, carrots, celery, leeks, and celery root until they caramelize, 10 to 15 minutes. Add the tomato paste and sauté until caramelized, 5 to 7 minutes. Add the red wine and reduce to a syrup consistency. Make a sachet by tying the thyme, bay leaves, and peppercorns in cheesecloth. Add the sachet, the chicken wings, and the chicken feet to the stockpot and cover with the ice. Bring to a simmer over medium heat and skim off all of the impurities and fats that rise to the top. Simmer over low heat, uncovered, for 5 hours, skimming every 30 minutes. Strain through a fine-mesh chinois and reduce to 1 quart. Strain again and chill over ice.

## CHICKEN STOCK

*Makes 1 gallon*
10 pounds chicken backs and necks
15 pounds ice cubes
1 cup diced leeks, white part only
1/2 cup diced celery
1/2 cup diced celery root
1/2 cup sliced shallots
1/2 cup diced fennel
5 white peppercorns
1 bay leaf
1 sprig thyme

Rinse the bones well under running water for 5 minutes. Place the bones in a 20-quart stockpot, top with the ice, and bring to a simmer over medium heat. Skim all of the impurities and fats off the top as it simmers. After the stock is skimmed, add the leeks, celery, celery root, shallots, and fennel. Make a sachet by wrapping the peppercorns, bay leaf, and thyme in a piece of cheesecloth. Add the sachet to the stock. Simmer, uncovered, for 3 hours, skimming every 30 minutes. Strain and chill over ice.

## DUCK JUS

*Makes 1 quart*
10 pounds duck carcasses, cut into 2-inch pieces
4 tablespoons duck fat
4 cups sliced onions
2 cups diced carrots
2 cups diced celery
2 cups diced leeks
2 cups diced celery root
5 tablespoons tomato paste
2 cups port
3 cups red wine
10 sprigs thyme
2 bay leaves
25 peppercorns
3 pounds chicken feet
2 gallons Chicken Stock (see above)

Preheat the oven to 375°F. Line 2 large rimmed baking sheets with parchment paper. Spread the duck bones in a single layer on the baking sheets and roast the bones in the oven until golden brown, 1 hour to 1 hour and 15 minutes, turning the bones over once after 20 minutes. Melt the duck fat in a 20-quart stockpot over high heat. Sauté the onions, carrots, celery, leeks, and celery root in the duck fat until they caramelize, about 7 to 10 minutes. Add the tomato paste and sauté until caramelized, 5 to 7 minutes. Add the port and reduce by half. Add the red wine and reduce to syrup consistency. Make a sachet by tying the thyme, bay leaves, and peppercorns in cheesecloth. Add the chicken feet, carcass bones, and sachet to the stockpot and cover with the Chicken Stock. Bring to a simmer over medium heat and skim the stock of all impurities and fats that rise to the top. Simmer, uncovered, over low heat for 5 hours, skimming every 30 minutes. Strain through a fine-mesh chinois and reduce to 1 quart. Strain again and chill over ice.

## FISH FUMET

*Makes 1 gallon*
5 tablespoons canola oil
2 cups diced leeks, white part only
2 cups sliced button mushrooms
1 cup diced celery
1 cup diced celery root
1 cup sliced shallots
1 cup diced fennel
4 cups white wine
10 white peppercorns
1 bay leaf
12 pounds white fish bones, cut into 2-inch pieces, cleaned of all blood and thoroughly rinsed
10 pounds ice cubes

Heat the oil in a 20-quart stockpot over medium heat. Sweat the leeks, mushrooms, celery, celery root, shallots, and fennel until soft, about 10 minutes. Add the wine and reduce to 1 1/3 cups. Make a sachet by tying the peppercorns and bay leaf in a piece of cheesecloth. Add the sachet, fish bones, and ice. Bring to a simmer over medium heat and skim away any impurities or fats that rise to the surface. Simmer gently for 30 minutes, being careful not to boil. Remove from the heat and allow to rest for 10 minutes. Skim again and ladle the fumet out, straining through cheesecloth. Be sure not to disturb the fish bones so as to keep the stock clear. Chill over ice.

## LAMB JUS

*Makes 1 quart*
10 pounds lamb bones, cut into 2-inch pieces
1/4 cup canola oil
4 cups sliced onions
2 cups diced carrots
2 cups diced celery
2 cups diced leeks
2 heads garlic, peeled
1/2 cup tomato paste
4 cups red wine
10 sprigs thyme
25 black peppercorns
2 bay leaves
4 gallons Veal Stock (see page 357)

Preheat the oven to 375°F. Spread the lamb bones in a single layer on 2 large rimmed baking sheets and roast in the oven until golden brown, 1 hour to 1 hour and 15 minutes, turning the bones every 30 minutes. Heat the oil in a 20-quart stockpot over high heat. Sauté the onions, carrots, celery, leeks, and garlic until they caramelize, about 10 to 15 minutes. Add the tomato paste and sauté until caramelized, 5 to 7 more minutes. Add the red wine and reduce to a syrup consistency. Make a sachet by tying the thyme, peppercorns, and bay leaves in cheesecloth. Add the sachet and bones to the stockpot and cover with the Veal Stock. Bring to a simmer over medium heat and skim off all impurities and fats that rise to the top. Simmer over low heat, uncovered, for 4 hours, skimming every 30 minutes. Strain through a fine-mesh chinois and reduce to 1 quart. Strain again and chill over ice.

## LOBSTER STOCK

*Makes 1 gallon*
10 pounds lobster bodies
1/2 cup canola oil
2 cups sliced onions
1 cup roughly chopped carrots
1 cup diced celery
1 cup diced leeks
1 cup diced fennel
4 cloves garlic
1 cup tomato paste
1/2 cup Cognac
2 cups white wine
15 pounds ice cubes
5 sprigs thyme
5 sprigs tarragon
5 sprigs lemon verbena
20 white peppercorns

Clean the lobster bodies by removing the outer shell with the antennae and discarding. Using scissors, clean the lungs and legs off the sides of the body and cut the bodies into quarters. Heat the oil in a 20-quart stockpot over high heat. Sauté the lobster bodies until they are evenly browned, 10 to 12 minutes. Add the onions, carrots, celery, leeks, fennel, and garlic and sauté for 5 to 7 minutes, until they are tender. Add the tomato paste and sauté for 4 to 5 minutes. Add the Cognac and reduce to 2 tablespoons. Add the white wine and reduce to 1/2 cup. Add the ice, thyme, tarragon, lemon verbena, and peppercorns and bring to a simmer over medium heat. Skim off any impurities or fats that rise to the top. Simmer for 30 minutes and strain through a fine-mesh chinois. Reduce to 1 gallon, strain again, and chill over ice.

## RABBIT JUS

*Makes 1 quart*

1/4 cup canola oil
10 pounds rabbit carcasses, cut into
   2-inch pieces
2 cups sliced onions
1 cup diced carrots
1 cup diced celery
1/2 cup diced leeks
1/2 cup diced celery root
4 tablespoons tomato paste
4 cups red wine
10 sprigs thyme
25 peppercorns
2 bay leaves
2 gallons Chicken Stock (see page 356)

Heat the oil in a 20-quart stockpot over high heat. Add the rabbit bones and brown evenly over high heat, 7 to 10 minutes. Add the onions, carrots, celery, leeks, and celery root and caramelize for 7 to 10 minutes. Add the tomato paste and caramelize for 5 to 7 minutes. Add the red wine and reduce to glaze. Make a sachet by tying the thyme, peppercorns, and bay leaves in cheesecloth. Add the sachet and the Chicken Stock to the stockpot. Bring to a simmer over medium heat and skim away any fats and impurities that rise to the top. Simmer for 3 hours, skimming every 30 minutes. Strain through a fine-mesh chinois and reduce to 1 quart. Strain again and chill over ice.

## VEAL JUS

*Makes 1 quart*

20 pounds veal knuckle bones, cut into
   2-inch pieces
5 pounds veal feet, cut into 2-inch pieces
1/4 cup canola oil
4 cups sliced onions
2 cups diced carrots
2 cups diced celery
2 cups diced leeks
2 cups diced celery root
1/2 cup tomato paste
4 cups red wine
10 sprigs thyme
25 black peppercorns
2 bay leaves
30 pounds ice cubes

Preheat the oven to 375°F. Spread the veal bones and feet in a single layer on 2 large rimmed baking sheets and roast in the oven until golden brown, 45 minutes to 1 hour, turning the bones and feet after 30 minutes. Heat the oil in a 20-quart stockpot over high heat. Sauté the onions, carrots, celery, leeks, and celery root until they caramelize, 10 to 15 minutes. Add the tomato paste and sauté until caramelized, 5 to 7 minutes. Add the red wine and reduce to a syrup consistency. Make a sachet by tying the thyme, peppercorns, and bay leaves in cheesecloth. Add the bones and feet to the stockpot with the sachet and cover with the ice. Bring to a simmer over medium heat and skim the stock of all impurities and fats that rise to the top. Simmer over low heat, uncovered, for 5 hours, skimming every 30 minutes. Strain through a fine-mesh chinois and reduce to 1 quart. Strain again and chill over ice.

## VEAL STOCK

*Makes 1 gallon*

5 pounds veal bones
5 pounds veal breast, cut into 2-inch
   pieces
3 pounds veal feet, cut into 2-inch pieces
20 pounds ice cubes
1 cup sliced onion
1/2 cup diced celery
1/2 cup diced celery root
1/2 cup diced leeks, white part only
2 cups white wine
10 white peppercorns
5 sprigs thyme
1 bay leaf

Rinse the bones well under running water for 5 minutes. Place the bones, veal breast, and veal feet in a 20-quart stockpot. Cover with the ice and bring to a simmer over medium heat. Skim all of the impurities and fats off the top as it simmers. After the stock is skimmed, add the onion, celery, celery root, and leeks. Make a sachet by wrapping the peppercorns, thyme, and bay leaf in a piece of cheesecloth. Add the sachet to the stock. Simmer, uncovered, for 4 hours, skimming every 30 minutes. Strain and chill over ice.

## VENISON JUS

*Makes 1 quart*

15 pounds venison bones, cut into
   2-inch pieces
1/4 cup canola oil
4 cups sliced onions
2 cups diced carrots
2 cups diced celery
2 cups diced leeks
2 cups diced celery root
1/2 cup tomato paste
1 cup Cognac
4 cups red wine
10 sprigs thyme
2 bay leaves
25 black peppercorns
4 gallons Veal Stock (see above)

Preheat the oven to 375°F. Spread the venison bones in a single layer on 2 large rimmed baking sheets and roast the bones in the oven until golden brown, 1 hour to 1 hour and 15 minutes, turning the bones every 30 minutes. Heat the oil in a 20-quart stockpot over high heat. Sauté the onions, carrots, celery, leeks, and celery root until they caramelize, about 10 to 15 minutes. Add the tomato paste and sauté until caramelized, 5 to 7 minutes. Add the Cognac and reduce by half. Add the red wine and reduce to a syrup consistency. Make a sachet by tying the thyme, bay leaves, and peppercorns in cheesecloth. Add the sachet and the bones to the pan and cover with the Veal Stock. Bring to a simmer over medium heat and skim off all impurities and fats that rise to the top. Simmer over low heat, uncovered, for 5 hours, skimming every 30 minutes. Strain through a fine-mesh chinois and reduce to 1 quart. Strain again and chill over ice.

## SMOKED BUTTER
*Makes 4 cups*
3/4 pound (6 cups) applewood chips
1 pound (8 cups) charcoal
 (not briquettes)
2 pounds cold butter, diced (1 inch)

Soak the applewood chips in cold water for 5 to 10 minutes. Line the cooking surface of a large cast-iron skillet with aluminum foil. Place the charcoal in the pan and set over high heat until the coals are white-hot.

Place the diced butter in an even layer in a set over ice. Place the stacked pans onto the top rack of a cold oven. Once the coals are white, drain the applewood chips and place three quarters of them over the coals. Return the cast-iron skillet to the burner until the chips begin to smoke. Place the cast-iron skillet in the oven on the lowest rack, as far way as possible from the butter, which should stay as cold as possible during the smoking process. Smoke the butter for 45 minutes, checking the smoke level every so often. It may be necessary to add more wood chips. You can expect the butter to soften and even separate around the edges of the pan. As it does so, you can stir it back together with a spatula. After 45 minutes, stir all of the smoked butter together and then transfer it to an airtight container or vacuum-seal in a *sous vide* bag. Keep in the refrigerator for 2 to 3 days.

## SMOKED COUSCOUS
*Makes 12 1/2 cups*
5 cups Tomato Water (see page 371)
5 cups couscous
3/4 pound (6 cups) applewood chips, or
 more if needed
1 pound (8 cups) charcoal
 (not briquettes)
1 pound fresh chickpeas
Juice of 3 lemons
Salt
Olive oil

Bring the Tomato Water to a simmer and pour over the couscous in a heat-resistant bowl. Cover with plastic wrap and let steam for 20 minutes. Soak the applewood chips in cold water for 5 to 10 minutes. Wrap the cooking surface of a large cast-iron skillet in aluminum foil. Place the charcoal in the skillet over high heat. Leave on the flame until the coals are white-hot. Drain the applewood chips and place them on top of the charcoal. They should begin to smoke.

Spread the steamed couscous out on a rimmed baking sheet and place the baking sheet on the top shelf of a cold oven. Place the cast-iron skillet on the lowest rack of the oven, far away from the couscous. Smoke for 1 hour, checking the smoke level a few times throughout. It may be necessary to add more wood chips. In the meantime, bring a pot of salted water to a boil. Add the chickpeas and cook for 1 minute. Transfer to a bowl of ice water and, once cool, peel. Chill the smoked couscous and toss with the lemon juice, salt, olive oil, and the chickpeas. Refrigerate for up to 3 hours.

## SMOKED CRÈME FRAÎCHE
*Makes 1 cup*
1 cup crème fraîche
2 tablespoons lemon juice
2 teaspoons salt
3/4 pound (6 cups) applewood chips
1 pound (8 cups) charcoal
 (not briquettes)

In a small bowl, whisk together the crème fraîche, lemon juice, and salt. Transfer to a small pan over ice.

Soak the applewood chips in cold water for 5 to 10 minutes. Line the cooking surface of a large cast-iron skillet with aluminum foil. Place the charcoal in the pan and set over high heat until the coals are white-hot. Remove from the heat.

Drain the applewood chips. Place three quarters of the soaked chips on top of the coals and return the skillet to the burner until the chips begin to smoke. Place the skillet in the oven on the lowest rack. Place the bowl of crème fraîche on top of a tray of ice and place in the oven as far away as possible from the skillet. The crème fraîche should stay as cold as possible during the smoking process. Smoke for 2 hours, checking the smoke level every so often; the smoke should be heavy and constant. It may be necessary to add more wood chips. Remove the crème fraîche from the oven and transfer to an airtight container or vacuum-seal in a *sous vide* bag. Keep in the refrigerator for 2 to 3 days.

## SMOKED PORK JERKY
*Makes 1 pound*
1 pound pork loin
1 3/4 cups salt
3/4 pound (6 cups) applewood chips
1 pound (8 cups) charcoal
 (not briquettes)

Trim any excess fat off of the pork loin. Combine the salt and 1 gallon water in a large pot and bring to a boil over high heat. Cool over ice. Transfer to a nonreactive container and add the pork loin. Refrigerate, covered, overnight or for 8 to 9 hours. Cut the pork loin into 1 1/2 inch cubes and set on a roasting rack.

Preheat the oven to 200°F. Soak the applewood chips in cold water for 5 to 10 minutes. Line the inside of a cast-iron skillet with aluminum foil. Place the charcoal in the pan and set over high heat until the coals are white-hot. Remove from the heat.

Drain the applewood chips. Place three quarters of the soaked chips on top of the coals and return the cast-iron skillet to the burner until the chips begin to smoke. Place the skillet in the oven on the lowest rack. Place the roasting rack with the pork on the highest rack. Smoke for 1 hour with heavy smoke. Be sure to check on the smoke level every so often. It may be necessary to add more wood chips. Remove the pork and the pan with the coals from the oven, (or grill) and lower the temperature to 170°F. Return the pork to the oven for 8 to 10 hours. Remove from the oven, cool to room temperature, and vacuum-seal in individual *sous vide* bags. Store in the refrigerator for up to 1 week.

## SMOKED STURGEON
*Makes 1 1/2 pounds*
1 1/2 pounds sturgeon, center-cut loin
3 pounds salt
3/4 pound (6 cups) applewood chips
1 pound (8 cups) charcoal (not
 briquettes)

Place the sturgeon in a baking pan, cover it in the salt, and cure for 1 hour in the refrigerator. Rinse the sturgeon under running water and pat dry with paper towels. Place the sturgeon on a cooling rack set over a rimmed baking sheet and refrigerate, uncovered, overnight or for 8 to 9 hours. Transfer the sturgeon to a roasting rack.

Preheat the oven to 175°F. Soak the applewood chips in cold water for 5 to 10 minutes. Line the inside of a cast-iron skillet with aluminum foil. Place the charcoal in the pan and set over high heat until the coals are white-hot. Remove from the heat.

Drain the applewood chips. Place three quarters of the soaked chips on top of the coals and return the cast-iron skillet to the burner until the chips begin to smoke. Place the skillet in the oven on the lowest rack. Place the roasting rack with the sturgeon on the highest rack. Smoke for 45 minutes with heavy smoke. Be sure to check on the smoke level every so often. It may be necessary to add more wood chips. Remove the sturgeon from the oven, cool to room temperature, vacuum-seal in a *sous vide* bag, and store in the refrigerator for 2 to 3 days.

CRUMBLES,
GRANOLAS,
AND DOUGHS

## ALMOND CRUMBLE

*Makes 2 cups*
3/4 cup sugar
1/4 cup butter
2 tablespoons light corn syrup
1 cup whole blanched almonds
1 teaspoon salt
1/2 teaspoon baking soda

In a medium straight-sided pot, combine the sugar, butter, corn syrup, and 1/4 cup water and bring to a boil over medium heat. Cook to a light caramel and stir in the almonds, salt, and baking soda. Keep stirring to prevent the almonds from burning. Cook to a medium caramel and pour onto a baking sheet lined with parchment paper. Cool to room temperature. Pulse to a fine crumble in a food processor.

## BITTER ALMOND CRUMBLE

*Makes 4 cups*
1/3 cup sugar
2 egg yolks
1/4 cup butter, room temperature
3/4 cup flour
1/4 cup ground bitter almonds
1 teaspoon baking powder
1/2 teaspoon *fleur de sel*

Preheat the oven to 350°F. Line a baking sheet with parchment paper. In a stand mixer fitted with a whisk attachment, whip the sugar and egg yolks on high speed until pale ribbons form. Add the butter and whip until fully incorporated. Change to a paddle attachment, and add the flour, bitter almonds, baking powder, and *fleur de sel*. Mix until well incorporated. Turn out onto the prepared baking sheet and roll to 1/2 inch thick. Cut into 1 1/2-inch-wide strips.

Bake for 15 minutes, until lightly browned. Remove from the oven. Reduce the oven temperature to 175°F. Break the crumble into large pieces and dry in the oven until crispy, about 20 minutes. Cool to room temperature. Coarsely grind in a spice grinder.

## AMARETTI CRUMBLE

*Makes 2 cups*
3/4 cup almond paste, room temperature
2/3 cup sugar
1/3 cup bitter almonds
1 egg
1/2 cup flour

Preheat the oven to 325°F. Line a baking sheet with parchment paper.

In a food processor, mix the almond paste, sugar, bitter almonds, and egg until combined. Add the flour and 1 tablespoon water and continue to mix until thoroughly combined. Transfer the dough to a piping bag. Pipe cookies onto the prepared baking sheet, using 1 tablespoon of dough for each cookie. Bake until golden, about 25 minutes. Cool to room temperature. Reduce the oven temperature to 170°F. Coarsely chop the cookies and return to the oven to dry out until crunchy, about 20 minutes.

## BLACK PEPPER CRUMBLE

*Makes 4 cups*
1/2 cups sugar
3 egg yolks
1/2 cup butter, room temperature
3/4 cup flour
1 teaspoon *fleur de sel*
1/2 teaspoon black pepper
1/4 teaspoon baking powder

Preheat the oven to 350°F. In the bowl of a stand mixer fitted with the whisk attachment, combine the sugar and the egg yolks, mixing on high speed until a pale ribbon forms. Change to the paddle attachment. Add the butter and mix to combine.

In a bowl, combine the flour, *fleur de sel*, pepper, and baking powder. Add this mixture, in 3 parts, to the egg mixture. The dough will be very soft. Spread the dough to a 1/2-inch thickness on a rimmed baking sheet lined with parchment paper and bake for 7 minutes. Rotate the baking sheet and bake for an additional 7 minutes. Break the dough apart into chunks and return to the oven for 5 more minutes, until golden brown. Cool to room temperature and crumble by hand.

## CARROT-DUCK CRUMBLE

*Makes 4 cups*
1 carrot
1 teaspoon olive oil
3/4 teaspoon salt
1 pound duck skin
3 shallots
2 cups canola oil
1/2 teaspoon Madras curry powder
1/4 teaspoon ground cumin
1 pinch cayenne pepper

Preheat the oven to 200F.

Peel and thinly slice the carrot on a mandoline. Toss the carrot slices with the olive oil and season with 1/4 teaspoon of the salt. Lay out the carrot slices on a baking sheet lined with a silicone baking mat and bake until dried, about 1 hour and 30 minutes. Cool the carrot chips at room temperature and cut into 1/4-inch pieces.

Freeze the duck skin in 1 layer on a baking sheet. Grind while still frozen through the small die on a meat grinder or ask your butcher to do this for you. Combine the ground duck skin and 1 cup water in a medium straight-sided pan and simmer over medium-low heat until the water has evaporated, about 30 minutes. Drain off half of the rendered duck fat. Return the pan to the stove and continue to crisp the duck fat until golden brown, about 20 minutes. Drain the duck fat and cool the crisped skin to room temperature on paper towels. Once cooled, finely chop the duck skin and combine with the chopped carrot chips.

Peel and thinly slice the shallots on a mandoline. Combine the sliced shallots and canola oil in a large straight-sided pan and fry over medium heat, stirring constantly, until the shallots are golden brown, 20 to 25 minutes. Strain the shallots and drain on paper towels. Cool the shallots to room temperature and finely dice. Combine with the carrot chips and duck fat.

Season the duck fat mixture with the curry, cumin, cayenne, and the remaining 1/2 teaspoon salt.

## CELERY ROOT CRUMBLE

*Makes 1 cup*
1/2 pound celery root, peeled and diced (1/2 inch)
1/2 pound russet potatoes, peeled and diced (1/2 inch)
12 cups canola oil
1 tablespoon finely chopped black truffle
1 teaspoon salt

Place the celery root and potatoes in a blender and fill to the top with water. Blend until the mixture resembles coarse sand. Strain through a fine-mesh chinois and rinse under cold water to remove any excess starch. Transfer to a kitchen towel and wring out the excess water.

Heat the oil in a large pot over medium heat to 220°F. Add the celery root and potatoes and whisk continuously to break up the starch and prevent it from burning. Fry until golden. Strain through a fine-mesh chinois and drain on paper towels. While still hot, toss with the black truffles and salt. Allow the crumble to cool to room temperature.

## CHOCOLATE CHIP COOKIE CRUMBLE

*Makes 4 cups*
3/4 cup butter
2/3 cup sugar
1/2 cup dark brown sugar
1/2 teaspoon salt
1 egg
1/4 teaspoon vanilla extract
1 1/2 cups flour
1/2 teaspoon baking soda
6 ounces Valrhona Equatoriale chocolate (55 percent), chopped and frozen

Preheat the oven to 350°F. Line a rimmed baking sheet with parchment paper. In a stand mixer fitted with the paddle attachment, cream together the butter, sugar, brown sugar, and salt until incorporated and fluffy. Add the egg and vanilla extract and mix to combine. In a separate bowl, mix together the flour and baking soda. Add the dry ingredients to the butter mixture and mix until combined.

Spread the cookie dough onto the prepared baking sheet. Bake for 15 minutes, until golden brown. Allow to rest and cool. Once the dough is cool, break it up into large pieces and pulse the cookie pieces with the chopped chocolate to a pea-sized crumble in a food processor.

## CHOCOLATE COOKIE CRUMBLE

*Makes 4 cups*
2/3 cup sugar
1/4 cup butter
1/2 teaspoon salt
1 egg
1 teaspoon vanilla extract
1/3 cup flour
1/3 cup unsweetened cocoa powder

In a stand mixer fitted with a paddle attachment, cream the sugar, butter, and salt. Add the egg and vanilla extract and mix until incorporated. In a separate bowl, sift together the flour and cocoa powder and gradually add to the wet mixture. Mix on medium speed until fully incorporated, about 3 minutes. Roll the dough to 1/2 inch thick between 2 sheets of parchment paper and freeze for 3 hours.

Preheat the oven to 350°F. Transfer the dough to a baking sheet and remove the top sheet of parchment paper. Bake for 6 minutes. Reduce the oven temperature to 200°F. Cut the dough into pieces and dry out in the oven for 20 minutes. Grind in a spice grinder to a coarse powder.

## COCOA NIB CRUMBLE

*Makes 2 cups*
1 cup cocoa nibs
1 cup sugar
2 tablespoons butter
2 tablespoons corn syrup
1 1/2 teaspoons salt
1/2 teaspoon baking soda

Line a baking sheet with parchment paper. Toast the cocoa nibs in a small sauté pan over medium heat until fragrant, about 5 minutes, and keep them warm. In a medium saucepan, bring the sugar, butter, corn syrup, and 1/4 cup water to a boil. Cook the mixture until it is a light caramel. Add the salt and baking soda and mix well. Add the toasted cocoa nibs and cook for 1 minute. Pour onto the prepared baking sheet and allow it to cool completely to room temperature.

Grind in a food processor until coarsely ground. Be careful not to grind the crumble too fine, as it can become oily.

## COCONUT CRUMBLE

*Makes 2 cups*
1 cup sugar
4 tablespoons butter
2 tablespoons corn syrup
2 cups large coconut flakes
1 1/2 teaspoons salt
1/2 teaspoon baking soda

Combine the sugar, butter, corn syrup, and 1/4 cup water in a large straight-sided pan and boil over medium heat until lightly caramelized. Add the coconut flakes, salt, and baking soda and cook in the caramel for another minute. Pour onto a baking sheet lined with parchment paper and cool to room temperature. Grind the crumble in a food processor until it forms a coarse powder.

## EVERYTHING CRUMBLE

*Makes 3 cups*
2 cups bread flour
1/4 cup sugar
2 tablespoons sesame seeds
2 tablespoons poppy seeds
1 tablespoon salt
1 1/4 cups butter, room temperature
1/2 cup dried caramelized onions

Preheat the oven to 325°F. Line a rimmed baking sheet with parchment paper. Combine the flour, sugar, sesame seeds, poppy seeds, and salt in the bowl of a stand mixer. Incorporate the butter, mixing at medium-high speed. Spread the mixture onto the prepared baking sheet and bake for 20 minutes. Cool to room temperature. Pulse briefly in a food processor until pea-sized. Add the Dried Caramelized Onions.

## CHERRY GRANOLA AND CRUMBLE

*Makes 2 1/2 cups*
1 cup rolled oats
1/4 cup sliced almonds
2 tablespoons light brown sugar
2 tablespoons maple syrup
1 1/2 tablespoons olive oil
1/4 teaspoon salt
1 cup freeze-dried cherries

Preheat the oven to 325°F. Line a rimmed baking sheet with parchment paper. In large bowl, mix together the oats and almonds. In a small saucepan, bring the sugar, maple syrup, oil, and salt to a boil. Pour over the oat mixture and toss to combine. Spread the oats onto the prepared baking sheet and bake for 10 minutes, stirring often until lightly golden and dry. Cool completely. In a food processor, pulse the cherries with 1 cup of the granola. Transfer to an airtight container. Pulse the remaining granola and store in a separate airtight container.

## HAZELNUT CRUMBLE

*Makes 2 cups*
2/3 cup sugar
1/3 cup butter
1/4 cup corn syrup
1 1/2 cups hazelnuts
2/3 tablespoon salt
2/3 teaspoon baking soda

In a medium saucepan over medium heat, bring the sugar, butter, corn syrup, and 2 tablespoons water to a boil. Add the hazelnuts and cook the mixture until the sugar becomes a light caramel. Add the salt and baking soda and continue to cook until golden, about 1 minute or until 300°F. Pour onto a sheet of parchment paper and allow to cool completely to room temperature. Once cooled, break apart and blend in a food processor to a crumble.

## JUNIPER BERRY CRUMBLE

*Makes 4 cups*
1 tablespoon juniper berries
1/4 cup butter, room temperature
2 tablespoons sugar
1 1/4 cups bread flour
1/2 cup rye flour
1 1/2 tablespoons salt
1 tablespoon milk

Preheat the oven to 350°F. Line a baking sheet with parchment paper.

In a small sauté pan over medium heat, toast the juniper berries for 1 minute and allow to cool. Grind to a fine powder in a spice grinder. In a stand mixer fitted with a paddle attachment, cream together the butter and sugar until light and fluffy. Add the bread flour, rye flour, salt, and ground juniper and mix. Slowly add the milk and mix until small clusters begin to form. Turn out the dough onto the prepared baking sheet. Flatten the dough to 1/2 inch thick and bake until golden brown, about 20 minutes. Cool to room temperature. Once cool, pulse in a food processor to a coarse crumble.

## LAMB-APPLE CRUMBLE

*Makes 2 cups*
1 cup Simple Syrup (see page 371)
1 Lady apple
1 pound ground lamb fat
2 cups canola oil
3 shallots, peeled and thinly sliced
1 tablespoon finely sliced chives
1 teaspoon *vadouvan* curry spice
1/2 teaspoon salt

Preheat the oven to 200°F. In a small saucepan over medium heat, warm the Simple Syrup without bringing it to a boil. Thinly slice the apple on a mandoline and soak the slices in the warm Simple Syrup for 10 minutes. Drain the apple slices and spread them out in a single layer on a baking sheet lined with a silicone baking mat. Bake until crispy, about 1 hour and 30 minutes. Cool the apple chips to room temperature. Dice into 1/4-inch pieces.

Combine the lamb fat and 1 cup water in a medium straight-sided pan and simmer over medium-low heat until the water has evaporated, about 20 minutes. Discard half of the rendered fat. Return the pan to the stove and continue to crisp the lamb fat until golden brown, about 10 minutes. Drain and discard the liquid lamb fat and cool the crispy lamb fat on paper towels. Once cooled, finely chop the lamb fat and combine with the chopped apple chips.

Combine the canola oil and shallots in a large straight-sided pan and fry over medium heat, stirring constantly, until the shallots are golden brown, 12 to 15 minutes. The oil should reach 266°F. Strain the shallots, drain on paper towels, and cool to room temperature. Once cooled, chop the shallots into small pieces and combine with the apple chips and crispy lamb fat.

Season the mixture with the chives, *vadouvan* curry, and salt.

## LOBSTER CRUMBLE

*Makes 3 cups*

1 1/2 cups bread flour
1 cup almond flour
1/2 cups sugar
2 tablespoons salt
1 1/4 cup cold Lobster Butter (see page 370)

Preheat the oven to 325°F. Line a rimmed baking sheet with parchment paper. Mix the bread flour, almond flour, sugar, and salt in a stand mixer. Add the Lobster Butter, little by little, until a rough dough is formed. Turn the dough out onto the baking sheet and pat it down to create an even layer of dough. Bake for 18 minutes, until golden brown. Remove from the oven and cool to room temperature. Once cool, pulse in a food processor until you have a pea-sized crumble.

## OAT CRUMBLE

*Makes 2 cups*

1/4 cup duck fat
1/4 cup minced shallots
2 cups rolled oats
1/4 cup sugar
1 tablespoon salt
Leaves from 5 sprigs thyme

Preheat the oven to 200°F. Line a rimmed baking sheet with parchment paper.

Melt the duck fat in a large sauté pan over low heat. Add the shallots and sweat until translucent. Add the oats, sugar, salt, and thyme leaves, and toast for 2 minutes. Transfer the oats to the prepared baking sheet and bake for 2 hours. Cool completely to room temperature.

## ORANGE SHORTBREAD CRUMBLE

*Makes 2 cups*

1 cup plus 2 tablespoons flour
1/2 cup confectioners' sugar
1/2 cup butter
Zest of 1 orange
1/2 vanilla bean, split lengthwise and scraped

Preheat the oven to 350°F. Combine all of the ingredients in a stand mixer fitted with the paddle attachment. Mix on medium-high speed until the butter is fully incorporated but the dough is still crumbly. Transfer to a baking sheet lined with parchment paper and bake the crumble for 10 minutes. Remove from the oven and stir to break into smaller pieces. Return to the oven and continue baking until lightly golden brown, another 10 minutes. Cool the shortbread to room temperature.

## ORANGE SUCRÉE CRUMBLE

*Makes 4 cups*

1/2 cup butter
1/2 cup sugar
1/2 vanilla bean, split lengthwise and scraped
1/2 teaspoon salt
Zest of 1 orange
1 egg
3 cups flour

Preheat the oven to 350°F. In the bowl of a stand mixer fitted with the paddle attachment, cream together the butter and sugar. Add the vanilla bean seeds, salt, orange zest, and egg, mixing until smooth. Add the flour and mix until just combined. Refrigerate for 1 hour. Roll the dough to a 1/4-inch thickness and bake on a baking sheet lined with parchment paper until golden brown, 7 to 9 minutes. Cool the dough to room temperature and crush into a coarse crumble.

## PARSNIP CRUMBLE

*Makes 1 cup*

3 parsnips, peeled and diced (1/4 inch)
6 cups canola oil
2 teaspoons salt

Place the parsnips in a blender and fill to the top with water. Blend until the mixture resembles coarse sand. Strain through a fine-mesh chinois and rinse under cold water to remove any excess starch. Transfer to a kitchen towel and wring out the excess water. Spread in an even layer on a baking sheet to dry.

Heat the oil in a large pot over medium heat to 220°F. Add the parsnips and whisk continuously to break up the starch and prevent it from burning. Fry until golden. Strain through a fine-mesh chinois and drain on paper towels. While still hot, season with the salt. Allow the crumble to cool to room temperature.

## SUCRÉE CRUMBLE

*Makes 4 cups*

1/2 cup butter
1/2 cup sugar
1/2 vanilla bean, split lengthwise and scraped
1/2 teaspoon salt
1 egg
3 cups flour

Preheat the oven to 350°F. In the bowl of a stand mixer fitted with the paddle attachment, cream together the butter and sugar. Add the vanilla bean seeds, salt, and egg, mixing until smooth. Add the flour and mix until just combined. Refrigerate for 1 hour. Roll the dough to a 1/4-inch thickness and bake on a baking sheet lined with parchment paper until golden brown, 7 to 9 minutes. Cool the dough to room temperature and crush into a coarse crumble.

## PEANUT CRUMBLE

*Makes 2 cups*

1 1/2 cups sugar
1/2 cup butter
1/4 cup light corn syrup
1 1/2 cups shelled peanuts
2 teaspoons salt
3/4 teaspoon baking soda

Combine the sugar, butter, corn syrup, and 1/2 cup water in a medium saucepan and bring to a boil over medium-high heat. Stir in the peanuts and cook to a light caramel, stirring often to avoid burning the nuts. Add the salt and the baking soda and cook for another minute. Pour onto a baking sheet lined with parchment paper and cool to room temperature. Pulse to a fine crumble in a food processor.

## PISTACHIO CRUMBLE

*Makes 2 cups*

2/3 cup sugar
1/3 cup butter
1/4 cup corn syrup
1 1/2 cups shelled pistachios
2/3 tablespoon salt
2/3 teaspoon baking soda

In a medium saucepan over medium heat, bring the sugar, butter, corn syrup, and 2 tablespoons water to a boil. Add the pistachios and cook the mixture until the sugar becomes a light caramel. Add the salt and baking soda and continue to cook for 1 minute. The mixture should be golden brown and reach 300°F. Pour onto a sheet of parchment paper and allow to cool completely to room temperature. Once cool, break apart and blend in a food processor to a fine crumble.

## PORK-SHALLOT CRUMBLE

*Makes 1 cup*

1 pound ground pork back fat
2 cups canola oil
3 shallots, thinly sliced
1/2 teaspoon salt

Combine the ground pork fat with 1/2 cup water in a medium straight-sided pan and simmer over medium-low heat until the water has evaporated, 30 to 40 minutes. Drain off half of the rendered pork fat and discard. Return to the stove and continue to crisp the fat until golden brown, about 10 minutes. Strain, reserving the solids, and cool the crisped pork fat on paper towels. Once cooled, finely chop the pork fat.

Combine the canola oil and shallots in a large straight-sided pan and fry over medium heat, stirring constantly, until the shallots are golden brown, 12 to 15 minutes. The oil should reach 265°F. Strain the shallots and drain on paper towels. Cool the shallots to room temperature. Once cooled, chop the shallots into small pieces and stir into the crispy pork fat. Season with the salt.

## RYE CRUMBLE

*Makes 4 cups*
1/2 cup butter, room temperature
1/4 cup sugar
1 cup rye flour
1 cup bread flour
2 tablespoons caraway seeds
1 tablespoon plus 1 teaspoon salt
1 tablespoon milk

Preheat the oven to 325°F. Line a baking sheet with parchment paper.

In a stand mixer fitted with a paddle attachment, cream the butter and sugar together until smooth. Slowly incorporate the rye flour, bread flour, caraway seeds, and salt. Add the milk and continue to mix until small clusters of dough begin to form. Flatten out the dough to 1/2 inch thick on the prepared baking sheet. Bake for 20 minutes, until golden brown. Cool to room temperature. Grind to a powder in a spice grinder.

## CURRY GRANOLA

*Makes 2 1/2 cups*
1/2 cup bitter almonds
1 cup sugar
1/4 cup butter
2 tablespoons glucose syrup
1/2 teaspoon baking soda
1 1/3 cups peanuts
1 tablespoon salt
1/2 cup *feuilletine*
1/4 teaspoon Madras curry powder
1 1/2 teaspoons dehydrated onion
1/2 teaspoon lemon thyme
1/2 teaspoon Maldon salt

Preheat the oven to 325°F. Toast the bitter almonds on a baking sheet for 20 minutes. Cool and coarsely grind in a food processor. In a medium pot, combine the sugar, butter, and glucose and cook to a dark caramel. Add the baking soda. The caramel will bubble up and then settle again. Add the peanuts and salt and cook for 2 minutes, stirring constantly. Pour the peanut brittle onto a silicone baking mat and allow it to cool completely to room temperature. Once cooled, coarsely grind the peanut brittle in a food processor.

In a large bowl, toss 1 cup of the ground peanut brittle with the toasted bitter almonds, *feuilletine*, Madras curry, dehydrated onion, lemon thyme, and Maldon salt.

## PROVENÇAL GRANOLA

*Makes 3 cups*
2 cups puffed white rice cereal
1 cup pine nuts
1/4 cup finely grated Parmesan
1 tablespoon basil seeds
1 tablespoon salt
1 1/2 teaspoons *piment d'Espelette*
1 1/2 teaspoons minced garlic
2 quarts canola oil (for frying)
1 cup basil leaves
1/4 cup glucose syrup

Preheat the oven to 250°F. Line 2 rimmed baking sheets with parchment paper.

In a large mixing bowl, combine the puffed rice, pine nuts, Parmesan, basil seeds, salt, *piment d'Espelette,* and garlic. Heat the oil to 400°F in a large pot and very quickly fry the basil. Transfer the leaves to a paper towel to remove any excess oil. Add the fried basil leaves to the puffed rice mixture. Warm the glucose in a small pot until liquefied and pour over the rice mixture. Toss the granola together until evenly incorporated and spread onto one of the baking sheets. Bake for 20 minutes. Flip the entire tray of granola onto the second parchment-lined baking sheet and cook for 20 more minutes to bake evenly. Cool to room temperature.

## VADOUVAN GRANOLA

*Makes 4 cups*
3 tablespoons beluga lentils
3/4 cup rolled oats
1/2 cup canola oil
4 tablespoons wild rice
5 tablespoons chopped pistachios
2 cups puffed white rice cereal
1/2 cup honey
2 tablespoons *vadouvan* curry spice
1 1/2 tablespoons salt

Preheat the oven to 200°F. Cook the lentils in boiling salted water until tender, about 10 minutes. Drain and spread them out on a rimmed baking sheet lined with parchment paper to cool.

Mix the rolled oats with 3 tablespoons of the canola oil and place on a rimmed baking sheet lined with parchment paper. Toast in the oven for 35 minutes. Remove from the oven and allow to cool. Raise the over temperature to 275°F.

Place 1/2 teaspoon of the canola oil in a small sauté pan over high heat. Once the oil begins to smoke, add half of the wild rice. Stir the rice constantly for 20 seconds. The rice should puff up and be light to medium brown. Transfer to a paper towel to drain off excess oil and cool. Repeat with another 1/2 teaspoon of canola oil and the other half of the wild rice.

Combine the lentils, oats, wild rice, pistachios, and puffed white rice in a mixing bowl. Combine the honey, 1/3 cup of the canola oil, the *vadouvan* curry, salt, and 1 tablespoon water in a small pot, and bring to a boil. Once the mixture boils, pour over the dry ingredients and mix together thoroughly. Place on a 13-by-18-inch rimmed baking sheet lined with parchment paper. Toast in the oven at 275°F for 8 minutes. Remove from oven and flip onto a new baking sheet lined with parchment paper. Return to the oven and toast for another 8 minutes, until golden brown. Remove from oven and allow to cool. The granola can be stored in an airtight container for up to 5 days.

## BRIOCHE

*Serves 8*
2 3/4 cups bread flour
1/3 cup sugar
2 tablespoons fresh yeast
1 tablespoon *fleur de sel*
5 eggs
1 egg yolk
2 1/4 cups butter, room temperature, cut into cubes

Place the flour, sugar, yeast, and *fleur de sel* in the bowl of a stand mixer fitted with a dough hook. Mix at medium speed. In a separate bowl, whisk together 4 of the eggs, the egg yolk, and 1 tablespoon water. Gradually add the egg mixture to the dry ingredients. The dough will initially be like a loose batter; as the gluten develops, it will bind and start to pull away from the sides of the bowl. This process will take 15 to 20 minutes.

Once the dough pulls away from the sides of the bowl, add the butter, 1 cube at a time, and continue to mix until the dough appears silky.

Place the dough in a greased bowl, cover with plastic wrap, and proof for an hour at room temperature. Transfer to the refrigerator and proof for an additional hour. Punch down the dough and place a piece of plastic wrap directly on its surface. Refrigerate overnight.

Working quickly and using just a dusting of flour to keep the dough from sticking, shape the dough into a log and roll to fit the size of a 5 1/2-by-13-inch loaf pan. Spray the pan with vegetable spray and transfer the dough to the pan. Evenly press the dough to cover the bottom of the loaf pan completely. Cover with plastic wrap. Proof the loaf in a draft-free, warm area of the kitchen for 3 hours, or until doubled in size.

Preheat the oven to 325°F. Beat the remaining egg and brush the top of the loaf with the beaten egg. Bake the brioche for about 1 hour or until the temperature in the center reaches 204°F on a probe thermometer and the top is a dark golden brown.

## PASTA DOUGH

*Makes 1 pound*
1 teaspoon saffron
3 cups Italian-style 00 flour
9 egg yolks
1 teaspoon salt

Bring 1 cup water to a boil. Add the saffron and reduce the liquid to 1/4 cup. Strain. Place the flour on a stainless-steel or marble countertop and create a well in the middle. Into the center of the well, pour 2 1/2 teaspoons of the saffron water, the egg yolks, and salt. Using a fork, work from the center of the well to incorporate the wet ingredients into the flour, bringing the pasta dough together. Knead for 10 minutes, until the pasta is somewhat firm yet elastic. Depending on the humidity, you may need to incorporate a little extra flour to keep the pasta from being tacky. Wrap the dough tightly in plastic and refrigerate for 30 minutes.

## APRICOT SORBET

*Makes 4 cups*

3 quarts fresh, ripe apricots, pitted
    and diced
1 1/2 cups sugar
Juice of 1 lemon
1 teaspoon citric acid

In a food processor, puree the apricots with the sugar and lemon juice. Season the puree with the citric acid. Pass the puree through a chinois and chill. Freeze in an ice-cream maker.

## BLACKBERRY SORBET

*Makes 4 cups*

1/2 cup sugar
6 cups blackberries
Juice of 1 lemon
1/2 teaspoon citric acid

Combine 1 cup water and the sugar in small saucepan and bring to a boil. In a blender, puree the blackberries with the water-sugar mixture, lemon juice, and citric acid. Strain and chill. Freeze in an ice-cream maker.

## BUTTERMILK OLIVE OIL SORBET

*Makes 4 cups*

1 cup cream
1/2 cup glucose syrup
3/8 cup milk powder
1/4 cup sugar
1 1/2 tablespoons salt
1 tablespoon lemon zest
1/2 teaspoon lactic acid
3 1/2 cups buttermilk
1 cup extra-virgin olive oil

Heat the cream in a small saucepan over medium heat and dissolve the glucose, milk powder, sugar, and salt into it. Pour the mixture into a blender and blend with the lemon zest and lactic acid. Drizzle in the buttermilk and olive oil and continue to blend until smooth. Strain and chill. Freeze in an ice-cream maker.

## CARAMELIZED WHITE CHOCOLATE SORBET

*Makes 4 cups*

13 ounces Valrhona Ivoire chocolate
    (35 percent), chopped
5 tablespoons malted milk powder
2 teaspoons sugar
1/2 cup glucose syrup
2 teaspoons salt

Bring a large pot of water to a simmer over medium heat. Place the chocolate in a *sous vide* bag and vacuum-seal. Place the sealed bag in the simmering water and cook for approximately 3 hours, or until the chocolate takes on a medium caramel color. Rotate the bag every 30 minutes to ensure even color. Cool in an ice bath. Once the chocolate has solidified, remove it from the bag and chop it into small pieces. Reserve it in a dry, airtight container.

In a small bowl, stir together the malted milk powder and the sugar. In a saucepan over low heat, combine the glucose with 3 3/4 cups water, heating until the glucose is dissolved and the liquid is warm. Slowly add the sugar mixture to the warm liquid and heat to just under a boil. Place the chopped caramelized chocolate and the salt in a bowl and pour the hot liquid over them. Allow to sit for 1 minute, and, using a hand blender, blend until smooth. Strain through a chinois and freeze in an ice-cream maker while still warm to avoid a grainy texture.

## CASSIS SORBET

*Makes 4 cups*

1 1/2 cups sugar
3/4 cup glucose syrup
3 cups cassis puree (from frozen puree)

In a large saucepan over medium heat, combine the sugar, glucose, and 4 cups water until the sugar is melted. Stir in the cassis puree and continue to heat until incorporated. Chill over ice and freeze in an ice-cream maker.

## CHERRY SORBET

*Makes 4 cups*

8 cups stemmed and pitted fresh Bing
    cherries
1 cup sugar
1 tablespoon citric acid, or to taste

Toss the cherries with sugar and citric acid. Puree in a blender until smooth and strain through a chinois. Freeze the cherry puree immediately in an ice-cream maker. It is important to freeze it as soon as possible, as the cherry puree will oxidize and turn brown rather quickly at room temperature.

## CHOCOLATE SORBET

*Makes 4 cups*

1 cup plus 2 tablespoons sugar
1 pound Valrhona Caraïbe chocolate
    (66 percent), chopped
1 teaspoon salt

Bring 4 1/4 cups water and the sugar to boil in a saucepan over medium heat. Pour the liquid over the chocolate, allow to sit for 1 minute to melt, and then puree with a hand blender. Strain through a chinois. Freeze in an ice-cream maker while still warm to avoid a grainy texture.

## COCONUT SORBET

*Makes 4 cups*

2/3 cup sugar
1/4 cup glucose syrup
2 1/4 cups frozen coconut puree

Combine 2 cups water with the sugar and glucose syrup in a saucepan and dissolve over low heat. Add the coconut puree and stir to combine. Strain, transfer to a bowl, and chill over ice. Freeze in an ice-cream maker.

## COFFEE ICED MILK SORBET

*Makes 4 cups*

1 cup ground coffee
1 3/4 cups milk
1 3/4 cups half-and-half
1 cup sugar
3/4 cup glucose syrup
1 teaspoon salt

Preheat the oven to 300°F. Place the ground coffee on a baking sheet and roast in the oven for 8 minutes. In a medium bowl, combine the milk, half-and-half, and the roasted coffee. Stir well and refrigerate overnight. Strain the coffee mixture through a coffee filter. In a large saucepan over medium heat, warm the coffee milk with the sugar and glucose until they are dissolved in the liquid. Pass through a chinois and chill over ice. Season with the salt and freeze in an ice-cream maker.

## GREEN APPLE SORBET

*Makes 4 cups*

2 1/2 pounds Granny Smith apples (about
    7), peeled, cored, and sliced (about 10
    cups)
1/3 cup sugar
1/3 cup glucose syrup
2 teaspoons malic acid
1 1/2 teaspoons xanthan gum

Place the apples in a *sous vide* bag and vacuum-seal. Bring a pot of water to a boil and cook the bag of apples until tender, about 20 minutes. Remove the cooked apples from the bag and puree in a blender with the remaining ingredients until completely smooth. Strain the mixture through a fine-mesh chinois and chill over ice, stirring constantly. Freeze in an ice-cream maker.

## HAZELNUT SORBET

*Makes 4 cups*

3 cups whole hazelnuts (skin on)
1 1/4 cups sugar
1/3 cup glucose syrup
1/3 cup milk powder
2 tablespoons salt

Preheat the oven to 325°F. Spread the hazelnuts on a baking sheet and toast the nuts in the oven until they are dark brown, about 30 minutes. The sorbet will be more flavorful if the nuts are well toasted.

Once the nuts are toasted, bring 6 cups water to a boil in a saucepan and add the warm toasted nuts. Cover the pan and continue to simmer until the nuts are fully softened, about 2 1/2 hours.

Puree the softened hazelnuts in a blender until completely smooth and strain the liquid through a chinois. You should have 5 cups of hazelnut liquid. If not, add enough water to bring the liquid to 5 cups.

In a medium saucepan, combine the hazelnut liquid, sugar, glucose, and milk powder, and heat until melted and combined. Strain again and season with the salt. Chill over ice and freeze in an ice-cream maker.

## LEMON MINT SORBET

*Makes 8 cups*

1 quart half-and-half
1 quart milk, plus more if needed
4 cups gently packed lemon mint
   or lemon balm leaves
1 1/2 cups sugar
1/2 cup glucose syrup
1 teaspoon salt

In a medium saucepan over medium heat, heat the half-and-half and 4 cups milk to just under a boil. Remove from the heat and add the lemon mint or lemon balm. Steep for 30 minutes and then strain through a chinois. Measure the liquid and add enough milk so that you have 8 cups total. Heat the mixture in a medium saucepan to just under a boil, and add the sugar, glucose, and salt. Blend with a hand blender, strain, and chill over ice. Freeze in an ice-cream maker.

## MALTED MILK SORBET

*Makes 4 cups*

2 3/4 cups milk
2 3/4 cups half-and-half
1/2 cup sugar
1/2 cup glucose syrup
6 tablespoons malted milk powder
2 tablespoons salt

In a medium saucepan over medium heat, combine the milk, half-and-half, sugar, and glucose. Bring to a simmer. Add the malted milk powder and salt, and bring to a boil. Mix with a hand blender. Strain and cool over ice. Freeze in an ice-cream maker.

## MILK SORBET

*Makes 4 cups*

2 1/2 cups half-and-half
3/4 cup glucose syrup
1/3 cup honey
1 tablespoon salt
2 1/2 cups milk

Combine the half-and-half, glucose, and honey in a small saucepan over medium heat. Season with the salt. Bring to just under a boil. Add the milk and mix with a hand blender to combine. Strain and cool over ice. Freeze in an ice-cream maker.

## PASSION FRUIT–KAFFIR LIME SORBET

*Makes 4 cups*

1 cup sugar
1/4 cup glucose syrup
1/4 cup kaffir lime leaves, thinly sliced
1 2/3 cups frozen passion fruit puree

In a saucepan over low heat, combine 2 cups water with the sugar and glucose syrup to dissolve. Add the kaffir lime leaves and remove from the heat. Steep the leaves for 30 minutes. Add the passion fruit puree and stir to combine. Strain and freeze the sorbet in an ice-cream maker.

## PEPPERMINT SORBET

*Makes 4 cups*

2 cups gently packed peppermint leaves
2 1/4 cups sugar
2/3 cup milk powder
1/2 cup glucose powder
1/2 teaspoon salt

Bring a pot of water to a boil. Add the peppermint leaves and cook for 20 seconds. Transfer to a bowl of ice water and, once cold, squeeze out the excess moisture in a dry towel. Combine 4 cups water with the sugar, milk powder, glucose powder, and salt in a medium saucepan over medium heat to dissolve. Blend the blanched peppermint leaves and the water-sugar mixture in a blender. Strain though a chinois and chill over ice. Freeze in an ice-cream maker.

## ROASTED BANANA SORBET

*Makes 4 cups*

8 ripe bananas
3/4 cup sugar
1/2 teaspoon salt
3/4 teaspoon yuzu juice

Preheat the oven to 350°F. Place the unpeeled bananas on a baking sheet lined with parchment paper and roast the bananas until they are brown and the juices run out, about 30 minutes. Peel the roasted bananas and place in the blender with the sugar, salt, and 1 1/2 cups water. Puree until smooth and strain. Season with the yuzu juice. Chill over ice and freeze in an ice-cream maker.

## SHEEP'S MILK YOGURT SORBET

*Makes 4 cups*

3/4 cup sugar
3/4 cup glucose syrup
2 tablespoons milk powder
3 1/2 cups sheep's milk yogurt
3 tablespoons lemon juice
1/2 teaspoon salt

Combine 1 1/2 cups water with the sugar and glucose in a medium saucepan over medium heat and bring to a simmer. Add the milk powder, stir, and simmer for 2 minutes, until completely dissolved. Cool over ice. Add the yogurt, lemon juice, and salt, and mix with a hand blender. Strain through a chinois. Chill over ice until very cold and then freeze in an ice-cream maker.

## SPEARMINT SORBET

*Makes 8 cups*

1 quart half-and-half
1 quart milk
4 cups gently packed spearmint leaves
1 1/4 cups sugar
1/2 cup glucose syrup
1 teaspoon salt

Heat the half-and-half and milk in a large saucepan over medium heat to just under a boil. Remove from the heat, add 3 cups of the spearmint leaves, and infuse for 30 minutes. Meanwhile, bring a small saucepan of water to a boil. Add the remaining 1 cup spearmint leaves and cook for 20 seconds. Transfer to a bowl of ice water. Drain the blanched spearmint leaves and squeeze out the excess moisture with a dry towel. Strain the spearmint leaves from the milk mixture. In a blender, puree the blanched spearmint leaves with the spearmint-infused milk and the sugar, glucose, and salt, until light green and smooth. Strain and chill over ice. Freeze in an ice-cream maker.

## STRAWBERRY SORBET

*Makes 4 cups*

10 cups hulled and quartered
   strawberries
1 1/2 cups sugar
1 teaspoon citric acid

Combine the strawberries with the sugar and citric acid in a blender. Puree on high and then strain through a chinois. Freeze in an ice-cream maker.

## BROWN BUTTER ICE CREAM

*Makes 4 cups*

1/3 cup butter
4 tablespoons milk powder
4 cups milk
2/3 cup glucose syrup
11 egg yolks
1 cup sugar
1 tablespoon salt
1 1/2 teaspoons cornstarch
3/4 cup Brown Butter (see page 370)
2 tablespoons lemon juice

To make browned milk solids, melt the butter in a small saucepan over medium heat. Add the milk powder, stirring often as the milk solids begin to brown. When evenly browned, strain through a chinois, reserving the solids. Turn the solids out onto a paper towel and pat dry to remove any excess butter. Reserve the milk solids in a dry, airtight container.

In a blender, puree 1 cup of the milk with 1/3 cup of the browned milk solids until smooth. Transfer to a saucepan with the remaining 3 cups of milk and add the glucose. Set over low heat to dissolve the glucose. In a separate bowl, whisk together the egg yolks sugar, salt, and cornstarch until smooth. Slowly whisk the egg yolk mixture into the hot milk mixture and cook the crème anglaise until it reaches 180°F. Strain. With a hand blender, emulsify the Brown Butter into the crème anglaise and season with the lemon juice. Freeze in an ice-cream maker.

## CARROT ICE CREAM

*Makes 4 cups*

1 3/4 cups carrot juice
1 1/4 cups milk powder
1/4 cup trimoline
2 tablespoons glucose syrup
13 egg yolks
1 1/2 cups Carrot Puree (see page 350)

In a medium saucepan, combine the carrot juice, milk powder, trimoline, and glucose. Dissolve over low heat. Slowly whisk in the egg yolks, stirring constantly and being careful not to curdle the eggs. Cook to 83°F and then blend the mixture with a hand blender. Strain through a chinois and cool over ice. Fold in the Carrot Puree. Refrigerate for at least 2 hours before freezing in an ice-cream maker.

## CHOCOLATE TRUFFLE ICE CREAM

*Makes 6 cups*

3 1/2 cups milk
2/3 cup cream
1/2 cup milk powder
2 tablespoons glucose syrup
3/4 cup sugar
6 egg yolks
8.6 ounces (2 cups) Valrhona Araguani chocolate (72 percent), chopped
3 tablespoons Black Truffle Butter (see page 371)
3 tablespoons finely chopped black truffles
1 tablespoon salt

Combine the milk, cream, milk powder, and glucose syrup in a medium saucepan and warm over low heat. In a mixing bowl, whisk together the sugar and egg yolks. Slowly stream the warm milk mixture into the egg mixture, whisking constantly. Return to the saucepan and cook, stirring constantly, until the mixture reaches 180°F. Strain through a chinois.

With a hand blender, blend in the chocolate, Black Truffle Butter, chopped truffles, and salt. Chill over ice, stirring constantly. Freeze in an ice-cream maker.

## COFFEE ICE CREAM

*Makes 6 cups*

2 cups coffee beans
4 cups milk
1 cup cream
1/2 cup milk powder
6 egg yolks
2 tablespoons glucose syrup
3/4 cup sweetened condensed milk
2 tablespoons coffee extract, preferably Trablit
2 tablespoons instant espresso powder
1 tablespoon salt

Preheat the oven to 350°F. Spread the coffee beans on a baking sheet lined with parchment paper and roast the beans in the oven for 20 minutes. Grind the coffee beans in a food processor and transfer to a large mixing bowl. Add the milk and cream and steep the ground coffee for 30 minutes. Strain through a chinois.

Transfer the coffee milk to a medium straight-sided saucepan and warm over medium-low heat. Stir in the milk powder. In a mixing bowl, whisk together the egg yolks and glucose syrup. Slowly stir the warm coffee milk into the egg yolk mixture. Return the mixture to the saucepan and, stirring constantly, cook over low heat to 180°F. Stir in the condensed milk, coffee extract, espresso powder, and salt. Strain through a chinois and chill the mixture over ice. Freeze in an ice-cream maker.

## GRANNY SMITH APPLE ICE CREAM

*Makes 8 cups*

3 pounds Granny Smith apples, cored and thinly sliced
2 cups apple cider
2 tablespoons plus 1/2 teaspoon citric acid
3 1/2 cups milk
3 1/2 cups cream
1/4 cup glucose syrup
9 egg yolks
1 3/4 cups plus 1/2 cup sugar
1/4 cup Calvados
1 tablespoon salt
2 pounds Fuji apples, peeled, cored, and quartered
1/2 cup light brown sugar
Zest and juice of 1 lemon
1 vanilla bean, split lengthwise and scraped

Cook the Granny Smith apples with the apple cider and 1/2 teaspoon of the citric acid in a saucepan over medium heat until the apples are tender and broken down, about 30 minutes. While still hot, puree in a blender until smooth. In another large saucepan, warm the milk, cream, and glucose syrup. Whisk in the apple puree. In a large bowl, whisk together the egg yolks and 1 3/4 cups of the sugar until pale yellow ribbons form. Slowly whisk the milk mixture into the eggs and then return to the saucepan. Cook to 180°F and strain through a chinois. Add the remaining 2 tablespoons citric acid, the Calvados, and the salt. Chill over ice and freeze in an ice-cream maker.

Preheat the oven to 350°F. Combine the Fuji apples, brown sugar, the remaining 1/2 cup sugar, and the lemon juice in a roasting pan. Cover with aluminum foil and roast for about 45 minutes. The apples should be soft and the liquid at the bottom of the pan should be syrupy. Puree the roasted apples with the lemon zest and the vanilla bean seeds. Pass through a fine-mesh tamis. Cool over ice and transfer to a piping bag.

To create a swirl effect in the ice cream, cut a medium hole at the tip of the piping bag. Scoop 3 large spoonfuls of ice cream into the bottom of a bowl. Squeeze a thin layer of Fuji apple puree on top. Continue layering the ice cream and puree until both are used. Freeze until firm.

## MOZZARELLA ICE CREAM

*Makes 4 cups*

2 1/2 cups buffalo mozzarella
2 1/2 cups skim milk
1/4 cup trimoline
2 tablespoons dextrose powder
1 1/2 tablespoons salt
1/2 teaspoon guar gum (1.6 grams)
1/2 teaspoon xanthan gum (1.2 grams)
1/2 teaspoon lactic acid

Puree all of ingredients in a blender on high speed until the mixture becomes warm. Blend for 15 more seconds to achieve a smooth consistency. Chill over ice. Transfer to a Pacojet container and freeze until solid. Blend thoroughly in the Pacojet.

## PEA ICE CREAM

*Makes 4 cups*

1 1/4 cups milk powder
1/4 cup trimoline
2 tablespoons glucose syrup
13 egg yolks
1 1/4 cups Sugar Snap Pea Puree (see page 352)
2 tablespoons Spinach Puree (see page 354)

In a medium saucepan, combine 1 1/4 cups water, milk powder, trimoline, and glucose. Dissolve over low heat. Slowly whisk in the egg yolks, stirring constantly and being careful not to curdle the eggs. Cook to 83°F and then blend the mixture with a hand blender. Strain through a chinois and cool over ice. Fold in the Pea and Spinach Purees. Refrigerate for at least 2 hours before freezing in an ice-cream maker.

## PISTACHIO ICE CREAM

*Makes 4 cups*

2 1/4 cups shelled pistachios
6 cups milk
1 cup sugar
10 egg yolks
1 cup Pistachio Paste (see page 151)
1 tablespoon salt

Preheat the oven to 300°F. Place the pistachios on a rimmed baking sheet and toast in the oven for 8 to 10 minutes. In a saucepan, heat the milk and 1/2 cup of the sugar to just under a boil. Add the warm toasted pistachios, remove from the heat, and steep for 15 minutes. Puree the milk and pistachios in a blender and strain through a chinois. In a large bowl, whisk together the remaining 1/2 cup sugar, the egg yolks, and Pistachio Paste. Slowly whisk in the warm pistachio milk. Cook, stirring constantly, until the mixture to reaches 180°F. Strain through a chinois. Add the salt and chill over ice. Once chilled, freeze in an ice-cream maker.

## POPCORN ICE CREAM

*Makes 4 cups*

1 cup popcorn kernels
2 tablespoons canola oil
4 cups milk
3 cups cream
1/2 cup sugar
3 tablespoons glucose syrup
1 tablespoon salt

Place the kernels and oil in a deep pot over medium heat and cover. Periodically shake the pot to rotate the kernels and allow even popping. When the popping slows, remove the pot from the heat and allow the popping to finish. Be careful not to burn the popcorn. Bring the milk, cream, sugar, and glucose to just under a boil and pour over the popcorn. Cover and steep for 1 hour. Divide the mixture in half. Puree half of the base in a blender until smooth. Pour back into the remaining base, whisk well, and strain through a chinois. Blend the strained mixture again until smooth and strain once more. Season with the salt. Freeze in an ice-cream maker.

## POTATO ICE CREAM

*Makes 4 cups*

2 tablespoons canola oil
4 cups peeled and sliced (3/8 inch) russet potatoes
2 cups skim milk
2 cups whole milk
1/4 cup agave nectar
2 teaspoons salt
1/2 cup crème fraîche
2 tablespoons Brown Butter (see page 370)

Preheat the oven to 350°F. Heat the oil in large oven-safe sauté pan set over high heat. Add the potatoes and cook for 2 to 3 minutes, turning them in the oil. Place the pan in the oven and roast for 20 minutes, until the potatoes are golden brown. Remove the potatoes from the pan, draining and discarding any excess oil. In a large saucepan, combine the skim milk, whole milk, agave nectar, salt, and the roasted potatoes. Bring to a simmer. Remove from the heat, cover, and steep for 45 minutes. Strain, reserving the potatoes and their cooking liquid separately.

Measure 1 cup of the cooked potatoes and discard the rest. In a blender, combine the potatoes, their cooking liquid, the crème fraîche, and Brown Butter. Blend together until smooth and pass through a fine-mesh chinois. Cool the mixture over ice and, once cold, freeze in an ice-cream maker.

## SALTED CARAMEL ICE CREAM

*Makes 4 cups*

1 cup plus 1 tablespoon sugar
2 1/4 cups cream
2 cups milk
1/2 cup glucose syrup
10 egg yolks
2 teaspoons salt

Heat 3/4 cup of the sugar in a heavy-bottomed saucepan. Cook over medium heat until it is a deep caramel color. In a separate saucepan, warm the cream, milk, and glucose until hot. Deglaze the caramel with the warm cream mixture. In a separate saucepan, whisk together the yolks with the remaining 1/4 cup plus 1 tablespoon sugar. Slowly incorporate the warm cream mixture into the yolk mixture. Warm over medium heat, stirring constantly, until the mixture reaches 178°F. Strain through a chinois. Season with the salt and chill over ice. Freeze in an ice-cream maker.

## WHITE ASPARAGUS ICE CREAM

*Makes 4 cups*

1 1/4 cups milk powder
1/4 cup trimoline
2 tablespoons glucose syrup
13 egg yolks
1 1/2 cups White Asparagus Puree (see page 354)

In a medium saucepan, combine 1 1/4 cups water, milk powder, trimoline, glucose, and glucose. Dissolve over low heat. Slowly whisk in the egg yolks, stirring constantly and being careful not to curdle the eggs. Cook to 83°F and then blend the mixture with a hand blender. Strain through a chinois and cool over ice. Fold in the White Asparagus Puree. Refrigerate for at least 2 hours before freezing in an ice-cream maker.

## WHITE TRUFFLE ICE CREAM

*Makes 4 cups*

2 cups milk
2 cups cream
1/4 cup milk powder
8 egg yolks
1 cup sugar
1 teaspoon salt
2 tablespoons White Truffle Butter (see page 371)
1 tablespoon chopped white truffle

Combine the milk, cream, and milk powder in a medium saucepan and warm over medium-low heat. In a mixing bowl, whisk together the egg yolks, sugar, and salt. Slowly pour the warm milk mixture into the egg mixture, whisking constantly. Return the mixture to the saucepan and cook over medium heat, stirring often, until the mixture reaches 180°F. Strain through a fine-mesh chinois. With a hand blender, blend in the Truffle Butter and the white truffles. Chill over ice and freeze in an ice-cream maker.

## FROZEN LEMON YOGURT

*Makes 4 cups*

1 1/4 cups sugar
2/3 cup glucose syrup
2 1/2 cups Greek yogurt
1 3/4 cups lemon juice

In a medium saucepan, combine 1 cup water with the sugar and glucose syrup, and dissolve over medium heat to just under a boil. Transfer to a bowl and chill over ice. Blend in the Greek yogurt and the lemon juice. Freeze in an ice-cream maker.

# BUTTERS, ETC.

### BROWN BUTTER
*Makes 1 1/2 cups*
1 pound butter
5 sprigs thyme
2 cloves garlic, crushed but kept whole

Place the butter in a medium saucepan over medium heat. Simmer for about 40 minutes. At this point, the butter should be clear and a light caramel color. Continue to simmer the butter and whisk vigorously until the color is walnut brown.

Place the thyme and garlic in a chinois lined with cheesecloth. Strain the Brown Butter over the thyme and garlic.

### CLARIFIED BUTTER
*Makes 1 3/4 cups*
1 pound butter

Place the butter in a medium saucepan over medium heat. Simmer for about 30 minutes. Once the butter is clear, strain through cheesecloth to remove milk solids. Refrigerate in an airtight container until ready to use, for up to 1 week.

### LOBSTER BUTTER
*Makes 2 cups*
4 lobster bodies
1 tablespoon canola oil
2 tablespoons tomato paste
2 pounds butter
1/2 cup diced carrot
1/2 cup diced onion
1/2 cup diced celery
1 spring thyme
1 sprig tarragon
1 bay leaf
2 cups Chicken Stock (see page 356)

Separate the heads from the lobster bodies and trim off and discard the antennae. Clean the lobster bodies of all tomalley, reserving any roe. Trim off the lungs, or dead man's fingers, as they can add a fishy flavor; trim off the legs, as they may burn during cooking. Cut each body into 4 even pieces.

In a large pot, over medium heat, heat the canola oil until it just begins to smoke. Add the lobster bodies and heads to the pan and raise the heat to high. Sauté until they begin to toast and brown. Add the tomato paste and sauté with the lobster for 2 minutes. Lower the heat to medium and add the butter, carrot, onion, celery, thyme, tarragon, and bay leaf. Heat until the butter is melted and begins to simmer. Add the Chicken Stock and bring to a simmer. Simmer over low heat until all the Chicken Stock evaporates and the butter clarifies, about 1 hour and 15 minutes. Strain through a fine-mesh chinois, discarding the lobster solids, vegetables, and herbs. Cool to room temperature to allow the fat to separate. Chill in the refrigerator until the butter is solid. Remove the solid butter from the container, discarding any remaining liquid. Pat the butter dry with paper towels and place it in an airtight container. Store in the refrigerator for up to 1 week.

## BLACK TRUFFLE BUTTER
*Makes 4 cups*
4 cups butter, softened
1/3 cup chopped black truffle
1 tablespoon *fleur de sel*

In a stainless-steel mixing bowl, fold together the butter, truffle, and *fleur de sel*. Store in the refrigerator for 2 to 3 days and in the freezer for up to 2 weeks.

## WHITE TRUFFLE BUTTER
*Makes 2 cups*
1 pound butter, softened
1/2 cup chopped white truffle trim
1 tablespoon *fleur de sel*

Place the butter in a mixing bowl. Fold in the white truffle trim and *fleur de sel*. Store in the refrigerator for 2 to 3 days or in the freezer for up to 2 weeks.

## ELEPHANT GARLIC CHIPS
*Makes 30 to 40 chips*
2 cloves elephant garlic, peeled
1 cup milk
4 cups canola oil
1 teaspoon salt

Trim off the top and bottom of the garlic cloves. Punch them with a 1-inch ring cutter. Thinly slice the garlic cylinders on a mandoline. Place the sliced garlic in a saucepan with the milk and bring to a simmer. Remove from the heat and steep for 10 minutes. Strain out the garlic and discard the milk. Rinse the garlic under cold water and pat dry.
 Heat the oil to 275°F in a small sauté pan. Fry the garlic for about 45 seconds

or until pale blond. To test for doneness, remove 1 chip from the oil. As it cools, it should become crispy. Once the chips are ready, remove them from the oil with a slotted spoon. Drain on paper towels and season with the salt. Cool to room temperature and store in an airtight container for up to 12 hours.

## LOBSTER ROE POWDER
*Makes 1/4 cup*
1/2 cup fresh lobster roe

In a small saucepan, whisk together the lobster roe and 1 tablespoon water. Set over low heat until the roe is orange and begins to congeal, 3 to 4 minutes. Remove the cooked roe from the pot and place on a plastic-wrapped plate. Microwave the cooked roe at 30-second intervals for 2 minutes total. The roe will start to harden and puff. The resulting roe should be bright orange and brittle. Allow the roe to cool to room temperature before breaking into pieces. Grind the roe in a spice grinder until powdery. Store in an airtight container for up to 3 days.

## MAYONNAISE
*Makes 2 cups*
2 egg yolks
1 teaspoon lemon juice
1/2 teaspoon Dijon mustard
1 1/2 cups canola oil
1 teaspoon salt

Place the yolks, lemon juice, and Dijon mustard in the bowl of a food processor. With the processor running, slowly stream in the canola oil and continue blending until the mayonnaise is fully emulsified. Season with the salt. Store in the refrigerator for 2 to 3 days.

## CRUSTACEAN MAYONNAISE
*Makes 2 cups*
2 tablespoons lobster roe
3 egg yolks
1 tablespoon Dijon mustard
6 tablespoons canola oil
1 tablespoon lemon juice
1 tablespoon salt

In a small saucepan, whisk the lobster roe with 4 tablespoons water. Place the saucepan over medium heat, whisking constantly, until the roe is bright red, about 1 minute. Cool over ice. Blend the egg yolks, mustard, and a few drops of water in a food processor. Add the cooled lobster roe. In a very slow, thin stream, add the canola oil, blending constantly, until the mixture is thick. Season with the lemon juice and salt and store in the refrigerator for 2 to 3 days.

## SHALLOT CONFIT
*Makes 1 1/2 cups*
3 cups olive oil
8 medium shallots, peeled
2 cloves garlic
2 sprigs thyme
1 teaspoon salt

Preheat the oven to 250°F. Combine all of the ingredients in a small baking dish and cover with aluminum foil. Cook the shallots in the oven until they are tender and can be easily pierced with a fork, 1 hour and 45 minutes to 2 hours. Store the shallots with their oil and seasonings in a jar in the refrigerator for 2 to 3 days.

## SIMPLE SYRUP
*Makes 2 cups*
1 cup sugar

Combine the sugar and 1 cup water in a small saucepan over medium-high heat. Heat until the sugar is melted. Cool and store in the refrigerator until ready to use, up to 2 weeks.

## TOMATO WATER
*Makes 1 quart, depending on the ripeness of your tomatoes*
10 pounds ripe tomatoes
1 large bunch green basil
2 tablespoons salt

Rinse the tomatoes under cold running water. Trim off the stems and quarter. Combine with the basil in a mixing bowl and season with the salt. Prepare a colander with 10 layers of cheesecloth. Moisten the cheesecloth with cold water and press out any excess. Place the prepared colander in a deep bowl to catch the liquid as it drains. In 3 batches, puree the tomatoes and basil in a blender on high speed for 30 seconds. Pour over the cheesecloth. Drain overnight, covered, in the refrigerator. Reserve the clear Tomato Water, noting that it may be necessary to reduce it to intensify the tomato flavor.

## THE ELEVEN MADISON PARK GRANOLA
*At the end of dinner at Eleven Madison Park, we give our guests a jar of our granola.*
*Makes 6 cups*
2 3/4 cups organic rolled oats
1 cup unsweetened coconut chips
1 cup shelled pistachios
1/3 cup pumpkin seeds
1 tablespoon salt
1/2 cup light brown sugar
1/3 cup maple syrup
1/3 cup extra-virgin olive oil
3/4 cup dried sour cherries

Preheat the oven to 300°F. In a large mixing bowl, toss together the oats, coconut, pistachios, pumpkin seeds, and salt. In a small saucepan over low heat, warm the brown sugar, maple syrup, and olive oil until the sugar is just dissolved. Fold into the oat mixture, coating all of the dry ingredients as evenly as possible. Spread out onto a large rimmed baking sheet lined with parchment paper. Bake until dry and lightly golden, about 15 to 25 minutes, stirring the granola often to allow for even baking and drying. Remove from the oven and fold in the dried sour cherries. Allow to cool to room temperature before transferring to individual jars.

# TOOLS

*All tools may be found at JB Prince unless otherwise noted.*

## ACETATE
Acetate creates a very flat, smooth surface, allowing melted chocolate to stay shiny. It is also used when making gelées and tuiles because it's very easy to peel them from acetate.

## ADJUSTABLE RECTANGULAR CAKE RING
Used to create rectangular molds and cutters, an adjustable rectangular cake ring allows you to make almost any size square or rectangle. *Available from Pastry Chef Central.*

## ADJUSTABLE PASTRY CUTTER
Also known as a dough divider or bicyclette, an adjustable pastry cutter produces uniform strips of dough of almost any size, resulting in even portions and perfect squares or rectangles.

## CHINOIS
A chinois is a conical sieve that is used to strain soups, stocks, and sauces through fine mesh.

## CHOCOLATE SPRAY GUN
A chocolate spray gun is used in pastry applications to apply a layer of chocolate over any shape of confection, creating a smooth, even coating.

## $CO_2$ CARTRIDGES
$CO_2$ cartridges create carbonation through the introduction of carbon dioxide. As liquids are expelled through a canister charged with $CO_2$, the gas expands and carbonates the liquid.

## CRINKLE-CUT KNIFE
A crinkle-cut knife creates a decorative wave shape on fruits, vegetables, and seafood.

## CRYOVAC MACHINE
A Cryovac machine draws out air from a *sous vide* bag and vacuum-seals the contents. It can be used to seal proteins, which can then be cooked in a water bath. It is also used to vacuum-seal fruits and vegetables, compressing them and allowing for the infusion of flavors. *Available from Le Sanctuaire.*

## DEHYDRATOR
A dehydrator allows for the slow, even dehydration of fruits and vegetables at very low, gentle temperatures.

## DEMI-SPHERE MOLD
Also called a half-sphere mold, it is used to create perfectly rounded, smooth confections.

## FLUTED RING CUTTER
This cutter has a fluted edge, creating a decorative border.

## IMMERSION CIRCULATOR
An immersion circulator precisely controls the temperature of a liquid through circulation. Vacuum-sealed foods are cooked *sous vide* at specific temperatures to slowly and gently break down proteins and intensify flavor.

## LOLLIPOP MOLDS
Lollipop molds are instrumental in making uniformly shaped sweet and savory lollipops. *Available from Candyland Crafts.*

## MADELEINE MOLD
Madeleine molds give madeleines their distinctive shape.

## MANDOLINE
To slice fruits, vegetables, and even nuts to varying thicknesses, a Japanese mandoline (benriner) works best. A French mandoline is necessary to make *gaufrette* (waffled) potatoes.

## MEAT HOOKS
Meat hooks can be used to hang and dry meats in a refrigerator, providing ample air circulation. *Available from Chef Depot.*

## MICROPLANE
A microplane is the essential tool for grating everything from cheese to chocolate and can be used to zest any fruit.

## MINI-MUFFIN FLEX MOLDS (2 INCHES)
These flex molds can be used not only to make muffins but also to serve as molds for small cakes or rolls.

## $N_2O$ CATRIDGES
Whipped-cream canisters are charged with nitrous oxide ($N_2O$). As liquids are expelled through the canister, the $N_2O$ expands and whips them into foam.

## PACOJET
Used to make extremely smooth ice creams and sorbets, a Pacojet uses a blade to finely shave a frozen base. While an ice-cream maker is suitable for the production of most sorbets and ice creams, a Pacojet will create a uniformly smooth texture when an ice-cream maker cannot. *Available from Pacojet.*

## PARISIAN SCOOPS AND MELON BALLERS
Parisian scoops and melon ballers create spheres of various sizes from fruits, vegetables, ice creams, and sorbets.

## PASTA ROLLER
A pasta roller turns pasta dough into thin sheets of pasta that can then be cut into various shapes and sizes.

## PASTRY TIPS
Pastry tips are used in the piping of doughs, batters, meringues, curds, and pastry fillings. They are available with openings of various sizes to control the amount that is expelled through the tip.

## RING MOLDS AND ROUND CUTTERS
Available in a variety of diameters, ring molds and cutters can be used to create perfect circles.

## ROUND FLEX MOLDS (1 1/4-INCH FLAT)
These flat, flexible molds are used to make round disks.

## SILICONE BAKING MATS
Nonstick silicone baking mats are used to line baking sheets and provide a smooth surface. They are also used when working with sugar and chocolate and can withstand very high heat.

## SOUS VIDE BAGS
In order for proteins, fruits, and vegetables to be vacuum-sealed, they must first be placed in a food- and heat-safe *sous vide* bag.

## TAMIS
A tamis is a drum-shaped sieve that is used to strain purees and gels, giving them a smooth texture. *Available from Korin.*

## TRIANGLE OR TRIANGULAR MOLD (19 INCH)
This long triangular mold is used as a mold for triangular pates, terrines, and confections.

## TWO-PIECE MAGNETIC MOLDS (1-INCH DIAMETER)
By using magnets to create a seal, this mold joins two half-sphere molds to make perfectly round spheres.

## WHIPPED-CREAM CANISTER
A whipped-cream canister, filled and then charged with $CO_2$ or $N_2O$, is used to create foams, sabayons, and whipped creams.

# SOURCES FOR TOOLS

## CHEF DEPOT
www.chefdepot.net
630-739-5200

## KORIN
www.korin.com
800-626-2172

## PACOJET
www.pacojet.com
336-856-2919

## PASTRY CHEF CENTRAL
www.pastrychef.com
888-750-CHEF

## JB PRINCE
www.jbprince.com
800-473-0577

## LE SANCTUAIRE
www.le-sanctuaire.com
415-992-6855, ext. 103

# SOURCES FOR INGREDIENTS

## EGGS AND DAIRY

**ARAUCANA EGGS**
Lynnhaven Farm
845-744-6089
www.lynnhavennubians.com

**CASTELMAGNO CHEESE**
Murray's Cheese
888-692-4339, ext. 7
www.murrayscheese.com

**FRESH GOAT'S MILK CHEESES**
Lynnhaven Farm
845-744-6089
www.lynnhavennubians.com

**AGED GOAT'S MILK CHEESES**
Murray's Cheese
888-692-4339, ext. 7
www.murrayscheese.com

**HOBELCHÄS**
Quality Cheese Inc.
239-246-0523
www.qualitycheese.net

**LA FAISSELLE FROMAGE BLANC**
Vermont Butter & Cheese Creamery
www.vermontcreamery.com

**VACHERIN MONT D'OR**
Murray's Cheese
888-692-4339, ext. 7
www.murrayscheese.com

## NUTS AND OILS

**BITTER ALMONDS (ALSO CALLED APRICOT SEEDS OR APRICOT KERNELS)**
Asiachi
323-940-8888, ext. 115
www.asiachi.com

**MARCONA ALMONDS**
Murray's Cheese
888-692-4339, ext. 7
www.murrayscheese.com

**NUT OILS**
Huilerie Beaujolaise
212-366-4863
www.GigaChef.com

**OLIO NUOVO**
McEvoy Ranch
866-617-6779
www.mcevoyranch.com

## GRAINS AND BREAD

**FLOUR**
King Arthur Flour
800-827-6836
www.kingarthurflour.com

**BRICK DOUGH**
The Chefs' Warehouse
718-842-8700
www.chefswarehouse.com

**FARRO**
Cayuga Pure Organics
607-229-6429
www.cporganics.com

**PISTACHIO NUT BREAD**
Balthazar Bakery
212-965-1785
www.balthazarbakery.com

## PRODUCE

**BABY GREENS**
Blue Moon Acres
215-794-3093
www.bluemoonacres.net

**EDIBLE FLOWERS**
The Chef's Garden
800-289-4644
www.chefs-garden.com

## DRIED PRODUCE

**FERMENTED BLACK GARLIC**
Kalustyan's
800-352-3451
www.kalustyans.com

**FREEZE-DRIED FRUITS AND VEGETABLES**
Terra Spice Company
574-586-2600
www.terraspice.com

**UMEBOSHI (ALSO CALLED TSUBO UME)**
Available at Asian markets

**WHITE IRANIAN FIGS**
Saffron King
212-879-7480
www.saffronking.com

## PASTRY

**BITTER ALMOND EXTRACT**
L'Epicerie
866-350-7575
www.lepicerie.com

**COCOA BUTTER**
L'Epicerie
866-350-7575
www.lepicerie.com

**COCOA NIBS**
Valrhona
888-682-5746
www.valrhona-chocolate.com

**CHESTNUT HONEY**
L'Epicerie
866-350-7575
www.lepicerie.com

**DEXTROSE**
Terra Spice Company
574-586-2600
www.terraspice.com

**EDIBLE GOLD DUST AND LEAF**
L'Epicerie
866-350-7575
www.lepicerie.com

**EGG-WHITE POWDER**
L'Epicerie
866-350-7575
www.lepicerie.com

**FEUILLETINE**
L'Epicerie
866-350-7575
www.lepicerie.com

**FROZEN FRUIT PUREES**
L'Epicerie
866-350-7575
www.lepicerie.com

**GLUCOSE SYRUP OR POWDER**
L'Epicerie
866-350-7575
www.lepicerie.com

**GELATIN SHEETS**
L'Epicerie
866-350-7575
www.lepicerie.com

**ISOMALT**
L'Epicerie
866-350-7575
www.lepicerie.com

**POP ROCKS (UNFLAVORED; ALSO CALLED PASTRY ROCKS)**
Chef Rubber
702-614-9350
www.shopchefrubber.com

**PASTRY CREAM POWDER**
The Chefs' Warehouse
718-842-8700, ext. 20104
www.chefswarehouse.com

**PÂTE À GLACER BRUNE**
The Chefs' Warehouse
718-842-8700, ext. 20104
www.chefswarehouse.com

**POURED FONDANT**
L'Epicerie
866-350-7575
www.lepicerie.com

**TRABLIT COFFEE EXTRACT**
L'Epicerie
866-350-7575
www.lepicerie.com

**TRIMOLINE**
L'Epicerie
866-350-7575
www.lepicerie.com

**VALRHONA CHOCOLATE**
Valrhona
888-682-5746
www.valrhona-chocolate.com

## MEAT AND POULTRY

**CAUL FAT**
D'Artagnan
800-327-8246
www.dartagnan.com

**COCKSCOMBS**
D'Artagnan
800-327-8246
www.dartagnan.com

**DUCK FAT**
D'Artagnan
800-327-8246
www.dartagnan.com

**FOIE GRAS**
Hudson Valley Foie Gras
845-292-2500
www.hudsonvalleyfoiegras.com

**GUANCIALE**
Salumeria Biellese
212-736-7376
www.salumeriabiellese.com

**GUINEA FOWL**
D'Artagnan
800-327-8246
www.dartagnan.com

**HARE**
D'Artagnan
800-327-8246
www.dartagnan.com

**JAMÓN IBÉRICO**
Despaña
888-779-8617
www.despanabrandfoods.com

**LAMB**
Jamison Farm
800-237-5262
www.jamisonfarm.com

**MUSCOVY DUCKS**
D'Artagnan
800-327-8246
www.dartagnan.com

**PIG**
St-Canut Farms
450-712-4642
www.stcanutfarms.com

**PIG BLOOD**
D'Artagnan
800-327-8246
www.dartagnan.com

**QUAIL**
D'Artagnan
800-327-8246
www.dartagnan.com

**RABBIT**
D'Artagnan
800-327-8246
www.dartagnan.com

**SPANISH BLOOD SAUSAGE (ALSO CALLED MORCILLA)**
Despaña
888-779-8617
www.despanabrandfoods.com

**SQUAB**
D'Artagnan
800-327-8246
www.dartagnan.com

**SUCKLING PIG**
Four Story Hill Farm
570-224-4137

**VEAL TONGUE**
Four Story Hill Farm
570-224-4137

**VENISON**
Millbrook Venison Products
800-774-DEER

**WILD BOAR SHOULDER**
D'Artagnan
800-327-8246
www.dartagnan.com

## FISH AND SEAFOOD

**BALIK SALMON**
Petrossian
800-828-9241
www.petrossian.com

**FROG LEGS**
Gary's Seafood Specialties
877-345-9176
www.garyseafood.com

**OSETRA CAVIAR**
Petrossian
800-828-9241
www.petrossian.com

## SPICES

**BEET POWDER**
Terra Spice Company
574-586-2600
www.terraspice.com

**CITRIC ACID**
Terra Spice Company
574-586-2600
www.terraspice.com

**DHANA DAL**
Kalustyan's
800-352-3451
www.kalustyans.com

**HAWAIIAN SEA SALT**
Kalustyan's
800-352-3451
www.kalustyans.com

**MADRAS CURRY POWDER**
Kalustyan's
800-352-3451
www.kalustyans.com

**ORANGE BLOSSOM WATER**
Kalustyan's
800-352-3451
www.kalustyans.com

**PEPPERMINT (DRIED)**
L'Epicerie
866-350-7575
www.lepicerie.com

**PIMENT D'ESPELETTE**
Terra Spice Company
574-586-2600
www.terraspice.com

**PINK CURING SALT**
Terra Spice Company
574-586-2600
www.terraspice.com

**SAFFRON**
Saffron King
212-879-7480
www.saffronking.com

**SZECHUAN PEPPERCORNS**
Kalustyan's
800-352-3451
www.kalustyans.com

**TELLICHERRY PEPPER**
Kalustyan's
800-352-3451
www.kalustyans.com

**VADOUVAN CURRY SPICE**
Kalustyan's
800-352-3451
www.kalustyans.com

**VIOLET MUSTARD (ALSO CALLED PURPLE CONDIMENT MUSTARD)**
L'Epicerie
866-350-7575
www.lepicerie.com

## VINEGAR AND VINEGAR POWDERS

**BALSAMIC VINEGAR POWDER**
Terra Spice Company
574-586-2600
www.terraspice.com

**BANYULS VINEGAR**
The Chefs' Warehouse
718-842-8700, ext. 20104
www.chefswarehouse.com

**ICE WINE VINEGAR**
Minus 8 Vinegar
877-209-7634
www.minus8vinegar.com

**MALT VINEGAR POWDER**
Terra Spice Company
574-586-2600
www.terraspice.com

**RED WINE VINEGAR POWDER**
Terra Spice Company
574-586-2600
www.terraspice.com

**UMEBOSHI VINEGAR (ALSO CALLED UME VINEGAR)**
Kalustyan's
800-352-3451
www.kalustyans.com

**WHITE VINEGAR POWDER**
Terra Spice Company
574-586-2600
www.terraspice.com

## SEAWEEDS

**DULSE SEAWEED**
Mendocino Sea Vegetable Company
707-895-2996
www.seaweed.net

**KOMBU**
Available at Asian markets

**MENDOCINO BLADDERWRACK**
Mendocino Sea Vegetable Company
707-895-2996
www.seaweed.net

**MENDOCINO GRAPESTONE**
Mendocino Sea Vegetable Company
707-895-2996
www.seaweed.net

**RED TOSAKA NORI (ALSO CALLED
SALT-PACKED RED SEAWEED)**
Available at Asian markets

**SUCCULENT MIRU (ALSO CALLED
CODIUM FRAGILE)**
Mendocino Sea Vegetable Company
707-895-2996
www.seaweed.net

## TRUFFLES

**BLACK TRUFFLES**
Plantin
04-90-46-41-44 (France)
www.plantin.com

**TRUFFLE JUICE**
Plantin
04-90-46-41-44 (France)
www.plantin.com

**WHITE TRUFFLES**
Urbani Truffles
212-247-8800
www.urbanitrufflesonline.com

## OTHER

**AGAR-AGAR**
Terra Spice Company
574-586-2600
www.terraspice.com

**APPLE PECTIN**
Terra Spice Company
574-586-2600
www.terraspice.com

**COCO BEANS (ALSO CALLED
FRENCH NAVY BEANS)**
D'Artagnan
800-327-8246
www.dartagnan.com

**FOOD COLORING (OIL-BASED)**
Candyland Crafts
877-487-4289
www.candylandcrafts.com

**IOTA CARRAGEENAN**
Terra Spice Company
574-586-2600
www.terraspice.com

**MALIC ACID**
Terra Spice Company
574-586-2600
www.terraspice.com

**SHIRO SHOYU (ALSO CALLED
WHITE SOY)**
Available at Asian markets

**SOY LECITHIN**
Terra Spice Company
574-586-2600
www.terraspice.com

**TAPIOCA MALTODEXTRIN**
Terra Spice Company
574-586-2600
www.terraspice.com

**XANTHAN GUM**
Terra Spice Company
574-586-2600
www.terraspice.com

**YUZU JUICE**
Available at Asian markets

**YUZU KOSHO**
Available at Asian markets

# INDEX

Page numbers in *italic* refer to photographs.

# ACKNOWLEDGMENTS

Our families, in particluar Frank and Juliette Guidara; Brigitte and Roland Humm; and Geneén, Vivienne, and Justine Humm, have provided us with years of constant support and love, guiding us through the experiences that have brought us to where we are today.

Sandra Di Capua, our mâitre d', was the organizational force behind this book, driving the creative processes and helping to edit everything from recipes to narrative text. Her involvement was critical.

Bryce Shuman, our longtime sous chef, provided the tremendous culinary guidance necessary to produce this book. He played an instrumental role in the writing, editing, and testing of every recipe.

Sue Li tested and retested the recipes in this book, translating them from kitchen vernacular to more accessible cookbook vocabulary.

Sous chefs Lee Wolen and Tom Allan prepared all of the dishes for the photo shoots, working with Chef Humm and Francesco Tonelli to make gorgeous plates of delicious food.

Angela Pinkerton, our pastry chef, designs and develops all things sweet at the restaurant. Her hard work and creative input was essential in writing the pastry recipes for this book.

Abram Bissell and James Kent, the leaders of our kitchen team, inspire us every day with their ability and continued pursuit of excellence.

The rest of the sous chefs at Eleven Madison Park, Chris Flint, Patrick Hennessy, David Nayfeld, Julian Proujansky, and Mark Welker, all played a role in developing the dishes in this book. Their consistent passion and determination has helped make our restaurant what it is today.

Amy Livingston, our fabulous assistant, did all of the coordination that allowed us to work on this book while running a four-star restaurant.

Megan Vaughan, our service director, compiled all of the notes for "A Day in the Life" and "How Eleven Madison Park Works."

Juliette Cezzar is responsible for the graphic identity of our restaurant and the look and feel of this book. We are deeply indebted to her incredible aesthetic sensibility.

Michael Sand's editorial guidance led us from the idea of a book to an actual book.

Jayne Yaffe Kemp combed the entire manuscript with a fine-tooth green pencil. We admire her attention to the tiniest of details.

David Black, exceptional book agent, brought our book to Michael Sand and Little, Brown.

Copyright © 2011 by Daniel Humm and Will Guidara
Photographs copyright © 2011 Francesco Tonelli

Little, Brown and Company
Hachette Book Group
237 Park Avenue, New York, NY 10017
www.hachettebookgroup.com

First Edition: November 2011

Little, Brown and Company is a division of Hachette Book Group, Inc. The Little, Brown name and logo are trademarks of Hachette Book Group, Inc.

The publisher is not responsible for websites (or their content) that are not owned by the publisher.

Bitter almonds, their seeds, and extracts can be poisonous if not processed to remove toxic chemicals. Obtain processed bitter almonds for culinary use from a reliable source such as those listed in the back of the book. The use of liquid nitrogen should be undertaken with proper care as described in "How to Use This Book." The author and publisher specifically disclaim any liability, loss, or risk, personal or otherwise, incurred as a consequence, directly or indirectly, of the use and application of any of the contents of this book.

Cooking *sous vide* (under vacuum) can raise certain safety concerns. In order to avoid the risk of bacteria-related illness in those recipes that call for *sous vide* preparation, cook all meats at the specified temperatures for the specified amount of time.

Library of Congress Cataloging-in-Publication Data
Humm, Daniel.
    Eleven Madison Park : the cookbook / Daniel
        Humm, Will Guidara ; photography by Francesco
        Tonelli. — 1st ed.
    p. cm.
    Includes index.
    ISBN 978-0-316-09851-9 / 978-0-316-20952-6 (deluxe edition)
    1. Cooking, French. 2. Eleven Madison Park
        (Restaurant) 3. Cooking — New York
    (City) — New York. 4. Cookbooks. I. Guidara, Will. II.
        Title.
    TX719.H84 2010
    641.59747 — dc22                    2010053240

10  9  8  7  6

IM

Design by Juliette Cezzar / e.a.d.

Printed in China